# AGRICULTURAL LAW

## IN A NUTSHELL®

ROGER A. McEOWEN
Kansas Farm Bureau Professor of
Agricultural Law and Taxation,
Washburn University School of Law

WEST
ACADEMIC
PUBLISHING

*Nutshell Series, In a Nutshell* and the Nutshell Logo are trademarks registered in the U.S. Patent and Trademark Office.

West, West Academic Publishing, and West Academic are trademarks of West Publishing Corporation, used under license.

Printed in the United States of America

**ISBN:** 978-1-68328-257-0

# IN MEMORIAM

*This book is dedicated*
*To the Memory of my parents*
*H.D. (Mac) McEowen*
*7/19/18–1/26/77*

*and*

*Nedra R. McEowen*
*5/31/18–8/9/09*

*and my father-in-law*
*David L. Sprunger*
*1/1/35–11/19/13*

# PREFACE

Agricultural law is a dynamic field that began to develop as an area for study largely in the twentieth century. Over the past 60 years, agricultural law courses have been developed and are offered widely at land grant universities, law schools, junior colleges and two-year vocational-technical institutions.

Agricultural law covers a wide array of topics and issues that illustrate the many areas where agriculture intersects the law. The reader will note how the law often treats "agriculture" and "farmers" and "ranchers" in a unique manner. In many respects, agricultural law is "law by the exception" as the late Washburn Law School Professor James B. Wadley often said. But, the legal concepts and principles addressed in this Nutshell have application that is broader than simply to agriculture, and the reader will find that fact apparent.

This Nutshell is intended to introduce readers to the basic concepts that apply to many legal issues that have application to farmers, ranchers, rural landowners, and agribusinesses. The Nutshell is designed to be used as a supplement to courses and teaching materials involving the various aspects of the law that are addressed. The book is organized along the same lines and largely drawn from the author's larger treatise, *Principles of Agricultural Law*. However, this Nutshell does not include such key topics as farm income taxation, as well as farm estate and business planning which are included in the author's primary work. Perhaps an additional Nutshell will be developed on those topics in the future.

It is my hope that you find the material in this text enjoyable and much more than a mere academic exercise. This text addresses real-life issues faced by real persons. Agricultural law is reality, and students will benefit from having used this text in a course on agricultural law, as will others that are in the business of agriculture.

ROGER A. MCEOWEN

Topeka, Kansas
May 2017

# ACKNOWLEDGMENTS

I wish to acknowledge publicly the help that I have received, in putting this Nutshell together for you, the reader. Tammy Haggerty of Seneca, Kansas, was invaluable to me with her word processing skills and editorial comments as the preparation of the text progressed chapter by chapter. She made sure that the project met the various deadlines and spotted numerous textual and cosmetic items that needed my closer attention. In spite of the scope of the project and the time commitment needed, she remained a joy to work with throughout. Thanks also to her family for allowing her the time needed to help complete this project. Also, special notice is due her father, William ("Tom") McGinnis, who has attended numerous of my tax seminars over the years.

I am also grateful to the editorial staff of West Publishing Co. that worked on this project, and for the input of lawyers, fellow law school faculty members and the many farmers, ranchers and rural landowners that I come into contact with on a daily basis, for their common-sense insight into practical issues that the book needed to address.

# OUTLINE

# TABLE OF CASES

## References are to Pages

*TABLE OF CASES*

# AGRICULTURAL LAW

## IN A NUTSHELL®

# CHAPTER 1
# INTRODUCTION

## I. OVERVIEW

For a variety of reasons, the law views many aspects of agricultural production as significantly different from other industrial enterprises. As a consequence, in such situations general legal rules have been deemed inappropriate as applied to agriculture. For example, farm employers are not subject to many federal labor laws and in many states are not included within the scope of the state workers' compensation provisions. Agricultural cooperatives are generally exempt from federal antitrust constraints and therefore can engage in activities which are prohibited to nonfarm businesses. Likewise, the Uniform Commercial Code (UCC) has special provisions for goods which are designated as "farm products." Other UCC rules governing implied warranties on the sale of goods do not apply to some farm livestock sales, and in some states a farmer is not considered a merchant for many purposes under the UCC. In recent years, an entire section of bankruptcy law has been created specifically for farmers and ranchers. Also, all states offer protection to agricultural operations from nuisance lawsuits brought by disgruntled neighbors. In some states, however, the level of protection is greater than in other states. In addition, agricultural land in most states is now valued at agricultural use value, rather than fair market value, for purposes of ad valorem real property taxes. This may also be the case for purposes of federal estate taxes if the land and operation qualify for special use valuation under the federal tax code. Likewise, federal hazardous chemical legislation and water pollution programs currently have major farm exemptions. Sometimes, alleged farming operations are challenged under state and local zoning laws. In many states, agricultural activities are not subject to county zoning. This provides another incentive for landowners to have their activities construed as agricultural activities.

Several reasons are commonly cited as an explanation for the different legal treatment of farmers and ranchers from other similarly situated individuals. Farming and ranching is typically viewed as a unique way of life that is dependent upon natural forces occurring in an isolated rural environment. Historically, American society has generally accepted the notion that the success of a particular agricultural operation is dependent upon various factors that are beyond the owner's control. These factors may include matters such as the weather, price and availability of production inputs, and variation in consumer demand for individual agricultural products. Society has also tended to view farmers and ranchers as a uniquely stabilizing element in society because of their vital role in food and fiber production. The Jeffersonian ideal of "family farms", while not universally evidenced in reality, still remains a potent idyllic concept to many. Likewise, because farms and ranches need large amounts of land to remain productive, farms and ranches are a major source of aesthetically and psychologically pleasing open space. Thus, the unique view society often affords agriculture is generally very beneficial to farmers and ranchers from a legal perspective. In order to obtain preferential treatment under the law as a "farm" or "ranch", a particular agricultural operation must be engaged in agricultural activity. There are many agricultural activities that meet the broad definition of "agriculture", but it may not be easy, in any particular case, to determine whether an activity meets the definition of "agriculture." It is, therefore, usually necessary to examine what the enterprise produces, the resources used in the production process, the organization's economic structure, the technology involved in the methods of production, the operator's particular role, and the relationship between the operator and the resources used in the organization of the enterprise and production of the product.

## II. HISTORY AND SOURCES OF AMERICAN LAW

### A. BASIC SOURCES OF LAW

The United States Constitution is the primary source of all law in the United States. No state constitution or any law enacted by the Congress or a state legislative body, and no decision of any state or federal court, can be contrary to the constitution. Any legislative enactment or decision determined to be contrary to the constitution will be declared null and void. The constitution also provides for other sources of law. For example, Article I establishes the legislative branch of government, the United States Congress, and further specifically sets out its power and the limitations on those powers. Article II establishes the Office of the President of the United States and the executive branch of government and sets out the powers of and limitations on that branch of government. Section 2 of Article II also gives the President the power to make treaties. However, all treaties must be made with the advice and consent of the United States Senate. Once the Senate approves a treaty, it has the same force and effect as laws enacted by the United States Congress. Thus, a treaty concerning U.S. internal affairs is superior to any state law or any state constitution. *See, e.g., Apel v. Le Blanc,* 223 N.W.2d 305 (Mich. 1974). Article III creates the Judicial Branch of the national government and provides that the judicial power of the United States is vested in one supreme court and in as many inferior courts as the Congress may establish.

The Tenth Amendment to the Constitution provides that the powers not delegated to the United States by the Constitution or prohibited by it to the states are reserved to the states, respectively, or to the people. The effect of this amendment is to allow the states to govern themselves in all areas where the Constitution does not specify national regulation. Article I, Section 8 of the Constitution grants Congress the power to regulate commerce with foreign nations and among the several states, the power to establish post offices, the power to raise and support an army, the power to provide and maintain a navy, the power to coin money, and various other powers related to the operation of the national government. Many of the environmental laws, federal farm programs and other federal regulations that impact agriculture have their constitutional basis in the "commerce clause" of Article I, Section 8. However, each state retains the right to have its own state government govern internal affairs within the state. Thus, each state has a constitution establishing a state, county, and municipal legislative system, an executive system, and a court system. Consequently, the individual state constitutions are a primary source of state law, but may not conflict with the United States Constitution.

Another large body of law applicable to agriculture is created by the various regulations and pronouncements of administrative agencies, both national and state. A major concern of regulatory and administrative law is that many regulations that have the force of law are made by administrative agencies rather than legislatures comprised of elected representatives. Any appeal of an agency decision must generally be made to the same agency that rendered the initial decision. The administrative agencies are creatures of legislatures and are given specifically delegated tasks and functions by the legislative body that created them. Thus, in many instances the agency acts as legislator, jury and judge. This raises questions of fundamental fairness. In general, administrative remedies must be exhausted before a court hearing can be obtained. Administrative law requires an understanding of how an agency functions and how adverse decisions can be appealed within the agency itself. Often, this requires access to the operating rules and regulations of the particular agency.

## B.    STARE DECISIS

Over several hundred years, the courts in England decided thousands of cases using the common law. From these decisions came precedents, which are cases that set the pattern for the way future cases are to be decided. The practice of deciding new cases with reference to prior decisions became a cornerstone of the English and, later, American judicial systems. The doctrine, known as stare decisis, requires judges to attempt to follow the precedent established by previous legal decisions. However, courts are not bound by stare decisis. Sometimes judges decide that society has changed and that "public policy" requires a different rule of law to reflect those changes. However, changing a legal principle based on societal changes is commonly viewed as the proper domain only of state legislatures and the Congress. As a result, judges are usually reluctant to decide any particular case differently from well-established precedent.

Sometimes there is no precedent on which a judge may base a decision, or there may be conflicting precedents. Cases involving issues for which there is no established precedent are called cases of "first impression". In situations where there is conflicting precedent, a judge will often refer to past decisions that may be similar to the current case and decide the case by reasoning through analogy, or examining social factors that might influence the issues involved and considering what the fairest result would be. While the majority of cases are decided according to precedent, cases that overturn precedent often receive much publicity.

## III.  CLASSIFICATIONS OF LAW

### A.  SUBSTANTIVE LAW

Substantive law consists of constitutions, treaties, statutes, ordinances, judicial decisions, and regulations and decisions of administrative bodies. There are three general areas of substantive law: criminal law, civil law and the law of equity.

### 1.  Criminal Law

Criminal law encompasses national and state statutes and local ordinances that make the commission or omission of certain acts punishable by fine or imprisonment. In criminal law, the state or national government prosecutes the person who disobeyed the particular criminal statute on behalf of the people. The wrong being punished is a wrong against society. Thus, criminal law only attempts to fine or imprison the wrongdoer, but does not compensate an injured party for damages to property or personal injury.

### 2.  Civil Law

The civil law provides compensation or other remedies for personal injury or loss of property. Civil law involves statutory and case law and establishes the rights and duties of individuals to other individuals in society. Civil law encompasses tort law, contract law, property law and many other areas of the law where the remedy sought is monetary damages rather than punishment by fine or imprisonment.

### 3. Law of Equity

The law of equity provides a remedy in the event monetary damages from a civil lawsuit are not an appropriate remedy. Quite often this equitable relief is requested when the lawsuit involves objects that are unique, priceless or have great sentimental value for which monetary damages are either inappropriate or extremely difficult to determine. Common examples of equity cases involve lawsuits for rescission or reformation of a contract, suits to partition property, suits to quiet title to real estate, and suits for an accounting by one business partner against another. In these types of cases, the party bringing the lawsuit typically requests the court to take action (require the other party to perform) rather than simply award monetary damages. A unique feature of equity cases is that they are normally tried before the judge only and no jury is allowed. In most states, the same judge hears all civil matters, with the judge having the power to award monetary damages or fashion an equitable remedy.

## B. UNIFORM LAWS

Business transactions are commonly conducted across state lines. Because each state has the right to govern itself and the business within its boundaries so long as its law does not conflict with the United States Constitution or federal legislation, a business conducting operations in multiple states must be aware of and conform to different legal standards as it conducts business in multiple states. As a result, uniformity of state law, especially with respect to business transactions, became increasingly necessary. Today, most states follow laws that are the same in each jurisdiction with respect to most business transactions.

## IV.   COURT SYSTEMS

There are 52 court systems in the United States; each state has its own unique court system, the District of Columbia has its own independent system of courts; and there is a separate federal court system. United States Supreme Court decisions serve as controlling authority in each of the state and federal court systems.

### A.   STATE COURT SYSTEMS

There are at least three and sometimes four levels to a typical state judicial system. The lowest level often consists of specialty courts of limited jurisdiction. These courts typically have jurisdiction over civil cases that involve small monetary amounts, nonfelony criminal matters, and traffic cases where the accused is willing to plead guilty. Decisions of these courts may be appealed to a trial court of general jurisdiction which holds a new trial rather than simply reviewing the record from the specialty court. In some states, an appeal may be made directly

to an appellate court for review rather than for a
retrial.

The next highest level of court in most states is the
trial court with general jurisdiction. Often these
courts are called district courts or superior courts,
but in New York this court is referred to as the
supreme court. Usually, each county has only one
trial court with general jurisdiction, but urban
counties may have more. These courts are courts of
record wherein testimony and proceedings are
recorded and all pleadings are in writing.

The next highest level of court system in most
states is an appellate court that hears appeals from
judgments entered by the courts below it. In these
courts, no new evidence is presented and the court
simply reviews the record, testimony and decision of
the lower court. In cases brought before an appellate
court, the party making the appeal (appellant) is
alleging that the lower court committed some sort of
reversible error.

The highest level of state judicial systems is
commonly referred to as the state supreme court, the
supreme judicial court, the supreme court of appeals
or, in New York, the court of appeals. As the court of
last resort, this court is a reviewing court and does
not hold new trials. Obtaining a review in a
particular state's highest court is similar to the
procedure for obtaining review at the appellate court
level, but this court is the appellant's last chance of
appealing the case unless a United States treaty or
statute is involved or the appellant maintains that a
particular state statute conflicts with the United

States Constitution or other federal law. In that event, a party may submit a petition for a writ of certiorari which is a formal request for the United States Supreme Court to hear the case. The nine justices of the United States Supreme Court review the writ and determine whether the issue or issues involved are important enough to warrant a full hearing before the Court. If at least four of the nine justices determine that the case should be reviewed, then the writ is granted and the case is scheduled for a formal hearing.

Opinions of a particular state's court of appeals and supreme court are published in that state's supreme court or court of appeals reporter, and in a regional reporter that contains supreme court and appellate court decisions of other states from the same geographic region of the country. For example, opinions of the Kansas Supreme Court are published in the Kansas Reports, cited as "Kan." The same opinions are also published (as of 1997) in the Pacific Reporter, Second Series, cited as "P.2d." Many of the cases reproduced throughout this text are state court decisions. Each case citation refers to the particular state reporter (if published therein) and the appropriate regional reporter. The state and regional reporters are found in any law school library and in some undergraduate libraries. County courthouses usually maintain only a set of their particular state's reporters and regional reporter containing that state's Supreme Court and court of appeals opinions.

## B.   FEDERAL COURT SYSTEM

The federal court system is a four-tier system with the lowest tier consisting of certain specialty courts such as the Court of International Trade, the United States Court of Federal Claims, the United States Tax Court and courts that hear appeals from decisions of certain federal administrative agencies. Appeals from these courts are made directly to either the United States Court of Appeals for the federal circuit, or the applicable federal circuit court of appeals, a third-tier appellate level court. The United States Bankruptcy Courts are also first-tier level courts, but appeals of bankruptcy court decisions are to appropriate federal district courts, second-tier courts. Bankruptcy court opinions are found in the Bankruptcy Reporter, cited as "B.R."

The next highest court level in the federal system contains the federal district courts. There are ninety-four federal district courts. These are courts of national jurisdiction and are located in every state. These courts have general jurisdiction concerning federal law and have the authority to hear civil, criminal and equitable cases. These courts also have the power to enforce their decisions by issuing court orders resulting in fines and/or imprisonment. Opinions of the federal district courts are reported in the Federal Supplement, cited as "F. Supp." or Federal Supplement, second series, cited as "F. Supp. 2d" (beginning in 1998). Other second-tier courts handle disputes involving the Federal Trade Commission, the National Labor Relations Board, and certain other national administrative agencies.

The administrative agencies are limited in jurisdiction to cases involving their specialty area and are limited in their power to enforce their decisions. Appeals from the federal district courts are filed with the appropriate federal circuit court of appeals for the appropriate circuit. The circuit courts of appeal also have the authority to approve and enforce agency decisions by court order.

The third tier in the federal court system contains the United States Circuit Courts of Appeals. There are 13 of these courts throughout the country, including eleven circuit courts, a federal circuit court and a circuit court for Washington, D.C., both located in Washington, D.C. These courts are reviewing courts similar to state level appellate courts and no new evidence may be submitted to them. Hearings held before these courts are not trials, but are reviews of the lower court's decision. A circuit court's jurisdiction is limited to only those cases occurring in lower courts within the particular circuit court's geographical area. The federal circuit, however, hears appeals from any case across the country that involves subject matter within its jurisdiction and cases from the United States Court of Federal Claims and the United States Court of International Trade. The D.C. Circuit hears appeals from the United States Tax Court involving tax cases arising in Washington, D.C., administrative agencies and the federal district court for the D.C. districts. Opinions of the Circuit Courts of Appeals are located in the Federal Reporter, Federal Reporter second series, cited as "F.2d," or Federal Reporter third series, cited as "F.3d" (beginning in 1997).

The highest tier in the federal court system is the Supreme Court of the United States. This is the court of final resort for appeal in any case. Usually, the Supreme Court is only a reviewing court, but the Constitution authorizes the Supreme Court to be a trial court in cases involving certain public officials and in cases where a state is a party. The Constitution, however, does not require the Supreme Court to exercise its power of original jurisdiction. Generally, the Supreme Court will only review cases where the issues involved are of considerable public concern or where there is a split of opinion among two or more federal circuit courts of appeal. Opinions of the United States Supreme Court are recorded in the United States Reports, cited as "U.S."

## V.　CIVIL PROCEDURE

Procedural law establishes the rules and standards for determining disputes in courts. A large body of law involves the procedural aspects of trying a case in the judicial system. Much of the procedural aspects of the cases included throughout this text has been eliminated.

## VI.　ENFORCING A JUDGMENT

Judgments are typically enforced in one of three ways. One way is for the prevailing party to levy execution on the losing party's property. The losing party's nonexempt property may be sold at public sale with the proceeds being applied against the judgment. A second method of execution is for the prevailing party to have the wages of the losing party garnished in accordance with state or federal law. Not all wages are subject to garnishment. A third manner in which a judgment may be enforced is for the prevailing party to secure a lien against the losing party's property. As for the losing party's real estate, the lien prevents the losing party from selling and giving clear title to the real estate without first paying the claim. In some instances, the property may be sold through an additional court process to enforce the claim. If the debtor owns property in states other than where the verdict was entered, the judgment may be enforced against the losing party's property in those other jurisdictions. The other states are required under Article IV of the United States Constitution to honor the judgment rendered in the other state.

## VII.  LEGAL RESEARCH

Legal research primarily involves finding the law, and making sure that the law that is found is current and has not been repealed by statutory enactment or reversed by subsequent legal decision. Primary sources of the law include the federal and state constitutions and opinions of the various federal and state courts. Other primary sources of the law include federal and state statutes and federal and state regulations.

Sources of secondary legal authority include legal treatises (such as this text), law reviews and legal encyclopedias such as American Jurisprudence (Am. Jur.), Corpus Juris Secundum (C.J.S.) and various state digests. These sources of secondary legal authority can be used to find primary authority. Once primary authority is located, it is always necessary to ensure it is still good law.

# CHAPTER 2

# CONTRACTS

## I. CONTRACT FORMATION— THE COMMON LAW

### A. OFFER AND ACCEPTANCE

A contract is generally formed when one party makes an offer and a second party accepts the offer. While a contract may be made in any manner sufficient to show agreement, at the very heart of contract law is the determination of the parties' intent to contract. Conduct by both parties that recognizes the existence of a contract is usually sufficient to establish a contract for sale. In all cases, however, a showing of mutual assent is necessary an enforceable contract. In many cases, there is little doubt as to what is an offer and what is an acceptance. If the offeror (the person making the offer) has clearly manifested a willingness to enter into a contract in such a way that the other party, the offeree, knows that assent is all that is necessary to cement the deal, and the offeree accepts, the requisite mutual assent exists. The best approach is to be unambiguous and state expressly whether a communication is intended to be an offer, acceptance, or merely an invitation to deal. For example, in *Lucy v. Zehmer,* 196 Va. 493, 84 S.E.2d 516 (1954), the defendant argued that his acceptance of the plaintiff's offer to buy his farm was made in jest. The plaintiff took the defendant seriously and the court held that a valid contract existed. However, in

*Anderson v. Backlund,* 159 Minn. 423, 199 N. W. 90 (1924), a landlord made statements to a tenant that induced the tenant to increase the stocking rate on a particular pasture. When a drought occurred and the cattle died, the tenant sued for breach of contract. The court held that the landlord's comments were too indefinite to result an enforceable contract.

Thus, the importance of the parties' intention (or lack of intention) that the contract be legally enforceable depends largely upon the context of the agreement. In general, transactions entered into in a business context raise a presumption that the parties intended the agreement to be legally enforceable.

## B.   SOLICITATIONS

Orders, advertisements and unilateral reward notices all demonstrate the various circumstances in which a contract may arise. For orders taken by salesmen, the order is generally only an offer and can be revoked until accepted by the home office. Unilateral reward notices are ordinarily considered to be offers and lapse in a reasonable time. The reward can be collected by a person rendering the specified performance only if such person knew of the offer at the time of performing, unless the reward offer is made by a governmental entity. In that case, any person performing the requested service is entitled to the reward even if the person had no idea the reward was being offered. Advertisements, including catalogs and circulars, are usually only invitations to deal and are not offers which can be accepted. Sometimes, however, an advertisement for

the sale of goods constitutes an actual offer. *See, e.g.,*
*Lefkowitz v. Great Minneapolis Surplus Store, Inc,*
251 Minn. 188, 86 N.W.2d 689 (1957).

## C.   OTHER COMMON LAW REQUIREMENTS

Case law in some states requires that a valid
binding contract be characterized by competent
parties, subject matter, legal consideration, mutual
agreement, and mutual obligation. For example, in
*Tyson Foods, Inc. v. Archer, et al.,* 356 Ark.136, 147
S.W.3d 681 (2004), the court struck down an
arbitration clause in a pork production contract due
to lack of mutual obligation. A separate contract
clause gave Tyson Foods, Inc. the right to take
possession of the hogs and proceed directly to court
upon the producer's breach of any of the contract
terms, but required the producer to submit any
claims to arbitration. However, if an arbitration
clause is unambiguous and is applicable to all
contracting parties, the mutuality requirement of
*Archer* is satisfied. See also *H&C Ag Services, LLC v.
Ohio Fresh Eggs, LLC, et al.,* No.6–15–02, 2015 Ohio
App. LEXIS 3615 (Ohio Ct. App. Sept. 14, 2015).

## II.  APPLICATION OF UCC
## ARTICLE 2 TO CONTRACTS

### A.   SCOPE OF ARTICLE 2

Article 2 of the Uniform Commercial Code pertains
to the sale of goods. "Goods" includes all things that
are movable, as well as timber, minerals or the like
and permanent type buildings if the seller severs

them from the land. If such items are to be severed by the buyer, they are classified as "interests in land." These transactions are handled as if the land were being sold, and Article 2 does not apply. Growing crops, temporary or movable buildings and other items that can be moved without materially harming the realty are also considered goods under the UCC as are animal products while still on or in the animal, and the unborn young of animals.

Article 2 also applies to contract involving goods that are provided along with services or real estate if the goods are a predominant factor of the contract. *See, e.g., Embryo Progeny Associates v. Lovana Farms, Inc.,* 203 Ga. App. 447, 416 S.E.2d 833 (1992).

## III. CONTRACT FORMATION UNDER THE UCC

### A. CONTRACTS INVOLVING MERCHANTS

When two parties are negotiating for the sale of goods, the offeror may promise to keep the offer open for a certain period of time. Before enactment of the UCC, the offer was revocable at any time before acceptance unless the offeree had purchased an option to keep the offer open. Under the UCC, however, a merchant's firm written offer is irrevocable for the time stated in the offer or, if no period is stated, for a reasonable time not to exceed three months

Frequently, an acceptance contains terms that are in addition to or different from the offer. Before enactment of the UCC, the common law required an acceptance to mirror the offer and not attempt to change it in any way. This was termed the "mirror image" rule and, if an acceptance tried to add new terms not already implied in the offer, it was not an acceptance, but a counteroffer. Under the UCC, however, an offer may be accepted in any manner or medium reasonable under the circumstances. For example, even though an offer might be made by letter sent through regular mail, acceptance under the UCC could be by electronic mail, facsimile or telephone. The offeror may, however, specify a particular means of acceptance. Likewise, if an offer calls for prompt or current shipment of goods, the offer can be accepted either by a prompt promise to ship the goods or by an actual shipment of the goods.

---

**Example 1:**

Tex Johnson, a South Dakota rancher, writes to a cattle feeder and offers to sell 500 head of yearling steers at $165 per hundred, delivered. The cattle feeder replies, "Accept your offer. Deliver the cattle in ten days and I will pay you three weeks from now when I ship a load of fat steers to Omaha."

Under the UCC, if both parties are merchants, the additional terms become part of the contract unless Tex notifies the cattle feeder within a reasonable time that the terms are objectionable, or unless the new terms materially alter the contract. Tex could prevent such terms from becoming a part of the contract by wording the contract so that the power of acceptance is limited to the precise words of the offer. However, if either or both parties are not merchants, the additional terms are ignored unless Tex chooses to accept them. The contract consists of the terms on which the writings of the parties agree.

———————

An acceptance may also be worded so that it is conditional on the person making the original offer accepting the additional conditions in the acceptance. For a contract to result, the person making the original offer must agree to the additional conditions.

## B.   AUCTION SALES

The UCC regulates auction sales in harmony with the general principles of contract law as established by the common law. As a result, an auction sale contract is enforced, as is true of any other contract, according to its terms.

Many agricultural goods are sold at auction. In an auction sale, the auctioneer is the seller's agent. The auctioneer is selected by the seller, is remunerated by the seller, is to act in the seller's interest and, to a degree, is subservient to the seller's wishes. Until the auctioneer signals that the sale has been consummated, the auctioneer is exclusively the seller's agent and functions in a principal-agent relationship. The auctioneer's authority and liability depend upon the nature and extent of the agency conferred on the auctioneer by the seller. If the auctioneer exceeds the scope of authority, the auctioneer does not bind the owner of the property. As an agent of the seller, the auctioneer must exercise ordinary care and skill in the performance of duties undertaken. An auctioneer may be held accountable to the seller for any secret profits received by the auctioneer as a result of the sale which are not disclosed to the seller. For instance, in *In re Wilson Freight Co.*, 30 B.R.971 (Bankr. S.D. N.Y. 1983), the court held that the auctioneer could not be held liable to the highest bidder for tractors because the auctioneer was acting as the seller's agent and never became a party to any contract that may have been formed with the high bidder.

The fundamental rule at common law and under the UCC is that a bid at an auction constitutes an offer to buy. A contract is formed when the auctioneer signals acceptance by the fall of the auctioneer's hammer or by some other act. If a bid is made while the hammer is falling in acceptance of a prior bid, the auctioneer has the discretion to reopen the bidding or declare the goods sold. A bidder may retract a bid until the auctioneer's announcement of completion of the sale. But a bidder's retraction does not revive any previous bid.

Auctions may be held either "with reserve" or "without reserve." These terms relate to the seller's right to withdraw the goods if dissatisfied with the bids received. In an auction conducted "with reserve," the seller or the auctioneer has the right to reject all bids if desired. In an auction conducted "without reserve," the seller does not have the right to withdraw goods and the goods must be sold to the highest bidder even if only one bid is made. An article or lot cannot be withdrawn unless no bid is made within a reasonable time. Under the UCC, all auctions are presumed to be "with reserve" unless it is expressly announced to the contrary. For auctions conducted without reserve, the seller is committed to the sale once a bid has been entered, regardless of the level of bidding or the seller's notion of the property's true value. In a without reserve auction, the seller is the offeror, the bidder is the offeree and a contract is formed when a bid is made, subject only to a higher bid being made. For auctions conducted with reserve, a bid is an offer, and a contract is formed when the seller accepts the bid. Acceptance in a with-reserve auction is usually denoted by the fall of the auctioneer's hammer, but UCC § 2–328(2) states that a sale may be completed "in any other customary manner." This permits a seller to reject the highest bid even after the auctioneer's hammer falls or the auctioneer otherwise ends the auction. For example, in *Bradshaw v. Thompson,* 454 F.2d 75 (6th Cir. 1972), the court noted that the seller of a horse could have withdrawn the horse from sale even after the auctioneer's hammer fell, but only before the horse was taken from the sale ring. But, when the horse was removed from the sale ring after being sold, all title and interest passed to the purchaser and a contract was formed. Likewise, in *Johnson v. Herman,* No. CX-98-946, 1998 Minn. App. LEXIS 1390 (Minn. Ct. App. Dec. 22, 1998), the Minnesota Court of Appeals reversed a lower court finding that a contract existed for the sale of a farm at auction and remanded the case to the trial court for a determination of trade custom.

At an auction, a seller may bid on the seller's own goods only if the right to do so is reserved in advance. Except at a forced sale, if the auctioneer knowingly receives a bid on the seller's behalf or the seller makes a bid, and notice has not been given that liberty for such bidding is reserved, the buyer may at the buyer's option void the sale entirely or take the goods at the price of the last good-faith bid before the completion of the sale. However, the seller must have an obligation to sell to the highest bidder before the bidder has a right to take the goods at the price of the last good-faith bid.

In some instances, the consequences of a seller not giving notice of an intention to bid can go beyond the bidder's remedies of avoiding the contract or taking the goods at the price of the last good-faith bid. If the seller acts with a malicious intent to inflate the bids and injure other bidders, punitive damages may be awarded.

While Article 2 of the UCC does not apply to real estate sold at auction, some courts have applied by analogy the various rules of Article 2 to real estate auctions. For example, *Well v. Schoeneweis,* 101 Ill. App. 3d 254, 427 N.E.2d 1343 (1981), involved an action for specific performance of a sale of farmland brought by the highest bidder at a public auction against the seller. The court, while noting that Article 2 did not apply to real estate auctions, stated that the rules for real and personal property were identical and that the lower court did not err in relying on Article 2 for arriving at its judgment. Similarly, in *Pitchfork Ranch Co. v. Bar TL,* 615 P.2d 541 (Wyo. 1980), the court noted that even though Article 2 did not apply to real estate sales, its auction sale provisions were useful.

## IV. REQUIREMENT THAT CONTRACTS BE IN WRITING

In the United States, every state, except Louisiana adopted and retained a statute of frauds (including a right of first refusal and settlement agreements involving real estate). Typically, these laws require a writing that create or transfer any interest in land (including a right of first refusal and settlement agreements involving real estate), except leases for a term not exceeding one year. The statute of frauds also applies to contracts that are not to be performed within one year from the making, and certain contracts of estate executors.

**Note:** With the advent of electronic communication, courts were faced with numerous situations involving the issue of whether the electronic communication satisfied the Statue of Frauds. Now numerous states have statutes that address the matter.

While contracts for the sale of land must be in writing to been enforceable, the law is also concerned about the potential for fraud by the sellers of real estate. Thus, the courts have created an exception to the Statute of Frauds designed to address a seller's attempt to breach an oral sales contract. This exception, known as "partial performance," applies when the buyer has taken steps which undeniably indicates reliance on the existence of an oral contract, and the seller would have prevented such steps from having been taken had there not been a contract. Elements indicating the existence of partial performance include the buyer making substantial permanent improvements to the land with the seller's knowledge that relate to the contract; the buyer assuming actual and exclusive possession of the property; and whether enforcing the Statute of Frauds would unjustly enrich the seller and inflict undue harm on the buyer. Generally, the party attempting to remove a contract from the Statute of Frauds under the partial performance exception bears the burden of establishing the existence of an oral contract and at least one of the elements of the exception.

The writing requirement for sales of goods is now found in a state's version of § 2–20 of the UCC. The Official version adopted by most states, is applicable only when the goods have a price of $500 or more. In addition, under UCC § 1–206 there is an overall statute of frauds for every contract involving a contract for the sale of personal property having a value in excess of $5000. Thus, for personal property except "goods" a contract not enforceable beyond $5000 unless there is some writing signed by the party against whom enforcement is sought.

**Note:** In any particular state, statutes may require certain kinds of contracts to be in writing.

## A. MERCHANT'S CONFIRMATORY MEMO RULE

Under the UCC, unwritten contracts between merchants are enforceable if a writing in confirmation of a proposed contract is received within a reasonable time unless written notice of objection to the contents of the writing is given within ten days. *UCC § 2–201(2).* Thus, the effect of this "merchants" exception is to take from a merchant who receives a writing in confirmation of contract the statute of frauds defense if the merchant does not object to the confirmation. In any event, the sender of the written confirmation must be able persuade a jury that a contract was in fact made orally, to which the written confirmation applies.

---

**Example 2:**

In December of 2016, Albert Black, a Kansas wheat farmer, telephoned his local elevator for a price quote. During their telephone conversation, Albert and the elevator agreed that Albert would sell the elevator 25,000 bushels of Grade #1 wheat (60# test weight) at the December price next July, with performance to be completed no later than July 3, 2017. The elevator sent Albert a written confirmation asking that it be signed and returned within ten days. Albert did not sign the written confirmation.

Because of poor growing conditions and a resulting small wheat crop, the July 2017 wheat price was substantially higher than the December 2016 price. Albert refused to perform in accordance with the forward contract, preferring instead to sell his wheat crop at the higher current market price. The elevator sued to enforce the forward contract. As a defense, Albert asserted the UCC statute of frauds.

If Albert is a merchant with respect to the kind of goods contemplated in the forward contract (wheat), Albert will be bound by the oral contract entered into over the telephone with the elevator in December of 2016. If it is determined that Albert is not a merchant, the elevator might be able to recover if it can establish that it changed its position in reliance on Albert's conduct, that Albert knew or reasonably should have known the elevator would sell the forward contract, or can demonstrate that nonperformance by Albert was based on Albert's desire to benefit from a higher market price.

———

A significant consideration is whether a particular farmer or rancher is a merchant. A "merchant" is defined as one who deals in goods of the kind being sold, or one who by occupation holds himself or herself out as having knowledge or skill peculiar to either the goods involved or the practice of buying and selling such goods. Courts are divided on the issue of whether a farmer or rancher is a merchant, with the outcome depending on the jurisdiction and the facts of the particular case. Unfortunately, in many instances, farmers and ranchers cannot know with certainty whether they are merchants without becoming involved in legal action on the issue.

Courts consider several factors in determining whether a particular farmer is a merchant. These factors include (1) the length of time the farmer has been engaged in marketing products on the farm; (2) the degree of business skill demonstrated in transactions with other parties; (3) the farmer's awareness of the operation and existence of farm markets; and (4) the farmer's past experience with or knowledge of the customs and practices unique to the marketing of the product sold.

## B.   THE STATUTE OF FRAUDS

Even if a particular contract for the sale of goods fails to satisfy the requirements of the statute of frauds, it is nonetheless enforceable if the goods are to be specially manufactured for the buyer and are not suitable for sale to others in the ordinary course of the seller's business. Likewise, if the seller, before notice of repudiation is received and under circumstances which reasonably indicate that the goods are for the buyer, has made either a substantial beginning of their manufacture or commitments for their procurement, the contract is enforceable even if it is oral. In addition, a contract not complying with the statute of frauds is enforceable if the party against whom enforcement is sought admits in a pleading, testimony or otherwise in court that a contract for sale was made, but the contract is not enforceable beyond the quantity of goods admitted. In addition, a contract failing to satisfy the statute of frauds is enforceable if payment has been received or the goods have been received and accepted.

In general, oral agreements that materially modify a written contract governed by the Statute of Frauds are not enforceable under the UCC. However, not all modifications are prohibited. Many states apply the doctrine of promissory estoppel to forbid reliance on the Statute of Frauds as a defense to the validity of oral contract modifications. In these jurisdictions, courts hold that if one party, to their own detriment, reasonably relies on another's oral promise to reduce an oral agreement to writing, the failure to create such a writing does not prevent the relying party from taking the modification out of the Statute of Frauds as a defense to the validity of oral contract modifications. In these jurisdictions, courts hold that if one party, to their own detriment, reasonably relies on another's oral promise to reduce an oral agreement to writing, the failure to create such a writing does not prevent the relying party from taking the modification out of the Statute of Frauds.

## C.  THE STATUTE OF FRAUDS
AND AUCTION SALES

If goods having a price of $500 or more, or real property, are sold at auction, the statute of frauds must be satisfied. While the auctioneer is authorized to sign a memorandum of sale on behalf of both parties, this authority is limited and expires soon after the sale has been made. Any memorandum, however, must reasonably identify the subject matter of the contract, the identity of the contracting parties, and any essential terms.

The statute of frauds also applies to loans for the purchase of agricultural land at auction sales. Absent a writing, a purchaser cannot enforce an alleged oral loan agreement when it cannot be performed within one year.

## D.  THE STATUTE OF FRAUDS AND
AGRICULTURAL LEASES—NON-UCC ISSUES

An agricultural lease is a contract as well as a conveyance of an interest in real property. Because a lease is a contract, the terms of the lease are interpreted and enforced using contract law principles. As such, it is important that both parties to the lease understand the content of their lease agreement and the laws that affect it. Likewise, if the lease is oral (and the majority of agricultural leases are oral), particular state statutes automatically become a part of the lease by implication. Parties to a lease are presumed aware of existing statutes, and regulations when entering into a contractual lease arrangement. An exception may exist, however, where the parties have shown an intention contrary to the provisions in state laws governing leases.

As indicated above, all states have statutes requiring a signed writing before most transactions involving interests in real property are enforceable. While these statutes of fraud vary from state to state, oral farm leases for a period of one year are generally enforceable. However, in some states, a one-year oral farm lease to commence in the future is unenforceable. This is the situation that arises, for example, when an oral promise is made on June 1 to rent land for one year beginning on the next September 1. Other jurisdictions take a more common sense approach and simply require that the tenant take possession within one year of the making of the oral lease.

Part performance by the tenant to an agricultural lease may constitute an exception to the statute of frauds in many jurisdictions. For example, an oral agricultural lease might be removed from the requirements of the statute of frauds if payment of consideration (whether in money or in goods or services) has been made, the lessee has taken possession, or the lessee has made valuable improvements to the land. Planting a crop can be a valuable improvement for purposes of part performance.

Promissory estoppel may also be applied as an exception to the Statute of Frauds where the party seeking to enforce an oral contract can show detrimental reliance on the alleged contract.

If a tenant takes possession of the land for an indefinite time period under an oral lease, but with rental payments to be made on a periodic basis, courts may conclude that an enforceable tenancy was created for the period of the rental payment and that the lease continued until terminated by proper statutory notice.

## 1. Agricultural Leases as Personal Services Contracts

Another issue that can arise under an oral agricultural lease is what happens when either the tenant or landlord dies during the lease term. If the landlord dies, the outcome is fairly straightforward. The landlord's heirs assume the responsibilities that the decedent had before death. If the lease is to be terminated, the heirs will have to follow the appropriate state statute for terminating the tenancy. If the tenant dies, however, the outcome may be different. Some courts hold that a state statute specifying that executors and administrators have the same remedies and are subject to the same liabilities as the decedent applies to an oral agricultural lease with the result that the lease continues upon the tenant's death. Other courts hold that the lease is a contract for services to be performed exclusively by the tenant and no one else. If the tenant dies, these courts hold that the oral contract ends and no notice of termination as might be required by state statute is necessary. This outcome, however, may be different if a cash lease is involved. *See, e.g., Wilson v. Fieldgrove,* 280 Neb. 548, 787 N.W.2d 707 (2010).

# V.  THE UCC AND CONTRACT PROVISIONS

## A.  QUANTITY

Normally, the parties to a sales agreement specify clearly the essential details such as price, quantity sold, time and place of delivery and any product warranties. However, under the UCC, all terms except quantity may be implied. A statement of quantity is essential. Quantity may be stated in specific terms such as bushels of corn or head of cattle, or in terms of a seller's total output or a buyer's requirements. Output and requirements contracts involving the sale of goods are governed by § 2–306 of the UCC, which imposes certain conditions if quantity is stated with respect to the output of a seller or the requirements of a buyer to prevent one party from taking unfair advantage of price changes. Section 2–306 contains three requirements: (1) the quantity must be such as would occur in good faith; (2) the quantity must not be unreasonably disproportionate to an estimate, if stated; and (3) the quantity must not be unreasonably disproportionate to any normal output or requirement of the recent past in the absence of an estimate. The "good faith" provision is designed to eliminate any lingering questions of indefiniteness or mutuality and is intended to include (in the case of merchants) the notion of "commercial standards of fair dealing."

Over the years, two primary issues have surfaced with respect to output and requirements contracts. One issue involves the question of how much product a requirements buyer is entitled to demand. In general, the code entitles the buyer to the buyer's good faith requirements. The buyer is not permitted to insist on unneeded goods—that is not good faith. If there is a stated estimate, the buyer is not entitled to any quantity unreasonably disproportionate to the estimate. Similarly, if there is no estimate or maximum or minimum stated in the contract, the buyer may demand only "any normal or otherwise comparable prior requirements." This is generally held to mean an amount reasonably foreseeable at the time of contracting. If the requirements are measured by a particular plant, a normal (as opposed to a sudden) expansion undertaken in good faith would ordinarily be proper. For requirements contracts containing a fixed price, one should always take into consideration whether the market price had increased greatly.

Another issue that has arisen over the years with respect to output and requirements contracts is whether a requirements buyer may diminish or terminate the buyer's requirements. In essence, this issue boils down to whether a requirements buyer

may go out of business so that the buyer has no
requirements or whether the buyer may simply
change the buyer's way of doing business so that
there is a reduction in the level of requirements or
perhaps their total elimination. Under the UCC, a
requirements buyer is permitted to go out of business
or change the method of doing business if it is in good
faith. This is the case even if the reductions are
highly disproportionate to normal prior requirements
or stated estimates. In general, the issue is one of
good faith. Putting in more modern equipment, for
example, so that the buyer has fewer requirements is
not considered bad faith.

## B.   PRICE

Price may be specified or may be left for
determination at a later time. In such instances, the
buyer is required to pay a "reasonable" price which is
determined in accordance with the circumstances.
*UCC § 2–305.* A reasonable price may be measured
by the market price, and in the event there is no
market price, the reasonable price may be
determined by actual cost plus a reasonable profit, or
any other economic and legal means of valuation.

## C.   DELIVERY

If a contract fails to state a time for the delivery of
goods, a reasonable time is assumed. As for the place
of delivery, the key determination is when the risk of
loss or damage to the goods shifts from the seller to
the buyer. In general, the place of delivery is the
seller's place of business (or the location of the goods

if different from the place of business) unless specified otherwise in the contract. For instance, if the contract specifies F.O.B. (free on board) the seller's place of shipment, the seller must bear the risk and expense of placing the goods in the carrier's possession for shipment to the buyer. Conversely, if the contract specifies F.O.B. the place of destination, the seller is under a duty to transport the goods to that place at the seller's own risk and expense and there deliver the goods to the buyer. Unless the contract specifically provides, a buyer need not pay until the goods are received and the buyer has the right to inspect the goods before making payment.

In recent years, the use of fixed-price forward contracts has gained popularity among grain producers. Forward contracts are of several types, but one of the most often used varieties is a sale agreement that binds the farmer to deliver a specified quantity of grain at a future date. The farmer takes the risk that the commodity price will not rise before delivery is required under the contract. This is usually the case as commodity prices tend to decline during harvest months as new crops come onto the market. The buyer usually covers the price risk by selling an identical amount of the commodity to a third party or by use of hedges in the futures market. Forward contracting can be a sound marketing tool provided that the amount of the crop forward contracted is limited, in general, to a modest proportion of a normal crop above crop insurance carried.

In the event growing conditions lead to smaller than expected crop yields, a particular producer could find himself or herself in a position of having hedged more than he or she is able to harvest with a resulting inability to deliver against the contract. The buyer in this situation is allowed to "cover" by purchasing substitute goods and charge the extra cost back to the seller. Another concern is the tendency of some producers to use a provision in the so-called "hedge to arrive" (HTA) contract that allows the transaction to be rolled forward several months when prices are expected to be lower. If the market continues to climb during this period, some buyers (elevators) may experience a severely weakened liquidity position and may exhaust their line of credit for margin calls.

A potentially serious problem with the "continuous forward roll" of HTA contracts is that they often make the delivery requirement unclear and may be illegal under Commodity Futures Trading Commission (CFTC) regulations that ban trade options (an off-exchange derivative) on agricultural commodities. Under the Commodity Exchange Act (CEA), the CFTC may exercise jurisdiction over futures contracts, or "transactions involving contracts of sale of a commodity for future delivery. *7 U.S.C. § 2(a)(1)(A)*. Cash forward contracts, however, are specifically carved out of the CFTC's jurisdiction by 7 U.S.C. § 1a(19), which excludes from the definition of "future delivery" any sale of any cash commodity for deferred shipment or delivery. Unfortunately, the CEA does not define the terms at issue. Thus, determination of whether a particular contract is futures contract or a spot transaction requires on examination of the features of each contract. Typically, the litigation involving HTA contracts reveals that the courts tend to uphold, as legal cash forward contracts, those contracts that contemplate actual physical delivery of a commodity (at a specific time) and the farmer (as the seller of grain who is engaged in the business of farming) has sufficient commodity on hand or a reasonable expectation of being able to produce the amount specified in the contract.

## VI.  AGRICULTURAL LEASE PROVISIONS— COMMON LAW CONCERNS

### A.  IN GENERAL

Most states do not have detailed legislation governing the rights and duties of farm tenants and landlords, although statutes exist in many states setting out rights and duties under residential leases. Where farm lease statutes do exist, they tend to be limited to matters such as termination of tenancies, assignment of leases, landlord's lien for rent, and duty to control noxious weeds. Where common law rules remain in effect, they concern such things as removable fixtures, permanent improvements, rights of entry for a landlord or new tenant, lease termination, rights of the tenant to harvest crops after the lease expires, and liability for rent in case of a natural disaster.

## B.  THE DOCTRINE OF EMBLEMENTS AND "AWAY-GOING" CROPS

An emblement is a crop growing on the leased premises, and the "doctrine of emblements" gives a former tenant (or the tenant's estate) rights to the growing crop if the land if the former tenant can establish that (1) the tenancy was for an uncertain duration; (2) the termination of the lease was due to either an "act of God" or the lessor's act and occurred without the tenant's fault; and (3) the crops were planted during the tenant's right of occupancy. Relatedly, an "away-going crop" is a crop that is growing upon the termination of a land lease. Thus, under the doctrine, if a tenancy ends without the fault of the tenant before a growing crop is harvested, the tenant is entitled to the tenant's share of the crops upon harvest. An exception exists, however, if the lease has a fixed expiration date and the crops cannot be harvested before the expiration date.

Often, the doctrine of emblements is limited to annual crops that are harvested from the leased premises, rather than crops that are produced, after an initial maturation process of several years. Thus, the fruit of fruit trees has been held *not* to come within the confines of the doctrine. Christmas trees may also be outside the doctrine.

The doctrine of emblements may also be involved when the landlord dies during the term of the lease and a growing crop exists (an "act of God" can include the landlord's death). Entitlement to the crop is fairly clear when the landlord owns a fee simple interest in the leased land—the landlord's heirs succeed to the landlord's share of the crop. However, if the landlord owns less than a fee simple interest in the leased land the outcome may be different. Under the common law, a life tenant cannot make a lease for a longer period than for the tenant's life unless the remaindermen agree. Thus, when a lease is involved, upon the life tenant's death the tenancy becomes a tenancy at will and can be terminated by a demand for possession (i.e. in accordance with state law). Thus, with respect to the doctrine of emblements, the question is whether the deceased landlord's estate or the holder of the remainder interest is entitled to the landlord's share. In *Finley v. McClure,* 222 Kan. 637, 567 P.2d 851 (1977), the landlord owned only a life estate interest in certain farm ground and leased it on shares to a tenant. The landlord died before the growing wheat crop was harvested, and the court held that the landlord's crop share was a personal asset of the landlord entitling the landlord's estate to the landlord's crop share on the basis that growing crops are personal property. The Nebraska Supreme Court has reached a similar conclusion. However, the Colorado Supreme Court has held that the remainderman is entitled to the landlord's share on the theory that title to growing crops is in the lessee, rent is not due until harvest (under a crop share lease), and upon harvest the remainderman has a present interest in the land. The Oregon Court of Appeals has followed the Colorado approach. Some states, such as Illinois, have statutes governing the apportioning of rent when a life tenant landlord dies with a growing crop in the ground.

Of course, parties to an agricultural lease can avoid the application of the doctrine of emblements or the away-going crop doctrine by addressing the issue in a written lease.

## C.   COMMON LEASE PROVISIONS

### 1.  Crop and Livestock Leases

It is advisable for the parties to an agricultural lease to be as thorough as possible in covering all areas that might lead to a conflict. While it is impossible to anticipate potential trouble areas with complete accuracy, the following is a suggested list of provisions that a written lease involving agricultural land should address.

1.   Names of the parties involved.

2.   Date the lease agreement is entered into.

3.   The rental amount.

4.   Legal description of the property being rented.

5.   Length and termination of the tenancy including the beginning and ending dates of the lease.

6.   When the rental amount is to be paid and in what amount.

7.   Any limitations on the tenant's use of the land with respect to particular farming practices.

8.  Whether the landlord or the tenant decides to participate in federal farm programs.

9.  The landlord's right to enter the premises.

10. Whether the tenant or the landlord decides the crops to be planted.

11. Whether the landlord or the tenant decides what type of agricultural chemicals to use on the leased premises and whether any particular chemicals are not to be used.

12. The tenant's right to improvements placed on the land during the tenancy.

13. Whether the tenant or the landlord is responsible for hired labor.

14. Whether the tenant or the landlord is responsible for accidents occurring on the leased premises.

15. Whether the tenant has the right to hunt on the leased premises and whether the tenant or the landlord can give permission to third parties to hunt on the leased premises.

16. Tenant's rights in the event of condemnation of the leased premises.

17. Tenant's acts that, if committed, would constitute a default of the lease.

18. For livestock leases, the stocking rate.

19. Whether the tenant or the landlord is responsible for control of noxious weeds.

20. Compensation of the tenant for permanent improvements.

21. Whether the tenant or the landlord is to carry insurance for the buildings on the leased premises.

22. How amendments or alterations to the lease are to be made.

23. A statement that a partnership between the landlord and tenant is not to be created by the lease agreement.

24. Whether subleasing is permitted.

25. Whether the landlord or tenant is responsible for maintaining and repairing fences.

26. What results if either the landlord or the tenant fails to perform as required by the lease.

27. What results if either the landlord or the tenant files bankruptcy.

28. Whether the landlord or tenant is to purchase crop insurance either through a private carrier or through the government.

29. For crop share leases, the percentage of share for the landlord and tenant; the responsibility for payment of input expenses; the responsibility for reserving storage space in public warehouses; the name (landlord's or tenant's) under which the crop will be stored; and (for tax

planning purposes) whether the landlord's material participation is required.

30. Whether the tenant has an option to purchase the land if the landlord decides to sell during the period of the tenancy.

## 2. Oil and Gas Leases

For oil and gas leases, the following provisions are recommended:

1. If the mineral owner is not the surface owner, a specification that the lessee's extraction method can be through a borehole only.

2. A provision barring all strip mining and other methods that substantially destroy the surface.

3. A specification of those substances included in the lease to the exclusion of others, i.e., "all petroleum and natural gas and related hydrocarbons except coal, lignite and uranium."

4. A provision concerning the right to underground disposal of salt water in abandoned wells on the property.

5. A specification of the lessee's route of ingress and egress to existing roadways on the leased premises.

6. Whether new roadways built by the tenant must be removed when the lease terminates.

7. Whether cattleguards are required and whether the tenant or landlord will maintain locked gates.

8. A provision specifying how close a well can be located to a dwelling.

9. A provision requiring all pipelines to be buried below plow depth in cultivated areas.

10. Whether the tenant has the right to caliche found on the leased premises free of charge for the construction of drill sites and roads.

11. A provision specifying the timeframe within which the tenant's structures must be removed after the lease expires or is forfeited.

12. Whether prior consent is necessary before seismic or other geophysical operations may be conducted.

13. A minimum royalty provision.

14. Whether the landlord has free usage of gas for domestic and/or agricultural purposes.

15. Whether the tenant has free use of water, oil and gas produced on the leased premises.

16. A provision pertaining to surface damage.

17.  Whether the lessee has the right to consolidate the leased premises with adjoining leased tracts.

18.  A provision specifying whether the tenant is required to pay for damages caused by the tenant's operation to growing crops, terraces, fences, gates and other items on the leased premises.

19.  A clear specification of how the royalty to be paid the lessor is to be computed.

## 3. Wind Energy Leases

For wind energy leases, the following provisions are recommended:

1.  A clause limiting the land subject to the agreement.

2.  A clause defining the term of the agreement and what events trigger early termination.

3.  If an automatic renewal clause is included, such a clause should be drafted narrowly (from the landowner's perspective) with any renewal periods granted only upon payment of additional compensation.

4.  A clause addressing how long the land can be tied up without any construction of a wind energy facility, and the land use restrictions applicable during the pre-construction phase.

5. If land use restrictions apply during the pre-construction phase, a clause should be included compensating the landowner for the reasonable value of the restrictions.

6. A clause requiring a minimum payment to the landowner if few or no turbines are constructed.

7. A clause specifying whether the developer can assign the agreement.

8. A clause limiting the landowner's obligations to the mortgagee if the landowner consents to a mortgage by the developer.

9. A clause detailing the landowner's rights concerning usage of the property.

10. A clause specifying how taxes and utilities are to be handled.

11. A clause requiring the removal of all improvements the developer makes upon termination of the agreement.

12. If the land is enrolled in a U.S.D.A. program, a clause should be included that requires the developer to indemnify the landowner for any lost government payments or the imposition of any penalties.

13. If the property is condemned, the agreement should specify how the

condemnation award will be allocated between the parties.

14. The agreement should specify the liabilities of the parties for actions of third parties that enter the premises.

## 4. Hunting Leases

Perhaps the most important consideration for landowners considering leasing their land for hunting concerns potential liability sustained or caused by hunters on the property. All states have some version of a recreational use statute which provides liability protection to landowners that allow others to come on the premises for recreational purposes, which includes hunting. However, under some state statutes, the landowner cannot charge a fee to receive the statutory liability protection. In addition, other statutory requirements may have to be satisfied.

A hunting lease is not technically a "lease" but rather a license to use the property for hunting purposes. It is a mere contract right to use the property for that specific purpose as defined by the parties. Thus, it is important for the parties to reduce their understanding to writing and include in the written contract certain key components such as a clear identification of the parties, a property description, the types of hunting allowed and when it is allowed, termination provision and any options for renewal, liability waiver and indemnification language, and payment terms.

## VII.  WARRANTIES

Because livestock, feed, seed or pesticides are goods, sales and other transactions involving such goods result in the creation of warranties. These warranties can be either express or implied. Express warranties are stated as part of the sales agreement and become part of the basis of the bargain, but implied warranties are read into the sales agreement by the UCC, absent specific language or circumstances excluding warranties. A sales agreement may result in the creation of two types of implied warranties: the implied warranty of merchantability and the implied warranty of fitness for a particular purpose.

### A.   EXPRESS WARRANTIES

Express warranties generally result from explicit statements made by the seller and are the most common way of imposing liability on sellers of agricultural products. Once an express warranty has been made, it is very difficult to disclaim and, in general, an express warranty cannot be limited. Under the UCC, an express warranty can be created in three ways. In each case, it is important that the event creating the express warranty occur at a time when the buyer could have relied upon it.

The first way an express warranty can be created is for the seller to make "any affirmation of fact or promise" that relates to the goods and becomes part of the basis of the bargain. The warranty is that the goods will conform to the affirmation or promise. Oral or written statements concerning the goods that the buyer relies on in purchasing the goods can create an express warranty. In agricultural sales, express warranties usually involve the seller's oral or written statements concerning the goods. If the statements become "part of the basis of the bargain," that is, if they tend to induce the buyer to make the purchase, they may be considered express warranties. But, statements do not create an express warranty if they are statements of opinion, honestly held, or merely commendation of the goods ("puffing talk"). *See, e.g., Schmaltz v. Nissen,* 431 N.W.2d 657 (S.D. 1988); *Tyson v. Ciba-Geigy Corp.,* 82 N.C. App. 626, 347 S.E.2d 473 (1986); *Fulton v. Vogt,* 583 N.W.2d 673 (Wis. Ct. App. 1998).

At some point a statement moves from being merely an opinion and becomes an express warranty because the buyer reasonably understands that only an opinion is involved. For example, a statement by the seller that "all of my cows are bred," or "all of my hay is of the highest quality" or "my tractor is in good shape" could create an express warranty that the goods (cows or hay) will conform to the particular affirmation or promise. Likewise, statements contained in product labels may be deemed to create express warranties.

An express warranty can also be created if the seller provides "any description of the goods" that becomes part of the basis of the bargain. The warranty is that the goods will conform to the description. Similarly, an express warranty can be created if the seller displays a "sample or model" of the goods. If the sample or model becomes part of the basis of the bargain, the warranty is that all of the goods will conform to the sample or model. *See, e.g., Dakota Grain Co., Inc. v. Ehrmantrout,* 502 N.W.2d 234 (N.D. 1993). The UCC creates a presumption that any sample or model is intended to become a basis of the bargain. To prevent a sample or model from creating an express warranty, the presumption must be rebutted by the seller.

In general, express warranties are not subject to exclusion or modification and, once made, are very difficult to disclaim or limit. The UCC requires that "[w]ords or conduct relevant to the creation of an express warranty [be construed as consistent with] words or conduct tending to negate or limit warranty . . . wherever reasonable . . . [and] negation or limitation is inoperative to the extent that such construction is unreasonable.

> **Note:** While it is difficult for an express warranty to be disclaimed once created, it may not be created if it doesn't become a basis of the bargain between the parties. For example, the statement by a tractor seller that the tractor was in "excellent condition" and "field ready" did not become a basis of the bargain with the buyer because the buyer inspected the tractor, determined it was in need of some repairs and was familiar with tractors based on his experience. *See, e.g., Chinn v. Fecht,* No. 3–14–0320, 2015 Ill. App. Unpub. LEXIS 20 (Ill. Ct. App. Jan. 9, 2015).

Parties to sales contracts should exercise caution when reducing oral agreements to writing with the intent of making the written contract the final agreement between the parties. Oral statements may inadvertently be omitted from a later writing, but could have served as the basis of the bargain. As such, an express warranty could have been created orally, but eliminated by a subsequent writing omitting the relied upon oral statements. The best approach may be to ensure that all previously negotiated terms are included in any subsequent written agreement.

Any representations made by a company, its employees, consultants or agents pertaining to a product, whether oral or written, can potentially be treated as express warranties. Thus, an important part of any loss prevention program is to closely monitor any representations made and provide training concerning appropriate representations.

## B.  IMPLIED WARRANTIES

Implied warranties are imposed by law to assure a fair result and fulfill the buyer's expectations that an acceptable product is being purchased. There are two types of implied warranties; the implied warranty of merchantability and the implied warranty of fitness for a particular purpose.

## 1.  Implied Warranty of Merchantability

The UCC holds merchants to a higher standard of business conduct than other participants to sales transactions. In every sale by a merchant who deals in goods of the kind sold, there is an implied warranty that the goods are merchantable. The warranty of merchantability exists even if the seller made no statements or promises and did not know of any defect in the goods. In order for goods to be merchantable, they must be goods that:

(a)  pass without objection in the trade under the contract description;

(c)  in the case of fungible goods, are of fair average quality within the description;

(d)  are fit for the ordinary purposes for which such goods are used;

(e)  run, within the variations permitted by the agreement, of even kind, quality and quantity within each unit and among all units involved;

(f)  are adequately contained, packaged, and labeled as the agreement may require;

(g)  conform to the promises or affirmations of fact made on the container or label if any.

Requirements (a) through (c) above are most often encountered in agricultural sales, with much of the focus on whether the goods are fit for the ordinary purposes for which they are used. The ordinary purpose standard is breached when goods are not reasonably safe or when they cannot be used to meet their normal functions. *See, e.g., Latimer v. William Mueller & Son* 149 Mich. App. 620, 386 N.W.2d 618 (1986); *Eggl v. Letvin Equipment Co.,* 632 N.W.2d 435 (N.D. 2001).

Requirement (d) involves bulk purchases and specifies that goods sold in bulk must be of an even kind, quality and quantity.

Requirements (e) and (f) pertain to goods that are sold in containers or packaging, and reflect an overlap between express warranties and the implied warranty of merchantability. They are especially important in sales of labeled goods, such as feed, seed or pesticides. Some courts have suggested that statements on labels or containers create both an express and an implied warranty.

Merchantability also involves the standard of merchantability in the particular trade. Usage of trade is defined as "any practice or method of dealing having such regularity of observance in a place, vocation or trade as to justify an expectation that it will be observed with respect to the transaction in question." If a product fails to satisfy industry standards, an implied warranty of merchantability may arise. *See, e.g.,* in *Kassab v. Central Soya,* 432 Pa. 217, 246 A.2d 848 (1968).

Even if a particular farmer does not qualify as a "merchant," known product defects must be disclosed to a potential buyer. Every seller with knowledge of defects must fully disclose defects that are not apparent to the buyer on reasonable inspection. This duty arises out of the underlying rationale behind the implied warranty of merchantability, which is to assure that the buyer is getting what is being paid for, and the UCC's requirement that market participants operate in "good faith."

The UCC warranty provisions also apply to sales transactions involving livestock and have attracted considerable attention in livestock agriculture in recent years. In a series of cases in the 1970s, courts applied the UCC implied warranty provisions to the sale of livestock as goods. The livestock industry strongly reacted and successfully lobbied for an exclusionary provision limiting the application of implied warranties in livestock sales. Some version of the statutory exclusion now exists in about half of the states, especially those states where the livestock industry is of major economic importance. The statutes are of three general types: those that exempt sellers from implied warranties in all situations, those providing that no implied warranty exists unless the seller knew the animals were sick at time of sale, and those providing an exemption if certain conditions are met. The Iowa statute excludes implied warranties if certain disclosures are made concerning the animals.

The statutory exclusion of warranties in livestock sale transactions applies only to implied warranties; express warranties are not affected. Express warranties can still be made in livestock transactions and may be particularly important in transactions involving breeding livestock. Many sellers tend to make statements that might rise to the level of an express warranty in order to induce buyers to conclude the sale. Such statements can become a part of the basis of the bargain and create an express warranty enforceable against the seller.

The typical statutory exclusion also is inapplicable in situations where the seller "knowingly" sells animals that are diseased or sick. However, it is likely to be difficult for a livestock buyer to prove that the seller knew animals were diseased or sick at the

time they were sold. Under the UCC, a seller
" 'knows' or 'has knowledge' of a fact when the seller
has 'actual knowledge' of it." Thus, in order to
overcome the statutory exclusion, the buyer must
prove (most likely by circumstantial evidence) the
seller's actual knowledge regarding the animal's
disease or sickness.

Under most state exclusionary statutes, the
meaning of "diseased or sick" is unclear. For instance,
in breeding animals, the failure to provide offspring
may result from recognizable diseases or from
defects, often genetic, that historically have not been
considered diseases. It is uncertain whether the
statutory exclusion of implied warranties applies in
circumstances involving genetic defects. Presently,
no court in a jurisdiction having the exclusion has
addressed the issue. Similarly, uncertainty exists
with respect to the application of the exclusion to the
sale of semen or embryo transfers, which are
increasingly common in the livestock industry.
Arguably, the livestock exclusion does not apply to
semen sales since semen is not "livestock."

## 2. Implied Warranty of Fitness for a Particular Purpose

A second implied warranty that can arise in a sales
transaction is that the goods are fit for the buyer's
particular purpose. *UCC § 2–315.* This warranty
arises when the seller has reason to know of the
buyer's particular purpose for purchasing the goods
and the buyer relies on the seller's skill or judgment
to select or furnish suitable goods. Unlike the implied

warranty of merchantability, the implied warranty of fitness for a particular purpose can be imposed on any seller (except possibly for seed and livestock, and except for a finance lessor) regardless of whether the seller is a merchant. This warranty exists if the facts surrounding the sale are such that the seller should realize that the buyer wishes to utilize the goods for a particular purpose and the buyer relies on the seller's skill and judgment in furnishing suitable goods for that particular purpose. The seller need not have actual knowledge of the particular purpose for which the goods are intended or that the buyer is relying on the seller's skill or judgment. The sale of specialty feeds is particularly susceptible to a claim that an implied warranty of fitness for a particular purpose has arisen. Specialty feeds are typically fed to animals with unique needs, and courts generally presume that sellers know those needs.

Even though a buyer cannot clearly establish reliance on the seller's skill or judgment to furnish suitable goods, some courts have still allowed a damaged buyer to recover. For example, in the case reproduced below, the plaintiff was a sophisticated buyer with considerable experience in grain and hogs, and there was little evidence that he relied on the skill and knowledge of the seller to select the particular feed corn involved that turned out to be contaminated with vomitoxin. The court, nevertheless, permitted recovery under a warranty of fitness theory for the death of the plaintiff's hogs after eating the contaminated corn.

A " 'particular purpose' differs from the ordinary purpose for which the goods are used. . . ." The rationale is that the implied warranty of merchantability covers basic uses for goods, whereas the implied warranty of fitness for a particular purpose covers a buyer's specific use. This does not mean that a sale contract cannot include both an implied warranty of merchantability and an implied warranty of fitness for a particular purpose. If both warranties are created, the UCC provides that "any question of fact as to which warranty was intended by the parties to apply must be resolved in favor of the warranty of fitness for particular purpose. . ."

## C.   DISCLAIMING IMPLIED WARRANTIES

In order to disclaim or modify an implied warranty of merchantability, the seller's "language must mention merchantability and in case of a writing must be conspicuous. . . ." Oral disclaimers of implied warranties of merchantability must use the word "merchantability," and in written disclaimers, the disclaiming language must be conspicuous within the written document. A disclaimer of an implied warranty of fitness for a particular purpose must be in writing.

The UCC specifically provides three ways in which all implied warranties can be excluded. First, unless the circumstances indicate otherwise, all implied warranties are excluded by expressions like "as is," "with all faults" or other language which in common understanding calls the buyer's attention to the exclusion of warranties and makes plain that there is no implied warranty. *See, e.g., Rayle Tech, Inc. v. DEKALB Swine Breeders, Inc.,* 133 F.3d 1405 (11th Cir. 1998). *But see, Snelten v. Schmidt Implement Co.,* 269 Ill. App.3d 988, 647 N.E.2d 1071 (1995).

The second manner in which an implied warranty can be excluded is when the buyer, before entering into the contract, examines the goods or a sample or a model as fully as desired or refuses to examine the goods. In this instance, there is no implied warranty with regard to defects which an examination should have revealed to the buyer. The third way an implied warranty can be excluded is by course of dealing, course of performance or usage of trade. The seller's relationship with the buyer, industry practice or usage of trade can exclude an implied warranty. For example, if the parties have previously engaged in contracts for the sale of livestock or feed with all previous contracts containing a disclaimer provision, or the industry practice is to limit liability, implied warranties may be excluded.

At the federal level, the Magnuson-Moss Warranty Federal Trade Commission Improvement Act *(15 U.S.C. §§ 2301–2312)* precludes the disclaimer or modification of any implied warranty created by state law when a consumer product supplier makes any written warranty with respect to a product. The implied warranties can only be limited to the duration of the express warranties, unless the express warranties are designed as a "Full Warranty," in which case the implied warranties cannot be limited even in their duration. Thus, the only way for a consumer product supplier to avoid extending implied warranties is to not provide any express warranties. Also, laws in some states prohibit sellers in consumer transactions from excluding, modifying or limiting implied warranties of merchantability or fitness. Any such limitation is usually considered void unless the buyer knew of the defect before purchasing and this knowledge became part of the basis of the sale. The only exceptions are for sales of livestock for agricultural purposes (as indicated above) and sales of seed for planting. In seed sale transactions, the Federal Seed Act (FSA) allows the seed sellers to use disclaimers, limited warranties, or non-warranty clauses in invoices, advertising or labeling. However, the FSA does not permit such limitation on warranties to be used as a defense in any criminal prosecution or other civil proceeding based on the FSA. As a result, seed purchasers may be faced with label disclaimers limiting liability to the price of the seed. Courts are split on the validity of such disclaimers with most courts invalidating them only if liability results from the seller's own negligence or intentional violation of the law.

Both express and implied warranties extend to any natural person in the family or household of the buyer or who is a guest in the buyer's home, if it is reasonable to expect that the person would use, consume or be affected by the goods.

## D.   ONE-SIDED CONTRACTS

Even if all of the UCC's requirements for language and form of disclaimer have been satisfied, a court may still refuse to enforce the disclaimer if the court determines that the seller is attempting to avoid the seller's basic obligations of "good faith, diligence, reasonableness and care," or that the disclaimer is "unconscionable" or that it is against "public policy." Most of the problems in this area involve printed form disclaimer of warranties. *See, e.g., Henningson v. Bloomfield Motors, Inc.,* 32 N.J. 358, 161 A.2d 69 (1960).

Questions of enforceability sometimes arise concerning contract clauses that place a limitation on damages. *See, e.g., Mullis v. Speight Seed Farms, Inc.,* 234 Ga. App. 27, 505 S.E.2d 818 (1998); *but see, Brunsman v. DEKALB Swine Breeders, Inc.,* 138 F.3d 358 (8th Cir. 1998).

## 1.  Agricultural Production Contracts

Agricultural production contracts also raise concerns about one-sidedness and unconscionable terms. These contracts generally provide for the raising of livestock, birds or crops with the farmer supplying the facilities and labor and the integrator supplying the livestock, birds or seeds and the feed and other supplies. The integrator generally retains title to the livestock, birds or crops and the contract generally establishes the amount paid to the farmer by the quantity and quality of the final product. Many of these contracts are forms drafted by the integrator, with no terms negotiated by the parties. Such contracts may be held to be contracts of adhesion and could be held void depending upon whether the factual circumstances demonstrate unconscionability. *See, e.g.,* Okla. Att'y Gen. Op. No. 2001–17 (Apr. 11, 2001). In any event, contracts of adhesion will be interpreted against the drafter.

Agricultural production contracts commonly contain an arbitration clause requiring the parties to submit any contract dispute to an arbitrator before going to court. Such provisions may violate state law. *See, e.g.,* in *Tyson Foods, Inc. v. Archer, et al.,* 356 Ark. 136, 147 S.W.3d 681 (2004). In addition, a provision was included in the 2002 Farm Bill prohibiting confidentiality clauses in agricultural production contracts.

## 2. Genetically Modified Organism (GMO) Contracts

Companies owning the intellectual property rights to GMO seeds require farmers to sign grower technology agreements to gain access to the seed. By signing an agreement, a farmer also agrees to be bound by the seed company's requirements and guidelines for using the GMO technology. Typically, the agreements are applied as part of the seed purchase and farmers are not given the opportunity to negotiate the agreements. Indeed, most technology agreements are triggered upon the opening of a bag of seed and state that if a farmer wishes not to be bound by the terms of the agreement the seed bags must be returned unopened to the seed dealer. Some common provisions in GMO technology agreements include the following:

1.   A clause stating that the farmer agrees to
     use the technology for the planting of a
     single crop.

2.   A clause prohibiting the saving of the seed
     or the supplying of the seed to anyone else.

3.   A clause requiring the payment of a
     technology fee.

4.   A provision allowing the seed company to
     review the farmer's FSA crop reporting
     information including acreage history,
     Form 578, aerial photographs, insurance
     claim documentation and dealer/retailer
     invoices for seed and chemical transactions.

5.   A provision allowing the company holding
     the intellectual property rights in the seed
     access to any records and receipts relevant
     to the grower's performance under the
     agreement.

6.   A clause stating that the agreement has no
     time limit.

7.   A clause giving the company the right to
     enter the grower's fields to conduct
     inspections to ensure that the grower is
     complying with the agreement, including
     the monitoring of refuge practices.

8.   A clause placing the burden on the grower
     to ensure that GMO grain is kept out of
     markets where it is not authorized.

9. A clause limiting the company's liability and resulting damages related to performance problems with the GMO seed.

10. A clause specifying the governing law to be applied when interpreting the contract.

11. A clause providing for remedies upon breach, including the payment of attorney's fees.

## VIII.   CONTRACT PERFORMANCE

### A.   RISK OF LOSS

If the seller is a merchant, the risk of loss generally passes to the buyer upon receipt of the goods. If the seller is not a merchant, however, the risk of loss generally passes to the buyer upon tender of delivery. Where the contract authorizes the seller to ship by carrier, and the contract does not require the seller to deliver the goods to a particular destination, the risk of loss passes to the buyer when the goods are delivered to the carrier. If the seller is required to deliver the goods to a particular destination, the risk of loss passes to the buyer when the goods are there tendered so as to enable the buyer to take delivery. If the goods fail to conform to the contract, the risk of loss remains with the seller until acceptance or the nonconformity is cured.

### B.   RIGHT OF INSPECTION

The buyer has a right of inspection of the goods before payment unless the delivery is cash-on-delivery (C.O.D.) or the contract requires payment before inspection.

## C.   COMMERCIAL IMPRACTICABILITY

A seller is excused from timely delivery of goods if performance becomes commercially impractical because of unforeseen circumstances. However, if a farmer fails to deliver a crop because drought, hail or other weather has destroyed it, the farmer is generally not excused from performance unless the contract called for the crop to be grown on a specified geographic area (such as a 160-acre tract) and weather damage reduces the amount available for delivery. *UCC § 2–615, Comment 9. See, e.g., ConAgra, Inc. v. Bartlett Partnership,* 248 Neb. 933, 540 N.W.2d 333 (1995); *Larsen v. Grabowski,* No. A-95-013, 1996 WL 119509 (Neb. App. Mar. 19, 1996).

## D.   ADEQUATE ASSURANCE

A sales contract imposes an obligation on both the seller and the buyer that each party's expectation of receiving performance will not be impaired. When reasonable grounds for insecurity arise (determined by reference to commercial standards) with respect to the performance of either the seller or the buyer, the insecure party may, by written demand, seek adequate assurance of due performance of the other party. *UCC § 2–609(1).* Until adequate assurance is received, the insecure party may, if commercially reasonable, suspend any performance for which the insecure party has not already received the agreed upon return. If the contract involves merchants, the reasonableness of grounds for insecurity and the adequacy of any assurance offered is determined in accordance with commercial standards. A demand for adequate assurance must be commercially reasonable.

A party feeling insecure should proceed cautiously when making a demand for adequate assurance. *See, e.g., Farmers Cooperative Elevator v. Heyes*, No. 23493 (Dist. Ct. for Kossuth County, Iowa, Dec. 23, 1997); *Land O'Lakes, Inc. v. Hanig* 610 N.W.2d 518 (Iowa 2000); *Shields Pork Plus, Inc. v. Swiss Valley Ag Service,* 329 Ill. App. 3d 305, 767 N.E.2d 945 (2002).

The failure of a party on whom a proper demand for due performance has been made to provide assurance of due performance within a reasonable time (not to exceed 30 days) results in repudiation of the contract. *UCC § 2–609(4).*

## IX.  REMEDIES UPON BREACH OF CONTRACT

### A.  BUYER'S REMEDIES

### 1.  Right of Rejection

A buyer has a right to reject goods that do not conform to the contract. Under the UCC, a buyer may reject nonconforming goods if such nonconformity substantially impairs the contract. A buyer usually is not allowed to cancel a contract for only trivial defects in goods. *See, e.g., Hubbard v. UTZ Quality Foods, Inc.* 903 F. Supp. 444 (W.D. N.Y. 1995).

## 2. Right to "Cover"

The traditional measure of damages for a seller's total breach of contract is the difference between the market price and the contract price. *See, e.g., Tongish v. Thomas,* 251 Kan. 728, 840 P.2d 471 (1992). The UCC retains this rule, UCC § 2–713(1), but also allows an aggrieved buyer to "cover" by making a good faith purchase or contract to purchase substitute goods without unreasonable delay. *UCC § 2–712(1).* The buyer that covers is entitled to recover from the seller the difference between the cost of cover and the contract price. *UCC § 2–712(2).*

---

**Example 3:**

Assume the same facts as set forth in Example 2 except that Albert Black signed and returned within ten days of receipt the written confirmation sent by the elevator. Assume that the December 2016 price for wheat was $5.50 per bushel. Because of poor growing conditions, Albert's wheat crop only yielded 17,500 bushels which Albert delivered to the elevator pursuant to the forward contract. Will Albert be excused from delivery of the additional 7,500 bushels of wheat as required under the forward contract? Likewise, what, if any, is the elevator's remedy? Assume the July 2017 market wheat price is $6.45 per bushel.

Albert will be excused from delivery of the additional 7,500 bushels of wheat as required under the forward contract only if the forward contract legally described the land on which the crop was to be grown and it was clear that Albert was selling the output of that tract. However, even if the contract does specifically describe the acres where the crop is to be grown, Albert will be required to deliver whatever he produces. He will only be relieved from the shortfall. As for the elevator's remedy, the elevator will be able to "cover" by taking the difference between the July 2017 market wheat price and the December 2016 price times the number of bushels of shortfall (7,500 × $.95 = $7,125). That amount can be charged to the seller.

---

Most of the agricultural cases concerning "covering" focus on the difference between the goods purchased as cover and the goods called for in the contract (cover goods must be like-kind substitutes), and the timeframe within which cover was carried out (there must be no unreasonable delay). *See, e.g., Erie Casein Company, Inc. v. Anric Corporation* 217 Ill. App. 3d 602, 577 N.E.2d 892 (1991); *Trinidad Bean and Elevator Co. v. Frosh,* 1 Neb. App. 281, 494 N.W.2d 347 (1992).

## 3.  Right of Specific Performance

If the goods are unique, the buyer may obtain possession of the goods by court order. This is known as specific performance of the contract. Contracts for the sale of real estate or art work, for example, are contracts for the sale of unique goods and the buyer's remedy is to have the contract specifically performed. Monetary damages can be awarded to a contracting party along with specific performance if it can be shown that damages resulted from the other party's failure to render timely performance.

## 4. Nonconforming Goods

A buyer has a right before acceptance to inspect delivered goods at any reasonable place and time and in any reasonable manner. The reasonableness of the inspection is a question of trade usage and past practices between the parties. If the goods do not conform to the contract, the buyer may reject them all within a reasonable time and notify the seller, accept them all despite their nonconformance, or accept part (limited to commercial units) and reject the rest. Any rejection must occur within a reasonable time, and the seller must be notified of the buyer's unconditional rejection. The buyer's right of revocation is not conditioned upon whether it is the seller or the manufacturer that is responsible for the nonconformity. *UCC § 2–608.* The key is whether the nonconformity substantially impairs the value of the goods to the buyer.

A buyer rejecting nonconforming goods is entitled to reimbursement from the seller for expenses incurred in caring for the goods. The buyer may also recover damages from the seller for nondelivery of suitable goods, including incidental and consequential damages. If the buyer accepts nonconforming goods, the buyer may deduct damages due from amounts owed the seller under the contract if the seller is notified of the buyer's intention to do so. *See, e.g., Gragg Farms and Nursery v. Kelly Green Landscaping* 81 Ohio Misc. 2d 34; 674 N.E.2d 785 (1996).

## 5. Timeframe for Exercising Remedies

The UCC allows buyers a reasonable time to determine whether purchased goods are fit for the purpose for which the goods were purchased, and to rescind the sale if the goods are unfit. Whether a right to rescind is exercised within a reasonable time is to be determined from all of the circumstances. *UCC § 1–204.* The buyer's right to inspect goods includes an opportunity to put the purchased goods to their intended use. Generally, the more severe the defect, the greater the time the buyer has to determine whether the goods are suitable to the buyer.

### B. SELLER'S REMEDIES

The seller may refuse delivery to an insolvent buyer or refuse delivery unless payment is made in cash. Goods shipped to an insolvent buyer may be stopped in transit. If the insolvent buyer has received the goods, the seller may reclaim them by making a demand within ten days for their return. If a solvent buyer fails to make a payment when due or repudiates the contract, the seller may stop delivery of goods in transit. Once a buyer accepts goods conforming to the contract, the goods cannot be returned and the buyer is obligated to pay the price when due. An action may be brought for the contract price upon nonpayment. Goods which the buyer has wrongfully refused to accept may be sold by the seller to someone else. Unfinished goods intended to be completed for the particular contract may be similarly treated. Resale of goods by the seller may be either at a public or private sale. The seller may recover damages from the buyer for wrongful nonacceptance of goods or for repudiation of the contract. The measure of damages is usually the difference between the contract price and the market price at the time and place of tender of delivery, or the profit which the seller would have made under full performance of the contract by the buyer. Sometimes the seller is entitled to the contract price plus any incidental damages incurred as a result of the buyer's breach.

## C. LIQUIDATED DAMAGES

A contract may provide for specific damages to be paid in the event of breach by either party. The specified amount must be reasonable at the time of contract formation or in the light of the anticipated or actual harm caused by the breach. Additional factors for determining whether the specified damage amount is reasonable concern the difficulties of proving actual loss and the inconvenience of otherwise obtaining an adequate remedy. However, terms that fix an unreasonably large amount of liquidated damages are void as a penalty.

## D. HANDLING DEPOSITS AFTER BREACH

If the seller justifiably withholds the delivery of goods because of the buyer's breach, the buyer is entitled to receive back the amount by which the deposits or payments exceed the sum specified under a reasonable liquidated damage provision, or 20% of the amount for which the buyer is obligated or $500, whichever is smaller.

## X.   STATUTE OF LIMITATIONS

Actions founded on written contracts must be brought within a specified time, generally five to ten years. For unwritten contracts, actions generally must be brought within three to five years. In some states, however, the statute of limitations is the same for both written and oral contracts. A common limitation period is four years. Also, by agreement in some states, the parties may reduce the period of limitation for sale of goods but cannot extend it.

# CHAPTER 3
# SECURED TRANSACTIONS

## I. OVERVIEW

Most of the legal issues arising from agricultural financing transactions are governed by Article 9 of the Uniform Commercial Code (UCC). In general, security interests in personal property are governed by Article 9.

The typical farmer or rancher utilizes three types of financing: long term, intermediate, and short term. Long term financing is used for buying land and improvements. Intermediate term financing is commonly used to purchase equipment, breeding livestock and smaller buildings. Short term financing is used for covering operating and production expenses and some equipment purchases. Farmers and ranchers borrow heavily from both public and private sources. The primary sources for long term real estate loans are insurance companies, private individuals and the Farm Credit System. Operational financing typically is provided by commercial banks, the Farm Credit System, vendors of inputs (feed, seed, fertilizer and chemicals) and the Farm Service Agency (formerly the Farmers Home Administration (FmHA)).

There are two categories of farm debt: real estate debt and debt not associated with real estate. Debt not associated with real estate, if it is secured, is usually secured by collateral such as crops, livestock and farm equipment, and is governed by Article 9.

Article 9 treats all security interests in personal property under the same set of rules. Before the UCC was enacted, most states had numerous security devices. These included chattel mortgages that secured loans for livestock, fertilizer, seed, feed and equipment; conditional sales contracts that were often used in the purchase of farm equipment and durable consumer goods; assignments of accounts receivable; and pledges. These antiquated devices can still be used under the UCC, but their effect is to create a "security interest." Before enactment of the UCC, some confusion existed over which device applied in a particular case. Article 9 eliminates much of the confusion by establishing a law of chattel security designed for modern day problems and applicable to purchase money transactions as well as loans against existing property, but some states have altered certain sections of Article 9.

## II. SECURED TRANSACTION BASICS

### A. SCOPE OF ARTICLE 9

#### 1. Overview

Occasionally, a lender loans money on an unsecured basis with the lender's security based solely on the borrower's reputation and promise to repay. More likely, however, a lender will require collateral to make sure the borrower repays the loan. Usually, the lender requires the borrower to sign a written agreement giving the lender legal rights to the collateral (such as the borrower's crops, livestock or equipment) if the borrower fails to repay the loan.

The situation where personal property or fixtures are used to secure payment of a debt or the performance of an obligation is called a secured transaction. Secured transactions under Article 9 of the UCC involve personal property and fixtures including loans on crops, livestock, inventories, consumer goods and accounts receivable. Article 9 does not govern mortgages on real estate purchases. Instead, mortgages on real estate are governed by different state laws dealing specifically with mortgages.

---

**Example 1:**

John Jones loaned Sally Smith $5,000. To secure the debt, Sally granted a security interest in her livestock. If Sally fails to repay the loan, John can exercise his rights as a secured party under Article 9. This means that John can take possession of the livestock, prepare them for resale or otherwise dispose of them in accordance with Article 9, and apply the proceeds to the debt that Sally owes.

---

Article 9 also applies to transactions that create a security interest in personal property or fixtures by contract. These include pledges, assignments, chattel mortgages, chattel trust deeds, factor's liens, equipment trusts, condition sales, trust receipts, other liens or title retention contracts or leases or consignments intended as security. *See, e.g., Herrington Livestock Auction Co. v. Verschoor,* 179 N.W.2d 491 (Iowa 1970).

Revisions to Article 9 have expanded the scope of Article 9 to also include payment intangibles and promissory notes. While accounts were covered under the former version of Article 9, the revisions expand the definition of an "account." For example, under the revisions an installment land contract is an "account" and is not a general intangible. That means that a creditor must describe it as an account and must perfect by filing a financing statement describing the collateral as the payments to be made under the contract (and not as a payment intangible or general intangible). So, while Article 9 does not apply to real estate transactions where real estate itself is the only collateral, it does apply to real estate transactions involving payments under an installment land contract as a contract for deed. *See, e.g., In re Huntzinger,* 268 B.R. 263 (Bankr. D. Kan. 2001).

The Revised Article 9 also applies to consignments and to agricultural liens.

## 2. Application to Leases

Difficult questions may also arise in attempting to determine whether a security interest arises when a lease is involved. For example, a lease may be a "true" lease (governed by Article 2A of the UCC) or it may, in fact, be a lease "intended as security" (in which event it is within the scope of Article 9, and must be perfected like all other security interests). In theory, the distinguishing characteristics of a lease and a security interest are easy to identify. If a seller of goods retains a security interest to secure the unpaid purchase price, the buyer receives the property and can keep it unless the buyer later defaults. The secured creditor (seller) can proceed against the goods only if the debtor defaults, but only to the extent of the unpaid debt. Thus, the secured party has only a limited contingent interest in the goods. Under a lease, however, the lessor always retains an interest in the leased property. When the lease expires, the goods return to the lessor. If the lessee defaults during the lease term, the lessor can retake possession of the goods, but is not required to dispose of the goods (by entering into a new lease).

Whether a lease is intended as security is to be determined by the facts of each case. The focus is on the nature and economics of the transfer, rather than on the parties' intent (*UCC § 1–201, Comment 37*). The fundamental economic component of a lease is that the lessor maintains a residual interest in the goods. Thus, the terms of a particular transaction should be analyzed to determine whether the lessor is really being compensated for that residual interest. For instance, if the transaction is structured such that the lessee becomes the owner of the goods at the end of the lease term without paying additional funds, the transaction is really a disguised secured transaction because the original amount paid under the "lease" fully compensated the "lessor" for the complete interest in the goods *See, e.g., In re Zaleha,* 159 B.R. 581 (Bankr. D. Idaho 1993).

The inclusion of an option to purchase does not, by itself, make the lease one intended for security. However, if the option price is nominal and the lessee cannot terminate the lease, the transaction creates a security interest. *See, e.g., In re Buehne,* 321 B.R. 239 (Bankr. S.D. Ill. 2005). Courts from several jurisdictions have held that permitting a lessee to apply 85% or more of the lease payments against the purchase price makes the lease one "intended for security," and, therefore, it must be perfected in the same manner as other security interests in order to have priority against the conflicting interests of third parties.

---

**Example 2:**

Tex Johnson leased some farm equipment to Jiggs Black. The lease provided that Jiggs could apply 85% of the lease payments against the purchase price. Tex did not file a financing statement or otherwise perfect. After entering into the lease, Jiggs filed bankruptcy. The bankruptcy trustee takes the leased goods free from the lease and Tex loses his rights in the goods, because the lease was "one intended for security" and should have been perfected under Article 9 as a security interest in order to have priority with respect to the trustee in bankruptcy.

---

Under the "economic realities" test, if items are leased with options to purchase and it would be foolish for the lessee not to exercise one or more of the options at the end of the lease term, the lease will be construed as a lease intended for security and is within the scope of Article 9. *See, e.g., In re Super Feeders, Inc.,* 236 B.R. 267 (Bankr. D. Neb. 1999). Lessors that are unsure whether a particular lease is a "true" lease or a lease "intended as security" should file a financing statement using the terms "lessor" and "lessee" instead of "secured party" and "debtor."

While the filing of the financing statement will not, by itself, determine whether or not the lease is intended as security, if it is determined for other reasons that the lease is intended as security, the security interest should be perfected by filing. In any event, improper classification could lead to a conversion action. *See Towe Farms, Inc. v. Central Iowa Production Credit Assoc.*, 528 F. Supp. 500 (S.D. Iowa 1981).

### 3. Consignment Situations

Frequently, it is difficult to determine whether an Article 9 security interest is involved in consignment situations. A consignment involves the delivery of goods to a person for sale, where the seller maintains a place of business at which the seller deals in goods of the kind involved under a name other than the name of the person making delivery, and title is retained by the seller until payment or resale. In a consignment situation, the goods delivered will be subject to the claims of the merchant's creditors unless the supplier (consignor) complies with any applicable law providing for a consignor's interest or the like to be evidenced by a signed writing establishing that the person conducting the business is generally known by his creditors to be substantially engaged in selling the goods of others, or complies with the perfection provisions of Article 9. In that event, the consignor may file a financing statement using the terms "consignor" and "consignee" instead of "secured party" and "debtor," and the filing of such a financing statement should not of itself be a factor in determining whether or not the consignment is intended as security. However, if it is determined for other reasons that the consignment is a secured transaction, the security interest will be perfected by the filing.

## B.   DEFINITIONS

### 1.  Security Agreement

A security agreement is a written agreement between a borrower and a lender that gives the lender an interest or a legal right (known as a security interest) in the borrower's property. Another way to think of a security interest is that it is the right of the lender to take the property described in the agreement if the loan is not repaid according to the agreement. Similarly, if a seller retains title to goods, all the seller has is a security interest in the goods. Thus, a security agreement is simply an agreement that creates or provides for a security interest. In most jurisdictions, specific "words of grant" are not required. All that is necessary is evidence of intent to create a security interest.

Under Revised Article 9, the debtor need not sign the security agreement. While a debtor may sign the security agreement, the debtor must "authenticate" a record containing the security agreement. Authentication can be made by the debtor signing a writing containing a security agreement that identifies the debtor, or by the debtor sending an electronic message containing a security agreement in an encrypted form that identifies the debtor as the sender. An authenticated agreement, however, is not required if the security) and the collateral is not a certificated security. The same is true if the collateral is a certificated security in registered form delivered to the secured party pursuant to the secured party, pursuant to the debtor's security agreement, or the collateral is deposit accounts, electronic chattel paper, investment property or letter-of-credit rights and the secured party has control pursuant to the debtor's security agreement. Thus, when the debtor has possession of the collateral, the debtor must have authenticated a security agreement that provides for a description of the collateral and, if the security interest covers timber to be cut, a description of the land covered. *UCC § 9–203(b)(3)(A).*

The function of the security agreement is to establish rights as between the debtor and the secured party (the creditor). Because several security interests may arise in the same collateral, priority of a security interest as against other creditors in the same collateral is vital to protect a creditor's claim against the collateral upon the debtor's default. A sample security agreement appears at the end of the chapter.

## 2. Security Interest

A security interest is created by the security agreement and is an interest or legal right in personal property or fixtures to secure payment or performance of an obligation. Thus, a security interest constitutes the lender's right to take the property pledged as collateral upon the debtor's default. It is, in essence, a contract designed to memorialize the agreement between the parties and make clear, if default occurs, what the secured party can repossess. A special type of security interest, known as a purchase money security interest (PMSI), is taken or retained by the seller of property to secure payment of the purchase price. A PMSI can also be obtained by a financing agency when it provides funds for the buyer to acquire specific property.

There is also a unique limited PMSI that a creditor can obtain in crops that are to be grown. A perfected security interest in crops for new value, that is given to enable the debtor to produce the crops during the growing season and given not more than three months before the crops become growing crops by planting or otherwise, takes priority over an earlier perfected security interest to the extent that such earlier interest secures obligations due more than six months before the crops become growing crops by planting or otherwise, even though the person giving new value had knowledge of the earlier security interest. *UCC § 9–312(2)*. The purpose of this provision is to permit farmers to obtain financing to allow planting of a current crop in circumstances where current lenders will not advance funds to enable the farmer to put in a crop.

## 3. Financing Statement

A financing statement is a brief document describing the collateral and must be filed as a public record in order to perfect the lender's security interest. A financing statement includes a brief description of the collateral, name and address of the lender and borrower, and other information concerning the extent of the security interest. Under the revisions, the debtor does not have to sign a financing statement. In general, there are no requirements that the financing statement be witnessed or acknowledged except when filed as part of real estate records in the office of the county recorder. The financing statement serves as notice to the public that the lender may have a security interest in property that the borrower owns. However, a financing statement is, by itself, insufficient to grant a security interest. A sample financing statement appears at the end of this chapter.

Under Revised Article 9, wrongful filing of a financing statement (filing by a party not entitled to make the filing) is not legally effective and subjects the filing party to a $500 penalty and liability for actual damages. Also, a failed financing statement can be amended to add collateral or a debtor if—(1) the debtor authorizes the filing in an authenticated record; (2) the creditor holds an agricultural lien that has become effective at the time of filing and the financing statement covers only collateral in which the person holds an agricultural lien; or (3) the debtor authorizes the filing of an initial financing statement and an amendment covering the collateral described in the security agreement and proceeds of collateral, whether or not the security agreement expressly covers proceeds.

## 4. Debtor

A debtor is the person owing payments or other performance of the obligation secured, including the seller of accounts or chattel paper.

## 5. Collateral

Collateral is the property (personal property or fixtures, but not real estate) which is subject to a security interest, including accounts and chattel paper that have been sold.

## 6. Buyer in the Ordinary Course of Business

A buyer in the ordinary course is a person who, in good faith, and without knowledge that the sale is in violation of the ownership rights or security interest of a third party in the goods, buys in the ordinary course from a person in the business of selling goods of that kind. *UCC § 9–201(9).* The significance of being a buyer in the ordinary course of business (BIOC) is that such person takes free of a security interest in inventory items created by that person's seller even though the security interest is perfected, and the buyer acquired all title that the transferor had power to transfer. For example, assume an individual would like to buy a tractor from the local implement dealer. The buyer wants to buy the tractor free and clear of any interest that the dealer may have given to one of its creditors in its inventory. If the implement dealer gave a security interest to the bank in its inventory, including the tractor in question, the buyer will take free and clear of the bank's interest in the tractor if the buyer is a buyer in the ordinary course of business.

It is critical to remember that there are *two* requirements set forth under UCC § 9–320: (1) the buyer must be a BIOC; and (2) the buyer's seller must have created the security interest involved. The following examples illustrate the application of the requirements.

––––––––––––

**Example 3:**

Frank bought a combine from a local dealer and granted a credit company a security interest in the combine. The credit company filed a proper financing statement with the Secretary of State. Frank then sold the combine to Sally. The credit company is not informed of the sale, and Frank later defaults on his obligation to the credit company. The credit company later learns that Sally has the combine and files a repossession action against Sally. The credit company will get the combine because Sally is not a BIOC (she didn't purchase the combine from someone engaged in the business of selling goods of that kind).

**Example 4:**

Assume the same facts as in Example 3 except that instead of selling the combine to Sally, Frank trades the combine to another dealer and that dealer sells the combine to Sally. Frank then defaults on his obligation to the credit company. The credit company learns that Sally has the combine and files a repossession action against her. The credit company will get the combine because Sally's seller did not create the security interest involved.

## 7. Fixture

The term "fixture," is not defined under Article 9. Article 9 simply states that goods are "fixtures" when they become so related to particular real estate that an interest in them arises under real estate law. Article 9, however, does contain extensive priority provisions that apply to real estate fixtures once the goods do actually become fixtures. An examination of a particular jurisdiction's real estate law regarding fixtures is necessary.

## C.   EFFECTIVENESS OF THE SECURITY AGREEMENT

## 1. Against the Debtor

## *i.  The Need to Properly Identify the Debtor*

For a security agreement to be effective against the debtor, one of two initial requirements must be met; either the collateral must be in the possession of the secured party or the agreement must be in writing, authenticated by the debtor, and reasonably identify the collateral. The basic rule is that the description must provide adequate guidance for the person doing the repossessing.

For business debtors, the security agreement must contain the debtor's correct name. For instance, if the debtor is a partnership or a corporation, the individual signing the security agreement on behalf of the entity must indicate that they are signing in their capacity as a partner or shareholder. However, most courts will not invalidate a security agreement if the debtor is sufficiently identified. *See, e.g., Mountain Farm Credit Service, A.C.A. v. Purina Mills, Inc.,* 119 N.C. App. 508, 459 S.E.2d 75 (1995).

## 2. Attachment

To be effective against the debtor, a security interest must also "attach." Under Article 9, three requirements must be satisfied for attachment to occur: (1) the parties to the transaction must agree to create a security interest; (2) the secured party must give something of value to the debtor, such as a loan of money; and (3) the debtor must own or have rights in the collateral.

---

**Example 5:**

Farmer Jones and Last National Bank of Dry Gulch executed a security agreement on July 10. On July 15, bank loaned Farmer Jones money. Attachment occurred on July 15. That is the first point in time when all of the requirements for attachment are satisfied.

## *i. Giving of Value*

Most of the litigation concerning attachment focuses on whether the secured party has given value to the debtor concerning past indebtedness or sufficiency of future advances. The UCC specifies that a person gives value for rights if the person acquired the rights in return for a binding commitment to extend credit or as security for, or in total or partial satisfaction of, a pre-existing debt, or in return for consideration sufficient to support a simple contract.

## ii. Rights in the Collateral

Sometimes an issue arises concerning whether the debtor owns the property or has rights in the collateral, especially when the property is owned in co-tenancy, or the collateral is grown or produced in accordance with a production contract.

> **Note:** The burden of proof to establish sufficient rights in collateral generally lies with the party asserting the security interest but, in some states, possession of the collateral by the debtor creates a presumption that the debtor owns the property which shifts the burden of proof to the debtor to prove ownership.

While the revisions to Article 9 provide that the debtor must have rights in the collateral or the power to transfer rights in the collateral to a secured party, the revisions do not define the term "rights." While "rights" does not necessarily mean "title," ownership of property gives the owner rights in the collateral while mere possession does not. *But, a debtor need not be an owner to be able to create an enforceable security interest.*

> **Note:** Under some state law provisions, possession of the collateral, accompanied by the contingent right of ownership, is sufficient for a security interest to attach under UCC § 203(b)(2). Likewise, state law may also provide that constructive possession is adequate to allow a lien to attach.

What is not clear is the precise point between actual ownership and mere possession where the debtor's relationship with the collateral establishes rights in the collateral sufficient to create a security interest.

A contractual right of ownership generally constitutes sufficient rights in the collateral. However, under a production contract, the producer no longer makes many of the daily operational decisions. Instead the processor controls the production-to-marketing cycle and has 24-hour access to the producer's facility. Farmers usually enter into production contracts in order to lock in a guaranteed price regardless of the prevailing market price. An important question, however, from a financing standpoint, is whether a producer operating under a production contract has a sufficient ownership interest in the products produced under contract for a security interest in the products to attach. Similar questions arise under consignment situations and livestock grower contracts involving feedlots. If the arrangement is merely that of a bailment, the debtor does not have a sufficient interest in the goods for a security interest to attach. A bailment occurs when goods are delivered (by a bailor) to another person (known as a bailee) for the performance of a specific objective, with the goods to be returned to the bailor upon completion of that objective. Arguably production contracts, consignment arrangements and feedlot grower contracts only constitute a bailment of the goods. Thus, an attempted security interest in the bailed goods would not attach because the debtor would not have rights in the collateral. Compare *In re Joy* 169 B.R. 931 (Bankr. D. Neb. 1994) with *National Livestock Credit Corp. v. First National Bank of Harrah* 503 P.2d 1283 (Okla. 1972).

The "rights" issue can also arise in the cattle feeding setting and can, depending on the particular facts, result in the court's finding that the feedlot operator did not have sufficient rights in the cattle placed in the feedlot to grant a security interest in the cattle. The "rights" issue is necessarily fact-dependent and a different result may be reached in a different case. For good example of the "rights" issue in the cattle feeding setting, see *American Bank & Trust v. Shaull,* 678 N.W.2d 779 (S.D. 2004).

Revised Article 9 applies to most consignment situations. Under the revisions, a "consignment" is defined as a transaction, regardless of its form, in which a person delivers goods (other than consumer goods) for the purpose of a sale and the merchant (i) deals in goods of that kind under a name other than the name of the person making delivery, (ii) is not an auctioneer, and (iii) is not generally known by its creditors to be substantially engaged in selling the goods of others. *UCC § 9–102(a)(20).* Transactions which create a security interest to secure an obligation are not "consignments." Unless a consignor perfects a security interest in the consigned goods, the consignee has rights and title in the consigned goods "identical to those the consignor had or had power to transfer." *UCC § 9–319(a).* The rights, if any, of a consignee when a consignor perfects a security interest in the consigned goods is left to non-UCC law. Thus, under the revisions, it is crucial that a party which delivers possession of farm products to another for raising or fattening perfect a security interest in the farm products in order to protect itself against a challenge from the grower's secured creditors.

For farm property owned in co-tenancy, a security agreement is effective as to the entire property only if all of the co-tenants sign the security agreement.

### iii.   Attachment of After-Acquired Property

Article 9 gives the debtor a broad power to commit after-acquired property to secure an obligation. *UCC § 9–204(a)*. This is accomplished with a security agreement that contains language providing that the transaction is secured by certain collateral regardless of when it is acquired by the debtor. Such a provision is usually called an "after-acquired property" clause because it allows a security interest to extend to property the debtor acquires after the loan or other secured transaction is made.

---

**Example 6:**

On June 1, Farmer Joe granted First Bank a security interest in all of Joe's equipment, including any equipment that Joe acquired after June 1. On August 1, Joe bought more equipment from the local implement dealer on "open account" (meaning that the implement dealer did not retain a PMSI in the equipment to secure the purchase price). Because First Bank has a security agreement claiming a security interest in Joe's after-acquired equipment, the bank's security interest will attach to the equipment Joe purchased on August 1.

———————

After-acquired property clauses are common in agriculture. An after-acquired property clause gives additional protection to a creditor and allows a creditor to extend funds to a debtor based not only on the collateral that the debtor presently owns, but also property that the debtor acquires in the future that comes within the terms of the after-acquired property clause. For example, a farm or ranch debtor can use the prospective commercial value of unborn animals and unplanted crops as a basis for obtaining funds. But remember, for the security interest to "attach," the debtor must have rights in the collateral. This requirement is particularly important with respect to after-acquired property. In general, no security interest attaches to after-acquired property until the property comes into existence and the debtor acquires rights to it. Most courts hold that a debtor has no rights in crops until they are planted or otherwise become growing crops, the young of livestock until they are conceived, or fish until caught.

Several courts have held that crops received by a debtor under a 1983-style payment-in-kind (PIK) program are subject to a security agreement that covers after-acquired property. In essence, a PIK certificate allows a farmer to have access to government supplies of a particular commodity. Other courts have held otherwise. The major issue in these cases is whether an enforceable security interest can be taken in generic commodity certificates. For livestock, some authorities suggest that a security interest in adult livestock plus an after-acquired property clause will not cover all increases. A security interest in an adult animal does not normally cover presently conceived but unborn young unless specifically included in the security agreement since the debtor has a present, separate interest in the unborn young. This problem was eliminated in the 1972 version of the UCC. By its very nature, an after-acquired property clause cannot include a present interest. Therefore, to cover all increase the security agreement should specifically mention the adult animal, all presently conceived but unborn young, and all increase not yet conceived.

> **Note:** It is possible that an after-acquired property clause could cause the security interest to attach to crops grown in the future even if the secured creditor does *not* advance additional funds to finance the planting of those crops.

Certain special rules exist pertaining to after-acquired property. For instance, a security interest in after-acquired property of a bailee's creditor does not attach to goods which are subject to bailment. For consumer goods (household goods), an after-acquired property clause includes only after-acquired property that is acquired within ten days after the secured party gives value. Commercial tort claims are also not subject to after-acquired clauses, and an after-acquired property clause does not prevail in bankruptcy if the property was obtained within 90 days of the bankruptcy filing and no purchase money security interest was involved.

A similar concern exists with respect to a creditor's rights in after-acquired property if a borrower desires to obtain funds in increments. In that case, the funds may be spread over a period of time, rather than in one lump sum. This allows additional loans to be made on the same collateral. The UCC provides that future advances to the debtor may be covered by one security agreement. Thus, a new agreement need not be executed each time an advance is made. However, to ensure that a security agreement covers future advances, the document evidencing a subsequent advance should refer to the original agreement.

---

**Example 7:**

Beth borrowed $10,000 from Farmers' Bank and granted the bank a security interest in her cattle to secure the loan. The security agreement contained a future advance clause allowing the bank to advance additional money to Beth with the cattle standing as security for the new advance as well as the first loan of $10,000. If Farmers' Bank loans Beth an additional $5,000, the bank will have a security interest in the cattle totaling $15,000.

---

The courts are split on the issue of whether a security agreement that does not contain an after-acquired property clause can still cover after-acquired collateral. In cases involving inventory and accounts where the trade expects inventory and accounts to be sold and collected and then replaced, the courts generally apply a rebuttable presumption, based on the nature of the overturning assets, that a security interest in inventory and accounts receivable includes after-acquired property. Conversely, in cases where the collateral is equipment and the description was "all equipment" with no specific reference to after-acquired equipment, the presumption that collateral will turnover does not apply. Thus, most courts hold that after-acquired equipment is not covered. A description of "all farm products" might be held to be subject to the rebuttable presumption rule inasmuch as they are similar to inventory in the hands of a farmer.

Revised Article 9–108 takes no position on the issue, noting instead that the question is one of contract interpretation.

## 3. Against Third Parties

### *i. Perfection*

Under Article 9, the term "perfection" describes the process that a secured party must take to make a security interest effective against third parties, particularly the debtor's general creditors or their representative in an insolvency proceeding. Perfection requires that the public somehow receive notice of the transaction. Once the parties to a loan or sale have agreed that the transaction is to be secured by the debtor's personal property, it becomes necessary to inform others that the property is subject to a security interest. For example, a banker would not want to make a loan using a farmer's next corn crop as security if the farmer had already borrowed elsewhere on the same collateral.

Perfection of a security interest in collateral is necessary to have an interest ahead of "a person who becomes a lien creditor without knowledge of the security interest and before it is perfected." A lien creditor includes a creditor with a levy or attachment against the property involved, an assignee for the benefit of creditors, or a receiver in equity or a trustee in bankruptcy. The secured party must perfect to prevent these people from making priority claims against the collateral. A secured party who has provided the purchase-money, credit or loan (which enabled the debtor to purchase the collateral) does have a ten-day grace period within which to perfect a security interest and still beat out lien creditors, but as a rule the secured party must perfect before the lien creditors or lose priority.

An unperfected security interest is subject to the priorities of all perfected security interests even though the perfected party knew of the prior unperfected security interest. For unperfected security interests, a buyer of the collateral wins if the buyer gives value and receives delivery without knowledge of another party's attempt to create a security interest in the collateral, and before such interest is perfected.

**Example 8:**

On February 1, Farmer Jones borrowed money from Second State Bank, and pledged a tractor as collateral for the loan. The bank and Jones executed a security agreement. On February 2, Farmer Jones sold the tractor to Farmer Brown. Brown paid Jones the full asking price. On February 3, Second State Bank filed a financing statement. On February 4, Brown took delivery of the tractor purchased from Jones. On February 5, Jones defaulted on the loan from Second State Bank. As between Second State Bank and Farmer Brown, Second State Bank would receive the tractor because Brown did not take possession of the tractor until after the bank perfected (by filing a financing statement). If Brown had received possession of the tractor before the bank filed, Brown could keep the tractor.

An unperfected security interest can also be subject to a buyer in the ordinary course of business (BIOC). A BIOC for some types of goods takes ahead of an unperfected security interest in the same goods. A buyer in the ordinary course (BIOC) is generally defined as a person who purchases goods in good faith, and without knowledge that the sale is in violation of the ownership rights or security interest of a third party in the goods. A BIOC also takes the goods free of a perfected security interest provided that the BIOC purchased the goods from a person who is in the business of selling those particular goods.

## ii. Methods of Perfection

There are three general methods of perfection that have widespread application to agriculture: (1) possession of the collateral, (2) filing a financing statement, and (3) automatic perfection.

### a. Possession of Collateral

One method of perfection is for the creditor to take possession of the collateral. If a creditor takes possession of the collateral, the public is deemed to know of the creditor's claim to the property and the security interest is, therefore, perfected. Perfection by possession is often not satisfactory for tangible property because the debtor or buyer wants possession and the creditor may find it inconvenient or costly to take possession of the property. However, taking possession may be an acceptable method of perfecting a security interest in intangible goods such as stocks or bonds.

### b. Filing

Normally, a security interest in tangible property is perfected by filing a financing statement or by filing the security agreement as a financing statement. Indeed, filing a financing statement usually is the only practical way to perfect when the debtor is a farmer or rancher. An effective financing statement merely indicates that the creditor may have a security interest in the described collateral and is sufficient if it provides the name of the debtor, gives the name and address of the secured party from which information concerning the security interest may be obtained, gives the mailing address of the debtor and contains a statement indicating the types or describing the items of collateral.

> **Note:** An adequate description of the collateral is critical if there is to be attachment and perfection. This is an important point that can arise in an agricultural context with respect to real estate, livestock and equipment that can be used either directly in agricultural production activities or merely indirectly.

The name of the debtor is the key to the notice system and priority. The financing statement is indexed under the debtor's name. If the debtor is a registered organization, only the name indicated on the public record of the debtor's jurisdiction or organization is sufficient. *See, e.g., In re EDM Corporation,* 431 B.R. 459 (B.A.P. 8th Cir. 2010).

But, federal tax liens appear not to be subject to the same exact match standard. The test is whether a reasonable searcher would find the lien notwithstanding the use of on abbreviation. Under UCC § 9–506, a financing statement is effective even if it has minor errors or omissions unless the errors or omissions make the financing statement seriously misleading. A financing statement containing an incorrect debtor's name is not seriously misleading if a search of the records of the filing office under the debtor's correct legal name, using the filing office's standard search logic, if any, discloses the financing statement filed under the incorrect name. However, some states have regulations defining the search logic to be used and may require that the debtor's name be listed correctly.

Under the revisions to Article 9, a legal description of the land need not be contained in the security agreement and financing statement if crops serve as the collateral. A description of the real estate is only required if the security interest covers timber "to be cut." *UCC § 9–203(b)(3)(A).*

Note: For a creditor to perfect a security interest in real estate with standing timber that is not under contract, the creditor must record a mortgage in the underlying real estate. If the timber is under contract, the creditor must file a financing statement. In that event, the secured creditor's interest will be subject to a mortgage that has already been recorded.

As for Christmas trees, many state statutory provisions treat them as "crops" that are personal property. Thus, a security interest with Christmas trees pledged as collateral must reasonably identify the collateral such that a third party could locate where the trees are growing. Also, the general rule is that a creditor with a perfected security interest in crops has priority over a perfected real estate lien covering crops.

The revisions state that a financing statement is sufficient if it provides the name of the debtor, the name of the secured party or representative of the secured party and "indicates the collateral covered by the financing statement." In addition, the revisions provide that a description of personal property or real property is sufficient if it "reasonably identifies" what is described. A description of collateral reasonably identifies the collateral if it identifies the collateral by (i) specific listing; (ii) category; (iii) a type of collateral defined in the UCC (other than commercial tort claims or, in the case of a consumer transaction, consumer goods, security entitlements, securities accounts or commodity accounts); (iv) quantity; (v) computational formula; or (vi) any other method where the identity of the collateral is objectively determinable.

With respect to cattle, the custom in many farming areas is to identify cattle by ear tags. Sometimes ear tags can contain an incorrect identification number or may fall off. If a certain number of cows are listed in a financing statement that are identified by ear tag numbers that are either incorrect or where the ear tags no longer exist, a question could arise as to whether the collateral description is adequate. *See, e.g., In re Baker,* 511 B.R. 41 (Bankr. N.D. N.Y. 2014); see also *In re Taylor,* 2011 Bankr. LEXIS 863 (Bankr. E.D. Ky. Mar. 4, 2011).

Although the secured party may file either a financing statement or the security agreement, there are several reasons why filing a financing statement may be preferable. For example, the security agreement may not meet the minimum requirements of a financing statement. A security agreement usually contains a maturity date, in which case the effectiveness of the financing statement would cease 30 days thereafter. On the other hand, a filed financing statement is effective for five years unless a shorter maturity date is specified. Upon lapse of a financing statement 60 days after the maturity date, the security interest becomes unperfected. If the security agreement is filed, there is an inference that only the items described are intended to be affected, not later items of the same kind of collateral. The inference is to the contrary if a separate financing statement is filed. It may be preferable to file a financing statement in the event it is likely that the parties might object to having all of the contents of the security agreement made public. In addition, a financing statement may be filed before a security agreement is made or a security interest otherwise attaches.

Another crucial aspect of perfection by filing is that the financing statement must be filed in the proper location to be effective. Indeed, the key to determining how to perfect is the correct classification of the collateral. The proper place to file varies from state to state. However, the key to proper filing is correct classification of the collateral. Collateral arising from an agricultural operation might be classified as equipment, farm products, inventory or documents of title. Indeed, much agricultural collateral can be classified in multiple ways. For instance, milk from cows located on a dairy farm could be farm products or inventory.

---

**Example 9:**

Don Drake is in the egg production business. The chickens are housed in production units on his farm. Each production unit is a large building that contains three concentric circles of caged hens, seven tiers high. Don converted almost all of his existing pasture and cropland when he switched from crop farming to the egg production business. In addition, there always are eggs in Don's possession. To have an enforceable security interest in the chickens and eggs as collateral, a creditor should describe them in the security agreement and financing statement exactly as they are: chickens, eggs and farm products. If they are described only as farm products, a court may determine that they are inventory based on the nature of Don's business. In that event, the creditor's interest would not be effective against third parties. Courts in some states have determined that confinement poultry enterprises are not agricultural operations.

---

For farm equipment that has been pledged as collateral, Revised Article 9 (which all states have adopted) provides for central filing of financing statements with the office of a designated state officer (typically the Secretary of State). The only local filing of financing statements occurs in the real estate records for fixtures—items of personal property that become physically part of the real estate, and are treated as part of the real estate until severed from it. Under the pre-revision version of Article 9, a creditor attempting to obtain a security interest in equipment used in farming operations had to file in the county of the debtor's residence, or if the debtor was not a state resident, the county where the goods were kept. Failure to file the financing statement in the proper office could result in the loss of both priority and the security interest itself. Thus, a premium was placed on the proper classification of collateral because the proper filing location often depended upon the type of collateral involved in the secured transaction.

Under the pre-revision Article 9 rules, no single set of standards emerged as the criteria for deciding whether "equipment [is] used in farming operations." Instead, an "actual use" test seemed to be the closest statement of a standard for the determination of the issue. If the equipment was used directly to perform tasks customarily done on farms, then it was likely that a court would find that the equipment was used in farming operations. *See, e.g., In re K.L. Smith Enterprises, Ltd.,* 2 B.R 280 (D. Colo. 1980), for a case that illustrates the hazards of using language in agricultural lending that is drawn from documents or lending practices appropriate for nonfarm financing. *But see, In re Blease,* 24 U.C.C. Rep. 450 (D. N.J. 1978). For a case where the court adopted a narrow view of "farming operations" that would probably exclude "factory type" production systems for livestock, Also see *National City Bank, Norwalk v. Golden Acre Turkeys, Inc.,* 65 Ohio 3d 371, 604 N.E.2d 149 (1992).

Three classifications are typically encountered when dealing with crops and livestock—farm products, inventory and documents of title. Filing rules for farm products vary from state to state, but can be classified into three general categories. In most states, the secured party must file a financing statement in the county of the debtor's residence. This is known as local filing. If growing crops or crops to be grown are the collateral and the land is located in a county other than that of the debtor's residence, the secured party must file a second financing statement in the county where the land is located. The secured party may also have to double file if the debtor is incorporated and the land upon which crops are or will be growing is located in a county other than the corporation's place of business.

Some states require central filing for farm products. In these jurisdictions, all financing statements must be filed in one office—typically the Secretary of State's office—to be effective. *See, e.g., In re Stevens,* 307 B.R. 124 (Bankr. E.D. Ark. 2004). A few states use a combination of local and central filing. However, regardless of whether a particular jurisdiction follows local or central filing it is important that the secured party correctly describe the collateral. If the creditor files a financing statement that describes the collateral improperly, even though the financing statement is filed in the correct office, the description is defective and the security interest is not perfected.

Harvested crops are farm products so long as they are on the farm. While harvested crops are on the farm, they remain in the possession of a person engaged in farming. However, once the crops move off the farm and into storage at the elevator, the crops are no longer in the physical possession, at least, of the farmer. To complicate matters, the grain is usually intermingled with grain from other farmers. The UCC is unclear on whether harvested crops stored off the farm continue to be farm products or whether they become inventory. It is clear that if a nonfarmer holds crops for sale, the goods are inventory. The lesson for creditors attempting to take a security interest in crops that are stored off the farm may be to treat harvested crops and animals off the farm as both farm products and inventory.

In states that follow central filing where all security financing statements are to be filed in a designated state office, the central filing requirement does not apply for security interests involving unextracted minerals, standing timber or fixtures. Those are usually filed in a county office because land titles may be involved. Also, security interests involving consumer goods are usually filed locally. The reason for state-level filing is the difficulty in knowing which counties to check for filings. That is an especially important point for far-flung farming or other business operations.

The revisions to Article 9 modified the definition of farm products so as to expressly include products of aquaculture in addition to crops produced on vines, trees or bushes, and to eliminate the existing requirement that the goods be in the "possession" of a debtor engaged in farming operations in order for the goods to be "farm products." The phrase "farming operation" is defined to mean the "raising, cultivating, propagating, fattening, grazing, or any other farming, livestock, or aquacultural operation." Thus, "farming operations" is now broadly defined such that the focus is placed on the ultimate product of the enterprise rather than the debtor's involvement in the operation to determine if goods are "farm products." The elimination of the requirement that the goods be in the "possession" of a person engaged in farming operations will result in harvested crops and livestock being deemed farm products if the debtor is engaged in farming operations regardless of whether the debtor has actual physical control over the goods.

The revisions have also removed the requirement for local filing for crops in order to simplify perfection and avoid traps for the unwary. Revised UCC § 9–501(a)(2) provides for central filing for all financing statements other than in the case of timber to be cut or fixtures. In such cases, the appropriate filing office is the office designated for the filing or recording of a mortgage on real property.

Especially in those states that do not follow central filing, it is absolutely critical to classify properly the goods that are subject to a security interest. If a creditor files in the wrong location, the creditor's interest will only be good against those persons having actual knowledge of the contents of the financing statement. The interest will not be good against other creditors that obtain an interest in the collateral, even though they filed later. If in doubt, filing at multiple locations is a prudent strategy. Financing statements that are properly filed continue to be effective even though the debtor's residence, place of business, or location of the collateral change.

### c. Automatic Perfection

In some cases, perfection can occur without filing. For PMSIs in consumer goods (except for fixtures and motor vehicles that are required to be licensed), the "purchase money person" (the seller or the financing agency that provided the cash or credit which the debtor used to buy the collateral) is given the benefit of an "automatic" perfection as soon as that person's security interest attaches to the collateral. Attachment occurs if the debtor executes and files a security agreement at the time the debtor received possession of the consumer goods or within 20 days thereafter. A PMSI perfected in this manner has priority over certain buyers such as a buyer not in the ordinary course, lessees and lien creditor interests which arise between the time the security interest attaches and the time of filing. Even without filing and with the debtor in possession of the consumer good, the seller or financing agency will still be protected against nearly all other possible claimants—lien creditors, other general creditors, the trustee in bankruptcy, another dealer to whom the collateral was given, or a buyer who had knowledge of the security interest.

Even though perfection is automatic without filing, filing may be desirable to give a higher priority to the perfected security interest against a bona fide purchaser (BFP). A BFP who purchases consumer goods that are subject to a creditor's security agreement takes the goods free and clear of the unfiled PMSI if the BFP buys without knowledge of the unfiled security interest for value, and for his or her own personal, family or household purposes. If the holder of a purchase money security interest does file, such filing prevails even against a BFP. Thus, buyers of consumer goods from other individuals should check filing records to make sure that the item they are buying is indeed "free and clear" of another party's security interest.

---

**Example 10:**

On July 1, Drysdale Department Store sold a refrigerator to Joan and took a PMSI in the refrigerator to secure the purchase price. The PMSI was evidenced by a security agreement, which Joan signed on July 14. The department store did not file a financing statement. On August 1, Joan borrowed money from Usery State Bank and granted the bank a security interest in the refrigerator.

Drysdale's security interest in the refrigerator is prior to Usery State Bank's security interest even though Drysdale did not file a financing statement. However, if Joan were to sell the refrigerator to her neighbor, Jane, and Jane buys the refrigerator without knowledge of the prior unfiled (but perfected) PMSI, gives value and the purchase is for her own personal, family or household purposes, Jane would prevail over Drysdale Department Store. Thus, if Drysdale wants their security interest to be perfected even against Jane, they should file a financing statement.

---

The revisions to the UCC treat PMSIs in livestock similarly to PMSIs in inventory. In addition, such security interests extend to all proceeds rather than just identifiable cash proceeds. This is an important distinction because livestock sellers are often paid a few days after delivery of livestock and, therefore, may have noncash proceeds in the form of a receivable. Under Revised UCC § 9–324(d) provides that a PMSI in livestock that are farm products has priority over a conflicting security interest in the same livestock and in their identifiable proceeds (subject to the rights of a lender with a security interest in deposit accounts) and "identifiable products in their unmanufactured states." In order to qualify for the PMSI, several requirements must be satisfied. These requirements are that the PMSI must be perfected when the debtor receives possession of the livestock, the purchase money secured party must send an authenticated notification to the holder of the conflicting security interest, the holder of the conflicting security interest must receive the notification within six months before the debtor receives possession of the livestock, and the notification must specify that the purchase money secured party has or expects to acquire a PMSI in livestock of the debtor and describes the livestock. See *Zink v. Vanmiddlesworth,* 300 B.R. 394 (N.D. N.Y. 2003).

----

**Example 11:**

On January 15, Bluestem Bank loans money to Sam and Sam grants the bank a perfected security interest in all livestock presently owned or after-acquired. On February 15, Ralph sells cattle to Sam, and Sam signs a promissory note, a security agreement and a proper financing statement. Ralph files the financing statement on February 18. Sam has possession of the livestock at all times and defaults on both obligations. Under the prior version of the UCC, Ralph would defeat the bank because he held a PMSI in non-inventory and filed within 20 days of Sam taking possession of the livestock. However, under Revised Article 9, the bank would win because Ralph did not notify the bank or file before Sam obtained possession of the livestock.

### iii. Continuation Statement

Revised Article 9 provides that financing statements properly filed under the prior version of Article 9 remain effective to perfect the security interest until the sooner of—(1) the expiration of such financing statements (usually five years from filing) or (2) June 30, 2006. In order to preserve the relative priority of prior financing statements, the secured creditor must file by the earlier of these two dates a special type of financing statement created by Revised Article 9 called the Initial Financing Statement in Lieu of Continuation Statement (referred to as an "In Lieu Filing"). In Lieu Filings must reference the prior financing statement (and multiple financing statements may be referred under a single In Lieu Filing) and contain an appropriate collateral description. In Lieu Filings need not be signed by the debtor and may be filed anytime during the effectiveness of a pre-Revised Article 9 filed financing statement. In Lieu Filings are effective for five years from their filing date. A sample "In Lieu of" continuation statement appears at the end of this chapter.

A continuation statement may be filed to avoid lapse of a financing statement. A continuation statement may be filed within six months before the five-year termination date of the filing of the financing statement. At least two courts have held that a continuation statement must be filed within the six-month period. *See, e.g., NBD Bank, N.A. v. Timberjack, Inc.,* 208 Mich. App. 153, 527 N.W.2d 50 (1994); *In re Isringhausen,* 151 B.R. 203 (Bankr. S.D. Ill. 1993). In these cases, the secured parties filed continuation statements just before the six-month window for filing a continuation statement allowed under § 9–403(2) of the UCC. The creditors did not file additional continuation statements within the six-month window and the court held the security interests to be unperfected.

As noted above, the general rule is that a continuation statement may be filed within six months before the five-year termination date of the filing of the financing statement. However, because financing statements effective under the prior version of Article 9 remain effective under Revised Article 9 until the earlier of five years from the time of filing or June 30, 2006, the five-year window may be shortened for certain filings as illustrated in the following example.

———————

**Example 12:**

Ag Credit Co. filed a financing statement under the prior version of Article 9 on November 1, 1996. The financing statement expires on November 1, 2001. Ag Credit Co. renewed the financing statement by filing a continuation statement within six months of November 1, 2001—on May 1, 2001. The continuation statement was filed before the Revisions to Article 9 became effective on July 1, 2001. The filing of the continuation statement has the effect of extending the expiration date of the financing statement until November 1, 2006. Under Revised Article 9, the financing statement lapses on the earlier of November 1, 2006, or June 30, 2006. Thus, the financing statement lapses on June 30, 2006. As a result, the six-month window for filing the continuation statement is shortened to the time period of May 1, 2006, through June 30, 2006.

--------

The example illustrates that creditors may need to check closely the expiration date of financing statements to determine if the period for filing continuation statements is shortened by virtue of the transitional rule. While some states have taken legislative action to clarify that the customary six-month continuation window and five-year effective period remain in effect for pre-Revised Article 9, some states have not. Litigation concerning the precise interpretation of the transitional rule in states that have not amended the Revised Article 9 transitional rule may result.

In general, a continuation statement must be signed by the secured party, identify the original statement by file number, and state that the original financing statement is still effective. The continuation statement must contain all of the information contained in the original financing statement. A routine continuation statement extends the life of an initial financing statement measured from the date of filing of the initial financing statement, rather than as of the filing date of the continuation statement itself. A sample continuation statement appears at the end of the chapter.

## iv.  *Termination Statement*

Except for consumer goods, whenever there is no outstanding secured obligation and no commitment to make future advances, incur obligations or otherwise give value to the debtor, the secured party must, on receipt of an authenticated demand by the debtor, send the debtor a termination statement stating that a security interest is no longer claimed under the financing statement. A secured party failing to send such a termination statement within ten days after demand may be fined and held liable for other damages to the debtor. Revised Article 9 permits the *debtor* to file a termination statement in situations where the secured party was required to file or provide the termination statement, and has failed to do so. In that event, the termination statement filed by the debtor must indicate on it that the debtor authorized the filing of the termination statement. The termination statement must identify, by its file number, the initial financing statement to which it relates and indicate that either it is a termination statement or that the identified financing statement is no longer effective.

For financing statements covering consumer goods after there is no outstanding security obligation and no commitment to make advances, incur obligations or otherwise give value, then within one month whether requested or not, or within ten days following written demand by the debtor, the secured party must file a termination statement. The same penalty of $100 plus any actual loss caused to the debtor is imposed for failure to comply.

If a financing statement covering farm products is filed, then within 60 days, or within ten days following written demand by the debtor, after there is no outstanding secured obligation and no commitment to make advances, incur obligations or otherwise give value, the secured party must file a termination statement. The same penalty applies as is noted above.

A secured party may, by a signed statement, release all or part of any collateral described in a filed financing statement. If it is all released, it will be treated as a termination statement.

## D.   PERFECTION AGAINST PROCEEDS

The security interest created by a security agreement is a relatively durable lien. The collateral may change form as the production process unfolds. Fertilizer and seed become growing crops, animals are fattened and sold, and equipment is replaced. The lien follows the changing collateral and in the end may attach to the proceeds from the sales of products, at least up to ten days after the debtor receives the proceeds. In other words, a security interest in proceeds is automatically perfected if the interest in the original collateral was perfected. However, a security interest in proceeds ceases to be automatically perfected ten days after the debtor receives the proceeds.

Many items of collateral are intended to be sold in the normal course of business. This is true whether the collateral is inventory, feeder cattle, or other property. Before enactment of the UCC, once such collateral was sold, the creditor was unsecured. Not only was the security interest lost in the collateral itself, but no security interest attached to the note, check, account receivable or money given in payment. Article 9, however, provides an extensive and careful coverage for security interests in proceeds. Proceeds are generally defined as whatever is received upon the sale, trade-in or other disposition of the collateral covered by the security agreement. Money, checks and similar items are "cash proceeds" while all other proceeds are "noncash proceeds." The general intent of Article 9 is to give the secured party with a security interest in collateral a similar security in anything which the debtor received from third parties in exchange for that collateral. In general, unless the debtor was authorized to make the sale or exchange of the collateral, a secured party can elect to pursue the collateral in the hands of a third party as well as the proceeds in the hands of the debtor. However, the general rule is subject to several exceptions, including the buyer in the ordinary course of business (BIOC) who buys goods (usually from a dealer's inventory). This BIOC takes the goods free and clear of a security interest created by the seller, even though that interest is perfected and even though the BIOC knows of the interest. No specific reference to proceeds is required in the security agreement. Indeed, the attachment of a security interest in collateral automatically gives the secured party an interest in the proceeds if they are identifiable.

## 1. Classification of Government Farm Program Payments

In agricultural settings, "proceeds" of crops or livestock can take several forms. These can include federal farm program deficiency payments, storage payments, diversion payments, disaster relief payments, insurance payments for destroyed crops, Conservation Reserve Program payments and dairy herd termination program payments, among other things. This is significant in agriculture because of the magnitude of the payments. In fact, in debt enforcement or liquidation settings, the federal payments are often the primary or only form of money remaining for creditors to reach.

> **Note:** Two courts have held that the Federal Crop Insurance Act (FCIA) preempts UCC Article 9. Thus, according to these courts, the exclusive method for a creditor to obtain a lien in undisclosed proceeds is through the FCIA authorized assignment process. See *In re Duckworth,* No. 10–83603, 2012 Bankr. LEXIS 1219 (C.D. Ill. Mar. 22, 2012)*; In re Cook,* 169 F.3d 271 (5th Cir. 1999).

In general, for governmental agricultural payments to qualify as proceeds, three conditions must be met: (1) the crop must have been planted; (2) the crop must have been lost or destroyed; and (3) the government payment being claimed must have been received by the producer for the lost or destroyed crop.

Regardless of the classification of farm program payments that a jurisdiction adopts, a creditor must always comply with applicable UCC requirements for the creation, attachment, and perfection of a security interest in the payments. In any event, however, the most effective manner for a creditor to perfect a claim against a farmer's federal farm program payments is to include specific references to federal farm program benefits in the security agreement.

Under the revisions to Article 9, the definition of "general intangibles" has been amended to specifically include government program payments and benefits. For example, Revised UCC § 9–102(a)(2) includes in its definition of an "account" the right to payment, whether or not earned by performance (i) for property that has been or is to be sold, leased, licensed, assigned or otherwise disposed of, (ii) for services rendered or to be rendered, and (iii) for a policy of insurance issued or to be issued.

## E. PRIORITIES AMONG SECURITY INTERESTS

If a debtor gives a security interest in the same collateral to two or more creditors, and the interests are perfected, it may be necessary to determine which one has priority. If the interests are perfected by filing, priority is determined by the time of filing. The creditor who filed first, wins. Therefore, because a financing statement may be filed before a security agreement is signed or the security interest attaches, a cautious creditor may wish to file early. If one or both are perfected in some manner other than filing, priority is determined by the time of perfection.

**Example 13:**

Frank James applied for a $10,000 loan from First Bank on June 1, and pledged his tractor as collateral. On June 2, First Bank filed a financing statement. On June 3, Frank obtained a $20,000 loan from Second Bank pledging the same tractor as collateral. Second Bank filed a financing statement on June 3. First Bank loaned money to Frank on June 10. On October 31, Frank defaulted on both the June 3 and June 10 loans.

Whether First Bank or Second Bank has priority depends on which one filed first. Because perfection was by filing, the first creditor to perfect wins. In this instance, because First bank filed before Second Bank, First Bank has priority. This is the case even though First Bank's interest did not attach until June 10, the date it loaned money to Frank.

If none of the secured parties is perfected, priority is determined by the order of attachment.

As an exception to the first-to-file rule, a PMSI, even though perfected by filing later than a perfected secured party having an interest in after-acquired property, can take priority.

## 1. PMSI in Crops

Under the former version of the UCC, a special rule existed for a PMSI in crops. However, Revised Article 9 removes the rule and does not replace it. A provision dubbed the "model provisions for production-money priority," which was designed as a substitute for Revised UCC § 9–312(2), is found in Appendix II to the Revised Article 9, but is not being enacted into law by most of the states which have enacted Revised Article 9. To qualify for priority under the Appendix provision, the production-money secured party must notify the earlier-filed secured party before extending the production-money credit. The notification affords the earlier secured party the opportunity to prevent subordination by extending the credit itself.

## 2.  PMSI in After-Acquired Property

The priority of a perfected security interest in after-acquired property can be displaced by a PMSI if certain procedures are followed. For collateral other than inventory, the holder of a PMSI has priority over a conflicting security interest in the same collateral or its proceeds if the PMSI is perfected at the time the debtor receives possession of the collateral or within 20 days thereafter. The UCC does not define the term "possession". In general, however, possession occurs when the recipient physically acquires the property, except for situations involving a sale on approval or an option to purchase. In those situations, possession occurs when the down payment is delivered or the option is exercised (in other words, the person became a debtor). Sometimes a question can arise concerning whether a particular arrangement actually involves a sale on approval.

---

**Example 14:**

Slim Chance would like to buy a new tractor, but Slim had earlier signed a security agreement containing an after-acquired property clause with Last Straw Bank covering all equipment subsequently acquired. The security interest of Last Straw Bank could be displaced by a PMSI if the PMSI is perfected at the time Slim receives possession of the new tractor or within 20 days thereafter.

**Example 15:**

Community Bank holds a perfected security interest in Barb Dwire's equipment as well as after-acquired equipment. On July 16, Dover Farm Equipment Company sold and delivered to Barb a tractor, retaining a PMSI. If Dover perfects within 20 days of July 16 (on or before August 5), Dover will have priority over Community Bank. If Dover perfects after August 5, Community Bank will have priority.

---

For inventory collateral, the PMSI must be perfected at the time the debtor receives possession of the inventory and the holder of the prior security interest must be notified of the PMSI. There is no 20-day rule for inventory financing.

### 3. PMSI in Livestock Rule

The revisions to Article 9 treat PMSIs in livestock similarly to PMSIs in inventory. But, there is no need for a subsequent lender to perfect (by giving authenticated notice) if the debtor never has possession of the livestock. *First National Bank v.*

*Lubbock Feeders,* 183 S.W.3d 875 *(Tex. Ct. App. 2006).* In addition, a PMSI in livestock extends to all proceeds rather than just identifiable cash proceeds.

Revised UCC § 9–332(a) provides that a transferee of money takes the money free of a security interest unless the transferee acts in collusion with the debtor in violating the rights of the secured party. Revised UCC § 9–332(b) provides that a transferee of funds from a deposit account takes the funds free of a security interest in the deposit account unless the transferee acts in collusion with the debtor in violating the rights of the secured party. A "deposit account" means a demand, time, savings, passbook, or similar account maintained with a bank. For example, assume a farmer obtains a loan and grants the lender a security interest in the farmer's crops, and upon harvesting the crops, sells them and deposits the check in the farm checking account at the bank. Further, assume that the farmer draws a check on the farm account payable to the local elevator for fertilizer expenses used to produce the crop, and then defaults on the loan from the lender. The result, under the UCC, is that the elevator takes free of the lender's security interest unless the bank acted in collusion with the farmer in violating the lender's rights. The UCC does not define "collusion" for purposes of this provision.

## F. USING CROPS AS FEED—THE "IDENTIFIABLE PROCEEDS" PROBLEM

If both a farmer's crops and livestock are items of collateral for the same lender, the lender does not usually object to use of the crops as feed. The lender's filed financing statement describing the crop and animals would give sufficient notice of the continuing lien and preserve an interest in the disappearing feed. However, where one lender has a lien on the crops that are fed and another has a lien on the animals that eat the crops as feed, a so-called "split line" of credit, the outcome is not completely clear. If rules as to commingling apply, a perfected security interest in the feed which loses its identity by becoming part of the animal ranks equally with other perfected security interests in the animals according to the ratio that the cost of the assets to which each interest originally attached bears to the total cost of the resulting animal. However, the Nebraska Supreme Court determined in a 1988 decision that the commingling of feed rule does not apply to feed where there is no evidence that the feed was fed to livestock. *Beatrice National Bank v. Southeast Nebraska Cooperative,* 230 Neb. 671, 432 N.W.2d 842 (1988).

The application of the commingling rule has not been entirely clear in court decisions. In one case, the court held that the feeding of grain to cattle that was pledged as collateral under a security agreement terminated the creditor's security interest in the grain, *First National Bank of Brush v. Bostron,* 39 Colo. App. 107, 564 P.2d 964 (1977). However, in another case, the debtor raised cattle that were owned by third party investors and the court determined that the creditor's security interest in the crops that were fed to the cattle continued in cattle proceeds under either Article 9 or because the feeding was considered to be a sale of the crops to the investors. *In re Pelton,* 171 B.R. 641 (Bankr. W.D. Wis. 1994).

The "identifiable proceeds" problem may also be a concern to a creditor in the event the debtor files bankruptcy. *See, e.g., Pitcock v. First Bank of Muleshoe*, 208 B.R. 862 (Bankr. N.D. Tex. 1997).

A properly perfected security interest in crops prevails over the rights of the holder of the underlying real estate unless the real estate owner had filed a UCC financing statement on unsevered crops as part of the real estate.

## G.   FIXTURES

For fixtures, the first secured party to record either a security interest in the fixtures or a real estate mortgage has first priority. This means that a fixture filing will prevail over a subsequent real estate interest, but that the converse is also true. In some states, a security interest in personal property that becomes a fixture takes priority over a secured interest in the real property. If a secured party wishes to have a security interest that has priority over those with an interest in the real estate, three tests must be met:

1.   It must be a purchase money security interest;

2.   The security interest must be perfected by a fixture filing or a real estate mortgage before the goods become fixtures or within ten days thereafter; and

3.   The debtor must have an interest of record in the real estate or be in possession of the real estate.

Whether a good is a fixture depends on how firmly the goods are attached to the real estate and how easy it is to remove them, how the operation of the goods is related to the use of the land, the relationship of the parties involved, and whether the goods would reasonably be expected to be sold with the land.

## H.   UNPERFECTED SECURITY INTERESTS

An unperfected security interest takes priority over claims of general creditors but not of lien creditors without knowledge of the security interest. Priority between two or more unperfected security interests is determined in order of attachment of the security interest.

## III.   RIGHTS OF PURCHASERS ACQUIRING PROPERTY SUBJECT TO A SECURITY INTEREST

## A.   DEBTOR'S RIGHT TO SELL COLLATERAL

Frequently, the parties specify in the security agreement whether the debtor is authorized to sell or dispose of the collateral without the secured party's permission. If the debtor is so authorized, the purchaser takes the property free and clear of the security interest. If the debtor is not authorized to sell the collateral, but does so anyway, a buyer of the collateral takes subject to the creditor's security interest unless the buyer can demonstrate that the creditor has a history of allowing secured goods to be sold even without giving the debtor written authorization. *See, e.g., Mercantile Bank of Springfield v. Joplin Regional Stockyards, Inc.,* 870 F. Supp. 278 (W.D. Mo. 1994).

## B.   INVENTORY PROPERTY

In general, the UCC rules governing the rights of purchasers in secured property vary depending upon the type of property purchased. Thus, the appropriate inquiry when determining the relative rights of purchasers attempting to acquire property that is subject to a security interest requires analysis of the transaction by the type of collateral involved.

For inventory property, a buyer in the ordinary course of business takes free of a security interest even though perfected and even though the purchaser knows of its existence. Goods are inventory if they are held for immediate resale or ultimate use in the ordinary course of business. This rule is based on commercial necessity and permits relatively unhindered buying and selling of inventory property. "Inventory" does not include farm products, but does include other goods that are held for sale or lease or to be furnished under contracts of service, or goods that are raw materials, work in process or materials that are used or consumed in a business.

## C.   FARM PRODUCTS

For farm products, the majority rule has been (until changed by federal law in 1986) that a buyer in the ordinary course of business from a seller engaged in farming operations did not take free of a perfected security interest unless evidence existed of a course of past dealing between the secured party and the debtor from which it could be concluded that the secured party gave authority to the debtor to sell the collateral. Thus, a farmer's sale of secured farm products did not cut off the creditor's right to follow farm products into the hands of buyers, such as grain elevators. This meant that when a farmer failed to settle with secured parties, buyers of farm products sometimes had to pay twice unless the buyer could show that the secured party gave the debtor authority to sell the collateral. This special treatment for farm products was believed to be justified on the basis of the unique manner in which many agricultural goods are marketed. Because farmers typically market farm products through agents or sell to financially sophisticated buyers, it was deemed reasonable to expect these parties to understand the need to check for filed financing statements. Likewise, it was presumed to be generally known that farm lenders expected payment when farm products were marketed given the fact that most farm operations are cyclical and do not generate regular cash flow. Thus, farm lenders commonly have all of their expectations focused on a single sale of a collateralized crop.

Effective December 23, 1986, the Food Security Act of 1985 (1985 Farm Bill) "federalized" the states' farm product rules. This gave the states two options—adopt a prescribed central filing system or follow an "actual notice" rule. Thus, under the federal rule, if a BIOC buys a farm product that has been "produced in a state" from a seller engaged in farming, the BIOC takes the farm product free of any security interest created by the seller unless:

1.   Within one year before the sale of the farm products, the buyer has received written notice of the security interest from the secured party (the direct notice exception);

2.   The buyer has failed to pay for the farm products; or

3.   In states which have established a central filing system, the buyer has received notice from the Secretary of State of an effective filing of a financing statement (EFS) or notice of the security interest in the farm products and has not obtained a waiver or release of the security interest from the secured party (the central filing exception).

   In states that had not adopted the special central filing system, secured creditors could require debtors involved in farming operations to provide a list of buyers, commission merchants and selling agents to or through whom the debtor may sell the farm products collateral. Where such a clause was included in a security agreement, the farmer-debtor could not sell collateral to or through a party not on that list unless the farmer-debtor notified the secured creditor of the new party within seven days before the sale or paid the proceeds of the sale to the secured party within ten days after the sale. Violation of this rule subjected the farmer-debtor to a fine of the greater of $5,000 or 15% of the value or benefit received from the sale of the collateral.

To comply with the direct notice exception, a secured creditor had to send the farm products purchaser a written notice listing (1) the secured creditor's name and address; (2) the debtor's name and address; (3) the debtor's social security number or taxpayer identification number; (4) a description of the farm products covered by the security interest and a description of the property; and (5) any payment obligations conditioning the release of the security interest. The description of the farm products had to include the amount of the farm products subject to the security interest, the crop year, and the counties in which the farm products are located or produced.

Under central filing, the secured creditor must file a financing statement containing the same information as required in the written notice under the direct notice exception, except the secured creditor need not include crop year or payment obligation information. Also, notwithstanding errors contained in the financing statement, a financing statement in a central filing state remains effective so long as the errors "are not seriously misleading." However, there is no "substantial compliance" rule with respect to the direct notice exception. A secured creditor must comply strictly with the requirements of the direct notice exception.

Under the farm products rule, a question arises as to whether a buyer in a direct notice state that buys farm products that were produced in a central filing state is subject to a filing in an EFS central notice state. 7 U.S.C. § 1631 says the answer to that question is "yes" but does not define what "produced in" means. Is the phrase restricted in meaning only to production activities or does it also include marketing of the farm products? One court has held that "produced in" means "the location where farm products are furnished or made available for commerce." *See, e.g., Great Plains National Bank v. Mount,* 280 P.3d 670 (Colo. Ct. App. 2012).

The 2002 Farm Bill made several changes in the federal farm products rule. Under the legislation, a financing statement is effective if it is signed, authorized or otherwise authenticated by the debtor. A financing statement securing farm products needs to describe the farm products and specify each county or parish in which the farm products are produced or located. Also, the required information on the security agreement must include a description of the farm products subject to the security interest created by the debtor, including the amount of such products where applicable, crop year, and the name of each county or parish in which the farm products are produced or located.

**Note:** Under Revised Article 9, "farm products" means goods, other than standing timber, with respect to which the debtor is engaged in a farming operation and which are:

- Crops grown, growing or to be grown, including crops produced on trees, vines and bushes; and aquatic goods produced in aquacultural operations;

- Livestock, born or unborn, including aquatic goods produced in aquacultural operations;

- Supplies used or produced in a farming operation; or

- Products of crops or livestock in their unmanufactured states.

"Farming operation" means raising, cultivating, propagating, fattening, grazing or any other farming, livestock or aquacultural operation. As such, the revised definition of "farm products" eliminates the provision explicitly requiring the collateral to be in the possession of a person engaged in a farming operation.

## D.   RIGHTS OF FARMER IN FAILURE OF ELEVATOR

In general, a buyer of grain from an elevator in the ordinary course of business takes free of claims under warehouse receipts. Warehouse receipts and scale tickets constitute prima facie evidence of ownership in commodities unless there is a statute to the contrary. Commingled grain that is stored in an elevator is owned in common by the persons storing the grain in the elevator. The warehouseman is severally liable to each owner of grain commingled in the elevator. Where the warehouseman has issued receipts and scale tickets representing more grain than stored in the elevator, only holders of duly negotiated receipts have an interest in the remaining grain. When an elevator fails, there usually is less grain stored in the elevator than there are claims for grain. In this situation, the holders of negotiated receipts and scale tickets share pro rata in the remaining grain.

**Example 16:**

The maximum capacity of the Dry Gulch, Colorado, elevator is 150,000 bushels. Tom Tiller stored 46,500 bushels, Dan Druff stored 13,500 bushels, and Natalie Dressed stored 90,000 bushels. The elevator went bankrupt when there were only 78,000 bushels stored. A pro rata distribution will result in Tom receiving 24,180 bushels, Dan 7,020 bushels, and Natalie 46,800 bushels.

In bankruptcy, unsecured claims of grain producers, up to $6,150 per producer, are allowed for grain or the proceeds of grain against a debtor owning or operating a grain storage facility.

Under the UCC, a farmer who is not paid or who is given an insufficient funds check may reclaim the goods upon demand made within ten days after receipt. The bankruptcy rule is similar but requires that the request be in writing. The UCC, but not the Bankruptcy Code, waives the ten-day provision if misrepresentation of solvency has been made to a seller in writing within three months before delivery.

## E. RIGHTS OF CASH SELLERS OF LIVESTOCK AND POULTRY

Under the Packers & Stockyards Act, any packer having average purchases exceeding $500,000 is to hold all inventories, receivables and proceeds from the sale of meat, meat food products and livestock products in trust for the benefit of all unpaid cash sellers of livestock. The trust protects cash sellers of livestock and poultry by making their rights to specific assets of the packer (or live poultry dealer) legally superior to the interests of any secured lenders to whom the packer offered those assets as collateral for loans. For cash sellers of livestock and poultry to a packer on a live basis, the packer owes payment by the close of the next business day following purchase and transfer of possession. For livestock sold on a "grade and yield" basis, the packer owes payment by the close of the next business day after determination of the purchase price. An unpaid seller must notify the packer *and* the nearest Packers and Stockyards Program (P&SP) regional office within 30 calendar days after payment was due to preserve the protection of the trust. An unpaid seller must notify the packer and P&SP of their claim within 15 business days immediately after the day the seller receives notice that the payment instrument was dishonored. An express agreement in writing can operate as a waiver of the seller's right to next-day cash payment for livestock. An implied agreement or a course of dealing in which the livestock seller has tolerated delays in payment are insufficient for a waiver.

At a minimum, the written trust claims should include the following information:

- The packer or live poultry dealer's name and contact information;

- The seller or grower's name and contact information;

- The date of the transaction(s) in which the packer or live poultry dealer failed to pay for livestock or poultry;

- The date the seller or grower received notice that one or more payment instruments from the packer or live poultry dealer were dishonored (if applicable);

- The amount of money the packer or live poultry dealer owes the claimant for livestock or poultry; and

- Any other information necessary to support the seller or grower's trust claim.

## IV. DEFAULT BY THE DEBTOR

Upon a debtor's default, a secured party may look to the collateral for a full, or at least partial, satisfaction of the obligation. An unsecured lender, in contrast, must rely on the debtor's general credit and may collect from the debtor's property only after first obtaining a judgment. If an unsecured creditor does receive a judgment, the county sheriff can be requested to carry out an execution against the collateral. Typically, the creditor does not know the nature and extent of the debtor's property. Thus, the debtor usually first requests that the sheriff carry out a general execution. This requires the sheriff to go to the debtor and demand payment. If the debtor refuses, the creditor can ask the court for permission to levy on particular items of the debtor. The sheriff then carries out a second execution on these items, collects the property, and conducts a sheriff's sale of the items to recover the amount of the judgment. The sheriff's sale is a public sale and must be preceded by any statutorily required notice. If the property does not bring enough to fully satisfy the judgment, the creditor can get another execution and go after other property of the debtor. However, some of the debtor's property may be exempt from execution so that the debtor has some property available to support the debtor and the debtor's family. Statutorily, exempt property varies from state to state, but common exemptions exist for the homestead, insurance proceeds and funds contained in certain retirement plans.

If fixtures are involved as the subject of the security interest, a secured party who has priority over all owners and incumbrancers of the real estate may remove the fixture, but is obligated to reimburse the owner or incumbrancer of the real estate (who is not the debtor) for any damages to the property because of removal other than a reduction in value of the property because the fixture is no longer there.

## A.   RIGHT TO POSSESSION

Unless otherwise agreed, a secured party has the right to take possession of the collateral upon default without judicial process if this can be done without breach of the peace. If the peace would be breached, the secured party must commence a legal action. The UCC does not define the phrase "breach of the peace." In general, the phrase is construed to mean that the creditor can recover the collateral unless the debtor objects or protests. If the debtor voluntarily relinquishes the property upon default, the creditor is entitled to utilize "self-help." If self-help fails or the debtor objects to the creditor's attempt to repossess the collateral, the creditor must bring a court action known as a replevin action. If the creditor repossesses the collateral over the debtor's objection, the creditor may be found liable for conversion.

If the security agreement provides, the secured party may require the debtor to assemble the collateral and make it available to the secured party at a place to be designated by the secured party which is reasonably convenient to both parties. If the collateral is large or it would be expensive or impractical to remove it from the debtor's premises, the secured party may render the collateral unusable and dispose of it directly from the obligor's premises.

## B.   RIGHT AND DUTY TO DISPOSE OF COLLATERAL

### 1.  In General

Upon a debtor's default, a secured party can repossess the collateral and may sell (either by public or private sale), lease or otherwise dispose of the collateral either in its existing condition or following any commercially reasonable preparation or processing. If the debtor has paid 60 percent of the cash price of a PMSI in consumer goods or 60 percent of the loan in the case of another security interest in consumer goods and has not signed, after default, a statement renouncing or modifying the debtor's right, a secured party who has taken possession of the collateral must dispose of the collateral within 90 days after possession or suffer liability to the debtor. In all other situations, the secured creditor may, after repossessing the collateral, retain the collateral in full satisfaction of the debt unless the debtor objects within 21 days of receipt of notice of the creditor's intent to retain the collateral. If the creditor does retain the collateral, the security interest is discharged along with any liens that are subordinate to such interest. If the collateral is not worth the amount that is owed against it, the creditor is not entitled to the deficiency.

## 2. Commercial Reasonableness

If the creditor disposes of the collateral, every aspect of the secured party's disposition of the collateral, including the method, manner, time, place and other terms must be commercially reasonable. If collateral is not disposed of in a commercially reasonably manner, the liability of a debtor or a secondary obligor for a deficiency may be limited.

Unless the collateral is perishable or threatens to decline speedily in value or is of a type customarily sold on a recognized market, the creditor must give the debtor reasonable notification of the time and place of any public sale, private sale or other intended disposition of the collateral unless the debtor, after default, has signed a waiver of notification of sale. The revisions to Article 9 did not change existing law with respect to the statutory language for the recognized market exception.

If the repossessed collateral fails to bring enough at sale to cover the creditor's claim, the creditor may bring a legal action against the debtor for the amount of the deficiency. To recover the deficiency, the sale of the collateral must have been made in a commercially reasonable manner. Proof that a greater amount could have been obtained for the collateral by its disposition at a different time or in a different method is not alone sufficient to preclude the secured party from establishing that the disposition was commercially reasonable. But, a low sales price suggests the court should scrutinize carefully all the aspects of the disposition to insure each aspect was commercially reasonable. Ultimately, the issue of whether the disposition of collateral was commercially reasonable is one of fact. Courts consider a number of factors to evaluate whether collateral was disposed of in a commercially reasonable manner. These factors include whether the secured party tried to obtain the best price possible, whether the sale was private or public, the condition of the collateral and any efforts made to enhance its condition, the advertising undertaken, the number of bids received and the method used in soliciting bids.

The secured party may buy repossessed collateral at a public sale and may also buy the collateral at a private sale if the goods are of a type customarily sold in a recognized market or of a type which is the subject of widely distributed standard price quotations.

## 3. Revised Article 9

Under the Revisions to Article 9, in non-consumer deficiency cases, the secured party need not prove compliance with the default provisions unless compliance is placed in issue. If compliance is placed in issue, the secured party has the burden to show compliance. If the creditor cannot prove compliance, the rule is that the failure will reduce the secured party's deficiency to the extent that the failure to comply affected the price received for the goods at the foreclosure sale. Under the revisions, the value of the collateral is deemed to equal the unpaid debt and the noncomplying creditor is not entitled to a deficiency, unless the creditor seeking a deficiency proves by independent evidence that the price produced at sale was reasonable. Thus, the creditor must prove what the collateral would have been sold for at a commercially reasonable sale and that this amount is less than the unpaid debt.

While Revised Article 9 does not define "commercially reasonable," Section 9–611(c) provides that in a commercial transaction notice must be given to debtors, secondary obligors, any person who has given the foreclosing creditor notice of a claim, and any other secured party that holds a perfected security interest in the collateral. When consumer goods are involved, notice need only be given to debtors and secondary obligors.

## C.   PROCEEDS OF DISPOSITION

If the creditor sells the collateral, the proceeds of disposition are applied in a specific order. The expenses of repossession are paid first. This includes the cost of conducting a sale or other disposition of the assets including the reasonable expenses of retaking, holding, preparing for sale or lease, selling, leasing and the like and, to the extent provided for in the agreement and not prohibited by law, the reasonable attorney's fees and legal expenses incurred by the secured party. Next, the proceeds of disposition are applied against any amount due for the security interest under which the disposition is made. After that, the proceeds are applied in satisfaction of third party security interests if written notification of demand therefore is received before distribution of the proceeds has been completed. Any remaining amounts are paid to the debtor. Thus, because expenses of repossession diminish what would otherwise remain for the debtor, the debtor has a strong incentive to cooperate with the sale and may even allow the sale to occur on the debtor's premises. Conversely, if there is any deficiency, the debtor is liable unless the secured party has agreed otherwise.

## D.   EFFECT OF CREDITOR'S DISPOSITION OF PROPERTY

When collateral is disposed of by a secured party after default, the disposition transfers to a purchaser for value all of the debtor's rights in the collateral and discharges the security interest and any subordinate interest or lien. When property is disposed of by public sale, if the purchaser has no knowledge of any defects in the sale and if the purchaser does not buy in collusion with the secured party, other bidders or the person conducting the sale, the purchaser then takes free of all rights and interests even though the secured party fails to comply with all of the requirements of the UCC. A purchaser at a nonpublic sale also takes free of all rights and interests even though the secured party fails to comply with all of the requirements of the UCC if the purchaser acts in good faith. Alternatively, a secured party may reduce the defaulted claim to judgment and enforce the security interest as a judgment creditor. The judgment lien supporting a levy made on the collateral by virtue of an execution based upon the judgment relates back to the date of perfection of the security interest in the collateral.

## E.   DEBTOR'S RIGHT TO REDEEM

Before a creditor is permitted to dispose of the collateral, a debtor must be given a reasonable time in which to redeem the collateral after receiving notice of default. At any time before the secured party has disposed of the collateral, entered into a contract for its disposition or discharged the obligation by retaining the property, the debtor or any other secured party or lienor has the right to redeem by tendering full payment of the obligation plus interest and expenses incurred by the secured party because of the default, including attorneys' fees to the extent provided in the agreement and not prohibited by law unless otherwise agreed in writing after default. The right to redeem may be waived only if it is so agreed upon between the parties in writing after default. For consumer loans, the debtor must be in default for ten days before notice may be given. Once notice is given, the consumer has 20 days to cure the default.

## F.   SECURED PARTY'S LIABILITY FOR FAILURE TO COMPLY WITH THE CODE

A secured creditor is liable for the actual damage caused by the creditor's failure to follow UCC default rules. If it can be established that the secured party is not proceeding in accordance with the provisions of the UCC on default, disposition may be ordered or restrained on appropriate terms and conditions. If the disposition has occurred, the debtor, or any person entitled to notification, or any person whose security interest has been made known to the secured party before the disposition, has a right to recover from the secured party any loss caused by a failure to comply with the UCC rules on default. If the collateral is consumer goods, the debtor has a right to recover in any event an amount not less than the credit service charge plus 10% of the principal amount of the debt or the time price differential plus 10% of the cash price.

## V.   STATUTORY PRIORITY RULES

### A.   GENERAL PRIORITY RULES FOR LIENS

A lien gives the lienholder an enforceable right against certain property that can be used to pay a debt or obligations of the property's owner. Most states have laws that give particular parties a lien by statute in specific circumstances. Statutory liens have generally taken priority over UCC perfected security interests. The rationale behind statutory liens is that certain parties who have contributed inputs or services to another should have a first claim for payment. For example, Section 9–310 of the UCC states:

"When a person in the ordinary course of his business furnishes services or materials with respect to goods subject to a security interest, a lien upon goods in the possession of such person given by statute or rule of law for such materials or services takes priority over a perfected security interest unless the lien is statutory and the statute expressly provides otherwise."

Section 9–104 of the UCC states that Article 9 does not apply to a landlord's lien or to a lien that is given by statute or other rule of law for services or materials except as provided in § 9–310 of the UCC concerning priority of such liens. This means that there has been no filing requirement that must be satisfied before a landlord's lien or other statutory lien can attach and be perfected. Statutory liens automatically apply once the requirements of the particular statute have been satisfied. Priority conflicts between nonpossessory agricultural liens (including landlords' liens) and perfected Article 9 security interests are settled under the common law on a case-by-case basis, sometimes leading to inconsistent treatment in the courts. In general, nonpossessory liens tend to be viewed as "secret liens" and do not fare well against perfected security interests.

In general, the rights of purchasers of farm commodities are subject to any existing landlord's lien. A landlord's lien on crops to satisfy payment of rent prevails over those competing claimants that have actual or constructive notice of the lien. In most of the jurisdictions that recognize landlord's liens, no filing or notice is required; the lien is automatic if rent is unpaid. However, Illinois, in 1983, modified the priority scheme for landlord's liens by providing that a good faith purchaser takes crops free of the landlord's lien unless, within the six months before the purchase, the landlord provides written notice of the landlord's lien to the purchaser. A landlord, for land rented in Illinois, may require the tenant, before the sale of any crop grown on the rented land, to disclose the names of persons to whom the tenant intends to sell crops where that requirement has been imposed. The tenant may not sell the crops to anyone not disclosed to the landlord as a potential buyer of the crops.

In some states (such as Kansas and North Dakota), a cash-rent landlord does not get a priority lien on the crops. Instead, a secured lender has priority. This does not mean that a landlord's lien is unavailable. However, a security agreement should be signed and a financing statement filed if the crops are to be collateral for payment of cash rent. A perfected security interest is good against purchasers of farm products as well as other creditors.

While a landlord's lien on crops for unpaid rent for land on which the crops were produced was not covered under former Article 9, it is covered under the uniform version of Revised Article 9. But, some states have made non-uniform amendments to Article 9's treatment of agricultural liens.

A statutory landlord's lien is ineffective in the event of bankruptcy and can be avoided by the trustee in bankruptcy. Therefore, the landlord should create and perfect a security interest to secure the payment of rent in the case of a cash rent lease in order to prevail in bankruptcy. But remember, for a security agreement to attach, the debtor must have rights in the collateral. If a tenant gives a security interest in "all crops raised" on a tract of land, the tenant has rights to only the tenant's portion of the crop.

In addition to the landlord's lien, many states recognize other priority liens by statute. These liens are generally available for persons who provide materials and services to ensure that they will get paid. Some of these statutory liens apply to agriculture. For example, some statutes recognize an agister's lien which is essentially a landlord's lien for payment of rent in livestock lease situations. Typically, the landlord must file a claim in the appropriate county office to perfect an agister's lien. In many of these same jurisdictions, a similar lien is available to those who feed and care for livestock. This type of lien is important in the custom feedlot industry, and generally applies if the bill remains unpaid for 60 to 90 days. After that, the lienholder may sell the livestock and apply the proceeds against the indebtedness.

Other statutory liens may include grain harvesting liens, mechanic's liens, forwarding and commission merchant's liens, artisan's liens, veterinarian's liens and warehouseman's liens.

## B. AG SUPPLY DEALER LIENS

Some states provide statutorily for an agricultural supply dealer's lien. The theory behind this type of lien is that parties who supply necessary inputs such as seed, feed, fertilizer, chemicals and petroleum products should have a method whereby they are assured of payment for the inputs supplied to agricultural producers. Several state legislatures passed agricultural supply dealer lien statutes during the farm debt crisis of the 1980s when an extraordinarily high number of farm and ranch operators went bankrupt and all of their property was claimed subject to perfected security interests under Article 9, leaving the supply dealer as an unsecured creditor with large unpaid bills.

Agricultural supply dealer lien statutes are rather complex, but most follow a common procedure. One common type gives an ag commodity dealer that sells an ag product a lien on the ag product or its sale proceeds. However, a question may arise concerning the viability of the lien when the ag product is consumed by livestock. *See, e.g., Farmers National Bank v. Green River Dairy, LLC,* 318 P.3d 622, 155 Idaho 853 (2014).

With respect to crop input suppliers, when a farmer or rancher attempts to purchase supplies on credit or on open account, the supplier can obtain a lien on the crops produced with such inputs. Under the Iowa statute, for example, the supplier must discover what other parties, if any, have a security interest in the purchaser's crops or livestock. *Iowa Code § 570A.* The supplier is required to contact these creditors and inquire about the purchaser's financial abilities. This puts the creditors on notice that the supplier may be attempting to take a statutory lien. The creditors can either agree to finance the purchase or send the supply dealer the buyer's financial records. If the creditors refuse to extend credit, the supply dealer can make the sale and obtain a lien by filing in the appropriate office, usually the Secretary of State's office. The lien is effective at the time of the purchase and is "perfected" by the filing of a financing statement within 31 days of the purchase. The lien applies to crops related to the purchased supply or livestock consuming the feed sold to the farmer by the dealer. The amount of the lien is the amount owed to the dealer for the "retail cost of the agricultural supply, including labor." The lien is perfected for the amount of supplies that the debtor buys from the supplier within 31 days before the supplier files the financing statement. The lien also extends to the proceeds of the input(s) supplied. The perfected lien does not continue nor does it cover future advances. If additional supplies are sold to a debtor after the initial 31-day period, another financing statement must be filed within 31 days of sale to perfect the lien for those additional supplies that are provided. For a case construing the statute, see *Oyens Feed Supply, Inc. v. Primebank,* 808 N.W.2d 186 (Iowa 2011).

Most state statutes provide that an agricultural supply dealer lien is superior to subsequently filed Article 9 security interests, and of equal priority to Article 9 interests already in existence.

A question can arise under a state's supply dealer lien statute concerning the total amount of inputs that the lien secures. *See, e.g., Tracy State Bank v. Tracy-Garvin Cooperative,* 573 N.W.2d 393 (Minn. Ct. App. 1998).

Because statutory liens grant "super priority" status only to the extent that they are perfected, it is important that a party seeking to gain super priority status understand the particulars of the statutory lien and follow the requirements to perfect the lien as intended.

## C.   REVISED ARTICLE 9 AND AGRICULTURAL LIENS

### 1.  Rules for Perfection and Priority

Revised UCC § 9–109(a)(2) applies Revised Article 9 to "an agricultural lien." Every state except Kansas includes this coverage. An "agricultural lien" is defined to mean "an interest, other than a security interest, in farm products which secures payment or performance of an obligation for goods or services furnished in connection with the debtor's farming operation or rent on real property leased by a debtor in connection with its farming operation." The lien must be created by statute in favor of a person that in the ordinary course of business furnishes goods or services to a debtor in connection with the debtor's farming operation, or in favor of a person that leased real property to a debtor in connection with debtor's farming operation. In addition, the effectiveness of the lien must not depend on the person's possession of the personal property.

An agricultural lien is perfected when the lien is effective under the statute creating it and a proper financing statement has been filed centrally.

Priority conflicts between a security interest and an agricultural lien depend on the state statute creating the lien. If the state statute creating the agricultural lien does not state a priority rule, the normal priority rules of Article 9 apply. Thus, perfected security interests have priority according to time of filing or perfection, whichever occurs first, unless the statute creating the lien specifically provides otherwise.

A perfected agricultural lien has priority over a conflicting unperfected security interest or agricultural lien. The first security interest or agricultural lien to attach or become effective has priority if a conflicting security interest or agricultural lien is unperfected. If a statute under which an agricultural lien is created provides that the agricultural lien has priority over a conflicting security interest or agricultural lien in the same collateral, that statute governs priority if the agricultural lien is perfected. As for conflicts between a lien creditor and an unperfected agricultural lien, the lien creditor defeats an unperfected agricultural lien holder.

## 2. The Landlord's Lien

A significant impact of the coverage of agricultural liens is that a landlord lien for unpaid rent of land used in a farming operation is now covered by Article 9. Thus, a landlord lien on crops for unpaid rent on land on which the crops are produced is not subject to the perfection, priority and enforcement rules of Revised Article 9.

If a landlord's lien exists on a crop and the tenant sells the crop without paying rent, it is critical to determine whether the statute creating the lien provides that the lien continues in proceeds. Revised Article 9 refers to an "agricultural lien, but not to "proceeds." Consequently, the negative inference is that proceeds of collateral subject to an agricultural lien are not covered by Revised Article 9. Indeed, Comment 2 to Revised UCC § 9–302 provides that Revised Article 9 does not deal with proceeds of collateral subject to an agricultural lien because no agricultural lien on proceeds arises under Article 9. But, an argument can be made that the UCC's silence is not a basis for preventing an agricultural lien's attachment to proceeds of sold property that was subject to an agricultural lien. Indeed, Comment 9 to Revised UCC § 9–315 states that Article 9 does not determine whether a lien extends to proceeds of farm products encumbered by an agricultural lien. If the proceeds are themselves farm products on which an agricultural lien arises under law, then the lien provisions of Article 9 apply to the proceeds in the same way in which they would have applied if the farm products had not been proceeds.

Importantly, a landlord's lien can be avoided by a trustee in bankruptcy. Thus, landlords that are uncertain about the financial status of a tenant should require cash up front.

## 3. Summary

In summary, several points can be made about Revised Article 9 and agricultural liens. First, an agricultural lien must be created by state law. Second, all agricultural liens must be perfected by filing a proper financing statement centrally—there no longer can be secret agricultural liens. Third, statutes without a priority rule will be controlled by Article 9 priority rules. Finally, the statute can provide for "super priority" agricultural liens, but they will be subject to the perfection and enforcement rules of Article 9.

# CHAPTER 4
# BANKRUPTCY

## I. OVERVIEW

In the United States, the opportunity for financially distressed debtors to file for bankruptcy is assured by Art. I, Sec, 8of the United States Constitution. Thus, bankruptcy is a matter of federal law.

The U.S. bankruptcy system is governed by two objectives—(1) a "fresh start" for poor but honest debtors who can obtain a discharge for some (but not all) debts; and (2) a policy of fairness for the unsecured creditors. The secured creditors are assured of receiving the value of their collateral. Bankruptcy provides a procedure by which the unsecured creditors share in the debtor's assets on a basis of fairness and equality.

On April 20, 2005, President Bush signed into law the largest overhaul of the Bankruptcy Code since 1978. The Bankruptcy Abuse Prevention and Consumer Protection Act of 2005 largely impacts consumer bankruptcy, but has provisions affecting corporations, farmers and small businesses.

## II. TYPES OF BANKRUPTCY

### A. LIQUIDATION

Debtors who have no hope of paying off their debts, and who wish to be free of their obligations, may file for "liquidation" bankruptcy. That procedure is governed by Chapter 7 of the Bankruptcy Code. This is known as "straight bankruptcy." The debtor turns over all assets to the bankruptcy court, receives back the assets that are exempt from creditors, and obtains a discharge from all dischargeable debts. Some obligations such as alimony, taxes and student loans are not dischargeable on social policy grounds. Student's loans are only dischargeable if not discharging the loan would result in an undue hardship to the debtor.

## B.   REORGANIZATION

Federal bankruptcy law also provides for rehabilitation or reorganization of debtors as an alternative to liquidation.

Chapter 11, the general reorganization provision, enables a debtor to enter into an agreement with creditors under which all or part of the business continues and the debts of the business are restructured. Approval of the plan by creditors is required as well as approval of the bankruptcy court. In general, creditors must receive as much as they would receive on liquidation.

Chapter 12, provides a reorganization option tailored to the unique needs of farm and ranch businesses. Secured debts are written down to the value of the collateral with the remaining debt from the secured obligations treated as unsecured debt. The debtor is required to apply all income above family living expense and the needs of the business to the plan. Unsecured debt remaining after the plan's three to five-year period is generally discharged. This chapter focuses on Chapter 12 bankruptcy.

Under Chapter 13, individual wage earners and small businesses with regular income develop a plan under which debts are paid over time from income and the debtor is discharged from remaining debts as provided under the plan.

A bankruptcy reorganization case is generally dismissed if the debtor dies while the reorganization plan is in effect. However, the parties involved may petition the bankruptcy court to continue administration of the case. The court will not dismiss the case if it determines that further administration is possible and is in the best interests of the parties.

## III.  WHO CAN BE A DEBTOR?

Individuals, partnerships, corporations and other types of business entities are eligible to file bankruptcy. Cooperatives are not specifically mentioned in federal bankruptcy law but are treated as corporations for bankruptcy filing purposes.

A joint case can be filed voluntarily by a husband and wife. A joint case has occasionally been allowed involving a corporation and the corporation's sole shareholder where the corporation was formed to operate the business owned by the debtor.

Generally, a decedent's estate may not be a debtor in bankruptcy. If a Chapter 7 case has already been commenced when the debtor dies, the case is to proceed to liquidation as if the debtor had not died. In the event a Chapter 11, 12 or 13 case has been commenced at the debtor's death, the case is to be dismissed unless further administration is possible and would be in the best interests of the parties.

The 2005 Act provides that, to be a debtor, a person must receive a briefing from an approved credit counseling agency outlining the opportunities available for credit counseling and assisting in a budgetary analysis. The credit counseling requirement has been held applicable to Chapter 12 farm debtors. *See, e.g., Bogedain v. Eisen,* No. 06–11831, 2006 U.S. Dist. LEXIS 59926 (E.D. Mich. Aug. 24, 2006).

## IV.  INVOLUNTARY BANKRUPTCY

The vast majority of bankruptcies are filed voluntarily by the debtor. However, U.S. bankruptcy law provides also for involuntary bankruptcy by action of the creditors against a person. The term "person" is defined to include corporations, partnerships and other business entities.

In general, a creditor of an insolvent debtor may petition to have a debtor adjudged an involuntary bankrupt (Chapter 7 or Chapter 11) if the creditors' claims total at least $15,775 more than the value of any security held by the creditor and the claim is not subject to a bona fide dispute. At least three creditors (who collectively hold unsecured claims aggregating at least $15,775 that are not contingent or the subject of a bona fide dispute) must join in the petition if the debtor has 12 or more creditors. Involuntary bankruptcy proceedings are available only for liquidations (Chapter 7) and for Chapter 11 reorganizations. They may not be commenced in the case of Chapter 12 or Chapter 13 debtor rehabilitation plans.

Upon the filing of an involuntary petition, the creditor must establish that the debtor is not paying its debts as the debts become due. The standard is satisfied where the debtor regularly misses a significant number of payments to a creditor or regularly misses payments that are significant in amount in relation to the size of the debtor's operations. Once an involuntary petition is filed and served on the debtor, the debtor has 20 days to file an answer before the court enters the order for relief. Under the 2005 Bankruptcy Act, an individual can only be a debtor upon completion of a "briefing" from a nonprofit budget and credit counseling agency. An individual who has not had a credit briefing cannot voluntarily or involuntarily be a debtor. Thus, it is anticipated that bankruptcy judges granting involuntary petitions will also order credit counseling as a routine matter.

Under 11 U.S.C. § 303(a), an involuntary case *cannot* be brought against a "farmer" or a "family farmer." *11 U.S.C. § 101(20)* defines a "farmer" as a "person that received more than 80 percent of such person's gross income during the taxable year of such person immediately preceding the taxable year of such person during which the case under this title concerning such person was commenced from a farming operation owned or operated by such person." "Farming operation" is defined in 11 U.S.C. § 101(21) as including "farming, tilling of the soil, dairy farming, ranching, production or raising of crops, poultry, or livestock, and production of poultry or livestock products in an unmanufactured state." This definition of "farming operation" is not an exclusive list of all farming activities, and the definition is not limited to those activities listed in the statute. As a result, the courts have wrestled with how to determine what constitutes "farming" and "farming operation" and what is income from farming both in the context of the exemption from involuntary proceedings and in the context of eligibility for Chapter 12 bankruptcy. *See, e.g.,  In re Blanton Smith Corp.,* 7 B.R. 410 (Bankr. M.D. Tenn. 1980).

In general, the courts have developed two tests when examining the debtor's income for the purpose of determining what percentage of that income is from farming. One of the tests examines the circumstances around the debtor's income in order to achieve an equitable result. *See, e.g., In re Watford* 898 F.2d 1525 (11th Cir. 1990).

In *In re Vecchione,* No. 13-42201-MSH, 2013 Bankr. LEXIS 4978 (Bankr. D. Mass. Nov. 20, 2013), the court referenced *Watford* for the proposition that other activities not specifically mentioned in 11 U.S.C. § 101(18) can qualify as a farming operation. However, the court determined that the debtor was not a "family farmer" engaged in farming operations for at least two years since he started growing pumpkins and watermelons. The court held that agritourism is not "farming" within either the letter or the spirit of 11 U.S.C. § 101(18). The court noted that, by the debtor's logic, Disneyland would be a farming operation because it was built on land that had formerly been an orange grove.

Another test (known as the "Tax Code test") has developed from the fact that the term "gross income from a farming operation" is not defined in the Bankruptcy Act. Under this test, courts use the definition of gross income under I.R.C. § 62(a), and then determine what percentage of that gross income is derived from farming operations. Applying this test, one court found that the occupant of a country residence (who received $1500 per month from the practice of law and $40 from farming) could not modify a security interest in the residence since it was solely a residence and not a "farm." *In re Bailard,* 4 B.R. 271 (Bankr. E.D. Va. 1980). *See also In re Sharp,* 361 B.R. 559 (B.A.P. 10th Cir. 2007). Also, under the "tax code test," the Eighth Circuit has held that income from a cash rent lease did not constitute "gross income from a farming operation." *In re Armstrong,* 812 F.2d 1024 (8th Cir. 1987), *cert denied,* 485 U.S. 925 (1987). But, the court allowed the proceeds from the sale of farm machinery to be included in farm income. A dissenting judge would have vacated the bankruptcy court's opinion and remanded the case for a determination of whether, under the totality of the circumstances, the leased land was part of the debtor's ongoing farming operation or whether it was a distinct and separate venture.

In a later case, *In re Ross,* 270 B.R. 710 (Bankr. S.D. Ill. 2001), the creditor moved to dismiss the debtor's Chapter 12 petition arguing that the debtor failed to qualify as a family farmer because income received from the sale of land in the year before filing was nonfarm income which, when added to other nonfarm income, exceeded the limitation on nonfarm income for a Chapter 12 filing. The debtor argued that the land sale proceeds were farm income and pointed to *Armstrong* as authority insomuch as *Armstrong* allowed income from farm machinery sales to count as farm income. The court, however, distinguished the case from *Armstrong* in that the debtors did not sell the land as part of a plan to save the remaining farm as a business. The court noted that the land had been held for investment or speculation, and that the debtor had characterized the sale as acreage from a real estate development. The debtor's counsel also stated that it was the debtor's good fortune that a golf course had been built across the road. Thus, the implication was that the debtors sold the land, not to save a failing farm, but to take advantage of a business opportunity. *See also, In re Teolis,* 419 B.R. 151 (Bankr. D. R.I. 2009).

In a 2013 case, the court followed the "Tax Code" definition of gross income in determining whether the 50 percent test was satisfied. *In re Perkins,* No. 13–31277, 2013 Bankr. LEXIS4539 (Bankr. E.D. Tenn. Oct. 30 2013). The court determined that the debtors derived at least 50 percent of their gross income from farming in 2010 and 2011 from farming operations. Thus, the debtors qualified as eligible to file Chapter 12, but their reorganization plan was ultimately denied confirmation for other reasons. In a 2014 case, the debtor was not eligible for Chapter 12 under the "totality of the circumstances." None of the debtor's family resided on the farm, the debtor was not involved in growing crops or raising livestock and he was not subject to the inherent risks of farming. *In re McLawchlin*, No. 13–37887, 2014 Bankr. LEXIS 2455 (Bankr. S.D. Tex. Jun. 5, 2014).

**Note:** A debtor's status as a farmer is an affirmative defense that the debtor must plead and prove in order for the status of "farmer" to be available to the debtor. Failure to plead the affirmative defense waves the defense.

## V.  COMMENCING A VOLUNTARY BANKRUPTCY CASE

A debtor can initiate a bankruptcy case by filing a voluntary petition and paying a filing fee. The filing is sometimes termed the "order of relief." A debtor then has the duty to—(1) file a list of creditors; (2) file schedules of assets and liabilities, current income and expenses and a statement of financial affairs; (3) indicate intentions within 30 days of filing or by the meeting of creditors, whichever is earlier, as to retention or surrender of property, exemptions and affirmation of debts; (4) cooperate with the trustee; (5) surrender property and recorded information regarding property of the bankruptcy estate; and (6) appear at a hearing to consider the discharge of debts.

In addition, under the 2005 Bankruptcy Act, the debtor must provide a certificate of credit counseling; evidence of payment from employers, if any, received 60 days before filing; a statement of monthly net income and any anticipated increase in income or expenses after filing; tax returns for the most recent tax year; tax returns filed during the case (including returns for prior years that had not been filed when the case began; and a photo I.D. (upon the trustee's request). Failure to provide the documents within 45 days after the petition has been filed (with the possibility of a 45-day extension) results in automatic dismissal of the case.

## A.   THE AUTOMATIC STAY

The filing of a bankruptcy petition automatically halts a wide range of conduct by the debtor or with respect to the debtor's property. This is called the "automatic stay." The automatic stay prohibits—(1) initiating or continuing a lawsuit against the debtor; (2) actions to obtain possession of property of the bankruptcy estate; (3) actions that create, perfect or enforce liens or security interests against property of the bankruptcy estate; (4) actions to collect, assess or recover claims before the petition was filed; (5) the set-off of debts owing to the debtor; (6) continuing or commencing litigation in the U.S. Tax Court concerning the debtor; or (7) discontinuing or altering service by a utility merely because the debtor has initiated a bankruptcy case unless the debtor fails to furnish adequate assurance of payment, by deposit or security, within 20 days of bankruptcy filing.

The automatic stay does not prevent several types of actions, however—(1) criminal actions against the debtor; (2) collection of alimony, separate maintenance or child support from property that is not part of the estate; (3) the perfection of a security interest if, under state law, the perfection of the security interest will date back to a date before the bankruptcy petition was filed (this provision is immensely important to merchants); (4) litigation by a governmental unit to enforce a policy or regulatory power; (5) enforcement by a governmental unit of a judgment obtained in an action enforcing a policy or regulatory power; (6) set off of mutual debts and claims that arose out of transactions in commodity futures, options for commodities and securities or other leveraged transactions; (7) litigation by the Secretary of Housing and Urban Development to foreclose a mortgage or deed insured under the National Housing Act covering a property of five or more units; (8) issuance of a notice of tax deficiency by a governmental unit; (9) use of cash, securities or other property held to secure a repurchase agreement to set off or settle a claim arising from the repurchase agreement; (10) action by a lessor of non-residential real estate to regain possession of the property from the debtor, where the lease has expired; and (11) presentment of a negotiable instrument and giving notice and protesting dishonor of such an instrument.

Transactions before bankruptcy filing may be reviewed and action taken to negate an advantage gained by a particularly diligent creditor or insider. The bankruptcy trustee has broad powers to examine pre-filing transactions; to disavow contracts, including unexpired leases; prevent third parties from terminating advantageous contracts; prevent acceleration of debts and, in some instances, to extend the term and reduce the rate of interest on secured and unsecured loans; and use property of a creditor during a reorganization proceeding.

The Bankruptcy Act of 2005 limits the application of the stay or provides that it does not go into effect in situations indicating bad faith or abusive filing. For example, the stay terminates after 30 days if there is a filing by an individual in Chapter 7, 11 or 13 (but not Chapter 12) within 1 year after the prior case (under any Chapter) was dismissed (except for a case refiled under another Chapter after a dismissal of a Chapter 7 case based on the means test). A party in interest (including the debtor) may move to extend the stay and show that the filing is in good faith. A case is presumed to be in bad faith for this purpose if more than one case was pending in Chapters 7, 11 or 13 and at least one such case was dismissed for failure to file required documents without substantial excuse, to provide adequate protection, or to complete a plan, and there is no showing that the debtor's financial situation has changed so as to allow a final discharge or completion of a plan. If two or more cases under any Chapter were dismissed during the prior year, the automatic stay does not go into effect at all until the court so orders after a hearing and a demonstration that the filing was made in good faith. The same bad faith factors are also applicable to this determination. The law also provides that the stay will terminate if the debtor does not timely file (i.e., within 30 days after the petition date) its statement of intent with respect to property subject to a security interest and timely (i.e. within 30 days after the first date set for the meeting of creditors) complies with the stated intention. The court may extend the stay upon the motion of the trustee if the property is of the value to the estate and adequate protection is afforded to the creditor.

## B.   LIFTING THE AUTOMATIC STAY

As noted above, the filing of the bankruptcy petition activates the automatic stay which halts most actions against the debtor and also prevents the debtor from disposing of the property. The creditors often respond quickly with a plea to the bankruptcy court for the automatic stay to be lifted. The arguments typically emphasize that the collateral is not being properly cared for (animals not being fed, cows not being milked), the collateral is declining in value (machinery continues to be used by the debtor and is suffering normal wear) or the land is dropping in value (soil is eroding, buildings not being properly maintained). If the bankruptcy court is convinced that the creditors' allegations are true, the court may require the debtor to provide "adequate protection" to the creditors. The debtor has three options for meeting an adequate protection order:

- Making periodic cash payments to the extent of any decrease in value of a creditor's interest in the debtor's property.

- Providing an additional or replacement lien to compensate for any decrease in value of the creditor's interest in the debtor's property.

- Granting any other form of relief that gives the creditor with an interest in the property the "indubitable equivalent" of such interest.

All three possibilities are often beyond the debtor's reach. Usually, the debtor's cash flow doesn't permit additional cash payments to offset declines in collateral value. Moreover, all of the debtor's property is often fully covered with at least one obligation (if not more), so providing a lien on unencumbered property is out of the question.

If the debtor is unable to respond, the court may order the automatic stay lifted as to designated assets and the creditor can take action to obtain the collateral to satisfy the obligation. Otherwise, the automatic stay continues until it is no longer useful, the bankruptcy estate is closed or dismissed, a discharge of the debtor's obligations is granted or, for reorganization bankruptcy, a plan of reorganization is confirmed.

In addition, the automatic stay can be modified "for cause."

For reorganization bankruptcies, creditors may scrutinize the debtor's property and ask the court to declare that some items are not "necessary for effective reorganization." The courts are in some disagreement as to whether the term means that the property is essential to operation of a farm and there is a reasonable probability of successful rehabilitation of the debtor's business within a reasonable time or whether it means only that the property is essential to operation of the farm.

If the court determines that specific items of property are not necessary for an effective reorganization, and the debtor lacks equity in the property, the automatic stay may be terminated as to those assets.

## C.   EXEMPT PROPERTY

The U.S. legal system has a long history of allowing debtors to hold specified items of property exempt from creditors (unless the exemption is waived). This, in effect, gives debtors a "head start" in becoming reestablished after suffering economic reverses. Typically, one of the largest and most important exemptions is for the homestead.

Initially even the exempt property is included in the debtor's estate in bankruptcy but the exempt assets are soon returned to the debtor. Only nonexempt property is used to pay the creditors.

Because of the availability of exemptions, debtors may be tempted to convert nonexempt property (such as cash) into exempt assets prior to bankruptcy filing. There is no general prohibition on such conversions, but courts closely examine attempted conversions with respect to the adequacy of the purchase price and the bargaining position of the parties involved. If the primary purpose of the move is to hinder, delay or defraud creditors, the conversion can be challenged.

---

**Example 1:**

Willard will soon be filing bankruptcy. Willard owns wheat and cattle free of any security interests, and sells these items to pay off the loan on his pickup and reduce the balance due against his farm home. Willard will claim his pickup and farm home exempt in the bankruptcy, and will be able to keep the automobile free of all security interests, and the farm home subject to a reduced mortgage.

**Example 2:**

John and Marcia's financial situation is rapidly worsening and they will soon be filing bankruptcy. As a result, they give $25,000 worth of cattle to their son in order to avoid losing the cattle to creditors in the bankruptcy proceedings. Because their son paid nothing for the cattle and the parties are related, the court may set the transfer aside as fraudulent.

---

Actual intent to defraud must generally be present, but a court may infer actual intent from the circumstances of the debtor's conduct. In other words, a debtor could engage in actual fraud as defined by 11 U.S.C. § 548(a)(1)(A) or constructive fraud under 11 U.S.C. § 548 (a)(1)(B). In addition, the funds used to acquire exempt assets must not be from the sale of collateral or as a result of wrongdoing by the debtor. In addition, some states have enacted limits on acquiring some types of exempt property (notably life insurance policies) within a specified time before bankruptcy filing.

**Note:** Exemptions are authorized under both state law (with the states varying significantly in their generosity to debtors) and federal law. Federal bankruptcy law, however, permits states by legislation to prohibit the use of federal exemptions. Thirty-thee states have acted to prohibit the use of federal exemptions. Debtors in those states can only use exemptions provided under non-bankruptcy law.

In general, that means such debtors are limited to state law exemptions.

## 1. Federal Exemptions

Under federal bankruptcy law, exemptions can be claimed in 11 categories:

- Up to $23,675 in value of property used by the debtor (or dependent of the debtor) as a residence.

- Up to $3,775 in value of one motor vehicle.

- All items that are household furnishings, household goods, wearing apparel, appliances, books, animals, crops or musical instruments held by the debtor or a dependent of the debtor primarily for personal, family or household use up to $600 per item and up to an aggregate of $12,625.

- Up to $1,600 in total value of jewelry held for personal, family or household use.

- A "wild card" exemption in any property of $1,250 plus up to $11,850 of the amount not used for the exemption for the debtor's residence.

- Up to $2,375 in total value of implements, professional books or tools of the trade of the debtor or a dependent of the debtor.

- Any unmatured life insurance contracts owned by the debtor except for credit life insurance.

- Up to $12,625 in dividends, interest or loan value of certain other life insurance.

- Professionally prescribed health aids.

- The debtor's right to receive certain benefits and payments, such as social security, unemployment compensation, public assistance, veteran's benefits, disability, alimony and child support needed for support, annuities, stock bonus or similar plans and some pensions, and payments under a qualified stock bonus, pension, profit sharing, annuity or similar contract or plan on account of illness, disability or death, age or length of service to the extent reasonably necessary for the support of the debtor or a dependent of the debtor.

- The debtor's right to receive, or property that is traceable to an award under a crime victim's reparation law, a payment on account of the wrongful death of an individual of whom the debtor was a dependent to the extent reasonably necessary for the debtor's support and any dependent of the debtor; a payment under a life insurance contract insuring an individual of whom the debtor was a dependent; up to $23,675 of monetary damages for bodily injury, not including pain and suffering or compensation for actual pecuniary loss of the debtor or a dependent of the debtor.

*11 U.S.C. § 522(d).*

## 2. State Law Exemptions

Each of the 50 states has developed a unique list of exemptions available to debtors. 18 states and the District of Columbia allow debtors to choose between their state exemptions or the federal exemptions. The remaining states have chosen to "opt-out" of the federal exemptions. Under the 2005 Bankruptcy Act, to be able to utilize a state's exemptions, a debtor must have resided in the state for 730 days preceding the bankruptcy filing. If the debtor did not reside in any one state for 730 days immediately preceding filing, then the debtor may use the exemptions of a state in which the debtor resided for at least 180 days immediately preceding filing. If those requirements cannot be met, the debtor must use the federal exemptions.

The Iowa list is included here for illustrative purposes.

- Wedding or engagement ring owned and received by the debtor or the debtor's dependents on or before the date of marriage, up to $2,000; $7,000 if purchased after marriage or within the last two years.

- Other jewelry of the debtor and the debtor's dependents, up to $2,000.

- One shotgun and either one rifle or musket (of unlimited value).

- Burial plot not exceeding one acre.

- Insurance policies:

- ○ The interest of an individual in any accrued dividend or interest, loan or cash surrender value of or any other interest in a life insurance policy owned by the individual if the beneficiary is the individual's spouse, child or dependent. *The amount of the exemption is not to exceed $10,000 in the aggregate for insurance acquired within two years of the date execution is issued or exemptions are claimed.*

- ○ Life insurance benefits payable to the spouse, child or dependent of the individual are exempt from creditors.

- ○ Amounts paid under an accident, health or disability insurance policy are exempt to the insured or, in the case of the insured's death, to the spouse, child or dependent of the insured.

- ○ Up to $15,000 in the aggregate of the avails of all matured policies of life, accident, health or disability insurance payable to the surviving spouse, child or dependent for debts of the beneficiary contracted prior to the death of the insured is exempt.

- Professionally prescribed health aids for the debtor or a dependent of the debtor are exempt.

- The debtor's rights are exempt in social security, unemployment or any public assistance benefits; veteran's benefits; disability or illness benefits; alimony, support or separate maintenance benefits reasonably necessary for the support of the debtor and dependents of the debtor and pension, annuity or similar plans or contracts on account of illness, disability, death, age or length of service, to the extent necessary for the support of the debtor and any dependents of the debtor.

- Personal property as follows:

  o Up to $7,000 in musical instruments, not including radios, television sets, or record or tape players, held primarily for personal, family or household use of the debtor or a dependent of the debtor; appliances, household furnishings, clothing, other personal property.

  o One motor vehicle, up to $7,000 worth of equity.

  o For debtors in bankruptcy, the debtor's interest in accrued wages and state and federal tax refunds as of the date of bankruptcy filing, not to exceed $1000 in total.

- Contributions and assets, including the accumulated earnings and market increases in value in various retirement plans or contracts.

- If the debtor is engaged in any profession or occupation other than farming, the implements, professional books or tools of the trade of the debtor or a dependent of the debtor, are exempt not to exceed $10,000 in total.

- If the debtor is engaged in farming and does not exercise the delay in enforcement of a deficiency judgment, any combination of the following not to exceed $10,000 in total is exempt:

- o Implements and equipment reasonably related to a normal farming operation. This exemption is in addition to the exempt motor vehicle.

- o Livestock and feed for the livestock reasonably related to a normal farming operation. *In re Sadler,* 327 B.R. 654 (Bankr. N.D. Iowa 2005).

- If the debtor is engaged in farming agricultural land, foreclosure occurs and a deficiency judgment is issued against the debtor, and the debtor does not exercise the delay in enforcement of the deficiency judgment, the "disposable earnings" of the debtor are exempt from garnishment to enforce the deficiency judgment after two years from entry of the deficiency judgment. However, earnings "paid to the debtor directly or indirectly by the debtor" are not exempt.

- U.S. government pensions are exempt.

- Workers' compensation benefits are exempt.

- The household is exempt except for debts contracted before its acquisition, those for which the homestead was encumbered by written contract after all other property is exhausted and debts incurred for improvement of the homestead. The homestead includes a dwelling house used as a home by the owner not to exceed one-half acre if within a city or 40 acres otherwise. If the value is less than $500, the homestead may be enlarged to reach that amount.

> **Note:** Under the 2005 Bankruptcy Act, the debtor may only exempt up to $160,375 (The amount is adjusted for inflation) of equity value in a homestead that was acquired within the 1,215-day period before the bankruptcy filing, but the calculation of that amount does not include any equity that has been rolled over during that period from one house to another within the same state. Also, the $160,375 limitation does not apply to the residence of a "family farmer." But, the limitation does apply if the debtor has engaged in certain criminal conduct or violated securities laws. Also, to the extent the homestead was obtained through fraudulent conversion of nonexempt assets during the 10-year period before filing, the exemption is reduced by the amount attributable to the fraud.

- Private libraries, family bibles, portraits, pictures and paintings not to exceed a value of $1000 in the aggregate are exempt.

- An amount is exempt not to exceed $100 in the aggregate in any cash on hand, bank deposits, credit union share drafts or other deposits or other personal property not otherwise specifically provided for.

- The debtor's interest, not to exceed $500 in total of:

  o Any residential rental deposit held by a landlord as a security deposit, as well as any interest earned on the deposit as a result of a statute or rule requiring that the deposit be placed in an interest-bearing account.

- Any residential utility deposit as well as interest earned on the deposit as a result of a statute or rule requiring that the deposit be placed in an interest-bearing account.

- Any rent paid to a landlord in advance of the date under any unexpired residential lease.

If a choice is available, a debtor can select the exemption category that would be most advantageous. Spouses who file a joint petition are each entitled to take their own exemptions and each spouse must select the same exemption category *if the state has not acted to prohibit the use of federal exemptions. See, e.g., In re Zimmel,* 185 B.R. 786 (Bankr. D. Minn. 1995).

**Note:** The 2005 Bankruptcy Act exempts tax-exempt retirement funds regardless of whether the debtor elects state or federal exemptions. Shortly before the 2005 Bankruptcy Act was signed into law, the U.S. Supreme Court in *Rousey v. Jacoway,* 540 U.S. 320 (2005), held that IRAs are exempt from the bankruptcy estate under *11 U.S.C. § 522(d)(10)(E)* because they confer a right to receive payment based on age and are similar to other plans or contracts that are statutorily exempt. The 2005 Bankruptcy Act, however, limits the exemption for IRAs (including Roth IRAs) to a $1,000,000 cap as adjusted for inflation. Presently, the cap is $1,283,025. But, eligible rollovers are protected without limitation. An inherited IRA does not, however, constitute "retirement funds" and, as such, is *not exempt* from creditors. That is the case for debtor's residing in states that have not opted out of the use of the federal exemptions, and debtors that reside in states that have opted out of the federal exemptions having statutory language that does not specifically exempt inherited IRAs.

## 3. "Tools of the Trade"

In agricultural bankruptcies, one of the more important exemptions listed above is for "tools of the trade." 11 U.S.C. § 522(f) permits the avoidance of non-possessory, non-PMSIs in "implements, professional books, or tools of the trade of the debtor or the trade of a dependent of the debtor" when the security interest impairs an exemption to which the debtor would have been entitled but for the security interest. Conceivably, many farm assets could qualify as a tool of the trade. For example, some courts have held that livestock held for breeding purposes, large items of farm equipment, and draft horses, are tools of the debtor's trade. Generally, courts focus on the functional use of an asset in the debtor's business in determining whether the asset is a tool of the debtor's trade. In any event, the debtor must be actively engaged in a farming business to exempt farm assets as tools of the trade. That raises a question as to whether off-farm employment affects the tools-of-the-trade exemption. In any event, to be considered as an exempt tool of the debtor's trade, the debtor must have a reasonable prospect of continuing in or returning to the farming business.

> **Note:** Generally, a tool of the trade must be tangible personal property that is used in the debtor's business. However, in a case involving debtors that operated a photography business that sold digitally manipulated landscape photographs, the court held

that their digital images and website were exempt tools-of-the-trade under state (KS) law (*Kan. Sta. Ann. § 60–2304(e)*). *In re Macmillan,* No. 14–40965, 2015 Bankr. LEXIS 61 (Bankr. D. Kan. Jan. 9, 2015).

## 4. Lien Avoidance

Another important aspect of claiming exemptions is that a debtor can avoid some kinds of liens and most security interests on exempt property. Thus, security interests can be avoided in—

- Exempt household furnishings, household goods, wearing apparel, appliances, books, animals, crops, musical instruments and jewelry. For such property, the items must be "held primarily for the personal, family or household use of the debtor or a dependent of the debtor" in order for liens to be voidable.

- Exempt implements and professional books and tools of the trade of the debtor or a dependent of the debtor and professionally prescribed health aids of the debtor or a dependent of the debtor, to the extent the security interests are not purchase money security interests and would impair the exemption.

The Bankruptcy Code allows a case to be reopened for cause and a lien avoidance motion to be granted so long as creditors will not be prejudiced.

In *In re Liming,* 797 F.2d 895 (10th Cir. 1986), the court allowed a debtor to avoid a lien on a tractor used in the debtor's farming business even though the loan for which the tractor was pledged as collateral was obtained by use of a false financial statement.

# VI.   CHAPTER 7 BANKRUPTCY (LIQUIDATION)

A Chapter 7 bankruptcy case calling for liquidation can be initiated by filing a voluntary petition and paying filing fees ($335.00 effective June 1, 2014). The debtor must file a list of creditors, a schedule of assets and liabilities, current income and expenses and a statement of financial affairs. A farmer would most likely utilize Chapter 7 if there is no intent (or hope) of continuing the farming operation. Chapter 7 bankruptcy is the quickest and least expensive form of bankruptcy available to debtors.

## A.   MEETING OF CREDITORS

Once a voluntary petition is filed, the bankruptcy court appoints an interim trustee to preside over the debtor's affairs. The interim trustee takes possession of the debtor's property, operates the debtor's business and, in general, performs the same functions as the permanent trustee.

At the first meeting of creditors, the creditors can elect a trustee and a creditor's committee. If a trustee is not elected at that time, the interim trustee serves as trustee.

The debtor is required to appear before the creditors and answer questions under oath about the debtor's property and business affairs.

**Note:** Under the 2005 Bankruptcy Act, the debtor must provide a certificate of credit counseling and repayment plan from an approved agency within 180 days of filing (unless incapacitated, disabled or on active duty in a military zone), pay stubs within 60 days of filing, itemized monthly net income, the most recent federal income tax return, evidence of any qualified education savings accounts and/or tuition programs, and a photo ID (upon the trustee's request).

A creditor is not required to file a proof of claim with the court or the trustee in order to be paid by the bankruptcy estate. But a creditor must file a proof of claim to be eligible for a priority in the distribution of the debtor's assets if the creditor is not listed in the schedules submitted to the court.

## B.   DISTRIBUTIONS OF PROPERTY

In Chapter 7 bankruptcy liquidations, the major concern is who receives the debtor's assets (other than the exempt assets which are returned to the debtor).

In general, property subject to a lien or other security interest is used to satisfy the obligation. Trustees in bankruptcy often "abandon" property to the debtor where the property value is less than the amount owed. The creditors are then free to obtain the property through foreclosure or other creditor action. Remember, one of the major objectives of bankruptcy is to treat unsecured creditors fairly. If an asset in bankruptcy is worth less than what is owed on it, the secured creditors are in line to receive the property's value. Hence, there is no reason for the property to remain in the bankruptcy estate. Abandonment moves such assets out of the bankruptcy estate and back to the debtor's hands temporarily so that the creditors can take action to obtain the property. Later in this chapter, we will examine an important income tax issue that arises when property is abandoned.

- For other property, the order of distribution is specified in federal bankruptcy law. *11 U.S.C. § 507.*

- Allowed administrative expenses of the bankruptcy estate are paid first.

- Next in line are unsecured claims arising after an involuntary petition in bankruptcy is filed and before an order for relief is granted or a trustee is appointed.

- Unsecured claims for wages, salaries and commissions are entitled to a high priority up to $11,725 per creditor.

- Unsecured claims for contributions to employee benefit plans come next up to $11,725 per employee less any amount paid as a priority claim as a wage, salary or commission.

- Grain producers are eligible for a sixth priority distribution up to $6,150 per producer for unsecured claims for grain or the proceeds of grain against a debtor owning a grain storage facility. A similar priority is allowed for unsecured claims of fishermen, up to

$6,150 per fisherman, against a debtor owning a fish produce storage or processing facility. This was authorized by Congress in response to urging by farmers for some relief when grain storage facilities file bankruptcy and farmer-owned grain is held in the facility.

In addition, a bankruptcy court must, upon the request of a grain producer who is a creditor of a bankrupt grain storage facility, expedite the determination of the interests in the disposition of grain held by the facility.

- A priority is accorded for up to $2,600 per claim on unsecured claims for money deposited with the debtor for purchase or lease of property or services that were not delivered or provided.

- A priority is available for alimony, child support and separate maintenance.

- Unsecured tax claims of government, including income taxes, property taxes, gross receipts taxes, excise taxes and employment taxes, are given an eighth priority position.

- Claims for death or personal injury resulting from the operation of a motor vehicle or vessel if such operation was unlawful because the debtor was intoxicated from using alcohol or other drugs.

- The next highest priority goes to general unsecured creditors who have filed claims in a timely fashion or were excused for late filing.

- Distribution is then made to unsecured creditors who were not excused for late filing.

- Claims for unpaid fines and penalties are paid next.

- Creditors are then paid interest at the legal rate from the date of petition filing.

- Finally, any remaining funds are paid to the debtor. Typically, debtors receive nothing in a liquidation distribution. Indeed, unsecured creditors often receive no more than five to ten percent of their obligations.

## C.  DISCHARGE OF DEBTS

A major feature of bankruptcy in the United States, as noted above, is discharge of indebtedness. This makes possible the "fresh start" for debtors.

Only individual debtors are entitled to a discharge. Corporations and other artificial entities in a liquidation proceeding are typically left with no assets and can be dissolved.

In general, only debts that arose before bankruptcy filing are dischargeable. However, not all debts are in line for discharge and not all debtors are eligible for discharge.

### 1. Debts Ineligible for Discharge

Several categories of debts are not eligible for discharge:

- Taxes entitled to a preference (normally those within the last three years), for which a return was not filed or was filed late, or for which a fraudulent return was filed or which the debtor tried to evade, are not dischargeable. Penalties on non dischargeable taxes are likewise not dischargeable. A federal income tax lien against exempt property is not discharged in bankruptcy although the debt for the taxes, penalties and interest secured by the lien may be discharged in bankruptcy. The exempt property may be subject to foreclosure and sale to pay the tax lien.

- Debt incurred to pay state and local taxes is not discharged.

- Fines, penalties and forfeitures payable to a governmental unit that are not compensation for pecuniary loss are not dischargeable, nor is debt incurred to pay fines and taxes.

- Student loans that are insured, guaranteed or funded by a government unit, for-profit entity and non-governmental entity unless the loan was "due and payable" more than five years before the filing of bankruptcy are ineligible for discharge.

- Claims neither listed nor scheduled by the debtor in time to permit the creditor to file a timely proof of claim cannot be discharged.

- Alimony and child support are not discharged.

- Nonsupport obligations incurred from divorce or separation are not discharged.

- Claims based on the receipt of money, property or services by fraud, false pretenses or a materially false written statement concerning the debtor's (or an insider's) financial condition intentionally made to deceive creditors are not in line for discharge.

- Claims based on fraud or defalcation while the debtor was acting in a fiduciary capacity or based on embezzlement or larceny are not eligible for discharge.

- Claims based on willful or malicious injury are not dischargeable.

- Debts that were (or could have been) listed in a prior bankruptcy proceeding and were not discharged in the earlier proceeding because of the debtor's acts or conduct are not eligible for discharge.

- Claims owed to a single creditor aggregating more than $600 for luxury goods and services incurred by an individual on or within 90 days of filing the bankruptcy petition cannot be discharged.

- Cash advances aggregating more than $875 that are consumer credit under an open end credit plan if incurred on or within 70 days before filing the bankruptcy petition (per line of credit) are not in line for discharge.

- Claims arising from a judgment entered against the debtor for operating a motor vehicle, vessels or aircraft while legally intoxicated are not eligible for discharge.

- Homeowner association, condominium and cooperative fees are not discharged.

- Debt associated with pension and/or profit sharing plans is not dischargeable.

- In general, a debtor is denied discharge for fraudulent conduct within one year of filing the bankruptcy petition or during the bankruptcy case or for failure to explain a loss of assets or preserve sufficient recorded information concerning the debtor's financial condition or business transactions.

## 2. Debtors Ineligible for Discharge

Some debtors, because of their conduct, may not be eligible for discharge. A discharge may be denied for a debtor who:

- Fraudulently transferred, destroyed or concealed property within one year before the petition was filed or as to property of the estate after the petition was filed;

- Unjustifiably concealed, destroyed, falsified or failed to keep records;

- Knowingly or fraudulently gave a false oath or account;

- Failed to satisfactorily explain a loss or deficiency of assets;

- Refused to obey a court order; or

- Committed any of the above in connection with a case concerning an insider within one year prior to filing the petition.

## 3. Frequent Discharge

The Bankruptcy Act of 2005 addresses the process of filing Chapter 7 bankruptcy to discharge unsecured debts followed by a Chapter 13 filing to handle secured debt, generally a mortgage. Under the Act, the time between subsequent Chapter 7 discharges is expanded from six to eight years. Debtors must also wait two years after receiving a Chapter 13 discharge to refile, or four years if the debtor received a discharge under Chapter 7, 11 or 12. The stay terminates 30 days after the petition is filed if a previous Chapter 7, 11 or 13 case was filed and dismissed with the preceding year. A history of previous filings gives rise to a rebuttable presumption under various circumstances including a presumption of bad faith against any creditor who received relief from the automatic stay pending when the case was dismissed.

## VII. CHAPTER 11 BANKRUPTCY (REORGANIZATION)

Chapter 11 of the Bankruptcy Code is the general reorganization provision for individuals and firms operating a business. In general, "any person" except a governmental unit may be a debtor in a Chapter 11 case. There is no debt limit associated with Chapter 11. Farmers are eligible for Chapter 11, although Chapter 12 bankruptcy was specifically designed and enacted for the reorganization of farm and ranch business. A major drawback of Chapter 11 is the relatively short time the debtor has to overcome existing financial problems, and an absolute priority rule that prohibits debtors from retaining ownership of their property unless unsecured creditors receive 100 percent of their claims. However, farmers and ranchers with only temporary financial problems and who desire to continue the operation may find Chapter 11 useful.

## VIII. CHAPTER 12 BANKRUPTCY (REORGANIZATION)

Under 1986 amendments to the Bankruptcy Act of 1978, Congress created Chapter 12 bankruptcies for "family farmers." The Act was scheduled to expire on October 1, 1993, was extended numerous times before being made a permanent part of the Bankruptcy Code by the Bankruptcy Act of 2005, effective July 1, 2005.

Chapter 12 bankruptcy can only be initiated voluntarily. The filing fee is $275.00 (as of June 1, 2014).

## A.  THE DEBTOR

### 1. Family Farmer

To be eligible for Chapter 12 bankruptcy, a debtor must be a "family farmer" or a "family fisherman" with "regular annual income." The term "farming operation" includes farming, tillage of the soil, dairy farming, ranching, production or raising of crops, poultry, or livestock, and the production of poultry or livestock products in an unmanufactured state. *11 U.S.C. § 101(21)*. A "family farmer" is defined as an individual or individual and spouse who earned more than 50 percent of their gross income from farming either for the taxable year preceding the year of filing or during the second *and* third tax years preceding filing, and whose aggregate debts do not exceed $4,153,150 (as of April, 2016). In addition, more than 50 percent of the debt must be debt from a farming operation that the debtor owns or operates.

**Note:** "Farming operation" includes farming, tillage of the soil, dairy farming, ranching, production or the raising of crops, poultry or livestock, and the production of poultry or livestock products in an unmanufactured state. *11 U.S.C. § 101 (21)*. A few courts have addressed the issue of whether a tree farm is a "farming operation" for purposes of Chapter 12. One court has held that logging is a farming operation, and that the income from timber harvesting is included in farm income when timber harvesting occurs on a sustained yield basis and is part of an integrated farming operation. *In re Sugar Pine Ranch,* 100 B.R. 28 (Bankr. D. Ore. 1989). Another court, however, criticized such an expansive view and determined that even if a tree farm qualified as a farming operation, the debtor in the case also processed the trees at a sawmill which disqualified the debtor's operation from being a farming operation. *In re Miller,* 122 B.R. 360 (Bankr. N.D. Iowa 1990). In yet another case, the court denied confirmation of the reorganization's plan largely because the testimony about the amount of plantings was contradictory, no harvesting had yet occurred, and only slight tree farming activity had occurred. *In re McMahon Family Limited Partnership,* No. 12-373144-svk, 2013 Bankr. LEXIS 2771 (Bankr. E.D. Wisc. Jul. 10, 2013*).*

For a "family fisherman" (defined as an individual engaged in a commercial fishing operation) the 50 percent test must be satisfied in the tax year preceding the year of filing and the aggregate debt limitation is $1,868,200. In addition, at least 50 percent of the debtor's aggregate, non-contingent, liquidated debts (excluding a debt for the principal residence of such individual or such individual and spouse unless such debt arises out of farming operation), on the date the case is filed, must have arisen out of a farming operation owned or operated by the debtor or the debtor and debtor's spouse. *11 U.S.C. § 101(18).* To meet the test of arising out of the farming operation, the debt must be directly related to the farming operation.

Closely-held corporations, business trusts (but not other trusts), cooperatives, and partnerships in which more than 50 percent of the stock or equity is held by one family or by one family and the relatives of the members of such family can be a "family farmer" if: (1) the family or relatives conduct the farming operation; (2) more than 80 percent of the value of its assets are related to the farming operation; (3) its aggregate debts do not exceed $4,153,150 for a farming operation; ($1,924,550 for a fishing operation) and not less than 50 percent (80 percent for a fishing operation) of its "aggregate non-contingent liquidated debts (excluding a debt for one dwelling which is owned by such corporation or partnership and which a shareholder or partner maintains as a principal residence, unless such debt arises out of a farming operation), on the date the case is filed, arose out of the farming operation owned or operated by such corporation or such partnership;" and (4) if the corporation issues stock, it is not publicly traded.

There is no requirement that 50 percent or more of the corporation's or partnership's gross income be from farming, but the debtor corporation must be conducting a farming operation. Problems can arise if the corporation leases land on a yearly cash rent basis. The income under the lease must be commensurate with the risks of the farming operation in order for the corporate landlord to qualify for Chapter 12 relief. The required level of risk may be achieved under a cash lease with a rent adjustment clause for poor or nonexistent crops.

### i. Gross Income from Farming

To be eligible, more than 50 percent of an *individual* debtor's gross income must come from farming in either the year before filing or in both the second and third tax years preceding filing. This provision seeks to disqualify tax shelter and recreational farms from Chapter 12 protection. The farm income test is to be applied at the time of bankruptcy filing. This means that the determination of whether a debtor is a farmer that is engaged in farming is made at the time the bankruptcy petition is filed. Likewise, the determination of whether the debtor has the intent to continue farming is made at the time of filing also. 11 U.S.C. § 101(18) says that a "family farmer" is an individual and spouse "engaged in a farming operation. . ." But see *In re Williams,* No. 15-11023(1)(12), 2016 Bankr. LEXIS 1804 (Bankr. W.D. Ky. Apr. 22, 2016).

Gross income from farming has been held to include government program payments, proceeds of the sale of farm equipment, and income from rental of farm equipment where the lessor has some risk in the farm operation. However, income from the sale of farmland and income from custom farming, even if performed for the debtor's farm operation, is not included in gross income from farming.

Income from farming has also been held to include income from breeding, raising and selling of bred and raised horses but not income from horse training and showing. However, in one case, where the horse riding operations were combined with dairy operations, both sources of income were included in gross income from farming. Similarly, a cattle rancher's income from hauling cattle for third parties was farm income where the hauling was found to be related to the debtor's own operations, and, in another case, the income from the debtors' timber operation was farm income where the debtors sold their own timber, lived in a traditional farm setting, had traditional farm equipment, and were subject to the same risks inherent in an ordinary farming business.

Although income from cash leasing of farmland is not included in gross income from farming, a corporate farm debtor has been allowed to file in Chapter 12 even though a majority of the farmland would be cash leased. Generally, cash rent income is not income from a farming operation that counts toward the 50 percent test. The basic test is whether the lessor is subject to the risks from farming under the lease. For example, in *In re Maynard*, 295 B.R. 437 (Bankr. S.D. N.Y. 2003) the debtor operated a farm as an S corporation which leased the land from the debtor. The debtor's pre-petition farm income consisted entirely of the rent from the corporation. The rents were held to be income from farming to the debtor because no rent was paid if the corporation lacked income, the debtor was actively involved in the farming operation, the rent came from farming operations, and the debtor continued to farm the property after bankruptcy. However, in *In re Easton*, 118 B.R. 676 (Bankr. N.D. Iowa 1990), an individual farm debtor was allowed to file a Chapter 12 bankruptcy where farmland was cash leased to the debtor's son and the court found that the lease was part of the total family farm operation. Income from crop-share leases is generally considered to be gross income from farming unless the lessor has no participation in the operation of the farm.

## ii. Debts Arising from Farming

As mentioned above, two debt restrictions must be satisfied for a debtor to proceed under Chapter 12: (1) aggregate debt must not exceed $4,153,150 (as of April 1, 2016); and (2) at least 50 percent of the aggregate non-contingent liquidated debts on the date the case is filed must arise out of the farming operation. The debt limit test is applied at the time the petition is filed. In general, a debt "arises out of a farming operation" if it has some connection to the debtor's farming operation. For example, a farmer's debts secured by nonfarm property may be considered in the aggregate farm debt if the loan proceeds are used directly for or in the farm operation such that the debt arises out of the farming operation.

In *In re Roberts,* 78 B.R. 536 (Bankr. C.D. Ill 1987), the debtor inherited a farm from her mother. Approximately 46 percent of the scheduled debts represented taxes and attorney fees arising from the inheritance. The court held the taxes and fees were directly linked to the farming operation because they had to be paid to allow the debtor to keep the farm.

For a farmer whose debts exceed $4,153,150, it is apparently not possible to file initially under Chapter 11, sell some assets and reduce debt and then convert to Chapter 12, which is otherwise permissible; the $4,153,150 limitation is applied when the case is filed.

If a husband and wife file a joint petition, the $4,153,150 limit is not doubled.

## 2. Debtor in Possession

Under Chapter 12, a farmer remains in possession of estate property unless removed "for cause," i.e., for fraud, dishonesty, incompetence or gross mismanagement of the affairs of the debtor either before or after commencement of the case. Remaining in possession of estate property is a Chapter 12 debtor's most fundamental right, and is consistent with the purpose of Chapter 12 to permit debtors to save their farm and pay their creditors over time with funds generated from future earnings.

While a Chapter 12 debtor remains in possession of estate property, the debtor is subject to the supervisory oversight of a standing trustee. The trustee is always in the background and can remove the debtor from possession if the debtor commits fraud, dishonesty, incompetence, or gross mismanagement.

### B.   THE TRUSTEE

A trustee is appointed in every Chapter 12 case. A Chapter 12 trustee's duties are similar to those under Chapter 13. Specifically, a trustee under Chapter 12, is directed to

(1)   be accountable for all property received;

(2)   ensure that the debtor performs in accordance with intention;

(3)   object to the allowance of claims which would be improper;

(4)  if advisable, oppose the discharge of the debtor;

(5)  furnish requested information to a party in interest unless the court orders otherwise;

(6)  make a final report;

(7)  *for cause and upon request,* investigate the financial affairs of the debtor, the operation of the debtor's business and the desirability of the continuance of the business;

(8)  participate in hearings concerning the value of property of the bankruptcy estate; and

(9)  ensure that the debtor commences making timely payments required by confirmed plan.

In specifying the duties of trustees, Chapter 12 modifies the duty applicable to trustees under other chapters of the Bankruptcy Code to "investigate the financial affairs of the debtor." Chapter 12 authorizes an investigative role for trustees, as noted above, "for cause and on request of a party in interest. . . ." Thus, it would appear, in a routine case where there is no fraud, dishonesty, incompetence or gross mismanagement, the debtor should be allowed to reorganize without significant interference from the trustee.

The compensation of trustees is not to exceed 10 percent of payments made under the debtor's plan for the first $450,000 of payments. The trustee collects the fee from payments received under the plan. After the aggregate amount of payments made under the plan exceeds $450,000, the fee is not to exceed 3 percent.

Except as provided in the plan or in order confirming the plan, the trustee is to make payments to creditors under the plan. Courts have generally recognized that payments on fully secured claims that the bankruptcy plan does not modify can be paid directly to the creditor, as can claims not impaired by the plan. However, for claims that are impaired, courts are divided as to whether a court may approve direct payments to creditors. The issue of who actually disburses the debtor's payments is important to the trustee because the trustee is entitled to a statutory commission only on funds actually received from the debtor pursuant to the reorganization plan. In *In re Wagner,* 36 F.3d 723 (8th Cir. 1994), the court noted that the Bankruptcy Code does not prevent a debtor from making payments directly to creditors. As a result, the court focused on the specific language of the reorganization plan to determine if such direct payment was possible.

In early 2000, the Eighth Circuit Court of Appeals reaffirmed its position taken in *Wagner. Haden v. Pelofsky,* 212 F.3d 466 (8th Cir. 2000).

## C.  THE REORGANIZATION PLAN

### 1.  Filing the Plan

A Chapter 12 debtor has an exclusive 90-day period after filing for Chapter 12 bankruptcy to file a plan for reorganization unless the court grants an extension. A court may grant additional time only if circumstances are present for which the debtor should not fairly be held accountable.

The contents of every Chapter 12 plan must satisfy four requirements. A plan must—

(1) provide for submission of all future earnings of the debtor to control of the trustee for execution of the plan or the portion of future earnings as is necessary for execution of the plan;

(2) provide for full payment on a deferred basis of all priority claims unless the creditor agrees to lesser payment;

(3) if the plan classified different claims, provide for the same treatment of all claims within a class unless a claim holder agrees to less favorable treatment; and

(4) provide for payment of trustee's fees.

A Chapter 12 plan may contain certain optional provisions. A plan may—

(1) designate a class or classes of unsecured claims and treat consumer claims differently from other unsecured claims if the debtor is liable on such claims with another individual;

(2) modify the terms of repayment of secured and unsecured debt;

(3) provide for the curing or waiving of a default;

(4) provide for concurrent payment of secured and unsecured claims;

(5) provide for the curing of a default within a reasonable time and maintenance of payments during the case of a secured or unsecured claim on which a final payment will be due after the final payment under the plan;

(6) provide for assumption, rejection or assignment of executory contracts and unexpired leases;

(7) provide for the payment of part or all of a claim from property of the estate;

(8) provide for the sale of estate property or distribution of estate property to creditors with an interest in the property;

(9) provide for the payment of allowed secured claims over a period greater than the term of the plan consistent with the rights of secured creditors; and

(10) provide for the vesting of estate property in the debtor or any other entity upon or after confirmation of the plan.

In general, a plan may not provide for payments over a period longer than three years unless the court "for cause" approves a longer period, but the court may not approve a plan longer than five years.

However, plans longer than five years are utilized in cases where the debtor must make significant payments to unsecured creditors based on a liquidation analysis.

## 2. Plan Confirmation

Unless the time limit is extended by the court, the confirmation hearing is to be concluded not later than 45 days after the plan is filed. The court is required to confirm a plan if—(1) the plan conforms to all bankruptcy provisions; (2) all required fees have been paid; (3) the plan proposal was made in good faith without violating any law; (4) unsecured creditors receive not less than the amount the unsecured creditors would receive in a Chapter 7 liquidation; (5) each secured creditor either (a) accepts the plan, (b) retains the lien securing the claim (with the value of the property to be distributed for the allowed amount of the claim, as of the effective date of the plan, to equal not less than the allowed amount of the claim), or (c) the creditor receives the property securing the claim; and (6) the debtor will be able to comply with the plan. Also, under a provision added by The Bankruptcy Act of 2005, an individual Chapter 12 debtor must be current on post-petition domestic support obligations as a condition of plan confirmation.

### i. *Feasibility of the Reorganization Plan*

If the court determines that the debtor will be unable to make all payments as required by the plan, the court may require the debtor to modify the plan, convert the case to a Chapter 7, or request the court to dismiss the case. *See, e.g., In re Honeyman,* 201 B.R. 535 (Bankr. D. N.D. 1996).

### ii. Good Faith Proposal

As noted above, the Chapter 12 plan must be proposed in good faith. Good faith can be viewed as practically synonymous the requirement that the plan be feasible. *See, e.g., In re Lockard,* 234 B.R. 484 (Bankr. W.D. Mo. 1999).

### iii. Funding the Reorganization Plan

One court has held that the Bankruptcy Code does not require that a farmer who meets the pre-petition farm income test must have sufficient farm income to fund the Chapter 12 plan. *In re Sorrell,* 286 B.R. 798 (Bankr. D. Utah 2002). That same result was reached in *In re Williams,* No. 15–11023(1)(12), 2016 Bankr. LEXIS 1804 (Bankr. W.D. Ky. Apr. 22, 2016). 11 U.S.C. § 101(19) requires a debtor to have regular income sufficient enough to enable the debtor to make plan payments, and that its definition of "family farmer with regular income" which means that the income only be sufficiently stable and regular to enable the debtor to make plan payments. It does not require the income to be generated from farming activities.

Another court has held that a Chapter 12 debtor whose reorganization plan proposed the debtor's discontinuing farming and enrollment of all of the debtor's farmland in the Conservation Reserve

Program was not ineligible for Chapter 12 relief. *In re Clark,* 288 B.R. 237 (Bankr. D. Kan. 2003).

### iv.   The "Cram-Down" Rule

Under plan confirmation provisions, a debtor may be able to reduce secured obligations to the value of the collateral and restructure the debt secured by a lien on the amount of the value of the property with the debt amortized to pay the lienholder the present value of the secured claim.

---

**Example 3:**

Assume a debtor has one asset, a farm, purchased for $750,000 of which $500,000 was financed with a first mortgage. The land plummeted in value to $350,000 and the debtor filed Chapter 12 bankruptcy. With court approval, it may be possible to write down the $500,000 of debt to the value of the collateral ($350,000) with the other $150,000 then treated as unsecured debt. The debtor must apply all available income (after business expenses and family living expenses) to paying the unsecured debt during the term of the plan only if the trustee or an unsecured creditor object to payment of less than all available income to the trustee for payments to unsecured creditors. *11 U.S.C. § 1225(b)(1)(B).* After the completion of payments under the plan, the remaining unsecured debt is discharged. The secured debt of $350,000 may be reamortized over a reasonable time period at a reasonable rate of interest.

## 3. The Disposable Income Requirement

An unsecured creditor who objects to confirmation may block confirmation unless the court finds that the unsecured creditors receive full value for their claims or the plan provides that all of the debtor's projected disposable income (over the three-year or longer period of payment) will be applied to make payments under the plan. Because it is unlikely that a Chapter 12 debtor is able to pay unsecured debt in full, even over an extended period of time, the debtor's plan will need to include a provision committing all of the debtor's disposable income over the term of the plan to unsecured claims. Disposable income is defined as income received by the debtor that is not reasonably necessary for the maintenance or support of the debtor or a dependent of the debtor or for the payment of the debtor's business expenses. *11 U.S.C. § 1225 (b)(2).*

While it appears from the statutory language that the issue of whether the debtor's disposable income is committed to payments under the plan is to be determined at the time of plan confirmation, some courts have held that the issue of disposable income can be litigated again at the debtor's discharge hearing. Under that approach, the debtor must defend the payment of all actual disposable income over the term of the plan in order to receive a discharge, even if the debtor had paid all amounts projected for disposable income at confirmation and provided for in the confirmed plan. The split of authority on the issue resulted in a provision being included in the Bankruptcy Act of 2005 barring the

retroactive assessment of the debtor's disposable
income. While the amendment bars courts from
assessing disposable income on a retroactive basis,
plan modifications are still allowed in the event that
the debtor's income turns out to be greater than
anticipated when the plan was originally confirmed.
The amendment also gives the debtor the sole
authority to increase disposable income where the
result of such increase would be to increase the
amount of payments to unsecured creditors required
for a particular month so that the aggregate of such
payments exceeds the debtor's disposable income for
such month. Likewise, the amendment provides that
the plan may not be modified in the last year of the
plan by anyone except the debtor, to require
payments that would leave the debtor with
insufficient funds to carry on the farming operation
after the plan is completed.

## 4. Determining "Present Value"

For Chapter 12, unless a secured creditor agrees
otherwise, the creditor is entitled to receive the
value, as of the effective date of the plan, equal to the
allowed amount of the claim. Thus, after a secured
debt is written down to the fair market value of the
collateral, with the amount of the debt in excess of
the collateral value treated as unsecured debt which
is generally discharged if not paid during the term of
the plan, the creditor is entitled to the present value
of the amount of the secured claim if the payments
are stretched over a period of years.

---

**Example 4:**

A debtor owes $300,000 on farmland that has declined in value to $200,000. If needed to make the debtor economically and financially stable, the $300,000 debt may be written down to $200,000 with the $100,000 treated as unsecured debt. If the $200,000 obligation is rescheduled over 30 years, with no interest on the unpaid balance, the creditor has not received the "present value" of the $200,000 claim.

**Example 5:**

Using the same facts as in Example 4, if the creditor is assured interest on the unpaid balance of 20 percent per year, the creditor will ultimately receive substantially more, in present value terms, than $200,000.

## *i. Meaning of "Present Value"*

Basically, present value represents the discounted value of a stream of expected future incomes. "Present value" is defined as a term of art for an almost self-evident proposition: a dollar in hand today is worth more than a dollar to be received in a day, a month or a year hence."

Thus, the stream of income received in the future is discounted back to present value by the discount rate, *r*. The determination of present value is highly sensitive to the discount rate. By doubling the discount rate, the present value of an income producing asset is cut in half; reducing the discount rate by half doubles the value of an income producing asset.

### a.    Determining the Appropriate Discount Rate

Several different approaches have been used in Chapter 12 bankruptcy cases (and nearly identical situations in Chapters 11 and 13 cases) to determine the discount rate.

In 2004, however, the U.S. Supreme Court, in *Till v. SCS Credit Corporation*, 541 U.S.465 (2004), addressed the issue in the context of a Chapter 13 case that has since been held applicable in Chapter 12 cases. In *Till,* the Court held that the proper interest rate was 9.5 percent. That rate, the Court noted, was derived from a modification of the average national loan rate to account for the risk that the debtor would default. The Court's opinion has been held to be applicable in Chapter 12 cases. While the Court noted that courts using a formula approach have typically added 1 percent to 3 percent to the prime rate as a reflection of the risk of nonpayment, the Court did not adopt a specific percentage range for risk adjustment. However, it would seem appropriate for courts to assign a risk/uncertainty factor of zero to three percentage points for particular farm and ranch operations with most operations falling into the one to two percentage point premium category. For operations posing unusually small risks of default, a risk premium of less than one could be appropriate. Highly risky ventures could merit a risk premium in excess of two percentage points. It is anticipated that bankruptcy courts familiar with the farm enterprises in the area could readily assign the risk premium without the benefit of expert assistance.

## D.   CONVERSION AND DISMISSAL

### 1.  Debtor's Right to Convert

A Chapter 12 case can be converted by the debtor only to a Chapter 7 liquidation. Property that the debtor acquires after commencement of the Chapter 12 case becomes property of the new Chapter 7 bankruptcy estate. Similarly, crop proceeds earned before conversion but during pendency of bankruptcy are part of the new Chapter 7 bankruptcy estate. Cases may be converted from Chapters 11 and 13 to Chapter 12 upon request of the debtor if conversion is "equitable."

### 2.  Debtor's Right to Dismiss

A court, upon request of the debtor, may dismiss a Chapter 12 case at any time, unless the case had been converted from Chapter 7 or 11. This right can be exercised by the debtor at any time during the Chapter 12 case and may not be waived.

### 3.  Conversion or Dismissal for Cause

A court may, upon request of a party in interest and after notice and a hearing, dismiss a case under Chapter 12 or convert the case to Chapter 7 "upon showing that the debtor has committed fraud in connection with the case." A court may dismiss an action for cause at the request of a party in interest after notice and hearing for the following grounds—

(1)   unreasonable delay or gross mismanagement by the debtor that is prejudicial to creditors;

(2)   nonpayment of required fees and charges;

(3)   failure to file a plan in a timely manner;

(4)   failure to commence making timely payments required by confirmed plans;

(5)   denial of confirmation of a plan and denial of a request made for additional time for filing another plan or a modification of a plan;

(6)   material default by the debtor with respect to a term of a confirmed plan;

(7)   termination of a confirmed plan by reason of the occurrence of a condition specified in the plan;

(8)   continuing loss to or diminution of the estate and absence of a reasonable likelihood of rehabilitation or;

(9)   involvement as a debtor in an existing bankruptcy case.

In *In re Zurface,* 95 B.R. 527 (Bankr. S.D. Ohio 1989), the court converted a farm debtor's Chapter 12 case to a Chapter 7 upon finding that the debtor committed fraud with the intent to prejudice creditors.

## E.   PROTECTION OF FARMER INTERESTS

### 1.  Authority to Operate the Farm Business

A debtor in possession is given express authority to operate the farm business. However, as we have already noted, creditors have the right to insist on adequate protection of their interests and request relief from the automatic stay.

## 2. Authority to Sell Property

A trustee, after notice and a hearing, is allowed to sell portions of farmland and farm equipment free of security interests in the property. Any encumbrance on the property will attach to the proceeds of the sale. This enables debtors to downsize their farming operations.

## 3. Adequate Protection

In bankruptcy, the filing of the petition operates as an automatic stay against creditor actions. A secured creditor is barred from taking action against the collateral, as in foreclosure, unless the automatic stay is lifted. The primary basis for lifting the automatic stay is lack of adequate protection for the creditor such as where the collateral is being worn out, used up, disappearing or is otherwise declining in value.

Adequate protection in Chapter 12 bankruptcy may be provided by the debtor through—

(1)  periodic cash payments to the secured creditor by the trustee when the debtor's action results in a decrease in the value of the property securing a claim or of an entity's ownership interest in property;

(2)  providing an additional or replacement lien to the creditor to the extent the stay, use,

sale, lease or grant results in a decrease in the value of property securing a claim or of an entity's ownership interest in property;

(3) payment to the creditor for the use of farmland of "reasonable rent customary in the community where the property is located, based on the rental value, net income and earning capacity of the property;" or

(4) granting such other relief, other than compensation allowable as an administrative expense, as will "adequately protect the value of property securing a claim or of such entity's ownership interest in property."

## F.   DISCHARGE

As soon as practicable after completion by the debtor of all payments under the plan, unless the court approves a written waiver of discharge by the debtor after the order for relief, the court is to grant the debtor a discharge of all dischargeable debts provided for by the plan except for non-dischargeable debts. *11 U.S.C. § 727.*

At any time after confirmation of a plan and after notice and a hearing, the court may grant a discharge to a debtor who has not completed payments under the plan if—(1) the debtor's failure to complete payments is due to circumstances for which debtor should not justly be held responsible; (2) the value, as of the effective date of the plan, of property actually distributed under the plan on account of each allowed unsecured claim is not less than the amount that would have been paid on the claim under Chapter 7 liquidation; and (3) modification of the plan "is not practicable."

A trustee may object to discharge on various grounds including the fact that the debtor did not apply all disposable income on the plan, or failed to explain the loss of assets. Likewise, a debt is not dischargeable if the debtor acts, with respect to the debt, in a manner that willfully *and* maliciously injures a creditor. *See, e.g., 11 U.S.C. § 523(a)(6). Russell,* 262 B.R. 449 (Bankr. N.D. Ind. 2001). Malice requires conduct that is targeted at the creditor, at least in the sense that the conduct is certain or almost certain to cause financial harm.

## G.  MODIFICATION OF PLANS

A Chapter 12 plan may be modified, at the request of the debtor, the trustee or the holder of an unsecured claim, at any time after confirmation of the plan and before completion of payments. *11 U.S.C. § 1229(a).* A modification enables the debtor to make adjustments in his or her financial obligations when the debtor's financial situation has changed. However, a modified plan must meet all of the requirements for plan confirmation. In *In re Pearson,* 96 B.R. 990 (Bankr. D. S.D. 1989), the court held that a bankruptcy trustee could not obtain modification of a confirmed plan upon discovering that the debtors had unintentionally valued their land at 10 percent of its value. In *In re Cook,* 148 B.R.

273 (Bankr. W.D. Mich. 1992), the debtors won $6 million in the Michigan state Lottery and had their confirmed plan modified to provide for full payment to general creditors.

## H.  TAX PROVISIONS

### 1.  No Separate Tax Entity

As originally enacted, Chapter 12 did not create a separate tax entity for Chapter 12 bankruptcy estates for purposes of federal income taxation. This precludes debtor avoidance of potential income tax liability on disposition of assets as may be possible for individuals who file Chapter 7 or 11 bankruptcy. *See, e.g., In re Lindsey* 142 B.R. 447 (Bankr. W.D. Okla. 1992).

### 2.  Non-Priority Provision

The 2005 Bankruptcy Act allows a Chapter 12 debtor to treat claims arising out of "claims owed to a governmental unit" as a result of "sale, transfer, exchange, or other disposition of any farm asset used in the debtor's farming operation" to be treated as an unsecured claim that is not entitled to priority under Section 507(a) of the Bankruptcy Code, provided the debtor receives a discharge. *11 U.S.C. § 1222(a)(2)(A).* The amendment attempted to address a major problem faced by many family farmers filing under Chapter 12 where the sale of farm assets to make the operation economically viable triggered gain which, as a priority claim, had to be paid in full before payment could be made to general creditors. Even though the priority tax claims could be paid in full in deferred payments under prior law, in many instances the debtor did not have sufficient funds to allow payment of the priority tax claims in full even in deferred payments. That was the core problem that the 2005 provision was attempting to address.

### i. Timing of Asset Sales

Nothing in the legislation specifies *when* the property can be disposed of to be eligible for unsecured claim status. Of course, the taxing agencies must receive at least as large an amount as they would have received had the claim been a pre-petition unsecured claim. On this issue, the United States Court of Appeals for the Eighth Circuit has ruled that a debtor's pre-petition sale of slaughter hogs came within the scope of the provision, and that the provision changes the character of the taxes from priority status to unsecured such that, upon discharge, the unpaid portion of the tax is discharged along with interest or penalties. *In re Knudsen, et al. v. Internal Revenue Service,* 581 F.3d 696 (8th Cir. 2009). The court also held the statute applies to post-petition taxes and that those taxes can be treated as an administrative expense. Such taxes can be discharged in full if provided for in the Chapter 12 plan and the debtor receives a discharge. Upon the filing of a Chapter 12, a separate taxpaying entity apart from the debtor is not created. That is an important point in the context of the 2005 amendment. The debtor remains responsible for tax taxes triggered in the context of Chapter 12. The amendment, however, allows non-priority treatment for claims entitled to priority under *11 U.S.C. § 507(a)(2)*. That provision covers administrative expenses that are allowed by 11 U.S.C. § 503(b)(B) which includes any tax that the bankruptcy estate incurs. Pre-petition taxes are covered by 11 U.S.C. § 507(a)(8). But, post-petition taxes, to be covered by the amendment, must be incurred by the bankruptcy estate such as is the case with administrative expenses. Indeed, the IRS position is that post-petition taxes are not "incurred by the estate" as is required for a tax to be characterized as an administrative expense in accordance with 11 U.S.C. § 503(b)(1)(B)(i), and that post-petition taxes constitute a liability of the debtor rather than the estate. The U.S. Circuit Courts of Appeal for the Ninth and Tenth Circuits agreed with the IRS position, *Hall v. United States,* 617 F.3d 1161 (9th Cir. 2010), *cert. granted,* 564 U.S. 1003 (2011); *United States v. Dawes,* 652 F.3d 1236 (10th Cir. 2011) and the U.S. Supreme Court also agreed. *Hall v. United States,* 132 S. Ct. 1882 (2012).

## ii. "Farm Asset Used in Farming"

The 2005 provision, by the language of the statute only applies to a "farm Asset used in the debtor's farming operation." So, to qualify for non-priority treatment, taxes must satisfy two tests: (1) they must be taxes derived from the sale of a "farm asset," and (2) the farm asset must have been used in the debtor's farming operation. On this issue, in one case, the IRS took the position that the dissolution of a farm partnership caused by a bankruptcy filing amounted to a sale of a "partnership interest" rather than the sale of "farm assets" which, therefore, would not be entitled to non-priority treatment in accordance with the statutory provision. However, the court determined that the provision applies to the sale of farm assets in general, including capital assets used in farming, and that the sale of a farm partnership interest constituted the sale of a "farm assets." *In re Hemann,* No. 11-00261, 2013 Bankr. LEXIS 1385 (Bankr. N.D. Iowa Apr. 3, 2013). Because the underlying assets that were sold were farm assets that were used in a farming operation, they were covered by the provision. The court noted the Eighth Circuit's opinion and that the U.S. Supreme Court had not overruled the Eighth Circuit's opinion on the issue of the definition of "farm assets" for purposes of the 2005 statutory amendment. In another case, the court held that the debtors' tax liability attributable to the prepetition sale of farm assets that was reported on lines 13 and 14 of Form 1040 (long-term capital gains derived from Schedule D (sale of land) and Part I of Form 4797 (sale of swather), and ordinary gains from Parts II and III of Form 4797 (sales of business property—breeding livestock, equipment, shed and land) was eligible for non-priority treatment. *In re Keith,* No. 10-12997, 2013 Bankr. LEXIS 2802 (Bankr. D. Kan. Jul. 8, 2013). However, the prepetition sales of feeder cattle and crop sales did not qualify for non-priority treatment because, while they were farm assets, they were not used in the debtors' farming operation. Instead, they were end products of the debtors' farming operation with the tax attributable to the sale of the assets reported on Schedule F. Likewise, the debtors' receipt of crop insurance proceeds and federal crop disaster payments were the equivalent of income from the sale of farm products and were not entitled to priority treatment.

### iii.  Computation  of  Priority  and  Non-Priority Tax Claims

The 2005 provision also makes no mention of how the amount of priority and non-priority tax claims is to be computed. Operationally, if a Chapter 12 bankruptcy filer has liquidated assets used in the farming operation within the tax year of filing or liquidates assets used in the farming operation after Chapter 12 filing as part of the Chapter 12 plan, and gain or depreciation recapture income or both are triggered, the plan should provide that there are will be no payments to unsecured creditors until the amount of the tax owed to governmental bodies for the sale of assets used in the farming operation is ascertained. The tax claims are then added to the pre-petition unsecured claims to determine the percentage distribution to be made to the holders of pre-petition unsecured claims as well as the claims of the governmental units that are being treated as unsecured creditors not entitled to priority. That approach assures that all claims that are deemed to be unsecured claims would be treated equitably.

To accurately determine the extent of the priority tax claim under the non-priority provision, it is necessary to directly relate the priority tax treatment to the income derived from sources that either satisfy the non-priority provision or do not satisfy it. There are two basic approaches for computing the priority and general unsecured tax claims—the proportional or marginal allocation method. The proportional method (which is the IRS approach) divides the debtor's ordinary farming income by the debtor's total income and then multiplies the total tax claim by the resulting fraction. That result is then subtracted from the debtor's total tax liability with the balance treated as the non-priority part of the tax obligation. Conversely, under the marginal approach, the debtor prepares a pro-forma tax return that omits the income from the sale of farm assets. The resulting tax liability from the pro forma return is then subtracted from the total tax due on the debtor's actual return. The difference is the tax associated with the sale of farm assets that is entitled to non-priority treatment. A shortfall of the proportional method is that it merely divides the debtor's tax obligation by applying the ratio of the debtor's priority tax claim to the debtor's total income and then dividing the total tax claim. That mechanical computation does not take into account any deductions and/or credits that impact the debtor's final tax liability and which are often phased-out based on income. Instead, the proportional method simply treats every dollar of income the same. The result is that the proportional method, as applied to many debtors, will significantly increase the debtor's adjusted gross income and the priority tax obligation. The most recent court decision on the issue has, like earlier cases, rejected the proportional method in favor of the marginal method. *In re Keith,* No. 10–

12997, 2013 Bankr. LEXIS 2802 (Bankr. D. Kan. Jul. 8, 2013).

### 3. Planning Points

If a debtor determines post-confirmation that, to insure financial and economic viability, assets used in the farming operation must be liquidated, the Chapter 12 plan could be modified to allow the sale of assets so long as the modified plan made provision to make payments to the taxing bodies in an amount that would equal or exceed what would have been received had it been a pre-petition unsecured claim. Upon entry of the Chapter 12 discharge, the claim of the governmental body for taxes on the sale of assets used in the farming business would also be discharged. If the debtor does not receive a Chapter 12 discharge, the taxing bodies are free to pursue the debtor as if no bankruptcy had been filed, assessing and collecting the tax and all penalties and interest allowed by law.

The 2005 Act also specifies that a Chapter 12 plan may provide for less than full payment of all amounts owed for a claim entitled to priority under 11 U.S.C. § 507(a)(1)(B) (a higher priority classification for domestic support obligations assigned to governmental units) only if the plan provides that all of the debtor's projected disposable income for a five-year period beginning on the date that the first payment is due under the plan will be applied to make payments under the plan.

## IX.   INCOME TAXATION IN BANKRUPTCY

For individuals under Chapter 12 or 13 bankruptcy and for partnerships and corporations under all bankruptcy chapters, the debtor continues to be responsible for the income tax consequences of business operations and disposition of the debtor's property. However, for individuals under Chapter 7 or 11 bankruptcy, a new tax entity is created at the time of bankruptcy filing. The legislation creating Chapter 12 did not create a separate tax entity for Chapter 12 filers for federal income tax purposes. Thus, payment of all the tax triggered in bankruptcy is the responsibility of the debtor.

## A.   BANKRUPTCY ESTATE AS NEW TAXPAYER

The creation of the bankruptcy estate as a new taxpayer, separate from the debtor, highlights the five categories of taxes in a Chapter 7 or 11 case.

**Figure 1. Categories of Income Taxes in Bankruptcy**

| | | | **Category 4**<br>Taxes paid as administrative expenses in bankruptcy |
|---|---|---|---|
| **Category 1**<br>Taxes more than 3 years back | **Category 2**<br>Taxes within last 3 years | **Category 3**<br>Taxes in first short year | **Category 5**<br>Taxes in second short year |
| Dischargeable | Priority claim but not dischargeable | Priority claim but not dischargeable | Debtor's responsibility |

Jan. 1                    Date of                    Dec. 31
                          filing

Category 1 taxes are taxes where the tax return was due more than three years before filing. These taxes are dischargeable unless the debtor failed to file a return or filed a fraudulent return. Category 2 taxes are the taxes due within the last three years. These taxes are not dischargeable but are entitled to an eighth priority claim in the bankruptcy estate, ahead of the unsecured creditors. Category 3 taxes are the taxes for the portion of the year of bankruptcy filing up to the day before the day of bankruptcy filing. If the debtor's year is closed as of the date of filing, the taxes for the first year, while not dischargeable, are also entitled to an eighth priority claim in the bankruptcy estate. If the debtor's year is not closed, the entire amount of taxes for the year of filing are the debtor's responsibility.

Category 4 taxes are the taxes triggered on or after the date of filing and are the responsibility of the bankruptcy estate. Taxes due are paid by the bankruptcy estate as an administrative expense. If the taxes exceed the available funds, the tax obligation remains against the bankruptcy estate but does not return to the debtor.

Category 5 taxes are for the portion of the year beginning with the date of bankruptcy filing (or for the entire year if the debtor's year is not closed) and are the responsibility of the debtor.

## 1. Election to Close the Debtor's Tax Year

In general, the bankrupt debtor's tax year does not change upon the filing of bankruptcy. But, debtors

having non exempt assets may elect to end the
debtor's tax year as of the day before the filing.

Making the election creates two short tax years for
the debtor. The first short year ends the day before
bankruptcy filing and the second year begins with
the bankruptcy filing date and ends on the
bankrupt's normal year-end date. If the election is
not made, the debtor remains individually liable for
income taxes for the year of filing. But, if the election
is made, the debtor's income tax liability for the first
short year is treated as a priority claim against the
bankruptcy estate, and can be collected from the
estate if there are sufficient assets to pay off the
estate's debts. If there are not sufficient assets to pay
the income tax, the remaining tax liability is not
dischargeable, and the tax can be collected from the
debtor at a later time. The income tax owed by the
bankrupt for the years ending after the filing is paid
by the bankrupt and not by the bankruptcy estate.
Thus, closing the bankrupt's tax year can be
particularly advantageous if the bankrupt has
substantial income in the period before the
bankruptcy filing. Conversely, if a net operating loss,
unused credits or excess deductions are projected for
the first short year, an election should not be made in
the interest of preserving the loss for application
against the debtor's income from the rest of the
taxable year. But, in any event, if the debtor does not
act to end the tax year, none of the debtor's income
tax liability for the year of bankruptcy filing can be
collected from the bankruptcy estate. Likewise, if the
short year is not elected, the tax attributes (including
the basis of the debtor's property) pass to the

bankruptcy estate as of the beginning of the debtor's tax year. Therefore, for example, no depreciation may be claimed by the debtor for the period before bankruptcy filing. That could be a significant issue for many agricultural debtors.

---

**Example 6:**

Sam Tiller, a cash method taxpayer, on January 26, 2004, bought and placed in service in his farming business, a new combine that cost $402,000. Sam is planning on electing to claim $102,000 of expense method depreciation on the combine and an additional $150,000 (50 percent of the remaining depreciable balance) of first-year bonus depreciation as well as regular depreciation on the combine for 2004. However, during 2004, Sam's financial condition worsened severely due to a combination of market and weather conditions. As a result, Sam filed Chapter 7 bankruptcy on December 5, 2004.

If Sam does not elect to close the tax year, the tax attributes (including the basis of his property) will pass to the bankruptcy estate as of the beginning of Sam's tax year (January 1, 2004). Therefore, Sam would not be able to claim any of the depreciation for the period before he filed bankruptcy (January 1, 2004, through December 4, 2004).

## 2. Tax Attributes

If the debtor acts to end the tax year (which must be done with the filing of the tax return for the first short year, by the 15th day of the fourth full month after the end of the month bankruptcy is filed), the debtor's tax attributes pass to the bankruptcy estate at the time of filing. The tax attributes include net operating loss carryovers, credit carryovers and capital loss carryovers as well as the features associated with the debtor's property including income tax basis figures. In the event the debtor does not act to end the year, the tax attributes pass to the bankruptcy estate as of the beginning of the debtor's year (usually January 1). Obviously, the decision to close the year carries highly important tax consequences.

### 3.  Bankruptcy Estate

The transfer of property to the bankruptcy estate does not, in itself, trigger adverse tax consequences. The estate reports income and claims deductions and credits as if the debtor had continued in the same business.

The administrative expenses of bankruptcy are allowed as deductions in the bankruptcy estate.

The bankruptcy estate is allowed one personal exemption, the deductions of an individual and the basic standard deduction and is taxed at the rates applicable to a married taxpayer filing separately.

An income tax return, Form 1041, must be filed by the trustee or debtor in possession if gross income exceeds the exemption amount plus the basic standard deduction ($10,400 in 2017).

### 4.  Abandonment

As discussed earlier in this chapter, if any item of property passing into the bankruptcy estate is worth less than what is owed on it as secured debt, the trustee may "abandon" the property back to the debtor. The secured creditor is then free to remove the property from the debtor through foreclosure or otherwise to satisfy the debt owed to the secured creditor.

A major concern is whether the bankruptcy estate or the debtor pays the resulting income tax liability.

---

**Example 7:**

A debtor has one asset, a bin of shelled corn worth $60,000 but with a security interest in the corn held by the local bank for $75,000. The trustee abandons the bin of corn back to the debtor.

- With the "deflection" theory, the bin of corn never enters the bankruptcy estate and, instead, is deflected back to the debtor. The debtor must report the gain on the corn and pay the tax.

- Under the "entrapment" theory, the $60,000 of gain on the corn is triggered as the corn is transferred back to the debtor and the gain is trapped in the bankruptcy estate which must pay the tax.

---

The minority approach follows the entrapment theory. *See, e.g., In re A.J. Lane & Co., Inc.,* 133 B.R. 264 (Bankr. D.Mass. 1991).

Under the minority approach the deflection theory pins the tax liability on the debtor. *See, e.g., In re Olson,* 930 F.2d 6 (8th Cir. 1991).

## B.   DISCHARGE OF INDEBTEDNESS

An important part of debt resolution is the income tax consequences to the debtor. Actually, there are two major categories of income tax consequences—(1) gain or loss if property is transferred to the lender in satisfaction of indebtedness and (2) possible discharge of indebtedness income to the extent debt discharged exceeds the fair market value of property given up by the debtor.

### 1.  Nature of the Debt—Recourse or Nonrecourse

The handling of discharge of indebtedness income depends upon whether the debt was recourse or nonrecourse. With recourse debt, the collateral stands as security on the loan. If the collateral is insufficient, the debtor is personally liable on the obligation and the debtor's non exempt assets are reachable to satisfy any deficiency. The bulk of farm and ranch debt is recourse debt.

Here's how it looks graphically:

## Figure 2. Income Tax Treatment of Discharge of Indebtedness Income

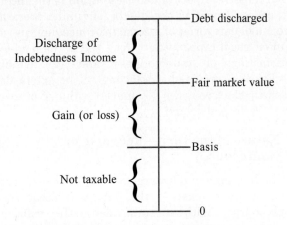

If property is given up by the debtor, the income tax consequences involve a two-step process. Basically, it is as if the property is sold to the creditor, and the sale proceeds are applied on the debt. First, there is no gain or loss (and no other income tax consequence) up to the income tax basis on the property. The difference between fair market value and the income tax basis is gain or loss. There is no relief from gain—even if the taxpayer is insolvent. This is the end of the first step in the process— treated as a hypothetical sale on the debt being discharged. Second, if the indebtedness exceeds the property's fair market value, the difference is discharge of indebtedness income.

---

**Example 8:**

I. M. Poor transferred to a creditor an asset with a fair market value of $60,000 and the creditor discharged $75,000 of indebtedness for which I. M. is personally liable. I. M.'s income tax basis in the asset is $40,000.

The $40,000 return of basis would be without income tax consequence. The difference between basis and fair market value of the property ($20,000) would be taxed as if the property were sold and may produce ordinary income or capital gain depending on the nature of the asset involved.

I. M. would have income from discharge of indebtedness equal to the difference between the fair market value of the asset and the amount of indebtedness discharged ($15,000).

---

As noted below, there are several relief provisions that a debtor may be able to use to avoid the general rule that discharge of indebtedness amounts are income.

For nonrecourse debt, the collateral stands as security on the obligation. But if the collateral is worth less than the balance on the debt, the debtor does not bear personal liability on the obligation. Therefore, the creditor must look solely to the collateral in the event of default. Very little farm and ranch debt is nonrecourse, except perhaps for some installment land contracts and commodity loans from the Commodity Credit Corporation to the extent that the debtor may pay off the loan with a sufficient amount of an eligible commodity having a price support value equal to the outstanding value of the loan (or less than the value of the loan in the case of a "marketing assistance loan"). Handling nonrecourse debt involves a simpler one-step process. Fair market value is ignored, and the entire difference between the income tax basis of any property involved (and transferred to the creditor) and the amount of debt discharged is gain (or loss). There is no discharge of indebtedness income.

---

**Example 9:**

Cybil purchased an unimproved farm in 1981 for use in her farm business for $200,000 on contract. In 1987, Cybil forfeited the contract to the seller as a time when the balance due on the contract was $140,000 and the fair market value of the farm was $100,000. Cybil was solvent at the time.

Cybil would have a $60,000 loss. The fair market value of the property is not relevant. The gain or loss is computed by examining the difference between Cybil's income tax basis (purchase price), and the amount of the liability discharged.

---

The IRS has prescribed special rules for handling Farmers Home Administration loans (redesignated as part of the Farm Service Agency in 1994).

## 2.  Handling Discharge of Indebtedness Income

The general rule is that discharge of indebtedness produces ordinary income. *I.R.C.  § 61(a)(12).*

However, there are five exceptions to the general rule.

### i. *Bankruptcy*

Debtors in bankruptcy need not report discharge of indebtedness income as income on their tax return. However, debtors in bankruptcy must reduce their tax attributes (including operating losses and investment tax credits carried forward) and reduce the income tax basis of their property. Losses are reduced dollar for dollar; credits are reduced $1 for $3 ($1 of credit offsets $3 of discharge of indebtedness income). To preserve net operating losses and tax credit carryovers, a debtor may elect to reduce the basis of depreciable property before reducing other tax attributes.

### ii. *Insolvent Debtors*

Debtors who are insolvent but not in bankruptcy likewise do not have income to report from discharge of indebtedness. But, again, insolvent debtors must reduce tax attributes and reduce the income tax basis of property. It is handled much like debtors in bankruptcy make the calculations. However, the amount of income from discharge of indebtedness that can be excluded from income is limited to the extent of the debtor's insolvency. If the amount of debt discharged exceeds the amount of the insolvency, income is triggered as to the excess. Thus, for the rule of insolvent taxpayers to apply, the taxpayer must be insolvent both before and after the transfer of property and transfer of indebtedness.

The determination of the taxpayer's solvency is made immediately before the discharge of indebtedness. "Insolvency" is defined as the excess of liabilities over the fair market value of the debtor's assets. Both tangible and intangible assets are included in the calculation. Likewise, both recourse and nonrecourse liabilities are included in the calculation, but contingent liabilities are not. The separate assets of the debtor's spouse are not included in determining the extent of the taxpayer's insolvency. Historically, the courts have held that property exempt from creditors under state law is not included in the insolvency calculation. However, the IRS ruled in mid-1999 that property exempt from creditors under state law is included in the insolvency calculation. The Tax Court agreed in early 2001 and again in 2007.

### iii.  Real Property Business Debt

Taxpayers other than C corporations can elect to exclude from gross income amounts realized from the discharge of "qualified real property business indebtedness." Instead, the income tax basis of the property is reduced.

The provision does not apply to farm indebtedness.

### iv.  Solvent Farmers

For all debtors other than farmers, once solvency is reached there is income from discharge of indebtedness. For solvent farm debtors, however, the discharge of indebtedness arising from an agreement between a person engaged in the trade or business of farming and a "qualified person" to discharge "qualified farm indebtedness" is eligible for special treatment. A special procedure for reducing tax attributes and reducing the basis of property is available to the debtor.

A "qualified person" is someone who is "actively and regularly engaged in the business of lending money and who is not somehow related to or connected with the debtor." "Qualified farm indebtedness" means indebtedness incurred directly in connection with the operation by the taxpayer of the trade or business of farming and 50 percent or more of the average annual gross receipts of the taxpayer for the three proceeding taxable years (in the aggregate) must be attributable to the trade or business of farming. In many instances, the presence of off farm income can make qualifying for the solvent farm debtor rule difficult.

In *Lawinger v. Commissioner,* 103 T.C. 428 (1994), the court held that a cash rent landlord was not a person engaged in the trade or business of farming and that the discharge of indebtedness was not discharge of qualified farm indebtedness.

If the requirements are met, a solvent farm debtor first reduces tax attributes in the following order:

- Net operating loss of the taxable year and any carryover losses to that year.

- General business credits (including investment tax credits carried over to that year).

- Minimum tax credit

- Capital losses for the year and capital losses carried over to that year.

- Passive activity loss and credit carryovers.

- Foreign tax credits

Again, losses reduce discharge of indebtedness income dollar for dollar. One dollar of credits reduces $3 of discharge of indebtedness income.

After the reduction of tax attributes, solvent farm debtors reduce the income tax basis of property used in a trade or business or held for the production of income in the following order—

- Depreciable property.

- Land used or held for use in the trade or business of farming.

- Other qualified property.

An election can be made to reduce the basis of depreciable property first, before reducing the tax attributes. This may help to preserve the tax attributes for later use.

If, after tax attributes and property basis is reduced, discharge of indebtedness remains, the remainder is income.

## 3. Primary Residence Indebtedness

Legislation enacted in 2007 permits up to $2 million of acquisition indebtedness that is forgiven on a mortgage attributable to the taxpayer's principal residence to be excluded from gross income. The provision expired at the end of 2016.

## 4. Purchase Price Adjustment

For solvent taxpayers who are not in bankruptcy, any negotiated reduction in the selling price of assets does not have to be reported as discharge of indebtedness income. To be eligible, the debt reduction must involve the original buyer and the original seller.

---

**Example 10:**

B purchased 320 acres of land from A in 1990 for $300,000. Earlier this year, unable to make any of the principal payments, B succeeded in convincing A to reduce the selling price to $200,000. The amount of the reduction, $100,000, would be discharge of indebtedness income except for this special provision. B must reduce the basis by $100,000 which could pose a problem for assets depreciated out or depreciated already to a low level.

---

Sometimes, a question arises concerning whether the seller has adverse tax consequences from the forgiveness. For example, before 1980, a common practice among farm and ranch families was to sell some land to the children and set the payments up at $10,000 per year and write the $10,000 amount off at Christmas. (As we will see in Chapter 8, this would not generate any federal gift tax liability because of the present interest annual exclusion.) The Internal Revenue Code, since 1980, has made it clear that any cancellation or forgiveness of payments must be treated as though received by the seller. *I.R.C. § 453B.* However, the IRS has ruled in a private letter ruling that forgiveness of payments to help a financially troubled debtor does not result in income to the seller. *Ltr. Rul. 8739045, June 30, 1987.*

# CHAPTER 5
# REAL PROPERTY

## I. OVERVIEW

In many farming and ranching operations, the real estate is the primary asset in terms of value. The ownership, possession and transfer of real property give rise to many legal issues. This chapter addresses issues associated with the nature and ownership of real property, and the legal issues resulting from the transfer of title to an interest in real property, including the income tax aspects of transferring real estate. Other legal issues arising from the ownership and use of real property (such as land use conflicts and environmental issues) are covered elsewhere in this book.

## II. NATURE AND OWNERSHIP OF REAL PROPERTY

The term "real property" includes generally land and whatever is erected, growing upon or affixed to it. The term includes, for most purposes, items such as fences, buildings, tile lines, mineral deposits and air rights. Water rights have generally been considered as property. However, in some states (such as Kansas), a water right is a right to use water and is not a right to own.

### A. ESTATES IN LAND

Land ownership includes two separate estates in land—the surface estate and the mineral estate. The

mineral estate can be severed from the surface estate
with the result that ownership of the separate estates
is in different parties. In some states, the mineral
estate is dominant. That means that the mineral
estate owner can freely use the surface estate to the
extent reasonably necessary for the exploration,
development and production of the minerals beneath
the surface. If the owner of the mineral estate has
only a single method for developing the minerals,
many courts will allow that method to be utilized
without consideration of its impact on the activities
of the surface estate owner. But, under the
accommodation doctrine, if alternative means of
development are reasonably available that would not
disrupt existing activities on the surface those
alternative means must be utilized.

Clearly, when land ownership is split into a surface
estate and a mineral estate, many important legal
issues can arise.

## 1. The Fee Simple

A "fee simple absolute" is the largest ownership
interest possible in land. A fee simple denotes
ownership of potentially infinite duration. For
example, if O owns Blackacre and conveys it to A, the
document referencing the conveyance would read
"from O to A in fee simple absolute." A fee simple
absolute is inheritable by either lineal or collateral
heirs, generation after generation, but is freely
transferable, either inter vivos (during life) or by will
(at death), free of any claim of the transferor's heirs.
However, if the owner of a fee simple absolute should

die intestate (without a will) and without natural
heirs, the estate will pass to the state by "escheat."

A fee simple interest can also be structured such
that the interest lasts only until the occurrence of a
designated event. For example, the fee simple owner
of Blackacre could convey Blackacre to "A Church for
so long as the land shall be used be used for church
purposes," or to "A Church until the land shall cease
to be used for church purposes." The qualifying
language is called a "special limitation" and the
estate determinable continues only until the
designated state of affairs ceases or the designated
event occurs, at which time the estate simply expires.
Thus, a fee simple determinable is a "smaller" estate
than a fee simple absolute because the special
limitation may cause the fee simple determinable to
expire even though the owner of that estate has not
died without heirs capable of taking by intestate
succession. The residue of the fee simple absolute
owned by the person who created the fee simple
determinable may be retained by such person (or
such person's heirs, if the fee simple determinable is
created by will), or it may be simultaneously
transferred to a third person by a "gift over." When
the residue of the fee simple absolute is retained by
the person creating the fee simple determinable (or
his heirs), such person is said to retain a possibility
of reverter. When the residue is simultaneously
transferred to a third person by a "gift over," the
interest obtained by the third person is an executory
future interest.

When the state of affairs upon which a fee simple determinable is limited ceases to exist or the designated terminating event occurs, the fee simple determinable expires by operation of law, without the necessity of any action by the person who owns the possibility of reverter or executory interest which constitutes the residue of the fee simple absolute. As a result, the owner of the possibility of reverter or executory interest, has an immediate right to possession of the property and may immediately bring an action to recover its possession.

Today, estates in fee simple determinable are rarely encountered in commercial transactions except that oil and gas leases often contain special limitations creating estates in fee simple determinable. In addition, estates in fee simple determinable are sometimes created when land is given to charitable, religious or educational institutions.

Another type of fee simple subject to a qualifying limitation is a fee simple subject to a condition subsequent. A conveyance of Blackacre "from O to A provided, however, that the land hereby conveyed shall be used for no other purpose than as agricultural land" gives A a fee simple subject to a condition subsequent, and gives the grantor (O) a right to "reenter" the land and oust the grantee or successors in interest if a breach of the condition should occur. However, many courts hold that words of condition, standing alone, are ambiguous and that the grantor who omits any express provision for reentry, termination, or forfeiture may be found to have intended to create only a personal covenant, a real covenant or equitable servitude, an easement, an equitable charge or a trust, rather than a defeasible estate. Thus, if a grantor desires to create a fee simple subject to a condition subsequent, the language creating the instrument should expressly provide for reentry and termination of the estate granted upon breach of the stated condition. When such a provision is included in the conveyancing instrument, most courts will find that a fee simple subject to a condition subsequent is created.

As is the case with fee simple determinables, estates in fee simple subject to a condition subsequent are rarely created in commercial transactions, but they are still sometimes created when land is given to charitable, religious or educational institutions.

Another type of fee simple interest similar to a fee simple determinable and a fee simple subject to a condition subsequent is the fee simple subject to an executory limitation. This type of interest is a fee simple estate which, upon the happening of a designated event, will automatically pass to a designated person other than the person who created the defeasible estate or such person's successors in interest. For example, A could convey Blackacre either by deed or by will "to B and his heirs, but if B shall die leaving no surviving children, then to C and his heirs." The effect of such a conveyance or devise is to give B a present fee simple subject to a shifting executory limitation and to give C an executory interest in fee simple.

## 2. The Life Estate

A life estate is an interest in land which is not terminable at any fixed time, but cannot last longer than the life or lives of one or more persons. For example, an instrument conveying Blackacre "from O to A for life," gives A an interest in the land as long as A is alive. Upon A's death, the land may pass to whomever A directs under the terms of A's will. A life estate may also be coupled with a remainder interest. A remainder interest is a future interest which can become a present possessory interest only upon the expiration of some prior interest or interests, usually a life estate. A remainder can be either vested or contingent. For example, if O transfers Blackacre "to A for life, remainder to B," if B is alive and ascertainable at the time of the conveyance, B has a vested remainder. If the transfer is "from O to A for life, remainder to the heirs of B," the unborn and unascertained heirs of B have a contingent remainder.

The use of the life estate and life estate-remainder arrangements is common in agricultural families. However, if not structured properly, a life estate can create a very inflexible interest in the life estate holder. For example, if father leaves the farmland to mother for life with a remainder to the children, upon the father's death (assuming he dies first), mother has the right to live on the land, but if the land is too expensive to maintain or too far from town, mother cannot sell the property unless all of the remainder holders consent. These problems can be avoided with careful planning including the use of powers of appointment and/or leaving the property to a trustee in trust for mother for her life with a remainder to the children. The trustee has the power of sale and can dispose of the property if appropriate.

A reversion specifies the ownership interest remaining after conveyance of an interest to another, and becomes possessory upon expiration of the granted interest. For example, if O conveys Blackacre "to A for life, reversion to O," O has a reversionary interest in the property. An estate for years is an interest in property, the duration of which is specifically fixed in the conveyancing instrument. Most oral agricultural leases involve reversions. However, a lease may also be structured as an estate for years. For example, if O transfers Blackacre "to A for one year," A has an estate for the duration of one year. A lease creates a continuing relationship between landlord and tenant. The obligations of the landlord and tenant are fixed by the lease terms (covenants) and the drafting of those terms requires careful thought and foresight.

## 3. Agricultural Leases as Estates in Land

An agricultural lease represents an estate in land for a definite period of time that is fixed in advance. The time of commencement, term and time of termination of the lease must be specified. If such items are not specified in a written lease, state law controls the lease's duration and establishes the procedure for terminating the lease.

In most states, oral agricultural leases are generally presumed to be tenancies from year to year that automatically renew for another one year period if proper notice is not given to terminate the lease. However, evidence with respect to the period of time for which rent is to be paid, or of a contrary intent expressed through either past practice or land custom may also be considered. For a landlord to terminate properly the tenant's rights under an oral lease, state statutes must be followed. However, state notice of termination statutes typically do not apply to a tenant that becomes a tenant from year to year by occupying the premises after the expiration of the term fixed in a written lease. In this situation, the notice of termination of the tenancy usually must fix the termination to take place on the same day and month specified in the original lease under which the tenant first occupied the premises. However, the landlord will likely be required to give the tenant notice a prescribed amount of time before the termination date.

If a landlord gives notice to terminate an oral agricultural lease after the tenant has prepared the ground for planting a crop, the landlord is typically required to reimburse the tenant for the fair and reasonable value of the tenant's services furnished. This value may include the cost of any fertilizers, herbicides, and/or pest control substances applied to the land. If the tenant plants a fall seeded crop before receiving notice that the tenancy will terminate the following spring, the tenant is typically permitted to harvest the crop. However, if the landlord provides statutory notice of termination before the tenant plants a fall seeded crop, the landlord is entitled to the entire crop.

State law typically specifies the procedure that must be followed for terminating an oral agricultural lease. For example, in Kansas, written notice must be served upon the tenant at least 30 days before March 1, specifying that the lease ends on March 1 or, with respect to fall planted crops, on the earlier of harvest or August 1. *Kan. Stat. § 58–2506(a).* Perhaps the best way to send notice is by registered or certified mail addressed to the tenant at the tenant's usual place of residence. In that case, the tenant must sign a receipt upon receiving the notice.

### i. The Importance of Leasing to Agriculture

Leasing is of primary importance to agriculture. Leasing permits farmers and ranchers to operate larger farm businesses with the same amount of capital and assists beginning farmers and ranchers in establishing a farming or ranching business.

Leasing is also important in terms of its relation to a particular farm or ranch family's estate plan. For example, with respect to Social Security benefits for retired farm-landlords, pre-death material participation under a lease can cause problems. A retired farm-landlord who has not reached full retirement age (66 and two months in 2017) may be unable to receive full Social Security benefits if the landlord and tenant have an agreement that the landlord shall have "material participation" in the production of, or the managing of, agricultural products.

While material participation can cause problems with respect to Social Security benefits, material participation is required for five of the last eight years before the earlier of retirement, disability or death if a special use valuation election is going to be made for the agricultural real estate included in the decedent-to-be's estate. *I.R.C. § 2032A.* The solution, if a family member is present, may be to have a nonretired landlord not materially participate, but rent the elected land to a materially participating family member or to hire a family member as a farm manager. Cash leasing of elected land to family members is permitted before death, but generally not after death. The solution, if a family member is not present, is to have the landlord retire at age 65 or older, materially participate during five of the eight years immediately preceding retirement, and then during retirement rent out the farm on a nonmaterial participation crop-share or livestock-share lease.

Leases can also have an impact on a producer's eligibility for farm program payments. In general, to qualify for farm program payments, an individual must be "actively engaged in farming." For example, each "person" who is actively engaged in farming is eligible for up to $125,000 in federal farm program payments each crop year. A tenant qualifies as actively engaged in farming through the contribution of capital, equipment, active personal labor, or active personal management. Likewise, a landlord qualifies as actively engaged in farming by the contribution of the owned land if the rent or income for the operation's use of the land is based on the land's production or the operation's operating results (not cash rent or rent based on a guaranteed share of the crop). In addition, the landlord's contribution must be "significant," must be "at risk," and must be commensurate with the landlord's share of the profits and losses from the farming operation.

A landowner who cash leases land is considered a landlord under the payment limitation rules and may not be considered actively engaged in farming. In this situation, only the tenant is considered eligible. Under the payment limitation rules, there are technical requirements that restrict the cash-rent tenant's eligibility to receive payments to situations in which the tenant makes a "significant contribution" of (1) active personal labor and capital, land or equipment; or (2) active personal management and equipment. Leases in which the rental amount fluctuates with price and/or production (so-called "flex" leases) can raise a question as to whether or not the lease is really a crop-share lease which thereby entitles the landlord to a proportionate share of the government payments attributable to the leased land. Under Farm Service Agency (FSA) regulations, a lease is a "cash lease" if it provides for only a guaranteed sum certain cash payment, or a fixed quantity of the crop (for example, cash, pounds, or bushels per acre). *7 C.F.R. § 1412.504(a)(2)*. All other types of leases are share leases. Beginning, with the 2009 crop year, FSA has taken the position that a tenant and landlord may reach any agreement they wish concerning "flexing" the cash rent payment and the agreement will not convert the cash lease into a share-rent arrangement.

## ii. Allocation of Risk Between Landlord and Tenant

As mentioned above, leasing arrangements are generally differentiated by the allocation of risk between the landlord and tenant. While this is a function of the type of lease involved, risk allocation is also dependent upon the terms of a written lease agreement or common law principles for oral leases. For example, a clause common in many leases requires the tenant to farm the land in accordance with good farming practices (i.e., not commit waste on the premises). *See, e.g., Keller v. Bolding,* 2004 N.D. 80, 678 N.W.2d 578 (2004). As a result, an understanding of the potential legal and economic risks involved in a leasing relationship and the negotiation of lease terms are very important. *See, e.g. K&M Enterprises v. Pennington,* 764 So. 2d 1089 (La. Ct. App. 2000).

## iii. Custom Farming Arrangements

In the agricultural sector, agreements other than leases are sometimes utilized which authorize a person to come onto the owner's premises to conduct farming operations. For instance, some farming and ranching operations utilize employees, while other operations hire a farm management company or an individual as an independent contractor with compensation based on a certain number of dollars per acre to prepare, plant, cultivate and harvest. Custom cutters provide combine crews that follow the harvest each year from Texas to Canada.

Usually, those who hire custom cutters treat them as independent contractors from a legal perspective.

While the status of a tenant or independent contractor is usually clear, the status of a cropper is less clear. A cropper occupies a legal position somewhere between the status of a tenant and an employee or independent contractor. A person is likely to be a cropper and not a tenant when the landowner supplies land and all the inputs, controls the operation of the farm and pays a portion of the crop to the person who actually raises and harvests the crop. A cropper, unlike a tenant who has a possessory interest in the leased premises and control over the farming operation, only has permission to be on the land. A cropper does not have any legally enforceable interest in the crops and has only a contract right to be compensated in-kind for the cropper's labor. While a tenant is entitled to proper notice of lease termination, a cropper has no interest in real property to terminate. When a question arises with respect to the status of the parties, courts attempt to determine the intent of the parties as evidenced by the terms of the written or oral contract, circumstances surrounding the agreement, the action of the parties and the type of farming operation. Typically, no single factor controls. Instead, an examination of all the factors is necessary in most situations to determine the status of the parties. Indeed, most courts do not find controlling the parties' characterization of the arrangement. But if a landowner gives exclusive possession of a farm to another party, some courts have held that act to establish a landlord-tenant relationship. As for croppers, a court could find them to be employees instead of independent contractors under a state workers' compensation law.

## B.    OTHER INTERESTS IN LAND

### 1.  Easements and Profits

A landowner may give rights in the owner's real estate to another person without creating an "estate." For example, an easement does not give the holder of the easement a right of possession, but a right to use or to take something from someone else's land. To the holder of the easement, the easement is a right or interest in land, but to the owner of the real estate subject to the easement, the easement is an encumbrance upon that person's estate. Easements may take several forms and are common in agricultural settings. For example, O, owner of Blackacre, may grant to A, owner of Whiteacre, a right-of-way over a specified portion of Blackacre for passage to and from Whiteacre. A has an easement over Blackacre appurtenant to Whiteacre. The right-of-way is the most common easement, but there are many others including an easement of flowage over Blackacre for surface waters from Whiteacre, a right to flood Blackacre by waters backed up by a dam on Whiteacre, or a right to have the soil on Blackacre retained in such condition that it continues to support the buildings on Whiteacre. In essence, the easement gives A the right to use Blackacre for specified purposes, as distinguished from a right to possess Blackacre.

The specific terms of an easement apply in determining what type of use can be made of the easement. If the instrument creating the easement is silent, the easement is presumed to last forever and a presumption of normal development arises. For example, if X owns Blackacre and Y owns adjacent Whiteacre, and X has an easement across Whiteacre, if X sells out to a developer, Y cannot enjoin cars coming across Whiteacre unless it is excessive or the easement is deemed to benefit land other than Blackacre.

### i. Easements in Gross and Appurtenant Easements

An easement may be either an easement in gross or an appurtenant easement. An easement "in gross" is one whose benefits serve the holder only personally instead of in connection with such person's ownership or use of any specific parcel of land. For example, easements held by utility companies, street easements, and railroad easements are easements in gross. An easement in gross is a non-assignable personal right that terminates upon the death, liquidation or bankruptcy of its holder. An easement that is "appurtenant" is one whose benefits serve a particular parcel of land. An appurtenant easement becomes a right in that particular parcel of land and passes with title to that land upon a subsequent conveyance. Examples of appurtenant easements include walkways, driveways and utility lines that cross a particular parcel and lead to an adjoining or nearby tract. In Wyoming, a water right becomes appurtenant to the land upon which the water is used, and the ditch, water pipe, or other conduit for the water becomes attached to the land and is necessary for the beneficial enjoyment of the land. *See, e.g., Rennard v. Vollmar,* 977 P.2d 1277 (Wyo. 1999).

Determining whether an easement is one in gross or is appurtenant depends upon the circumstances of each particular situation. Courts generally prefer appurtenant easements. The particular classification matters when the question is whether the easement in question is assignable or whether it passes with the title to the land to which it may be appurtenant.

### ii. Affirmative and Negative Easements

An easement is either an affirmative easement or a negative easement. Most easements are affirmative and entitle the holder to do certain things upon the land subject to the easement. A negative easement gives its holder a right to require the owner of the land subject to the easement to do or not to do specified things with respect to that land. Thus, negative easements are synonymous with covenantal land restrictions and are similar to certain "natural rights" that are incidents of land ownership. These include riparian rights, lateral and subjacent support rights, and the right to be free from nuisances. However, most American courts reject the English "ancient lights" doctrine and refuse to recognize a negative easement for light, air and view. *See, e.g., Fontainebleau Hotel Corp. v. Forty-Five Twenty-Five, Inc.* 114 So.2d 357 (Fla. App. 1959). However, if a property owner's interference with a neighboring owner's light, air or view is done maliciously, the court may enjoin such activity as a nuisance. *See, e.g., Coty v. Ramsey Associates, Inc.* 149 Vt. 451, 546 A.2d 196 (1988).

A concept related to an easement is that of a profit. For example, O, owner of Blackacre, could grant to A a right to enter Blackacre to cut and remove timber. A is said to have a profit in Blackacre—a right of severance which will result in A's acquiring possession to the severed thing. The general distinction between an easement and a profit is that an easement allows some use to be made of the land subject to the easement, while profits allow some substance to be severed and removed from the land subject to the profits. In most instances, a profit is accompanied by an easement, either an express easement or an implied easement. For example, a profit to remove any substance from land must carry with it access over the burdened land sufficient to reach, work and remove the substance.

Easement and profit rights generally include the right to improve the burdened land, perhaps only to a gravel road, but perhaps to erect and maintain more substantial structures, such as bridges, pipelines, and even buildings that facilitate use of the easement or profit. Sometimes a question arises as to whether a point is reached at which structures become so substantial that the rights become those of occupation and possession instead of just use. In answering this question, courts look at the circumstances as a whole instead of the labels the parties use. In general, the existence of permanent, substantial structures is viewed as an estate rather than an easement or profit. Other interesting situations arising in agricultural settings involve rights to enter another person's land to remove things that the landowner may not own. Examples include rights to fish in a stream, hunt for wild animals or take water from a stream or spring.

A concept related to easements and profits is that of a license. A license is a term that covers a wide range of permissive land uses which, unless permitted, would be trespasses. For example, a hunter who is on the premises with permission is a licensee. The distinction between a license and an easement or profit is that a license can be terminated at any time by the person who created the license. For example, permission to hunt may be denied. Conversely, easements and profits exist for a fixed period of time or perpetually and are rights in land. A license is only a privilege. Likewise, easements and profits are interests in land while licenses are not, and licenses may be granted orally, but because easements and profits are interests in land, they are subject to the statute of frauds and must be in writing.

### iii. Implied Easements

An easement may also be implied from prior use or necessity, or arise by prescription. An implied easement may arise from prior use if there has been a conveyance of a physical part of the grantor's land (hence, the grantor retains part, usually adjoining the part conveyed), and before the conveyance there was a usage on the land that, had the two parts then been severed, could have been the subject of an easement appurtenant to one and servient upon the other, and this usage is, more or less, "necessary" to the use of the part to which it would be appurtenant, and "apparent." An easement implied from necessity involves a conveyance of a physical part only of the grantor's land, and after severance of the tract into two parcels, it is "necessary" to pass over one of them to reach any public street or road from the other. No pre-existing use needs to be present. Instead, the severance creates a land-locked parcel unless its owner is given implied access over the other parcel.

### iv. Prescriptive Easements (Adverse Possession)

Acquiring an easement by prescription is analogous to acquiring property by adverse possession. If an individual possesses someone else's land in an open and notorious fashion with an intent to take it away from them, such person (known as an adverse possessor) becomes the true property owner after the statutory time period (anywhere from 10 to 21 years) has expired. For an easement by prescription to arise, the use of the land subject to the easement must be open and notorious, adverse, under a claim of right, continuous and uninterrupted for the statutory period. If use is permissive, the adverse possession statute is never tolled. Also, it is generally not possible to assert an adverse possession claim against the government.

For example, assume that A owns Blackacre, and that B owns adjacent Whiteacre. A drives across a portion of Whiteacre to reach A's garage on Blackacre. A does this five days a week for 22 years. B then puts up a barbed wire fence in A's path. If A can show an adverse use of Whiteacre and that A's use was continuous for the full statutory period, and that A's use was visible and notorious or was made with B's acquiescence, A will have a prescriptive easement over Whiteacre. However, acquiescence does not mean permission. If A receives permission from B to cross Whiteacre, the prescriptive period never begins to run and no prescriptive easement will arise.

Adverse possession (prescriptive easement) statutes vary by jurisdiction in terms of the requirements a person claiming title by adverse possession must satisfy and the length of time property must be adversely possessed.

Once title is successfully obtained by adverse possession, the party obtaining title can bring a court action to quiet title. A quiet title action ensures that the land records properly reflect the true owner of the property.

### v. *Termination of Easements*

An easement may be terminated in several ways. Merger, also referred to as unity of ownership, terminates an existing easement. For example, assume that A owns Blackacre and B owns adjoining Whiteacre. B grants A an easement across Whiteacre so that A can acquire access to Blackacre. Two years later, A buys Whiteacre in fee simple. Because A now owns both tracts of real estate, the easement is terminated.

An easement may also be terminated by a release. If the easement was for a duration of more than one year, the release must be in writing to be effective and comply with all of the formalities of a deed.

An easement may also be terminated by abandonment. Mere intent to abandon is not effective to terminate the easement. Instead, abandonment can only occur if the holder of the easement demonstrates by physical action an intent to permanently abandon the easement. Mere words are insufficient to cause an abandonment of the easement. For example, assume that an easement holder builds a barn in such a manner that access to the easement is blocked. This action would be sufficient to constitute abandonment of the easement.

An easement may also be terminated by estoppel where there is reasonable reliance by the owner of the servient tenement who changes position based on assertions or conduct of the easement holder. For example, assume that A tells B that A is releasing the easement over B's property. As a result, A doesn't use the easement for a long time. B then builds a machine shed over A's easement. In this situation, the easement would be terminated by estoppel and A could not reassert the existence of the easement after the machine shed has been built.

An easement may also be terminated by prescription where the owner of the servient tenement possesses and enjoys the servient tenement in a way that would indicate to the public that no easement right existed.

## 2. Ownership and Use of Abandoned Railways

The General Railroad Right-of-Way Act of 1875 (*43 U.S.C. § 934*) provided railroad companies "right[s] of way through the public lands of the United States." However, over time, a certain amount of railroad trackage has been abandoned for rail use. For those farmers and ranchers owning agricultural land adjacent to railroads, the abandonment of an active rail line presents a number of real property issues.

During the nineteenth century, many railroad companies acquired easements from adjoining landowners to operate rail lines. In some instances, railroads acquired a fee simple interest in rights-of-way and in those situations, can sell or otherwise dispose of the property. In most situations, however, a railroad was granted an easement for railroad purposes, usually acquired from adjacent property owners. In that event, the abandonment of the line automatically terminates the railroad's easement interest, and the interest generally reverts to the owners of the adjacent land owning the fee simple interest from which the easement was granted. After abandonment, state law controls the property interests involved. Once abandonment occurs, federal law does not control the property law questions involved. The only exception is if the United States retained a right of reverter in the abandoned railway. Under the Abandoned Railroad

Right of Way Act, (*43 U.S.C. § 912*) land given by the United States for use as a railroad right-of-way in which the United States retained a right of reverter must be turned into a public highway within one year of the railroad company's abandonment or be given to adjacent landowners. Subsequently, the Congress enacted the National Trails System Improvement Act of 1988 under which those lands not converted to public highways within one year of abandonment revert back to the United States, not adjacent private landowners.

Under the Railroad Revitalization and Regulatory Reform Act of 1976, the Secretary of Transportation is authorized to prepare a report on alternate uses for abandoned right-of-ways. The Secretary of the Interior can offer financial, educational and technical assistance to local, state and federal agencies. In addition, the Interstate Commerce Commission (ICC) is authorized to delay disposition of railroad property for up to 180 days after an order of abandonment, unless the property is first offered for sale on reasonable terms for public purposes including recreational use. The National Trails System Act amendments of 1983 authorized the ICC to preserve for possible future railroad use, rights-of-way not currently in service and to allow interim use of land as recreational trails. Effective January 1, 1996, the Congress replaced the ICC with the Surface Transportation Board (STB), and gave the STB authority to address rail abandonment and trail conversion issues.

The 1983 amendments allow railroads to transfer inactive railroad corridors to qualified organizations for interim use as trails until such time as the rights-of-way are needed for future rail service, on the condition that the organizations operating the corridors as trails assume all legal and financial responsibility for the corridors. This is known as railbanking.

Under the 1983 amendments, a railroad must follow a certain procedure if it desires to abandon a line. For example, the railroad must obtain the STB's permission for either a permanent abandonment or temporary discontinuance. The STB will grant either a permanent abandonment or temporary discontinuance based on the possible future public convenience and whether a "qualified person" wishes to operate a trail on the line. If a trail operator exists, such person must agree to manage the trail, take legal responsibility for the trail and pay any taxes on the trail. The STB engages in a three-stage process for railroad abandonment. A railroad must file an application with the STB and notify certain persons of its planned abandonment. The application must state whether the right-of-way is suitable for recreational use. In addition, the application must notify government agencies and must be posted in train stations and newspapers giving the public a right to comment. The STB then determines whether "present or future public convenience and necessity" permit the railroad to abandon. A trail organization then must submit a map and agreement to assume financial responsibility and the STB will then determine whether the railroad intends to negotiate a trail agreement. If such a determination is made, the STB will issue a "certificate of interim trail use" or a certificate of abandonment. The parties have 180 days to reach this agreement. If no agreement is reached, the line is abandoned. Abandonment of a railroad right-of-way cannot occur without the prior authorization of the STB. But, once abandonment occurs, the STB no longer has any jurisdiction over the issue.

Before passage of the 1983 amendments, it was clear that when a railroad ceased line operation and abandoned the railway, the easement interest of the railroad in the line reverted to the adjacent landowners of the fee simple. However, the 1983 amendments established a more detailed process for railroad abandonment and gave trail organizations the ability to operate an abandoned line. While most railroads hold a right-of-way to operate their lines by easement specifying that the easement reverts to the landowner upon abandonment, after passage of the 1983 amendments, a significant question is when, if ever, abandonment occurs. One court has held that the public use condition on abandonment does not prevent the abandonment from being consummated, at which time STB jurisdiction ends, federal law no longer preempts state law, and state property law may cause the extinguishment of the railroad's rights and interests.

A more fundamental issue is whether a preclusion of reversion to the owner of the adjacent fee simple is an unconstitutional taking of private property. This question was answered in 1990 when the United

States Supreme Court upheld the 1983 amendments on constitutional grounds. The court reasoned that because there was no abandonment of the rail line by the railroad at issue in the case, the ICC retained jurisdiction over the rail line. In addition, the court held that it was a legitimate governmental purpose to preserve rail lines for public recreation. However, the Supreme Court did not conclude in *Preseault* that no compensable taking occurs when a rail line is converted to a trail, because the court noted that a landowner may obtain compensation by filing an action in the United States Court of Federal Claims. Indeed, the Court of Federal Claims ruled that the government must pay the landowners $234,000 plus 15 years of interest, plus attorney fees for a strip of land less than 500 feet long that was taken to form part of a bicycle trail. *Preseault v. United States,* No. 90–4043L, 2001 U.S. Claims LEXIS 274 (Fed. Cl. May 22, 2001); 52 Fed. Cl. 667 (2002).

Takings claims that arise from the conversion of a railroad line to a trail are analyzed under a three-part test: (1) a determination of the type of property interest that the railroad owned (e.g., an easement or a fee simple interest); (2) if the property interest was an easement, a determination of whether the terms of the easement limited use only for railroad purposes or whether the terms allow for future use as a public recreational trail; and (3) if the railroad acquired a "broad enough" easement under applicable state law, a determination of whether the easements terminated before the alleged taking with the result that the property owners at the time held fee simple ownership interests unencumbered by the easements.

In late 2002, the United States Court of Federal Claims awarded $410,000 to 13 landowners along Missouri's Katy Trail. *Moore, et al. v. United States,* 54 Fed. Cl. 747 (2002). While the court's opinion does not call into question the validity of the 1983 amendments, it does clarify that compensation must be paid to landowners whose private property has been taken for a public purpose when, under state law, abandoned rail lines revert to adjacent landowners. In 2011, the court determined that a taking had *not* occurred upon abandonment of a railroad line because, under state law, the deeds at issue transferred a fee simple absolute to the railroad rather than an easement. *Thompson, et al. v. United States,* 101 Fed. Cl. 416 (2011). Similarly, in 2013, the court held that the Federal Government was liable for an unconstitutional taking under the Fifth Amendment to the extent that the railroads involved in the case had been granted easements and the government converted the rail line to trail usage under the National Trail Systems Act. *Burgess, et al. v. United States,* 109 Fed. Cl. 223 (2013). However, where the deeds in issue transferred a fee interest in the rail line to the railroad rather than an easement, the court dismissed the takings claims because the fee owners of the adjacent lands could not prove that they held sufficient property interests to establish a takings claim.

In 2014, the Supreme Court held that fee simple ownership of an abandoned railroad right of way vested in the owner of the surrounding tract, not in the United States, which had claimed a reversionary interest. *Marvin M. Brandt Revocable Trust, et al. v. United States,* 134 S. Ct. 1257 (2014).

## III. FORMS OF CO-OWNERSHIP OF LAND

A fee-simple interest in land may be held in co-ownership either as tenancy in common, joint tenancy, tenancy by the entirety or as community property. For property held as tenants in common, each tenant owns an undivided interest in the whole property. Each tenant's interest may be sold or mortgaged, and upon a tenant's death, that tenant's interest passes to their heirs or under the terms of the deceased tenant's will. A tenant may obtain partition of the property or sale and partition of the proceeds. The party seeking partition must present sufficient evidence that a partition is possible. If sufficient evidence is not presented, the court may determine that the property is indivisible and must be sold. In general, partition and sale will be ordered if partition-in-kind would greatly prejudice one owner.

For property owned in joint tenancy with right of survivorship, each joint tenant owns an undivided interest in the whole property and each tenant's interest may be sold or mortgaged. However, upon death of a joint tenant, that person's interest passes to the surviving tenant or tenants. Passage of a deceased joint tenant's interest is not controlled by that person's will unless the decedent was the sole surviving tenant. Thus, the survivorship feature of joint tenancy precludes the use of the life-estate remainder arrangement as to the nonmarital portion of a decedent's estate.

---

**Example 1:**

Juanita and Wanda own an 80-acre tract of land as joint tenants with right of survivorship. Wanda would like for her daughter Cathy to own Wanda's interest in the real estate upon Wanda's death. To further that objective, Wanda has her attorney prepare a will that devises her interest in the real estate to Cathy.

Wanda dies. Wanda's will is not effective to control the disposition of Wanda's interest in the real estate. Because of the survivorship feature of the joint tenancy, Juanita receives Wanda's interest, and owns the entire interest in the property. Cathy does not receive any interest in the tract.

---

Joint tenancy may be destroyed by transfer, sale, contract to sell, partition or by agreement. If any of those events occurs, the property is then held by the owners as tenants in common. The standard words for creating a joint tenancy are "to A and B as joint tenants, with right of survivorship, and not as tenants in common." If the language in a conveyancing instrument is unclear as to whether tenancy in common or joint tenancy is intended, a tenancy in common is presumed. Thus, if joint tenancy is intended, the conveyancing instrument must specifically mention the right of survivorship.

Tenancy by the entirety is a special form of spousal joint tenancy between spouses that is recognized in nineteen states and the District of Columbia. In these jurisdictions, a conveyance or devise to husband and wife is presumed to create a tenancy by the entirety, unless language in the conveyancing instrument indicates otherwise. However, courts in some jurisdictions hold that when a married couple receives property through intestate succession (the state distributional scheme where the decedent dies without a will) they take as tenants in common. Tenancy by the entirety property can be conveyed or mortgaged, and is terminated by a conveyance of the entire interest of one spouse to the other spouse. When one tenant dies, the surviving spouse usually becomes the sole owner of the property.

Ten states (AZ, CA, ID, LA, NV, NM, TX, WA, & WI; AK is an "opt-in state) recognize another form of marital property ownership known as community property. Community property law is based on a philosophical premise that husband and wife are equals. Thus, during marriage they form a type of marital partnership. In these jurisdictions, all property acquired during marriage is community property. However, property that either spouse acquires before marriage remains that spouse's separate property. Likewise, any property acquired during marriage by gift, or inheritance is also the separate property of the particular spouse receiving the property. In the community property jurisdictions, each spouse can dispose of all of his or her separate property by will, and can dispose of one-half of the community property.

## IV. TRANSFERRING TITLE TO AND INTERESTS IN REAL PROPERTY

### A. SHORT-TERM CONTRACT FOR SALE OF LAND—ELEMENTS

### 1. Names of Parties and Type of Ownership

A short-term contract for the sale of land should specify the names of the parties and whether ownership is to be tenancy in common, joint tenancy, tenancy by the entirety or in the name of an entity such a partnership, corporation, trust or estate.

### 2. Signed Writing

As a general rule, agreements creating or transferring an interest in real property must be in writing and be signed by the grantor of the interest. In general, several exceptions to the writing requirement are recognized. These include leases for a term not exceeding one year, transactions where a part or all of the purchase price has been paid, and transactions where possession has been given.

### 3. Legal Description of Land

To be effective to pass an interest in land, the Statute of Frauds requires that an instrument transferring an interest in real property must describe adequately the land conveyed. The conveyancing instrument, known generally as a real estate deed, must contain a description of the land such that the property being conveyed can be located by reference to the deed. Most instruments transferring interests in real property refer to the property by legal description. The description defines a series of boundary lines on the earth's surface which delineate a two-dimensional geometric figure. The land described is limited horizontally by the geometric figure and theoretically extends from the earth's center to the sky.

Several methods are utilized to specify the boundary lines. The government survey is the form of legal description that dominates in the central and western United States and involves reference to congressional townships where the property is mapped out on a grid in accordance with Base Lines and Principal Meridians. The Base Lines run east and west on a true parallel of latitude, and the Principal Meridians run along a longitude. There are thirty-six sets of Base Lines and Principal Meridians in the contiguous forty-eight states. Additional lines that are parallel to each Base Line are spaced out approximately every six miles and divide the land into "Townships." Similarly spaced, parallel to each Principal Meridian at six mile intervals, are north-south lines that divide the land into "Ranges." The sets of parallel lines are perpendicular to each other and intersect to form townships which are tracts of land six miles square containing approximately 23,040 acres. A line of townships running north and south is called a range, and the ranges are numbered east and west from the meridian. Each township in a range is also numbered north and south from the base line. Each township is further divided into thirty-six "sections" each of approximately one square mile and containing 640 acres. The sections are numbered boustrophedonically beginning with Section 1 in the northeast corner and running west to the range line, and in the next row to the south proceeding west to east. This procedure is followed until Section 36 is reached which is in the southeast corner of the township. Each section can be further divided into halves, quarters and in even smaller amounts of property.

Real estate descriptions contained in deeds are properly read backwards from right to left. The following example demonstrates the language used to convey an interest in real estate where the land is described by reference to the public survey system.

**Example 2:**

Sam Tiller is considering purchasing a tract of Nebraska land for a price of $250,000. The legal description is as follows:

All of Section 5, and the NW1/4 of Section 6, T18N, R32W of the Sixth Principal meridian, McPherson County, Nebraska.

The description contains 800 acres. A section contains 640 acres. Sam would own the NW1/4 of Section 6, or a 160-acre tract. Sam also would own Section 5, or another 640 acres. Combined, the description contains 800 acres.

Much land in the eastern part of the United States has not been surveyed under the government survey system. Instead, real estate is described either by metes and bounds or courses and distances. A metes and bounds legal description begins at some geographic point of beginning. References are typically made to identifiable and permanent objects or locations. A courses and distances description is based on a surveyor's notes. It makes reference to a starting point and specifies the direction and length of lines there from. In other words, an identified starting point is given and the boundaries are traced from that point as so many feet, or rods, etc. Commonly, a courses and distances description is combined with a metes and bounds description. The following is an example of a metes and bounds property description.

## 4.  Selling Price and Time of Payment

A short-term contract for sale of land usually contains a provision specifying the selling price and time of payment. Commonly, buyers prefer a contract provision allowing them to avoid the contract if acceptable financing cannot be obtained. Thus, unless the buyer has a loan commitment in writing, the buyer may wish to negotiate for a provision permitting the contract to be voided if financing cannot be obtained on reasonable terms. Likewise, the selling price should be clearly specified along with a definite indication of the date for the closing of the transaction, payment of purchase price and date of possession.

## 5.  Real Estate Taxes

Another common element of a short-term contract for sale of land is a specification of how real property taxes are to be apportioned between the seller and buyer. In many states, property taxes are assessed and payment made in arrears. For farms, property tax liability is often allocated by crop year so that the party with possession bears the property tax burden (with the same time delay from assessment to payment). Thus, the party deriving the benefit, bears the tax burden.

## 6. Risk of Loss

A short-term contract for sale of land usually contains a provision specifying which party bears the risk of loss from fire or other casualty. Generally, the buyer bears the risk of loss from fire or other casualty. However, both the buyer and the seller have an insurable interest in the property and may carry insurance. In most situations, however, the contract specifies what insurance is to be carried, who pays the premiums, and who receives the proceeds upon occurrence of the insured events. Typically, insurance premiums continue to be paid by the seller until closing and possession. However, if the seller and the buyer are insured with a single policy, usually the proceeds are made payable to the parties (seller and buyer) as their interests appear. However, the buyer may want to negotiate for a provision making the proceeds payable to the buyer to be used to repair, replace or rebuild the damaged or destroyed property and, if not so used, to reduce the principal balance due.

## 7.  Personal Property

A short-term land sale contract typically specifies whether any personal property is to be included in the sale, the purchase price of such property and how and when the amounts are to be paid.

## 8.  Quality of Title and Real Estate Deeds

Another common element of a short-term land sale contract concerns specification of the quality of title to be received by the buyer. For buyers, it is very important to ensure that the quality of title desired is actually obtained. The title to real property is affected by prior transfers and transactions involving the property. For attorney-abstract transactions, the abstract of title contains a summary of information which is on file pertaining to the property. An abstract contains a record of all previous owners. Although not absolutely necessary for transfer of real property, the abstract is a valuable aid in examining the title to a tract of real estate.

Opinions on marketability of title are provided to the buyer by the buyer's attorney. The buyer's attorney examines the land records (called a title search) and renders an opinion concerning marketability. The attorney is not a guarantor of the title, however. If the attorney's opinion as to marketability was not arrived at negligently, the attorney is not liable to the buyer if title eventually proves to be defective. With the "attorney method," the attorney reviews the documents or file and prepares a title opinion for the buyer.

Purchasers can protect themselves against defects in title in many states by purchasing title insurance. A title insurance policy specifies the extent of the protection given to the purchaser. Where title insurance is used, the buyer typically makes a one-time premium payment on title insurance which indemnifies the buyer in the event title defects arise and disturb the buyer's ownership rights. However, the only defects insured against are ones that would be easily discoverable by a search of the land records. The policy does not provide the buyer any more protection than an attorney's opinion. However, the title insurance company may have greater financial resources to satisfy claims when compared with the financial resources of an attorney who conducted a negligent search of the real estate records.

Some states permit title registration. This is a judicial determination of interests in the property with an accompanying assurance of good title to the buyer. In the jurisdictions permitting title registration, registration is only optional and the record system is still available. Defects in title can often be corrected by affidavit or quit claim deed. However, in some instances, a lawsuit may be necessary to "quiet title" to the property. Suit to quiet title is costly and is only done as a last resort to cut off any claims against the property.

### i. General Warranty Deed

The highest quality of title to real estate is evidenced by a general warranty deed. With a general warranty deed, the grantor warrants the title against defects arising at any time before the transfer—even before the seller became associated with the land. With a general warranty deed, the seller warrants that the seller owns the property; that the seller can convey the property, and that the seller will defend the buyer against claims of third persons.

### ii. Special Warranty Deed

With a special warranty deed, the grantor warrants the title against defects that arose only after the grantor acquired the land, but not against defects arising before that time. Buyers of land should be particularly careful in accepting a special warranty deed if there are any potential environmental problems associated with the real estate. The Comprehensive Environmental Response Compensation and Liability Act (CERCLA) (more commonly referred to as the "superfund" law) holds as a "potentially responsible party" current owners of land where hazardous waste has been dumped at any time in the past. It is easy to confuse special and general warranty deeds, and believe that a specially warranted title provides greater protection to a buyer than does a general warranty deed.

### iii. Quitclaim Deed

With a quitclaim deed, the grantor merely transfers whatever interest the grantor has in the property and does not warrant against defects in title. Another form of quitclaim deed is a fiduciary deed (the type of deed given by trustees, executors and other fiduciaries).

### iv. Recording the Deed

Recordation of the deed protects the owner's rights. While a deed need not be recorded to be valid between the buyer and the seller, recording is mandatory in several states. However, recording a deed protects the purchaser's interest in the property with respect to other individuals. A nominal fee is typically charged for recording a one-page deed, with an additional amount charged for each additional page or fraction thereof. In some states, installment contracts are routinely recorded. In other states, recording only occurs if the buyer is not going to take possession.

#### a. The Delivery Requirement

In general, a deed must be delivered to be effective to pass title. However, intention to make delivery is the controlling element in determining whether a purported delivery is effective to transfer the real estate. Thus, while no particular form of delivery or ceremony is necessary, any event that clearly manifests the grantor's intent to deliver is effective to convey title. Thus, it is not necessary for a physical transfer of the deed to take place if the grantor has the present intent to part with legal control of the property. Conversely, a physical transfer of the deed is not effective to convey title if the delivery is not completed with the requisite intent.

---

**Example 3:**

Sid executes a deed with the present intent to convey title to Sam. Sam, however, does not accept delivery. Sid thereupon puts the deed in his dresser drawer. Sid subsequently dies with the deed remaining in the drawer. The result is that Sam has title to the real estate because Sid had the present intent to deliver the deed.

---

Because of the requirement of a present intent to deliver, any conveyance where the grantor intends to withhold from the grantee complete ownership until the performance of some condition or the happening of some event is a conditional delivery and is ineffective to convey the associated real estate. For example, a deed delivered to a third party with instructions upon the grantor's death is ineffective to transfer title. A deed cannot be used to transfer property at death as can a will unless the will requirements are met. The formalities for deeds and wills are different. As a result, a deed that fails to transfer title because the grantor did not have the present intent to deliver is seldom treated as a valid will even if the grantor's intent would be furthered. *See, e.g., Giefer v. Swenton,* 23 Kan. App. 2d 172, 928 P.2d 906 (1996).

## 9. Rights of Seller upon Buyer's Default

A short-term contract for sale of land usually contains a provision specifying the seller's rights upon the buyer's default. This element will be discussed more fully later in this chapter.

## B.   REAL ESTATE MORTGAGES

### 1.  In General

A farmer or rancher can obtain financing for the agricultural operation by pledging certain personal property or fixtures as collateral for a loan. The lender gains a security interest in the collateral to secure repayment in the event that the debtor fails to repay the loan. These transactions are governed by Article 9 of the UCC. However, Article 9 does not apply to real estate. A mortgage is what gives the lender an interest in the real estate to secure repayment of the loan. A mortgage establishes an obligation from the mortgagor (owner of the mortgaged property) to the mortgagee (holder of the mortgage). Deeds of trust are generally handled the same as mortgages. The mortgage gives the mortgagee a security interest in the land to assure performance of the obligation. Recording is critical to protect the mortgagee's security interest ahead of all other creditors and subsequent transferees and the order of recordation establishes the priority of mortgages.

The mortgagor remains liable on the obligation until released or the obligation is paid. At that point, the mortgagee surrenders the mortgage and executes a discharge of the mortgage, which is recorded. If the mortgagor deeds his or her equity interest to another, the mortgagee retains the security interest in the land and the obligation against the original mortgagor. A novation (voluntary agreement among the seller, buyer and mortgagee) releases the original mortgagor from liability.

For property acquired "subject to" the seller's mortgage, the buyer pays the seller the difference between the amount of the mortgage and the selling price, but does not assume a personal obligation to pay the mortgage debt. The buyer makes payments on the mortgage as they become due in order to protect the buyer's equity. A buyer who "assumes" the seller's mortgage pays the seller the difference between the amount of the mortgage and the selling price, and also agrees to be liable for the mortgage debt personally. Thus, it is generally best for sellers to not permit a third party to take over their mortgage. If the third party subsequently defaults, the seller will remain liable. However, if the third party assumes the seller's existing mortgage, the third party is liable upon default. Presently, many mortgages specify that upon sale, the lender may either call the entire outstanding debt due or accept the new purchaser at the same or a different interest rate and under the same or different mortgage terms.

## 2. Remedies Available to Mortgagees upon Default

A mortgagee has available certain remedies upon the mortgagor's default. For instance, the mortgagee may take action to foreclose the mortgage and cut off the mortgagor's interest in the property after passage of a statutorily required period of time in which the debtor may "redeem" the property. In some states, foreclosure is by court action only with a successful foreclosure action cutting off any other party's rights in the property that are inferior to the lender's rights. The property is then sold at a foreclosure sale typically conducted by the county sheriff with the proceeds first applied against the expenses of sale and the mortgagee's claim, with any remaining amount paid to the mortgagor.

At any time before the foreclosure sale, a holder of an obligation junior to the mortgagee may pay the holder the amount secured, with interest and costs, together with any other liens of the holder that are paramount to the junior lienholder and obtain an assignment of the mortgage holder's interest. The junior lienholder may then proceed with foreclosure or discontinue the foreclosure action at the option of the junior lienholder.

Other liens on the property sold are to be paid off in accordance with their order of priority. If the amount secured by the lien is not yet due, a rebate of interest fixed by the court must be made to the holder, or the holder's lien on the property is postponed to those of a junior date. If none, the balance is paid to the mortgagor. If the proceeds of sale do not satisfy the mortgagee's obligation, the deficiency may be obtained from the mortgagor's other property not exempt from execution under a general execution unless the parties have stipulated otherwise.

Foreclosed property can typically be redeemed by the mortgagor within one year from the date of sale by paying the amount of the obligation plus costs and interest. If the mortgagor has paid less than a prescribed amount of the original indebtedness (typically 25–33%), the court may be authorized to set a shorter redemption period. Also, the redemption period may be extended for equitable reasons. During the redemption period, the debtor possessing the property is entitled to rents and profits from the property unless the property is being wasted. The redemption period generally cannot be waived if the mortgaged instrument is secured by agricultural land. In many jurisdictions, the debtor/owner of the property has the sole redemption right during the first several months. During the next several months, creditors may redeem from each other. For any remaining period, the redemption right is exclusively the debtor's. The cost of redemption equals the sale price of the property plus taxes, interest and other costs.

## 3. Mortgage Foreclosure Moratoria

As a result of the financial crisis caused by the Great Depression of the 1930s, a total of 28 states enacted mortgage foreclosure moratoria of various types. Most of the statutes had expired or had been repealed by the 1980s. All of the statutes, however, involved an attempt to slow down or cushion the impact of real estate mortgage foreclosures. The farm debt crisis of the 1980s spawned a second round of moratorium statutes in some of the states most deeply affected by sharply declining land values. However, in some of these states, such as Kansas, the state courts declared the particular state statute an unconstitutional violation of the restriction placed on the state to interfere with contracts. *Federal Land Bank of Wichita v. Bott,* 240 Kan. 624, 732 P.2d 710 (1987).

## C.   SPECIAL RULES FOR FSA LOANS

The Farm Service Agency (FSA) (formerly the Farmers Home Administration (FmHA)) is an agency within the United States Department of Agriculture (USDA) and is funded with taxpayer dollars. Presently, over 40 percent of all agricultural loans are held by the Farm Credit System and FSA. The FSA limits the type of person eligible to borrow from it. For example, eligible borrowers must be engaged primarily or directly in farming or ranching in the United States, be a United States citizen, have training or farming experience to assure success in farming, own or operate an enterprise not larger than a family farm, and be unable to obtain credit elsewhere.

Under the Agricultural Credit Act of 1987, lenders participating in the guaranteed farm loan program are required to enter into an agreement with the FmHA to delay foreclosure until 60 days after a determination as to whether the borrower is eligible for the interest rate buy-down program and the FSA (FmHA) is directed to avoid losses on loans, with priority consideration to writing down the loan principal and interest and setting aside debt whenever those procedures would facilitate keeping the borrower on the farm or ranch. To be eligible for restructuring assistance, the loan must meet several conditions. For example, the delinquency must be beyond the borrower's control, the borrower must have acted in good faith, and the borrower must present a preliminary plan with reasonable assumptions indicating that the borrower will be able to meet necessary family living and operating expenses and service all remaining debt. In addition, the recovery for FSA must be equal to or greater than the recovery from foreclosing or liquidating. Borrowers are also entitled to below market interest rates on restructured loans of approximately five percent or less.

A borrower receiving restructuring assistance is only required to service the debt to the value of the collateral which is typically below fair market value. Thus, a borrower's loan can be written down to the point that the "net recovery value" of the restructured debt is equal to or greater than the net recovery value of the collateral securing the debt. That is the amount of the current appraised value of the collateral less the estimated administrative, legal and other expenses associated with liquidation of the loan and disposition of the collateral. A new promissory note is executed for each note rescheduled or reamortized, and a borrower must enter into a shared appreciation agreement (SAA) for all write-downs involving real properties as collateral. The IRS position is that the borrower realizes discharge of indebtedness income to the extent the old debt balance exceeds the buyout amount even when an SAA is part of the restructuring arrangement.

If a feasible debt restructuring plan cannot be worked out with FSA, a debtor is permitted to buy the collateral at its net recovery value if the net recovery value of the secured property exceeds the net recovery value of a restructured loan supported by the debtor's cash flow. The debtor must execute an SAA and agree to pay in full the difference between the net recovery value of the property and the property's fair market value (as of the date of the agreement) if within ten years the property is conveyed for an amount greater than the net recovery value. The Tax Court has ruled that a borrower recognizes discharge of indebtedness income in the year of the buy-back of the collateral. *Jelle v. Comm'r,* 116 T.C. No. 6 (2001).

Previously discharged FSA debt is subject to recapture under provisions included in the Agricultural Credit Act of 1987. Shared appreciation agreements (SAAs) (up to a ten-year term) are authorized. Debt recapture occurs if, at the time a recapture triggering event occurs, the property pledged as security has appreciated in value. The appreciation recapture for FSA is set at 75 percent of the appreciation in the property's value (up to the amount of the debt forgiven) if the recapture triggering event occurs during the first four years, 50 percent thereafter. Recapture occurs either at the end of the term of the agreement, on conveyance of the property, on repayment of the loan or when the borrower ceases farming operations.

Under regulations promulgated in 1992, property value was to be determined by the amount a typical purchaser would justifiably pay for the property based on its income potential in its customary use for agricultural purposes. The regulation was revised in 2000 such that the value of property subject to an SAA was to be determined based on the property's rental value. *See, e.g., Davies v. Johanns,* 477 F.3d 968 (8th Cir. 2007), *rev'g,* 409 F. Supp. 2d 1150 (W.D. Mo. 2006).

In 1999, the FSA issued interim regulations amending the SAA requirements to allow borrowers with agreements ending in 1999 and 2000 who have not paid their obligation or made arrangements to pay and cannot pay the amount due, to have all or part of the obligation suspended for one year. The suspension can be renewed up to two times. During any period of suspension, the obligation accrues interest at the federal borrowing rate. The FSA finalized the regulations in 2000, with the final regulations allowing the value of some capital improvements made during the term of the SAA to be deducted from recapture, changing the maturity period of future SAAs from 10 years to five years, and reducing the interest rate on SAA loans to the Farm Program Homestead Protection rate. In a separate provision, the Agricultural Appropriations Act of 2000 contains a provision allowing the USDA to amortize for up to 25 years the recapture amounts from terminated SAAs. The interest rate may not exceed the rate applicable to a loan to reacquire homestead property less 100 basis points.

The 2002 Farm Bill authorizes the restructuring of recapture amounts that were amortized at the time the amounts became due. Existing regulations authorize restructuring provided the borrower has other program loans, for a term not exceeding 25 years from the original amortization agreement. Thus, the provision expands existing regulations to allow restructuring of recapture amounts for individuals who do not have other program loans outstanding.

In choosing restructuring alternatives, priority is to be given principal and interest write-down if lenders involved agreed to participate in the restructuring plan or in state mediation. Even without participation by other lenders, FSA is to write-down principal and interest if that is the least cost alternative for FSA. In general, the mandate of the FSA is that if a lender, through restructuring, would receive as much as through foreclosing, restructuring must be undertaken.

Proposed regulations were issued on May 23, 1988, implementing the provisions of the Agricultural Credit Act of 1987 applicable to FSA. The regulations identify five categories of borrowers for purposes of debt servicing relief. For Phase I borrowers, the objective is to keep the borrower in business paying at regular rates and on regular terms. Before loans get behind schedule, loans may be rescheduled or reamortized. For Phase II borrowers, if the borrower cannot be kept in business paying regular rates and "after having extended terms to the maximum extent allowable," FSA may lower interest rates and defer principal. For Phase III borrowers, after delinquency for 180 days, the process is activated of determining the best net recovery for FSA while trying to keep the farmer on the farm. Debt principal may be written down. An appraisal of collateral and a sound and accurate calculation is needed to determine whether the best net recovery for FSA is in write-down of the debt and continuation of the farming operation or in liquidation of the collateral. For Phase IV borrowers, when a borrower's debts cannot be restructured and liquidation is required, the borrower has the right to purchase the collateral securing the FSA debt at net recovery value. Both before and after acceleration, the borrower can settle the debt by conveying the property, either by sale to another farmer or voluntary conveyance to FSA, or through foreclosure. For Phase V borrowers, FSA takes the property into inventory with the farmer given the opportunity to use the preservation service programs and reacquire the property and continue farming under the lease-back/buy-back program. The farmer may elect to use the homestead retention program rather than the lease-back/buy-back.

As a result of public outcry over large write-offs with some exceeding $1 million, legislation was enacted in 1990 as part of the 1990 Farm Bill that limits the number of write-downs per borrower to one for loans made after January 7, 1988. Loans made on or before that date are considered made after that date for this purpose if a restructuring, write-down or recovery buy out is provided after that date. In addition, a lifetime debt forgiveness limitation of $300,000 of principal per borrower is established.

The 1996 Farm Bill contained several provisions limiting FSA lending activity. Under the 1996 legislation, a borrower may not receive more than one debt forgiveness on a direct loan. Borrowers who have received debt forgiveness on a direct or guaranteed loan may not receive a direct or guaranteed loan other than a farm operating loan for paying annual farm or ranch operating expenses.

The 1996 law also provides for a cutoff of FSA loans by revisiting a 1992 amendment that phased out operating loans for long time borrowers. Under the 1992 law, if a borrower had obtained an operating loan for five or more years, or a guaranteed loan for 10 or more years, a loan was not to be made to the borrower after the fifth year occurring after October 28, 1992. The regulations interpreted the provision to mean that the borrower had five years of eligibility after October 18, 1992, and a year did not count if no operating loans were outstanding as of that year.

Under the 1996 rule, if a farmer or rancher, as of October 28, 1992, had received a direct or guaranteed operating loan during each of 10 or more previous years, the borrower is eligible to receive a *guaranteed* operating (but not a direct) loan during five additional years. Those five additional years ran from October 28, 1992. If loans were outstanding during each of those years, it appears that time would run out for the borrower for even guaranteed loans on October 28, 1997.

As for farm ownership loans, the 1996 legislation provides that if, as of April 4, 1996, a farmer or rancher had a direct farm ownership loan

outstanding for less than five years, a loan is not to
be made after April 4, 2006. In the event a borrower
had a direct farm ownership loan outstanding for five
years or more, as of April 4, 1996, a loan was not to
be made after April 4, 2001.

The 1996 law also specifies that direct operating
loans are not to be made to a borrower who is
delinquent on any direct or guaranteed loan. This
provision became effective on the date of enactment,
April 4, 1996.

The Debt Collection Improvement Act of 1996
amended existing legislation in an attempt to crack
down on those who become delinquent with respect
to nontax debts owed to the federal government.
Under the provision, if a nontax debt to the federal
government is delinquent, the individual or firm is
ineligible for federal assistance including direct
loans, loan insurance, loan guarantees, commodity
loans and loan deficiency payments. The statutory
provision only refers to denial of the right to obtain
"a loan . . . or loan insurance or guarantee. . . ," but
the FSA issued a Notice on March 24, 2000, stating
that ". . . producers with any federal delinquent
nontax debt may not obtain commodity loans and
LDPs," and advised state and county FSA offices that
". . . LDPs are 'in lieu' of loans." The FSA county
offices were ordered to "not make loans or LDPs to
producers who they are aware have federal
delinquent nontax debt." Thus, the administrative
interpretation by FSA made it clear that the
ineligibility went well beyond "a loan . . . or loan
insurance or guarantee" administered by FSA. The

legislation provides that the provision can be waived "by the head of a federal agency," and that the Secretary of the Treasury has the authority to exempt, "at the request of an agency, any class of claims." However, an amendment attached to the fiscal year's 2001 agriculture appropriations bill provided that proceeds from LDPs and marketing loans can be credited to a farmer's delinquent loans.

The 2002 Farm Bill deletes the requirement that a direct loan may not be made to a farmer or rancher who has operated a farm or ranch for five years or more. Also, under the 2002 Act, limited liability companies, joint operations and trusts are specifically included as eligible entities for purposes of USDA farm ownership loans, farm operating loans and emergency loans. However, the legislation does not define "joint operation" or "joint operations." Those terms are less well known and less precise than "joint venture" which is a form of general partnership. In addition, the legislation does not include limited liability partnerships (LLPs) in the amendment.

## D.   RESTRUCTURING FARM CREDIT SYSTEM LOANS

The Farm Credit System is a federally chartered and regulated cooperatively owned lending institution. Under provisions added by the Agricultural Credit Act of 1987, not later than 45 days before a system institution begins foreclosure proceedings, the borrower is to be notified that the loan may be eligible for restructuring. The decision to restructure is to be based on five factors: (1) whether the lender's cost to restructure is less than the cost of foreclosure; (2) whether the borrower is applying income above necessary and reasonable living and operating expenses; (3) whether the borrower has the necessary financial capacity and management skills; (4) whether the borrower's operation can be made viable; and (5) whether restructuring is consistent with sound lending practices.

If the potential cost to restructure a loan is less than or equal to the potential cost of foreclosure, the loan is to be restructured. The cost of restructuring is to include the present value of interest income and principal foregone, reasonable and necessary administrative expenses, whether the borrower has presented a restructuring plan and cash flow analysis, and whether the borrower has provided complete and current financial statements. The cost of foreclosing is to include the difference between the loan balance and the liquidation value of the loan, taking into consideration collateral value and repayment capacity. Also included in determining the cost of foreclosing is the estimated cost of maintaining the loan as a nonperforming asset, the estimated cost of administrative and legal actions necessary to foreclose and dispose of the property, the estimated change in value of the collateral until expected disposition of the collateral, and all other costs incurred as a result of foreclosure for loan liquidation.

Each Farm Credit System district was directed to develop a policy within 60 days for restructuring distressed loans.

## E.   INSTALLMENT LAND CONTRACTS

Two types of contracts are often involved in the sale of agricultural land. One type, sometimes referred to as a "contract for sale of land," contemplates passage of a deed after a relatively short period of time during which the marketability of title is determined and financing is arranged. Various legal aspects of this type of contract have already been addressed in this chapter. A second type, referred to as the "installment land contract" is an instrument for long-term financing of land purchases.

Under an installment land contract, the seller is the financier rather than a commercial lender. Title generally remains in the seller until a specified part or all of the payments of principal and interest have been made, at which time the buyer is entitled to receive a deed. The down payment is also usually low, quite often less than 20% of the purchase price. Beginning farmers and other farmers with minimal amounts of cash find this feature of the installment land contract favorable. The buyer is also normally given possession, even though the general rule is that possession follows legal title. In most cases, the party in possession pays real property taxes and assessments, and the buyer typically has an obligation to insure the premises either at the time the contract is entered into or at the time of possession. In addition, most of the provisions found in a short-term contract also appear in an installment land contract.

The payment clause in an installment contract involving agricultural land is of primary importance. Principal and interest payments should be set at manageable levels, and the timing of the payments is also critical. Usually, annual or semi-annual payments are desired. Monthly payments are not practical unless the buyer is operating a dairy farm or otherwise has a flow of income on a monthly basis. There are several methods of computing principal and interest payments under an installment land contract. Under a standard plan, fixed annual payments of principal and interest are made. A larger portion of each succeeding payment represents principal and a smaller portion represents interest. Under the "Springfield Plan", fixed principal payments are made annually with declining interest payments on the unpaid balance as payments are made over time. The total payment decreases with each succeeding payment. The Springfield Plan is the plan most often used for purchases of agricultural land. Under an increasing payment plan, which is rare and is limited almost exclusively between related parties, the total payment of principal and interest increases with each payment made. This plan may be helpful to buyers anticipating difficulty in meeting payment obligations the first few years after purchase. Other payment provisions may include a pre-payment privilege, variable payment plans where the payment size depends upon prices, yields or income, and an acceleration clause which requires that all remaining payments become due if the buyer defaults. If land contracts are foreclosed, the same rules apply as govern foreclosure of real estate mortgages including moratorium provisions.

An installment land contract involving cropland should clearly specify whether the buyer or the seller is entitled to crops planted but not harvested at the time the contract is entered into. Clear specification can avoid a battle over ownership to growing crops. For instance, in *United States v. Newcomb*, 682 F.2d 758 (8th Cir. 1982), a perfected security interest in growing crops given by the buyer under an installment land contract was held to be superior to the seller's claim under the installment sale contract. To remedy this problem Revised Article 9 of the UCC treats growing crops as "goods." Thus, Article 9 is the exclusive statutory mechanism under which a lender can obtain a security interest in crops. *See, e.g., Revised UCC 9–105(1)(h)*. Likewise, it may be prudent to include a contract provision concerning seller reimbursement for land preparatory expenses if the contract is consummated before planting.

In the event of the purchaser's default under an installment land contract, the seller may have the contract foreclosed in the same manner that a mortgage is foreclosed. In this event, the property is sold to satisfy the debt. The seller may also opt to have the contract rescinded by mutual agreement with the buyer, or the seller may obtain a judgment for the amount of the debt. In some instances, the rights of the buyer under the contract may be forfeited. Upon forfeiture, the buyer loses rights in the property and the property reverts back to the seller. Forfeiture is a distinguishing characteristic of the installment land contract and is only available to the seller if the seller still has title. However, in some states, the seller may only take advantage of the statutory procedure for forfeiture if the contract provides expressly for forfeiture as a remedy. In these states, buyers are typically allowed a reasonable time in which to cure the default before the seller can require forfeiture.

Other beneficial provisions in an installment land contract include a clause specifying whether the buyer is responsible for maintaining improvements on the property, a clause listing acceptable farming methods to be utilized during the contract term and a clause detailing how the proceeds will be split if a portion or all of the farm is condemned or a utility obtains an easement across the premises.

## V.   INCOME TAX ASPECTS OF PROPERTY TRANSFERS

### A.   INCOME TAX BASIS AND THE COMPUTATION OF GAIN

For purposes of computing gain or loss on the sale or exchange of property, the general rule is that gain is recognized to the extent of the difference between the property's adjusted basis and the amount realized on sale or exchange. Losses incurred on the sale of personal assets (such as a residence) are generally not deductible.

The income tax basis of property depends upon whether the property was purchased, received by gift, or received by inheritance or under the terms of a decedent's will. The basis of purchased property is ordinarily its cost, which includes the amount of any mortgages and other obligations on the property. The basis of property acquired by gift is generally the donor's basis. The donor's basis simply carries over into the donee's hands. Thus, gifted property is said to have a "carryover" basis. However, the basis of gifted property may be increased by the amount of gift tax paid if the market value of the gift exceeds the donor's basis. For gifts made after 1976, the increase in basis is limited to the gift tax attributable to the net appreciation on the gift.

---

**Example 4:**

In 1997, Bill Jones gave a tract of Illinois farmland to his daughter, Jennifer. At the time of the gift, the land was worth $100,000. Bill's basis in the land at the time of the gift was $20,000. Bill paid federal gift tax of $15,600 incident to the transfer. Under the "carryover" basis rule, the basis of the land in Jennifer's hands is $20,000. However, the basis can be increased by the amount of gift tax that Bill paid attributable to the net appreciation on the gift. The computation is as follows:

1. Adjusted basis (Bill's hands).................. $20,000

2. FMV at time of gift................................. 100,000

3. Appreciation (attributable to Bill)........... 80,000

4. Line (3) ÷ Line ............................................ 280%

5. Gift tax paid.............................................. 15,600

6. Gift tax attributable to net appreciation
on the gift...................................................... 15,600

$$x \quad .80$$

$$\overline{\quad \$12,480 \quad}$$

$$\$20,000$$

$$+12,480$$

Jennifer's basis = $32,480

---

For property acquired by gift, if the fair market value of the property is less than the donor's basis, the donee's basis is fair market value at the time of the gift for purposes of determining loss only.

The basis of property received by inheritance or under a will is the value of the property at the time of the decedent's death as determined for federal estate tax or state inheritance tax purposes. However, appreciated property transferred within one year of death does not receive a new income tax basis if the donor or the donor's spouse receives the property or its proceeds back after death. A couple of planning avenues may be available to avoid the impact of this rule. These include gifting the property to the decedent-to-be and receiving the property back upon the decedent's death more than a year later, or gifting the property to a terminally ill spouse and having the spouse devise the property to family members.

The "unadjusted basis" of property is adjusted upward for improvements made and is adjusted downward for depreciation allowable. Capital improvements to property increase the basis by the cost of such additions or alterations. Allowable depreciation reduces the basis regardless of whether the taxpayer actually deducted the amounts. *I.R.C. § 1016.*

The difference between the adjusted income tax basis and selling price is taxable gain.

Items that produce income in respect of decedent (IRD) do not receive adjustments to income tax basis at death. This is a major exception to the step-up (or step down) in basis rule for inherited property. IRD property is property that is close to being earned at the time of the decedent's death, but is not actually earned before death. Income in respect of decedent is income earned at the time of death, but not reportable on the decedent's final income tax return because of the decedent's particular method of accounting. Thus, IRD property typically includes any income accrued at the date of death for a cash basis decedent/taxpayer. IRD property includes Series E bond interest, share rents in the hands of a nonmaterially participating farm landlord, qualified retirement accounts, and installment sale obligations such as land contracts. In general, the gain is reported the same as the decedent would have done if living. An income tax deduction is permitted when the gain is recognized for the federal estate tax attributable to inclusion of income in respect of decedent items in the estate.

## B.   OPTIONS FOR POSTPONING OR AVOIDING THE RECOGNITION OF GAIN ON SALE OR EXCHANGE OF REAL PROPERTY

There are several potential tax planning strategies available for postponing or avoiding gain recognition on the sale or exchange of real property. Each strategy involves unique qualification requirements that must be satisfied.

### 1. Exclusion of Gain on Sale of a Principal Residence

exclude up to $250,000 ($500,000 for married persons filing jointly or for a surviving spouse that sells the marital home within two years of the pre-deceased spouse's death) of gain on the sale of a personal residence. A "residence" can include a houseboat, house trailer or the house or apartment that the taxpayer is entitled to occupy as a tenant-stockholder in a cooperative housing corporation, but does not include personal property that is not a fixture under state law. *Treas. Reg. § 1.121.1(b)(1).* To be eligible for the exclusion, the taxpayer (which can include a bankruptcy estate) must have owned the home and used it as a principal residence for periods aggregating two or more years during the five-year period ending on the date of sale. In addition, the taxpayer must not have used the new exclusion for the gain on the sale of a principal residence within the two-year period ending on the date of the sale. Thus, the exclusion is allowed no more frequently than once every two years. For taxpayers that fail to meet the requirements because of a change in place of employment or a change in health or unforeseen circumstances, they will be allowed to exclude gain up to a fraction of the maximum allowable exclusion on an otherwise qualifying sale of the principal residence. The excludible amount is the portion of the gain that would have been excluded but for the two-year requirements equal to the portion of the two-year period the above conditions are satisfied. The following example illustrates the application of the rule.

---

**Example 5:**

On May 25, 1997, Mark and Marcia sold their home in Detroit for $700,000, net of sales commissions. They had lived in the home for 22 years and had a $220,000 basis in the home. They moved to Ft. Wayne, IN, and are looking for a new home.

They can avoid recognition of all of the $480,000 gain on the Detroit home, regardless of the amount they spend on the Ft. Wayne home, or whether they buy a home in Ft. Wayne at all.

---

Gain realized on the sale of a principal residence does not qualify for the exclusion to the extent of depreciation allowed or allowable with respect to business use or rental of the principal residence for periods after May 6, 1997.

If both spouses satisfy the requirements of I.R.C. § 121, they can each claim a $250,000 exclusion, regardless of whether they file separately or jointly and regardless of whether they own the homes separately or jointly. However, spouses can combine their $250,000 exclusions even though one of them does not meet the two-year ownership requirement if they file a joint return for the year of sale, either or both of the spouses meets the two-year ownership requirement, and neither spouse has used the new exclusion in the previous two-year period.

Regulations finalized in late 2002 address the eligibility of vacant land for the exclusion. Under the regulations, vacant land can be treated as part of the principal residence if it is adjacent to land containing the principal residence, the taxpayer sells or exchanges the dwelling in a sale or exchange that meets the requirements to the exclusion within two years before or two years after the date of sale or exchange of the vacant land, the taxpayer owned and used the vacant land as part of the taxpayer's principal residence, and the requirements have otherwise been met for the exclusion with respect to the vacant land. *Treas. Reg. § 1.121–1(b)(3).*

Under the new provision, ownership and use by a deceased spouse is attributed to the surviving spouse. For example, assume that a married couple moves into the home that the husband had owned and lived in before the marriage. Shortly after moving into the home, the husband died and the surviving spouse became the owner. The surviving spouse can add the time her deceased husband owned and used the house to the time she owned and used the house for purposes of meeting the two-year requirement. If she sells the home within two years of the husband's death, she would be entitled to the $500,000 exclusion. Also, if a residence is held by a trust, a taxpayer is treated as the owner and the seller of the residence during the period that the taxpayer is treated as the owner of the trust or the portion of the trust that includes the residence under the grantor trust rules applicable to the residence.

Taxpayers who owned a home as of August 5, 1997, and sell it in the two-year period beginning on August 5, 1997, can exclude a portion of the gain on the sale, even if they did not meet the two-year ownership and use requirements. The portion they can exclude is calculated in the same manner as if the sale was a result of a change in health or employment, or other unforeseen circumstances.

The I.R.C. § 121 exclusion does not apply to property acquired in a like-kind exchange within the prior five-year period beginning with the date of property acquisition. The provision is designed to counter situations where (1) the property is exchanged for residential real property, tax-free, under I.R.C. § 1031; (2) the property is converted to personal use; and (3) a tax-free sale is arranged under I.R.C. § 121. However, if like-kind exchange treatment applies to the residence, the homeowner may also be able to benefit from exclusion of gain. In early 2005, IRS published guidance on coupling the I.R.C. § 121 exclusion with like-kind exchange procedures. The impact of the guidance is that, for farm residences, the amount of the allowable exclusion will more than cover the gain involved. In other situations, the new procedure may allow deferral of realized gain into replacement property. The five-year ineligibility period also applies to exchanges by the taxpayer or by any person whose basis in the property is determined by reference to the basis in the hands of the taxpayer (such as by gift).

## 2. Involuntary Conversion

Another way to avoid tax on the gain incurred on the sale or exchange or real property arises in the event the property is condemned. *I.R.C. § 1033.* Involuntarily or compulsorily converted agricultural real estate may be condemned by the government in exercise of its eminent domain power which allows the government to "take" private property for a public purpose (such as building a road) so long as "just compensation" is paid to the landowner. Condemnation or sale under threat of condemnation of an asset used in the business or a capital asset held more than one year is an involuntary conversion. Gains on involuntary conversions are not recognized if the taxpayer purchases other property similar or related in service or use within a specified time. The replacement property must be acquired within two years (three years for real property taken by condemnation or seizure) after the close of the first taxable year in which the taxpayer has actual or constructive receipt of the proceeds from the condemnation. The basis rules are generally the same as the rollover rules under former I.R.C. § 1034. For real property used in a trade or business or held for the production of income or investment, the replacement may be with property of a like kind.

## 3. Like-Kind Exchange

Generally, an exchange of property for other property is treated as a sale. However, no gain or loss is recognized if property held for productive use in a trade or business or for investment is exchanged for property of a like-kind to be held either for productive use in a business or for investment. However, the rule does not cover stock in trade, other property held primarily for sale, stocks or bonds. The new property is treated as a continuation of the original property. With respect to the trade of tangible personal property, such as farm machinery, the Treasury Regulations determine if property is like-kind by reference to being within the same product class. Also, property is of a like-kind to property that is of the same nature or character. Like-kind property does not necessarily have to be of the same grade or quality. In addition, for intangible assets, the determination of like-kind must be made on an asset-by-asset basis. Thus, a like-kind trade can involve a bull for a bull, a combine for a combine, but not a combine for a sports car or a farm or ranch for publicly traded stock.

**Note:** If a transaction qualifies as a like-kind exchange, the replacement property is treated as a continuation of the original investment and neither gain nor loss is recognized until (if ever) the replacement property is sold. Gain, however, is recognized to the extent of any boot or unlike property received in the exchange.

With respect to real estate, a much broader definition of like-kind applies. Virtually any real estate used for business or investment can be exchanged for any other real estate if the exchanger continues to use the replacement property for business or investment. Thus, agricultural real estate may be traded for residential real estate and a leasehold interest can be exchanged for a fee interest if the leasehold interest is of at least 30 years. However, if bare farmland is traded for farmland with depreciable structures on it, tax issues can arise. Many farm depreciable buildings and structures are I.R.C. § 1245 property. For example, commodity storage facilities and single-purpose agricultural structures are I.R.C. § 1245 property, as are irrigation systems, drainage tile, and other improvements to farm real estate. If property with an I.R.C. § 1245 depreciation recapture attribute is disposed of in an I.R.C. § 1031 exchange, the I.R.C. § 1245 depreciation recapture must be recognized to the extent that the replacement property has insufficient I.R.C. § 1245 property. IRS Form 8824 provides a location for reporting the I.R.C. § 1245 depreciation recapture if non-I.R.C. § 1245 property is received in exchange.

**Note:** Water rights that are limited in duration are not considered like-kind to a fee interest in land, *Wiechens v. United States,* 228 F. Supp. 2d 1080 (D.

Ariz. 2002). But, if the water rights are limited only as to annual use the IRS has ruled that they are of sufficient like-kind to a fee interest in land to qualify the transaction for like-kind exchange treatment. *Ltr. Rul. 200404044, Oct. 23, 2003.*

An exchange may qualify for the like-kind exchange treatment even if the replacement property is received after the relinquished property has been given up. This is known as a non-simultaneous (deferred) exchange, and a qualified intermediary (Q.I.) is to be used to facilitate the exchange. The Q.I., pursuant to a written agreement with the taxpayer, holds the proceeds from the sale of the relinquished property in trust or an escrow account. This is done to ensure that the taxpayer is not in constructive receipt of the sale proceeds. The Q.I. takes title to the property that is sold (the relinquished property).

**Note:** The Q.I. cannot be related to the taxpayer (including ancestors or lineal descendants), or have had a financial relationship with the taxpayer in the immediate two years preceding the close of the transaction. *Treas. Reg. § 1.1031(k)–(3).* See also *Blangiardo v. Comm'r,* T.C. Memo. 2014–110.

After the relinquished property is transferred, replacement property must be identified within 45 days, and the replacement property must be received within 180 days (or by the due date for the income tax return, including extensions, if this is earlier). Rules were announced in 2000 allowing the replacement property to be acquired before disposition of the property relinquished if the 45-day and 180-day rules are observed. For exchanges between related parties, if either party transfers the property within two years of the transaction, the exchange is taxable. Exceptions are provided for transfers because of the death of either party, the transfer is because of involuntary conversion or the principal purpose was not tax avoidance.

An exchange may also be a "reverse" exchange. With a reverse exchange, the taxpayer receives the replacement property *before* the transfer of the relinquished property. Often, a reverse exchange is facilitated by a "parking" transaction or a "build-to-suit" transaction where the replacement property is "parked" with an exchange facilitator that holds title to the replacement property, usually until improvements to the property are completed. While the Code doesn't address reverse exchanges and regulations haven't been developed to provide guidance, the IRS did issue a safe harbor in 2000 for such transactions. *Rev. Proc. 2000–37, 2000–2 C.B. 308.* Under the safe harbor, the Q.I. must hold the property for the taxpayer's benefit and be treated as the beneficial owner for federal tax purposes. In addition, for the safe harbor to apply, the IRS said that the 45-day and 180-day requirements must be met. The IRS made no comment on the tax treatment of "parking" transactions that don't satisfy the safe harbor. But, a major difference between the safe harbor and the Treasury Regulations governing deferred exchanges is that, under the safe harbor, the Q.I. must take title and beneficial ownership of the replacement property. In a deferred exchange, the Q.I. only need "facilitate" the exchange. That doesn't require taking legal title. Later, in 2004, the IRS tightened the safe harbor so that it didn't apply to taxpayers who acquire replacement property that the taxpayer or a related party owned before the exchange. *Rev. Proc. 2004–51, 2004–2 C.B. 294.*

Clearly, with Rev. Proc. 2004–51, the IRS didn't want taxpayers to use reverse exchanges to reinvest proceeds from the sale of one property into improvements to other real estate that the taxpayer had previously owned. For example, assume that a farmer owns a tract of land that is not in close proximity to his primary farming operation and has become inconvenient to operate. Thus, the farmer wants to sell the tract and use the proceeds to build a livestock facility on other land that he owns that is adjacent to his farming operation. In an attempt to structure the transaction in a manner to qualify as a tax-deferred exchange, the farmer transfers title to the land where the livestock facility will be built to a Q.I. The farmer provides the financing and the Q.I. has the livestock facility built. The farmer then transfers the tract that he desires to dispose of to the Q.I. and the Q.I. sells it and uses the sale proceeds to retire the debt on the livestock facility. Because the farmer owned the land on which the livestock facility was built before the exchange occurred, Rev. Proc. 2004–51 would operate to bar the transaction from tax-deferred treatment. *But see, Estate of Bartell v. Comr.,* 147 T.C. No. 5 (2016).

In a like kind exchange, no gain or loss is recognized and the basis in the new property is the same as the basis of the property given up. However, if any cash boot is paid, the taxpayer must recognize gain on the transaction to the extent of the cash received.

---

### Example 6:

Ken Brown traded a 160-acre tract of farmland which he originally purchased for $100,000 for 120 acres of other farmland worth $150,000. Ken also received $15,000 in cash with the trade.

| | |
|---|---:|
| Value of property received | $150,000 |
| Cash and other property received | 15,000 |
| | $165,000 |
| Less basis in property given up | 100,000 |
| Realized gain | $65,000 |
| Recognized gain | $15,000 |
| | |
| Basis in property given up | $100,000 |
| less cash received | $15,000 |
| | $85,000 |
| Gain recognized | 15,000 |
| Basis in property received | $100,000 |

---

If a single item of property is traded for multiple like-kind properties, the basis of the property given up is allocated to the properties received in accordance with their respective fair market values on the date of the exchange.

## C.   INCOME TAX ASPECTS
## OF INSTALLMENT SALES

### 1. Installment Reporting of Gain

In general, gain or loss must be recognized at the time of sale. However, under the installment method, a seller can defer tax and recognize gain for any particular tax year in proportion to the amount of installments received. *I.R.C. § 453.* This allows the seller to spread the income tax liability over the entire term. Installment contracts are also beneficial because the periodic payments can be available to the seller for retirement income, a security interest may be retained in the property and the buyer has control and beneficial enjoyment of the property. However, if the seller may outlive the term of the contract, income problems could result if the payments were being used for living expenses.

Installment reporting of gain is automatic for eligible property. An election not to have installment reporting apply must be made on or before the due date (including extensions of time) for filing the income tax return for the year in which the sale occurs. Once an election is made, it can only be revoked with the consent of the IRS. In addition, installment reporting only applies to gain and not to loss upon sale of real property.

When real property is sold on an installment basis, part of each payment received represents gain and part represents a nontaxable return of the taxpayer's basis in the property. The amount of principal reported as income for any year is determined by the "gross profit percentage" which is based upon the gross profit on the entire transaction and the total contract price. "Gross profit" is the selling price less the adjusted income tax basis. The selling price is computed without a reduction for any existing mortgage and/or selling expenses. The "total contract price" is the amount to be paid by the buyer and does not include a mortgage except to the extent the mortgage exceeds the income tax basis. The remaining amount of each principal payment is a nontaxable return of basis. Interest received is taxable as ordinary income.

The reporting of gain from an installment sale of real property involves a four-step process. The first step is to subtract the seller's adjusted basis in the property from the selling price. This yields the "gross profit." In making this computation, expenses of sale are added to the basis of the property. The total contract price is computed next. The total contract price is the amount the buyer pays less indebtedness. The indebtedness must be "qualifying indebtedness" that is functionally related to the property. Debt incident to the sale, such as legal fees, does not count. The "gross profit percentage" is determined next by dividing the gross profit by the total contract price. The fourth step is to multiply each payment received by the gross profit percentage, with the result being the amount of gain to be reported for the year.

**Example 7:**

Wilbur Jones is retiring from farming, but has no heirs interested in continuing the operation. As a result, Wilbur decides to sell his farm to Tom Tiller in 2012 for $1,325,000. Wilbur agrees to sell the farm on an installment basis, and agrees to take annual payments of $66,250 for twenty years with no down payment. Wilbur's basis in the farm is $360,000, and he owns the farm debt-free. The computational process for reporting gain is as follows:

Step 1 (calculate gross profit)

| | |
|---|---|
| Selling price | $1,325,000 |
| Less: Basis | (360,000) |
| Expenses of sale | (26,500) |
| Gross profit | $938,500 |

Step 2 (determine the total contract price)

| | |
|---|---|
| Selling price | $1,325,000 |
| Less: Qualifying indebtedness | 0.00 |
| Total contract price | $1,325,000 |

Step 3 (compute the gross profit percentage)

$$\frac{\text{Gross profit}}{\text{Total contract price}}$$

$$= \frac{\$938,500}{\$1,325,000}$$

$$= .7083$$

Step 4 (calculate amount of each payment received reportable as gain)

Amount received in 2012 ...................... $66,250.00

Gross profit percentage .............................. × .7083

Amount reportable as gain .................... $46,924.88

Amount representing
nontaxable return of basis .................... $19,325.12

---

## 2. Minimum Interest Rules

Under an installment sale, a part of each principal payment is treated as interest rather than sales price if interest of less than the prescribed "test rate" is specified. *I.R.C. § 483*. Thus, installment obligations are subject to a minimum test rate of interest. Where the amount of seller financing in a transaction is $5,717,400 or less for 2017, under the general rule, the test rate is the *lesser* of 9 percent or 100 percent of the applicable federal rate (AFR). When the amount of seller financing is more than $5,717,400 for 2017, the test rate is 100 percent of the AFR. The 9 percent test rate is not available for new property that would have been eligible for investment tax credit, and any seller financing provided in connection with a sale-lease-back transaction must use a test rate of 110 percent of the AFR. The threshold amount is indexed for inflation and the AFR is determined on a monthly basis. In general, both parties are required to account for the interest in seller-financed transactions under the accrual method of accounting. However, if the amount of seller financing is $4,083,800 or less for 2017, both parties may elect to account for interest under the cash method of accounting. The figure is indexed for inflation and the election to report interest on the cash method of accounting is unavailable to dealers or those on the accrual method of accounting.

For sales of land between family members, to the extent that the sales price does not exceed $500,000 during a calendar year, the minimum interest rate is the lower of 6% compounded semi-annually or the AFR. Also, the use of a rate other than a market rate of interest creates a gift. The amount of the gift is the discounted present value of the difference between the market rate of interest and the interest actually charged.

"Payments in the year of sale" include a down payment or other payment in a prior year. The year of sale is generally the year in which the benefits and burdens of ownership pass from seller to buyer. Usually this involves the transfer of possession unless title passes before any other transfer of benefit, in which case the year of title passage is the year of sale. If the seller's indebtedness taken over by the buyer exceeds the income tax basis of the property, the excess is considered a payment in the year of sale.

The buyer may claim depreciation from the date of possession. Recaptured depreciation is taxed to the seller in the year of sale. Depreciation recapture is involved when gain is realized on disposition of depreciable property. The recapture of depreciation is instantaneous.

---

**Example 8:**

Hammond Beans acquired a tract of farmland and associated buildings on an installment basis in 1992. The purchase price was $100,000. Hammond sold the tract in 1997 for $100,000. During Hammond's period of ownership, Hammond took $40,000 of depreciation on the buildings subject to Section 1250 recapture ($10,000 of which is in excess of what straight line depreciation would have been).

Thus, upon the sale of the land and buildings in 1997, Hammond will recognize $40,000 of gain. Of that amount, $10,000 is reportable as depreciation recapture and $30,000 is capital gain. The $10,000 of depreciation recapture is reported in the year of sale even if Hammond receives nothing under the contract in the year of sale.

---

## 3. Disposition of the Contract by the Seller

Sale, gift or other disposition or satisfaction of an installment obligation results in recognition of gain. The privilege of income deferral by installment reporting is generally personal to the party electing the installment method and does not outlast the period during which the obligation is held. In essence, almost anything the seller does will trigger tax liability with the amount of gain or loss being the difference between the basis of the installment obligation at the time of disposition and either the amount realized upon the sale or the fair market value of the obligation at the time it is disposed of other than by sale.

There are two exceptions where transfer does not require gain recognition. The first exception applies if disposition results on account of death. In the event of death of the seller within the term of the contract, the tax is not immediately due, but the installment contract does not receive a new basis. Payments received after death are treated as income in respect of decedent and the recipient reports the income in the same manner as the decedent would have done if living. Disposition of an installment obligation to the obligor after death of the seller results in taxable gain for the deceased seller's estate to the extent of the obligor's ownership share. The other exception is for transfers by one spouse to another or a transfer between ex-spouses because of divorce. In this case, the transferee is taxed on the installment obligation just as the transferor would have been taxed.

### *i. Cancellation of the Contract*

Cancellation of an installment obligation is treated as a taxable disposition of the obligation by the holder. The amount of the gain is the difference between the fair market value of the obligation and its basis, if the parties are not related. Thus, if the seller forgives or cancels the obligation to pay amounts due, the result is the same as a disposition of the obligation. In the event the parties are related, the gain is the difference between the face amount and the basis of the obligation. Fair market value of the obligation is treated as not less than its face value. The IRS has ruled that cancellation of principal in a debt restructuring involving an installment sales contract does not result in income tax consequences to the seller.

### ii. Pledging the Contract

The tax consequences are also unfavorable if the seller takes the contract to a lender and pledges the contract on a new loan. In that event, the entire amount of the loan proceeds is treated as a payment on the contract. This is a tremendous blow to a seller trying to dispose of an installment obligation. However, the result is otherwise if the interest rates and maturity date differ and the taxpayer does not part with a substantial portion of the ownership rights in the obligation. Pledging of an installment obligation results in the net proceeds of the secured indebtedness being treated as a payment received for installment obligations above $150,000 except for personal use property and farm property.

### iii. Related Party Rules

For sales between closely related parties, disposition of the property by the purchaser within two years of the original transaction may result in taxable gain to the original seller except for: (1) transfers because of involuntary conversion; (2) transfers after the death of the installment seller or purchaser; (3) sale or exchange of stock to the issuing corporation; or (4) transfers where it is established to the satisfaction of the IRS that the disposition did not have, as one of its principal purposes, income tax avoidance.

The disposition of a contract to children in exchange for annuity payments constitutes a taxable disposition. For a disposition by gift, the donee's income tax basis presumably would be the fair market value of the obligation inasmuch as the donor's basis would be increased by virtue of the taxable disposition. A tax-free exchange to a corporation or partnership does not trigger taxability with respect to the installment obligations transferred. All potential depreciation recapture on installment sales of real or personal property is taxed to the seller in the year of sale.

For sales of depreciable property between related persons (limited to entities), the deferred payments are deemed received in the taxable year of sale. Family members are not included in the definition of "related parties". An exception is provided if income tax avoidance is not a principal purpose.

## 4. Apportioning Purchase Price on Acquisition of Real Property

Upon purchase of real property which includes land, depreciable property and a personal residence, the purchase price as the tax basis should be allocated among the items in proportion to the fair market value at the time of the acquisition. The basis so determined for each item governs for purposes of depreciation and for computing gain or loss on sale. For multiple asset acquisitions involving "assets which constitute a trade or business" for purposes of determining the transferor's basis in the assets and the gain or loss of the transferor, the basis is to be allocated to cash and cash-like items, certificates of deposit, government securities and other marketable stock or securities; other tangible and intangible assets; all "section 197 intangibles" except for goodwill and going concern value; and good will and going concern value (in that order) in proportion to fair market values.

# VI. PROPERTY TAX ASPECTS OF REAL PROPERTY OWNERSHIP

In most states, real property is listed and valued every two years. In each year in which real property is not regularly assessed, the assessor lists and assesses any real property not included in the previous assessment and any improvements made since the previous assessment. Normal and necessary repairs up to a threshold amount per building per year do not increase the taxable value. The tax rate, typically expressed in dollars per $1,000 of actual value, is applied against actual value or a percentage of actual value. Actual value is usually the "fair and reasonable market value" of the property. "Market value" is defined as the result of a "fair and reasonable exchange in the year in which the property is listed and valued between a willing buyer and a willing seller, neither being under any compulsion to buy or sell and each being familiar with all the facts relating to the particular property."

In general, the actual value of agricultural property is to be determined on the basis of productivity and net earning capacity on the basis of use for agricultural purposes. This typically results in lower valuation for real property tax purposes for agricultural property than nonagricultural property. Thus, to obtain favorable tax treatment, the parcel an question must be used as farm or ranch land for agricultural purposes in accordance with the particular state statute. While agricultural dwellings are typically valued as rural residential property and are assessed at the same percentage of actual value as other residential property, the lower "use" valuation of agricultural real estate when compared with nonagricultural real estate has spawned numerous cases constructing the boundary of tie definition of "agricultural land" and "agricultural activities."

In some states, such as Nebraska, the value of agricultural land is based on prevailing market value instead of the land's income-producing capability. This can cause valuations to increase substantially when investors buy tracts nearby at inflated values, or land is purchased other than in arm's-length transactions.

Assessed property value may also be reduced upon evidence of environmental contamination or restrictions on land use. For example, in one Pennsylvania case, the presence of oil contamination reduced the assessed value of a parcel of real estate from $2.4 million to $1 million. *In re B.P. Oil Company, Inc.,* 159 Pa. Commw. 414, 633 A.2d 1241 (1993); *Bergen County Associates v. Borough of East Rutherford,* 265 N.J. Super 1, 625 A.2d 524 (1992) *certification denied,* 134 N.J. 428, 634 A.2d 528 (1993).

Assessed values may also be reduced because of external environmental factors even if a particular parcel experiences no environmental contamination or land use restrictions. *See, e.g., Salk v. Metamore Township,* Doc. No. 89167 (Mich. Tax. Trib., Nov. 5, 1995); *Adkins v. Thomas Solvents Co.,* 487 N.W.2d 715 (Mich. 1992); *Livingston v. Jefferson County Board of Equalization,* 10 Neb. App. 934, 640 N.W.2d 426 (2002).

In some states, such as Washington, assessors are statutorily required to take into account any environmental factors affecting property value, and account for the fact that uncertainty surrounding health hazards on an adjoining property may make prospective buyers demand a substantial price discount for potential risks associated with the property. *Wash. Rev. Code § 84.40.030 (1996).*

## VII. SPECIAL INCOME TAX PROBLEMS FOR SELLERS OF ASSETS

### A. MODIFICATION OF CONTRACT TERMS

Sellers attempting to write down contracts in order to assist troubled buyers can take advantage of an enormous latitude in the tax code that allows the modification of contracts without triggering negative tax consequences. In general, a modification resulting in a deferral of the principal due and an increase in the interest rate does not result in a taxable disposition. The substitution of a mortgage contract, in an amount equal to the unpaid balance of the purchase price, payable on the same terms and conditions of payment as the balance of the installment obligation, results only in a change in the type of security and does not constitute a satisfaction or disposition of the installment obligation. If the buyer sells the property and the seller agrees to a "novation", there apparently is no disposition. Likewise, no disposition occurs on release of a blanket mortgage to facilitate sale of individual land parcels. If there is a substantial change in the terms of the obligation, the current rules on minimum interest rates apply, however.

## VIII.  REPOSSESSION OF PROPERTY SOLD UNDER AN INSTALLMENT SALE

### A.   REPOSSESSION OF LAND

A special exception exists under I.R.C. § 1038 that is very favorable to sellers repossessing land under an installment sale. The provisions governing the calculation and reporting of gain on repossession of real property are mandatory if the transaction comes within the statute. In applying the rules, it is immaterial whether the seller realized a gain or sustained a loss on the sale of the real property or whether it can be ascertained at the time of sale whether a gain or loss occurred. It is also immaterial what method of accounting the seller used in reporting gain or loss from the sale or whether at the time of reacquisition the property has increased or decreased in value since the time of the original sale. However, the rules do not apply if the disposition constitutes a tax-free exchange of the property. In addition, for the special rules to apply the debt must be secured by the real property.

## 1. Calculating Gain on Repossession of Real Property

On repossession, whether voluntary or involuntary, the amount of gain recognized is the lesser of—(1) the amount of cash and the fair market value of other property received before the reacquisition (but only to the extent such money and other property exceeds the amount of gain reported before the reacquisition); or (2) the amount of gain realized on the original sale (adjusted sales price less adjusted income tax basis) in excess of the gain previously recognized before the reacquisition and the money or other property transferred by the seller in connection with the reacquisition.

Amounts of interest received, stated or unstated, are excluded from the computation of gain. Because the provision is applicable only when the seller reacquires the property to satisfy the purchaser's debt, it is generally inapplicable where the seller repurchases the property by paying the buyer an extra sum in addition to cancelling the debt. The rules generally are applicable, however, if the seller reacquires the property when the purchaser has defaulted or when default is imminent even if the seller pays additional amounts. The provisions on repossession of real property do not apply except where the indebtedness was secured by the real property. Therefore, reconveyance of property by the obligor under a private annuity to the annuitant would appear not to come within the rules. The following example illustrates these points.

---

### Example 9:

On January 2, 1997, Burt DuLapp sold farmland to Ernie Pyle for $150,000 on an installment basis. Burt acquired the land in 1960. The contract called for $15,000 down and payments of $15,000 per year for nine years. Burt's adjusted income tax basis in the property at the time of sale was $30,000. Burt received the down payment and the first regular payment for the following year, with all payments reported whereupon Burt proceeded to forfeit Ernie's interest in the property. The four-step computational procedure produces the following results:

Step 1: Calculate the amount of cash and the fair market value of the property received before the reacquisition.

| | |
|---|---|
| Year of sale | $15,000 |
| Following year | $15,000 |
| Total | $30,000 |

Step 2: Subtract the gain returned as income for the period before the acquisition.

| | |
|---|---|
| Total contract price | $150,000 |
| Less adjusted basis | 30,000 |
| Gross profit | $120,000 |

Fraction reported as gain:

Gross profit / Total contract price =
$120,000 / $150,000 = 80%

Gain before application of second limitation:

Money and other property received ............ $30,000

Less: Gain reported ($30,000 x .80) ............ <u>$24,000</u>

$6,000

Step 3: Determine the second limitation on amount of gain.

Sales price of property ............................... $150,000

Less: Adjusted basis
at time of sale .................................... $30,000

<u>$24,000</u>

Gain returned as income
before acquisition ............................ <u>$54,000</u>

Limitation on amount of gain ...................... $96,000

Step 4: Determine the lesser figure from Step 2 or Step 3 as the amount of gain resulting from reacquisition ............................................................. $6,000

---

**Note:** If an installment sale involves the personal residence along with the farmland complications can arise if the seller reacquires the property and had excluded the gain attributable to the personal residence under I.R.C. § 121. Unless the personal residence is re-sold within a year of the reacquisition, the gain excluded under I.R.C. § 121 is, essentially, recaptured in accordance with I.R.C. § 1038. *See, e.g., Debough v. Comm'r,* 142 T.C. No. 17 (2014).

The character of the gain from reacquisition is determined by the character of the gain from the original sale. For an original sale reported on the installment method, the character of the reacquisition gain is determined as though there had been a disposition of the installment obligation. If the sale was reported on the deferred payment method, and there was voluntary repossession of the property, the seller reports the gain as ordinary income. If the debts satisfied were securities issued by a corporation, government or political subdivision, the gain would be capital gain.

Once the seller has reacquired the property, it is important to determine the seller's basis in the reacquired property. The adjusted income tax basis for the property in the hands of the reacquiring seller is the sum of three amounts—(1) the adjusted income tax basis to the seller of the indebtedness, determined as of the date of reacquisition; (2) the taxable gain resulting from reacquisition; and (3) the money and other property (at fair market value) paid by the seller as reacquisition costs.

The holding period of the reacquired property, for purposes of subsequent disposition, includes the holding period during which the seller held the property before the original sale plus the period after reacquisition. However, the holding period does not include the time between the original sale and the date of reacquisition.

The provisions on reacquisition of property generally apply to residences or the residence part of the transaction. However, the repossession rules do not apply if—(1) an election is in effect for an exclusion on the residence and (2) the property is resold within one year after the date of reacquisition.

If those conditions are met, the resale is essentially disregarded and the resale is considered to constitute a sale of the property as of the original sale. In general, the resale is treated as having occurred on the date of the original sale. An adjustment is made to the sales price of the old residence and the basis of the new residence. If not resold within one year, gain is recognized under the rules for repossession of real property. An exclusion election is considered to be in effect if an election has been made and not revoked as of the last day for making such an election. The exclusion can, therefore, be made after reacquisition. An election can be made at any time within three years after the due date of the return.

No bad debt deduction is permitted for a worthless or a partially worthless debt secured by a reacquired personal residence, and the income tax basis of any debt not discharged by repossession is zero. Losses are not deductible on sale or repossession of a personal residence. When gain is not deferred or excluded, the repossession of a personal residence is treated under the general rule as a repossession of real property. Adjustment is made to the income tax basis of the reacquired residence.

Under the 1980 amendments, the estate or beneficiary of a deceased seller is entitled to the same nonrecognition treatment upon the acquisition of real property in partial or full satisfaction of secured purchase money debt as the deceased seller would have been. The income tax basis of the property acquired is the same as if the original seller had reacquired the property except that the basis is increased by the amount of the deduction for federal estate tax which would have been allowable had the repossession been taxable.

Also, the nonrecognition provision on repossessions of land does not apply to a former shareholder of a corporation who receives an installment obligation from the corporation in a liquidation when that shareholder, upon default by the buyer, subsequently receives the real property used to secure the obligation.

## B.   REPOSSESSION OF PERSONAL PROPERTY UNDER INSTALLMENT SALE

The tax consequences of repossession of personal property originally sold under an installment sale are much more painful to the seller when compared to the rules applicable to repossession of real property. In these situations, the relief provisions of I.R.C. § 1038 do not apply. Upon repossession, the seller realizes gain or loss in the year of repossession, the same as though the note or other obligation had been sold.

### 1. Voluntary Repossessions

For voluntary repossessions (those where the purchaser, upon being unable to make payment, voluntarily agrees to return the property to the seller in full satisfaction of the outstanding debt), the gain or loss is determined by the difference between the fair market value of the repossessed personal property (determined as of the date of repossession) and the seller's income tax basis in the purchaser's note or other obligation that is satisfied by the repossession. The seller's basis in the obligation is the face value of the purchaser's note (contract price less the principal payments made under the contract) minus the unrealized profit (the percentage of profit times the unpaid principal balance). The seller must adjust this basis figure for any other amounts collected or costs incurred in repossession. The following example illustrates these points.

---

**Example 10:**

Bob Upp sold a tractor for $30,000 on an installment basis. Bob's income tax basis in the tractor at the time of sale was $18,000. The gain of $12,000 was reported with a 40% gross profit percentage. The buyer defaulted when the outstanding balance was $20,000 and the fair market value of the tractor was $16,000. Bob offered to cancel the outstanding obligation if the purchaser would return the tractor. The purchaser agreed to return the tractor. The amount of gain that Bob must recognize upon repossession is calculated as follows:

FMV of property when repossessed ....................$16,000

Less seller's basis in obligation given up:

    Original contract price .......... $30,000

    Less payments received .......... 10,000

    Balance ................................. $20,000

    Less unrealized profit
    ($20,000 x .40) ........................... 8,000

                       $12,000 ........... (12,000)

Balance..................................................................4,000

Less repossession costs........................................... 1,200

Recognizable gain .................................................$2,800

---

The character of the gain or loss is the same as on the original sale. If the obligation arose from a sale by a dealer to a customer, gain or loss on repossession is ordinary income, the amount can be shown (on the dealer's income tax return and in the dealer's books) as an adjustment to the cost of goods sold. For a gain, purchase cost would be decreased; for a loss, purchase costs would be increased. If the original property was I.R.C. § 1231 property (property used in the trade or business), it would be shown on Form 4797 with a separate sheet showing the computation of gain or loss. If the original sale involved a capital asset and it was nonbusiness property, it would be shown on Schedule D with a separate sheet showing the computation of the gain or loss.

## 2. Involuntary Repossessions

An involuntary repossession or foreclosure occurs when the purchaser is in default and is unwilling to return the property to the seller. The foreclosure sale or other action by the seller may involve bidding by the original seller or by a third party to reacquire the property. The original seller may buy back the property or a third party may purchase the property and turn over the proceeds to the seller. If the original seller regains the property, it is assumed the seller paid the current fair market value for the property. In either case, the fair market value of the property at the time of sale may not be sufficient to cover the outstanding debt. In that event, the seller may obtain a deficiency judgment against the original purchaser for the remaining debt. If the seller receives only a partial payment of the debt; the original purchaser remains liable for the balance as evidenced in the deficiency judgment.

The gain or loss is computed using the same procedure as in a voluntary repossession.

---

**Example 11:**

Assume the same facts as in Example 10 (sale of tractor for $30,000, seller's income tax basis of $18,000, gain of $12,000 had been reported with a 40 percent gross profit percentage) except that the property was not returned voluntarily. The seller took action under the UCC default rules, and had the property sold at a foreclosure sale. A third party purchased the property for $16,000 with the proceeds turned over to the seller in partial satisfaction of the $20,000 outstanding at the time of the obligation. A deficiency judgment for $4,000 in favor of the seller was obtained for the remaining amount of the obligation. The gain on the repossession is calculated as follows:

FMV upon repossession ......................................$16,000

Less seller's basis in obligation given up:

        Original contract price.............. $30,000

        Less payments received ............ $10,000

        Balance ...................................... $20,000

        Less deficiency judgment.............. 4,000

| | | |
|---|---|---|
| Balance ...................................... | $16,000 | |
| Less unrealized profit ($16,000 x .40) .............................. | 6,400 | |
| Balance ...................................... | $9,600 | (9,600) |
| Less repossession costs ....................................... | | (1,200) |
| Recognized gain.................................................... | | $5,200 |

The seller received $16,000 (the cash received). The income tax basis in the amount received is $9,600 (60 percent of the $16,000 face value). The gain of $6,400 is adjusted downward by the costs of repossession which were $1,200. The result is $5,200 of recognized gain.

When comparing the involuntary repossession situation set forth in Example 11 with the voluntary repossession situation of Example 10, note that the involuntary repossession produced a recognized gain of $5,200 whereas in the voluntary repossession of Example 10, the seller cancelled the entire outstanding debt of $20,000, but only $16,000 of the outstanding debt was cancelled in this example. The buyer remained liable for the $4,000 balance of the outstanding obligation because of the deficiency judgment. If and when the entire deficiency judgment amount of $4,000 is paid, the seller must report $1,600 of gain. Of the $4,000 received, 60 percent or $2,400 would be a tax-free return of basis and would be deductible as a bad debt deduction when worthless.

----

The income tax basis of the reacquired property in the hands of the seller for purposes of a subsequent disposition (or for depreciation) would be the fair market value of the property at the time of the involuntary repossession adjusted for the interim period. The income tax basis is the same whether repossession is voluntary or involuntary.

When an involuntary repossession occurs, a bad debt deduction is allowable if the outstanding debt is greater than the fair market value of the item repossessed by the seller. The timing and nature of the bad debt deduction depend upon whether the excess debt over the fair market value of the item received is uncollectible and whether the seller is a dealer in personal property. If the seller is not a dealer in personal property, a bad debt deduction is allowed in the year the remaining debt becomes completely worthless.

A bad debt deduction is allowed a dealer only if the property is not repossessed, as demonstrated in the following example.

---

**Example 12:**

Assuming the same facts as in Example 11, where the seller obtained a deficiency judgment for the remaining indebtedness of $4,000, if the entire $4,000 is determined to be uncollectible, the $2,400 of seller's basis in the obligation (60 percent × $4,000) would be allowable as a bad debt deduction.

The bad debt deduction in the previous example equals the difference between the gain reported in Example 10 of $2,800 and the gain reported in Example 11 of $5,200. Thus the final income tax consequences should be the same for a voluntary and involuntary repossession.

## IX.   RESCISSION OF CONTRACT

Rescission refers generally to the cancellation of a contract. Rescission can occur as a result of innocent or fraudulent representation, mutual mistake, lack of legal capacity, an impossibility to perform a contract not contemplated by the parties, or duress and undue influence. Rescission may be mutual—all of the parties to the agreement agree (in writing) to terminate their respective duties and obligations under the contract. Rescission may also be unilateral—where one party to the agreement seeks to have the contract cancelled and the parties restored to the position they were in economically at the time the agreement was entered into.

An innocent as well as intentional misrepresentation may serve as the basis for a unilateral rescission of contract. To be successful on such a claim, the plaintiff must have justifiably relied on a false statement, which was material to the transaction. The rule prevents parties who later become disappointed at the outcome of their bargain from capitalizing on any insignificant discrepancy to void the contract.

There is a split of authority regarding a buyer's duty to investigate a seller's fraudulent statements, but the prevailing trend is toward placing a minimal duty on the buyer. With respect to land sale transactions, the general rule is that a seller's defense that the buyer failed to exercise due care is disallowed if the seller has made a reckless or knowing misrepresentation. However, the defense is typically allowed if the buyer's fault was so negligent that it amounted to a failure to act in good faith and in accordance with reasonable standards of fair dealing. So, in general, a purchaser of land may rely on material representations of the seller and is not obligated to ascertain whether such representations are truthful. *See, e.g., Boyle, et al. v. McGlynn, et al.,* 814 N.Y.S.2d 312 (2006). This principle can be applied in similar agricultural land sale transactions where plans are being made for the development of any activity that could be considered a nuisance.

## X.　BAD DEBT DEDUCTION

### A.　ELEMENTS NECESSARY FOR DEDUCTIBILITY

An income tax deduction is allowed for debts which become worthless within the taxable year. For a bad debt to be deductible, there must be a debtor-creditor relationship involving a legal obligation to pay a fixed sum of money. A bad debt deduction may be claimed only if there is an actual loss of money or the taxpayer has reported the amount as income. Maintaining good records is the key. *See, e.g., Vaughters v. Commissioner,* T.C. Memo. 1988–276.

To be deductible, the debt must be proved to be worthless with reasonable steps taken to collect the debt. Bankruptcy is generally good evidence that at least part of the debt is worthless, but the debtor's technical insolvency may not be. It is not necessary to resort to legal action if it can be shown that a judgment would not be collectible, however.

A deduction may only be claimed in the year a debt becomes worthless. A debt becomes worthless when there is no longer any chance it will be paid. It is not necessary to wait until the debt is due to determine its worthlessness.

Any recovery of a bad debt or part of a bad debt allowed as a deduction in a prior year is includible in gross income in the year of recovery except to the extent excluded.

A debt may be totally or partially worthless. A debt is a totally worthless bad debt if the taxpayer is unable to collect what is still owed even though some of the debt had been collected in the past. The amount remaining to be paid is eligible for a bad debt deduction. Factors indicating total worthlessness include the debtor being in a serious financial position, insolvency, lack of assets, ill health, or bankruptcy.

## B. BUSINESS BAD DEBTS

Bad debts may be business bad debts or nonbusiness bad debts. Corporations have only business bad debts. Business bad debts are deducted directly from gross income while a nonbusiness bad debt is reported as a short-term capital loss when it becomes totally worthless.

A business bad debt relates to operating a trade or business and is mainly the result of credit sales to customers or loans to suppliers, clients, employers or distributors. A bad debt deduction may be taken for accounts and notes receivable only if the amount had been included in gross income for the current or prior taxable year. While this largely limits bad debt deductions to accrual-basis taxpayers, a business bad debt deduction for a cash basis taxpayer is possible. For example, a business loan may go sour and the obligation may become worthless. A business bad debt is one that is incurred in the taxpayer's trade or business. In money lending situations, the business of the taxpayer must be lending money.

## C.   NONBUSINESS BAD DEBTS

Nonbusiness bad debts are bad debts not acquired or created in the course of operating the taxpayer's a trade or business, or a debt the loss from the worthlessness of which is not incurred in the taxpayer's trade or business. Thus, a noncorporate taxpayer's bad debts may be either business or nonbusiness bad debts. To be deductible, nonbusiness bad debts must be totally worthless; partially worthless nonbusiness bad debts are not deductible. Nonbusiness bad debts are deductible only as short-term capital losses and are reported on Schedule D, Form 1040. As such, they are not as valuable as business bad debts.

## D.   GUARANTEES

If payment of another's debt is guaranteed, a bad debt deduction may be claimed by the guarantor if payment is made under the guarantee. To qualify for a deduction these guarantees must meet one of two conditions—(1) the guarantee must have been entered into for profit with the guarantor receiving something in return; or (2) the guarantee must be related to the taxpayer's trade, business or employment. In many instances, these requirements can be very difficult to satisfy. For example, most guarantees are entered into as an accommodation. In addition, the amount that the guarantor receives in return must be a reasonable amount under the circumstances. With respect to the requirement that the guarantee be related to the taxpayer's trade, business or employment, the IRS particularly scrutinizes intra-family arrangements and generally holds that for parents guaranteeing a child's debt, the parent is not in the trade or business of guaranteeing loans. Instead, the parent typically is in the trade or business of farming or some other enterprise. *See, e.g., Lair v. Commissioner,* 95 T.C. 484 (1990).

The loss may be either from a business or be a nonbusiness bad debt depending upon the facts of the situation. To qualify as a business bad debt, the taxpayer must show that the reason for guaranteeing the debt was closely related to the taxpayer's trade or business. If the reason for making the guarantee was to protect the taxpayer's investment but not as part of the taxpayer's trade or business, a guarantee may give rise to a nonbusiness bad debt. Guarantees made as a favor to friends where the taxpayer received nothing in return do not give rise to a deduction.

Since a guarantor is only secondarily liable and becomes liable only on the principal's default and notice, a release of the guarantor before becoming primarily liable does not appear to involve discharge of indebtedness income. In the event a guarantor has become primarily liable, release of the guarantor would seem to produce the possibility of discharge of indebtedness income.

Likewise, a deduction may be available for interest paid by a guarantor after the primary obligor is discharged in bankruptcy.

## E.   REPORTING BAD DEBTS

A bad debt deduction must be explained on the income tax return with a statement attached that shows a description of the debt, the name of the debtor, the business or family relationship between the creditor and debtor, if any, the date the debt became due, efforts made to collect the debt and basis upon which the decision was made that the debt was worthless. For business bad debts, the amount claimed as a deduction should be reported on Form 1120 or 1120-S in the case of a corporation. The amount of deduction attributable to a business bad debt should be reported on Form 1065 for partnerships and Form 1040 for bad debts incurred in relation to a trade or business as an employee. The amount claimed as a deduction for a business bad debt for individuals carrying on the business of farming as a sole proprietor are reported on Schedule F of Form 1040. For individuals carrying on a trade or business other than farming as a sole proprietor, business bad debts are reported on Schedule C of Form 1040.

Nonbusiness bad debts for individuals are deducted on Form 8949 as a short-term capital loss, with various notations. A separate line should be used for each bad debt. For losses of a decedent's estate that are associated with the decedent's debts, they are nonbusiness debts unless they were closely related to the decedent's trade or business at the time they became worthless. In addition, a nonbusiness bad debt, to generate a deduction, requires a separate detailed statement attached to the return.

Nonbusiness bad debts for partnerships are entered on Schedule D, Form 1065 in the same manner as above shown for Schedule D, 1040, for individuals.

## XI. RECOVERIES FROM SETTLEMENTS AND COURT JUDGMENTS

Recoveries from out-of-court settlements or as a result of judgments obtained may fall into any one of several categories. Quite clearly, damages received on account of personal physical injury or physical sickness is excluded from income. *I.R.C. § 104(a)(2)*. Thus, amounts received on account of sickness or mental distress may be received tax-free if the sickness or distress is directly related to personal injury. As the regulations point out, nontaxable damages include "an amount received (other than workmen's compensation) through prosecution of a legal suit or action based on tort or tort-type rights, or through a settlement agreement entered into in lieu of such prosecution." *Treas. Reg. § 1.104–1 (1970)*. However, recoveries representing punitive damages are taxable as ordinary income regardless of whether they are received on account of personal injury or sickness. The enactment also made it clear that damages not attributable to physical injury or physical sickness are includible in gross income. In many lawsuits, there is almost always some lost profit involved and recovery for lost profit is ordinary income. For recoveries in connection with a business, if the taxpayer can prove that the damages received were for injury to capital, no income results except to the extent the damages exceed the income tax basis of the capital asset involved. The recovery is, in general, a taxable event except to the extent the amount recovered represents a return of basis. Recoveries representing a reimbursement for lost profit are taxable as ordinary income.

Most actions brought by farmers or ranchers against lenders or others involve an element of lost profit and some involve recovery of basis. Therefore, there is likely to be at least a partially taxable event. The proper characterization of recoveries is vitally important. In addition, there may be a discharge of indebtedness involved and, in some instances, the transaction may be characterized as a "sale" of property to the creditor.

If the amount of an award or court settlement includes contingent attorney fees, the portion of the award representing contingent attorney fees is includible in the taxpayer's gross income. For fees and costs paid with respect to a judgment or settlement of a case involving discrimination in employment or the enforcement of civil rights, attorney's fees and other costs are deductible.

# CHAPTER 6

# COOPERATIVES

## I. OVERVIEW

Many farmers and ranchers belong to one or more agricultural cooperatives, commonly referred to as co-ops. A co-op is a business entity that distributes its income to its members in accordance with a member's use of the co-op. This feature distinguishes a co-op from the partnership or corporate form of doing business.

Rarely does the business transacted by a single farmer or rancher have an impact on prices paid for inputs or an impact on prices received upon sale of farm or ranch products. As a consequence, co-ops are designed to give farmers and ranchers the benefits of group action in the production and marketing of agricultural commodities, and in obtaining supplies and services. Thus, a primary objective of co-op formation is to provide members with some economic market power.

The primary function of a co-op is the allocation of economic benefits, either in the form of net savings or net earnings, to the member-patrons based on the quantity of business done with the member-patrons rather than on the amount of investment in or services provided to the organization as is the case with corporations and partnerships. However, cooperatives resemble other businesses in certain respects. Co-ops have similar physical facilities, perform similar functions, and must follow sound business practices. Co-ops usually incorporate under state laws (although the state statutes are specifically designed for cooperatives). Co-ops draw up bylaws and other necessary legal papers. Members elect a board of directors. But, co-ops are distinctively different from other businesses with respect to their purpose, ownership, control and distribution of benefits.

Most co-ops are characterized by democratic ownership and control by users, limited returns to capital, return of net income or margins to users on the basis of use and the obligation of users to provide equity or ownership financing. Democratic control means that a member has one vote regardless of the degree of that member's patronage or stock investment. However, some states permit voting based upon a member's patronage and stock investment. In those jurisdictions, the power of a single member is usually limited by allowing the member to cast no more than a small percentage of total qualified votes, typically less than 3 percent, but in some states the percentage is higher.

Most states have statutory limits specifying the maximum rate of return on investment capital. In many jurisdictions, an 8 percent rate is established as the maximum return, but some states establish much higher limits. These statutes are premised upon the general idea that an agricultural co-op is not designed as a for-profit, investment vehicle.

The feature that co-op profits are distributed in accordance with a particular member's use (also known as patronage) runs concurrent with a goal of maximizing members' interests and the notion that the co-op is an extension of the farm or ranch business. To accomplish this objective, a co-op attempts to market patrons' commodities at the highest possible price and purchase quality inputs at the lowest possible cost. The resulting savings (usually referred to as net income rather than profits) belong to the patrons and are distributed to them at least annually, usually in the form of patronage refunds, though not necessarily all in cash. Typically, at least 20 percent is paid out as a cash patronage refund and the balance is invested in the user's name as a retained patronage refund. The retained portion is redeemed at a later time, usually when the user has stopped using the cooperative.

## II.  NATURE OF CO-OPS

Co-ops are voluntary business organizations chartered by state law that enable persons to join together for mutual help, joint purchasing, and collective marketing for the benefit of the members. Agricultural co-ops tend to be either marketing co-ops or supply co-ops although some carry on both functions. A marketing co-op is designed to assist in the marketing of its members' agricultural products. A supply co-op is designed to secure supplies and equipment needed by the membership at the lowest possible per unit cost. Many local grain co-ops combine the marketing and supply functions and may provide services such as grain storage and drying, fertilizer application and feed grinding and mixing. There are also service co-ops, such as rural electric and telephone co-ops, which provide services that might otherwise be unavailable to rural residents.

## A.   MARKETING CO-OPS

A marketing co-op either functions as a purchaser of its members' products at the prevailing market rate or as a pooling agency. If the co-op purchases its members' products, the products may be then commingled with similar products for resale. At the end of the taxable year, the results of the co-op's activities will determine whether any net earnings have been realized. These earnings are allocated to each patron on the basis of the patron's percentage of input. The patron then receives his or her share of the earnings as a patronage refund.

If the co-op functions as a pooling agency, individual farmers or ranchers, as well as farm or ranch corporations, LLCs and partnerships, contract with the co-op to sell their product at a prescribed contract price, less an amount for marketing cost based on volume. All of the production for a particular season is then "pooled" and marketed. In this situation, the co-op does not enjoy net earnings. Participants receive all of the pool proceeds in accordance with the marketing agreement, less amounts contributed to the capital of the co-op on a per-unit basis. These amounts are referred to as "per-unit retains." The per-unit retains are held as capital of the co-op and are redeemed or repurchased in the same manner as deferred patronage allocations. Pooling arrangements are characterized by a sharing of risks, expenses and revenues with payment of an average price. Marketing pools tend to be heavily utilized by milk, fruit, vegetable and nut cooperatives.

In a marketing co-op, members may agree to market their products through the co-op by the use of marketing contracts. While this practice is seldom used by grain marketing and farm supply co-ops throughout the Midwest, in other jurisdictions marketing contracts may require the members to sell all or any specified part of their production through the co-op for a specific period of time, usually not to exceed ten years. In general, exclusive co-op marketing contracts are valid so long as they conform to the usual requirements of contract law. Generally, the co-op's obligations under the contract are to sell the product and return the sale price to the member, deducting expenses and other costs as specified in the agreement.

Another type of marketing co-op, known as a bargaining co-op, bargains collectively for its members by acting as their agent. Bargaining co-ops generally do not take physical possession of agricultural products. The actual sale of the product may be made by the member to the buyer, but on terms agreed to by the co-op. This type of marketing co-op is almost exclusively used by dairy farmers and vegetable producers.

In recent years, value-added or "new wave" cooperatives have been formed in certain parts of the United States, primarily the upper Midwest and northern plains. A value-added or "new wave" cooperative is a closed or defined membership cooperative requiring investment up front in direct proportion to use with the cooperative engaged in processing, production, marketing or input manufacturing.

## B.   SUPPLY CO-OPS

A supply co-op purchases the products needed by its members, such as machinery parts, fertilizer, feed or petroleum products, at wholesale prices. Large, regional co-ops may own and operate fertilizer manufacturing plants, feed mills, oil refineries and other production plants. These products are then sold to the members as they need them. Net earnings at the end of the accounting period are distributed to the members as patronage refunds, based upon the volume of business transacted by the member with the co-op. Some portion of these refunds may be deferred and retained by the co-op, to be paid to the members at a future date as an equity redemption.

Most local agricultural co-ops perform both marketing and supply functions and are "buy-sell" organizations that do not typically use marketing contracts. In addition, most agricultural co-ops are capital stock organizations. Many of the co-ops that began as nonstock co-ops, issuing member certificates to their patrons, have now converted to stock co-ops.

## III.   FORMATION OF CO-OPS

The process for forming an agricultural co-op resembles the process for establishing an S or C corporation. For example, articles of incorporation must be prepared pursuant to a state statute governing co-op formation. However, several factors are unique to the formation of a co-op.

Many states limit membership in an agricultural co-op to "agricultural producers." Co-op membership is achieved either through purchasing a share of stock or a membership certificate, depending upon whether the co-op is a stock or nonstock co-op, or through using the co-op and receiving retained patronage refunds or per-unit capital retains. The objective for producers is to take advantage of the benefits of co-op membership as a user, rather than to seek a return on investment. For investment obtained through stock purchase, the cost of shares or certificates is usually nominal, and they are usually not classified as securities. Only a small amount of co-op membership is achieved through purchased equity.

Bylaws are adopted and may require members to patronize the co-op. In some co-ops, a member's commitment to market through the co-op is set out in a marketing agreement, the legal effect of which may be governed by statute.

Co-op members elect directors. The directors hire the manager or chief executive officer. In most states, directors must be co-op members. Similar to corporations, directors of co-ops who violate statutory or common law duties or who violate rules established in the governing documents of the co-op can incur personal liability. Liability issues facing co-op directors are discussed in greater detail later in this chapter.

Upon formation, a co-op is affected by many statutes that do not apply to regular business corporations. Likewise, special provisions govern co-op taxation, the status of co-op financial instruments under state and federal securities laws, the special treatment of agricultural co-ops under antitrust laws, and the eligibility to borrow from farm credit system (FCS) banks. These and other statutes are important not only to the formation of an agricultural co-op, but to its ongoing operation.

The following table summarizes the usual steps of co-op formation.

---

## Table 1: Sequence of Events—Co-Op Formation

1. Local producers meet to discuss potential economic benefits of doing business as a co-op and determine the interest in and need for a co-op.

2. If a majority of producers vote to transact business through a co-op, a steering committee in established.

3. The steering committee analyzes market supply and demand and cost data.

4. A meeting is held to discuss the results of the data obtained in Step 3.

5. A business plan is developed.

6. The necessary legal papers for incorporation are prepared.

7. Bylaws are adopted and ratified.

8. A board of directors is elected.

9.  A membership drive is conducted.

10. Capital is acquired.

11. A manager is hired or designated.

12. Facilities are acquired.

13. Operations begin.

---

## IV.  MANAGEMENT

A co-op is characterized by two levels of management. The board of directors is the policymaking body and board members are elected from within the membership by members to represent them in overseeing the co-op's business affairs. Most state statutes require five to nine members to be elected to the board. The directors establish policy, report to members, give direction to the manager, and are accountable to the membership for their actions in conducting business affairs. Among major responsibilities, the board hires the manager (chief executive officer) and retains an independent auditor to evaluate the co-op's financial condition.

The manager supervises and coordinates day-to-day operations by managing human capital and physical resources. The manager supervises and coordinates business activity, develops plans to reach objectives, and takes steps to carry out board policy on a daily basis.

## V.  FINANCIAL STRUCTURE

Because co-ops are typically characterized by limited returns to invested capital, no appreciation on equity capital and limited liquidity of equity investment, they are not particularly attractive to outside investment capital. As a result, co-ops must use unique methods to raise capital and operating funds. For example, to begin or expand operations, a typical co-op is capitalized by seeking capital investments from members, retaining patronage funds, or borrowing debt or capital, or a combination of each of the three methods.

### A.  STOCK AND MEMBERSHIP PURCHASES

Members help finance co-ops by purchasing common stock, preferred stock, membership certificates, bonds, promissory notes or debentures. This involves a mix of equity and debt financing. The purchase of a share of common stock or a membership certificate may be a prerequisite to voting membership. Since the purchase price is almost always minimal (usually from $25 to $100), common stock and membership certificate sales usually do not constitute major sources of capital for agricultural co-ops.

### B.  PATRONAGE BASED FINANCING

Patronage based financing is the most important source of equity financing for almost all agricultural co-ops. This financing is generated either through the co-op's issuance of per unit retains or written notices of allocation of retained patronage refunds.

The less widely used of the two methods, per unit retains, is particularly suited to certain marketing co-ops. Pursuant to bylaws or an agreement with each member, the co-op deducts and retains a set amount per unit marketed from the payment due the member, such as 15 cents per bushel or 25 cents per hundred weight. The co-op's net earnings are not used in calculating the retain. The effect is to capitalize the co-op while giving patrons a documented equity interest. At the end of the year, each member is given a statement indicating the amount of capital invested through per-unit retains. If certain IRS rules are followed, per-unit retains, whether paid in cash or certificate form, are income to patrons, but not income to the co-op. These are called qualified per-unit retains.

A much more common method of equity financing is directly related to the co-op's net earnings. Net earnings are derived from the members, belong to the members and are refunded at least annually to the members on the basis of the members' patronage. These earnings are called "patronage earnings" or "patronage refunds." Patronage is usually calculated on the basis of dollar volume of business transacted with the co-op. Without an agreement to the contrary, co-ops distribute net patronage earnings to members at least annually. Part is paid in cash and part is retained as new equity investment. When patronage refunds are not paid in full in cash, the co-op is generally authorized to make refunds to patrons in the form of written notices of allocation (commonly called retained patronage refunds). In practice, a large percentage of a typical agricultural co-op's net earnings are retained for equity funding. Similar to per-unit retains, patronage refunds can be taxed as income to the patron recipients, but not to the co-op. These are called qualified retained patronage refunds.

To take advantage of the federal tax strategy just described, the annual refund to each member must be paid at least 20 percent in cash with the balance in qualified patronage retain certificates or qualified written notices of allocation. The objective is to pass 100 percent of patronage earnings as patronage refunds in cash or certificates to patrons so that they, rather than the co-op, will be subject to income tax on such amounts. As a result, net earnings are taxed only once. However, there is no prohibition against capitalization of a co-op by issuing nonqualified written notices of allocation. Patronage refunded in the form of written notices exceeding 80 percent would fall into this category as would refunds not based entirely on patronage. For example, a co-op might issue nonqualified allocations in a year when its other taxable income is low and then redeem in a later tax year when other income is high. This strategy can be used only with the patron's consent. Amounts represented by the 80 percent plus notices are included in the co-op's taxable income in the year of issuance, there being no pass-through to patrons. However, when nonqualified notices are redeemed in a subsequent tax year, the member has taxable income while the co-op takes a deduction. Thus, regardless of whether the distribution of net income is in a qualified or nonqualified form, the end result is that the income is taxed once and the member pays the taxes.

Over time, a co-op member's equity interest can grow to tens of thousands of dollars. Members are allowed to slowly "earn" their equity investment over time by large stock redemptions are generally not made unless the co-op has enough profits to create "new" equity to replace "old" equity. Termination of membership, withdrawal, or expulsion rarely requires forfeiture of a member's equity, but also rarely triggers immediate redemption. Bylaw provisions, unless overridden by state statute, still govern redemption of equity for continuing members. Where the bylaws are silent concerning treatment of former members, provisions in some state statutes allow former members more immediate redemption rights than those of continuing members. While it might seem appropriate to redeem equity when a member ceases active farming or ranching, or dies, some co-ops do not have earnings and liquid assets sufficient to make such disbursements. Consequently, co-op directors generally have great discretion to redeem patronage refunds and per-unit retains upon a member's retirement or death. Unless there has been an abuse of that discretion, courts generally support decisions of directors not to repurchase stock or redeem patronage refunds and per-unit retains, even if the request is made by a member's estate.

Generally, third parties such as a member's creditors, a member's trustee in bankruptcy, or a member's divorced spouse cannot compel a co-op to take action that the member could not compel. In bankruptcy, for example, the member's interest may vest in the trustee, but the co-op will not be required to make immediate payment. However, where the debtor, during the pendency of the bankruptcy, receives cash payments from the co-op based on pre-petition farming operations, the payments will be property of the bankrupt estate. When the bankrupt farmer member is a corporation, the trustee in the bankruptcy may argue that bylaws or current practices requiring payment upon the death of an individual patron should also apply in cases of corporate "death."

## C.   BORROWED CAPITAL

Eligible agricultural co-ops have access to certain FCS banks for long-term capital improvement loans and short-term operating loans. The Agricultural Credit Act of 1987 continued the lending authority of FCS banks, and, subject to certain conditions, gave new authority to finance co-op partnerships, joint ventures and subsidiaries.

To be an eligible borrower, a co-op must transact at least 50 percent of its business with members. In addition, 80 percent of the voting control of an eligible co-op must be held by "farmers, producers or harvesters of aquatic products, or eligible co-op associations." This percentage is reduced to 60 percent for certain service co-ops, as well as for certain farm supply co-ops. Eligible co-ops must observe the one-member one-vote rule, or *set and hold* dividends on stock or membership capital at or below a rate of return currently approved by the Farm Credit Administration.

While co-ops borrow from FCS banks and other lenders, interest rates are generally lower for CCC price support loans. For certain commodities, CCC loans can be made to co-ops whose members have placed their commodities in a marketing pool with title in the co-op. The co-op can hold the commodities until prices improve, but can immediately pass-through to members a part of CCC loan proceeds. To the extent that some of the loan money stays temporarily with the co-op, the need for the co-op to borrow short-term at more expensive rates may be eliminated or at least reduced.

## VI.  LIABILITY OF CO-OP DIRECTORS TO MEMBER-SHAREHOLDERS AND OTHERS

A member's level of responsibility for a cooperative's functions and procedures varies depending on the size of the association. Generally, in many small cooperatives, individual members share most of the responsibilities of the cooperative's operation. In larger cooperatives, most of the operational functions are conducted by a board of directors that is elected by the membership. A cooperative's board of directors functions generally the same as a corporate board of directors, with board membership restricted to members of the cooperative and usually comprised of between five and nine members. Because a cooperative board tends to function similarly to a corporate board, most courts tend to apply the principles of corporate law to cases involving cooperatives and their directors.

Co-op directors have the same fiduciary duties of obedience, loyalty and care that corporate directors have. Fiduciary duties are duties assigned to or incumbent upon someone who is a trustee or in a position of trust, such as a co-op director. The duty of obedience requires directors to comply with the provisions of the incorporating statute, articles of incorporation, bylaws, and all applicable local, state and federal laws. The duty of loyalty requires directors to act in good faith, and the duty of care requires directors to act with diligence, care and skill. Both the duty of loyalty and the duty of care are dependent upon the particular state's statutory or common law standard of director conduct.

The complexities of the laws affecting co-ops and the "prudent person" standard for the duties of loyalty make it difficult for directors to know their responsibilities. The growing awareness of corporate responsibilities and the increased litigiousness of society coupled with difficult economic conditions suggest that directors and their co-ops should know the duties of corporate directors, officers and nondirector management to avoid legal challenges and problems associated with inadequate or unprofessional director performance.

## A.  OBEDIENCE TO ARTICLES OF INCORPORATION, BYLAWS, STATUTES AND LAWS

Upon the acceptance of the office of director, a director is responsible for performing all duties involved in directing the co-op within the limits of the law. Failure to obey the applicable articles of incorporation, bylaws, state statutes or federal laws may result not only in co-op liability, but also in the liability of directors for illegal or "ultra vires" acts.

### 1.  Illegality

Directors engaging in an act, or permitting the co-op to engage in action, that violates the articles of incorporation, bylaws, state co-op statute, other state law, federal law, or public policy may incur liability for damages. Damages from such liability normally accrue only to the co-op. However, directors causing their co-op to engage in illegal actions may be personally liable for culpable mismanagement for violating their duty of care by failing to attend to co-op activities or neglecting their decision making responsibilities.

### 2.  Ultra Vires

Board of director actions that are not within the powers conferred by the co-op's articles or bylaws are "ultra vires." When a director acts outside of the scope of authority as established in the co-op's articles, bylaws or applicable state statute to the injury of the co-op, the director may be liable to the co-op for the resulting damage. Directors may be liable for ultra vires acts both in jurisdictions that consider a co-op director to be a fiduciary or trustee and in jurisdictions that consider a co-op director to be an agent of the co-op. The non-timely return of member equities is a frequent subject for an allegation that the co-op has acted beyond the scope of its powers.

## B.   FIDUCIARY DUTY OF OBEDIENCE, LOYALTY AND CARE

The fiduciary duty of obedience, loyalty and care requires co-op directors to discharge the duties of their respective positions in good faith. To satisfy the duty of obedience, a director must comply with the cooperative's articles of formation, bylaws and all applicable local, state and federal laws. In general, good faith includes doing what is proper for the co-op, treating stockholders and patrons fairly, and protecting the shareholders' investments in a diligent, careful and skillful manner. The duty of loyalty is the fiduciary duty that is most often litigated. The duty of loyalty requires directors to avoid conflicts of interest, not to take advantage of corporate opportunities for personal gain (such as self-dealing and insider trading), to treat the co-op and the shareholders fairly, and not to divulge privileged information.

### 1.  Conflicts of Interest

A conflict of interest arises between a director and a co-op when a director has a material personal interest in a contract or transaction that either affects the co-op or includes the co-op as a party. In general, a director's duty of loyalty requires interested directors to disclose any conflict of interest between themselves and their co-op. Also, conflict issues may arise in situations involving capitalization of the cooperative, redemption rights of members and preferential treatment in insolvency.

An obvious conflict of interest between a co-op and its directors is director compensation. At common law, directors were not entitled to any compensation or salary. However, most state co-op statutes now allow co-ops to provide remuneration to their directors or to provide for director remuneration through provisions in the articles of incorporation or bylaws. These provisions enable interested directors to approve compensation for their work for and service to the co-op.

A conflict of interest may also arise from marketing and purchasing contracts between the directors and their co-op. Such contracts generally do not pose a problem for co-op directors because most state co-op statutes contain a provision precluding any contract for profit between a co-op and a director that differs in any way from the business relations accorded regular members or from terms current in the particular director's district. Under this statutory requirement, directors cannot enter any contract for profit that is not made available to other members.

A director may also create a conflict of interest by taking a directorship position with a second co-op or corporation. If a co-op director also serves as a director of a second business organization which transacts business with the co-op, there may be a conflict of interest which should be disclosed to both businesses.

Where directors have discretion concerning the payment of dividends or deviation from normal business practices, there may be a conflict if the directors' decision operates to the directors' benefit and the detriment of other parties or members. This could occur, for instance, where the directors decline to pay dividends on preferred stock held by members or nonmembers because the co-op's earnings are returned to active patrons.

## 2. Corporate Opportunities

A co-op director's duty of loyalty prevents a director from personally taking advantage of opportunities that would also be of value to the co-op unless the co-op chooses not to pursue the particular opportunity. This is known as the corporate opportunity doctrine and applies to business opportunities that the director learns about by reason of the director's position with the co-op. The corporate opportunity doctrine usually requires two conditions to be met before there may be director liability. First, the director must have appropriated a business opportunity rightfully belonging to the co-op. Second, there must be a violation of the director's fiduciary duty of loyalty in appropriating the opportunity.

## 3.  Fairness

A director must act fairly when making decisions or taking actions that affect the competing interests of the co-op, its stockholders or patrons, or minority holders of co-op interests. Fairness may also involve the open and fair disclosure of information from both the co-op and its directors to the co-op and its directors, stockholders and patrons. In general, a co-op's bylaws are a contract between the members and the co-op which imposes on the board of directors an implied duty of good faith and fair dealing in its relationship with its members.

Co-op directors may breach their duty of fairness in providing for the payment of dividends to current members or in redeeming co-op equities of former members. Where directors have the authority to either allocate net earnings as patronage refunds or pay dividends on preferred stock, the failure to pay dividends on stock could be unfair. The injustice arises because the preferred stockholder is not receiving any return on money invested in the co-op. Director discretion in the redemption of co-op retained equities also may be a breach of loyalty if the directors provide different treatment for different persons or classes of members or patrons. For example, some courts have ruled unfair a board of directors' refusal to redeem certificates when other certificates had been redeemed upon demand. The Iowa Supreme Court, has construed state co-op law to held that a co-op's board of directors did not breach any fiduciary duties by giving priority as to the redemption of preferred stock to deceased natural members and retirees, not informing members of its retirement policy and selling supplies to a competing co-op without member consent. *Mitcheville Cooperative v. Indian Creek Corp.* 469 N.W.2d 258 (Iowa 1991).

### 4. Confidentiality

The fiduciary relationship existing between a director and co-op includes the duty of confidentiality. This duty prohibits a director from disclosing privileged information. Lawsuits against directors for the breach of this duty are rare. The federal and state securities acts, with their strict provisions concerning the nondisclosure of certain information, constitute more demanding legislation which may affect the directors' duty of confidentiality.

## C.   DUTY OF CARE

Co-op directors have a duty to act carefully in directing co-op affairs. This duty varies from state to state but, in general, requires directors to use that degree of diligence, care and skill which an ordinarily prudent person would exercise under similar circumstances and in the same position. Arguably, a co-op director's duty of care should be more stringent than the duty of care of corporate directors, but most states impose the same duty of care on co-op and corporate directors.

The duty of care, however, may not be the same for any two directors since the duty is subjective and depends upon the background, qualifications, knowledge and expertise of the individual director as well as the particular circumstances and responsibilities of the director's position. Thus, the facts and circumstances of each case determine how much care a director must use in fulfilling directorship responsibilities. Typically, the duty of care is subdivided into four categories. These categories are (1) attention to co-op matters; (2) reliance on officers and employees; (3) delegation of duties; and (4) decision making—the Business Judgment Rule.

## 1.  Attention to Co-Op Matters

Directors must attend to co-op matters in a timely fashion as required by state common law or statute. These duties require directors to attend meetings, follow the articles and bylaws, be cognizant of the various laws affecting the co-op and comply with their provisions, appoint and supervise officers and employees, and perform any other matters that reasonably require the directors' attention. The main issue for consideration is the standard of attention required. Usually, this is determined by reference to a particular state's corporation laws.

## 2.  Reliance on Officers and Employees

This duty concerns the ability of a director to rely on information, reports, statements or financial data prepared or presented by co-op officers or employees. Directors may not rely upon information from others unless the directors have first made a good faith inquiry into the accuracy and truthfulness of the information. Directors should take special care to be fully informed, when approving payment of dividends or making distributions of net income or assets, since there may be personal liability for any wrongful · distribution or payment.

## 3. Delegation of Duties

The board of directors manages co-op affairs. Administrative functions are performed by the co-op's executives and managers. The board of directors should be able and willing to delegate duties to provide for the business operations of the co-op.

Directors must have authority for delegating their duties. This authority may be statutory or may come from the co-op's articles of incorporation or bylaws. However, the delegation of authority does not relieve the board from responsibilities imposed by law.

## 4. Decision Making—The Business Judgment Rule

Directors, in the performance of their management functions, may make decisions that prove to be unpopular or disadvantageous for the co-op. The Business Judgment Rule is a defense that a director may assert against personal liability where the director has fulfilled the duty of care. The Business Judgment Rule protects disinterested directors from member lawsuits in much the same manner as tort law protects professionals from malpractice. If a board of directors decision proves to be unwise or unprofitable, the directors will not be personally liable unless the decision was not made on the basis of reasonable information or was made without any rational basis whatsoever.

Three common types of conduct which the Business Judgment Rule does not protect include self-dealing, lack of knowledge and personal bias. A director self deals when the director has a material personal interest in a co-op contract, transaction or business decision. Directors are also personally liable when they fail to consider all relevant information readily available in making a decision. A requirement that directors make their business decisions in good faith without personal bias or favoritism may be an issue where co-op directors have discretionary power to redeem the retained equities of former patrons. Most co-op directors have an interest in the retained equities of former patrons because the equities constitute an interest-free investment in the co-op. This investment operates to increase the net earnings of the co-op and the funds available for patronage refunds. By declining to redeem the retained equities of former patrons, the directors, if they are current patrons, are able to increase their own patronage refunds. Thus, directors have a personal interest in any decision concerning the redemption of retained equities of non-patrons, and the Business Judgment Rule does not apply.

## D.   COMMON LAW LIABILITY

### 1.  Fraud

Co-op members, or former members if the cause of action occurred during their membership, who are dissatisfied with the management of the co-op may institute an action against the co-op and its directors for fraud. For example, director action that conceals information that should be disclosed to co-op members constitutes fraud. *See, e.g., Parish v. Maryland & Virginia Milk Producers Association Inc.,* 250 Md. 24, 242 A.2d 512 (1968), *cert. denied* 404 U.S. 940 (1971).

### 2.  Conversion

Co-op directors may also be sued for conversion. Such examples may include approving chattel mortgages which result in the loss of members' property. The absence of director authorization or inaction involving a wrongful property transfer is a defense which may shield defendant directors from liability for conversion.

### 3.  Tort

Corporate directors may also be sued in tort for personal injury or damages resulting from their negligent or intentional acts.

### 4.  Corporate Waste

Co-op directors may also be sued for the waste of corporate assets. While courts generally do not interfere with directors' management of a co-op, one court stated that "directors will be held liable if they permit the funds of the corporation or the corporate property to be lost or wasted by their gross or culpable negligence."

## 5.  Nuisance

The directors of co-ops that create offensive odors, dust, noise or other pollution may be named in lawsuits brought by neighbors seeking to stop the offensive activity. For example, in one California case, resident homeowners sued a co-op that manufactured fertilizer from cow manure and against three of its directors to enjoin the co-op's operations as a nuisance. *Rynsburger v. Dairymen's Fertilizer Co-op., Inc.,* 266 Cal. App. 2d 269, 72 Cal. Rptr. 102 (1968).

## E.    SHAREHOLDER DERIVATIVE SUITS

A stockholder's cause of action in a derivative suit consists of two basic elements: (1) an actionable wrong to the corporation perpetrated either by outsiders or insiders; and (2) the wrongful refusal of the corporation's management to bring an action to rectify the wrong.

Most co-ops are subject to shareholder derivative suits in the same manner as corporations. These suits may be authorized either by state co-op law, by a similar provision in the state's corporation law or under the state's common law. Any person bringing a derivative action must satisfy the requirements of state law.

A shareholder derivative action may be brought to correct a broad range of conduct of outsiders, directors, officers or other insiders. The derivative remedy extends to mismanagement, misappropriation of corporate assets, dilution of stockholder equity by improper issuance of additional stock, and a variety of other actions which adversely affect the value of the aggregate of stockholder ownership. A committee of disinterested directors may be able to have a derivative action dismissed if the committee concludes that the suit is without merit.

## VII.  INCOME TAX TREATMENT OF CO-OPS AND THEIR MEMBERS

### A.  IN GENERAL

A co-op may exclude certain items from gross income through specifically allowed deductions. This special tax status afforded co-ops, reflects Congress' view that co-ops are designed to operate at cost and that "profits" belong to members. The approach is similar in effect to viewing the co-op as a partnership for tax purposes. A co-op can have the benefit of additional exclusions from gross income if it satisfies certain requirements. Depending on whether patronage refunds are from a marketing co-op or a supply co-op, the refunds received by members will be treated either as taxable income or as a reduction of expenses.

A cooperative can also reduce its taxable income by claiming a deduction for net income derived from most production activities. The amount of the deduction is the lesser of 9 percent of the cooperative's qualified production activities income, 9 percent of the cooperative's taxable income computed without regard to the deduction and 50 percent of Form W-2 wages that the cooperative pays during the tax year. The amount of the cooperative's deduction is calculated at the cooperative level and passes through (in whatever amount the cooperative chooses) to members of the cooperative where it is not limited by the member's adjusted gross income or Form W-2 wages.

## B.   TAXATION OF CO-OP MEMBERS

Patronage refunds received by a co-op member are taxable income if the merchandise or product marketed or purchased concerns the business of the farmer. Patronage refunds from a marketing co-op are fully taxable as additional revenue received for a farm product. Patronage refunds from a supply co-op are treated as a reduction in expenses for farm supplies.

When a patronage refund takes the form of a rebate on the cost of something the farmer uses in the farming business, the question is whether the purchased article was a current expense or a capital investment. If it was a current expense, such as seed or feed bought in a prior year producing a dividend in the current year, the farmer might deduct from the costs of seed and feed in the current year the amount of the "rebate" from the previous year, or may simply report the refund as income on the "patronage refunds" line and then deduct the full outlay for seed and feed in the ordinary manner. Either procedure produces the same tax. However, if the refund or rebate relates to a capital asset or property used in the trade or business, an adjustment should be made to the cost of the property.

A co-op member includes in gross income the cash, the stated amount of "qualified" written notices of allocation, and the fair market value of other property (excepting nonqualified written notices of allocation) received as a patronage refund (or a nonpatronage distribution from a tax-exempt co-op). A notice is "qualified" if (1) 20 percent of the total refund of which it is a part is paid in cash or by qualified check, and (2) it is redeemable in cash within 90 days of issue or the distributee has consented to report it as income. Consent may be made in writing or by membership in an organization after it adopts a bylaw requiring such consent, or by endorsing and cashing a "qualified" check paid as part of the patronage dividend or distribution. A "qualified" check is imprinted with a statement that endorsement and cashing of the check constitutes the payee's consent to report the accompanying written notices of allocation as income. If a written notice of allocation is not "qualified," it is not income to the patron when issued. A co-op member reports income when the item is redeemed, sold, or disposed of. If the recipient dies, the decedent's successor reports the income upon receipt. Distribution of cash patronage refunds, qualified cash patronage refunds and qualified per-unit retains as well as redemption of nonqualified patronage refunds and nonqualified per-unit retains create taxable income to recipients and a deduction from taxable income to the co-op.

A co-op member may suffer a loss if a taxable allocation is redeemed for less than its face value. This loss is an ordinary loss arising from the member's trade or business if the member had joined the co-op to facilitate business activities. *Rev. Rul. 70–64, 1970–1 C.B. 36.* Similarly, co-op members notified in writing by a farmers' co-op that their outstanding marketing credits have been cancelled to offset excessive marketing advances paid them in a prior year are entitled to an ordinary loss in the year in which they were notified. The loss is measured by the difference between the stated amount included in income in the earlier year and the amount received upon redemption. On the other hand, losses on equity interests in a co-op that were purchased or acquired in a transaction that did not involve allocated patronage earnings are properly characterized as capital losses.

It is possible for a co-op to be a member and patron of another co-op. Farmer patrons may belong to a local co-op which is in turn a member of a regional co-op which may be a member of a larger co-op. The patronage refunds simply pass down through the structure. However, each co-op makes its own decision as to how much income to distribute to its patrons, and is generally not obligated to pass all earnings from one level to the next level.

## C.   TAXATION OF THE CO-OP

Agricultural co-ops satisfying certain prescribed requirements do not include in gross income patronage refunds and per-unit retains paid in money, other qualified property, qualified written notices of allocation, or qualified per-unit retained certificates. These distributions are "qualified" as deductions from taxable income of the cooperative and patrons are taxed on such distributions, including those amounts paid in the form of equity in the co-op. Thus, this type of a co-op must separate patronage from nonpatronage-sourced income, and is taxed like an ordinary corporation with respect to nonpatronage-sourced income, but like a partnership with respect to patronage-sourced income. In other words, nonpatronage-sourced income is fully taxable to the co-op and is fully taxable to the patron if paid out in dividends. Patronage-sourced income is taxed only once, usually to the patron.

An agricultural co-op may acquire even more favorable tax treatment by making an election under I.R.C. § 521 to be treated as a "tax exempt" association. This election entitles the co-op to additional deductions for distributions to stockholders and patrons from nonpatronage earnings. *I.R.C. § 1382(c)*. "Nonexempt" co-ops may allocate and deduct only income arising from business conducted with patrons, but only if they satisfy certain Internal Revenue Code requirements. *See I.R.C. § 1388(a)*. With these additional exclusions, a § 521 co-op is likely to have little, if any, taxable income. Such a co-op, as a practical matter, is "exempt" from federal income tax. More on this point in a moment.

## 1. Nonexempt Co-Ops

For an agricultural co-op to receive the basic benefits of co-op taxation, it must be "operating on a cooperative basis." For many years, the IRS position was that a co-op did not operate on a co-op basis if more than 50 percent of its business was with nonmembers. *See, e.g., Rev. Rul.* 72–602, *1972–2 C.B. 150*. In 1978, the Eighth Circuit Court of Appeals ruled against the IRS 50 percent test and held that business conducted with patrons could be handled under the special co-op tax rules but that nonmember business was to be handled under general corporate tax rules. *Conway County Farmers Association v. Comm'r*, 588 F.2d 592 (8th Cir. 1978).

In early 1992, the IRS issued a ruling in which it spelled out seven factors (three fundamental and four additional) for consideration in determining whether an organization is "operating on a cooperative basis." *Ltr. Rul. 9219030, Feb. 7, 1992.* The three fundamental factors are: (1) subordination of capital; (2) democratic control; and (3) operation at cost. With respect to subordination of capital, the organization must limit the financial return it pays on its contributed capital. While not required, democratic control is present if each member has one vote regardless of the size of the member's investment or the amount of business the member does with the co-op. The organization is deemed to operate at cost if, at least annually, the organization returns the excess of revenues over related costs to patrons in proportion to the volume or value of business conducted with each patron.

The four additional factors are: (1) joint effort; (2) minimum number of patrons; (3) limited business conducted with nonmembers; and (4) liquidating distributions. A joint effort is present if the organization is engaged in some joint effort actively with, for, or on behalf of its members. A minimum number of patrons is defined as sufficient membership to form a "mutual joinder of interest" in the risks and benefits of the co-op effort. Similarly, the amount of business conducted with nonmembers must be limited. In 1993, the IRS issued a ruling formally revoking the 50 percent test. *Rev. Rul. 93–21, 1993–1 C.B. 188, modifying Rev. Rul. 72–602, 1972–2 C.B. 510.* Consequently, a co-op operating on a for-profit nonpatronage basis with nonmembers is no longer automatically precluded from co-op income tax treatment. Substantial nonmember business transactions is not fatal to co-op tax treatment, but is one factor for consideration. As for liquidating distributions, present and former members must participate on a proportionate basis in any distribution of the organization's assets. Revenue rulings and reported cases distinguish between organizations performing functions consistent with a corporation-shareholder relationship and those organizations offering a true co-op patron relationship.

**Example 1:**

A group of farmers established a co-op to purchase raw products, blend them and sell fertilizer to members for use in their farming operations. This is an association operating on a co-op basis. However, if nonfarm investors purchase the capital stock of a for-profit fertilizer corporation, then the classic corporation-shareholder relationship exists. After the sale, the corporation does not sell fertilizer to farmers. Instead, it sells sacked lots to each shareholder and then markets that product to farmers on behalf of those shareholders. The IRS and the courts have refused to recognize this type of organization as consistent with "operating on a cooperative basis."

The Internal Revenue Code also requires that amounts refunded to patrons (members and nonmembers) be paid pursuant to valid, pre-existing obligations requiring the co-op to pay each patron from the net earnings of the co-op's patronage business. Effective for distributions in taxable years beginning after October 22, 2004, the net earnings of a cooperative are not to be reduced by amounts paid during the tax year as dividends on capital stock or other proprietary capital interests of the organization to the extent the articles of incorporation or bylaws or other contract with patrons provide that such dividends are in addition to amounts payable to patrons derived from business done with or for patrons during the taxable year.

Co-ops operating on a co-op basis, whether nonexempt or exempt, may exclude from gross income for tax purposes patronage dividends or refunds paid in money, other property, per-unit retains and qualified written notices of allocation. Qualified written notices of allocation must reveal how much of the patronage refund is being retained by the co-op for capital accumulation purposes. If all IRS technical requirements are met and at least 20 percent of patronage dividends for the tax year are paid to patrons in cash, the co-op can exclude from its income the total patronage refund. This assumes that the patron has consented to the inclusion in his or her income of the entire amount. This consent may be given in a written agreement, by a member becoming subject to pertinent bylaws, or by endorsement when the patron cashes a qualified check for the 20 percent or larger percentage being paid out in cash.

Note: To be able to deduct patronage dividends, a cooperative may provide notice via email or by posting to the cooperative's website instead of mailing the notice via regular U.S. mail.

Co-ops that operate on a co-op basis deduct per-unit retains that are allocated or distributed to patrons in the form of qualified per-unit retained certificates. As with patronage refunds, the patron must consent to the arrangement which creates tax liability for the patron where no cash is received, as when qualified per-unit retain certificates are issued. Unlike patronage refunds, no cash payment needs to accompany issuance of per-unit retain certificates to be qualified.

Another tax issue that has plagued co-ops in recent years has been IRS efforts to treat interest income on temporarily invested excess funds as nonpatronage-sourced income subject to tax. Generally, a co-op's interest and rental income are not patronage-sourced. However, interest and rental income can become patronage-sourced when generated by activities integral to bona fide co-op functions, but is not patronage-sourced when generated by for-profit ventures incidental to co-op functions. *See, e.g., CF Industries, Inc. v. Commissioner*, 995 F.2d 101 (7th Cir. 1993).

The IRS will continue to challenge earnings made by co-ops on investments of excess or reserve funds. Cooperatives investing excess or reserve funds in a manner which will produce a return should be exceedingly careful to establish a justifiable business reason for the investment that relates to the co-op's ordinary business.

The IRS has also taken the position in litigation that capital gains and losses of nonexempt agricultural cooperatives are always to be classified as non-patronage. But, that view has been rejected in favor of a test determining whether each item of gain or loss was realized in a transaction that either directly related to the cooperative's enterprise or facilitated the accomplishment of the cooperative's marketing, purchasing, or service activities on behalf of its patrons. *Farmland Industries v. Comm'r*, T.C. Memo. 1999–388, *acq.*, I.R.B. 2001–13, 920.

In 1997, the Eleventh Circuit Court of Appeals held that a nonexempt co-op's redemption of qualified notices of written allocation at less than face value did not result in taxable income to the co-op of the difference between the face value and the discounted value. *Gold Kist, Inc. v. Commissioner,* 110 F.3d 769 (11th Cir. 1997).

### *i. Deductibility of Losses*

For interests in cooperative representing retained patronage dividends, redemption of qualified written notices of allocation at less than the stated amount on issuance produces an ordinary loss. The loss is measured by the difference between the stated amount that was included in income in an earlier year and the amount received upon redemption. Ordinary losses can be used to reduce ordinary income without limit.

For transactions that do not involve allocated patronage dividends, but instead involve the taxpayer's investment in stock of the cooperative, the outcome is a capital gain or capital loss. An equity interest in a cooperative is not eligible for treatment as a trade or business gain or loss under I.R.C. § 1231. That's because a "trade or business" is defined as "property used in the trade or business, of a character which is subject to the allowance for depreciation . . . held for more than 1year, and real property used in the trade or business held for more than 1 year. . . ." Cooperative stock is neither depreciable property nor real property.

For members of a cooperative that incur a write-down of equity, if the equity was based on patronage, the nature of the loss is an ordinary loss. However, for a cooperative that had triggered gains or losses from the sale of facilities, the tax treatment is based on whether each item of gain or loss was realized in a transaction that either directly related to the cooperative's enterprise or facilitated the cooperative's activities on behalf of its patrons. If that test is met, the write-down of equity produces an ordinary loss; if that test is not met, the write-down produces a capital loss. The Tax Court rejected the IRS argument that capital gains and losses never qualify as patronage income. *Farmland Industries v. Comm'r.*, T.C. Memo. 1999–388.

The appropriate Code section for the deduction of losses depends on whether the loss is properly characterized as a loss from worthless securities or a bed debt. The two are mutually exclusive inasmuch as the bad debt deduction provision is specifically made inapplicable to a debt which is evidenced by a security as defined in the worthless securities provision.

Although the regulations do not provide guidance on whether stock in a cooperative is subject to treatment as a worthless security, the Tax Court has allowed losses on cooperative stock to be deducted under the worthless security rules.

Under the worthless securities rules, the cost or other basis of stock is deducted in the year that the stock becomes totally worthless. No deduction is allowed for partially worthless stock. A loss from worthless stock that is a capital asset is generally subject to the limitation on capital losses. Note that if any security which is not a capital asset becomes wholly worthless during the year, the loss is an ordinary loss.

Therefore, it would seem that stock in a cooperative which was acquired as an investment, and which does not involve retained patronage is a capital asset and is subject to treatment as a worthless security. However, whether an interest in a cooperative representing retained patronage is subject to the worthless securities rules depends upon whether the interest is a capital asset. The fact that the Internal Revenue Service in *Rev. Rul. 70–64* allowed ordinary loss treatment on such an interest would indicate that an interest in a cooperative representing or including retained patronage is not considered a capital asset. Rev. Rul. 70–64 specifically noted that the ordinary loss in that ruling was deductible under the worthless securities provision, I.R.C. § 165.

If an interest in a cooperative is not considered subject to the worthless securities rules, on the grounds that the interest in the cooperative that represents retained patronage is not a "security" within the meaning of the worthless securities provision, any loss may be allowable as a bad debt deduction. In that event, a deduction is available if the debt becomes wholly worthless during the year. Only a bona fide debt qualifies for a bed debt deduction. A bona fide debt is a debt arising from a debtor-creditor relationship based upon a valid and enforceable obligation.

For losses involving worthless securities, only the basis of "wholly worthless" securities is deductible in a taxable year. Losses involving a cooperative in reorganization bankruptcy (Chapter 11) would seem *not to be deductible until there is a formal determination that the securities are indeed worthless.*

It would seem that losses on interests in a cooperative, representing retained patronage, may be classified as business bad debts. While partially worthless bad debts are deductible as business bad debts, it is necessary to show that the deductible amount was "charged off" during the year. Bankruptcy is generally good evidence that at least part of a debt is worthless. But, for a cooperative in reorganization bankruptcy, a bad debt deduction may not be claimable until formal action is taken by the bankruptcy court declaring that the debt has, indeed, been "charged off."

### ii. Income Tax Effects of Bankruptcy

The general rule is that if a cooperative cancels or redeems at a discount stock distributed to a member as a patronage-sourced dividend, the cooperative receives taxable income from the cancellation or redemption to the extent of the value of the stock or discount. However, if as part of the liquidation plan, the cooperative does not cancel or redeem the stock, the cooperative does not recognize income from the bankruptcy.

### 2. "Exempt" Co-Ops

An agricultural co-op meeting the requirements of I.R.C. § 521 may request and receive a "letter of exemption." The advantage of § 521 status is the availability to the co-op of two additional deductions from gross income: dividends paid on capital stock paid to patrons; and distributions of nonpatronage income allocated to patrons based on patronage with the co-op. With respect to distributions of nonpatronage income, it is clear that a § 521 co-op can exclude from gross income rents and interest passed on to patrons on the basis of patronage whether or not the rents and interest are patronage sourced.

A farmer's co-op that qualifies under I.R.C. § 521 is considered an "exempt" organization. To qualify for exempt status certain requirements must be satisfied. The primary requirements for qualification are as follows:

(1) The organization must be:

    (a) An association of farmers, fruit growers, livestock growers, dairymen, or others of like kind.

    (b) "Organized and operated on a cooperative basis," to

    (c) market the products of members and other producers, or purchase supplies and equipment for the use of members and other patrons.

(2) If the organization has capital stock:

    (a) The dividend rate must be fixed not to exceed the legal rate of interest in the state of incorporation, or 8 percent a year, whichever amount is greater, based upon the value of the consideration for which the stock was issued; and

(b) Substantially all of the stock, except nonvoting preferred, must be owned by producers who market their products or purchase their supplies and equipment through the association.

(3) Financial reserves must be restricted to reserves that are required by state law or that are reasonable for any necessary purpose. The reserves, in addition, must be allocated to the accounts of patrons unless the co-op includes the reserves in computing taxable income.

(4) The value of products marketed or purchased for nonmembers may not exceed that for members, and a purchasing co-op may not purchase for persons who are not members or producers more than 15 percent of the value of the co-op's total purchases. Business conducted for or with the United States government is disregarded in determining whether the 50 percent and 15 percent tests are met.

(5) Nonmembers must be treated the same as members in business transactions, with respect not only to the allocation of patronage refunds to the accounts of patrons, but also to pricing, pooling, or payments of sales proceeds, in prices of

supplies or equipment, and in fees charged for services.

(6)  The organization must keep permanent business records, reflecting business transactions with members and nonmembers, including distributions to them.

With respect to the requirement that the organization must be a "an association of farmers', fruit growers', or like association," court cases and IRS rulings restrict the exemption to agricultural co-ops. For instance, a co-op formed to market fish produced by members in privately owned warehouses qualified for the exemption. *Rev. Rul. 64–246, 1964–2 C.B. 154.* Also exempt was an agricultural co-op formed to produce and market range grasses on land owned or leased by members for grazing its herd of breeder cattle and for grazing cattle of others during the peak growing season. *Rev. Rul. 75–5, 1975–1 C.B. 166.* However, a co-op which marketed fish not produced on farms by members was not exempt. *Rev. Rul. 55–611, 1955–2 C.B. 270.* Co-ops that have been held to be not exempt because they were not of "like kind" include co-ops for advertising agents, co-ops owning and operating apartment houses, co-ops engaged in scavenger services and sale of junk as well as co-ops organized by persons engaged in the lumber business for the purpose of marketing building materials on a co-op basis.

In order to qualify for the exemption, a co-op must be organized and operated on a co-op basis. Usually, faulty organization is not fatal to tax exempt status when the association is clearly operating on a co-op basis.

To be operating on a co-op basis and satisfy the requirements of I.R.C. § 521, the co-op must market products for member and nonmember producers, or purchase supplies and equipment for them. Members and nonmembers must be treated similarly and the co-op must return to them the sales proceeds from their products, less necessary marketing expenses, based upon the value or quantity of their products sold. Necessary expenses are those incurred in connection with processing, manufacturing, or distributing co-op products, as well as the expenses associated with the handling, packaging, and servicing of supplies and equipment purchased by the co-op for members and patrons. As for the requirement of equal treatment, the exemption will be denied if the co-op charges a higher price for a certain group of members and nonmembers than it does for other members and nonmembers, even though only a small percentage of sales is at the higher price. In addition, the co-op must not market more for nonmembers than it does for members in terms of value.

An exempt co-op's function must be to market or purchase for its members. Other activities are permissible when they are incidental to the co-op's function, and are designed to increase the co-op's efficiency in performing its exempt activities, or when necessary to fill outstanding orders, such as emergency purchases from outsiders. This "emergency purchase exemption" is typically not available where a co-op makes advance contracts in excess of the normal expected members' production. In addition, the IRS and the courts take a narrow view of what constitutes "emergency purchases" and require that purchases be made for the sole purpose of meeting pre-existing obligations instead of for investment or profit purposes. *See, e.g., Hills Mercantile Co.,* 22 BTA 114 (1931). Exempt status was also denied for a co-op whose principal activities were caretaking and harvesting of citrus groves. *Philips Cooperative v. Comm'r,* 17 T.C. 1002 (1951). In essence, to qualify for the exemption when purchasing supplies and equipment, a co-op must treat members and nonmembers alike, and purchase for them at cost, plus necessary expenses.

An exempt co-op may not conduct more than half of its marketing business for nonmembers, and not more than 15 percent of total purchases may be from those who are neither members nor producers. Members include those who participate in the profits *and* management of the co-op. *Treas. Reg. § 1.521–1(a)(3) (1965).* Thus, the status of patrons as members or nonmembers determines whether the marketing or purchasing limitations are violated. This, in turn, affects a co-op's exempt status. Likewise, a patron's status as a producer determines whether a co-op qualifies under the purchasing limitations and stock ownership restrictions.

Marketing for nonmembers on a co-op basis by an exempt co-op is restricted to "other producers" of the marketed products. The IRS defines a producer as one who, as owner or tenant, bears the risks of production and cultivates, operates, or manages the farm for gain or profit. In essence, if the producer is engaged in the trade or business of farming, he or she will be deemed to be a producer for purposes of being a co-op member. A person who receives a rental (either in cash or in-kind) which is based upon farm production is engaged in the trade or business of farming and is a producer. Generally, a person who receives a fixed rental or other fixed compensation without reference to production is not a producer. A shareholder of a farm corporation does not qualify as a producer solely because the corporation is engaged in farming. Only if the shareholder bears the risks of production individually will the shareholder qualify.

An exempt co-op may issue capital stock, but its dividend-interest income must be fixed not to exceed 8 percent (or the legal rate of the state of incorporation, if higher) of stock purchase price. Substantially all of the stock must be owned by "producers" who either purchase or sell through the co-op. Nonvoting preferred stock is not counted when owners are not entitled to profits other than fixed dividends. For marketing co-ops, substantially all of the stockholders must be current patrons as well as producers if the co-op is to elect and maintain exempt status. In a 1969 Eighth Circuit Court of Appeals case, the court noted that Congress did not intend exempt status to be granted if the producers marketed their products or purchased their supplies through the co-op only at such times as they found expedient. *Cooperative Grain & Supply Co. v. Comm'r,* 407 F.2d 1158 (8th Cir. 1969). The IRS has ruled that the "substantially all" requirement is satisfied if at least 85 percent of all of the capital stock (excluding nonvoting preferred) is held by producers. The Eighth Circuit Court of Appeals in a later decision held that, for purposes of the 85 percent test, the determination of stock ownership is made on the basis of whether the patron had the right to vote at the annual shareholder's meeting following the close of the taxable year. *Farmers Cooperative Co. v. Comm'r,* 822 F.2d 774 (8th Cir. 1987).

In order to qualify for exempt status, a co-op cannot have any taxable income for its own account in excess of authorized reserves or surplus. However, a co-op can accumulate a reserve required by state law, or a reasonable reserve or surplus for a necessary purpose (e.g., erection of business facilities, purchase of machinery, and amortization of loans incurred for such expenditures).

To elect and maintain exempt status, the co-op must distribute patronage refunds to nonmembers on the same basis as members with certain exceptions. IRS regulations illustrate this requirement with an example of a milk producer's co-op engaged in the collecting and disposing of milk products. The co-op distributes the proceeds, less necessary operating expenses, among the producers on the basis of either the quantity or the value of milk or butterfat in the milk furnished by producers. The co-op is exempt so long as the business proceeds are distributed on a proportionate basis.

A co-op need not distribute patronage refunds to nonmember producers in cash, so long as their shares can be determined from its records and the shares are applicable to purchased stock or membership. Likewise, the co-op can distribute nondeductible written notices of allocation (to all patrons) when the distribution is for less than $5. Similarly, the co-op can distribute nondeductible allocations to non-consenting patrons. Also, the co-op can pay less interest (or dividends) on nonqualified written notices of allocation held by non-consenting patrons, than on qualified allocations issued to consenting patrons. Similarly, the co-op can pay less interest and dividends on per-unit retained certificates issued to non-qualifying patrons than it pays on the certificates issued to qualifying patrons, but the difference must be reasonably related to the co-op's tax disadvantage from the nonqualified allocations issued to non-consenting patrons and certificates issued to non-qualifying patrons. Otherwise, the co-op cannot discriminate between non-consenting and consenting patrons or non-qualifying and qualifying patrons when making distributions or when redeeming nondeductible written notices of allocation.

A co-op, to be exempt, must keep permanent business records reflecting business transactions with and distributions to members and nonmembers. A co-op must file Form 1028 with the IRS in order to request the exemption.

## D.   THE DOMESTIC
## PRODUCTION DEDUCTION

I.R.C. § 199 allows taxpayers to claim a deduction on their income tax return based on their net income from most production activities in the United States. The domestic production activities deduction (DPAD) for tax years beginning after 2009 is limited to the lesser of:

- 9% of the qualified production activities income (QPAI);

- 9% of the entity's taxable income without regard for I.R.C. § 199 (modified adjusted gross income for individual taxpayers); and

- 50% of Form W-2 wages paid during the year by the taxpayer that are allocable to domestic production gross receipts (DPGR)

QPAI equals domestic production gross receipts (DPGR) reduced by the sum of the following:

- Cost of goods sold (CGS) allocable to DPGR;

- Other deductions and expenses directly allocable to DPGR; and

- A share of other deductions and expenses that are not directly allocable to DPGR or another class of income

QPAI for many farmers is the sum of their net income reported on Schedule F (Form 1040), Profit or Loss from Farming, and net gain from sale of raised livestock reported on Form 4797, Sales of Business

Property. However there are exceptions to this general rule.

DPGR are receipts derived from the lease, rental, license, sale, exchange, or other disposition of qualifying production property that is manufactured, produced, grown, or extracted by the taxpayer in whole or in significant part within the United States. Qualifying activities include cultivating soil, raising livestock, and fishing as well as storage, handling, and other processing (other than transportation activities) of agricultural products.

For many farmers, the 50% of wages limitation is the major limiting factor on their DPAD. Many farmers have little or no paid labor. In addition, wages for which withholding is not required are excluded from "Form W-2 wages." Thus, wages paid in commodities, wages paid for agricultural labor to a child of the proprietor that is under age 18 or to a child under age 18 who is the child of all the partners in a partnership, and compensation paid in the form of nontaxable fringe benefits are not included in "Form W-2 wages."

The DPAD can be confusing for members of cooperatives. Unlike the treatment of owners of other pass-through entities such as partnerships and S corporations, the DPAD deduction for products sold by a cooperative is calculated at the entity level and the cooperative can elect to pass part or all of the DPAD through to its members based on their patronage. Because the DPAD is calculated at the cooperative level and the deduction passes through to the members of the cooperative, the deduction on the member's tax return is *not* limited by the member's adjusted gross income or Form W-2 wages.

A cooperative engaged in marketing agricultural and horticultural products is treated as having produced any products that are produced by its patrons and marketed by the cooperative. In determining the pass-through DPAD, the cooperative's taxable income and QPAI are computed without taking into account any deductions for patronage dividends, per-unit retain allocations, and nonpatronage distributions under I.R.C. § 1382(b) and (c).

This rule led many cooperatives to take a closer look at how they characterized their payments to members for the members' commodities. That characterization depends on the member agreement with the cooperative. The IRS was asked to examine several agreements, and began issuing private letter rulings on the matter in 2008. IRS has taken the position that payments a cooperative makes to its members for their commodities are advance per unit retains payments in money (PURPIM). Consequently, a cooperative does not have to deduct those payments from their DPGR to compute their QPAI. The result is that a cooperative's ability to treat the payments for commodities as PURPIM significantly increases the cooperative's QPAI and potentially the DPAD the cooperative can elect to pass-through to its members.

The DPAD is a deduction only against patronage-sourced income. The DPAD cannot be computed by aggregating patronage and nonpatronage-sourced income. Since cooperatives compute gross patronage-sourced income for DPAD purposes without deducting PURPIMS, patronage-sourced income is higher than it otherwise would be which gives cooperatives an advantage over corporations. In *CCM 20131802F (Feb. 27, 2003),* a Subchapter T cooperative computed its DPAD by aggregating income from both patronage and nonpatronage sources. Nonpatronage sources had negative QPAI and would have resulted in DPAD of zero if calculated separately from income derived from patronage sources. Thus, by calculating patronage and nonpatronage sourced income together, the cooperative was able to use half of its nonpatronage wages when computing its DPAD. The IRS, citing *Farm Service Cooperative v. Comr.,* 619 F.2d 718 (8th Cir. 1980), noted that a cooperative cannot deduct W-2 wages from nonpatronage activities against income from patronage-sourced income. Thus, the cooperative had to perform separate DPAD calculations for both patronage and nonpatronage activities.

Similarly, in *CCM 20132701F (May 16, 2013),* a large, integrated and diversified agricultural concern that was also a Subchapter T cooperative, operated both a grain marketing and agricultural supply cooperative. It marketed grain on a patronage basis for its members which included both farmers and local grain cooperatives. It treated all payments made to members and nonmembers for grain as purchases and not as PURPIMS. Thus, the grain purchases became part of the cooperative's cost of goods sold. In late 2009, IRS issued a PLR to the cooperative that said that the grain payments to members and eligible nonmember patrons were PURPIMs, and that the cooperative's DPAD was to be computed without taking a deduction for grain payments to the members and eligible nonmember patrons. The cooperative then sought IRS guidance concerning whether its increased DPAD caused by the reclassification of purchases to PURPIMs (which had the effect of reducing the cooperative's nonpatronage income for the year) could offset the cooperative's nonpatronage-sourced income. However, the IRS determined that because the enhanced DPAD was entirely attributable to the cooperative's patronage grain business it could only be used to offset patronage-sourced income. The DPAD resulting from the reclassification was inherently patronage-based. As such, the enhanced DPAD amount could only be used to reduce patronage-sourced income, not nonpatronage-sourced income.

## VIII. ANTITRUST LAWS

In 1890, the Congress adopted legislation designed to prevent monopolies or any conspiracy to restrain trade (the Sherman Act). The treatment afforded agricultural co-ops under the antitrust laws of the United States has had an impact on their organization and operation.

### A. THE SHERMAN ACT

The Congress passed the Sherman Act of 1890 as a federal response to the shortcomings of the common law approach to regulating trade restrictions. Although the Act used certain common law terminology such as "restraint of trade" and "conspiracy", it was not meant simply to incorporate the existing common law into federal law. The Congress viewed the Sherman Act as a new body of law, largely free of common law origins. The Sherman Act gave federal courts the jurisdiction to develop a "new common law" of competitive behavior by elaborating and refining the meaning of "old common law" terms. This "new common law" became a uniform, national law, superseding the numerous state rules then in effect.

The Sherman Act went far beyond the common law by establishing absolute prohibitions on certain conduct (punishable as crimes), invoking the equity power of federal courts to restrain violations, and providing for effective private damages actions. Section 1 of the Sherman Act makes unlawful (and criminal) "every contract, combination ... or conspiracy in restraint of trade" in interstate or foreign commerce. Section 2 prohibits monopolizing, attempts to monopolize, and combinations or conspiracies to monopolize any part of interstate or foreign commerce. Early amendments designed to exempt arrangements, agreements, or combinations among persons engaged in horticulture or agriculture made with the view of enhancing the price of agricultural or horticultural products failed to pass. As a result, in 1908, the United States Supreme Court interpreted the Sherman Act to include agricultural and labor organizations since Congress had failed to specifically exempt them from coverage under the Act. *Loewe v. Lawlor,* 208 U.S. 274 (1908). In 1911, the Sixth Circuit Court of Appeals determined that a combination of farmers was prohibited by the Sherman Act. *Steers v. United States,* 192 Fed. 1 (6th Cir. 1911). An association of tobacco farmers had "pooled" tobacco and withheld it from the market in an effort to bring about higher prices. Certain nonmembers of the association attempted to ship their tobacco to market, but were prevented by other farmers. The Court of Appeals determined this action to be illegal under the Sherman Act as a "direct and absolute restraint [upon interstate commerce], bearing no reasonable relation to lawful means of accomplishing lawful ends."

The courts interpreted the Sherman Act to mean that more serious anti-competitive practices, such as price fixing and agreements not to compete were unlawful per se. With the so-called per se offenses, reasonableness is not a factor.

While the Congress recognized the unique problems of farmers in connection with obtaining adequate prices for agricultural products and provided in several appropriations bills that no part of the funds appropriated for enforcement of the Sherman Act could be used for prosecution of agricultural co-ops, prosecution of co-ops in state courts as violations of state antitrust laws continued. As state legislatures attempted to exempt agricultural co-ops from antitrust statutes, many early state laws granting co-ops exemptions from antitrust laws were held unconstitutional.

## B.   THE CLAYTON ACT

The Clayton Act was enacted in 1914. Section 3 prohibits sales on the condition that the buyer not deal with competitors of the seller ("tie-in" sales, exclusive dealing arrangements, and requirements contracts) where the effect "may be substantially to lessen competition or tend to create a monopoly" in any line of commerce. Section 4 of the Act allows private parties injured by violations of the Sherman and Clayton Acts to sue for three times the amount of damages. Congress also clarified the status of agricultural co-ops and labor unions under the antitrust laws, with Section 6 of the Clayton Act basically exempting labor unions and agricultural organizations from the Sherman and Clayton Acts. Section 6 of the Clayton Act declares that the antitrust laws do not forbid the "existence and operation" of agricultural co-ops that did not have capital stock and were not operated for profit. This section further provides that the antitrust laws were not to be construed so as "to forbid or restrain individual members of such organizations from lawfully carrying out the legitimate objects" of the co-ops. Co-ops and their members were not to "be held or construed to be illegal combinations or conspiracies in restraint of trade." To come within the protection of Section 6, the farmer co-op had to be formed "for purposes of mutual help; the co-op could not have capital stock and the co-op could not be operated for profit." Section 6 refers only to co-ops not having capital stock. Thus, associations of producers having capital stock did not come within the antitrust exemption contained in Section 6, and the status of agricultural co-ops under the federal antitrust laws remained unclear.

## C.   THE CAPPER-VOLSTEAD ACT

The Capper-Volstead Act was enacted in 1922 with the purpose of remedying two problems encountered under Section 6 of the Clayton Act. While Section 6 of the Clayton Act provided a basic exemption for agricultural organizations from application of the Sherman and Clayton Acts, it limited the exemption to organizations that did not have capital stock and, furthermore, Section 6 did not specifically sanction certain co-op marketing activities.

The Capper-Volstead Act provides that "persons engaged in the production of agricultural products as farmers, planters, ranchmen, dairymen, nut or fruit growers, may act together in associations, corporate or otherwise, with or without capital stock, in collectively processing, preparing for market, handling, and marketing in interstate and foreign commerce, such products of persons so engaged." *7 U.S.C. § 291 (2008).* As such, the Act extended the Section 6 Clayton exemption to capital stock agricultural co-ops comprised of agricultural producers. These co-ops can have marketing agencies in common and their members can make the necessary contracts and agreements to effect such purposes. However, agricultural co-ops must be operated for the mutual benefit of the members and no member of the association can be permitted more than one vote because of the amount of stock or membership capital owned, or the co-op cannot pay dividends on stock or membership capital in excess of 8 percent per year. Most co-ops comply with both requirements as a matter of practice or because their state statute requires both. In addition, the co-op is prohibited from dealing in the products of nonmembers to an amount greater in value than are handled by it for members. Without these special provisions, agricultural marketing co-ops probably could not exist. The member farmers likely would be engaged in prohibited price fixing.

The grant of immunity from antitrust charges is further limited by Section 2 which empowers the Secretary of Agriculture to issue cease-and-desist orders when an organization exempt from antitrust restrictions is found to be monopolizing or restraining trade, to the extent that the price of any agricultural product is unduly enhanced. While this does not give the Secretary of Agriculture primary or exclusive jurisdiction over such organizations, they can still be sued under the antitrust laws for exceeding the exemption granted.

An agricultural co-op must satisfy two requirements in order to be shielded by the Capper-Volstead Act from antitrust liability. First, the organization must be involved in the "processing, preparing for market, handling, or marketing "of the agricultural products of its members. Thus, the exemption has been held not to apply to the activities of firms or persons operating packing houses. *Case-Swayne Co. v. Sunkist Growers, Inc.,* 389 U.S. 384 (1967), *reh'g denied,* 390 U.S. 930 (1968). Second, the organization claiming to be immunized from liability must be composed of "members" that are "producers of agricultural products" or cooperatives composed of such producers. As such, the exemption does not cover the activities of an association consisting in part of persons engaged in "production" and in part of persons not so engaged. *In re Mushroom Direct Purchaser Antitrust Litigation,* 621 F. Supp. 2d 274 (E.D. Pa. 2009). See also *National Broiler Marketing Association v. United States,* 436 U.S. 816 (1978); *In re Fresh and Process Potatoes Antitrust Litigation,* 834 F. Supp. 2d 1141 (D. Idaho Dec.2011).

Even if the Capper-Volstead Act Section 1 exemption applies and a particular co-op qualifies for the exemption, the exemption does not legalize activities which are coercive, such as boycotts aimed at forcing nonmembers to join the co-op. While co-op price fixing has been held to be permissible under the Capper-Volstead Act Section 1 exemption, a boycott to force nonmembers to adhere to prices established by the co-op has been held to not be within the scope of the exemption.

Permissible activities allowed by Capper-Volstead include agricultural producers acting together in associations to collectively process, prepare for market, handle and market products. Producers in one association can agree on marketing practices with producers of another association by informal means, by use of a common marketing agent, or through a federation. Capper-Volstead co-ops are not totally exempt from the scope of the antitrust laws. A Capper-Volstead co-op may lose its limited antitrust exemption if it conspires or combines with persons who are not producers of agricultural products. For example, a dairy co-op combined with labor officials, municipal officers and other non-producers to seek control of the supply of fluid milk in the Chicago area by paying to producers artificially high noncompetitive prices. Any immunity that the dairy co-op might have had under Section 6 of the Clayton Act or under Section 1 of the Capper-Volstead Act was lost. *United States v. Borden Co.,* 308 U.S. 188 (1939).

Similarly, Section 2 of Capper-Volstead does not protect co-ops that unduly enhance prices of agricultural products. That is particularly the case if price enhancement is the result of production limitations. As noted above, the Capper-Volstead Act allows agricultural producers to act together to process, prepare for market, handle and market an agricultural product after it has been planted and harvested. Thus, by it terms, the Capper Volstead Act does not apply to production limitations, acreage limitations or collusive crop planning.

While the Secretary of Agriculture can enforce Section 2 by investigating complaints of undue price enhancement, there has not yet been a case where the evidence has been deemed sufficient to warrant a hearing. The U.S. Department of Justice, the Federal Trade Commission, and private parties may bring actions against a co-op when the alleged conduct is not protected by Capper-Volstead or in the first instance when the co-op failed to meet the Capper-Volstead organizational requirements.

## D.  OTHER LAWS GRANTING LIMITED IMMUNITY TO AGRICULTURAL CO-OPS

### 1.  The Cooperative Marketing Act

The Cooperative Marketing Act of 1926 permits agricultural producers and their associations to legally acquire and exchange past, present and prospective data concerning pricing, production and marketing. This information may also be exchanged through "federations" of co-ops and by or through a common agent "created or selected" by the producers, co-op, or federation.

### 2.  The Robinson-Patman Act

In general, the Robinson-Patman Act prohibits sellers from charging different prices for commodities of "like grade and quality" if the effect of the discrimination "may be substantially to lessen competition or tend to create a monopoly". However, price discrimination is lawful if the price differential is justified by savings in the cost of manufacture, sale or delivery resulting from the differing methods or qualities in which such commodities are sold or delivered to such purchasers or the price difference is the result of changed market conditions. It also provides that co-op patronage refunds will not be characterized as illegal rebates with respect to sellers of products.

### 3.  The Agricultural Marketing Agreement Act

Under the Agricultural Marketing Agreement Act of 1937 (AMAA), the Secretary of Agriculture

(Secretary) is authorized "to enter into marketing agreements with processors, producers, associations of producers, and others engaged in the handling of any agricultural commodity or product thereof in interstate or foreign commerce or which "directly burdens, obstructs, or affects" such commerce. *7 U.S.C. § 608b (2008).* A marketing agreement is a formal, but voluntary agreement between the Secretary and handlers of a particular agricultural commodity. The purpose of a marketing agreement and order is "to establish and maintain such orderly marketing conditions for agricultural commodities in interstate commerce as will establish" reasonable prices which farmers receive for their agricultural commodities. Marketing agreements affect the quality, size and quantity of an agricultural commodity shipped to markets and are essentially self-help mechanisms to advance the economic interests of the industry. Marketing agreements exist for a wide variety of agricultural crops including raisins grown in California, avocados grown in Florida, and papayas grown in Hawaii. The AMAA provides that "[t]he making of any such agreement shall not held to be a violation of any of the antitrust laws of the United States, and any such agreement shall be deemed to be lawful."

## 4. The Agricultural Fair Practices Act

The Agricultural Fair Practices Act (AFPA) makes it unlawful for either a processor or a producers' association to engage in practices that interfere with a producer's freedom to choose whether to bring products to market individually or to sell them through a producers' coop. The AFPA does not prohibit other discriminatory practices by handlers, nor does it require them to deal with or bargain in good faith with a co-op. The AFPA preempts certain provisions of state agricultural marketing and bargaining laws.

# CHAPTER 7
# CIVIL LIABILITIES

## I. OVERVIEW

Tort law is concerned with substandard behavior, and its objective is to establish the nature and extent of responsibility for the consequences of tortious (wrongful) conduct. Tort law is divided into three general areas on the basis of the type of activity that produced the particular problem. An intentional tort is the intentional action that results in injury to another person or their property leading to recovery. A privileged tort is a tort that is justified by particular circumstances and is associated with a defense that negates liability. In other words, even if all of the facts necessary to a successful case can be proved, there are additional facts present sufficient to establish a privilege to commit the tort. A tort may also be committed negligently. Negligence is a fault system designed to provide a measure of compensation and to serve as a deterrent.

These cases, in an agricultural context, may involve such situations as employer/employee relationships, fence and boundary disputes, crop dusting and many other similar situations.

## II. INTENTIONAL TORTS

By its very nature, an intentional tort implies that the person committing the tort intended his or her action to injure another person or damage their property, or expected that result. Intent, however, is broader than a desire or purpose to bring about physical results. It extends not only to those consequences which are desired, but also to those which the actor believes are substantially certain to follow from what the actor does. For instance, a person who fires a bullet from a gun into a neighbor's home may fervently pray that the bullet will hit no one, but if the person knows there is a substantial certainty that firing a gun into a house may result in harm, the person will be deemed to have intended that consequence. However, mere knowledge and appreciation of a risk short of substantial certainty does not constitute intent. A person who acts with the belief or consciousness that the act will cause an appreciable risk of harm to another person may be negligent, and if the risk is great, the conduct may be characterized as reckless or wanton, but it is not an intentional wrong. Consequently, the distinction between intent and negligence is a matter of degree, and it is up to the jury to weigh the facts to determine whether the defendant intended or could have reasonably expected the resulting harm. Historically, the courts have drawn the line at the point where the known danger ceases to be only a foreseeable risk which a reasonable person would avoid, and becomes in the mind of the actor a substantial certainty.

The intent that tort liability is concerned with is not necessarily a hostile intent or a desire to do any harm. Rather, it is an intent to bring about a result which will invade the interests of another in a way that the law forbids, either by statute or by case law. Consequently, a person may be held liable for any resulting injury or damage although intending nothing more than a good-natured practical joke, or honestly believing that the act would not injure the plaintiff, or acting under the belief that it is for the plaintiff's own good.

## A. INTENTIONAL INTERFERENCE WITH A PERSON

### 1. Assault

An assault is an act, neither consented to nor privileged, that places another person in apprehension or fear of harmful or offensive contact. An assault can be committed without any physical contact. For instance, it may be an assault to shake a fist under another person's nose, to aim or strike at another with a weapon, or to hold the weapon in a threatening position, to rise or advance to strike another person, to surround another person with a display of force, to chase another in a hostile manner, or to do anything that puts another person in fear or apprehension of such person's continued well-being.

Usually, an assault is a tort that constitutes a breach of civil law. However, an assault can be both a civil and criminal wrong in certain situations. For instance, placing a person in apprehension or fear of harmful or offensive contact is an assault, but carrying through with that threat and actually causing physical injury might constitute a crime. The distinction between a civil wrong and a criminal wrong is that a criminal wrong is a breach against the state to which the state is a party. A civil wrong simply involves two persons or more, and the only involvement of the state is to establish rules for resolving the matter between the parties. Tort law is not concerned about the criminal aspect of a particular action.

To recover on an assault claim, the plaintiff need not prove actual damages. The damage award is limited only by what the judge will allow or the jury will return, is not limited to fixed or actual damages, and punitive damages may apply. However, the size of a damage award does depend upon the facts. Sometimes a judge and jury will determine that there was an assault, but reward only a nominal amount if they believe the damages were insignificant. Conversely, courts have awarded a large amount of damages in cases where the judge or jury determined that the plaintiff suffered great psychological trauma by being placed in fear or apprehension of personal harm.

## 2. Battery

A battery is an act that, either directly or indirectly, is the legal cause of an offensive touching of another person that is neither consented to nor privileged. Sometimes a battery is referred to as a completed assault. However, an assault need not precede a battery, and an assault can be committed without a battery.

While the recovery in these cases is often limited to actual damages, actual damages are extremely difficult to prove and the reward is whatever the judge will allow or the jury will return.

## 3. False Imprisonment

False imprisonment is the confinement of another person within fixed boundaries (such as a grain bin or bank vault), no matter how short the duration, provided the confinement was neither consented to nor privileged and the person was conscious of the confinement. False imprisonment is an intentional tort and can include actual, nominal, or punitive damages depending on the facts proven.

## B.   INTENTIONAL INTERFERENCE WITH REAL PROPERTY

## 1. Trespass

Trespass is the unlawful or unauthorized entry upon another person's land that interferes with that person's exclusive possession or ownership of the land. The tort of trespass is conceptually related to the tort of nuisance except that a nuisance is an invasion of an individual's interest in use and enjoyment of land rather than an interference with the exclusive possession or ownership of the land.

The law governing trespass to land is particularly important to farmers and ranchers because real estate plays a significant role in the economic life of the typical farmer or rancher.

A trespass consists of two basic elements: (1) intent and (2) force. Most jurisdictions do not impose absolute liability for trespass. Instead, proof of intentional invasion, reckless or negligent conduct, or inherently or abnormally dangerous activity is required. In these jurisdictions, proof of intent to commit a trespass is not necessary. Rather, the plaintiff must show that the trespasser either intended the act that resulted in the unlawful invasion or acted so negligently or in such a dangerous manner that willfulness can be assumed as a matter of law. A minority of jurisdictions still follow the common law approach holding an individual liable for any interference with the possession of land, even if that interference was completely unintentional. In these jurisdictions, it is immaterial whether the act was done accidently, in good faith, or by mistake.

Trespass also involves an element of force. Liability for trespass may result from any willful act, whether the intrusion is the immediate or inevitable consequence of a willful act or of an act that amounts to willfulness.

At its most basic level, a trespass is the intrusion on to another person's land without the owner's consent. However, many other types of physical invasions that cause injury to an owner's possessory rights abound in agriculture. These types of trespass include dynamite blasting, flooding with water or residue from oil and gas drilling operations, erection of an encroaching fence, unauthorized grazing of cattle, or raising of crops and cutting timber on another's land without authorization, among other things. In general, the privilege of an owner or possessor of land to utilize the land and exploit its potential natural resources is only a qualified privilege. The owner or possessor must exercise reasonable care in conducting operations on the land so as to avoid injury to the possessory rights of neighboring landowners. *See, e.g. Faulk v. Gold Kist, Inc.,* 599 So. 2d 23 (Ala. 1992); *Ream v. Keen* 112 Or. App. 197, 828 P.2d 1038 (1992).

A trespass claim could also arise if a farmer plants genetically modified crops with knowledge that the genetic traits from the crops would likely enter a neighbor's property, and genetic drift does in fact occur, causing harm to the neighbor's crop. Thus, if damage can be proven due to the intentional invasion of a GMO trait through pollen or other means onto another person's land, a trespass to land claim would exist. But, the plaintiff would have to show that particulate matter invaded the property, as opposed to something in the seed or a failure to clean equipment. Presently, there has not been a case of pollen drift involving GMO crops litigated to an appellate-level court on a trespass claim. However, cases involving comparable situations have been litigated. *See, e.g., Martin v. Reynolds Metal*, 342 P.2d 790 (Or. 1959); *Hall v. Deweld Mica Corp.*, 93 S.E.2d 56 (N.C. 1956); *Stevenson, et. al. v. E.I. Dupont de Nemours & Co.,* 327 F.3d 400 (5th Cir. 2003); *In re Tennessee Valley Authority Ash Spill Litigation,* 2012 U.S. Dist. LEXIS 122231 (E.D. Tenn. Aug. 23, 2012); *Johnson, et al. v. Paynesville Farmers Union Cooperative Oil Co.,* 817 N.W.2d 693 (Minn. 2012).

> **Caution:** In recent years, numerous anti-pesticide organizations have been established. Some of these organizations hold training sessions to provide equipment and teach rural residents and small

organic growers how to monitor and test for any pesticide levels on their property. As more individuals regularly monitor for trespass about which there may have been no previous knowledge or effects, courts are likely to see more of these types of cases being brought even in the absence of compensable damages or injury.

Historically, the courts viewed a person's ownership of land as extending directly above and below the property surface, and interference with that possession was actionable. Today, courts limit the notion of absolute ownership above the land's surface. A temporary invasion of a landowner's air space by aircraft is privileged if it does not unreasonably interfere with the possessor's enjoyment of the real estate. However, most courts recognize as actionable unlawful invasions of the subsurface. A mineral estate in land, like a surface estate, is real property. The oil and gas beneath the soil are considered a part of the overlying real estate. Each landowner who owns the subsurface interest separately, distinctly and exclusively owns all of the oil and gas under the land and is provided the usual remedies against trespassers who remove the minerals or destroy their market value.

## C.   INTENTIONAL INTERFERENCE WITH PERSONAL PROPERTY

### 1.  Trespass to Chattels

A trespass need not necessarily involve real estate, but may also involve personalty. The tort of trespass to chattels is defined as an intentional and unjustified interference with the possession of another person's chattel. The essence of an action for trespass to chattels is injury to possession, and actual physical force is not required. Instead, any unlawful use of, or interference with, the possession of another person's chattel, no matter how slight, constitutes an actionable trespass. The measure of damages is the actual diminution in the value of personal property caused by the interference.

## D.   INTENTIONAL DISPARAGEMENT OF FOOD PRODUCTS

The common law has long recognized a cause of action for tortious interference with business relations. *See, e.g., Tuttle v. Buck*, 107 Minn. 145, 119 N.W. 946 (1909).

Since 1991, a number of states have enacted legislation designed to protect perishable agricultural food products from false and malicious statements. The belief is that perishability makes the market value of food products especially vulnerable to false statements, and that the traditional common law product disparagement cause of action did not adequately address this vulnerability. Presently, thirteen states have enacted food disparagement statutes with several more states considering similar legislation. While no two state statutes are precisely identical, the food disparagement legislation exhibits similar provisions. Prominent statutes exist in Texas, Florida, Arizona and South Dakota.

The major issue concerning the food disparagement statutes is whether such legislation is unconstitutional as an abridgement of the First Amendment's protection of the freedom of speech. The common law action for tortious interference with business relations generally requires the plaintiff to prove that (1) the statement was communicated or published to a third person; (2) the statement played a material and substantial part in inducing others not to deal with the plaintiff; (3) the statement was false; and (4) the defendant acted with wrongful intent or malice. Some courts require the plaintiff to establish that the publication of the statement would cause harm, that the harm was intended or that the defendant knew the statement was false but published the statement in reckless disregard of its truth or falsity.

Courts deciding cases involving food disparagement statutes will most likely require plaintiffs to prove a statement's falsity. Arguably, state statutes that do not require a plaintiff to prove a statement's falsity are unconstitutional.

## III.   PRIVILEGED INVASION

### A.   SELF-DEFENSE

The extent of the self-defense privilege depends upon where it is exercised. An individual attacked in the home is entitled to use such force in self-defense as includes taking a life, if necessary, and need not retreat from the attacker. There is no duty to flee the home or otherwise retreat from the attacker. Any force that is reasonable and necessary under the circumstances is permissible. If the attack occurs away from the home, however, an attempt must be made to "retreat to the wall" before bodily injury can be inflicted or a life can be taken.

Outside of the home, if, under the circumstances, a "reasonable person" would believe that it is not reasonable to retreat, there is no duty to retreat. However, if an escape is possible, it must be attempted before a person is privileged to stand their ground and use such force as could lead to great bodily injury or death. In all cases, the jury determines the reasonableness of the belief after the fact.

## B.   DEFENSE OF PROPERTY

Agricultural property tends to be frequently exposed to those who might want to steal, damage or destroy. In general, to protect property from such things as vandalism and theft, the owner of the premises normally has a right to use such force (except for the taking of life or infliction of great bodily injury) as is reasonably necessary to protect the property. An individual is not privileged to use force in defending property in excess of that reasonably believed to be necessary and cannot use such force as is likely to lead to great bodily injury or death. *See, e.g., Katko v. Briney,* 183 N.W.2d 657 (Iowa 1971).

Occasionally, farmers and ranchers are required to defend their livestock from harm caused by trespassing dogs. Many states have adopted statutes that permit dogs to be killed if they are caught in the act of worrying, chasing, maiming or damaging domestic animals. It is critical to follow the specifics of the applicable state statute allowing the killing of trespassing dogs. *See, e.g., Grabenstein v. Sunsted,* 237 Mont. 254, 772 P.2d 865 (1998) Failure to do so can result in a criminal charge of cruelty to animals. *See, e.g., State v. Walter,* 266 Mont. 429, 880 P.2d 1346 (1994). In any event, the evidence must be sufficient to show that the dogs were engaged in the statutorily-enumerated conduct that authorized their killing.

Most state "dog-kill" statutes are only designed to protect livestock-type animals. Typically, they provide no protection for dogs shot in the act of harming wildlife, domestic pets, or even other family members.

## C.   ARREST

A private citizen who is not a peace officer may make a "citizen's arrest," but the right to make an arrest is very limited and it is usually unwise to exercise the right. It is generally preferable to call the sheriff, highway patrol or city police and have them make the arrest. Law enforcement officers have greater protection against a charge of unlawful arrest than private citizens.

Under the law of many states, a private citizen may make a citizen's arrest if a crime has been committed or attempted in their presence.

Most states have statutes providing that a citizen's arrest may be made if a felony has been committed *and* the person making the arrest has reasonable grounds for believing the person to be arrested has committed the act. There can be no question of reasonableness as to whether the crime was a felony. Peace officers generally have double reasonableness both as to whether a felony was committed and whether the person arrested committed the crime. For lesser crimes, even peace officers do not have double reasonableness.

### D.   RECLAIMING PROPERTY AND PRIVILEGED NECESSITY

While an individual usually does not have the right to enter another individual's property without permission, a person is generally privileged to enter another person's land to reclaim personal property put there without the personal property owner's tortious conduct or negligence. However, even with the privilege, the person is liable for any damages caused to the other person's property in the recovery process.

Sometimes because of the immediacy of the need to act, persons must enter the land of another without permission to prevent harm to other persons, property or things. This is considered a privileged necessity under the Restatement (Second) of Torts §§ 197 and 345 approach that some states have adopted. In these states, for example, if a person enters a landowner's property without permission but with the intent and purpose of preventing harm to the landowner's person, land or property, the entry is not a trespass but is a privileged entry. If the entrant is injured during such an entry, principles of reasonable care and comparative fault apply. *See, e.g., Wrinkle v. Norman,* 301 P.3d 312 (Kan. 2013). States that have not adopted the Restatement approach may still view the entry in such situations as a trespass.

## IV. LIABILITY TO PERSONS ENTERING ONE'S PROPERTY

### A. IN GENERAL

The liability of landowners or possessors of real property for injuries suffered by others while on the premises has traditionally depended upon the benefit that the entrant bestowed upon the owner or possessor. Traditionally, the law created a hierarchy of status. Under the historical approach, the adult trespasser is given the lowest status and the invitee and child trespasser the highest status. Mid-level status is given to social guests and licensees. Liability for injury to entrants is determined on the basis of the duty owed to the entrant in accordance with the entrant's status. A high duty of care is owed to invitees and child trespassers, while a relatively low duty of care is owed to an adult trespasser.

Since the mid-1960s, some states have shifted toward a general duty of care and away from a classification of status. While many jurisdictions still adhere to the traditional hierarchical approach, there is a significant amount of variability in the judicial opinions on the matter.

## B.   TRESPASSER

The adult trespasser is owed the lowest duty of care. A trespasser is a person who is on the premises without permission and who does not confer a benefit on the landowner or occupier. The hunter without permission is an example of a trespasser. Trespassers take the premises as they are. Landowners must refrain from willfully or wantonly injuring trespassers. However, once a landowner or occupier discovers a trespasser, the trespasser must be warned of any dangers, including hidden dangers, which exist on the land. Similar to the known trespasser rule, a minority of states utilize an exception to the rule of no liability to adult trespassers when the facts indicate that harm to trespassers should reasonably be anticipated by the landowner (or possessor) due to the maintenance of a potentially dangerous artificial condition. The exception applies if the owner or possessor knew or should have known of constant trespassing where the dangerous condition exists, that the condition was likely to cause serious harm to a trespasser, and that the trespasser would not likely discover the hazard. If those conditions are met, the owner or possessor must use reasonable care to warn trespassers of the condition.

## C.   CHILD TRESPASSER

Child trespassers are entitled to greater protection than adult trespassers. By nature, children lack mature judgment and generally cannot appreciate dangers that are inherent on the land on which they are trespassing. Thus, landowners must take extra precaution to prevent injuries that might arise from "attractive nuisances." Under the "attractive nuisance doctrine," if a landowner has a reasonable expectation that children will be attracted to the premises by a dangerous artificial condition on the land that the landowner could reasonably have expected would cause an unreasonable risk of serious bodily injury to children and the child trespasser was not mature enough to appreciate the danger of the artificial condition, trespassing children are elevated in status to that of a "licensee" or "invitee."

The attractive nuisance doctrine has a potentially wide application in agriculture. It is not unusual for many items of farm machinery to remain in the open rather than in an enclosed structure. These items are usually quite tempting to children to play in, on or around. *See, e.g., McGaughey v. Haines,* 189 Kan. 453 370 P.2d 120 (1962).

The attractive nuisance doctrine applies to children who are unable to appreciate the risk involved with dangerous artificial conditions on another person's land. As such, the doctrine may be found to apply to a teenager and not a small child or vice versa. The key is whether the particular child at issue was capable of understanding the inherent dangers involved. *See, e.g., Griffin v. Woodward,* 486 S.E.2d 240 (N.C. App. 1997).

Perhaps the greatest potential application of the attractive nuisance doctrine to farmers and ranchers concerns bodies of water. Undoubtedly, farm ponds attract children. Most of the courts that have considered the question have indicated that bodies of water are not attractive nuisances and that child trespassers will be treated the same as adult trespassers in terms of the duty that the owner or occupier of the real estate owes to them.

The attractive nuisance doctrine only applies to artificial conditions of the land. The doctrine does not apply to natural bodies of water. But, the "natural bodies of water" exception does not apply when the child is an "invitee." *See, e.g., Degel v. Majestic Mobile Manor, Inc.*, 129 Wash. 2d 43, 914 P.2d 728 (1996). Most of the courts that have considered the issue indicate that the remoteness of farm ponds is the key factor. For farm ponds located in remote areas, most courts hold that it would be an unfair burden on property owners and occupiers to have to shoulder liability for injury to child trespassers. For example, it may be prohibitively costly to maintain fences to keep young children out or adopt other safety measures. However, items associated with a remote farm pond may be an attractive nuisance

While the modern trend is that a pond or other body of water is likely not to be considered an attractive nuisance, the same reasoning does not necessarily apply to swimming pools. However, most of the litigated swimming pool cases have occurred in densely populated urban areas where there is a greater probability of trespassing children and may not be as costly to keep unwanted children away from the premises.

The reach of the attractive nuisance doctrine is demonstrated by the types of situations in which courts have held the doctrine is or could be applicable. *See, e.g., Louisville Trust Co. v. Nutting,* 437 S.W.2d 484 (Ken. Ct. App. 1996); *Harrison v. City of Chicago,* 308 Ill. App. 263, 31 N.E. 2d 359 (1941); *Novicki v. Blaw-Knox Co.,* 304 F.2d 931 (3rd Cir. 1962); *Menneti v. Evans Construction Co.,* 259 F.2d 367 (3rd Cir. 1952).

Conversely, in some cases the plaintiffs have been unable to recover under the attractive nuisance doctrine. *See, e.g., Franich v. Great Northern Railroad Co.,* 260 F.2d 599 (9th Cir. 1958); *Louche v. Silvestri,* 149 Conn. 373, 179 A.2d 835 (1962); *Hughes v. Star Homes Inc.,* 379 So. 2d 301 (Miss. 1980).

The scope of the attractive nuisance doctrine is restricted by the "allurement limitation" with the doctrine not applying if the child is already a trespasser on the defendant's land before noticing the object on the land which resulted in harm. *See, e.g., United Zinc & Chemical Co. v. Brit,* 258 U.S. 268 (1922).

## D.   LICENSEE

The licensee is afforded slightly higher status than that of a trespasser. A licensee is anyone on the premises with permission or acquiescence, but who does not bestow a benefit on the landowner or occupier. Perhaps the most common example of a licensee is the hunter with permission who does not pay a fee. While a landowner or occupier is not obligated to make the premises safe for a licensee, due care must be exercised to avoid injury to the licensee. In addition, a licensee is entitled to a warning of hidden dangers and hazards that the landowner or occupier knows about and the licensee cannot reasonably be expected to discover. For instance, a landowner or occupier cannot fail to warn of hidden dangers and deliberately direct a licensee to come into contact with those unexpected dangers without liability. Other than the duty of the landowner or occupier to notify of hidden dangers, the licensee takes the premises as it exists.

## E.   SOCIAL GUEST

The social guest enjoys slightly higher status than that of a licensee. A social guest is on the premises without conferring an economic benefit, but does confer a social benefit. A social guest might be able to recover from a fall on a highly-waxed floor, a faulty step or a poorly lighted stairway. If it can be established that the premises were carelessly maintained, a social guest is likely to recover.

## F.   INVITEE

A landowner or occupier owes the highest duty of care to an invitee. An invitee is a person on the premises for business purposes or for mutual advantage rather than solely for the benefit of the person entering the property. An invitee is a business guest such as a cattle buyer, milk truck driver, veterinarian or employee. Door-to-door salesmen can be classified as invitees once they have been greeted and asked inside.

The duty of care owed to a public official who enters another person's premises to discharge their duties can vary depending on the jurisdiction. Such persons do not neatly fit in either the licensee or invitee category. Some jurisdictions apply a "no-duty" rule, often referred to as the "firefighter's rule," that bars public officials from any recovery for injuries sustained in carrying out their public duties. However, recovery is available even in these jurisdictions where the injury does not result from a risk that is related to the public official's performance of his or her duties on the premises.

In general, a landowner or occupier, while not an insurer of an invitee's safety, owes an invitee a duty to make and keep the premises safe and to warn of existing dangers. Thus, the owner/occupier has a general duty to search out dangers and maintain a level of surveillance for risks that can befall a person who is on the premises as a business guest or invitee. *See, e.g., Baumler v. Hemesath,* 534 N.W.2d 650 (Iowa 1995), a farm employee sued the employer successfully for failure to provide a safe working area and to warn of danger. However, a landowner need not take action to routinely inspect undeveloped land that is used for agricultural purposes. *See, e.g., Bradshaw v. Smith, et al.,* No. 113,922, 2016 Kan. App. Unpub. LEXIS 686 (Kan. Ct. App. Aug. 19, 2016).

## G.    MODERN APPROACH TO TORT LIABILITY OF LANDOWNERS AND OCCUPIERS

Presently, a minority of states apply the rule that the owner or occupier owes a duty of "reasonable care under all of the circumstances" to all entrants. The cases are decided on a case-by-case basis with several factors considered such as the foreseeability of harm to the entrant, the magnitude of the risk of injury, the individual and social benefit of maintaining the condition, and the burden to the landowner or occupier in providing adequate protection. Another minority of jurisdictions retain the common law duty with respect to trespassers and all other unlawful entrants, but utilize a standard of reasonable care for all lawful entrants.

## 1. Liability for Injuries on Leased Premises

In general, a landlord is not liable for injuries to third parties that occur on premises that are occupied by a tenant. The reason for the rule is that the tenant has the possession over the leasehold premises during the tenancy and has control over what occurs on the leased property. However, there are at least six well recognized exceptions to this general rule. For example, if the landlord conceals dangerous conditions or defects that cause the third party's injury, then the landlord will be liable. Likewise, if conditions are maintained on the premises that are dangerous to persons outside of the premises, the landlord is liable for any resulting injury. A landlord will also be liable if the premises is leased for admission of the public or if the landlord retains control over part of the leased premises that the tenant is entitled to use. In addition, if the landlord makes an express covenant to repair the leased premises, but fails to do so resulting in injury, the landlord is liable. Similarly, a landlord is liable for injuries resulting from the landlord's negligence in making repairs to items located on the leased premises.

In general, a licensee or invitee of the tenant has no greater claim against the landlord than has the tenant. Thus, a landlord's duty to not wantonly or willfully injure a trespasser is usually passed to the tenant who has control of the property. However, a landlord can be held liable where the landlord knew of defects that were likely to injure known trespassers.

A landlord is usually not held responsible for injuries occurring on the leased premises caused by animals that belong to the tenant. Generally, it must be proven that the landlord had actual knowledge of the animal's dangerous propensities. *See, e.g., Bryant v. Putnam,* 908 S.W.2d 338 (Ark. 1995).

Another exception to the general rule of landlord non-liability for a tenant's acts is if the landlord knows that the tenant is harming the property rights of adjacent landowners and does nothing to modify the tenant's conduct or terminate the lease. In that situation, the landlord can be held liable along with the tenant. *See, e.g., Tetzlaff v. Camp, et al.,* 715 N.W.2d 256 (Iowa 2006).

## 2.  Recreational Use of Land

Recognizing the potential liability of owners and occupiers of real estate for injuries that occur to others using their land under the common law rules, the Council of State Governments in 1965 proposed the adoption of a Model Act to limit an owner or occupier's liability for injury occurring on the owner's property. The stated purpose of the Model Act was to encourage owners to make land and water areas available to the public for recreational purposes by limiting their liability toward persons who enter the property for such purposes. Liability protection was extended to holders of a fee ownership interest, tenants, lessees, occupants, and persons in control of the premises. Land which receives the benefit of the act include roads, waters, water courses, private ways and buildings, structures and machinery or equipment when attached to the realty. Recreational activities within the purview of the act include hunting, fishing, swimming, boating, camping, picnicking, hiking, pleasure driving, nature study, water skiing, water sports, and viewing or enjoying historical, archeological, scenic or scientific sites. Most states have enacted some version of the 1965 Model legislation.

An owner or occupier owes no duty of care to keep the premises safe for entry or use by others for recreational purposes, or to give any warning of dangerous conditions, uses, structures, or activities to persons entering the premises for such recreational purposes. Similarly, if an owner, directly or indirectly, invites or permits any person without charge to use the property for recreational purposes, the owner does not extend any assurance the premises are safe for any purpose, confer the status of licensee or invitee on the person using the property, or assume responsibility or incur liability for any injury to persons or property caused by any act or omission of persons who are on the property.

The protection afforded by the Model Act is not absolute, however. Should injury to users of the property be caused by the willful or malicious failure to guard or warn against a dangerous condition, use, structure, or activity, the protection of the act would be lost. Likewise, if the owner imposes a charge on the user of the property, the protection of the act is lost. The 1965 Model Act contained a specific provision that did not exempt anyone from liability for injury in any case where the owner of land charges a fee to the person or persons who enter or go onto the land for recreational purposes. Under most state statutes patterned after the Model Act, if a fee is charged for use of the premises for recreational purposes, it converts the entrant's status to that of an invitee. Some states (such as Wisconsin) establish a monetary limit on what a landowner may receive in a calendar year and still have the liability protection of the statute. The North Dakota statute provides immunity for landowners that invite the public onto their land for recreational rather than commercial purposes, with the distinction between the two classifications largely turning on whether a fee is directly charged. *Woody v. Pembina County Annual Fair and Exhitition Association,* 877 NW.2d 70 (N.D. 2016).

Many fee-based recreational use operations require guests to sign a form releasing the landowner from liability for any injury a guest may sustain while recreating on the premises. To be an effective shield against liability, a release must be drafted carefully and must be clear, unambiguous, explicit and not violate public policy. Courts generally construe release language against the drafter and severely limit the landowner's ability to contract away liability for its own negligence. Likewise, most courts that have considered the question have held that a parent cannot release a minor child's prospective claim for negligence. This has led some state legislatures to consider legislation designed to protect organizations while not allowing wrongdoers to escape liability for intentional or grossly negligent conduct.

Problems may also arise for persons who do not actually charge a fee, but have an expectation that there will be compensation. In general, the policy underlying the consideration exception in recreational use statutes is to retain tort liability where use is granted in return for an economic benefit. Since the potential for profit is thought sufficient to encourage owners who want to make commercial use of their land to open them to the public, the further stimulus of tort immunity is unnecessary and improper. Owners who derive economic benefit are in a position to post warnings, supervise activities and otherwise seek to prevent injuries. Such landowners can purchase liability insurance and spread the cost of accidents over all users of the land. For example, the farmer or rancher who nails a wooden box on a corner fence post and everyone knows that they are free to use the premises for recreational purposes, but they are expected to put something in the box when they leave, may lose the liability protection of the recreational use statute and elevate the status of entrants to that of an invitee or licensee. Most courts that have considered this issue have denied protection of a recreational use statute where there was a definite expectation of economic benefit on the landowner's part.

With increased interest by farm and ranch owners in providing recreational activities to generate additional income, some states have passed ag immunity laws designed to supplement the protection provided by recreational liability acts. In general, the various state statutes provide liability protection for landowners against the injury or death of a participant in a recreational activity arising from the "inherent risks" of the activity.

Recreational use statutes generally do not preclude legal claims based on negligent supervision. For example, in *Dickinson v. Clark*, 767 A.2d 303 (Me. 2001), the plaintiff was engaged in cutting and making firewood on the defendant's property and was injured while loading a wood splitter. The state recreational use statute covered the harvesting or gathering of forest products and would have shielded the defendant from liability for the plaintiff's injuries. As a result, the plaintiff alleged negligent supervision and instruction concerning the use of the wood splitter. The court held that the plaintiff's claim was not precluded by the recreational use statute inasmuch as the statute only precluded claims alleging premises liability, and allowed the case to proceed to trial on the negligent supervision claim.

## 3. Equine Activity Liability Acts

In recent years, nearly all states have enacted Equine Activity Liability Acts designed to encourage the continued existence of equine-related activities, facilities and programs, and provide the equine industry limited protection against lawsuits. *See, e.g. Germer v. Churchill Downs Management,* 201 So. 3d 721 (Fla. Ct. App. 2016). The laws generally require special language in written contracts and liability releases or waivers, require the posting of warning signs and attempt to educate the public about inherent risks in horse-related activities and immunities designed to limit liability. Under the typical statute, an "equine activity sponsor," "equine professional," or other person can only be sued in tort for damages related to the provision of faulty tack, failure to determine the plaintiff's ability to safely manage a horse, or failure to post warning signs concerning dangerous latent conditions.

Recovery for damages resulting from inherent risks associated with horses is barred, and some state statutes require the plaintiff to establish that the defendant's conduct constituted "gross negligence," "willful and wanton misconduct," or "intentional wrongdoing."

### 4. Agritourism Acts

Numerous states have enacted agritourism legislation designed to limit landowner liability to those persons engaging in an "agritourism activity." Typically, such legislation protects the landowner (commonly defined as a "person who is engaged in the business of farming or ranching and provides one or more agritourism activities, whether or not for compensation") from liability for injuries to participants or spectators associated with the inherent risks of a covered activity. The statutes tend to be written very broadly and can apply to such things as corn mazes, hay rides and even hunting and fishing activities. *See, e.g., Shore v. Maple Lane Farms, LLC,* 411 S.W.3d 405 (Tenn. Sup. Ct. 2013); *Forster v. Town of Henniker,* 167 N.H. 745 (2015).

On the liability issue, some state laws (such as the Illinois, Kansas, Maine and Oklahoma provisions) limit liability to situations where the landowner acted wantonly or with willful negligence, and exclude liability for injury arising from the inherent risks associated with an active farming operation. In many of the states that have agritourism statutes, the posting of specific signage is required to get the liability protection and, of course, the person claiming the protection of the statute must meet the definition of a covered person and the activity that gave rise to the liability claim must be a statutorily covered activity. Further, in some states (such as Iowa), liability release forms, at least with respect to minors, may be deemed to violate "public policy" (as decided by judges rather than the public).

Under some provisions, the landowner must post warning signs to receive the protection of the statute, and in some states the landowner must register their property with the state. In any event, it is important for landowners to become familiar with the particulars of state law.

## 5. Natural Conditions

The general rule has been that if a natural object on the premises (such as tree roots obscured by leaves or a hole in the ground) injured another person, the landowner was not liable. There was no duty to remedy a natural hazard. That was particularly the case with respect to rural land. But, over time, some states have modified the common law rule, particularly as applied to trees. *See, e.g., Pesaturo v. Kinne,* 161 N.H. 550, 20 A.3d 284 (2011). In such situations, tree owners owe a duty to ensure that their trees do not cause harm to people on adjacent property or to the adjacent property itself. Thus, instead of the attempting to draw a line between natural and artificial conditions, the modern trend is to decide cases involving damages caused by natural conditions based on general negligence principles.

## V.  NEGLIGENCE

### A.   IN GENERAL

The negligence system is a system designed to provide compensation to those who suffer personal injury or property damage. The negligence system is a fault system. In a few areas, such as automobile insurance (in some states) and workers' compensation, the concept of fault has been rejected, but a pure negligence system requires that fault be established.

For a person to be deemed legally negligent, certain conditions must exist. These conditions can be thought of as links in a chain. Each condition must be present before a finding of negligence can be obtained. The first condition is that of a legal duty giving rise to a standard of care. To be liable for a negligent tort, the defendant's conduct must have fallen below that of a "reasonable and prudent person" under the circumstances. A reasonable and prudent person is what a jury has in mind when they measure an individual's conduct in retrospect—after the fact, when the case is in court. The conduct of a particular tortfeasor (the one causing the tort) who is not held out as a professional is compared with the mythical standard of conduct of the reasonable and prudent person in terms of judgment, knowledge, perception, experience, skill, physical, mental and emotional characteristics as well as age and sanity. For those held out as having the knowledge, skill, experience or education of a professional, the standard of care reflects those factors. For example, the standard applicable to a professional veterinarian in diagnosing or treating animals is what a reasonable and prudent veterinarian would have done under the circumstances, not what a reasonable and prudent *person* would do.

If a legal duty exists, it is necessary to determine whether the defendant's conduct fell short of the conduct of a "reasonable and prudent person (or professional) under the circumstances." This is called a breach, and is the second element of a negligent tort case.

Once a legal duty and breach of that duty are shown to exist, a causal connection (the third element) must be established between the defendant's act and (the fourth element) the plaintiff's injuries (whether to person or property). In other words, the resulting harm to the plaintiff must have been a reasonably foreseeable result of the defendant's conduct at the time the conduct occurred. Reasonable foreseeability is the essence of causality (also known as proximate cause). *See, e.g., Land v. United States,* 35 Fed. Cl. 345 (1996).

Proximate cause can also be an issue (apart from negligence) with respect to coverage for an insured-against loss. *See, e.g., Griess & Sons v. Farm Bureau Insurance Co.,* 247 Neb. 526, 528 N.W.2d 329 (1995).

An individual will be held liable for harm that is reasonably foreseeable or reasonably expected to result from the defendant's actions. There must be a causal connection—a causal linkage—between the defendant's action and the plaintiff's harm. Conversely, a superseding cause is an intervening force that relieves an actor from liability for harm that the actor's negligence was a substantial factor in producing. Thus, negligence that is too remote from the subsequent injury bars liability."

Foreseeability may also be an issue with respect to the plaintiff. *Palsgraf v. Long Island Railroad Co.,* 248 N.Y. 339, 162 N.E. 99 (1928), is an example of an injury which was caused by an unbroken chain of events. However, the court ruled that it was not foreseeable to a reasonable and prudent person that the actions which triggered the chain of events could ultimately cause injury to the plaintiff. For a modern version of *Palsgraf, see Zokhrabov v. Park,* 963 N.E.2d 1035 (Ill. Ct. App. 2011).

It is possible that a negligent tort claim could be brought against a farmer that plants genetically modified crops if the crops cross-pollinate and contaminate a neighbor's conventional crop. For the neighbor to prevail in court, the neighbor would have to prove that the farmer had a duty to prevent contamination, that the duty was breached (e.g., failure to select seed properly, adhere to specified buffer zones, or follow growing and harvesting procedures), and that the breach of the duty caused the neighbor's damages, which were a reasonably foreseeable result of the farmer's conduct. To date, no appellate-level court has rendered an opinion in a negligence tort case involving genetically modified crops.

As noted above, the foreseeability of harm is generally a major factor that is considered in determining the existence of a duty. However, the Restatement (Third) of Torts states that the foreseeability of physical injury to a third party is not to be considered in determining whether there exists a duty to exercise reasonable care. One court has adopted the Restatement approach in holding that a landowner had a duty to exercise reasonable care to keep their premises in a manner that would not create hazards on adjoining roadways. *See, e.g., Thompson v. Kaczinski, et al.,* 774 N.W.2d 829 (Iowa 2009), *vac'g,* 760 N.W.2d 211 (Iowa Ct. App. 2008).

## B. DEFENSES TO NEGLIGENT TORTS

There are three basic defenses to negligent torts. They are: (1) contributory negligence, or comparative negligence, depending upon the rule of law adopted by the particular state; (2) assumption of risk; and (3) acts of nature.

## 1. Contributory Negligence

In some states, the defendant may assert a defense of contributory negligence by the plaintiff as a complete defense and thereby defeat recovery.

Historically, most states allowed contributory negligence as a defense. If the plaintiff was guilty of negligence, no matter how slight, the plaintiff could recover nothing from the defendant. In recent years, many states have viewed this rule as too harsh and have moved toward a system of comparative fault. Presently, the vast majority of states have adopted some form of a comparative fault system. Under a typical comparative fault system, a plaintiff can recover against a defendant if the plaintiff's comparative fault is not greater than the defendant's comparative fault (or the combination of defendants, if more than one). Thus, if the plaintiff's fault exceeds 50%, the plaintiff will not recover at all. However, if the plaintiff's comparative fault is less than 50%, the plaintiff's recovery will be reduced by the percentage of the plaintiff's fault.

There are two types of comparative fault statutes. One type is "pure" comparative fault in which the plaintiff can recover for his loss, so long as some fault is attributed to the defendant(s). The plaintiff's recovery is reduced by the plaintiff's allocation of fault. For instance, if the jury determines that the plaintiff had $1,000 in damages and was 95% at fault for a car accident and the defendant was 5% at fault, the plaintiff will recover $50 (5% of $1,000). The second type of comparative fault statute is a "modified" comparative fault statute. There are two interpretations of this type. In some states, if the plaintiff is at least as much at fault as the defendant, then the plaintiff will not recover any of his damages. So, if the plaintiff in these jurisdictions is more than 49% at fault, he will recover none of his damages. In other jurisdictions, the plaintiff cannot be more at fault than the defendant(s). This means if the plaintiff is 50% at fault or less, he will recover his damages reduced by his amount of fault.

## 2. Assumption of Risk

An assumption of risk defense may be a complete defense to a plaintiff's negligent tort action. When a person is aware of the danger in a particular situation, yet continues to maintain exposure to that danger and injury results, that person cannot complain of the defendant's negligence. Similarly, the assumption of risk defense applies to risks that are inherent in a particular situation.

## 3. Acts of Nature

An act of nature may also constitute a defense. If lightning strikes a large tree in a field, causing the tree to fall on and crush a neighbor's barn, the tree's owner would not be liable, because the proximate cause of the damage was an act of nature. The outcome could be different if the tree was known to be partially rotted and it was foreseeable that sooner or later the tree would fall in a storm. Similarly, if a tornado swept the tree into the neighbor's house, there would be no liability. If, however, the tree had been dead for an extended period of time and the owner simply failed to cut the tree down and remove it, an act of nature defense would likely be unavailable if the owner was aware (or should have been aware) of the tree's condition. In that event, the possibility that a windstorm would cause the tree to fall and do damage to others would be reasonably foreseeable.

## C. SPECIAL SITUATIONS

There are a number of instances where society has not been completely comfortable with a negligence approach from a policy perspective. In these situations, a recovery is either easier to obtain or more difficult than is usually the result under a negligence system. Today, many jurisdictions have modified the traditional negligence doctrine in certain special situations.

### 1. Guest Statutes

In states having a "guest statute," an owner or operator of a motor vehicle is typically excused from liability for injuries suffered by nonpaying guests riding with the driver unless the driver is intoxicated or reckless—mere ordinary carelessness is an insufficient ground for a lawsuit. Historically, that meant a nonpaying passenger assumed the risks associated with ordinary negligence.

Beginning in the 1970s, some state legislatures began repealing their guest statutes and, in other states, courts began to carve out exceptions to the laws. In addition, more than twenty state guest statutes have been challenged on constitutional grounds with a clear majority of them being found unconstitutional. Alabama is the only remaining state with a comprehensive guest statute.

## 2.  Good Samaritan Laws

An individual is not legally required to render aid to another person who is in peril, even though such assistance might be the humanitarian thing to do. However, if aid is rendered, but is rendered carelessly, the person providing the aid can be held liable for any resulting damages. Also, once an individual has begun to provide assistance to an individual in peril, there is a duty to continue until a replacement comes or the aid otherwise becomes unnecessary.

Presently, all states and the District of Columbia have a Good Samaritan law. A Good Samaritan law specifies that a person rendering aid and assistance to someone in peril without expectation of compensation can only be held liable for injuries resulting from recklessness or willful intent to injure. If compensation is received for assisting people in perilous situations, as would be the case of an emergency medical technician, a more stringent standard of care usually applies. As for hospital care, the Good Samaritan statutes generally fall into one of three categories—those that expressly exclude hospital care; those that expressly include hospital care; and those that contain no explicit provision one way or the other.

## 3. Bailments

A bailment occurs when physical possession of property is transferred to another individual for safe-keeping of when property is borrowed. If an injury results from the use of the bailed property, liability depends upon the type of bailment at issue. There exist at least six types of bailment situations: (1) gratuitous bailments for safekeeping; (2) bailment for the bailee's use; (3) a simple pawn; (4) bailment for hire; (5) bailment whereby the bailee agrees for a fee to operate or manage the thing bailed; and (6) the bailment of a thing to be managed by the bailee without compensation. A different standard of care applies in each type of situation. In general, however, the bailee is subject to a standard of care varying with the benefit derived from the bailment. For instance, a bailee is held to a standard of slight negligence where the loan is for the bailee's benefit or use, but is only held to a standard of gross neglect where the bailee undertakes safe keeping for the bailor. Where both parties benefit from the bailment, the usual standard is that of ordinary care.

## 4. Manufacturer's Liability

Since the early 1960s, manufacturer's liability law has changed greatly. The recent trend is away from a negligence approach and toward strict liability. In many instances, an injured party is not required to show that the manufacturer was negligent. While a strict liability approach is not the same as absolute liability, in many instances, manufacturer's liability has become so favorable for plaintiffs that many manufacturers have complained of the inability to afford liability insurance coverage.

Under the modern approach, the injured party is required to prove five elements in order to recover from a manufacturer on a product liability claim. First, the injured party must show that the defendant sold the product and was engaged in the business of selling the product. This requirement is typically easy to satisfy. Second, the injured party must show that the product was in a defective condition. This, likewise, is not usually very difficult to establish. Third, the injured party must show that the defective condition was unreasonably dangerous to an ordinary user during normal use. Normal use includes all intended uses and foreseeable misuses of the product. This requirement is somewhat more difficult to satisfy than the first two, and a few courts do not require this element. If this element is required, a product may be deemed to be unreasonably dangerous if the manufacturer fails to warn of dangers inherent in the product's normal use that is not obvious to an ordinary user. If the product bears an adequate warning, the product is deemed not to be in defective condition in those states whose product liability act follows Comment j of the Restatement (Second) of Torts § 402A. However, some states follow Comment j of the Restatement (Third) of Torts § 2, which provides that an adequate warning does *not* foreclose a finding that a product is defectively designed. In these states, a manufacturer cannot simply warn of open and obvious dangers. The belief in these states is that Comment j allows an adequate warning to absolve the manufacturer of its duty to design against dangers when a reasonably safer design could have been adopted that would have reduced or eliminated the risk remaining after a warning is provided. But, under either approach, foreseeable misuse of the product remains an issue. *See, e.g., Mallery v. International Harvester Company,* 690 So. 2d 765 (La. Ct. App. 1996).

The fourth element that an injured party must prove to recover from a manufacturer on a product liability claim is that the product was expected to reach the user without substantial change in condition and, in fact, did so. The fifth requirement is that the product defect was the proximate cause of the plaintiff's injury or damage. This requirement is the most difficult to show and involves proving one of the elements of negligence.

As mentioned above, the recent focus in product liability law has been on design defects.

### *i. FIFRA Preemption*

There are at least three situations that a particular farmer or rancher may face in which they will be limited in their ability to sue a manufacturer on a product liability claim. The first of these involves damages to persons or realty arising from the use of registered pesticides. The Federal Insecticide, Fungicide and Rodenticide Act (FIFRA) authorizes the Environmental Protection Agency to regulate pesticide sale and use. Under FIFRA, it is unlawful to use any registered pesticide in a manner inconsistent with its labeling. While this "label use" provision gives the EPA authority to assess civil penalties against producers that use pesticides improperly or damage the environment, it also limits the ability of injured parties to sue pesticide manufacturers on either an inadequate labeling or wrongful death theory. A significant question has been whether FIFRA preempts state law damage claims for pesticide-related agricultural crop injury and whether FIFRA preemption of damage claims is limited to the specific subjects that EPA reviews at the time it first approves a pesticide product's labeling.

FIFRA allows states to regulate the sale and use of federally registered pesticides to the extent the regulation does not permit any sales or uses prohibited by FIFRA, but a state cannot impose or continue in effect any requirements for labeling or packaging in addition to or different from what FIFRA requires. A significant legal question concerns the extent to which FIFRA preempts state common law tort claims on the basis that the claims impose labeling or packaging requirements in addition to or different from those imposed by FIFRA. A majority of courts have held that FIFRA preempts all common law tort claims that challenge the adequacy of pesticide labels. However, while most courts have held that FIFRA preempts state law claims for failure to warn, actual defective label claims, and claims for breach of express and implied warranties, the courts have recognized that FIFRA does not necessarily preempt all state law claims.

Overall, the courts have utilized different rationales for determining the extent of preemption of state common law and statutory claims. In 2005, the U.S. Supreme Court, in *Bates, et al. v. Dow Agrosciences LLC*, 544 U.S. 431 (2005), provided important guidance on how courts are to analyze FIFRA preemption claims in the future. The plaintiffs in *Bates* were 29 Texas peanut farmers who claimed that in the 2000 growing season their crops were severely damaged by the application of the defendant's pesticide. The farmers claimed that the defendant knew or should have known that the pesticide would stunt the growth of peanuts in acidic soils. However, the pesticide label stated that the pesticide was recommended in all areas where peanuts were grown. Before the 2001 growing season the defendant reregistered the pesticide with the EPA, and the EPA approved a supplemental label that specified that the product was not to be used on peanuts grown in soils with a high acidity level (pH of 7.2 or greater). After negotiations failed, the farmers gave notice of intent to sue under Texas law, and the defendant filed a motion for declaratory judgment in Federal District Court on the grounds that FIFRA preempted the farmers' claims. The farmers also brought tort claims based in strict liability and negligence, fraud, breach of warranty and violation of the Texas Deceptive Trade Practices-Consumer Protection Act. The District Court granted the defendant's motion, finding that FIFRA preempted the farmers' claims, and the U.S. Court of

Appeals for the Fifth Circuit affirmed. The Fifth Circuit reasoned that the farmers' claims were preempted because if the claims were successful, the defendant would be induced (as opposed to being actually required) to change its label. Accordingly, the farmers' successful claim would impose an additional "requirement" on the defendant under state law—something the states cannot do under FIFRA.

The Supreme Court began its analysis in *Bates* by noting that FIFRA preemption applies to state rules that: (1) establish a requirement for labeling or packaging that; (2) is in addition to or different from what FIFRA requires. The Court noted, therefore, that rules that require manufacturers to design reasonably safe products, use due care in conducting appropriate testing of their products, market products free of manufacturing defect, and to honor their express warranties or other contractual commitments are not preempted because they do not qualify as requirements for labeling or packaging. Thus, the Court ruled that the farmers' claims for defective design, defective manufacture, negligent testing and breach of express warranty were not preempted. The Court rejected the Fifth Circuit's "inducement" test as overbroad—that the farmers' claims were preempted because, if successful, the defendant would be induced to change the pesticide label. However, the Court ruled that the farmers' fraud and negligent-failure-to-warn claims were premised on common law rules that qualified as "requirements" for labeling or packaging. But, such claims are only preempted, the Court reasoned, if the state level common law rules establish requirements that are "in addition to or different from" FIFRA's standards. The farmers claimed that their claims based on fraud and failure-to-warn were not preempted because these common law duties were equivalent to FIFRA's requirements that a pesticide label not contain "false or misleading" statements, or inadequate instructions or warnings.

Ultimately, the Court ruled that it had not received sufficient briefing on whether FIFRA preempted the farmers' fraud and failure-to-warn claims brought under Texas law, and remanded the case to the Fifth Circuit for a resolution of those claims. In remanding on these claims, the Court emphasized that a state law labeling requirement must in fact be equivalent to a requirement under FIFRA to survive preemption. If, for example, the element of falsity contained in a Texas common law fraud action imposes a broader obligation than FIFRA's requirement that labels not contain "false or misleading statements," the action would be preempted to the extent of the difference. The Court also opined that state law requirements must be measured against any relevant EPA regulations that give content to FIFRA's misbranding standards. Likewise, the Court stated that jury instructions must ensure that nominally equivalent labeling requirements are genuinely equivalent such that a pesticide manufacturer should not be held liable under a state labeling requirement unless the manufacturer is also liable for misbranding under FIFRA.

In rejecting the "inducement" test of the Fifth Circuit and utilizing a "parallel requirements" test for determining FIFRA preemption, it is likely that more claims against pesticide manufacturers will survive preemption. It is no longer a valid ground for preemption that a state-based claim, if successful, would induce a manufacturer to change a label. Under the "parallel requirements" test, preemption applies only to claims that, if successful, would actually require a label to be changed. Thus, the key is whether applicable state law imposes broader obligations on pesticide manufacturers than does FIFRA.

> **Note:** Nothing in FIFRA precludes states from providing a remedy to farmers and state law claims can be asserted based on alleged FIFRA violations to the extent that the claims would not impose a requirement that is in addition to or different from FIFRA requirements. However, a federal claim cannot be asserted.

It is reasonable to believe that the Court's opinion will lead to additional litigation against applicators and other parties that have some connection with the activity that caused damages along with pesticide manufacturers, and may cause some state legislatures to reexamine state statutes governing pesticides with an eye toward conformity with FIFRA. In any event, the Court illustrated its preference against preemption without clear direction from the Congress.

## *ii. Alterations and/or Multiple Component Parts*

The second situation limiting the ability of injured farmers or ranchers to sue a manufacturer on a product liability claim is when purchased equipment is altered or when multiple component parts are purchased individually, but are then later combined to make a complete system. If the component parts are not defective, but when combined produce a defective system, the manufacturers of the component parts do not have a duty to warn or properly instruct about the use of the system. When purchased equipment is altered, the manufacturer is generally released from liability unless the manufacturer could have reasonably foreseen that purchasers would alter the equipment in the manner that resulted in injury.

## *iii. "Economic Loss" Doctrine*

The third situation limiting the ability of injured parties to sue a manufacturer on a product liability claim involves application of the "economic loss" doctrine. The doctrine bars tort claims that are not based on physical injury to the plaintiff or the plaintiff's property. Under the "economic loss doctrine" set forth in the Restatement (Third) of Torts § 21, product defects that damage only the product itself, or make the product useless are *not* within the domain of product liability law. Most courts hold that the doctrine applies equally to consumer purchasers as well as business purchasers (but that the doctrine does not apply to contracts that are predominantly for the provision of services). Consequently, these types of cases are to be decided under contract law, with contract-based damages. The question is what the purchaser contracted for— if what was purchased was insured, the insurance company is liable for the loss. The doctrine also applies to "other property" that is damaged if the damage was or should have been reasonably contemplated by the contracting parties.

## 5. Last Clear Chance to Avoid Injury

As originally applied, the last clear chance doctrine operated as a plaintiff's response to a defense of contributory negligence. The doctrine holds liable the party who had the last clear chance to avoid damage or injury to the other party. This doctrine imposes a duty upon one party to exercise care in avoiding injury to another party who has negligently placed themselves in danger. Invoking this doctrine requires knowledge of the plaintiff's presence, realization of peril, and an ability to avoid any resulting injuries.

The states are not in complete agreement on the application of the last clear chance doctrine. There are two basic schools of thought. The humanitarian school imposes a duty of reasonable diligence on persons to ascertain the predicament of an individual in peril and to take appropriate action to avoid injury to that person. Other jurisdictions follow what is known as a "discovered peril" approach, which means that if an individual happens to see another person in peril, there is a duty to try and avoid injury to that person. However, there is no duty to avoid injury because there is no duty to maintain a lookout for such persons.

Other states have abolished the last clear chance doctrine in its entirety and have subsumed it under the heading of proximate cause.

## VI.   STRICT LIABILITY

Some activities are deemed to be so dangerous that a showing of negligence is not required to obtain a recovery. Under a strict liability approach, the defendant is liable for injuries caused by the defendant's actions, even if the defendant was not negligent in any way or did not intend to injure the plaintiff. In general, those situations reserved for resolution under a strict liability approach involve those activities that are highly dangerous. When these activities are engaged in, the defendant must be prepared to pay for all resulting consequences, regardless of the legal fault.

### A.   WILD ANIMALS

In general, landowners are not strictly liable for the acts of wild animals on their property. But, some courts have held that a landowner could be found negligent with regard to the indigenous wild animals that are found on the landowner's property if the landowner knows or has reason to know of the unreasonable risk of harm posed by the animals.

If an individual keeps wild animals on his or her premises, the individual will be strictly liable for any damages that the animals cause to other persons or their property. In many jurisdictions, the owner or possessor of hard-hoofed animals, such as cattle, horses and donkeys, may also be strictly liable for injuries caused by those animals, at least if known to have a vicious propensity.

## B. DOGS AND OTHER DOMESTIC ANIMALS

Injuries or other damages caused by dogs are handled differently. The owner or possessor of a dog is normally not liable unless the owner knows the animal to be dangerous. *See, e.g., Rowlette v. Paul,* 219 Ga. App. 597, 466 S.E.2d 37 (1995). Historically, a dog was entitled to its first bite. The dog's owner would not be liable for injuries from the dog's bite until the dog had already bitten someone. Until the dog has bitten someone, it is not known to be dangerous. In recent years, many states have passed statutes changing the common law rule and holding a dog owner (or a person who "harbors" a dog) responsible for the injuries caused by the dog. An exception is usually made, however, for personal injuries caused by a dog if the defendant was trespassing or was committing an unlawful act at the time of the injury. Some state statutes also make a distinction on the basis of whether the dog would attack or injure someone without provocation. Also, under Restatement (Second) of Torts § 518, the owner of a domestic animal who does not know or have reason to know that the animal is more dangerous than others of its class may still be liable for negligently failing to prevent the animal from

inflicting an injury. Approximately 20 states follow
the Restatement approach.

Of importance to agriculture is that some state
"dog-bite" statutes contain a "working dog exception."
The exception contained in the Colorado statute, for
example, applies if the bite occurs while the dog is on
its owner's property or while the dog was working
under the control of its owner. *Legro v. Robinson*, No.
15CA0486, 2015 Colo. App. LEXIS 2041 (Colo. Ct.
App. Dec. 31, 2015), *on remand from Robinson v.
Legro,* No. 12SC1002, 2014 Colo. LEXIS 414 (Colo.
Sup. Ct. May 27, 2014).

## C.  MAINTAINING DANGEROUS CONDITIONS ON PROPERTY

Strict liability is imposed on persons responsible
for activities or conditions on their property that are
unreasonably dangerous and cause injury or damage
to other persons or their property. For example, if a
farmer or rancher decides to create a drainage ditch
with explosives, and the resulting rock debris causes
damages to a neighbor, the farmer will be strictly
liable.

## D.  UNNATURAL LAND USES

A strict liability approach for "non-natural" land use
activities has long applied. Today, the rule has been
extended to include most activities that are
extremely dangerous. *But see, Koger v. Ferrin,* 926
P.2d 680 (Kan. Ct. App. 1996).

Perhaps the most frequent application of the doctrine to agriculture is in situations involving the aerial application of pesticides and other chemicals to crops. See *Langan v. Valicopters, Inc.,* 567 P.2d 218 (Wash. 1977). Most states utilize a strict liability rule if damage occurs. A few states purport to require a showing of negligence, but, in reality, even in these jurisdictions it may be difficult for a farmer to escape liability if damage occurs. For example, in Arkansas, violation of aerial crop spraying regulations constitutes evidence of negligence and the negligence of crop sprayers can be imputed to landowners because aerial crop spraying is viewed as an inherently dangerous activity. *McCorkle Farms, Inc. v. Thompson,* 84 S.W.3d 884 (Ark. Ct. App. 2003).

Some courts have limited application of the strict liability rule and have found a defendant not liable for an abnormally dangerous activity in situations where the plaintiff was abnormally sensitive to the defendant's conduct. *See, e.g., Foster v. Preston Mill Co.,* 268 P.2d 654 (Wash. 1954).

Strict liability does not protect against "harms incident to the plaintiff's extraordinary and unusual use of land." This is similar to the modern trend in manufacturer's liability cases, where recovery is limited to instances where the defect in the manufactured product was the proximate cause of the injury or damage. Also, what is abnormally dangerous can depend on the circumstances and characteristics surrounding the complained-of activity. *See, e.g., Crosstex North Texas Pipeline, L.P.*

*v. Gardiner,* No. 15-0049, 2016 Tex. LEXIS 580 (Tex. Sup. Ct. Jun.24, 2016).

Arguably, if a farmer plants a genetically modified (GM) crop with knowledge that the crop is likely to cross-pollinate conventional crops in adjacent fields, the farmer could be held strictly liable for any resulting damages. The situation could be viewed as similar to the problem of pesticide drift. The damages in a cross-pollination case could include, among other things, loss of organic certification, costs associated with breaches of identity preserved crop contracts, and litigation costs of neighboring farmers who are sued by seed companies for "theft" of genetic intellectual property that was actually present in their fields due to wind and cross-pollination. *See, e.g., Monsanto v. Trantham,* 156 F. Supp. 2d 855 (W.D. Tenn. 2001); *Monsanto v. McFarling,* 302 F.3d 1291 (Fed. Cir. 2002); *cert. den.,* 545 U.S. 1139 (2005). But, if the GM crop at issue had already received appropriate regulatory approval, the plaintiff could be required to prove that the GM crop was unnatural or abnormally dangerous.

## E. CONVERSION

Conversion is the intentional and wrongful taking, detention or appropriation of another person's property. Contrary to a damage award in a trespass against chattel case, where actual damages must be shown, nominal damages may be awarded in a conversion action. The basis of a conversion suit is the wrongful deprivation of the owner's possessory right instead of the wrongful acquisition of the property. There exists some uncertainty as to what types of "property" may be the subject of conversion. However, it appears that so long as a specific and identifiable item of personal property having some value is converted, an action for conversion is appropriate. Real property cannot be the subject of a conversion action. Earth, sand, gravel and timber are considered part of the real estate only while they remain in their natural position in the ground. If they are wrongly severed and removed, however, they become personalty for which a conversion action is available. Fully matured crops can also be the subject of conversion, but growing crops cannot be converted because they cannot profitably be severed from the soil. Other property which may be the subject of conversion includes money (which can be described, identified, or segregated), checks, promissory notes, and life insurance policies.

Technically, conversion is a strict liability, rather than an intentional, tort. While there must be an intent to control the property, ignorance of the owner's right of title or the converter's lack of good faith are not requisites for liability. The only requirement for conversion is the exercise of unauthorized control over the owner's rights in the property. *See, e.g., First National Bank of Amarillo v. Southwestern Livestock, Inc.,* 859 F.2d 847 (10th Cir. 1988).

The measure of damages for conversion is the fair market value of the property at the time and place of conversion, with interest computed from the time of conversion until the entry of judgment. Even if the property is recovered, the owner may still sue and recover the reasonable value for the property's use and any loss in market value during the period of detention. Where converted chattels fluctuate in market value, the measure of damages is the highest market price of the property within a reasonable time after the owner has notice of the conversion. Additional damages may also be recovered upon proof of wrongful intent, knowledge, motive, mistake, or lack of good faith.

# VII.  OTHER LIABILITIES ARISING FROM LAND USE

## A.  NOXIOUS WEEDS

The liability of farmers and ranchers for the spread of weeds and other noxious vegetation onto adjoining land is governed by statute in almost all jurisdictions. Noxious weed laws create a duty on the part of owners, tenants, and other possessors of land to destroy noxious weeds or otherwise prevent their spread. A landowner's duty to control the spread of weeds (absent malicious intent to injure an adjoining landowner) only extends to weeds specifically listed in the applicable state noxious weed law. *Krug v. Koriel*, 23 Kan. App. 2d 751, 935 P.2d 1063 (1997).

A typical noxious weed statute delegates enforcement authority to state agriculture officials, as well as local boards and officials. A typical statute defines the type of noxious weed or other vegetation subject to regulation, establishes county weed control districts, authorizes the appointment of local weed control officials and specifies their authorities and duties, prescribes the duty of landowners to destroy weeds, establishes the procedure for giving notice to offending parties, and provides local control authorities with limited enforcement powers. Most state noxious weed statutes provide that weed control officials may assess the cost of removing weeds to the property owner rather than a tenant or other person in possession of the premises. Some statutes also impose criminal penalties for violations.

Most state noxious weed laws do not permit an injured landowner to recover civil damages for the spread of weeds from an adjoining owner's property. However, this does not prevent an injured party from suing to recover damages for the defendant's negligence in allowing weeds to overspread the plaintiff's land. *See, e.g., Collins v. Barker,* 668 N.W.2d 548 (S.D. 2003). In reality, however, obtaining a judgment may be rather difficult. An injured landowner must usually prove that the weeds were spread by the defendant's active negligence or willful conduct rather than by nature. While it may be possible for the plaintiff to prove negligence by the fact that the defendant was found guilty of violating a criminal weed control provision, there does not appear to be any authority directly on point.

An offended landowner may also be able to recover damages for the spread of noxious weeds onto their land from an adjoining landowner's premises by showing that the noxious weeds were destroyed negligently. *Kukowski v. Simonson Farm, Inc.,* 507 N.W.2d 68 (N.D. 1993).

## B.   NUISANCE

### 1.  In General

A nuisance is an invasion of an individual's interest in the use and enjoyment of land rather than an interference with the exclusive possession or ownership of the land. Nuisance law prohibits land uses that unreasonably and substantially interfere with another individual's quiet use and enjoyment of property. The doctrine is based on two interrelated concepts: (1) landowners have the right to use and enjoy property free of unreasonable interferences by others; and (2) landowners must use property so as not to injure adjacent owners.

The two primary issues at stake in any agricultural nuisance dispute are whether the use alleged to be a nuisance is reasonable for the area and whether the use alleged to be a nuisance substantially interferes with the use and enjoyment of neighboring land. *See, e.g., Bower v. Hog Builders, Inc.,* 461 S.W.2d 784 (Mo. 1970).

"Nuisance" and "negligence" are not the same thing. Operating a farming or ranching activity properly and having all requisite permits may still constitute a nuisance if a court or jury determines the activity is "unreasonable" and causes a "substantial interference" with another person's use and enjoyment of property. Whether a complained of activity, such as spreading manure, results in a "substantial" and "unreasonable" interference with another's property will depend on the facts of each case and the legal rules used in the particular jurisdiction.

Because each claim of nuisance depends on the fact of the case, there are no easy rules to determine when an activity will be considered a nuisance. In general, a court faced with a particular nuisance claim will consider several factors. Primary among these factors is whether the use complained of is a reasonable use that is common to the area or whether it is not suitable. Also important is whether the use complained of is a minor inconvenience which happens very infrequently or whether it is a regular and continuous activity. The nature of the property use being disturbed is also an important consideration. If the interference has a significant impact on the complaining party's use of their own property, such as the prevention of living in the complaining party's home, a nuisance will likely be found. Similarly, if the complained-of use is preventing another landowner's use of their property that is a vital part of the local economy, the court will balance the economics of the situation and most likely conclude that the complained of use constituted a nuisance. An additional important factor, but not conclusive in and of itself of the issue is whether the complained of use was in existence prior to the complaining party's use of their property which is now claimed to be interfered with. A related concern, if the activity generating the alleged nuisance was in existence prior to the complaining party moving into the vicinity, is whether the nuisance activity was obvious at the time the complaining party moved in. Many courts also attempt to balance the economic value to society of the uses in question. If the complained of use adds jobs and income to the local economy, the value to society of continuing the alleged nuisance may outweigh the negative impact it causes.

## 2. Remedies

The courts have much discretion in establishing an appropriate remedy for a nuisance. The most common remedy is for the court to stop (enjoin) the nuisance activity. However, most courts try to fashion a remedy to fit the particular situation. *See, e.g., Valasek v. Baer,* 401 N.W.2d 33 (Iowa 1987); *Spur Industries, Inc. v. Del E. Webb Development Co.,* 108 Ariz. 178, 494 P.2d 700 (1972).

## 3. Classifications of Nuisance

Nuisances are typically classified in two ways. A private nuisance is a civil wrong, based on a disturbance of rights in land. A private nuisance may consist of an interference with the physical condition of the land itself, as by vibration or blasting which damages a house, the destruction of crops, flooding, the raising of the water table, or the pollution of a stream or underground water supply. A private nuisance may also consist of a disturbance of the comfort or convenience of the occupant as by unpleasant odors, smoke, dust or gas, loud noises, excessive light, high temperatures, or even repeated telephone calls. The remedy for a private nuisance lies in the hands of the individual whose rights have been disturbed.

A public nuisance, on the other hand, is an interference with the rights of the community at large. A public nuisance may include anything from the obstruction of a highway to a public gaming house or indecent exposure. The normal remedy is in the hands of the state.

A nuisance can be classified as either temporary or permanent. A temporary nuisance is one that can be abated; a permanent nuisance cannot be abated. Damages can be awarded for a temporary nuisance if the complaining party can show that economically feasible techniques are available to the defendant to abate the nuisance to the degree where it is no longer a substantial interference with the plaintiff's use and enjoyment of their property, and the defendant has failed to utilize those techniques.

A nuisance may also be classified in terms of a nuisance per se which is a nuisance as a matter of law (such as by statute) under any circumstance. Relatively few nuisances are classified as a nuisance per se. A nuisance per accidens is an activity that only becomes a nuisance because of surrounding circumstances. For example, a lawfully operated feedlot may only become a nuisance because of peculiar environmental factors associated with it. Similarly, because an activity is lawful under state law means that it cannot be a nuisance per se.

Courts generally do not allow a nuisance suit to proceed on the basis of a claimed "anticipated nuisance." An activity is generally allowed to be conducted to determine if it can be operated in a fashion that does not constitute a nuisance. *See, e.g., Simpson v. Kollasch,* 749 N.W.2d 671 (Iowa 2008).

## 4. Potential Defenses Against Nuisance Actions

### i. In General

There are no common law defenses that an agricultural operation may use to shield itself from liability arising from a nuisance action. However, courts do consider a variety of factors, to determine if the conduct of a particular farm or ranch operation is a nuisance. Of primary importance are priority of location and reasonableness of the operation. Together, these two factors have led courts to develop a "coming to the nuisance" defense. This means that if people move to an area they know is not suited for their intended use, they should be prohibited from claiming that the existing uses are nuisances.

### ii. Right-to-Farm Laws

Every state has enacted a right-to-farm law that is designed to protect existing agricultural operations by giving farmers and ranchers who meet the legal requirements a defense in nuisance suits. The basic thrust of a particular state's right-to-farm law is that it is unfair for a person to move to an agricultural area knowing the conditions which might be present and then ask a court to declare a neighboring farm a nuisance. Thus, the basic purpose of a right-to-farm law is to create a legal and economic climate in which farm operations can be continued. Right-to-farm laws can be an important protection for agricultural operations, but, to be protected, an agricultural operation must satisfy the law's requirements.

Right-to-farm laws are of three basic types: (1) nuisance related; (2) restrictions on local regulations of agricultural operations; and (3) zoning related. While these categories provide a method for identifying and discussing the major features of right-to-farm laws, any particular state's right-to-farm law may contain elements of each category.

The most common type of right-to-farm law is nuisance related. This type of statute requires that an agricultural operation will be protected only if it has been in existence for a specified period of time (usually at least one year) before the change in the surrounding area that gives rise to a nuisance claim. These types of statute essentially codify the "coming to the nuisance defense," but do not protect agricultural operations which were a nuisance from the beginning or which are negligently or improperly run. For example, if any state or federal permits are required to properly conduct the agricultural operation, they must be acquired as a prerequisite for protection under the statute.

While right-to-farm laws try to assure the continuation of farming operations, they do not protect subsequent changes in a farming operation that constitute a nuisance after local development occurs nearby. *See, e.g., Flansburgh v. Coffey,* 370 N.W.2d 127 (Neb. 1985).

If a nuisance cannot be established a right-to-farm law can operate to bar an action when the agricultural activity on land changes in nature. *See, e.g., Dalzell, et al. v. Country View Family Farms, LLC,* No. 1:09-CV-1567-WTL-MJD, 2012 U.S. Dist. LEXIS 130773 (S.D. Ind. Sept. 13, 2012)*; Parker v. Obert's Legacy Dairy, LLC,* No. 26A05-1209-PL-450, 2013 Ind. App. LEXIS 203 (Ind. Ct. App. Apr. 30, 2013).

A second type of right-to-farm statute is designed to prevent local and county governments from enacting regulations or ordinances that impose restrictions on normal agricultural practices. This type of statute is usually contained in the state's agricultural districting law. Under this type of a statute, agricultural operations are required to be located within a designated agricultural district in order to be protected from nuisance suits. However, agricultural activities, even though they may be located in an agricultural district, must be conducted in accordance with federal, state and local law or rules in order to take advantage of the statute's protections. Some courts have held that state law preempts local governments from making siting decision for confined animal feeding operations. *See, e.g. Worth County Friends of Agriculture v. Worth County,* 688 N.W.2d 257 (Iowa 2004); *Adams v. State of Wisconsin Livestock Facilities String Review Bd.,* No. 2009AP608, 2012 Wisc. LEXIS 381 (Wisc. Sup. Ct. Jul. 11, 2012).

A third type of right-to-farm statute exempts (at least in part) agricultural uses from county zoning ordinances. The major legal issue involving this type of statute is whether a particular activity is an agricultural use or a commercial activity. *See, e.g., Lake County v. Cushman,* 40 Ill. App. 3d 1045, 353 N.E.2d 399 (1976); *Soil Enrichment Materials Corp. v. Zoning Board of Appeals of Grundy County,* 15 Ill. App. 3d 432, 305 N.E.2d 521 (1973); *People v. Husler,* 34 Ill. App. 3d 977, 342 N.E.2d 401 (1975). *Northville Township v. Coyne* 170 Mich. App. 446, 429 N.W.2d 185 (1988).

In some states, agricultural activities receive nuisance-type protection through zoning laws wholly separate from the protections of a right-to-farm statute. *See, e.g., Farmegg Products, Inc. v. Humboldt County,* 190 N.W.2d 454 (Iowa 1971); *Thompson v. Hancock County,* 539 N.W.2d 181 (Iowa 1995); *Kuehl v. Cass County,* 555 N.W.2d 686 (Iowa 1996),

A related question is whether ordinances ostensibly aimed at health and environmental concerns constitute zoning. *See, e.g., Enterprise Partners v. Perkins County,* 260 Neb. 650 (2000).

## VIII.  EMPLOYER'S LIABILITY FOR INJURIES TO EMPLOYEES

Two separate legal systems are utilized to determine an employer's liability for injuries to employees. The common law system involves certain employer-owed duties, the breach of which subjects the employer to suit for damages, unless a common law defense applies. Conversely, workers' compensation is a no-fault system that was developed near the beginning of the twentieth century.

## A.   EMPLOYMENT NOT COVERED BY WORKERS' COMPENSATION

Under the common law, in order to hold an employer liable for injuries suffered by employees, an employee must show that the employer breached a duty owed to the employee. An employer's liability to an injured worker depends heavily upon the employer's negligence. The employer bears certain common law responsibilities such as: (1) the duty to provide reasonably safe tools and appliances; (2) the duty to provide a reasonably safe place to work; (3) the duty to warn and instruct the employee of dangers which the employee could not reasonably be expected to discover; and (4) the duty to provide reasonably competent fellow employees.

### 1.  Duty to Provide Reasonably Safe Tools and Appliances

An employer has a duty to provide reasonably safe tools and appliances. For example, if a farmer or rancher as an employer sends an employee out to work with a dull ax and the ax head glances off and lacerates the employee's leg, the employer will be held liable. Likewise, if a truck with defective brakes is provided, or a tractor with a bad clutch or missing power takeoff shield is provided, and injury results, the employer will be held liable.

### 2.  Reasonably Safe Workplace

In agriculture, it can be quite difficult in many instances to provide a safe work environment for employees. The agricultural working environment is a nonstandard environment. A judge or jury is called on to review the factual situation and determine whether the work environment was *reasonably* safe given the conditions that the employer could control. For example, if employees are expected to carry bags of feed across a slick concrete floor, that is likely to be deemed an unsafe work environment. Also, an employer is under a duty to maintain a lookout for unsafe conditions and dangerous employee practices. See *Martensen v. Rejda Brothers, Inc.,* 283 Neb. 279, 808 N.W.2d 855 (2012).

## 3. Duty to Warn of Hidden Dangers

An employer is under a duty to warn employees of dangers that the employer knows the employees are not likely to discover. *But see, Suddath v. Parks,* 914 S.W.2d 910 (Tenn. Ct. App. 1995).

## 4. Duty to Hire Reasonably Competent Fellow Employees

An employer has a duty to avoid hiring any employee whom the employer should realize is unfit and poses a risk to fellow employees. Failure to exercise reasonable care in the hiring of employees exposes the employer to liability for any injuries a particular employee causes to fellow employees. Similarly, an employer may have a duty to terminate the employment relationship with a particular employee upon learning that the employee is incompetent and poses a risk to the safety of fellow employees.

## 5. Duty to Make Reasonable Rules for Conduct of Employees

An employer also bears a duty to set reasonable rules for work conduct. The extent of this duty depends upon the particular situation. For instance, if the employment involves the use of welding equipment, the employer is under a duty to establish rules that would protect an employee's eyes. Similarly, an employer may be under a duty to require employees to wear protective clothing when the employment involves handling of herbicides or pesticides. Likewise, if the employment involves the operation of machinery, the duty may be to prevent employees from wearing loose-fitting clothing, or to require the machinery to be stopped before it is cleaned.

## 6. An Employer's Common Law Defenses

If an employee sues the employer for injury allegedly arising from the employer's negligence based upon breach of any of the duties mentioned above, an employer may defend on the basis that no duties owed to the employee were breached. Alternatively, the employer may assert certain common law affirmative defenses to limit or bar recovery

### i. Assumption of Risk

If an employee is aware of the danger posed by a job-related hazard, the employee may be deemed to have assumed the risk of being injured. However, most courts refuse to apply the assumption of risk doctrine on the basis that where the employee's choice is between submitting to the danger or getting fired, the choice is not voluntary. But, if the employee's submission to the risk is "unreasonable", most courts still allow an employer to assert a contributory negligence defense. In agricultural employment situations, employees generally agree to assume the ordinary risks associated with the weather and being around animals. However, specific risks are not assumed. For example, if an employee is sent to unload a load of feed and the easiest way to do it is to walk across a wet concrete floor, the employee will be deemed to have assumed the risk associated with slipping on the wet floor. *See, e.g., Gullickson v. Torkelson Brothers, Inc.,* 598 N.W.2d 503 (N.D. 1999).

### ii. Negligence of a Co-Employee

If the employer has exercised due care in the selection and retention of employees and one employee commits an act of negligence that injures a fellow employee, the employer will not ordinarily be held liable. The injured employee, however, may look for redress from the employee actually causing the injury.

### iii. Contributory Negligence and Comparative Fault

As mentioned earlier in this chapter, some states may permit an employer to assert that the employer was contributorily negligent and thereby defeat recovery, or that the employee bears some fault to reduce the amount of damages.

## B.   EMPLOYMENT COVERED BY WORKERS' COMPENSATION

Before the advent of workers' compensation statutes, it was rare for an employee to recover for injuries sustained while on the job. By 1920, almost all industrial employment was covered by workers' compensation laws. Historically, agricultural employment has been exempt from coverage. Indeed, as recently as 1973 only about one-third of the states included agricultural employment under their workers' compensation statutes. In 1973, a national report was issued that called attention to the plight of injured agricultural employees. This report caused several states to extend workers' compensation coverage to agricultural employment. But, workers' compensation coverage may not apply to ag production contract transactions.

Workers' compensation is a no-fault system to provide recovery for employees injured in an employment situation. Because it potentially applies only ins employment situations, it may not apply in ag production contract transactions. *See, e.g., Winglovitz v. Agway, Inc.,* 667 N.Y.S.2d 509 (N.Y. App. Div. 1998).

Worker's compensation is a system of easy recovery where the plaintiff does not have to show that the employer was negligent. Instead, in order to recover on an injury claim under workers' compensation, the employee need only show (1) that the employee suffered an injury or illness; (2) that the injury or illness occurred while the employee was acting within the scope and course of employment; and (3) that the injury or illness was causally related to the employment. *See, e.g., Angleton v. Starkan, Inc.,* 250 Kan. 711, 828 P.2d 933 (1992).

While the no-fault aspect of workers' compensation laws is designed to make it easier for injured employees to recover, the amount of the recovery is fixed. Different types of injuries to different body parts are worth a specified amount of damages. Damages are reflected in terms of number of weeks of benefits. The more serious the injury, the larger the recovery. Occupational illnesses related to the employment can also serve as grounds for recovery under a workers' compensation statute.

Workers' compensation benefits are payable without a showing of fault for injuries or illness and most state statutes place benefits in five distinct categories. Benefits are predicated upon a loss of earning capacity caused by a disability that is a function of impairment. The first category is for temporary disability which, in most states, specifies that the injured employee can start receiving benefits beginning a specific number of days after the injury. Permanent partial disability applies, for example, if an employee loses a limb while acting within the scope and course of employment. There is a healing period of benefits related to permanent partial disability. Permanent total disability allows the injured employee to recover benefits for the remainder of the employee's life. A final category is for death benefits if an employee is killed while acting in the scope and course of employment. Benefits relate to the type of injury or illness and the employee's income level.

Each state specifies a maximum benefit level for each category of benefits. For example, a typical state statute may specify that the employee is entitled to 80 percent of the average weekly spendable earnings of the employee, but the benefit cannot exceed 200 percent of the average weekly wage for the state.

Employers cover the risk of having to pay workers' compensation benefits by taking out insurance. Most states have numerous workers' compensation carriers. Agriculture is a most hazardous occupation with worker's compensation insurance rates in the vicinity of 6–7 percent of the employer's payroll. Some states have reported that the workers' compensation coverage rate for agriculture are as high as 15 percent of the agricultural payroll. As a result, workers' compensation coverage is a costly benefit package for an agricultural employer.

If an employer does not carry workers' compensation insurance and hires employees that are covered by the state's workers' compensation law, the employer is still liable if an employee is injured in the scope and course of their employment. Thus, if a 21-year-old individual becomes permanently and totally disabled, the company will be required to pay benefits until retirement age which could amount to a huge liability for the employer. Thus, it is not prudent to conduct business without workers' compensation insurance if employees are covered by the state workers' compensation law.

Presently, nearly all states have extended workers' compensation coverage to agricultural employment, but specify a minimum annual payroll (usually $2,500 to $10,000) or a certain level of employment for coverage to be effected. In other states, employees engaged in agricultural-related work activities are not covered. *See, e.g., Larsen v. DB Feedyards, Inc., 648 N.W.2d 306 (Neb. 2002); Hanawalt v. Brown,* No. 2015-SC-000183, 2016 Ky. Unpub. LEXIS 14 (Ky. Sup. Ct. Mar. 17, 2016).

In some states, the exclusion of agricultural employment from workers' compensation has been challenged as an unconstitutional violation of the Equal Protection Clause on the basis that the distinction between "farm and ranch laborers" and "administrative and sales staff" is an irrational and distinction lacking any rational purposes. While the vast majority of states that have considered such a claim have rejected it, the New Mexico Supreme Court, in 2016, did strike down the exclusion for ag workers in the state workers' compensation statute. *Rodriguez, et al. v. Brand West Dairy, et al.,* 378 P.3d 13 (N.M. Sup. Ct. 2016), *aff'g,* 356 P.3d 546 (N.M. Ct. App. 2015).

## C.   OCCUPATIONAL SAFETY AND HEALTH ACT OF 1970

The Occupational Safety and Health Act (OSHA) of 1970 is an elaborate set of rules covering many employment situations and imposing stiff civil fines and criminal penalties for violations. OSHA covers every nonfarm employer, even those with only one employee. Under OSHA, an employer must comply with safety and health standards and must meet recordkeeping requirements. Employers with ten or fewer employees are exempt from some of the recordkeeping requirements. A sole proprietor and members of the sole proprietor's family are not covered.

Since 1976, funding has been withheld for enforcement of the Act relative to "any person who is engaged in a farming operation and employs ten or fewer employees." As a result, most farming operations are exempt from OSHA coverage. However, large agricultural operations are covered.

OSHA, as passed in 1970, provides that a state could take over enforcement of the law if the state adopted rules at least as stringent as the federal rules. In these states, OSHA is enforced by a state agency (typically the State Department of Labor) which operates in accordance with the federal guidelines.

Covered employers are subject to two basic requirements. First, an employer must comply with certain safety and health standards. For agricultural operations employing migrant labor, safety and health standards applicable to sanitation in temporary labor camps must be followed. Standards are also specified for storage and handling of anhydrous ammonia and other field pesticides, pulpwood logging operations, slow moving vehicle emblems, and machine guards. Tractors exceeding 20 horsepower that were manufactured after October 25, 1976, must comply with standards for roll-over protective structures. In addition, employers must give initial and annual instruction to employees pertaining to rollover hazards including how to securely fasten the seat belt (if applicable), instruct employees to avoid operating the tractor near ditches, embankments and holes, to reduce speed when turning, crossing slopes or operating on rough, slick or muddy surfaces, and to stay off slopes too steep for safe operation. The regulations also specify that the tractor driver must not permit other persons to ride on the tractor while it is in operation, and that the tractor should be operated smoothly with no sudden turns, starts or stops. The hitch should only be made to the drawbar and hitchpoints recommended by the tractor manufacturer, and when the tractor is stopped the brakes should be set securely and a parking brake should be utilized if one is available. A number of standards have also been proposed concerning farm and ranch shops with respect to electrical and other types of batteries as well as electrical, plumbing and other codes for agriculture.

Employers are also required to maintain certain records. An OSHA notice must be posted in a prominent place to inform employees of job safety and health protection under the act. Not posting or failing to post the notice in a prominent place subjects the employer to substantial fines. In addition, all reportable injuries and illnesses must be logged and a report filed. Major accidents (one or more fatalities or hospitalization of five or more employees) must be reported within 48 hours after the accident. OSHA violations subject an employer to monetary penalties on a daily basis. Willful violations by an employer that result in death of an employee is punishable by substantial fine or imprisonment up to six months. A second conviction doubles the penalties. An employee who believes his or her job situation constitutes eminent danger or threatens potential physical harm may request an inspection by sending a signed statement or completing a complaint form. An employee cannot be discharged from employment or disciplined for filing a complaint. OSHA is not designed to compensate injured employees; rather OSHA's purpose is to create a safe workplace for the employee.

## IX.   EMPLOYER'S LIABILITY TO THIRD PERSONS FOR ACTS OF EMPLOYEES

### A.   MASTER-SERVANT OR INDEPENDENT CONTRACTOR RELATIONSHIP

In certain situations, one person may be held liable for the tortious acts of another person based on a special relationship between the two. Such liability (called vicarious liability) exists even though the person held liable not have personally committed the act. An employer may be held vicariously liable for the tortious acts (usually negligent ones) committed by an employee. Thus, if an employee commits a tort during the "scope of employment", the employer will (jointly with the employee) be liable. This rule is often described as the doctrine of "respondeat superior", which means "let the person higher up answer." There are several explanations given for this doctrine, but the most convincing is that accidents arising directly or indirectly out of an enterprise ought to be paid for by the entrepreneur in question as a cost of doing business. In practicality, the employer may often have a "deep pocket" or have insurance, whereas the employee is frequently judgment-proof. Also, the necessary control by the employer for an employer-employee relationship to exist justifies liability. Furthermore, the employer is likely to be in a better position to obtain insurance against work-related accidents than is the employee.

Vicarious liability applies to torts committed by employees and generally not to those committed by independent contractors. *See, e.g., Coates v. Anderson,* 84 P.3d 953 (Wyo. 2004). Therefore, it is critical to determine whether a particular individual was an employee or an independent contractor. While no single factor is dispositive in all cases, an employee is generally one who works subject to the control of the employer. An employer may also be directly liable to a customer for breaching a duty of care owed to the customer to supervise its employees involved in service for hire or to supply its employees with safe and proper equipment. *See, e.g., Eischen, et al. v. Crystal Valley Cooperative,* 835 N.W.2d 629 (Minn. Ct. App. 2013). An independent contractor, on the other hand, although hired to produce a certain result, is not subject to the control of the employer while the work is performed.

In any given situation, there may not be any control over the manner of performance, but there may be control over the means of performance. Thus, individuals hiring other persons to accomplish certain tasks should clearly specify whether an employer-employee relationship is to result.

If the subordinate is free to execute the work without being subject to the direction of the principal as to details, that person is usually an independent contractor. A person engaging an independent contractor is generally not liable to third persons for the independent contractor's acts. However, if the work is such that, unless special precautions are taken, there will be a high degree of danger to others, the person hiring the independent contractor will be liable. This is an exception for "inherently dangerous" activities. A similar exception can apply for work that is not "ultra-hazardous" if it is performed without adequate precautions.

In some states, aerial crop spraying is considered evidence of negligence. In these situations, a plaintiff only needs to establish that aerial spraying occurred and damage resulted. A showing of negligence on the part of the individual spraying the crops is not necessary. However, the majority of states still require a showing of negligence before damages can be recovered. In the states not requiring a showing of negligence, the practical effect is to apply a strict liability rule. In these jurisdictions, delegation of the spraying task to an independent contractor does not eliminate a farmer's liability. This problem is so severe that most farm liability policies do not cover the aerial spraying or dusting of crops. The damage award in a crop dusting case is calculated on the basis of the difference between the crop yield that would have normally resulted and the yield actually obtained after the damage, adjusted for any reduction in costs, such as drying or hauling costs. Yield is based on the best evidence available.

A difficult question in the area of respondeat superior is whether, in a particular case, the employee was acting "within the scope of his employment" when the tort occurred. In general, the tort is within the scope of employment if the individual acted with the intent to further the employer's business, even if the means chosen were indirect, unwise, and perhaps even forbidden. Most courts hold that an employee will be deemed to be within the scope of employment even though the employee's intent to serve the employer is coupled with a separate personal purpose. *See, e.g., Fruit v. Schriener,* 502 P.2d 133 (Ala. 1972).

Most courts hold that if an accident occurs when the employee is traveling from home to work, the employee is not acting within the scope of employment. This seems correct because the employer usually has no "control" over the employee at that time. The result should be the same even if the employer pays the employee a mileage allowance for the trip, and also agrees to pay the employee's hotel expenses for an overnight stay. Likewise, where the employee is returning home after the day's business activities, most courts do not hold an employer liable if the employee commits a negligent act.

Interesting cases arise in situations involving an employee on a business trip who makes a short "side trip", or "detour", for the employee's own purposes. The traditional view has been that while the employee is on the first leg of a side trip, the employee is engaging in what is often called a "frolic and detour", and is thus not within the scope of employment. But, as soon as the employee begins to return towards the path of the original business trip, the employee is once again within the scope of employment, no matter how far afield the employee may be at that point. The recent trend, however, has been to take a less "mechanical" view of the "frolic and detour" problem. Most courts today hold that the employee is within the scope of business if the deviation is "reasonably foreseeable". Under this approach, the employee might be within the scope of employment even while heading toward the object of a personal errand, if the deviation was slight in terms of distance. But, if the deviation was large and unforeseeable, in terms of miles, then the employee is not within the scope of business even while heading back towards the business goal, at least until returning reasonably near to the original route the employee was supposed to take.

## X. LIABILITY FOR COMMUNICATION OF ANIMAL DISEASES

### A. TRESPASSING OR STRAYING ANIMALS

If an owner of diseased animals knows of an infection and knows that it would be communicated to other animals if contracted, some states hold the owner liable for damages caused by transmission of the disease. Knowledge that the animals were infected is typically an essential element. Once the animals' owner has knowledge of the disease, the owner is under a duty to take reasonable steps to ensure that the animals do not come into contact with healthy, uninfected livestock of anyone else. Knowledge that the animals were infected is typically an essential element. Several states by statute require restraint of animals that are known to have an infectious or contagious disease from running at large or coming into contact with other animals. These statutes have been enacted by the major livestock producing states.

Recovery may be prevented if the complaining party is contributorily negligent. Knowledge that animals running at large were infected coupled with the complainant's failure to attempt to prevent the infected animal from coming in contact with the complainant's own animals may preclude recovery. Moreover, allowing infected animals to remain on the complaining party's premises after being aware of their diseased condition may be a bar to damages.

## B.   LANDLORD'S DUTY REGARDING DISEASED PREMISES

Sometimes questions arise concerning a landlord's liability for diseased or contaminated premises when a tenant brings healthy animals to the premises. In most jurisdictions, the liability of the landlord depends largely upon the landlord's deceit to the tenant concerning the past presence of disease on the premises. Thus, if a tenant has healthy animals and brings those animals onto the landlord's diseased or contaminated premises and the animals become diseased themselves, it will be difficult for the tenant to recover against the landlord. Failure to disclose the diseased condition of the leased premises is usually not a basis for action. Instead, actual deceit is required. Therefore, if the tenant fails to ask whether the premises are disease or contamination free, the landlord is under no duty to disclose that fact to the tenant. *See, e.g., Wilcox v. Cappel,* 1996 WL 706782 (Neb. Ct. App. Dec. 3, 1996) However, if the tenant asks and the landlord responds less than fully or less than truthfully, actual deceit may be present and provide the tenant a basis for recovery.

The lesson for tenants is clear—if recovery is sought for damages against a landlord arising from defects in the leased premises, the tenant should make a thorough inspection of the property and ask questions. It is best to reduce the lease agreement to writing and specify which party is liable for damages resulting from disease or contamination.

## C.  DISPOSAL OF ANIMAL CARCASSES

All states have statutory requirements that must be satisfied in order to properly dispose of a dead animal. In most states, disposal must occur within 24 hours after death. By statute, states typically acknowledge that disposal may be by burying, burning or feeding the carcass to other livestock. The option of feeding the carcass to other livestock is typically only available if the animal did not die of a contagious disease. Disposal is also usually available to a licensed rendering company. The typical state statute requires direct delivery to the point of disposal with an exception often made for stops to load additional carcasses. Vehicles used to transport the carcass of an animal typically must be lined or other measures taken to prevent any leakage of liquid, and must be disinfected after each transport.

Most states prohibit certain methods of dead animal disposal. For instance, placing the carcass of dead animal in a water course or roadway is a misdemeanor in many states. Similarly, knowingly allowing a carcass to remain in such an area is also a misdemeanor. But, in most jurisdictions, cattle and horse carcasses may be moved from one farm to another if they are not diseased.

## XI. FENCE LAWS AND TRESPASSING LIVESTOCK

### A. FENCE LAW THEORIES

Historically, the common law required livestock owners to keep livestock on their own land, and failure to do so could subject the livestock owner to liability for trespass if the livestock entered another landowner's property. Thus, the livestock owner had the responsibility to "fence-in" livestock. Some states, primarily the western range states, statutorily changed the common law rule and required landowners to construct fences around their property before damages could be collected from the owner of trespassing livestock. This became known as the "fence-out" theory, and still exists in some western states. In a fence-out jurisdiction, if livestock trespass within a lawful enclosure, the livestock owner is strictly liable for the damages caused by the livestock. *See, e.g., Madrid v. Zenchiku Land & Livestock,* 51 P.3d 1137 (Mont. 2002). No proof of negligence is necessary.

In fence-in jurisdictions, if livestock escape through the owner's faulty fence, the owner is liable for any resulting damages. However, if the fence is in good shape, the livestock owner is generally not liable absent a showing of negligence. Evidence of negligence includes such things as gates having been left open, the fence being improperly constructed or maintained, knowledge that the animals were in heat requiring a stronger enclosure or a closer watch, or knowledge that the animals were outside their enclosure and the owner made no attempt to return them.

The same rules apply when livestock wander onto a public roadway and cause injury to a motorist. In fence-out jurisdictions, no duty is imposed on livestock owners to prevent livestock from wandering on to a public highway in an open area other than the general duty to take reasonable care. *See, e.g., Andersen v. Two-Dot Ranch, Inc.,* 49 P.3d 1011 (Wyo. 2002). In most fence-in jurisdictions, the animal's owner must be shown to have been negligent.

Some fence-in jurisdictions apply the doctrine of res ipsa loquitur in livestock/automobile collision cases. Res ipsa loquitur is a procedural technique that can be used to shift the burden of proof in a tort case. Literally, the doctrine means "the thing speaks for itself." In a tort case, the plaintiff normally bears the burden of proving that the defendant failed to act in a reasonable and prudent manner, that the accident was foreseeable, and that the resulting damage or injury was a proximate cause of the defendant's action. The basic premise of the doctrine is that it is obvious that the accident would not have happened had it not been for the defendant's negligence, but the plaintiff does not have access to information which would verify or prove such negligence. Thus, if the plaintiff can also show that the instrumentality producing the occurrence (i.e., cow on a public roadway) is under the exclusive control of the alleged wrongdoer, and the alleged wrongdoers cannot explain the circumstances, the plaintiff may plead res ipsa loquitur, and shift the burden to the defendant to prove that the defendant was not negligent. *Curtis v. Lein, et al.,* 169 Wash.2d 884, 239 P.3d 1078 (2010); *Roberts v. Weber & Sons, Co.,* 248 Neb. 243, 533 N.W.2d 664 (1995); *Coglazier v. Fischer,* No. A-95-858, 1996 Neb. App. LEXIS 226 (Neb. Ct. App. Nov. 5, 1996). But, some fence-in jurisdictions refuse to apply the doctrine. *See, e.g., Fisel v. Wynns,* 667 So.2d 761 (Fla. 1995).

Most of the jurisdictions following the fence-in theory provide an exception permitting livestock to be moved on a public roadway without violating state fence law. Most of these statutes permit animals to be moved on a public roadway as long as the animals are under control. However, control of livestock being moved on a public highway may be difficult to maintain in certain circumstances. It is advisable to have sufficient help in moving the livestock so as to maintain control and notify oncoming motorists of the livestock being moved.

## B. DISTRAINT

If a neighbor's animals trespass onto an adjoining property owner's land and the adjoining property owner's land is lawfully fenced, the adjoining owner may have a right to distrain the animals. Most state distraint statutes are quite specific and should be followed very carefully. Many statutes allow the person on whose property the animals have trespassed to hold the animals until their owner pays for the damages caused and the expenses of distraint. The cost of distraint is typically the reasonable cost of feeding and keeping the animals. The individual distraining the animals must give notice of the damages caused to the owner of the livestock and if the damages are not paid within a certain time period (usually five to seven days) after notice has been received, the landowner holding the animals may commence an action against the owner to recover damages. In some states, as an alternative to distraint, the county sheriff may hold the livestock in custody. This approach may be taken if the landowner simply desires to remove the livestock from his or her premises. Damages are not paid. The animals are simply removed from the premises.

## C. IMPREGNATING FEMALE ANIMALS

If a male animal escapes through or over a fence and breeds female animals, the owner of the male

animal is generally responsible for the damages
caused unless a deficient fence maintained by the
complaining party was a factor in the matter. The
measure of damages is generally the difference in
value of the female animals and their offspring if
bred to a male animal of their own station in life
compared to the value as bred to male animals in
question.

## D.   PARTITION FENCES

### 1.  Boundary by Acquiescence

By assumption, a partition fence is located on the
property line. In the event a partition fence is not
located on the property line, an erroneously located
boundary may become the true boundary after a
statutorily-specified number of years of acquiescence.
The "doctrine of practical location," as boundary by
acquiescence is known, typically arises where, as a
result of a dispute, one party occupies to a fence line
and the other party acquiesces in that occupation for
the required length of time. Another common
scenario that gives rise to application of the doctrine
is where adjoining landowners know that a
particular fence or line in a field is not the true
boundary, but do not know where the true boundary
is located. After the statutory period of usage of the
adjoining tracts in this manner, the fence or field line
can become the legal boundary. Boundaries believed
to be in error should be surveyed and, if not correctly
located, an objection filed before the statutory time
period has elapsed.

## 2. Adverse Possession

A concept related to acquiring title to property by acquiescence, known as adverse possession, occurs if an individual possesses continuously someone else's land in an open and notorious fashion with an intent to take it away from them. The adverse possessor becomes the true property owner after the statutory time period (typically between 5 and 21 years) has expired. The doctrine of adverse possession may be invoked, for example, when a stream changes location and an individual continues to farm up to the stream bank. *See, e.g., City of Lawrence v. McGrew,* 211 Kan. 842, 508 P.2d 930 (1973).

## 3. Location of Partition Fence

A partition fence can be built right on the property line with literally one-half of the post on one side and the other half on the other side. Once the fence is constructed, it becomes owned by the two adjoining owners in tenancy in common. The same principle can also apply to trees that are on the property line. *See, e.g., Young v. Ledford,* No. 2080473, 2009 Ala. Civ. App. LEXIS 554 (Ala. Ct. Civ. App. Nov. 6, 2009).

There are two situations where it is anticipated that there will be exceptions to the rule that a partition fence is built on the property line. One is where the adjoining landowners have agreed to maintain a private roadway or lane as a passageway between the two tracts. In such event, a fence can be built on either side of the lane serving as access. The other situation is where the adjacent tracts are separated by a water course, gorge, canyon or some other topographical characteristic making it impractical to build the fence on the property line. In these situations, the fence should be built as close as possible to the correct boundary location.

## E. DUTY TO BUILD AND MAINTAIN A PARTITION FENCE

State law (in "fence-in" jurisdictions) typically requires landowners to build and maintain partition fences on request. However, in some states, a landowner not wanting to enclose his or her land cannot be compelled to build or pay for an equal share of any partition fence. *See, e.g., Fogle v. Malvern Courts, Inc.,* 701 A.2d 265 (Pa. Supr. Ct. 1997), In other states, a landowner not wanting to pay the costs of constructing a fence must prove that the cost of construction will be greater than any value the fence will add to the land. *See, e.g., Wurzelbacher v. Colerain Township Board,* 105 Ohio App. 3d 97, 663 N.E.2d 713 (1995). This problem usually arises when one of the adjacent landowners raises livestock and the other adjacent landowner does not. Under the fence-in theory, a livestock owner is required to fence livestock in. *See, e.g., Estate of Wallis v. Snyder,* 659 N.E.2d 423 (Ill. Ct. App. 1995), However, the non-livestock owner who does not participate in the building or maintenance of a partition fence may be precluded from recovering for damages caused by trespassing animals coming across the boundary line. This serves to limit the fence-in theory, and has led to litigation.

Fencing statutes that impose a duty on an adjoining landowner without livestock to contribute to the building or maintenance of a partition fence have been upheld as constitutional. The claim has been made that such statutes amount to an unconstitutional taking of private property requiring compensation under the Fifth Amendment. *See, e.g., Choquette v. Perrault,* 153 Vt. 45, 569 A.2d 455 (1989); *Gravert v. Nebergall,* 539 N.W.2d 184 (Iowa 1995).

## 1. What Is a Legal Fence?

All state statutes prescribe the rules governing a legal fence. The most popular type of fence used in agriculture today is the "barbed wire" fence. State fencing statutes prescribe the number of wires, the spacing between the wires, the tension and strength of the wires, and the distance between the posts. An electric fence may or may not be a legal fence. Other types of fences such as a fence of stone, hedge, post and rails, post and palings, post and planks, palisades, rail or "worm" fences and turf fences may also be deemed a legal fence.

## 2. Division of Partition Fence Responsibility

In general, in states following the "fence-in" rule, the owners of adjoining lands are required to build and maintain in good repair all partition fences in equal shares. *See, e.g., Duncalf v. Ritscher Farms, Inc.,* 627 N.W.2d 906 (Iowa 2001). There are several methods for dividing fence responsibility, but only two hard and fast rules. One well established rule is that if the parties can agree between themselves, they can allocate responsibility. Preferably this is done with the parties entering into a written fence agreement that describes the property involved and the fence responsibility assigned to each tract. Such agreements may usually be recorded in a county office where the property is located. Once recorded, the agreement runs with the title to the underlying real estate and binds both present and successor owners of the property. In other words, agreements that are not filed publicly may be enforced only against a party to the agreement and those with notice of the agreement. Others are generally not bound by a predecessors' oral or unrecorded written agreement of which they had no notice. A second established rule is that if the prior property owners agreed to a particular division of fence responsibility, the owners may agree to accept the predecessors' division.

Other methods for dividing fence responsibility may include adopting what is commonly known as the "right hand" rule which is widely followed, but is not required by law unless decreed by the fence viewers (the officially designated arbiters of fence disputes locally) or specified in a fence agreement. Under the right hand rule, each owner standing on his or her property facing the fence agrees to build and maintain the right hand portion.

In the event a division for fence responsibility cannot be arrived at between the parties, problems of dividing fence responsibility may be resolved by the fence viewers. The fence viewers are usually the county commissioners of the county in which the land is located or members of the township governing board.

Most state statutes have a process that can be invoked to compel a landowner to build or repair a partition fence. The usual process first requires making a request of an adjoining landowner to repair his or her share of an existing fence or erect his or her share of a new fence. If the adjoining owner makes no effort to comply within a reasonable time, a written request should be made of the fence viewers to hear the dispute and make a determination. The fence viewers determine any maintenance responsibility and will establish a deadline for when the work is to be accomplished. If the work is not accomplished by the proper party, the fence viewers will have the other party make a deposit to cover the cost involved and will hire the work done and then charge the account to the noncomplying party in the form of additional property taxes.

## F.   HIGHWAY FENCES

In some states, it is conventional to expect landowners to build highway fences. However, some states today have resolved the issue by delegating to the state highway commission or department the responsibility to build and maintain highway fences. In addition, some states require double fences along the interstate. The farmer is responsible for maintaining the inner fence and the state department of transportation is responsible for maintaining the outer fence. The land in between sometimes creates serious problems with respect to weed control.

Highway fences, in states that have delegated to the state the responsibility to build and maintain, may not need to be livestock-tight fences on the basis that the purpose of a highway fence is to restrict vehicular access to the roadway, rather than keep livestock fenced in. However, in one case, the state supreme court held that the state department of transportation has a duty to maintain safe roadways which includes a duty to keep livestock off the roadway by maintaining highway fences. *See, e.g., Reynolds v. Kansas Dept. of Transportation,* 43 P.3d 799 (Kan. 2002), *rev'g,* 30 P.3d 1041 (Kan. Ct. App. 2001).

## G.   RAILROAD FENCES

Railroad fences produce many legal problems. Most of the legal problems associated with railroad fences have arisen since the mid-twentieth century in the advent of termination of rail lines and the abandonment of some stretches of railroad. Problems arise because the railroad is under a duty to build and maintain the fence on both sides of the railroad's right-of-way. The landowner does not typically have any responsibility to build or maintain railroad fences, even in certain situations when the railroad abandons the line, unless ownership of the abandoned line reverts to the adjacent landowner. *See, e.g., May v. Tri-County Trails Commission,* 220 Wis.2d 729, 583 N.W.2d 878 (1998).

In some states, if a railroad refuses to build or maintain a fence, it is a crime punishable with a cash fine for each offense. In other states, the landowner is given the right to build the fence and recover costs from the railroad with interest accruing at a specified rate plus any attorney's fees necessary to recover the cost. The type of railroad fence contemplated is the type of fence required to "turn" the landowner's stock.

Failure by a railroad to maintain a fence or "cattle" guard at a public road crossing makes the railroad liable, under strict liability rules, unless the animals were on the track through a willful act of the owner. Failure to pay such losses within a certain time frame (usually 30 days) after demand entitles the animals' owner to sue for recovery of damages plus court costs and attorney's fees.

# CHAPTER 8
# WATER LAW

## I.  OVERVIEW

Conflicts concerning water rights are not uncommon in agriculture, and the factors which may be relevant in solving such problems are numerous. Some of these factors include the significance of the source of the water involved. For example, if the water source is a navigable stream or lake that is of vital commercial importance to the country, diversion by adjoining landowners for agricultural purposes may damage not only other landowners on the watercourse, but also the economic development of the entire area. Conversely, the water source may be a non-navigable stream or lake, underground percolating water, or surface water that merely follows the natural drainage contours of the land. Other factors for resolution of water rights conflicts include the economic interests of the area and the importance of water in the furtherance of those interests.

In addition to federal statutory and regulatory provisions that govern water usage, each state regulates water use within its borders. As a result, both federal and state regulators enforce the statutes and promulgate regulations and guidelines as part of their regulatory programs.

## II.   NATURAL STREAMS AND LAKES

In the United States, three distinct legal systems exist that govern the right to use and consume water from natural streams and lakes: (1) the riparian system; (2) the prior appropriation system; and (3) the permit or administrative system. There is a close correlation between the legal system utilized in a particular jurisdiction and how plentiful water is in that jurisdiction. In general, the riparian system prevails in the Eastern United States where rainfall is usually plentiful. The prior appropriation and permit systems prevail in those states west of the Missouri River where rainfall is generally less in amount per year.

### A.   WATER RIGHTS IN NON-NAVIGABLE WATERS

#### 1.  Riparian Systems

The word riparian derives from the Greek for "ownership of the bank." A riparian owner is one who owns land on the bank of a watercourse, or one who owns the land along, bordering upon, bounded by, fronting upon, abutting or adjacent and contiguous to and in contact with the watercourse. In its strictest form, the riparian system rests on the proposition that the owner of land is entitled to have stream flows adjacent to the land flow naturally through or past the premises, neither diminished nor artificially augmented in quantity and unimpaired in quality. In other words, the water flow is to remain unchanged. The riparian system prevails or has prevailed to some degree in the 31 eastern states of the continental United States where there is usually an ample water supply.

Strictly applied, the riparian doctrine is not conducive to economic development because water cannot be withdrawn from a watercourse for a consumptive use. Early courts struggled with the strict application of the riparian doctrine in a time when the nation was growing and becoming more industrialized. Some of the early cases construed the riparian doctrine to allow an individual to use water to turn a millwheel as long as there was minimal evaporation as the millwheel revolved. However, irrigation was an impermissible consumptive use because it diminished what a downstream riparian would be entitled to have flow past their property. Similarly, if water was withdrawn for cooling purposes or to run a packing plant or some similar type of operation, it was deemed to be not in accordance with the strict application of the riparian doctrine.

The courts soon began to recognize the practicalities of development and that the strict application of the riparian doctrine was retarding economic development. Consequently, the courts developed a "reasonable use" application of the riparian doctrine that divided water usage in to natural uses that are necessary for survival (domestic use and livestock watering) and artificial uses, and upstream and downstream riparians. *See, e.g., Evans v. Merriweather,* 2 Ill. (3 Scam.) 491 (1842); *Edmonson v. Edwards,* 111 S.W.3d 906 (Mo.

Ct. App. 2003); *Atkinson v. Corson,* 289 S.W.3d 269
(Mo. Ct. App. 2009).

Artificial uses are those uses that increase comfort
and prosperity. Artificial uses can only be met once
natural uses have been satisfied. Artificial uses
include irrigation and manufacturing and, in some
states, municipal uses. A lower riparian can insist
that upper riparians curtail artificial uses in order to
provide water for the lower riparian's natural uses.
As between competing artificial uses, the courts
typically allow a use if it is reasonable. This theory of
reasonable     use     recognizes     some     permissible
restrictions on use, but permits water use if such use
is reasonable and if the use does not interfere with
other riparian owners. This theory evidences that the
interest of the riparian is not in the natural state of
the stream, but in the use of water that is actually
enjoyed. *See, e.g., Gehlen Brothers v. Knorr* 101 Iowa
700, 70 N.W. 757 (1897).

A concept similar to riparian rights, known as
"littoral rights," applies to lakes. An owner of a
lakeshore property is entitled to withdraw water
from the lake as long as the withdrawal does not
diminish the quantity or quality of water in the lake.

With respect to land conveyances, riparian rights
pass (without mention) in a deed to land. However, it
is believed that riparian rights can be severed from
the land by express conveyance. Because the riparian
doctrine generally restricts water use to riparian
land, holders of riparian rights can be expected to
apply water until the marginal return is equal to the
cost, which is likely to be at or near zero for some

uses. Non-riparians, despite high potential returns for water, are unable to acquire rights to use water unless transfers of riparian rights are permitted. In many states, the right of riparians to transfer water has been limited or denied. As a result, the riparian system typically fails to allocate water where the return is the highest and economic efficiency is, therefore, not promoted.

## 2. Prior Appropriation

Most of the United States west of the 100th meridian utilizes the prior appropriation system. The prior appropriation system is based on a recognition that water is more scarce, and establishes rights to water based on when water is first put to a beneficial use. The doctrine grants to the individual first placing available water to a beneficial use, the right to continue to use the water against subsequent claimants.

A significant issue in the western United States is the right of federal agencies to water on public land. For instance, the Nevada Supreme Court has ruled that the state water engineer must allow federal agencies to apply for water rights to unappropriated water on public grazing land. *United States v. State Engineer,* 27 P.3d 51 (Nev. 2001). However, Nevada law requires an applicant for stockwater rights to be able to put the water to beneficial use. Federal agencies do not own commercial livestock, and, therefore, cannot put water to beneficial use. Also, the U.S. Supreme Court has held that lands to which any right or claim of another attached is not public land. *Bardon v. Northern Pacific Railroad Co.,* 145 U.S. 535 (1882). That is an important point because the U.S. Court of Federal Claims has held, in a case involving a Nevada rancher, that ranchers have private property rights on their grazing allotment. *Hage v. United States,* 51 Fed. Cl. 570 (2002). Thus, grazing allotments are not "public lands" and the water rights on them are not unappropriated.

The prior appropriation, doctrine is referred to as a "first in time, first in right" system of water allocation. The oldest water right on a stream is supplied with the available water to the point at which its state-granted right is met, and then the next oldest right is supplied with the available water and so on until the available supply is exhausted. *See, e.g., Garetson Bros. v. Am. Warrior, Inc.,* 347 P.3d 687, 51 Kan. App. 2d 370 (2015), *rev. den.,* No. 14-111975-A, 2016 Kan. LEXIS 50 (Kan. Sup. Ct. Jan. 25, 2016), *remand decision at Haskell Co. Dist. Ct.,* No. 2012-CV-09 (Feb. 1, 2017). In order for a particular landowner to determine whether such person has a prior right as against another person, it is necessary to trace back to the date at which a landowner's predecessor in interest first put water to a beneficial use. The senior appropriator, in the event of dry conditions, has the right to use as much water as desired up to the established right of the claimant to the exclusion of all junior appropriators.

Water rights in a majority of the prior appropriation states are acquired and evidenced by a permit system that largely confirms the original doctrine of prior appropriation. The right to divert and make consumptive use of water from a watercourse under the prior appropriation system is typically acquired by making a claim, under applicable procedure, and by diverting the water to beneficial use. The "beneficial use" concept is basic; a non-useful appropriation is of no effect. What constitutes a beneficial use depends upon the facts of each particular case. *See, e.g., In re Water Rights of Deschutes River and Tributaries,* 134 Ore. 623, 286 P. 1049 (1930); Okla. Atty. Gen. Op. 99–21 (Jul. 21, 1999).

Some states require that a particular use not only be of benefit to the appropriator, but also be a reasonable and economic use of the water in view of present and future demands upon the source of supply.

In many prior appropriation states, barriers to transfer of water rights are as great as in riparian states. This is the case even though a prior appropriation water right is not as closely linked to land ownership as is a riparian right, and a prior appropriation right may be separately conveyed. In some states, especially the more arid western states, a water right is a right to use the water and is not a right to own the water. The water right is attached to the land on which the water is used, and can be severed from that land.

The prior appropriation system also does not deal with return flow problems caused by differing rates of consumptive use between different appropriators. For example, agricultural irrigation is approximately an 80 percent non-consumptive use. This means that about 80 percent of water appropriated for irrigation eventually returns to its source. However, industrial uses are typically more consumptive in nature although the use of water for cooling typically involves low rates of consumption. Strictly applied, the prior appropriation system does not concern itself with rates of consumptive use.

## 3. Permit (Administrative) Systems

A permit system of water allocation centralizes the allocation decision or decisions by placing the responsibility for allocating water among competing uses in the hands of an administrative agency, usually at the state level. The heart of such a system of water allocation is a permit. Presently, several eastern states and a few western states follow some form of an administrative system of water allocation.

The scope of the various state administrative systems, all of which are statutory, differs greatly. Some statutes purport to regulate only unused rights to water, leaving untouched water rights being exercised at the time of enactment, while other statutes purport to regulate only rights to groundwater. Other state statutes exclude certain water from regulation such as diffused surface water falling on one's own property and water that is put to a beneficial domestic use if the amount is less than a prescribed level on a daily basis. Several states, such as Iowa and Kansas, undertake to regulate all water within the state. The Iowa Act attempts to regulate not only unused rights to water, but water that is already subject to some kind of allocation.

Typically, permits are granted for a term (typically 10 to 25 years), and in most states, the holder of a water right may make application to the appropriate state office to change the place of use, point of diversion, or the use made of the water. When such an application is made, state law may allow additional limitations on consumptive use of the water subject to the permit to be made. *See, e.g., Wheatland Electric Cooperative, Inc. v. Polansky,* 46 Kan. App. 2d 746, 265 P.3d 1194 (Kan. Ct. App. Nov. 4, 2011). Also, a water right can be terminated for non-use. *See, e.g., Frick Farm Properties, L.P. v. Kansas Department of Agriculture,* 216 P.3d 170 (Kan. 2009), *aff'g,* 40 Kan. App. 2d 132, 190 P.3d 983 (2008).

Most permit systems are based largely upon those which originated in Colorado and Wyoming. A particular state's supervision and control is usually exercised through the chief engineer of the state Division of Water Resources or similar official, and through the courts. In some states, a board or department of the state government exercises control. In general, a water right is obtained by filing an application for a permit to appropriate water for beneficial use with the appropriate state officer. An application form has certain standard features that must be satisfied. For example, an application must typically be on the proper form; be accompanied by any required filing fee; give the name and mailing address of the applicant; specify the source of water supply, the proposed place of use, and, if for irrigation, the number of irrigable acres; provide a legal description of the location of the point of diversion or ask for a period of time to establish a point of diversion; enumerate the maximum rate at which water is to be diverted and the total quantity of water sought; and be signed by the applicant or authorized representative. A filed application receives a number and a priority date and time.

In most states, priority stems from the time of filing, rather than from final approval. However, in some states, the mere filing of an application does not insure that a permit will be issued. In these jurisdictions, the state official responsible for approving an application must determine that the application meets certain requirements. Typically required is water availability, that the proposed use neither impairs an existing water right nor unreasonably affects the public interest, that the proposed use is made in good faith and that the proposed use is for a beneficial purpose.

If an application is approved, the applicant will receive a document that can be filed with an appropriate county office in the county where the diversion is to occur. This document will specify the rate and quantity of water that can be diverted as well as the source of the water supply. In some states, recording of this document is necessary to establish priority as to conflicting water rights.

## B.   WATER RIGHTS IN NAVIGABLE WATERS

As between riparian owners, equality of benefits from flowing waters is sought and the rule is that each is entitled to the stream's natural flow, subject only to a reasonable use which much not substantially diminish the stream's quantity or impair its quality. A different right intervenes, however, with respect to navigable waters. While the early rule was that riparian owners on navigable streams had the same rights as riparian owners on non-navigable streams, early courts recognized that all riparian interests were subject to a dominant public interest in navigation. Most courts hold that a riparian owner of a navigable waterway does not have private rights in a stream or body of water which is appurtenant to his or her land, and, in short, no rights beyond that of any other member of the public. The only difference being that such a landowner is more conveniently situated to enjoy the privileges which all the public have in common, and that such person has access to the waters over his or her own land, which the public do not.

## III.  RECREATIONAL USE OF RIVERS AND STREAMS

### A.   PUBLIC ACCESS

In the United States, the individual states own the beds of navigable streams or lakes that flow or exist within their borders, and hold them in trust for their citizens. Under this public ownership concept, states may license use of the beds or lease rights to minerals found there. The right of the public to recreate over the bed can be asserted either because there is a federal navigational servitude or because the state has an expanded definition of navigability which allows more public uses than exist under federal law.

Under state law, the public's right to use rivers or lakes for recreational purposes is typically limited to those waters where the state owns the bed. For non-navigable streams, the title to the bed is held by the adjacent upland owner. Consequently, ownership of the bed is related to the concept of navigability. In general, navigability for title purposes is determined by the "natural and ordinary condition" of the water at the time of statehood. *See, e.g., Defenders of Wildlife v. Hull,* 199 Ariz. 411, 18 P.3d 722 (2001); *Oregon v. Riverfront Protection Association,* 672 F.2d 792 (9th Cir. 1982); *North Dakota ex rel. Board of University and School Lands v. Andrus,* 671 F.2d 271 (8th Cir. 1982); *Northwest Steelheaders Assoc., Inc. v. Simantel,* 112 P.3d 383 (Or. Ct. App. 2005).

It is not necessary that the watercourse be navigable in "interstate commerce." A water body can be navigable for title purposes but not for Commerce Clause purposes. *See, e.g., Utah v. United States,* 403 U.S. 9 (1971); *Hardy Salt Co. v. Southern Pacific Transportation Co.,* 501 F.2d 1156 (10th Cir 1974).

Although a federal test for bed title controlled the rights that states received upon joining the Union, state title tests are still important. When the states received title to the beds, they had the power to keep or dispose of them. Before several Supreme Court decisions which required federal law to be used in determining bed ownership, there were many state court decisions. These tests are still in use today and many conflict with federal law. When they do, federal law controls for title purposes (under the definition of "navigability"), but state law has been incorporated into this to determine what rights the state retains and what rights were granted to adjacent landowners. For example, some states (such as CO, IL, MS, NE and, perhaps, OR) keep title to watercourse beds only where there is a title influence.

Other states follow a rule of "navigability in fact" similar to the federal rule. These states include Arkansas, California, Florida, Idaho, Indiana, Iowa, Louisiana, Minnesota, Missouri, Montana, Nevada, Oklahoma, Tennessee, Utah, Washington and Wyoming. In these jurisdictions, the state retains title to watercourse beds only if the watercourse is navigable in fact. On the navigability test, see *The Daniel Ball,* 77 U.S. (10 Wall.) 557 (1870); *The Montello,* 87 U.S. (20 Wall.) 430 (1874); *United States v. Appalachian Electric Power Co.,* 311 U.S. 377 (1940) and *PPL Montana, LLC v. Montana,* 132 S. Ct. 1215 (2012).

The remaining states use other approaches. For example, Minnesota and North Dakota apparently use a pleasure boat test. *See, e.g., Lampray v. Metcalf,* 53 N.W. 1139 (Minn. 1893); *Roberts v. Taylor,* 181 N.W. 622 (N.D. 1921). In Texas, all rivers with an average width of 30 feet are navigable. In Massachusetts, Maine and New Hampshire, ponds over a specified minimum size (great ponds) are public. Other states, such as Michigan, use a saw log test. In early 2014, the New Mexico attorney general issued a non-binding opinion in which he took the position that a private landowner cannot prevent persons from fishing in a public stream that flows across a landowner's property if the stream is accessible without trespassing across privately owned adjacent lands. *Opinion No. 14–04 (Apr. 1, 2014)*. That opinion was based on New Mexico being a prior appropriation state and, as a result, unappropriated water in streams belongs to the public and is subject to appropriation for beneficial use irrespective of whether the adjacent landowner owns the streambed. Thus, the public has an easement to use stream water for fishing purposes if they can access the stream without trespassing on private property.

There are several other ways states have power over the water within their boundaries. Under its police power, a state may regulate its waters, whether or not they are navigable under the federal test, in order to protect the public's health, safety, and general welfare. Some western states claim ownership of all the water in the state, and as the owner, they claim the power to regulate. Other states limit their control to those waters considered navigable under bed ownership tests. As a result, state laws on public use of watercourses are a complex mix of cases and legislation.

## B. FENCING ACROSS A WATERCOURSE

Areas of concern for farmers and ranchers owning land adjacent to a watercourse include whether the public can use the surface, whether a public right of access exists, and whether there are public shoreline rights. These concerns are primarily related to issues pertaining to trespass, damage to property, and liability for injury.

One of the major issues is whether a landowner can fence across a watercourse. In general, if a landowner owns both banks of a non-navigable stream, the landowner has the same rights and powers over the stream as the landowner has over the adjacent land. This means that a fence may be constructed across the stream and other appropriate steps may be taken to protect property against trespass. However, if a stream is fenced with malicious intent to injure trespassers, and a trespasser is injured, most courts hold the landowner liable. Malicious intent is crucial. *See, e.g., Kansas ex rel. Meek v. Hays,* 246 Kan. 99, 785 P.2d 1356 (1990).

While the Kansas court rejected the idea of expanding recreational use by court decree, leaving the issue for the legislature, not all state courts have been as restrictive. *See, e.g., Arkansas v. McIlroy,* 268 Ark. 227, 595 S.W.2d 659 (1980). Similar conclusions have been reached by courts in California, Idaho, Michigan, Missouri, New Mexico, Ohio, Oregon, Washington and Wisconsin. Other states have expanded public use under a different approach. For instance, the Wyoming Supreme Court has held that the legislature could authorize the use of a stream by the public, and Minnesota and Indiana have statutes permitting the legislature to make such determinations. Similarly, Iowa and South Dakota have extended public use on grounds that relate to their interpretation of state ownership of some or all non-navigable stream beds. The Montana Supreme

Court, referring to the "public trust" has made all waters property of the state, regardless of stream bed ownership or navigability.

For navigable streams, a riparian owner's rights extend only to the high water mark, a point indicated by vegetation and the nature of the soil. Thus, a riparian owner is allowed to construct piers and wharfs in order to make use of the surface, but cannot fence across the stream.

## IV.  DIFFUSED SURFACE WATER

A second classification of water law concerns diffused surface waters. Many of the legal issues facing farmers and ranchers with respect to surface water relate to its disposal. Surface water is important because it is the chief supplier of water to surface streams and lakes.

By definition, diffused surface water lacks the elements of channel and constancy of flow which characterize streams and other watercourses. In general, diffused surface water is water that appears on the surface of the ground in a diffused state with no permanent source of supply or regular course. It usually is created by rain or snow, and has no substantial or permanent existence. Essentially, diffused surface water is water on the surface of the ground which is so undefined that it cannot be properly termed a watercourse. However, surface water is generally distinguished from flood waters that have escaped from a natural watercourse because of extraordinary circumstances.

## A.   RULES GOVERNING DRAINAGE OF SURFACE WATER

For agriculture, drainage of surface water is a significant legal issue. When surface water is sufficient, problems can arise concerning disposal of rainfall and/or melting snow which water-logs valuable fields and pastures forming bogs and sinkholes, thereby making cultivation difficult or impossible. In general, it has historically been wrongful for a landowner to disturb the existing pattern of drainage and thereby obstruct the flow of water from another's lands, or cast upon the lands of another more water than would naturally flow thereupon, or cause an usually high concentration of water in the course of drainage. However, three different legal theories may be utilized to resolve surface water drainage conflicts.

### 1.  English Rule—Absolute Ownership

The rule of absolute ownership, also known as the common enemy rule, is the oldest legal theory applicable to the use of surface water. This rule is based upon the theory that surface water is the enemy of every landowner and a property owner is given complete freedom to discharge surface waters regardless of the harm that might result to others. The owner is allowed to dispose of surface water in any manner that will result in the highest benefit to his or her land. In its original form, the common-enemy doctrine encouraged land development, but also encouraged conflict both between and among landowners. Today, most courts have modified this rule by importing into it qualifications based on concepts of reasonable use, negligence, and/or nuisance to prohibit discharges of large quantities of water onto adjoining land by artificial means in a concentrated flow, except through natural drainways. *See, e.g., Currens v. Sleek,* 138 Wash. 2d 858, 983 P.2d 626 (1999); *Mullins v. Greer,* 26 Va. 587, 311 S.E.2d 110 (1984).

## 2. Civil Law Rule

The civil law rule imposes liability upon one who interferes with the natural flow of surface water and thus invades another's interest in land. This rule is the opposite of the common enemy rule, and is phrased in terms of dominant and servient estates. This rule imposes a servitude upon the lower or servient estate which requires that it receive all waters which flow in the course of nature from the higher or dominant tract. The owner of the dominant tract cannot, however, do anything that would increase the natural drainage burden imposed upon the lower estate. *See, e.g., Mullen v. Natural Gas Line Company of America L.L.C.,* 801 N.W.2d 627 (Iowa Ct. App. May 25, 2011). Essentially, the civil law rule involves accepting the natural flow of water. While this rule minimizes conflict between and among landowners, it also discourages land improvement. As a result, some states have modified the civil law rule to accommodate artificial changes in the natural flow of surface water if the change is incidental to the normal use and improvement of land. These changes are most likely to be acceptable when the water empties into an existing natural watercourse.

However, substantial changes in natural drainage flows resulting in damages to an adjoining landowner are not permissible. This rule applies even in connection with governmentally approved soil conservation practices that substantially alter the natural flow of surface water. *See, e.g., O'Tool v. Hathaway,* 461 N.W.2d 161 (Iowa 1990).

The strict application of the civil law rule has also been modified by a so-called "husbandry" exception, and interference with natural drainage will be allowed if the interference is limited to that which is incidental to reasonable development of the dominant estate for agricultural purposes. *See, e.g., Callahan v. Rickey,* 93 Ill. App. 3d 916, 418 N.E.2d 167 (1981).

## 3. Reasonable Use Rule

Today, many jurisdictions have adopted the rule of reasonable use which attempts to avoid the rigidities of either the civil-law or common-enemy doctrines. Instead, the reasonable use rule determines the rights of the parties by an assessment of all the relevant factors with respect to interference with the drainage of surface waters. Under the reasonable use rule, a landowner is entitled to make a reasonable use of diffused surface water, with such use being a factual question for a jury. *See, e.g., Kral v. Boesch,* 557 N.W.2d 597 (Minn. Ct. App. 1996). The jury must determine whether the benefit to the actor's land outweighs the harm that results from the alteration of the flow of surface water onto neighboring lands. A landowner will be liable for damages only to the extent that interference with the flow of surface water is unreasonable. Determinations of reasonableness are questions of fact and depend upon such things as the degree or extent of harm, the foreseeability of damage, and the amount of care that was exercised to prevent damage. *See, e.g., Vokal v. Vokal,* No. A10–573, 2010 Minn. App. Unpub. LEXIS 1133 (Minn. Ct. App. Nov. 23, 2010); *Enderson v. Kelehan,* 223 Minn. 163, 32 N.W.2d 286 (1948).

## 4. Drainage Codes

In an attempt to address surface water drainage problems, many states have adopted statutory drainage codes whereby a landowner can institute drainage proceedings. State drainage codes authorize proceedings for construction, repair or improvement of agricultural drainage ditches. Such systems may involve several miles of open main ditch and laterals. Benefitted lands are assessed for benefits received. Any taking of land for physical construction is compensated as in eminent domain, although there is a setoff against benefits that accrue to the balance of the tract. Funding for construction typically is by sale of bonds by the ditch district or authority. Bonds are repaid with funds from special assessments against benefitted lands.

Ditch systems require maintenance. Some state drainage codes provide for funds from general revenues for minor maintenance such as cutting weeds, removing saplings, and repairing minor washouts. Major repairs are often funded in formal proceedings. Under many codes, a distinction is made between repairs and improvements. Whereas a repair seeks to restore the ditch to its original specifications, subject only to minor re-sloping of washouts, an improvement contemplates deepening and widening of all or parts of the ditch, installation of larger culverts, and perhaps the addition of a lateral over added lands. Improvement proceedings require constitutionally mandated notice and hearing as in original proceedings.

A significant problem for farmers and ranchers is that routine ditch maintenance can be blocked by laws designed to protect wetlands. As a result, drainage systems that have fallen into disrepair may be left to deteriorate.

## V.  UNDERGROUND WATER

In general, the law recognizes two types of underground water: (1) water that flows in known and defined subterranean watercourses; and (2) water that percolates and oozes through the ground in an unknown and undefined direction. The rights pertaining to utilization of underground water are determined first by determining the class to which the water belongs.

Without evidence to the contrary, all underground water is presumed to be percolating and oozing through the earth, and the burden of showing the existence of an underground stream is on the party desiring to avail themselves of the rules of distribution relating to surface streams. For example, a riparian landowner above an underground watercourse has riparian rights in the underground water if it can be shown that the underground water flows in a well-defined channel capable of delineation. This means that, in general, the underground water cannot be removed and later returned to the underground watercourse even though undiminished and/or unaugmented in quantity or quality.

## A.  RULES GOVERNING UTILIZATION OF GROUNDWATER

### 1.  Rule of Absolute Ownership—English Rule

The rule of absolute ownership (a.k.a. "rule of capture") grants absolute ownership of all underground water to the surface owner. The surface owner has a right to any amount of water that can be pumped. This rule is synonymous with the strict application of the riparian doctrine pertaining to above ground watercourses. The riparian doctrine originally applied to groundwater that flowed in a well-defined channel capable of being distinctly traced. The owner of the land overlying such subterranean water has riparian rights. Presently, no U.S. jurisdiction strictly applies the riparian doctrine to underground water, but Texas comes the closest. *See, e.g., Sipriano v. Great Spring Waters of America, Inc.,* 1 S.W.3d 75 (Tex. 1999). In addition, the Texas Court of Appeals has, citing its *Sipriano* opinion, applied the rule of capture to any migratory subsurface minerals that a landowner can produce absent malice or willful waste. *Petro Pro, Ltd, et al. v. Upland Resources, Inc.,* 279 S.W.3d 743 (Tex. Ct. App. 2007).

In 2012, the Texas Supreme Court held, on the basis of oil and gas law, that landownership in Texas includes interests in in-place groundwater. Accordingly, such groundwater cannot be taken for public use without adequate compensation guaranteed by Article I, Section 17(a) of the Texas Constitution. *The Edwards Aquifer Authority, et al. v. Day, et al.,* 369 S.W.3d 814 (Tex. 2012), *remand decision at The Edwards Aquifer Authority, et al. v. Bragg,* 421 S.W.3d 118 (Tex. Ct. App. 2013).

## 2. Reasonable Use Rule

Some states follow the "American rule" of reasonable use. Under this rule, each landowner is restricted to a reasonable exercise of his or her own rights and a reasonable use of that property in relation to the rights of other persons to use their property similarly. In essence, this involves application of a modified version of the riparian doctrine. Under this theory, a landowner has the right to as much underground water as needed for beneficial uses, but such water cannot be withdrawn if the use constitutes waste or injures another person or their property. *See, e.g., Brady v. Abbott Laboratories,* 433 F.3d 679 (9th Cir. 2005), *reh'g. den.,* 446 F.3d. 924 (9th Cir. 2006).

In some states, underground water cannot be removed and later returned to an underground watercourse even though undiminished.

The reasonable use rule is also important in the context of hydrologically-connected groundwater and surface water. This is particularly an issue in the western half of the United States where rainfall is relatively scarce and water for crops must come from either above ground rivers and streams or underground aquifers. When the above ground water sources are hydrologically connected to underground sources, and there is insufficient water for all users, the rights to the competing uses must be determined. The Restatement (Second) of Torts § 858 sets forth the reasonable use rule in this context as follows:

Liability for Use of Groundwater

(1) A proprietor of land or his grantee who withdraws water from the land and uses it for a beneficial purpose is not subject to liability for interference with the use of water by another, unless

    (a) the withdrawal of groundwater unreasonably causes harm to a proprietor of neighboring land through lowering the water table or reducing artesian pressure,

    (b) the withdrawal of groundwater exceeds the proprietor's reasonable share of the annual supply or total share of groundwater, or

    (c) the withdrawal of the groundwater has a direct and substantial effect upon a watercourse or lake and unreasonably causes harm to a person entitled to the use of its water.

In early 2005, the Nebraska Supreme Court, in a case of first impression, recognized a common-law right for interference with surface water against users of hydrologically-connected groundwater. *Spear T Ranch, Inc. v. Knaub et al.*, 269 Neb. 177 (2005). See also *Michigan Citizens for Water Conservation v. Nestle Waters North America, Inc.*, 269 Mich. App. 25, 709 N.W.2d 174 (2005). The court noted that the common law should acknowledge and attempt to balance the competing equities of groundwater uses with surface water appropriations, and that the Restatement sets forth the best approach to achieve this end. Under the Restatement approach, the court held, the burden of proof is on surface water users to show that the interference from groundwater users is direct and substantial. The court also ruled that the state groundwater appropriation statute (and corresponding regulations) did not abrogate the common law claim.

## 3. Prior Appropriation

Under the prior appropriation doctrine, the person who first puts groundwater to a beneficial use has a priority right over other persons subsequently desiring the same water. This doctrine is applied in many western states that also follow the prior appropriation doctrine with respect to surface water. In many of these states, appropriation rights are administered through a state-run permit system.

## 4. Correlative Rights

Several states follow, at least to a degree, the correlative rights doctrine. This doctrine requires reasonable use of groundwater with some notion of sharing between overlying landowners. *See, e.g., Koch v. Auperle,* 274 Neb. 52, 737 N.W.2d 869 (2007). In addition to correlative rights, priority rights control the appropriators who remove the water from the overlying land. The correlative rights doctrine is a modification of the riparian doctrine. Several states recognize correlative rights to an extent, with California being the most significant of these states.

## B.   STATE GROUNDWATER REGULATION

Some states regulate groundwater in tandem with surface water, thereby forming one water code. Other states, although possessing detailed surface water regulations, have enacted entirely separate codes to govern groundwater. In these states, the burden of integrating the total water resource rests with an administrator, and the courts must solve problems caused by conflicts between users from the different supplies.

Most groundwater codes provide for area determinations by a state agency in charge of groundwater administration. The primary administrative issues with respect to groundwater concern the issues of subsequent wells which lower the water level and thereby interfere with prior users, and whether a minimum groundwater level is necessary, and if it is, how the desired level should be established and maintained. These issues are of greatest concern in the western states where both surface and groundwater is relatively scarce.

In many states, wells for domestic watering purposes (i.e., the household and livestock watering) are exempt from the administrative process irrespective of the impact of such wells on senior water rights in a fully appropriated area. *See, e.g., Five Corners Family Farmers, et al. v. State,* 173 Wash.2d 296, 268 P.3d 892 (2011). In those states, all that is typically required is the filing of an application for a domestic well. No further notice or evaluation by the state is necessary. *See, e.g., Bounds v. State, et al.,* 306 P.3d 457 (N.M. Sup. Ct. 2013), *affn'g., Bounds, et al. v. State,* 149 N.M. 484, 252 P.3d 708 (N.M. Ct. App. 2010).

The states handle groundwater issues in different manners. Some states restrict new users from interfering with a prior user in any respect. This appears to be the approach in Colorado and Idaho. However, while the Idaho statute provides that prior appropriations shall be the criterion, it states that "a reasonable exercise of this right shall not block economic development of underground water resources." Other states view a groundwater appropriation right as only a right to take a certain quantity of water from the ground. The continuance of certain pumping levels or pressures is not part of the right acquired by a beneficial appropriator. This appears to be the approach of Oklahoma and Nebraska. *See, e.g., Bamford v. Upper Republican Natural Resources District,* 245 Neb. 299, 512 N.W.2d 642 (1994), *cert. denied,* 513 U.S. 874 (1994).

Some states, such as Oregon and Washington, follow a middle ground approach and curtail unlimited exploration concerning groundwater pumping, thereby granting to prior users a certain degree of stability and security in the maintenance of water levels.

A few states, such as Kansas, require that minimum desirable streamflow levels be maintained in certain rivers and streams. In order to secure a benefit from groundwater resources, a minimum level must be established within which it is economically feasible to pump water, and this level must be maintained by limiting withdrawals to the amount of natural or artificial recharge.

This approach allows excessive pumping until the minimum level is reached and then limits the amount of pumping to equal the rate of recharge. Other western and typically arid states, such as Colorado, New Mexico, Arizona and Wyoming, do not have provisions requiring minimum desirable streamflows. This difference in groundwater law between adjoining states has led to litigation concerning streamflow levels in watercourses that flow in and across state boundaries.

## VI.   BOUNDARY DISPUTES

Farmers and ranchers owning agricultural land adjacent to a watercourse may be faced with a changing property line due to shifts in the size and location of the watercourse. The property boundary may be slowly eroded away or may change suddenly as the result of a flood or similar natural disaster. In general, the location of the new boundary depends upon whether the watercourse is navigable or non-navigable, and how fast the change has occurred.

Typically, the description of the boundary of a watercourse bed is defined by state law. Most states use the ordinary high water line of the boundary, but a few states use the low water line as the boundary. This difference in definition may be significant in terms of access along navigable streams. If the water level in a stream fluctuates, the bed below the ordinary high water line may be exposed. This means that the owner of upland property, if the property ends at the ordinary high water line, is separated from the stream by a strip of public land during times of low water. The public may be entitled to access over this. If the low water line is used, a strip of public land will not appear adjacent to the stream, and there may not be any public use of the bank allowed.

## A.   ACCRETIONS AND AVULSIONS

An accretion occurs when soil is deposited in an area that was once under water, thereby creating new land. An accretion need not be continuous in the time sense. Alternatively, an avulsion is a change in a watercourse boundary that is not gradual or imperceptible. If a watercourse shifts bodily, taking a new course without removing piece by piece from its bank, it is said to shift by avulsion. *See, e.g., Anderson v. Cumpston,* 258 Neb. 891, 606 N.W.2d 817 (2000). Consequently, avulsion may be defined as a lateral movement discontinuous in the space sense.

In the time sense, the actual avulsion is almost instantaneous.

In general, slow changes (accretions) that occur through such things as erosion or any other similar process, results in a shift in the property boundary. Thus, a landowner whose property is being slowly eroded will have a constantly changing land area. If the change is rapid (avulsion), then the boundary lines do not shift, and ownership disputes should not arise. *See, e.g., Monument Farms, Inc. v. Daggett,* 2 Neb. App. 988, 520 N.W.2d 556 (1994); *Stop the Beach Renourishment, Inc. v. Florida Department of Environmental Protection, et al.,* 560 U.S. 702 (2010).

If a landowner owns property on both sides of a non-navigable stream, streambed is considered the exclusive property of the landowner subject to possible rights of public access. If a landowner owns land adjoining a non-navigable stream on one side of the stream only, the usual rule is that ownership of the bed extends to the middle thread or course of the main current of the stream—sometimes called the meander line. This general rule could be varied if a land description was sufficiently precise to indicate that the bed of the stream was expressly reserved or excepted from the property conveyed in the deed.

## VII.  WEATHER MODIFICATION SYSTEMS

### A.  IN GENERAL

The possibility of controlling the weather is of particular importance to agriculture because farming and ranching are highly weather sensitive occupations. Weather modification activities include the placing of substances in the atmosphere with the intention and for the purpose of producing artificial changes in the atmosphere's behavior. Weather modification activities are designed to achieve objectives such as augmenting precipitation, dispersing fog and suppressing hail.

The increase in state regulation of weather modification has coincided with the increase in weather modification activities. A majority of states have some form of regulatory program concerning the conduct of weather modification activities. There is a great deal of variation among the states in terms of the degree and type of regulation, but a licensing requirement and permit process are typical.

## 1.  Different Public Interests

Not all persons are benefitted in the same manner by a given type of weather. For example, additional rains may be welcomed by farmers and ranchers but not by weekend recreationists or vacationers. As long as the weather is the result of nature, there are usually no legal problems. However, once attempts are made to modify the weather, the potential for conflict is created. States such as Colorado, Illinois, Minnesota and South Dakota have attempted to provide for public input into the decision making process regarding weather modification by requiring public notice and input before a weather modification activity begins. This serves as an attempt to balance varied interests in weather modification activities.

## 2. Tort Liability Issues

Another important aspect of weather modification concerns the questions of liability for damages caused by weather resulting from weather modification activities. The general liability rule is to hold liable for damages the party who benefitted or was expected to benefit from the weather modification activity that gave rise to the particular harm. While this may produce heavy economic burdens in some instances when massive damage occurs, most states that regulate the conduct of weather modification activities require persons engaged in weather modification activities to have the financial ability to compensate for any damages to persons or property that result from weather modification activities. This is usually achieved by requiring prepaid insurance policies or bonds to cover potential liability.

Before an individual engaged in weather modification can be held liable for damages, the person who suffered injury must prove an injury to a legal right, and a causal relationship between the weather modification activity and the alleged damage. Recovery may be based on several theories including negligence in the conduct of the weather modification activity, trespass on the defendant's property, strict liability or private nuisance. However, it may be difficult for an individual to recover against a person engaged in weather modification because of the difficulty in establishing a causal link between the modifier's action and the resulting damages. As a result, some states, such as Pennsylvania and West Virginia, hold individuals engaging in weather modification activities strictly liable for any resulting damages. Colorado, while not applying a strict liability test, makes it negligence per se for an individual to fail to obtain a license or permit before conducting a weather modification activity.

# CHAPTER 9

# ENVIRONMENTAL LAW

## I. THE LEGAL BASIS OF ENVIRONMENTAL LAW

### A. STATUTORY LAW

Much of environmental law is based on federal and state statutes with administrative agencies at both the federal and state level given the authority to promulgate regulations interpreting the laws and enforcing their provisions. In many instances, a particular farmer or rancher who is found to be in violation of an environmental law will initially be dealing with the governmental administrative agency responsible for administering the statute alleged to have been violated. Typically, only after all applicable administrative remedies have been undertaken can an affected farmer or rancher obtain recourse in a court. Consequently, it is in a farmer or rancher's best interests to become familiar with the administrative procedures of any governmental agency having jurisdiction over any aspect of their operation.

The National Environmental Policy Act (NEPA) of 1969 was one of the first modern environmental statutes and remains one of the most important. *42 U.S.C. §§ 4321–4370b (2008).* NEPA was the Congress' response to nationwide pressure for the adoption of a national policy designed to protect the environment. Perhaps NEPA's most significant feature is that it requires government agencies to file an environmental impact statement (EIS) before taking any action that would have a significant environmental impact. An EIS must address the environmental cost and benefit of the proposed project, the optimal location for a new facility in terms of limiting adverse effects on the environment, and the use of best available technology to minimize risks. *See, e.g., Pacific Rivers Council v. United States Forest Service, et al.,* 689 F.3d 1012 (9th Cir. 2012), *withdrawing and replacing,* 668 F.3d 609 (9th Cir. 2012), *rev'g in part and aff'g in part,* No. 2:05-CV-00953-MCE-GGH, 2008 U.S. Dist. LEXIS 85403 (E.D. Cal. Sept. 18, 2008), *cert. granted,* 133 S. Ct. 1582 (U.S. 2013); *Union Neighbors United, Inc. v. Jewell,* 831 F.3d 564 (D.C. Cir. 2016).

NEPA has been held to apply to GMO crops. *Center for Food Safety, et al. v. Vilsack, et al.,* No. C 08–00484 JSW, 2009 U.S. Dist. LEXIS 86343 (N.D. Cal. Sept. 21, 2009), appellate decision at, *Center for Food Safety, et al. v. Vilsack,* 636 F.3d 1166 (9th Cir. 2011).

While NEPA does not have a significant impact on the typical farm or ranch operation, it does subject very large operations that require construction of major facilities to its regulatory scope. In addition, NEPA set the stage for an increased governmental involvement in the control of air and water pollution. These laws authorize the federal government to set national standards to which the individual states must adhere. However, the states are permitted to devise plans for their implementation and to submit these plans to the EPA administrator for approval. In order to be approved, however, the state plans must adhere to standards that are at least as strict as those of the federal government.

## B. COMMON LAW

Common law rules are designed to protect property owners from trespass and nuisance that diminish the value of their property. For example, under the common law rule of riparian rights as the doctrine relates to water pollution, downstream property owners have a right to undiminished water quality. If an upstream party pollutes and damages downstream property values, then the party downstream may bring a private nuisance action against the polluter. The remedy is payment of damages and/or an injunction. *See, e.g., Whalen v. Union Bag & Paper Co.,* 101 N.E. 805 (N.Y. 1913). In a later case, the court limited the rule in *Whalen* that a nuisance which results in substantial continuing damage must be enjoined. *Boomer v. Atlantic Cement Company, Inc.,* 26 N.Y.2d 219, 257 N.E.2d 870 (1970).

The common law doctrine of nuisance also provided recourse for the public against unwanted intrusions of pollution. Multiple parties showing evidence of damages by the same party could call on the state to bring an action. Again, the remedy was damages and/or injunction. *See, e.g., Georgia v. Tennessee Copper Co.,* 206 U.S. 230 (1907).

But, there are shortcoming to the common law nuisance approach for addressing environmental For example, a lawsuit is filed only after environmental damage has occurred and the defendant has committed capital to activity alleged to have caused the problem. In addition, the employment and economic survival of a particular community may be at stake if a polluting firm is forced to cease operations. Likewise, it may not always be possible to determine who is responsible for causing the pollution. Another drawback of the nuisance approach is that it may give a "license to pollute." Also, standing to sue may be a problem. Another drawback of the nuisance approach is that there is no direct effort at a benefit/cost analysis, and no particular plaintiff may have sufficient damage to warrant filing a lawsuit. In addition, the courts are generally ill-equipped to deal with nuisance types of problems.

## C. UNCONSTITUTIONAL "TAKINGS" ISSUES

### 1. Eminent Domain

The "takings" clause of the Fifth Amendment has been held to apply to the states since 1897. *See Chicago, Burlington and Quincy Railroad Co., v. Chicago,* 166 U.S. 226 (1897). In addition, the state constitutions of 47 states expressly prohibit the taking of private property for public use without just compensation (the exceptions are Kansas, North Carolina and Virginia). The Fifth Amendment states in part ". . . nor shall private property be taken for public use without just compensation." *"Just compensation" equals fair market value, generally in cash. For partial takings, "severance damages" may be awarded in addition to compensation for the part taken. See, e.g., Sharp v. United States,* 191 U.S. 341 (1903).

The clause has two prohibitions: (1) all takings must be for public use, and (2) even takings that are for public use must be accompanied by compensation. Historically, the "public use" requirement operated as a major constraint on government action. For many years, the requirement was understood to mean that if property was to be taken, it was necessary that it be used by the public—the fact that the taking was "beneficial" was not enough. Eventually, however, courts concluded that a wide range of uses could serve the public even if the public did not, in fact, have possession. Indeed, so many exceptions were eventually built into the general rule of "use by the public" that the rule itself was abandoned.

In 1954 and again in 1984, the U.S. Supreme Court demonstrated its willingness to define expansively "public use," and confirmed the ability of a state to use eminent domain power to transfer property outright to a private party, so long as the exercise of the eminent domain power is rationally related to a conceivable public purpose. But, in recent years, state courts have split on the issue of whether the government's eminent domain power can be exercised to take private homes and businesses for the development of larger businesses by private companies. The argument is that the larger businesses enhance "economic development" that increases jobs and tax revenue in the area and that this satisfies the Fifth Amendment's "public use" requirement. *See, e.g., Bailey v. Myers,* 206 Ariz. 224, 76 P.3d 898 (Ariz. Ct. App. 2003). The Michigan Supreme Court has ruled, however, that such exercise of the eminent domain power is proper only if (1) the private entities involved are public utilities that operate highways, railroads, canals, power lines, gas pipelines, and other instrumentalities of commerce; (2) the property remains under the supervision or control of a governmental entity; or (3) the public concern is accomplished by the condemnation itself (i.e., blighted housing has become a threat to public health and safety). *County of Wayne v. Hathcock,* 684 N.W.2d 765 (Mich. 2004).

In 2005, the Supreme Court clarified the difference among the states by again ruling that the eminent domain power can be exercised on behalf of a private party for economic development that benefits the public by increasing jobs and the tax base in the area. *Kelo, et al. v. City of New London,* 545 U.S. 469 (2005). Thus, if the exercise of eminent domain for a private party is done in conjunction with a development plan and does not involve obvious corruption, the taking will be allowed (and compensation will have to be paid). With the Court's most recent opinion, the Court is clearly deferring to states on the issue. If the condemnation of property is rationally related to a legitimate purpose of government, it will be approved. Likewise, states may restrict the exercise of eminent domain on behalf of private parties if they so desire. In the wake of *Kelo,* several states either amended the state statutory process for proceedings involving condemnation of private property, or have amended the state constitution. In addition, the Ohio Supreme Court has held that a taking providing nothing other than an economic benefit violates the Ohio constitution. *City of Norwood v. Horney,* 853 N.E.2d 1115 (Ohio 2006). The Court has also held that Ohio landowners have a property interest in the groundwater underlying their land such that governmental interference with that right can constitute a taking. *McNamara v. City of Rittman,* 838 N.E.2d 640 (Ohio 2005).

> **Note:** For constitutional takings purposes, "property" may include more than just the surface estate. For example, in *The Edwards Aquifer Authority, et al. v. Day, et al.,* 369 S.W.3d 814 (Tex. Sup. Ct. 2012), the Texas Supreme Court unanimously held, on the basis of oil and gas law, that landownership in TX includes interests in in-place groundwater. As such, water cannot be taken for public use without adequate compensation guaranteed by Article I, Section 17(a) of the TX Constitution. In the case, the plaintiffs were farmers that sought permit to pump underground water for crop irrigation purposes. The underground water at issue was located in the Edwards Aquifer and the plaintiffs' land was situated entirely within the boundaries of the aquifer. A permit was granted, but water usage under the permit was limited to 14 acre-feet of water rather than 700 acre-feet that was sought because the plaintiffs could not establish "historical use." The Court determined that the plaintiff's practice of issuing permits based on historical use was an unjustified departure from the Texas Water Code permitting factors.

## 2. Regulatory (Non-Physical) Takings

Much of environmental law involves limitations on an individual's use of their privately-owned property. Thus, a governmental body either enacts a statute or promulgates a regulation that restricts one's use of their property to protect identifiable environmental values deemed worthy of protection by society at large. The restriction on land use may even be so complete that, in effect, the restriction amounts to the government "taking" the property. The taking of private property involves a governmental entity seeking to acquire a recognized legal property right such as a fee, an easement or a leasehold, with plans to occupy or use the property taken with something such as a road, building or park. However, these regulatory restrictions on private property usage do not involve a physical taking. A nonphysical taking may involve the governmental condemnation of air space rights, water rights, subjacent or lateral support rights, or the regulation of property use through environmental restrictions. Thus, environmental laws and regulations substantially impacting private property rights can be examples of nonphysical takings that give rise to Fifth Amendment concerns. Since the property is not physically taken, a question arises as to when a defacto regulatory taking has occurred. The legal issue is the point at which an environmental regulation becomes so burdensome on land use that a compensable taking has occurred.

Many environmental laws and regulations at the state and local level are promulgated pursuant to the "police power". The Supreme Court, in 1837, recognized that state and local governments have an inherent power to protect the health, safety, welfare or morals of their people and that the reasonable exercise of this power does not violate the

Constitution. *Charles River Bridge v. Warren Bridge Co.*, 36 U.S. (11 Pet.) 420 (1837). This power came to be known as the "police power". However, until the 1930s, legislation and regulations that directly impacted fundamental constitutional rights such as those contained in the first ten amendments of the United States Constitution (known as the Bill of Rights) were generally struck down as unconstitutional. *See, e.g., United States v. Carolene Products Co.*, 304 U.S. 144 (1938).

However, since the Supreme Court's decision in *Carolene Products*, a sea change has occurred in the legal analysis of takings cases. Presently, almost all legislation enacted pursuant to a state or local government's police power is presumed to have a reasonable basis for enactment. In addition, courts generally tend to hypothesize reasons for a law's enactment if the legislative body responsible for enacting the law fails to state explicitly the reasons behind its judgment. *See, e.g., Williamson v. Lee Optical of Oklahoma, Inc.*, 348 U.S. 483 (1955), the court held that legislation restricting the use of property was to be treated like economic measures that do not involve a fundamental constitutional right. As such, legislation affecting property rights would not be struck down as unconstitutional if the legislation bore a rational relationship to a legitimate end of government such as protecting the public's health, welfare or safety. This reasoning permitted a tremendous expansion in the use of the police power and its impact upon property rights, as well as the eminent domain clause of the Fifth Amendment.

In a key case decided in 1978, the U.S. Supreme Court set forth a multi-factored balancing test for determining when governmental regulation of private property effects a taking requiring compensation. *Penn Central Transportation Co. et al. v. New York City*, 438 U.S. 104 (1978). However, in dictum in a 1980 opinion, *Agins v. City of Tiburon*, 447 U.S. 255 (1980), the Court stated that government regulation of private property "effects a taking if [it] does not substantially advance legitimate state interests. . . ." Since that time, some courts have held that government must provide compensation for a regulation of property unless it is able to prove that the regulation will substantially advance legitimate government interests—without regard to the other factors that a court would ordinarily weigh under the *Penn Central* test, such as the burden on the particular property owner and "reasonable expectations." But, in a 2005 case, *Lingle, et al. v. Chevron U.S.A. Inc.*, 544 U.S. 528 (2005), the Supreme Court confirmed that it is the multi-factored *Penn Central* test, rather than a "substantially advances" means/ends test, that generally governs the question whether a regulation of property requires just compensation.

The Court, in *Lingle*, left intact the rule that a taking occurs when land-use regulation completely eliminates the landowner's use of the property, and found a taking on that basis in *Lucas v. South Carolina Coastal Council*, 505 U.S. 1003 (1992). The *Lucas* case has two important implications for environmental regulation of agricultural activities. First, the *Lucas* court focused solely on the economic viability of the land and made no recognition of potential noneconomic objectives of land ownership. However, in the agricultural sector land ownership is typically associated with many noneconomic objectives and serves important sociological and psychological functions. Under the *Lucas* approach, these noneconomic objectives are not recognized. Second, under the *Lucas* rationale, environmental regulations do not invoke automatic compensation unless the regulations deprive the property owner of *all* beneficial use. On remand, the South Carolina Supreme Court determined that the landowner was entitled to compensation. *Lucas v. South Carolina Coastal Council,* 309 S.C. 424, 424 S.E.2d 484 (1992).

Under the *Lucas* approach, an important legal issue is whether compensation is required when the landowner has economic use remaining on other portions of the property that are not subject to regulation. In *Miller Brothers v. Michigan Dept. of Natural Resources,* 203 Mich. App. 674, 513 N.W.2d 217 (1994), the plaintiffs owned oil and gas rights in west central Michigan. In 1987, the director of the State Department of Natural Resources prohibited exploration for or development of oil and gas on the bulk of the plaintiff's property. The court focused solely on the landowner's use of the mineral interests involved to hold that the plaintiff's property had been taken. Even though a non-mineral interest land use possibility remained, the court held that the landowners were denied all economically viable use of the *mineral interest*. The court found it immaterial that all but one of the plaintiffs had extensive landholdings outside of the protected area.

The Supreme Court's opinion in *Lingle* also does not bar takings claims in situations involving "unconstitutional conditions" to property usage. *See, e.g. Nollan v. California Coastal Commission,* 483 U.S. 825 (1987); *Dolan v. Tigard,* 512 U.S. 374 (1994). *Nollan* and *Dolan* involved the special application of the "doctrine of unconstitutional conditions," which provides that the government may not require a person to give up the constitutional right to receive just compensation when property is taken for a public use in exchange for a discretionary benefit that has little or no relationship to the property. *Nollan* and *Dolan* involved permit conditions that required dedications of land that would allow permanent physical invasions by the public, and the Court ruled that these physical invasions, if unilaterally imposed, would constitute per se takings. The cases are inapplicable to impact fees and other permit conditions that do not involve physical invasions.

**Note:** In *Koontz v. St. Johns River Water Management District,* 133 S. Ct. 2586 (2013), the court held that the unconstitutional conditions doctrine espoused in *Nollan* and *Dolan* made no distinction between conditions precedent and conditions subsequent, and applies even though none of the plaintiff's property is actually taken. Thus, monetary exactions absent a physical taking of property are subject to takings scrutiny.

Also in a case decided in 2002, *Tahoe-Sierra Preservation Council, Inc. v. Tahoe Regional Planning Agency,* 535 U.S. 302 (2002), an association of property owners near Lake Tahoe brought a takings claim after a regional planning agency imposed a moratorium on development in the area. The court reasoned that *Lucas* only required analysis of regulatory taking claims as a categorical taking in the unusual case where there is a total prohibition on the beneficial economical use of property. The court held that a taking had not occurred because moratoria are essential land-use development tools and that the time it takes for a decision to be made should be protected. Three justices dissented, pointing out that the distinction between temporary and permanent prohibitions is tenuous and that takings in the case lasted almost six years. A separate dissent by Justices Thomas and Scalia argued that regulations prohibiting all productive uses of property are subject to *Lucas'* per se rule regardless of whether the property involved retains theoretical useful life and value if, and when, the "temporary" moratorium is lifted. The Court also made it clear that in evaluating whether a regulation works a taking, court must focus on the landowner's entire parcel of property. That means, for example, that regulation impacting only a portion of landowner's tract would not constitute a compensable taking. *See, e.g., Brace v. United States,* 72 Fed. Cl. 337 (2006).

Thus, after the Court's *Lingle* opinion, a landowner seeking to challenge a government regulation as an uncompensated taking of private property may proceed by alleging a "physical" taking, a *Lucas*-type total regulatory taking (*see, e.g., State v. Basford,* 119 So. 3d 478 (Fla. Sup. Ct. 2013), a *Penn Central* taking (*see, e.g., The Edwards Aquifer Authority v. Bragg,* No. 04-11-00018-CV, 2013 Tex. App. LEXIS 10838

(Tex. Ct. App. Aug. 28, 2013)), or a land-use exaction violating the *Nollan* and *Dolan* standards. *See, e.g., Kafka, et al. v. Montana Department of Fish, Wildlife & Parks, et al.,* No. 05–146, 2008 Mont. LEXIS 697 (Mont. Sup. Ct. Dec. 31, 2008).

A constitutional violation may also be found for a temporary taking. *Arkansas Game & Fish Commission v. United States,* 133 S. Ct. 511 (2012), *rev'g., and rem'g.,* 637 F.3d 1366 (Fed. Cir. 2011), remand decision at *Arkansas Game & Fish Commission v. United States,* 736 F.3d 1364 (Fed. Cir. 2013).

## D. THE "COMMERCE CLAUSE"

Much environmental legislation and regulation restricting private land use activities is created pursuant to the commerce clause of the United States Constitution. (*Article I Section 8*). Since the mid-1930s, the U.S. Supreme Court has interpreted the "commerce clause" in such a manner to give almost absolute power to the Congress to regulate commerce among the states. Thus, the vast majority of environmental legislation will survive constitutional attack except for the takings issue discussed above. However, in a 1995 Supreme Court opinion not involving environmental legislation, the court indicated that it was taking a narrower view of the Congress' authority to regulate commerce. *United States v. Lopez,* 514 U.S. 549 (1995). The Court adhered to its precedent in *Lopez* in *United States v. Morrison,* 529 U.S. 598 (2000), where the court otherwise required that actions must "substantially affect" interstate commerce to fall within the ambit of the commerce clause. However, later in 1995, the U.S. Supreme Court refused to hear a commerce clause case challenging the United States Army Corps of Engineers (COE) jurisdiction over isolated wetlands used by migratory waterfowl. *Leslie Salt Co. v. United States,* 55 F.3d 1388 (9th Cir. 1995), *cert. denied, Cargill, Inc. v. United States,* 516 U.S. 955 *(Thomas, J. dissenting).* But, in *United States v. Wilson,* 133 F.3d 251 (4th Cir. 1997), the court invalidated a COE regulation asserting jurisdiction over isolated wetlands based on potential, as opposed to actual, connections with interstate commerce. *See 33 C.F.R. § 328.3(a)(3).* However, in late 1999, the Seventh Circuit Court of Appeals upheld, against a *Lopez* challenge, a COE regulation over isolated wetlands actually used by migratory birds. *Solid Waste Agency v. United States Army Corps of Engineers,* 191 F.3d 845 (7th Cir. 1999), *cert. granted,* 529 U.S. 1129 (2000). The case was reversed, however, by the Supreme Court in early 2001. *Id.* 531 U.S. 159 (2001).

In *United States v. Olin Corp.,* 927 F. Supp. 1502 (S.D. Ala. 1996), the court invalidated the Comprehensive Environmental Response, Compensation and Liability Act (CERCLA) as an unconstitutional violation of the Commerce Clause. The court held that the contamination at issue was purely local in nature, and did not "substantially affect" interstate commerce as required under *Lopez.* In early 1997, however, the 11th Circuit Court of Appeals reversed the district court's opinion.    107 F.3d 1506 (11th Cir. 1997). In late 1998, the United

States District Court for the Eastern District of North Carolina upheld a federal regulation under the Endangered Species Act involving a prohibition against the taking of red wolves on private land against a commerce clause challenge. *Gibbs v. Babbitt*, 31 F. Supp. 2d 531 (E.D. N.C. 1998), *aff'd*, 214 F.3d 483 (4th Cir. 2000), *cert. denied*, 531 U.S. 1145 (2001).

The government can also regulate agriculture via the spending power (*United States v. Dierckman*, 201 F.3d 915 (7th Cir. 2000)), and legislation enacted pursuant to the spending power does not preempt state law on the same issue. *See, e.g. Citizens for Honesty and Integrity in Regional Planning v. County of San Diego*, 258 F. Supp. 2d 1132 (S.D. Cal. 2003).

## II.  FEDERAL REGULATORY APPROACH—AIR

### A.  CLEAN AIR ACT

#### 1. In General

The 1970 Clean Air Act amendments represented a major increase in the regulation of activities contributing to air pollution. This legislation created air quality control regions and made the individual states responsible for sustaining air quality in those regions. The states could regulate existing sources of pollution with less restrictive requirements. *See, e.g., State, ex rel. Cooper v. Tennessee Valley Authority, et al.*, 615 F.3d 291 (4th Cir. 2010). The amendments gave the EPA the authority to establish ambient air quality standards. The primary standards are designed to protect public health, while secondary standards are designed to protect public welfare from any known or anticipated adverse effects of pollutants on plants, animals, buildings and other materials but not impacts on people. At the time the ambient air quality standards were authorized, a time limit of three years was established to achieve the primary standards, and the secondary standards had to be achieved within a reasonable time with the possibility of extensions being granted for up to an additional two years with no consideration to be given to economic and technological feasibility. *Union Electric Company v. EPA,* 427 U.S. 246 (1976).

Under the Clean Air Act, all "major sources" of pollution must obtain an operating permit. *42 U.S.C. § 7661a(a) (2008).* A "stationary source" is defined by statute to mean "any building, structure, facility or installation which emits or may emit any air pollutant." *42 U.S.C. § 7411(a)(3) (2008).* There are presently six "criteria pollutants" (pollutants for which standards have been established). These are carbon monoxide, lead, nitrogen oxide, ozone, sulphur dioxide and particulate matter. A seventh pollutant is volatile organics (also known as hydrocarbons or VOCs) Volatile organics are the prime ingredient in the formation of ozone.

Pollutants must be identified and their effect on air quality measured. The EPA, in addition, must issue criteria and information as to how emissions of pollutants can be controlled. All of this requires an objective measurement of the pollutants. The EPA has great discretion under the Clean Air Act in determining the manner that it carries out the statutory provisions of the law. *See, e.g., National Environmental Development Association's Clean Air Project v. Environmental Protection Agency, et al.,* 686 F.3d 803 (D.C. Cir. 2012), *cert. den.,* 133 S. Ct. 983 (U.S. 2013).

In 1996, the EPA proposed regulations to further tighten clean air standards. The proposed standard for particulate matter focuses on particles smaller than 2.5 micrometers in diameter as compared to the present standard of ten micrometers. The proposed regulations were finalized in 1997, and it became likely that new nonattainment areas would be created that would significantly impact agricultural activities and result in higher compliance costs. Industry groups and several states challenged the new regulations. In 1999, the District of Columbia Circuit Court of Appeals invalidated the regulations on the basis that the EPA's powers under the Clean Air Act were too vague and amounted to an unconstitutional delegation of authority by the Congress. *American Trucking Associations, Inc., et al. v. United States,* 175 F.3d 1027 (D.C. Cir. 1999), *cert. granted sub. nom, American Trucking Associations, Inc., et al. v. Browner,* 530 U.S. 1202 (2000). However, the U.S. Supreme Court reversed on the delegation issue inasmuch as the Congress required EPA to set clean air standards at levels sufficient, but not more stringent than necessary, to protect public health. *Whitman v. American Trucking Associations, Inc.,* 531 U.S. 457 (2001). But, the Supreme Court did hold that the EPA acted unreasonably in implementing standards for all pollutants in nonattainment areas rather than imposing a specific plan for implementing ozone standard attainment schedules. The Supreme Court also remanded the case for the lower court to consider unaddressed challenges to the regulations. The issue on remand was whether the EPA reasonably exercised its discretion, and the court found that the EPA's decisions regarding particulate matter and ozone were rational and supported by the record. *American Trucking Associations, Inc., et al. v. Environmental Protection Agency*, 283 F.3d 355 (D. D.C. 2002).

The EPA moved to implement the standards by designating geographic areas that do not meet the standards. The D.C. Circuit Court of Appeals, in 2009, ruled that the EPA complied with the CAA and acted reasonably in establishing national ambient air quality standards for fine particulate matter. *Catawba County, et al. v. Environmental Protection Agency*, No. 05-1064, 2009 U.S. App. LEXIS 14948 (D.C. Cir. Jul. 7, 2009). States will then have to submit plans detailing how compliance will be achieved. The major impact of the new regulations on agriculture is expected to be in California. In 2004, California did enact a rule regulating emissions from transportation refrigeration units in trucks. The EPA approved the rule, and upon challenge a court approved the rule because it did not impermissibly amount to national regulation. Instead, the rule applied only in California and did not apply to vehicles that didn't operate in California. In addition, the court determined that the EPA had properly considered the costs of the rule. *American Trucking Associations, Inc. v. Environmental Protection Agency,* 600 F.3d 624 (D.C. Cir. 2010).

In 2009, the EPA began promulgating new pollution rules designed to diminish U.S. coal production. The rules were known as the Cross-State Air Pollution Rule, the Mercury and Air Toxics Standards for Utilities, the Cooling Water Intake Structures regulations and the Disposal of Coal Combustion Residuals rule. In 2012, however, a federal court invalidated the EPA's authority to implement the Cross-State Air Pollution rule. *EME Homer City Generation, L.P. v. Environmental Protection Agency, et al.,* 696 F.3d 7 (D.C. Cir. 2012), *cert. granted,* 133 S. Ct. 2857 (2013). The EPA rule imposed a cap and trade style program that expanded existing limitations on sulfur dioxide and nitrogen oxide emissions from coal-fired power plants in 28 "upwind" states. EPA claimed to have the authority to cap emissions that supposedly traveled across state lines. While the CAA grants the EPA authority to require upwind states to reduce their own significant contributions to a downwind state's non-attainment, the court noted that the rule could impermissibly require upwind states to reduce emissions by more than their own significant contributions to a downwind state's non-attainment. The court also held that the EPA failed to allow states the initial chance (as required by statute) to implement any required reductions with respect to in-state sources by quantifying a state's obligations and establishing federal implementation plans. The EPA admitted that the rule would cost the private sector $2.7 billion and force numerous coal-fired power plants to shut down.

## 2. Greenhouse Gas Emissions

In a 2007 opinion, a majority of the Supreme Court ruled that the EPA had offered "no reasoned explanation" for its refusal to regulate carbon dioxide and other emissions from new cars and trucks that contribute to climate change. *Massachusetts, et al. v. Environmental Protection Agency, et al.,* 549 U.S. 497 (2007). The CAA, EPA argued, did not give the agency the authority to address global climate change and that, in any event, executive policy specifically addressing global warming warranted the EPA's refusal to regulate in such area. However, the Court held that the plaintiffs had standing to challenge the EPA's denial of the plaintiffs' rulemaking petition, and EPA had the statutory authority to regulate emissions from new automobiles and that their decision to not regulate such emissions was arbitrary and capricious. The majority opinion does *not* require the EPA to change its position. However, EPA must demonstrate that whatever it chooses to do complies with CAA requirements. The Court stated that EPA must "ground its reasons for action or inaction in the statute."

With the opinion, the Court has laid the statutory foundation for the EPA to take action to regulate greenhouse gas emissions under the CAA. The Court's opinion could have important implications for the developing ethanol industry. Scientific studies have shown that the use of ethanol-blended fuels leads to increased levels of aldehydes and peroxyacyl nitrates which are presently unregulated under the CAA. Other studies have shown that while ethanol-blended fuel (specifically E-85) reduces the atmospheric levels of two carcinogens, benzene and butadiene, it increases formaldehyde and acetaldehyde, and significantly increases ozone, a prime ingredient of smog. Other studies have concluded that there is no evidence of climate change. *See, e.g., "Searching for Information in 133 Years of California Snowfall Observations,"* Journal of Hydrometeorology No. 3 (Jun. 2012) pp. 895–912.

**Note:** In litigation stemming from the 2007 U.S. Supreme Court opinion, the U.S. Circuit Court of Appeals for the D.C. Circuit upheld under an arbitrary and capricious standard the EPA's finding that carbon dioxide and other greenhouse gas emissions are a threat to public health and the environment. In 2009, the EPA had issued an "endangerment" finding determining that carbon dioxide is a pollutant in spite of the fact that it is a colorless, odorless, non-toxic gas that has no direct effect on human health and in spite of a lack of scientific consensus on the issue. The EPA's "endangerment" finding was upheld under the deferential standard accorded to governmental agencies on the basis that the EPA finding was not completely arbitrary and capricious even though the EPA could not provide a specific number at which GHGs cause "climate change," and even though Office of Inspector General, in 2011, released a report showing that the EPA failed to comply with federal data guidelines when providing its technical support document supporting its "endangerment" finding. *Coalition for Responsible Regulation, Inc., et al. v. Environmental Protection Agency, et al.,* 684 F.3d 102 (D.C. Cir. 2012).

Under the Obama Administration, the EPA (supported by the USDA) exempted "biogenic" carbon dioxide from carbon emissions requirements so as to exempt the ethanol fuel industry from carbon emissions regulations. However, in *Center for Biological Diversity, et al. v. Environmental Protection Agency, et al.,* 722 F.3d 401 (D.C. Cir. 2013), the court held that there was a complete lack of a statutory basis for exempting biogenic carbon dioxide from the carbon emissions requirements. The ruling will also apply to paper and lumber manufacturers.

The federal district courts that have addressed the issue have all held that climate change lawsuits involve non-justiciable political questions that are not suitable for court resolution. *See State v. American Electric Power Co., Inc.,* 406 F. Supp. 2d 265 (S.D. N.Y. 2005); *California v. General Motors Corp.,* No. 3:06-CV-05755-MJJ, 2007 U.S. Dist. LEXIS 68547 (N.D. Cal. Sept. 17, 2007); *Native Village of Kivalina, et al. v. Exxon Mobil Corporation, et al.,* No. C 08-1138 SBA, 2009 U.S. Dist. LEXIS 99563 (N.D. Cal. Sept. 30, 2009), *aff'd.,* No. 09-17490, 2012 U.S. App. LEXIS 19870 (9th Cir. Sept. 21, 2012); *United States v. EME Homer City Generation L.P., et al.,* 823 F. Supp. 2d 274 (W.D. Pa. 2011); *Loorz, et al. v. Perciaspepe,* No. 11-CV-2235, 2013 U.S. Dist. LEXIS 72301 (D. D.C. May 22, 2013). See also *Comer, et al. v. Murphy Oil USA, Inc.,* 839 F. Supp. 2d 849 (S.D. Miss. 2012), *aff'd.,* 718 F.3d 460 (5th Cir. 2013). The U.S. Supreme Court agrees. *American Electric Power Company, Inc., et al. v. Connecticut, et al.,* 564 U.S. 410 (2011). The public nuisance doctrine has also been held inapplicable to activities that the CAA regulates. *State v. Tennessee Valley Authority,* 615 F.3d 291 (4th Cir. 2010), *rev'g,* 593 F. Supp. 2d 812 (W.D. N.C. 2009).

## B.   ANIMAL FEEDING OPERATIONS

In early 2009, EPA, pursuant to the EPCRA, issued a final regulation regarding the reporting of emissions from confined AFO's. The rule applies to facilities that confine more than 1,000 beef cattle, 700 mature dairy cows, 1,000 veal calves, 2,500 swine (each weighing 55 pounds or more), 10,000 swine (each weighing less than 55 pounds), 500 horses and 10,000 sheep. The rule requires these facilities to report ammonia and hydrogen sulfide emissions to state and local emergency response officials if the facility emits 100 pounds or more of either substance during a 24-hour period.

## C.   PREEMPTION OF STATE COMMON LAW CLAIMS

In 1987, the United States Supreme Court ruled in *International Paper Co. v. Ouellete,* 479 U.S. 481 (1987), that the Clean Water Act (CWA) preempts lawsuits stemming from "non-source state law," meaning that it bars lawsuits alleging common law or statutory claims based upon the laws of states other than the state where the regulated discharges occur. Courts have uniformly found this to mean that the similar CAA also bars lawsuits alleging nuisance or negligence based upon the laws of states *other than the state where the emissions occur.* In *Ouellete,* the court reasoned that application of an affected state's law to an out of state source would undermine the important goals of efficiency and predictability in the permit system. Years later in *American Electric Power Co. v. Connecticut (AEP)*, 564 U.S. 410 (2011), the United States Supreme Court ruled that the CAA also preempts the application of federal common law. This holding, for example, bars a federal common law nuisance claim against the holder of a CAA permit. The United States Supreme Court, however, has never ruled on the question of whether the CAA preempts common law claims based in nuisance, trespass and negligence brought under the law of the state where the emissions occur.

Several lower federal court opinions have considered the issue of CAA preemption. In *Bell v. Cheswick Generating Station*, 734 F.3d 188 (3d Cir. 2013), *cert. den.* 134 S. Ct. 2696 (2014), the Third Circuit ruled that the CAA did not preempt state common law claims brought under the laws of the source state. Since *AEP*, *Bell* is the first and only federal court decision to hold that the CAA does not preempt common law nuisance claims allegedly arising from emissions regulated under the CAA. The *Bell* court focused on the text of CAA's savings clauses to determine that it was not unlike the CWA and that, as such, the Supreme Court's language in *Ouellette* controlled. However, the Fourth Circuit applied *Ouellette* in another way, ruling in *North Carolina ex rel. Cooper v. Tennessee Valley Authority*, 615 F.3d 291 (4th Cir. 2010), that a state law *is* preempted if it interferes with the methods by which the federal statute was designed to reach its goals. The Fourth Circuit found that public nuisance law in the *source* state was preempted by the CAA because the injunctive relief requested was a collateral attack on Congress's chosen process of determining appropriate standards and granting permits. The injunctive relief requested in the case would have cost the permit holder in excess of one billion dollars. The Fourth Circuit noted that if the injunction were allowed to stand it would encourage courts "to use vague public nuisance standards to scuttle the nation's carefully created system for accommodating the need for energy production and the need for clean air. The result would be a balkanization of clean air regulations and a confused patchwork of standards, to the detriment of industry and the environment alike."

The issue of whether the CAA preempts source state common law claims is ultimately a federal question. Nonetheless, federal question jurisdiction does not exist for issues raised only as a defense to a plaintiff's action comprising only state law claims on its face. As such, plaintiffs will continue to file common law and statutory claims. In *Freeman v. Grain Processing Corporation*, 848 N.W.2d 58 (Iowa 2014), the Iowa Supreme Court ruled that neither the CAA nor its Iowa counterpart (*Iowa Code 455B*) preempts state common law claims alleging negligence, nuisance or trespass.

## III. FEDERAL REGULATORY APPROACH—SOIL AND WATER

Water pollution is commonly divided into two categories: point source and nonpoint source. Point source water pollution is waste discharged into a water body from a specific and clearly discernable discharge point such as a pipe or ditch. Nonpoint pollution, on the other hand, is the diffuse discharge of waste into a water body where the specific source cannot be located, as with sediment or certain agricultural chemicals. Most agricultural water pollution is nonpoint source pollution. However, runoff from an animal feedlot can be construed as point source pollution.

### A. SOIL EROSION

The federal government has been concerned with the problem of soil erosion for many years. The two major agencies within the United States Department of Agriculture (USDA) that have substantial soil erosion responsibilities are the Natural Resource Conservation Service (NRCS) and the Agricultural Stabilization and Conservation Service (ASCS), now the Farm Service Agency (FSA). In general, the federal soil conservation programs are limited to conservation incentives in the form of technical assistance and cost sharing.

Many states also have soil erosion and sediment control statutes that require landowners to take certain actions designed to minimize soil erosion. In some states, such as Kansas, the burden is placed upon local county commissioners to take action designed to minimize soil erosion. Landowners occasionally have challenged the validity of such state laws on the basis that the statutes are an unconstitutional exercise of the state's police power. *See, e.g., Woodbury County Soil Conservation District v. Ortner,* 279 N.W.2d 276 (Iowa 1979).

## B.   CONSERVATION RESERVE PROGRAM

In 1985, the Congress enacted the Conservation Reserve Program (CRP) with the primary purpose of creating a program for long-term land retirement for marginally productive and erodible cropland. The CRP involves lease agreements between the government and the landowners under which the government makes an annual cash payment to the landowner (or landowner and tenant) for a minimum of ten years. *16 U.S.C. § 3831(e)(1).* These payments are designed to induce landowners of eligible land to remove the land from agricultural production and place it in cover to stabilize the topsoil. An important factor influencing the success of the CRP is that an acceptable degree of resource stewardship must be practiced to retain eligibility for government farm program benefits. The CRP, in effect, establishes a covenant between the landowner and the public in which the landowner pledges to take care of the land and the public agrees to provide substitute payments for the income that would otherwise be realized from the land.

## C.  CONSERVATION SECURITY/ STEWARDSHIP PROGRAM

The Conservation Security Program was established as part of the 2002 Farm Bill and provides payments to farmers and ranchers that practice good stewardship on agricultural land and implement new practices that improve existing conservation benefits. The CSP is an entitlement program (not a competitive sign-up as is the CRP) that is available to any agricultural landowner that develops an approved plan specifying the acceptable conservation practices to be utilized. The program is generally available for all cropland, grassland, prairie, improved pasture and rangeland in the United States. In general, land enrolled in the CRP, the Wetland Reserve Program and the Grassland Reserve Program is ineligible for the CSP.

The CSP was not reauthorized under the 2008 Farm Bill, but was changed to the Conservation Stewardship Program (CSP). It is a voluntary program that provides participants with an annual land use payment ($40,000 annual payment limit) for certain environmental benefits. Contracts are for a five-year term. Eligible land cannot simultaneously be enrolled in other conservation programs.

## D.  CLEAN WATER ACT

The CWA recognizes two sources of pollution. Point source pollution is pollution which comes from a clearly discernable discharge point, such as a pipe, a ditch, or a concentrated animal feeding operation. Under the act, point source pollution is the concern of the federal government. Nonpoint source pollution, while not specifically defined under the CWA, is pollution that comes from a diffused point of discharge, such as fertilizer runoff from an open field. Control of nonpoint source pollution is to be handled by the states through enforcement of state water quality standards and area-wide waste management plans. Under 1977 amendments, irrigation return flows are not considered point sources. *See, e.g., Pacific Coast Federation of Fishermen's Associations, et al. v. Glaser, et al.,* No. CIV S-2:11-2980-KJM-CKD, 2013 U.S. Dist. LEXIS 132240 (E.D. Cal. Sept. 16, 2013).

## 1. Point Source Pollution and the NPDES

The federal government controls point source pollution by means of a federal permit system. This federal permit system, known as the National Pollutant Discharge Elimination System (NPDES) is the chief mechanism for control of discharges.

The states are free to adopt their own equivalents of the NPDES, and most have done so. The CWA provides that the EPA "shall" transfer permit-issuing authority to a state if it meets nine statutory criteria which, taken together, establish that the state has authority under its own laws to administer an NPDES-type system. However, the Endangered Species Act mandates that each federal agency "shall," through consultation with the Secretary of the Interior, "ensure that any action authorized, funded or carried out by such agency . . . is not likely to jeopardize" an endangered or threatened species, or the species' habitat. In a 2007 opinion, the U.S. Supreme Court ruled that once the CWA's nine criteria are satisfied, transfer authority is non-discretionary (i.e., the EPA cannot deny a transfer application). To hold otherwise, the Court reasoned, would implicitly repeal the CWA transfer criteria and effectively add species conservation as a tenth criterion. *National Association of Home Builders v. Defenders of Wildlife,* 127 S. Ct. 2518 (2007).

No one may discharge a "pollutant" from a point source into the "navigable waters of the United States" without a permit from the EPA. The definition of "pollutant" has been construed broadly to include the tillage of soil which causes the soil to be "redeposited" into delineated wetlands constitutes the discharge of a "pollutant" into the navigable waters of the United States requiring an NPDES permit. *See, e.g., Duarte Nursery, Inc. v. United States Army Corps of Engineers,* No. 2:13-cv-02095-KJM-AC, 2016 U.S. Dist. LEXIS 76037 (E.D. Cal. Jun. 10, 2016) However, an NPDES permit is not required unless there is an "addition" of a pollutant to regulable waters. *See, e.g., Friends of the Everglades, et al. v. South Florida Water Management District, et al.,* 570 F.3d 1210 (11th Cir. 2009) *reh'g., den.,* 605 F.3d 962 (11th Cir. 2010), *cert. den.,* 551 U.S. 644 (2010). But, in 2014, the Federal District Court for the Southern District of New York vacated a corresponding EPA regulation on the basis that the rule violated the U.S. Supreme Court plurality opinion in *Rapanos v. United States,* 547 U.S. 715 (2006). The district court remanded the rule to the EPA, with instructions for the EPA to provide additional explanation with respect to its interpretation of the rule. *Catskill Mountains Chapter of Trout Unlimited, Inc., et al. v. United States Environmental Protection Agency, et al.,* No. 08-CV-5606 (KMK), 2014 U.S. Dist. LEXIS 42535 (S.D. N.Y. Mar. 28, 2014).

The NPDES system only applies to discharges of pollutants into surface water. However, groundwater produced in connection with methane gas extraction and discharged into a river has been held to be a "pollutant" within the meaning of the CWA, even if the water is unaltered during the process. *Northern Plains Resource Council v. Fidelity Exploration and Development Co.,* 325 F.3d 1155 (9th Cir. 2003), *cert. den. sub. nom., Fidelity Exploration and Development Co. v. Northern Plains Resource Council,* 540 U.S. 967 (2003). The discharge of water with pollutants from one distinct water body into another constitutes an addition of a pollutant under the CWA, requiring an NPDES permit. *Catskill Mountains Chapter of Trout Unlimited, Inc. et al. v. City of New York,* 451 F.3d 77 (2d Cir. 2006). The collected runoff from logging operations (i.e., mud and sediment that washes off logging roads) into forest and rivers has been held to be a point source discharge of stormwater associated with industrial activity requiring an NPDES permit. *Northwest Environmental Defense Center v. Oregon Forest Industry Council, et al.,* 617 F.3d 1176 (9th Cir. 2010).

Discharges of pollutants into groundwater are not subject to the NPDES permit requirement even if the groundwater is hydrologically connected to surface water. *See, e.g., Umatilla Water Quality Protective Association v. Smith Frozen Foods,* 962 F. Supp. 1312 (D. Or. 1997); *United States v. ConAgra, Inc.,* No. CV 96-0134-S-LMB, 1997 U.S. Dist. LEXIS 21401 (D. Idaho Dec. 31, 1997).

A CWA violation can be found without evidence of any observed discharges. *Waterkeeper Alliance, Inc. v. Hudson, et al.,* No. WMN-10-487, 2012 U.S. Dist. LEXIS 179962 (D. Md. Dec. 20, 2012). But, the plaintiff must conduct testing or sampling of the alleged contaminated water to provide the court with some evidence of a CWA violation.

Excluded from the definition of a point source pollutant are silvicultural pest control activities from which there is natural runoff. Also excluded from the definition of "pollutant" is "fill material." Fill material is subject to the permit requirement of the U.S. Army Corps of Engineers and does not also require an EPA NPDES pollution discharge permit. *See, e.g., Couer Alaska, Inc. v. Southeast Alaska Conservation Council, et al.,* 557 U.S. 261 (2009). Nonpoint source silvicultural activities such as nursery operations, site preparation, reforestation and subsequent cultural treatment, thinning, prescribed burning, pest and fire control, harvesting operations, surface drainage, or road construction and maintenance from which there is natural runoff are not subject to the NPDES system as point source pollutants. However, one court has held that the United States Forest Service Program of aerial spraying of national forest lands to control disease outbreak that would kill Douglas Fir trees by spraying insecticides directly into rivers which are waters covered by the CWA constitutes a point source pollutant subject to the NPDES permit requirement and is not exempt as a silvicultural pest control activity. *League of Wilderness Defenders/Blue Mountains Biodiversity Project v. Forsgren*, 309 F.3d 1181 (9th Cir. 2002). However, collected runoff from logging operations in the form of mud and sediment that washed off logging roads into forests and rivers is a point source discharge of stormwater associated with industrial activity requiring an NPDES permit under the CWA. *Northwest Environmental Defense Center, et al. v. Brown, et al.*, 640 F.3d 1063 (9th Cir. 2011). In *Decker v. Northwest Environmental Defense Center*, 133 S. Ct. 1326 (2013), the U.S. Supreme Court upheld the EPA's regulation that temporary logging roads do not involve "industrial" activity and, thus, an NPDES permit was not required for associated runoff. In late 2007, the EPA issued a final rule concluding that pesticides applied in accordance with the Federal Insecticide, Fungicide, and Rodenticide Act are exempt from the CWA's permitting requirements. However, in early 2009, the U.S. Circuit Court Appeals for the Sixth Circuit vacated the rule.

The CWA identifies concentrated animal feeding operations (CAFOs) as a point source of pollution subject to the NPDES. Thus, the EPA has issued effluent limitations and federal standards of performance for feedlots. But, an individual state may issue NPDES permits for discharges into navigable water within its jurisdiction if state programs are approved by the EPA. *33 U.S.C. § 1342(b) (2008).* Approval is limited to programs which are equal to or stricter than federal standards and which comply with EPA guidelines.

An animal feeding operation is a CAFO for purposes of the NPDES if either of the following criteria is met: (1) more than the numbers of animals specified in any of the following categories are confined—(a) 1,000 slaughter and feeder cattle; (b) 700 mature dairy cattle (whether milked or dry cows); (c) 2,500 swine each weighing over 55 pounds (10,000 swine each weighing less than 55 pounds); (d) 500 horses; (e) 10,000 sheep or lambs; (f) 55,000 turkeys; (g) 82,000 laying hens or broilers (if the facility has a continuous overflow watering); (h) 30,000 laying hens or broilers (if the facility has a liquid manure system); (i) 5,000 ducks (if the facility has a liquid manure handling system; 30,000 if the facility has something other than a liquid manure handling system); (j) 125,000 chickens other than laying hens; or (k) 1,000 animal units; or (2) more than the following numbers and types of animals are confined—(a) 300 slaughter or feeder cattle; (b) 200 mature dairy cattle (whether milked or dry cows); (c) 750 swine each weighing over 55 pounds; (d) 150 horses; (e) 3,000 sheep or lambs; (f) 16,500 turkeys; (g) 30,000 laying hens or broilers (if the facility has continuous overflow watering); (g) 9,000 laying hens or broilers (if the facility has a liquid manure handling system); (h) 1,500 ducks; or (i) 300 animal units; and either one of the following conditions are met: pollutants are discharged into navigable waters through a man-made ditch, flushing system, or other similar man-made device; or pollutants are discharged directly into waters of the United States which originate outside of and pass over, across, or through the facility or otherwise come into direct contact with the animals confined in the operation.

On January 12, 2001, EPA issued proposed rules designed to address water quality problems associated with livestock operations. The Final Rules were published on February 12, 2003, *68 Fed. Reg. 7176*, and became effective on April 14, 2003. Under the Final Rules, an animal feeding operation (AFO) is defined as a "lot or facility" where animals are confined for 45 days or more within a 12-month period, and on which crops are not grown during the normal growing season. CAFOs and AFOs are divided into three categories with large CAFOs defined as those confining more than a specified number of animals that discharge pollutants into water of the United States. All large CAFOs must apply for an NPDES permit unless it can demonstrate that it has no potential to discharge pollutants into regulable waters other than agricultural stormwater from land application areas. A CAFO that receives a "no potential to discharge" determination remains liable under the CWA for actual discharges without a permit. The Final Rules also require that all CAFO NPDES permits must include nutrient management plans, record keeping obligations (including maintenance of nutrient management plans), off-site manure transfer records and annual reporting of the number of animals in confinement and the amount of manure applied. In addition, each animal category must satisfy effluent limitation guidelines. Beef, dairy, swine and poultry operations must implement best management practices for the land application of manure based upon the nutrient management plan and subject to certain setback requirements, but are expressly allowed to discharge from the land application area so long as the waste is applied in accordance with a nutrient management plan. Horse and sheep CAFOs, however, cannot discharge except in an "overflow" event from a facility built to contain all wastes plus the runoff from a 10-year, 24-hour storm event.

Shortly after the Final Rules were published, environmental and agricultural industry groups sued challenging the Final Rules. The environmental groups challenged the Final Rules for failing to incorporate the nutrient management plans into NPDES permits, unlawfully applying the agricultural stormwater exemption to CAFOs, putting in place insufficient technological controls and not protecting water quality. The industry groups challenged the Final Rules as unlawfully extending the permit requirement to all large CAFOs and regulating runoff from land application areas in excess of EPA's authority. In *Waterkeeper Alliance, Inc., et al. v. United States Environmental Protection Agency,* 399 F.3d 486 (2d Cir. 2005), the court invalidated those provisions of the Final Rule that allowed permitting authorities to issue permits without reviewing the terms of the nutrient management plans, allowed permitting authorities to issue permits that did not include the terms of the nutrient management plans, and required CAFOs to apply for NPDES permits regardless of whether they had actual discharges. The court also directed the EPA to select a proper standard for pathogen reduction, clarify the new source performance standard, and clarify the basis for failing to promulgate water quality based effluent limitations for discharges other than agricultural stormwater discharges.

Note: In a case involving a West Virginia poultry CAFO, the EPA had issued an order that the CAFO obtain an NPDES permit for stormwater discharges on the basis that a regulable discharge occurred when dust, feathers and dander were released through ventilation fans and then came into contact with precipitation. *Alt, et al. v. United States Environmental Protection Agency,* No. 2:12-CV-42, 2013 U.S. Dist. LEXIS 65093 (W.D. W. Va. Apr. 22, 2013). Such discharges, EPA claimed, were not within the agricultural stormwater discharge exemption because the exemption only applied to land application areas where crops are grown. The CAFO was threatened with significant fines and challenged the EPA's position in court. In response, the EPA withdrew its order and motioned to dismiss the case. The court refused the EPA's motion, and later determined that that the litter and manure that washed from the CAFO to navigable water by precipitation were an ag stormwater discharge that was exempt from the CWA's NPDES permit requirement. *Alt v. United States Environmental Protection Agency,* 979 F. Supp. 2d 701 (N.D. W. Va. 2013).

As a result of the court's opinion, EPA published a proposed rule. *71 Fed. Reg. 37743, 37747.* The proposed rule specifies that permits issued before the court's opinion (June 27, 2005), and nutrient management plans required by those permits, continue in force until they are either modified, revoked, rescinded or terminated. Also, CAFOs with actual or proposed discharges must apply for a permit. CAFOs may voluntarily seek certification that they do not discharge. Doing so provides protection for accidental discharges. In other words, a certified but unpermitted CAFO would not be liable for failing to apply for a permit before an accidental discharge. In addition, nutrient management plans are subject to analysis by the permitting authority. Nutrient management plans are subject to administrative review before issuance of a notice of intent under a general permit. *40 C.F.R. § 122.23(h)*. In addition, permitting authorities must provide public notice of any proposal to grant coverage to the CAFO under the permit, and must make available for public review and comment the notice of intent that the CAFO submits, including the CAFO's nutrient management plan and the draft terms of the nutrient management plan to be incorporated into the permit. The proposed rule also requires that the nutrient management plan be a part of the permit application and be subject to review. Originally, CAFOs that are required to develop and implement a nutrient management plan had until July 31, 2007, to do so. However, the EPA issued a final rule, 72 Fed. Reg. 40245, on July 18, 2007, that established new deadlines for CAFOs to obtain NPDES permits and implement nutrient management plans. The new deadline was February 27, 2009, for "newly defined CAFOs (those operations that were not defined as

CAFOs until the EPA issued the 2003 CAFO final rule). February 27, 2009, was also the deadline for the filing of nutrient management plans for all permitted CAFOs. An application for an NPDES permit (and corresponding state permits) must include a nutrient management plan that incorporates limitations and standards required by federal regulations. *See 40 C.F.R. § 122.21(i)(1)*. The terms of a nutrient management plan must include the "field-specific rates of application properly developed . . . to ensure appropriate agricultural utilization of the nutrients." Changes to nutrient management plans are subject to review by the permitting authority and are subject to public review and comment.

Under the rules, a CAFO may have difficulty in determining whether it must apply for an NPDES permit. The rules call for a case-by-case determination of whether the CAFO does, or will, discharge from the production or land application area based on an objective assessment of the CAFO's design, construction, operation and maintenance. An unpermitted CAFO that previously discharged does not need to apply for an NPDES permit if it has taken steps to permanently fix the cause of the discharge. Similarly, a CAFO need not have an NPDES permit to claim the agricultural stormwater exemption for precipitation-related discharges from land application if it does not discharge or propose to discharge.

The final rule also specifies that a CAFO may obtain authority to discharge under a state's general permit, but each notice of intent under a general permit must include the information that is otherwise required for a permit. Because a CAFO's effluent limitation is specified in the CAFO's nutrient management plan, the only way a permitting agency can determine compliance with the CWA is to review each CAFO's plans for handling nutrients. The terms of a general permit are not sufficient to authorizing such discharges, so sufficient information must be included in a nutrient management plan to be part of a notice of intent.

In early 2011, the United States Court of Appeals for the Fifth Circuit vacated part of the CAFO rules. *National Pork Producers Council, et al. v. United States Environmental Protection Agency,* 635 F.3d 738 (5th Cir. 2011). The court invalidated the portion of the rules requiring CAFOs to receive an NPDES permit if they propose to discharge pollutants into navigable waters. The court held that the EPA could not impose a duty to apply for a permit on a CAFO before there was an actual discharge. However, the court did uphold the portion of the rules that required a CAFO to have a permit if it is discharging. The claim that the portion of the rules requiring all nutrient management plans to specify land application procedures exceeded the EPA's statutory authority was time-barred. In a final rule published on July 30, 2012, and effective the same day, the EPA eliminated its requirement that CAFOs are required to obtain a discharge permit for runoff from feedlots. The EPA also eliminated the requirement of voluntary reporting option for CAFOs that allowed CAFOs to certify that they did not discharge contaminated water from the CAFO in lieu of permitting.

A few days later, the Michigan Court of Appeals upheld state environmental rules governing CAFOs which required CAFOs to obtain a state-level NPDES permit even though the CAFO did not discharge or demonstrated no potential to discharge. *Michigan Farm Bureau, et al. v. Department of Environmental Quality,* No. 290323, 2011 Mich. App. LEXIS 589 (Mich. Ct. App. Mar. 29, 2011). While the state's rules were inconsistent with the federal rules and caselaw, the court determined that it was within the power of the EPA to grant the state the authority to administer its own NPDES program. Thus, the validity of the state CAFO regulations was to be addressed solely in accordance with state law which, in Michigan, gave the defendant the authority to pass regulations designed to protect state water resources from waste disposal. On that point, the court noted that the defendant had properly and sufficiently supported its claim that the rule at issue was necessary to protect the environment and that the rule was rationally related to the defendant's responsibility under state law to protect water resources from pollution.

As mentioned above, under the 1977 amendments to the CWA, irrigation return flows are not considered point source pollutants. *See, e.g., Hiebenthal v. Meduri Farms,* 242 F. Supp. 2d 885 (D. Or. 2002). In addition, agricultural stormwater discharges are excepted from the NPDES as nonpoint source pollutants. In EPA's proposed CAFO rule (*71*

*Fed. Reg. 37743, 37747*), discharges from land application are exempt as agricultural stormwater only if the CAFO has a nutrient management plan in place. The final rule requires unpermitted CAFOs with agricultural stormwater discharges to maintain documentation of their nutrient management plans. However, in *Concerned Area Residents for the Environment v. Southview Farm,* 34 F.3d 114 (2d Cir. 1994), the court held that a large New York dairy operation with extensive liquid manure spreading operations was a point source pollutant under the CWA because the farm itself fell within the definition of a CAFO and could not avail itself of the agricultural exemption for stormwater discharges.

In 1999, the United States District Court for the Eastern District of Washington ruled that the removal and land application of manure from livestock operations are integral parts of those operations and are, therefore, subject to CWA requirements. *Community Assoc. for Restoration of the Environment v. Henry Bosma Dairy,* 54 F. Supp. 2d 976 (E.D. Wash. 1999), *aff'd,* 305 F.3d 943 (9th Cir. 2002). See also *Water Keeper Alliance v. Smithfield Foods, Inc.,* No. 4:01-CV-27-H(3), 2002 U.S. Dist. LEXIS 21314 (E.D. N.C. Sept. 20, 2001).

In another case that is the first of its kind, the federal district court for the Eastern District of Washington kept alive a lawsuit filed by seven environmental groups alleging that the BNSF Railway Company violated the CWA. *Sierra Club, et al. v. BNSF Railway Co.,* No. 2:13-CV-00272, 2014 U.S. Dist. LEXIS 1035 (E.D. Wash. Jan. 2, 2014). The plaintiffs claimed that while transporting coal on its tracks "adjacent to" and "in proximity to" waters of the United States, the railway discharged coal dust without a permit through holes in its cars and through the open tops of its cars. The plaintiffs claimed that a federal discharge permit was required for such discharges, and that each and every rail car transporting the coal constitutes a "point source." In addition, the plaintiffs claimed that each discharge from each car on each separate day constitutes a separate CWA violation. The railway asked the judge to dismiss the claims that alleged the release of coal dust to land, not water, arguing that the plaintiff was not asserting that such pollution reached the water through a "confined, discrete conveyance." The plaintiffs asserted that they only needed to trace the pollutant back to a single, identifiable source, the coal cars. The court agreed that, regardless of where pollution originates, "a plaintiff must prove that the pollutant reached the water through a confined, discrete conveyance." Even so, the court denied the railway's motion to dismiss, and granted the plaintiff an opportunity to attempt to develop facts "to show that the railway illegally introduced pollutants into navigable waters without a permit." The court noted that the "issue appears to be whether coal from rail cars that falls onto land, rather than directly into the waters, offends the CWA." The court stated that it was giving the plaintiff an opportunity to develop facts that would allow their claims to either stand or fall, "based on the statutory definition of a point source discharge." The future success of plaintiffs' claims will likely depend on whether the court treats the coal dust like manure discharged onto fields near a river (which does create a point source discharge if ultimately flowing into the river) or like waste rocks that eventually make their way to surface waters from waste rock pits (which are not point sources under the CWA because the water seepage is "not collected or channeled").

In another point-source case, *Reynolds, et al. v. Rick's Mushroom Service, Inc., et al.,* 246 F. Supp. 2d 449 (E.D. Pa. 2003), the court held that a mushroom storage and processing facility that disposed of spent mushroom substrate at an off-site location after storing the substrate on-site for a year or more was a point source of pollution subject to the NPDES requirements. The court specifically noted the plaintiff's system of wastewater collection and spraying was very similar to systems implemented at CAFOs.

**Note:** In 2011, the defendant proposed a rule that would have required a CAFO to release comprehensive data providing precise CAFO locations, animal types and number of head as well as personal contact information including names, addresses, phone numbers and email addresses of CAFO owners. The proposed rule was withdrawn in 2012, with the EPA reserving the right to develop a similar rule in the future. The withdrawal was upheld on the basis that the EPA is owed even greater deference when it withdraws a rule and maintains the status quo. *Environmental Integrity Project, et al. v. McCarthy,* 139 F. Supp. 3d 25 (D. D.C. 2015).

The 2005 Energy Act specifies that an NPDES permit is not required for construction activities involving oil and gas interests.

## 2. Control of Nonpoint Source Pollution

Pollution from nonpoint agricultural sources, particularly that originating from soil erosion, is more extensive than pollution resulting from feedlot operations. But, because nonpoint source pollution is largely dependent upon local topographical conditions, the Congress believed it was best left to the control of the states through the continuing planning process required by § 303 (relating to water quality standards) and § 208 (areawide waste management plans) of the Clean Water Act. Also, in 1987, the Congress amended the CWA to establish a national nonpoint source program under § 319. States meeting preliminary criteria can receive federal grant money from EPA to address nonpoint source pollution.

While the § 208 planning process focuses on urban industrial pollution, it also applies to agricultural pollution and can be an effective means of controlling that problem. The CWA provides that areawide "208 plans" must identify sources of agricultural nonpoint pollution and the methods (including land use practices) that can be employed to prevent it. EPA regulations require that nonpoint source pollution be controlled through the application of the best management practices. *40 C.F.R. Part 35, Subpart G.* The EPA has suggested that best management practices for farms probably include such familiar soil conservation practices as the use of terraces, contour farming, and minimum tillage, as well as new techniques to be developed. The EPA stresses that studies have shown that good conservation practices can reduce sediment pollution from 50–90 percent.

**Note:** One court has held that the violation of state water quality standards could not occur without a discharge violation. *House of Raeford Farms, Inc. v. North Carolina Department of Environmental and Natural Resources*, 774 S.E.2d 911 (N.C. Ct. App. 2015).

Section 303 ("Water Quality Standards and Implementation Plans"), requires states to adopt water-quality standards, to the extent not previously done, and to carry forward those already adopted subject to EPA approval. Standards are to be set for both interstate and intrastate waters, and the standards must be updated periodically and submitted to EPA for review and approval. The standards are to take into account the unique needs of each waterway including "propagation of fish and wildlife" as well as "agricultural . . . and other purposes." Any state that fails to set water quality standards is subject to the EPA imposing its own standards on the state. Section 303 does not exempt any rivers or waters, but covers all waters to the full extent of federal authority over navigable waters. The states are to establish total maximum daily loads (TMDLs) for watercourses that fail to meet water quality standards after the application of controls on point sources. A TMDL establishes the maximum amount of a pollutant that can be discharged or "loaded" into the water at issue from all combined sources on a *daily* basis and still permit that water to meet water quality standards. *See, e.g., Anacostia Riverkeeper, Inc., et al. v. Jackson,* 713 F. Supp. 2d. 50 (D. D.C. 2010). A TMDL must be set "at a level necessary to implement water quality standards." *33 U.S.C. § 1313(d)(1)(C) (2008).* Historically, the EPA calculated TMDLs on an annual basis rather than a daily basis, approved TMDLs that achieve annual and seasonal (but not daily) water quality standards, and assigned wasteloads to categories of sources instead of to individual point sources. This approach was held to be reasonable due to the ambiguous nature of 33 U.S.C. § 1313(d) in *Friends of the Earth v. United States Environmental Protection Agency, et al.,* 346 F. Supp. 2d 182 (D. D.C. 2004). However, the case was reversed on appeal. *Friends of the Earth v. United States Environmental Protection Agency,* 446 F.3d 140 (D.C. Cir. 2006). The CWA does not define TMDL, but the EPA's regulations break it into a "waste load allocation" for point sources and a "load allocation" for nonpoint sources. TMDLs purpose is to limit the amount of pollutants in a watercourse on any particular date.

A significant question is whether the EPA has the authority to regulate nonpoint source pollutants under § 303 through the TMDL process and require reductions in nonpoint source discharges. This is an important issue for agriculture because the primary source of agricultural pollution is nonpoint source. Indeed, the TMDL requirements were challenged in early 2000 by farm interests as being inapplicable to nonpoint source pollution. *Pronsolino v. Marcus,* 91

F. Supp. 2d 1337 (N.D. Cal. 2000), *aff'd, sub. nom., Pronsolino v. Nastri,* 291 F.3d 1123 (9th Cir. 2002), *cert. denied,* 539 U.S. 926 (2003).The court, however, held that the TMDL requirements, as a comprehensive water-quality standard under the CWA, were designed to apply to every navigable river and water in the country. Although the court noted that the CWA applied TMDL to point and nonpoint sources differently, it stressed that TMDL was clearly authorized for nonpoint sources. Thus, according to the court, any polluted waterway— whether the source of pollution is point or nonpoint— is subject to TMDL requirements.

The case was affirmed on appeal, but the appellate court, in dictum, noted that the statute did not require states to actually reduce nonpoint source pollution flowing into these waters. The appellate court made clear that TMDL implementation of nonpoint source pollution is a matter reserved to the states. Thus, the court appeared to substantially limit the EPA's ability to require nonpoint source pollution reduction—the EPA can develop TMDLs that highlight the need for aggressive control of nonpoint source pollution, but cannot address nonpoint source pollution by itself. Where a state fails to establish TMDLs, the EPA has the power to implement them. *See, e.g., American Farm Bureau Federation, et al. v. United States Environmental Protection Agency, et al.,* No. 1:11-CV-0067, 2013 U.S. Dist. LEXIS 131075 (M.D. Pa. Sept. 13, 2013). The courts are usually highly deferential to the EPA's decision to leave the control of nonpoint source pollution up to the states even when TMDLs are involved. *See, e.g., Conservation Law Foundation v. United States Environmental Protection Agency,* No. 15-165-ML, 2016 U.S. Dist. LEXIS 172117 (D. R.I. Dec. 13, 2016). Likewise, an NPDES permit is only required when, after a TMDL is established, the EPA makes a determination that further controls on stormwater are needed. *See also Gulf Restoration Network v. Jackson,* No. 12-677, Section "A" (3), 2016 U.S. Dist. LEXIS 173459 (E.D. La. Dec. 15, 2016).

In 2002, EPA announced its Proposed Water Quality Trading Policy. *67 Fed. Reg. 34702 (May 15, 2002).* The policy is an attempt to foster pollution trading as a means to meet water quality goals. Trading would be used to implement a TMDL or provide a means for point sources to achieve water quality based permit requirements, but would not be available to satisfy technology-based affluent limitations. Trades would be enforced by incorporating either variable or alternate permit limits based on the level of reductions achieved in the trade, and would be based on fungible, clearly defined pollution reduction credits and allowances between different pollution sources (most likely between point and nonpoint sources). Reduction in agricultural water pollution is central to the trading scheme insomuch as EPA has suggested that procedures developed by NRCS be used to determine sediment loss from ag land be used for trading reductions in ag runoff.

In 2010, the EPA published a TMDL of nitrogen, phosphorous and sediment that can be released into the Chesapeake Bay watershed. The TMDL set forth a timetable for compliance by the affected states. In addition, states were required to determine how much agriculture had to reduce runoff by adopting new technology and conservation practices. The new rules were legally challenged in 2011 on the basis that the EPA lacked the authority to regulate individual pollutants from farmland and other specific sources, and that the EPA lacked the authority to regulate individual pollutants from farmland and other specific sources. In 2014, attorneys general from 21 states joined the lawsuit. In mid-2015, however, while the court held that likely economic injury in the form of higher compliance costs was sufficient to confer standing to challenge the TMDL, the court held that the EPA had acted within its authority under 33 U.S.C. § 1251(d) in developing the TMDL. *American Farm Bureau, et al. v. United States Environmental Protection Agency, et al.*, 792 F.3d 281 (3d Cir. 2015), *pet. for cert. filed,* U.S. Sup. Ct. (Nov. 6, 2015*).

Traditionally, the courts have not allowed disaffected persons to bring lawsuits on the basis of an alleged violation of a state water quality standard established in accordance with Section 303 of the CWA. The standards are generally believed to be too ambiguous and nonspecific. Only specific effluent limitations set forth in an NPDES permit have historically been subject to legal challenge. *But see, Northwest Environmental Advocates v. Portland,* 74 F.3d 945 (9th Cir. 1996), *cert. denied,* 518 U.S. 1018 (1996).

The Secretary of Agriculture, with the approval of the EPA, is authorized to establish programs to control nonpoint source pollution for improved water quality in those states or areas for which the EPA administrator has approved a waste management plan. *33 U.S.C. § 1288(j)(1) (2008)*. These programs are administered through the NRCS. Under this program, known as the Rural Clean Water Program, the Secretary may enter into five to ten year contracts with owners and operators of rural land for the purpose of installing and maintaining measures incorporating best management practices to control nonpoint source pollution. Under such contracts, landowners agree to manage their farms in conformity with a plan approved by a soil conservation district. If farmers agree to do this, the Secretary of Agriculture may provide technical assistance and share the cost of carrying out the practices set forth in the contract. Usually, such financial aid cannot exceed 50 percent of the total cost of the measures set forth in the contract; however, the Secretary may increase this proportion if it is determined that implementing the plan would principally benefit offsite water quality, and requiring the landowner to pay the matching share would impose so great a burden as probably to prevent the owner's participation in the program.

The 1996 Farm Bill created the Environmental Quality Incentives Program (EQIP) with the purpose of providing financial assistance to farmers and ranchers in meeting nonpoint source pollution requirements. The EQIP provides cost-share assistance for up to 75 percent of the cost of certain conservation practices, such as grassed waterways, filter strips, manure management facilities, capping abandoned wells, and wildlife habitat enhancement. Incentive payments can be made for up to three years to encourage producers to perform land management practices involving such matters as nutrients, manure, irrigation water, wildlife, and integrated pest management. The EQIP was reauthorized by the 2014 Farm Bill and a $450,000 per person/legal entity payment limit applies for 2014–2018.

## 3. Wetlands

Section 404 of the Clean Water Act makes illegal the discharging of dredge or fill material into the "navigable waters of the United States" without obtaining a permit from the Secretary of the Army acting through the Corps of Engineers (COE). Over the years, EPA has issued "compliance orders" to landowners and other parties when EPA believed that the land in issue contained wetlands subject to EPA's jurisdictional control. The issuance of a compliance order has the effect of freezing the affected party in place until a Section 404 permit is obtained. EPA has also taken the position that such orders do not give the affected party the right to a hearing or the ability to obtain judicial review because (in EPA's view) such orders are not "final agency action" that carries appeal rights with it. However, in *Sackett v. United States Environmental Protection Agency,* 132 S. Ct. 1367 (2012)*, rev'g.,* 622 F.3d 1139 (9th Cir. 2010), a unanimous Court held that the CWA does not preclude pre-enforcement judicial review of EPA administrative compliance orders. Preclusion, the Court held, would violate constitutional due process requirements. In 2015, the U.S. Court of Appeals for the Eighth Circuit held that a Corps of Engineers "preliminary determination" that the wetlands at issue on a tract that the owner sought to mine for peat has a "significant nexus" to a navigable river more than 100 miles away constituted a final agency action that could be appealed. *Hawkes Co., Inc., et al. v. United States Army Corps of Engineers,* 782 F.3d 994 (8th Cir. 2015), *rev'g.,* 963 F. Supp. 2d 868 (D. Minn. 2013), *cert. granted, United States Army Corps of Engineers v. Hawkes, Co., Inc.,* No. 15–290, 2015 U.S. LEXIS 7874 (U.S. Sup. Ct. Dec. 11, 2015). On further review, the U.S. Supreme Court unanimously affirmed. 136 S. Ct. 1807 (2016).

Until 1975, the Corps construed the term "navigable waters" to mean waters that were actually navigable. In accordance with regulations promulgated in 1975, the COE expanded its jurisdiction to "other waters" of the United States, including streams, wetlands, playa lakes, and natural ponds if the use, degradation or destruction of those areas could affect interstate commerce. However, by the early 1990s, the term "waters of the United States" was defined to mean "all waters which are currently used or were used in the past, or may be susceptible to use in interstate or foreign commerce. . . ." *33 C.F.R. § 328.3(a)(1).*

The COE issued new regulations in 1977 that defined wetlands as "areas that are inundated by surface or groundwater at a frequency and duration sufficient to support, and that under normal circumstances do support, a prevalence of vegetation typically adapted for life in saturated soil conditions. Wetlands generally include swamps, marshes, bogs and similar areas." *33 C.F.R. § 328.3(b)*. This definition was upheld by the United States Supreme Court in 1985. *United States v. Riverside Bayview Homes, Inc.,* 474 U.S. 121 (1985). Every pre-1989 COE regulatory guidance letter defined the phrase "under normal circumstances," with regard to vegetation, to mean vegetation that exists under the present characteristics of established use of a particular tract of land was farming, the "normal circumstance" of that land was as farmland. In January 1989, the COE adopted the *Federal Manual for Identifying and Delineating Jurisdictional Wetlands* which defined "under normal circumstances" to mean what vegetation would exist if the land was *not* disturbed to grow corn, soybeans or wheat. Consequently, established use on a particular tract of land became irrelevant. The Corps verified this definition in regulatory guidance letter 90–7 issued on September 26, 1990. Even though the Congress invalidated the 1989 manual in 1991 as not having been subjected to public review, the COE issued a memorandum on August 27, 1991, stating that the definition of "under normal circumstances" had been modified by the 1990 guidance.

A series of court decisions beginning in the mid-1970s also contributed to the COE's increasing jurisdiction over wetlands. *See, e.g., United States v. Holland,* 373 F. Supp. 665 (M.D. Fla. 1974)*; United States v. Ashland Oil & Transportation Co.,* 504 F.2d

1317 (6th Cir. 1974); *Natural Resources Defense Council v. Calloway*, 392 F. Supp. 685 (D. D.C. 1975). *See also, United States v. TGR Corp.*, 171 F.3d 762 (2d Cir. 1999); *Save Our Sonoran, Inc. v. Flowers*, 381 F.3d 905 (9th Cir. 2004). In 1983, the Fifth Circuit Court of Appeals held that the term "discharge" may reasonably be understood to include "redeposit" and concluded that the term "discharge" covered the redepositing of soil taken from wetlands such as occurs during mechanized land clearing activities. *Avoyelles Sportsmen's League, Inc. v. Marsh*, 715 F.2d 897 (5th Cir. 1983). In 1987, the COE's permit jurisdiction was held to extend to wetlands created by irrigation and flood control structures. *United States v. Akers*, 651 F. Supp. 320 (E.D. Cal. 1987). In *United States v. Sinclair Oil Co.*, 767 F. Supp. 200 (D. Mont. 1990), a Montana rancher was found liable under the CWA for removing fallen trees and large rocks from a river that flowed through his ranch. The court found that the redeposit of indigenous riverbed materials met the definition of "fill" and that the rancher's activities were subject to the CWA's permit requirements.

### i. Isolated and Nonadjacent Wetlands

Since 1975, the COE and the EPA have defined "waters of the United States" such that the agencies assert regulatory authority over isolated wetlands or wetlands not adjacent to "waters of the United States" if a link exists between the water body and interstate commerce. The courts have upheld the interpretation. *See, e.g., United States v. Byrd*, 609 F.2d 1204 (7th Cir. 1979). In 1985, an EPA internal memorandum concluded that CWA jurisdiction could be extended to include isolated wetlands that were or could be used by migratory birds or endangered species. In 1986, the COE issued memoranda to its districts explaining that the use of waters by migratory birds could support the CWA's jurisdiction. This view was initially upheld by the courts. *See, e.g., United States v. Sargent County Water Resource District,* 876 F. Supp. 1081 (D. N.D. 1992). However, the Seventh Circuit Court of Appeals held that the EPA's regulatory definition of "other waters" whose destruction could adversely impact interstate commerce did *not* include such isolated wetlands and was invalid. *Hoffman Homes, Inc. v. EPA,* 961 F.2d 1310 (7th Cir. 1992). In a final decision, the court held that isolated wetlands *actually used by* migratory birds presented a sufficient connection to interstate commerce to give the EPA and COE jurisdiction under the CWA. *Hoffman Homes, Inc. v. EPA,* 999 F.2d 256 (7th Cir. 1993).

In *Solid Waste Agency of Northern Cook County v. United States Army Corps of Engineers,* 191 F.3d 845 (7th Cir. 1999), *rev'd,* 531 U.S. 159 (2001) (SWANCC), suburban Chicago municipalities that selected a 533-acre abandoned sand and gravel pit containing excavation trenches for a 410-acre solid waste disposal site. The trenches had become permanent and seasonal ponds that were home to approximately 121 species of birds, including many endangered, water-dependent, and migratory birds. Because the proposal for the site required filling-in some of the ponds, the COE, asserting jurisdiction under the "migratory bird rule," refused to issue a permit in 1991 and 1994, citing a need to protect the habitat of the migratory birds. When the municipalities challenged the COE's jurisdiction, the District Court granted the COE's motion for summary judgment, and, on appeal, the Seventh Circuit held that the Congress had authority under the Commerce Clause to regulate intrastate waters and that the "migratory bird rule" was a reasonable interpretation of the CWA. *Solid Waste Agency v. United States Army Corps of Engineers*, 191 F.3d 845 (7th Cir. 1999).

The Supreme Court reversed, and held that the "migratory bird rule" exceeded the COE's regulatory authority. 531 U.S. 159 (2001), *rev'g*, 191 F.3d 845 (7th Cir. 1999). The Court held that the COE did not have jurisdiction over ponds that are not adjacent to open water. The Supreme Court's SWANCC decision seemed to indicate rather strongly that the COE did not have a legal basis to regulate isolated waters that did not have a substantive connection to interstate commerce. While "navigability" could be argued, the opinion did remove federal jurisdiction over private ponds and seasonal or ephemeral waters where the only connection with interstate commerce is migratory waterfowl. But, subsequent court opinions have indicated that other factors are relevant in determining whether the federal government can regulate isolated water where the potential connection with interstate waters is more than migratory waterfowl. Those factors include recreational use for interstate or foreign travelers, fish or shellfish habitat, or use of the water for industrial purposes by industries engaged in interstate commerce. In any event, federal jurisdiction over open waters that ultimately flow into interstate waters or waters that are navigable-in-fact remained after the Court's SWANCC opinion. The key question in any particular case was whether the isolated wetland had a sufficient connection with "waters of the United States" to be subject to the permit requirement of Section 404 of the CWA.

In 2006, the Supreme Court issued another opinion involving the question of federal regulation over isolated wetlands. *Rapanos, et ux., et al. v. United States Army Corps of Engineers,* 547 U.S. 715 (2006). Unfortunately, the Court failed to clarify the meaning of the CWA phrase "waters of the United States" and the scope of federal regulation of isolated wetlands. In addition, the plurality opinion also held that a wetland may not be considered "adjacent to" remote "waters of the United States" based merely on a hydrological connection. Thus, in the plurality's view, only those wetlands with a continuous surface connection to bodies that are "waters of the United States" in their own right, so that there is no clear demarcation between the two, are "adjacent" to such waters and covered by permit requirement of Section 404 of the CWA. Justice Kennedy authored a concurring opinion, but on much narrower grounds. In Justice Kennedy's view, the Sixth Circuit correctly recognized that a water or wetland constitutes "navigable waters" under the CWA if it possesses a significant nexus to waters that are navigable in fact or that could reasonably be so made. But, in Justice Kennedy's view, the Sixth Circuit failed to consider

all of the factors necessary to determine that the
lands in question had, or did not have, the requisite
nexus. Without more specific regulations comporting
with the Court's 2001 SWANCC opinion, Justice
Kennedy stated that the COE needed to establish a
significant nexus on a case-by-case basis when
seeking to regulate wetlands based on adjacency to
non-navigable tributaries, in order to avoid
unreasonable application of the CWA. In Justice
Kennedy's view, the record in the cases contained
evidence pointing to a possible significant nexus, but
neither the COE nor the Sixth Circuit established a
significant nexus. As a result, Justice Kennedy
concurred that the Sixth Circuit opinions should be
vacated and the cases remanded to the Sixth Circuit
for further proceedings.

**Note:** Under the rationale of *Marks v. United States,*
430 U.S. 188 (1977), Justice Kennedy's opinion is the
controlling opinion in the case. Under Marks, when
the Court fails to reach a majority opinion, the holding
of the Court is viewed as the position taken by the
concurring opinion rendered on the narrowest
grounds. In this case, that is Justice Kennedy's
concurring opinion. *But see, United States v. Johnson,*
467 F.3d 56 (1st Cir. 2006), *cert. den.,* 128 S. Ct. 375
(2007), where the court determined that by adhering
to Justice Kennedy's standard as the single
controlling test, there could be circumstances in
which a site would be within CWA jurisdiction due to
application of the "significant nexus" test, but that
same site would not be considered within CWA
jurisdiction, according to the plurality opinion. As
such, a site could be within CWA jurisdiction if it

satisfied either the plurality's standard or Justice Kennedy's standard.

The bottom line is that the Court injected enormous uncertainty into the law. This is illustrated by the court's opinion in *United States v. Chevron Pipeline Co.*, 437 F. Supp. 2d 605 (N.D. Tex. 2006). The case involved oil that spilled from a pipeline into a tributary of an intermittent stream which is connected to a creek that travels almost 24 miles before flowing into a river. The court found Justice Kennedy's test impossible to apply and held that, in accordance with prior Fifth Circuit caselaw, generally dry channels and creek beds do not create a significant nexus to navigable waters. But, a different court has used Justice Kennedy's rationale to find a significant nexus between isolated and navigable waters. *Northern California River Watch v. City of Healdsburg,* 457 F.3d 1023 (9th Cir. 2006), *cert. den.,* 552 U.S. 1180 (2008). Presently, however, every federal court applying *Rapanos* (including the First, Third, Seventh, Ninth and Eleventh Circuit Courts of Appeal) has concluded that the Corps may assert CWA jurisdiction over a given site if the site meets Justice Kennedy's test. *North California River Watch v. City of Healdsburg,* 496 F.3d 993 (9th Cir. 2007); *United States v. Johnson,* 467 F.3d 56 (1st Cir. 2006); *United States v. Robinson,* 505 F.3d 208 (11th Cir. 2007); *United States v. Gerke Excavating, Inc.,* 464 F.3d 723 (7th Cir. 2006); *Precon Development Corporation, Inc. v. United States Army Corps of Engineers,* 633 F.3d 278 (4th Cir. 2011); *United States v. Donovan,* 661 F.3d 174 (3d Cir. 2011). No court has held that if Justice Kennedy's test is met, but the plurality's test is not, no CWA jurisdiction exists. *See, e.g., United States v. Bailey,* 516 F. Supp. 2d 998 (D. Minn. 2007), *aff'd,* 571 F.3d 791 (8th Cir. 2009).

In April of 2011, the EPA issued proposed guidance concerning its jurisdiction over isolated wetlands under the CWA's dredge and fill provision. In the guidance, EPA claims jurisdiction over waters beyond that permitted by existing regulations by taking the position that it could claim jurisdiction over subject waters under *either* the test set forth in the *Rapanos* plurality opinion *or* the test established by Justice Kennedy. However, in a court decision issued about a month after the proposed guidance was issued, the court held that in determining the proper interpretation of the phrase "waters of the United States" for purposes of the federal government's jurisdiction under the CWA, Justice Kennedy's "significant nexus" text expressed in *Rapanos* is the only test to be used in determining jurisdiction. *United States v. Freedman Farms, Inc.,* 786 F. Supp. 2d 1016 (E.D. N.C. 2011).

In March of 2014, the EPA and the COE released a proposed rule defining "waters of the United States" in an attempt to significantly expand the agencies' regulatory jurisdiction under the CWA. Under the proposed rule, the CWA would apply to all waters which have been *or ever could be used* in interstate commerce as well as all interstate waters and wetlands. In addition, the proposed rule specifies that the agencies' jurisdiction would apply to all "tributaries" of interstate waters and all waters and wetlands "adjacent" to such interstate waters. The agencies also asserted in the proposed rule that their jurisdiction applies to all waters or wetlands with a "significant nexus" to interstate waters. Under the proposed rule, "tributaries" is broadly defined to include natural or man-made waters, wetlands, lakes, ponds, canals, streams and ditches if they contribute flow directly or indirectly to interstate waters irrespective of whether these waterways continuously exist or have any nexus to traditional "waters of the United States." The proposed rule defines "adjacent" expansively to include "bordering, contiguous or neighboring waters." Thus, all waters and wetlands within the same riparian area of flood plain of interstate waters would be "adjacent" waters subject to CWA regulation. "Similarly situated" waters are evaluated as a "single landscape unit" allowing the agencies to regulate an entire watershed if one body of water within it has a "significant nexus" to interstate waters. The proposed rule excludes from regulation certain artificially irrigated areas, artificial lakes and ponds used for stock watering, irrigation or rice growing, artificial swimming pools, small ornamental waters used primarily for aesthetic reasons and water-filled depressions incidental to construction activity. Also, existing exemptions for certain agricultural activities are retained along with 53 identified conservation practices.

The proposed rule became effective as a final rule on August 28, 2015 in 37 states, but a decision by a North Dakota federal district court judge blocked the rule from taking effect in the remaining 13 states. The lawsuit filed in that case and in other similar lawsuits across the country claimed that the rule exceeded congressional authority under the CWA, interfered with state sovereignty to regulate non-federal waters and that the EPA violated the Administrative Procedures Act (APA) when it issued the rule. At least one court issued a temporary injunction, and legislative efforts to rescind the rule were taken. On October 9, 2015, the U.S. Court of. Appeals for the Sixth Circuit issued a nationwide injunction barring the rule from being enforced anywhere in the U.S. In 2016, the Sixth Circuit ruled that it had jurisdiction to hear the challenge to the final rule. *Murray Energy Corp. v. United States Department of Defense,* 817 F.3d 261 (6th Cir. 2016). In early 2017, the Supreme Court of the United States decided that it would determine whether jurisdiction over the WOTUS rule belonged in the Sixth Circuit or in the federal district courts. *National Association of Manufacturers v. Department of Defense,* No. 15-3751, *cert. granted,* Jan. 13, 2017 (U.S. Sup. Ct.).

Thus, until the matter is resolved, the definition of "waters of the United States" is governed by the 1986 definition of the phrase and the "significant nexus" test of *Rapanos.*

### *ii. Exemption for "Normal Farming Activities"*

An exemption from the CWA § 404 permit requirement exists for "normal farming activities" such as plowing, seeding, cultivating, minor drainage, harvesting, upland soil and water conservation projects, construction or maintenance of farm ponds, irrigation ditches, maintenance of drainage ditches and construction or maintenance of farm roads not otherwise impairing navigable waters. *33 U.S.C. § 1344(f)(1) (2008). See, e.g., Coon, et al. v. Willet Dairy, LP, et al.,* 536 F.3d 171 (2d Cir. 2008), *aff'g,* No. 5:02-CV-1195 (FJS/GJD), 2007 U.S. Dist. LEXIS 51718 (N.D. N.Y. Jul. 17, 2007). In general, COE regulations limit the exemption to pre-established farming activities that do not bring a new area into farming or require modifications to the hydrological regime. *33 C.F.R. § 323.4(a)(1)(ii).* In addition, the EPA, not the COE, is the final authority to decide the scope of the exemption. 43 Op. Att'y. Gen. 15 (1979).

In general, the courts have narrowly construed the exemption to those situations where the agricultural activity is extremely minimal and no additional areas of "navigable waters" are brought into use. *See, e.g., United States v. Huebner,* 752 F.2d 1235 (7th Cir. 1985). As such, the exemption for agricultural activities applies only to prior established and continuing farming activities. *See, e.g., United States v. Cumberland Farms of Connecticut, Inc.,* 826 F.2d 1151 (1st Cir. 1987), *cert. denied,* 484 U.S. 1061 (1988). In addition, the burden of proof to establish that the exemption applies is on the particular farmer or rancher claiming the exemption. *United States v. Acquest Transit LLC,* No. 09-CV-055S, 2009 U.S. Dist. LEXIS 60337 (W.D. N.Y. Jul. 15, 2009). For example, the conversion of wetlands to fish farming ponds has been held to constitute a new use that is ineligible for the "normal farming activities" exemption. *Conant v. United States,* 786 F.2d 1008

(11th Cir. 1986). Also, filling to stabilize riverbanks and rechannel streambeds has been held not to fall within the scope of the exemption as normal ranching or upland soil and water conservation practices. *See, e.g., United States v. Zanger,* 767 F. Supp. 1030 (N.D. Cal. 1991).

Exempt activities are subject to a "recapture" provision that requires a permit if a discharge changes the use of the waters, impairs the waters' flow or circulation, brings an area of navigable waters into a use to which it was not previously subject, or reduces the reach of the waters. *33 U.S.C. § 1344(f)(2) (2008). See, e.g., Greenfield Mills, Inc. v. Macklin,* 361 F.3d 934 (7th Cir. 2004). Thus, only routine activities with relatively minor impacts on waters are exempt and the exemption will be lost if the activity is a new use and the activity reduces the reach or impairs the flow of water. *See, e.g., In re Carsten,* 211 B.R. 719 (Bankr, D. Mont. 1997); *People v. Appel,* 51 Cal. App. 4th 495, 59 Cal. Rptr. 2d 216 (1996).

In *United States v. Brace,* 41 F.3d 117 (3d Cir. 1994), the court held that the "normal farming activity" exemption only applied to activities occurring on the particular site in question regardless of the relationship to the activities occurring on the remainder of the land. For a similar case, see *United States v. Sargent County Water Resource District,* 876 F. Supp. 1090 (D. N.D. 1994).

### iii. Swampbuster

The conservation-compliance provisions of the 1985 Farm Bill introduced the concept of "swampbuster." Swampbuster denies federal farm program benefits to persons planting agricultural commodities for harvest on converted wetlands. As enacted, Swampbuster was only concerned with wetland conversion occurring after the date of the legislation's enactment and defined wetlands to exclude "playa lakes" and other temporarily flooded areas. In addition, local decision makers were given latitude to guard against unfair determinations. The report of the conference committee a week before the 1985 Farm Bill was signed into law stated that wetland conversion was considered to be "commenced" when a person had obligated funds or begun actual modification of a wetland.

The legislation charged the SCS with creating an official wetland inventory with a particular tract being classified as a wetland if it had (1) the presence of hydric soil; (2) wetland hydrology (soil inundation for at least seven days or saturated for at least 14 days during the growing season); and (3) the prevalence of hydrophytic plants under undisturbed conditions. In other words, to be a wetland, a tract must have hydric soils, hydrophytic vegetation and wetland hydrology. The presence of hydrophytic vegetation, by itself, is insufficient to meet the wetland hydrology requirement and the statute clearly requires the presence of all three characteristics. *B&D Land & Livestock Co. v. Schafer*, 584 F. Supp. 2d 1182 (N.D. Iowa 2008). The

SCS then developed a manual to communicate national and state wetland policy to SCS field staff. In June, 1986, the interim rules for Swampbuster were published in the Federal Register and evidenced general compliance with congressional intent and made no mention of "farmed wetland." Under the interim rules, wetland was assumed to be truly wet ground that had never been farmed. In addition, "obligation of funds" such as assessments paid to drainage districts, qualified as commenced conversions, and the Fish and Wildlife Service (FWS) had no involvement in ASCS or SCS decisions. In September of 1986, a proposal to exempt from Swampbuster all lands within drainage districts was approved by the chiefs of the ASCS, SCS, FmHA, FCIC and the Secretary of Agriculture. However, the USDA proposal failed in the face of strong opposition from the FWS and the EPA.

The final Swampbuster rules were issued in 1987 and greatly differed from the interim rules. The final Swampbuster rules eliminated the right to claim prior investment as a commenced conversion. Added were farmed wetlands, abandoned cropland, active pursuit requirements, FWS concurrence, a complicated "commenced determination" application procedure, and special treatment for prairie potholes. Under the "commenced conversion" rules, an individual producer or a drainage district is exempt from Swampbuster restrictions if drainage work began before December 23, 1985 (the effective date of the 1985 Farm Bill). If the drainage work was not completed by December 23, 1985, a request could be made of the ASCS on or before September 19, 1988, to make a commencement determination. Drainage districts must satisfy several requirements under the "commenced conversion" rules. A project drainage plan setting forth planned drainage must be officially adopted. In addition, the district must have begun installation of drainage measures or legally committed substantial funds toward the conversion by contracting for installation or supplies.

The final rules defined "farmed wetlands" as playa, potholes, and other seasonally flooded wetlands that were manipulated before December 23, 1985, but still exhibited wetland characteristics. Drains affecting these areas can be maintained, but the scope and effect of the original drainage system cannot be exceeded. *7 C.F.R. § 12.33(b)*. Prior converted wetlands can be farmed, but they revert to protected status once abandoned. Abandonment occurs after five years of inactivity and can happen in one year if there is intent to abandon. A prior converted wetland is a wetland that was totally drained before December 23, 1985. Under 16 U.S.C. § 3801(a)(6), a "converted wetland" is defined as a wetland that is manipulated for the purpose or with the effect of making the production of an agricultural commodity possible if such production would not have been possible but for such action. In *Clark v. United States Department of Agriculture,* 537 F.3d 934 (8th Cir. 2008), the court upheld an interpretation of the "converted wetland" definition that attributes conversion to a landowner that makes an area more suitable for farming rather than an interpretation that construed the statute to mean whether the subject property could possibly grow crops. If a wetland was drained before December 23, 1985, but wetland characteristics remain, it is a "farmed wetland" and only the original drainage can be maintained.

In *Boucher v. United States Department of Agriculture,* 149 F. Supp. 3d 1045 (S.D. Ind. 2016), the court determined that the NRCS followed regulatory procedures found in 7 C.F.R. § 12.31(b)(2)(ii) for determining wetland status on the land that was being farmed by comparing the land to comparable tracts that were not being farmed. The court also noted that existing regulations do not require site visits during the growing season and "normal circumstances" of the land does not refer to normal climate conditions but instead refers to soil and hydrologic conditions normally present without regard to the removal of vegetation. The court also determined that the ten-year timeframe between the preliminary determination and the final determination did not deprive the plaintiff of due process rights. As a result, the court granted the government's motion for summary judgment. Likewise, in *Foster v. Vilsack, 820 F.3d 330 (8th Cir. 2016),* the court determined that the defendant's method for determining hydrology by using aerial photographs taken when the tract was under normal environmental conditions was proper, given that the tract was drier than normal during the defendant's site visit and because the plaintiffs had tilled the tract such that it was not in its normal condition at the time of the site visit. The court also rejected the plaintiffs' claim that the defendant had relied on a comparison site too distant from the tract at issue that wasn't within the local area as the regulations required. The comparison site chosen was 40 miles away but was within the same Major Land Resource Area. As such, the comparison site satisfied the regulatory criteria contained in 7 C.F.R. § 12.31(b)(2) to find a similar tract in its natural vegetative state. Accordingly, the defendant's use of the comparison site was not arbitrary, capricious or contrary to the law.

Prior converted cropland continues to be a contentious issue. *See, e.g., New Hope Power Company, et al. v. United States Army Corps of Engineers,* 746 F. Supp.2d 1272 (S.D. Fla. Sept. 2010). In *New Hope,* the court held that the defendant had improperly extended its jurisdiction over prior converted croplands that are converted to non-agricultural use and where dry lands are maintained using continuous pumping.

Drainage activities on land designated as "farmed wetlands" have led to litigation. *See, e.g., Gunn v. United States,* 118 F.3d 1233 (8th Cir. 1997), *cert. denied,* 522 U.S. 1111 (1998), where the court upheld the government's regulatory definition of a "converted wetland," and determined that the land was not "prior converted wetland" (wetland converted to land capable of agricultural production before December 23, 1985) even though the land was initially drained in 1906. Indeed, the court noted that the farmland never became "converted wetland," but was "farmed wetland," because it retained wetland characteristics continuously from 1906 to 1992. Consequently, the drainage system was required to remain in its December 23, 1985, condition with the result that the land could not be farmed without the farmer losing eligibility for farm program benefits. The court reasoned that the 1992 drainage activity was unrelated to the 1906 drainage even though the "commenced conversion" regulations allow a farmer to demonstrate that conversion to wetlands occurred before December 23, 1985, through the commitment of substantial funds to another party for performance of drainage activities. The court reached this conclusion even though drainage district assessments had been paid on the land for decades.

Unfortunately, the *Gunn* court did not precisely address the issue of the original "scope and effect" of the 1906 drainage activities. Under USDA regulations, farmed wetland can be used as it was before December 23, 1985, and a hydrologic manipulation can be maintained to the same "scope and effect" as before December 23, 1985. The USDA is responsible for determining the scope and effect of original manipulation on all farmed wetlands. Arguably, if the 1906 drainage allowed crop production to occur on all of the land at issue *at that time*, then the effect of the 1906 drainage on the wetland was to convert it to crop production, and that status could be maintained by additional drainage activities after December 23, 1985. However, for farmed wetlands, the government has interpreted the "scope and effect" regulation such that the depth or scope of *drainage ditches, culverts or other drainage devices* be preserved at their December 23, 1985, level regardless of the effect any post-December

23, 1985, drainage work actually had on the *land* involved.

In *Barthel v. United States Department of Agriculture,* 181 F.3d 934 (8th Cir. 1999), the Eighth Circuit Court of Appeals invalidated the government's interpretation of the "scope and effect" regulation. The court held that a proper interpretation should focus on the status quo of the manipulated wetlands rather than the drainage device utilized in post-December 23, 1985, drainage activities.

In 1990, the Congress tightened the Swampbuster rules by adding a new provision which provided that "any person who in any crop year subsequent to November 28, 1990, converts a wetland by draining, dredging, filling, leveling, or any other means for the purpose, or to have the effect, of making the production of an agricultural commodity possible on such converted wetlands shall be ineligible for USDA farm benefits. *16 U.S.C. § 3821(b)–(c) (2008).* Thus, after the 1990 Swampbuster amendments, a person could become ineligible for USDA farm benefits either by (1) converting wetland and growing crops on the land if the conversion was accomplished after December 23, 1985, or (2) merely converting wetland after November 28, 1990, so that crops could be grown on the land. *See, e.g., United States v. Dierckman,* 201 F.3d 915 (7th Cir. 2000), *aff'g,* 41 F. Supp. 2d 870 (S.D. Ind. 1998). The rules were changed to also add a stronger penalty for wetland conversions. While converting a wetland before Nov. 28, 1990, resulted in only a proportional loss of benefits, conversion after that date results in the loss of *all* USDA benefits on *all* land the farmer controls until the wetland is restored or the loss is mitigated. *16 U.S.C. § 3821(c) (2008).*

After the 1990 Swampbuster rule change, the USDA took the position that activities that made ag production "possible" on converted wetland meant that any activity that made such land more farmable was prohibited. In its 1996 edition of the National Food Security Act Manual, the USDA's regulatory definition of a converted wetland (which the statute defines in 16 U.S.C. § 3821(c)) to mean any "manipulation which allows or would allow production of an agricultural commodity where such production was not previously possible, or making an area farmable more years than previously possible. . . ." The USDA's regulatory position was upheld by the U.S. Circuit Court of Appeals for the Eighth Circuit, *Clark v. United States Department of Agriculture,* 537 F.3d 934 (8th Cir. 2008), but has been rejected by the Federal District Court for the Eastern District of California. *Koshman v. Vilsack,* 865 F. Supp.2d 1083 (E.D. Cal. 2012).

Under the 1996 Farm Bill, a farmed wetland located in a cropped field can be drained without sacrificing farm program benefit eligibility if another wetland is created elsewhere. Thus, through "mitigation," a farmed wetland can be moved to an out-of-the-way location. In addition, the 1996 legislation provides a good faith exemption to producers who inadvertently drain a wetland. If the wetland is restored within one year of drainage, no penalty applies. The legislation also revises the concept of "abandonment." Cropland with a certified wetland delineation, such as "prior converted" or "farmed wetland" is to maintain that status, as long as the land is used for agricultural production. In accordance with an approved plan, a landowner may allow an area to revert to wetland status and then convert it back to its previous status without violating Swampbuster. Also, while there is an exception from the Swampbuster restrictions for prior converted wetland that returns to wetland status after December 23, 1985, as a result of specified events, 16 U.S.C. § 3822(b)(2)(D) (2008), the exception does not apply if the land had returned to wetland status before or as of December 23, 1985. *See Horn Farms, Inc. v. Johanns,* 397 F.3d 472 (7th Cir. 2005), *rev'g,* 319 F. Supp. 2d 902 (N.D. Ind. 2004), *cert. den.,* 547 U.S. 1018 (2006); *Maple Drive Farms Family Limited Partnership v. Vilsack,* No. 1:11-CV-692, 2012 U.S. Dist. LEXIS 176539 (W.D. Mich. Dec. 13, 2012).

Farm program payments are not forfeited for producing agricultural commodities on converted wetland if the land was determined to be farmed wetland or farmed wetland pasture and NRCS determines that the conversion would have only a minimal effect on the wetland functions and values of wetlands in the area. *16 U.S.C. § 3822(f); 7 C.F.R. § 12.31(d). See, e.g., Rosenau v. Farm Service Agency,* 395 F. Supp. 2d 868 (D. N.D. 2005); *Holly Hills Farm Corp. v. United States,* 447 F.3d 258 (4th Cir. 2006), *aff'g,* No. 3.04-CV-856, 2005 U.S. Dist. LEXIS 12875 (E.D. Va. Jun. 29, 2005).

## iv. The Interplay of Swampbuster and CWA § 404

In 1993, the COE and EPA adopted new regulations clarifying the application of CWA § 404 to land designated as wetland. The regulations specifically exempt prior converted wetlands from the definition of "navigable waters" for CWA purposes. *58 Fed. Reg. 45,008–48,083 (1993)*. Thus, prior converted cropland is not subject to the permit requirements of § 404 of the CWA. However, "farmed wetlands" remain within the COE's jurisdiction under § 404 of the CWA. While farmed wetlands remain within the COE's jurisdiction under § 404 of the CWA, the COE cannot bring civil enforcement actions for unpermitted discharges into wetlands. *United States v. Hallmark Construction Co.,* No. 97 C 3682, 1998 U.S. Dist. LEXIS 11892 (N.D. Ill. Jul. 23, 1998).

Farmed wetlands are essentially prior converted wetlands where wetland characteristics remain and are defined as "potholes and playas" with seven or more consecutive days of inundation or 14 days of saturation during the growing season and other areas with 15 or more consecutive days (or 10 percent of the growing season, whichever is less) of inundation during the growing season. *58 Fed. Reg. 45,032 (1993)*. Drainage can occur on land classified as prior converted so long as no additional farmed wetland is converted. In addition, the COE and/or EPA must agree to all NRCS wetland determinations, and determinations involving agricultural land that impact the COE's ability to regulate such land under the CWA are subject to COE approval. Similarly, the FSA cannot make wetland jurisdictional determinations that are binding on the COE or the EPA. *33 C.F.R. § 328.3(a)(8) (2008).*

In *United States v. Hallmark Construction Company,* 30 F. Supp. 2d 1033 (N.D. Ill 1998), a real estate developer attempting to develop farmland found itself caught in the federal government's wetlands web. The case is instructive for its discussion of the differences between farmed wetland and prior converted cropland, and the procedure involved in a wetlands dispute.

In 1993, the Clinton administration made a policy announcement specifying that the SCS was to be designated as the lead agency for determining whether agricultural land is wetland for both CWA and swampbuster program purposes. Procedures were to be developed jointly by the SCS, COE, EPA and FWS. In addition, SCS appeal procedures were to be utilized to contest wetland determinations, and the COE, in coordination with EPA, SCS and FWS was to develop a nationwide general permit for CWA purposes for discharges associated with "minimal effects" and "frequently cropped with mitigation" conversions determined by SCS and FWS to qualify agricultural wetlands for exemption from swampbuster sanctions. A new administrative appeal process for wetland determinations and permit denials under CWA § 404 was to be developed, and a deadline of 90 days was established for COE review and decision making on § 404 permit applications. The government's "minimal effects" regulation (*7 C.F.R. § 12.31(d)*) which places the burden on the landowner the duty to request and prove eligibility for a "minimal effects" determination has been upheld. *See Clark v. United States Department of Agriculture,* 537 F.3d 934 (8th Cir. 2008).

In 1998, the District of Columbia Circuit Court of Appeals affirmed the district court and held that the COE does not have permitting authority under the CWA over incidental fallback from wetlands dredging activities. *National Mining Assoc. v. United States Army Corps of Engineers,* 145 F.3d 1399 (D.C. Cir. 1998). But, the court was careful to make clear that it was not prohibiting the regulation of any redeposit, but only incidental fallback. The court expressed skepticism that "wetland soil, sediment, debris or other material ... undergoes a legal metamorphosis during the dredging process, becoming a 'pollutant' for purpose of the [CWA]." However, the court's decision hinged on the fact that fallback does not qualify as an "addition" of pollutants. The court noted that the removal of dredged material is governed by the Rivers and Harbors Act of 1899 rather than the CWA. On May 10, 1999, the COE and EPA issued a final rule removing the term "incidental fallback" from the definition of dredged material under § 404 of the CWA. As a result of the court's decision, the Corps and EPA proposed a new rule redefining the definition of "discharge of dredged material." The new regulatory definition became effective in January 2001. *40 C.F.R. § 232.2(1) (2008).* The new regulation was invalidated in 2007 as rendering a narrower definition of incidental fallback than was permissible by a good faith reading of the caselaw involving the issue. *National Association of Homebuilders, et al. v. United States Army Corps of Engineers, et al.*, No. 01–0274 (JR), 2007 U.S. Dist. LEXIS 6366 (D. D.C. Jan. 30, 2007).

In early 2000, the Fourth Circuit Court of Appeals, in *United States v. Deaton,* 209 F.3d 331 (4th Cir. 2000), rejected the reasoning of the D.C. Circuit and held that incidental fallback was subject to regulation under the CWA as the addition of a "pollutant." Similarly, in 2001 the Ninth Circuit held that deep plowing requires a CWA § 404 permit because it produced a "regulable redeposit" of the plowed soil and constituted incidental fallback. *Borden Ranch Partnership v. United States Army Corps of Engineers,* 261 F.3d 810 (9th Cir. 2001), *cert. granted,* 536 U.S. 903 (2002). On December 16, 2002, the U.S. Supreme Court issued a one-sentence opinion affirming the Ninth Circuit after deadlocking 4–4 on the case. 537 U.S. 99 (2002).

## *v. Wetlands Case Law Developments*

Wetlands issues have spawned a number of important cases critical to agricultural operations. The cases have involved issues such as the definition of "adjacent wetlands" subject to governmental regulatory jurisdiction under the CWA. *See, e.g., Hobbs v. United States,* 947 F.2d 941 (4th Cir. 1991), *cert. denied,* 504 U.S. 90 (1992); *Save Our Community· v. United States Environmental*

*Protection Agency,* 971 F.2d 1155 (5th Cir. 1992); *National Wildlife Federation v. Agricultural Stabilization and Conservation Service,* 901 F.2d 673 (8th Cir. 1990); and pre-enforcement judicial review of wetland determinations under the CWA. *See, e.g., Laguna Gatuna, Inc. v. Browner,* 58 F.3d 564 (10th Cir. 1995), *cert. denied,* 516 U.S. 1071 (1996); *See also, Heck v. United States,* 37 Fed. Cl. 245 (1997). *But see, Miller Brothers, v. Michigan Department of Natural Resources,* 203 Mich. App. 674, 513 N.W.2d 217 (1994).

Because the penalties for violating the wetland rules under the CWA involve criminal sanctions, a number of important cases in recent years have involved the incarceration of farmers and ranchers for wetland violations. *See, e.g., United States v. Johansen,* 93 F.3d 459 (8th Cir. 1996).

### vi. Wetland "Takings" Implications

Wetlands issues have given rise to numerous cases concerning takings implications with the basic question being how far governmental regulation of wetlands can go before such regulation constitutes a defacto regulatory taking of the private property involved. A primary question is whether the denial of a CWA § 404 permit constitutes a taking without just compensation in violation of the Fifth Amendment. *See, e.g., Loveladies Harbor, Inc. v. United States,* 28 F.3d 1171 (Fed. Cir. 1994); *Roberge v. United States,* No. 92–753L (Ct. Cl. 1994); *Florida Rock Industries v. United States,* 45 Fed. Cl. 21 (1999); *Laguna Gatuna, Inc. v. United States,* 50 Fed Cl. 336 (2001);

*Helnore v. Wisconsin Department of Natural Resources,* 694 N.W.2d 730 (Wis. Ct. App. 2005); *Good v. United States,* 189 F.3d 1355 (Fed. Cir. 1999), cert. denied, 529 U.S. 1053 (2000); *Palazzolo v. Rhode Island,* 533 U.S. 606 (2001), decision on remand at, No. WM 88–0297, 2005 R.I. Super. LEXIS 108 (R.I. Sup. Ct. July 5, 2005); *Lost Tree Village Corporation v. United States,* 115 Fed. Cl. 219 (2014).

## E. SAFE DRINKING WATER ACT

The Safe Drinking Water Act (SDWA) is designed to protect public drinking water supplies from contamination by setting maximum contaminant levels (MCLs). *42 U.S.C. §§ 300f et seq.* The SDWA's objective is to ensure that public drinking water supply systems satisfy minimum national standards for the protection of public health. The SDWA considers farms and ranches as public water supplies if they have over 15 service connections or regularly serve a minimum of 25 year-round residents over a period of at least 60 days a year. Thus, large farming and ranching operations may be subject to the SDWA requirements such as testing for chemicals enumerated in the Act.

The SDWA provides the EPA the authority to control activities occurring above an aquifer that serves as the sole source of a community's water supply if the activities may affect the quality of the water in the aquifer. For example, the Act is designed to prevent waste injection into sole-source aquifers containing groundwater with less than 10,000 parts per million total dissolved solids such as occurs when irrigation return-water is placed underground through dry wells. If the water is deemed to exceed a certain chemical level, the use of dry wells for underground disposal is restricted.

## F. SURFACE MINING CONTROL AND RECLAMATION ACT

The Congress established the Surface Mining Control and Reclamation Act (SMCRA) in 1977 to address environmental issues associated with surface coal mining. *See 30 U.S.C. § 1202(a).* The SMCRA regulates surface mining on prime farmland that has historically been used as cropland through a permit system and a series of performance standards. *30 U.S.C. §§ 1201 et seq. (2008).* The SMCRA requires that a person seeking to operate a mine on prime farmland receive a permit before engaging in operations. The permit will be granted only if the operator can demonstrate the technical capacity to restore the land, within a reasonable time after the completion of mining, to the productivity level of prime farmland in the surrounding area and to its original contour. Information concerning the pre-mining productivity of the land must be contained in the permit application.

The SMCRA holds as its primary objective the insuring that both mining operations and post-mining reclamation are accomplished in a fashion that does not contribute to the contamination of surface water or groundwater. As a result, the SMCRA regulates the disposal of mine tailings and hazardous additives that may be introduced during the ore-extraction process. The SMCRA also addresses the need to plan mining operations entailing disposals so that no significant disruption of natural patterns of surface water or groundwater flow occurs. As a result, most mining operations are located near a source of water. In addition, the SMCRA, despite its name, regulates all mines regardless of depth.

The Supreme Court upheld the SMCRA as constitutional in 1981 in a case involving a challenge to "steep slopes" coal mining limitations. *Hodel v. Indiana,* 452 U.S. 314 (1981). However, the denial of an SMCRA permit to mine an alluvial valley floor has been held to be an unconstitutional taking. *Whitney Benefits, Inc. v. United States,* 31 Fed. Cl. 116 (1994).

Since 2009, the EPA has attempted to use the SMCRA as a means of restricting the coal mining business by rejecting discharge permits for coal mining projects. However, the SMCRA provides only a limited role for the EPA in the process of reviewing state permitting programs for compliance with CWA water quality standards before approval by the Interior Department. The regulatory rejection of discharge permits for coal mining projects via final agency action, a federal court held in 2012, amounted to a usurpation of the Secretary of the Interior's and a state's permitting authority under the SMCRA. *National Mining Association, et. al. v. Jackson, et. al.,* No. 10–1220, 2012 U.S. Dist. LEXIS 106057 (D. D.C. Jul. 31, 2012).

## IV. FEDERAL REGULATORY APPROACH—LAND

### A. HAZARDOUS WASTE

#### 1. Comprehensive Environmental Response Compensation and Liability Act

The Comprehensive Environmental Response Compensation and Liability Act (CERCLA), which became law in late 1980, set as a goal the initiation and establishment of a comprehensive response and financing mechanism to abate and control problems associated with abandoned and inactive hazardous waste disposal sites. While CERCLA focuses on hazardous waste sites, it can have significant ramifications for agricultural operations because the term "hazardous waste" has been defined to include most pesticides, fertilizers, and other chemicals commonly used on farms and ranches. *See, e.g., 40 C.F.R. § 261.* As such, CERCLA liability is a concern any time that agricultural land is purchased or leased.

#### i. CERCLA Components

CERCLA sets up an information gathering and analysis system to allow state and federal governments to determine more accurately the danger level at various disposal sites and to develop cleanup priorities accordingly. *42 U.S.C. § 9604 (2008).* The EPA is authorized to designate as hazardous any substance which, when released into the environment, may present a "substantial danger" to public health and welfare, or to the environment.

*42 U.S.C. § 9604 (2008)*. The act requires notification of any release into the environment of these substances. The act requires owners and operators of hazardous waste storage, treatment, and disposal sites to provide EPA with notification of the volumes and composition of hazardous wastes that can be found at their facility, and of any known or possible releases. The EPA uses this information to develop a national priorities list (NPL) in order to prioritize hazardous waste sites from those most dangerous and in need of immediate cleanup to those least dangerous and not as urgently in need of cleanup.

With respect to releases of hazardous substances, CERCLA provides that any person in charge of a "facility" from which a hazardous substance has been released in a reportable quantity must immediately notify the National Response Center. *42 U.S.C. § 9603(a) (2008)*. A comparable state-level requirement also applies under the Emergency Planning and Community Right to Know Act. *See also 42 U.S.C. § 11004(a) (2008)*. Releases that exceed 100 pounds per day must be reported. A key question of major importance to agriculture is whether large-scale livestock/poultry confinement operations operated by individual growers pursuant to contractual arrangements with vertically integrated firms constitute a single "facility," or whether each confinement structure on a farm is a separate facility. In *Sierra Club, Inc. v. Tyson Foods, Inc.*, 299 F. Supp. 2d 693 (W.D. Ky. 2003), the court held that Tyson was an operator of the chicken farms at issue pursuant to the production contracts with growers and that an entire chicken farm site is a facility from which releases must be reported under CERCLA. In a later case, *Sierra Club v. Seaboard Farms, Inc.,* 387 F.3d 1167 (10th Cir. 2004), the United States Court of Appeals for the Tenth Circuit ruled similarly that the term "facility," as defined in CERCLA, meant any site or area where hazardous substances come to be located. As a result, a large-scale confinement hog operation was held to be subject to CERCLAs reporting requirements for ammonia emissions that exceeded the per-day limit for the operation as a whole, even though no single "facility" at the operation exceeded the limit.

CERCLA also established two funds: (1) the hazardous substance response trust fund ("Superfund") which is funded by taxes on crude oil and chemicals and finances the government's response costs and damage claims for injury to or destruction or loss of natural resources; and (2) the post-closure liability trust fund which is financed by taxes on hazardous wastes and out of which payments are made to cover the costs of response damages or other compensation for injury or loss to natural resources.

CERCLA also provides the federal government with authority to respond to emergencies involving hazardous substances and to clean up leaking disposal sites. The EPA is given authority to require parties responsible for contamination to clean up the contamination or reimburse EPA for the costs of remediation. If the liable or "potentially responsible party" cannot be found or cannot afford to pay, then

EPA may use the Superfund to clean up the contamination.

CERCLA also holds persons responsible for releases of hazardous material liable for cleanup and restitution costs.

Liability is strict, joint and several, and can be applied retroactively to those having no continuing control over the hazardous substance. However, liable parties at a multi-party Superfund site are *not* jointly and severally liable if a reasonable basis exists to apportion their liability. *See, e.g., Burlington Northern and Santa Fe Railway Co., et al. v. United States et al.,* 556 U.S. 599 (2009).

There are monetary limits on liability, however. The liability limits do not apply to willful misconduct or willful negligence or knowing violation of regulations.

### ii. Elements of Liability

The government must establish four elements to prevail against a party under CERCLA. For example, the government must establish that the site in question is a covered facility subject to CERCLA regulation. Under 42 U.S.C. § 9601(9)(B) (2008), a covered facility is defined as any site or area where a hazardous substance has been deposited, stored, disposed, or placed, or is otherwise located. The definition is broad enough to potentially include such things as buildings, structures, equipment and vehicles. The government must also establish that a release (other than air emissions) or threatened release of a hazardous substance has occurred (the term "hazardous substance" is broadly defined and a "release" is defined as "any spilling, leaking, pumping, pouring, emitting, emptying, discharging, injecting, escaping, leaching, dumping, or disposing into the environment (including the abandonment or discarding or barrels, containers, and other closed receptacles containing any hazardous substance or pollutant or contaminant)." *42 U.S.C. § 9601(22) (2008))* which caused the U.S. to incur "response costs." Response costs can include expenses incurred in waste removal, damages resulting from injury to or destruction or loss of natural resources, and costs associated with health assessment or health effects resulting from the contamination. *42 U.S.C. § 9607(a) (2008).* However, CERCLA doesn't necessarily give a subcontractor a right of recovery against the landowner. *Price Trucking Corp. v. Norampac Industries, Inc.,* No. 11-2917-CV, 2014 U.S. App. LEXIS 5093 (2d Cir. Mar. 18, 2014). Also, the government need not prove that a particular defendant's waste caused the government to incur response costs. *See, e.g., Outlet City, Inc. v. West Chemical Products, Inc.,* 60 Fed. Appx. 922 (3d Cir. 2003). In addition, the defendant must be a "covered person" (also termed a "potentially responsible party"). If the four elements are proved, the defendant is strictly liable (absent a statutory defense).

Typically, the government has little trouble establishing the first three elements. Consequently, most CERCLA litigation concerns the issue of whether the defendant is a "covered person" as

defined by CERCLA. A current owner or operator of
a "covered facility" is a covered person. This includes
such individuals as tenants, as well as bankers,
insurers and other lenders that finance the purchase
of the land, limited partners and stockholders,
officers and employees, and may also include
easement holders. Also deemed to be a "covered
person" is any owner or operator of the site at the
time of disposal, any person who arranged for
disposal or treatment of hazardous substances at the
site, and any person who transported hazardous
substances to the site. Persons or entities serving as
an executor, administrator, conservator or trustee
whether serving as an individual or as a corporate
fiduciary may also be deemed a "current owner or
operator" and, as such, be a "covered person." A
corporation's control over a subsidiary does not make
it an "operator" of a polluting facility owned or
operated by the subsidiary unless the corporate veil
can be pierced (under state law) to impose derivative
liability, but if the parent actively participates in and
exercises control over the operations of the facility,
the parent may be held directly liable. *United States
v. Bestfoods,* 524 U.S. 51 (1998). *See also, United
States v. Kayser-Roth Corp., Inc.,* 103 F. Supp. 2d 74
(D. R.I. 2000). On a similar note, a corporate officer
has been held not liable under CERCLA as the
operator of a contaminated site even though the
officer's corporation was found directly liable as a
consequence of conducting waste disposal activities
at the site. *Browning-Ferris Industries of Illinois v.
Ter Maat,* 13 F. Supp. 2d 756 (N.D. Ill. 1998), *aff'd on
this issue,* 195 F.3d 953 (7th Cir. 1999), *cert. denied,*

529 U.S. 1098 (2000). *But see, Carter-Jones Lumber Co. v. Dixie Distributing Co.,* 166 F.3d 840 (6th Cir. 1999), *cert. denied,* 533 U.S. 903 (2001). In a different case involving parent corporation liability, the Seventh Circuit Court of Appeals held that a subsidiary cannot sue its parent to recover CERCLA cleanup costs. *Truck Components, Inc. v. Beatrice Co.,* 143 F.3d 1057 (7th Cir. 1998) *reh'g, en banc, denied* 1998 U.S. App. LEXIS 11491 (7th Cir. Jun. 1, 1998). In a 1994 case, the court held that a conservator or executor could be held liable as an owner under CERCLA by virtue of leasing a ranch. *Castlerock Estates, Inc. v. Estate of Markham,* 871 F. Supp. 360 (N.D. Calif. 1994). *See also, City of Phoenix v. Garbage Services Co.,* 827 F. Supp. 600 (D. Ariz. 1993). Consequently, fiduciaries of property in current use may want to consider executing an indemnity agreement with the operator concerning indemnification for liability arising from environmental problems caused by the operator's use.

CERCLA provides that a landowner responsible for response costs at a particular site may seek contribution from other potentially responsible parties (such as a previous owner). However, in late 2004 the U.S. Supreme Court took a strict reading of the statutory provision at issue and ruled that a contribution action may be brought only during or following any civil action that has been brought under Sections 106 or 107 of CERCLA. *Cooper Industries, Inc. v. Aviall Services, Inc.,* 543 U.S. 157 (2004). Under CERCLA, there are actually two distinct and complementary remedies (with different qualification requirements) that allow private parties to recover expenses associated with cleanup costs—a contribution action under § 113(f)(1) and a cost recovery action under § 107(a). While a contribution action may be brought only during or after a civil action has been filed against the potentially responsible party, a private party that that has not been sued for cleanup costs may bring a cost recovery action against another party, including federal agencies, to recover cleanup costs voluntarily incurred. *United States v. Atlantic Research Corporation,* 551 U.S. 128 (2007). The Court left open the question, however, of whether a PRP that involuntarily incurs direct cleanup costs under a consent decree can bring an action against other PRPs under § 107 or § 113. That is an important question because liability under § 107 is joint and several and under § 113 it is not. In addition, the statute of limitations for each section is different. The U.S. Circuit Courts of Appeal, however, have determined that § 107 is not available in cases involving direct cleanup costs that are incurred by virtue of a consent decree. *See, e.g., Solutia v. McWane, Inc.,* 672 F.3d 1230 (11th Cir. 2012).

Also, as a result of the Supreme Court's 2009 opinion in *Burlington Northern and Santa Fe Railway Co., et al. v. United State, et al.,* 556 U.S. 599 (2009), liability under CERCLA as an "arranger" for the disposal of hazardous substances requires evidence of intent that the subject chemicals will be "disposed" of. *See, e.g., United States v. General Electric Company,* 670 F.3d 377 (1st Cir. 2012). How much intent and the kind of intent necessary to support liability are less clear. So, in any given Superfund clean-up action in the future, a greater share of liability for clean-up will probably fall on actual owners and operators of subject property. As for apportionment, the Court's opinion could mean that arrangers will be responsible for contamination that the arranger *actually caused*. That's clearly the case when a reasonable basis exists for apportioning liability. In those situations, liability apportioned to defunct entities will result in the associated costs for that portion of clean-up costs being borne by the government (the taxpaying public). So, the Court's opinion could result in fewer potentially responsible parties as "arrangers," greater potential liability for landowners and operators, more cases filed concerning "intent" as applied to disposal of hazardous waste and more litigation on the issue of whether a reasonable basis for liability apportionment exists. However, in *DVL, Inc. v. General Electric Company, et al.*, 811 F. Supp. 2d 579 (N.D. N.Y. 2010), the court held that the plaintiff need not establish a causal link between hazardous waste and incurred response costs to establish liability as an "arranger" for moving a hazardous substance from one tract to another under CERCLA. However, the court noted that the evidence must show that the defendant deposited hazardous waste at the site in question and that requirement wasn't satisfied in the present case involving lateral migration.

### iii. Secured Creditor Exemption

An exemption from liability is provided for secured creditors whose only interest in the contaminated property is that of the property serving as collateral for a loan the lender has advanced to the party operating the premises. However, the exemption does not apply if the lender becomes too involved in the daily management or operation of the polluted property. *See, e.g., United States v. Mirabile*, 15 Envtl. L. Rep. 20994 (E.D. Pa. 1985); *United States v. Fleet Factors, Inc.*, 901 F.2d 1550 (11th Cir. 1990), *cert. denied*, 498 U.S. 1046 (1991).

Effective September 30, 1996, CERCLA was amended by the Asset Conservation, Lender Liability, and Deposit Insurance Protection Act of 1996. *Pub.L. No. 104–208, §§ 2501–2505, 110 Stat. 3009–462 (1996).* This legislation clarifies both lender liability and fiduciary liability for the costs of cleaning up environmental hazards. The legislation significantly narrows the potential liability of lenders and fiduciaries for environmental cleanup costs, and covered all existing claims which had not been finally adjudicated as of September 30, 1996. *Id. § 2505.* The Act specifies that lender/fiduciary liability does not extend beyond the assets of the trust or estate being managed. However, assets within the particular trust or estate are still potentially subjected to the cost of environmental cleanup under CERCLA. The Act also defines "fiduciary" in a manner specifically excluding fiduciary relationships established for the purpose of avoiding liability for cleanup costs. *42 U.S.C. § 107(n)(5)(A)(ii)(II) (2008).* Thus, an individual could not put contaminated assets owned outright in a trust, name themselves as trustee, and expect to avoid personal liability and limit the share of cleanup costs to the trust assets. Under the Act, however, fiduciaries remain personally liable if they are liable independently for their ownership as a fiduciary of contaminated assets or actions taken as a fiduciary. Likewise, if an individual is both a beneficiary and a fiduciary with respect to the same property and receives benefits that exceed customary or reasonable distributions or compensation permitted under applicable law, the fiduciary remains liable for cleanup costs. Similarly, the limitation on liability does not apply if the fiduciary's own negligence contributes to the contamination. *42 U.S.C. § 107(n)(3) (2008).*

The Act also specifies that lenders will be liable for the cleanup of contaminated property only if they participate in the management of the business that operates on the property. *42 U.S.C. § 101(20)(E) (2008).* Participation in management is defined as the actual exercise of decision making control over the compliance with the environmental laws.

### iv. Pesticide Exemption

There can be no recovery of response costs or damages under CERCLA from the application of a pesticide product registered under the Federal Insecticide, Fungicide, Rodenticide Act (FIFRA). This is known as the "pesticide exemption." However, one federal court has construed the pesticide exemption narrowly to not apply to the application of pesticides to unauthorized crops and in a manner that caused off-site drift. *United States v. Tropical Fruit, S.E.*, 96 F. Supp. 2d 71 (D. P.R. 2000).

### v. *Proposed Exemption for Small Businesses*

In early 2002, legislation was signed into law providing CERCLA liability relief to small businesses that contribute minimal amounts of hazardous waste to superfund sites. The legislation provides a "de micromis" exemption for small businesses that dispose of less than 100 gallons of liquid or less than 200 pounds of solid hazardous material before April 1, 2001, at a site listed on the National Priorities List. The legislation also would exempt from CERCLA liability households or businesses that employ no more than 100 workers and that dispose of only municipal solid waste at a superfund site. If a small business is sued by a larger responsible party for costs to clean up a site at which both parties disposed of waste, the larger party must prove the small business is responsible. However, if the government sues a small business for cost recovery, the small business must prove its innocence.

### vi. *Defenses Against Liability*

"Covered persons" that are potentially responsible for payment of cleanup costs under CERCLA can raise certain statutory defenses. An "Act of God" defense may apply if it can be established that the hazardous substance is on the premises as a result of a natural disaster. A defense is also available for hazardous substances occurring on account of war.

Likewise, a defense can be asserted if the presence of the hazardous substance occurred by an act or omission of a third party other than an employee or someone with a contractual relationship with the defendant, provided that the defendant can establish the exercise of due care with respect to the hazardous substances concerned and that the defendant took precautions against foreseeable acts or omissions of any such third party and the consequences that could foreseeably result from such acts or omissions. As previously discussed, a defense is also available for secured creditors who do not manage the secured property and hold title only to protect a security interest. *See, e.g., In re DuFrayne,* 194 B.R. 354 (Bankr. E.D. Pa. 1996).

Perhaps the most important defense for farmers and ranchers is the "innocent purchaser" defense. The innocent purchaser defense may apply if the defendant purchased land not known at the time of purchase to contain hazardous substances, but which is later determined to have some environmental contamination at the time of the purchase or is contiguous to land not known at the time of the purchase to be contaminated. In addition, under EPA rules a party will still be deemed to be an "innocent purchaser" for property purchased after January 11, 2002, even if the purchaser buys property with knowledge of contamination so long as all disposal of hazardous substances occurred before the purchase.

A defendant attempting to utilize this defense must establish that the real estate was purchased after the disposal or placement of the hazardous substance, and that the defendant did not know and had no reason to know at the time of purchase that a hazardous substance existed on the property. In *1325 G Street Associates v. Rockwood Pigments, Inc.*, 235 F. Supp. 2d 458 (D. Md. 2002), the court held that a potentially responsible party may bring CERCLA cost recovery action if it can show non-responsibility for contamination at the particular site.

To utilize the "innocent purchase" defense, the buyer, at the time of purchase, must undertake "all appropriate inquiry" into the previous ownership and uses of the property in an effort to minimize liability. The phrase "all appropriate inquiry" generally depends upon the existence or nonexistence of five factors: (1) any specialized knowledge or experience on the part of the purchaser about the property; (2) the relationship of the purchase price to the value of the property if it was uncontaminated; (3) commonly known or reasonably ascertainable information about the property; (4) the obviousness of the presence or likely presence of contamination of the property; and (5) the ability to detect such contamination by appropriate inspection.

Under the EPA's bona fide purchaser (BFP) final rule, the purchase of contaminated real estate can occur without the purchaser acquiring Superfund liability. The first judicial interpretation of the regulatory requirements of the BFP defense occurred in late 2010. In *Ashley II of Charleston, LLC v. PCS Nitrogen, Inc. v. Ross Development Corp. et al.*, 746 F. Supp2d 692 (D. S.C. 2010), the court was faced with a case involving an $8 million clean-up on a 43-acre property that had previously been used as a fertilizer manufacturing plant. Remediation of the site required the removal of arsenic, lead, polycyclic aromatic hydrocarbons (PAH) contamination and the raising of pH levels at the site. Multiple parties were brought into the action and the court allocated clean-up responsibility to each party involved. The plaintiff obtained a Phase I Environmental Site Assessment (ESA) before buying the property, which identified some sumps and stained concrete pads as Recognized Environmental Conditions ("RECs"). However, the plaintiff did not do any testing around the sumps or the concrete pads to determine if the RECs had, in fact, caused a release. Some time thereafter, the plaintiff tore down some buildings on a parcel of the property which had covered sumps that previously contained hazardous substances. No testing was done around the sumps before removal of the buildings. The government brought a CERCLA cost recovery action and the plaintiff was assessed $194,232 in remediation costs as the current owner of the property. The plaintiff sought reimbursement (contribution) of that amount from various parties who had either owned or operated the site in the past. The plaintiff asserted the BFP defense as the basis for contribution from the prior owner and operators.

In analyzing the defense, the court required the plaintiff to prove eight elements of the defense by a preponderance of the evidence: (1) no disposal after acquisition; (2) conduct all appropriate inquiry; (3) report all subsequent releases; (4) exercise appropriate care; (5) fully cooperate and assist in providing access to the property; (6) have all appropriate institutional controls; (7) comply with all requests and subpoenas; and (8) have no affiliation with parties that are potentially responsible parties.

The court determined that the plaintiff had satisfied the "all appropriate inquiry", reporting, accessibility, institutional control and subpoena compliance elements of the BFP defense. However, the plaintiff did not satisfy the disposal after acquisition, exercise of appropriate care and affiliation elements. Thus, the court found that the plaintiff was a Potentially Responsible Party because it was the current owner of contaminated property and it did not satisfy the requirements of the BFP defense. The court then allocated the clean-up costs to the various parties. The plaintiff was allocated 5 percent of the entire costs of clean-up— approximately $400,000. The original owner was allocated 45 percent of the responsibility, and the plaintiff was entitled to 76 percent contribution from other prior owners and operators (which would also apply to any future remediations).

A purchaser of land can take several common-sense steps to help satisfy the "appropriate inquiry obligation". A title search should be made of the property. Any indication of previous owners that may have conducted operations that might lead to contamination should be investigated. Aerial photographs of the property should be viewed and historical records examined. Likewise, investigation should be made of any government regulatory files concerning the property. A visual observation of the premises should be made, soil and well tests conducted, and neighbors questioned. However, the execution of an environmental audit may be the best method to satisfy the "all appropriate inquiry" requirement. Some states have enacted legislation requiring the completion of an environmental audit upon the sale of agricultural real estate. Today, many real estate brokers, banks and other lenders utilize environmental audits to protect against cleanup liability and lawsuits filed under CERCLA. A sample environmental audit based on the Indiana statutory form is included in Appendix 14B at the end of this chapter.

A state statute of repose may also be available as a CERCLA defense. The U.S. Supreme Court has held that 42 U.S.C. § 9658 (which preempts statutes of limitations applicable to state-law tort actions in certain circumstances) does not preempt state statutes of repose. *CTS Corp. v. Waldburger,* 134 S. Ct. 2175 (U.S. 2014). The Court found that "preemption" in the statute was characterized as an "exception" to the regular rule that "the statute of limitations established under State law" applied.

### vii. Summary

In recent years, CERCLA has become subject to widespread criticism with the focus primarily centering on CERCLA's uncertain criteria for establishing liability. Because the statutory language is ambiguous in many instances, courts have been given little congressional guidance for interpreting CERCLA's provisions resulting in each and every possible interpretation being litigated.

## 2. Resource Conservation and Recovery Act

The Resource Conservation and Recovery Act (RCRA) of 1976 subjects hazardous material to federal regulation if it is solid waste. *42 U.S.C. § 6903(27)*. RCRA establishes a permitting scheme to regulate the disposal of hazardous waste and determine liability.

Under RCRA, solid waste is defined as "any garbage, refuse, sludge from a waste treatment plant, water supply treatment plant, or air pollution control facility and other discarded material . . . resulting from industrial, commercial, mining, and agricultural operations, and from community activities. . . ." The regulatory definition (for purposes of the permit requirement) of "solid waste" is narrower than the statutory definition (which applies to citizen suits brought to abate imminent hazards to health or the environment).

In general, RCRA is designed to address the problems related to hazardous waste disposal at local landfills. In general, waste must be discarded to be solid waste under RCRA. Accordingly, agricultural open burning practices are likely not a regulable activity under RCRA. *See, e.g., Safe Air for Everyone v. Meyer, et al.,* 373 F.3d 1035 (9th Cir. 2004), *cert. denied,* 544 U.S. 1018 (2005) the court determined that bluegrass residue from open burning was not "solid waste" under RCRA. *But see, Safe Air for Everyone, et al. v. United States Environmental Protection Agency,* 488 F.3d 1088 (9th Cir. 2007).

Hazardous waste must be "discarded" to be subject to regulation under the RCRA. In one case, The court refused to grant the defendants (several dairy operations) summary judgment on the basis that the over-application (and allegedly improper application) of manure to fields, and the leakage of manure from lagoons constituted a "discarding" of hazardous waste. *Community Association for Restoration of the Environment, et al. v. Bosma Dairy, et al.,* No. 13-CV-3019-TOR, 2013 U.S. Dist. LEXIS 87758 (E.D. Wash. Jun. 21, 2013); see also, *Community Association for Restoration of the Environment v. Cow Palace, LLC,* 80 F. Supp. 3d 1180 (E.D. Wash. 2015). But, road salt used on streets is not "solid waste" because it is not "discarded." *Krause v. City of Omaha,* No. 15-2985, 2016 U.S. App. LEXIS 3018 (8th Cir. Feb. 22, 2016).

RCRA was amended in 1984 to establish a comprehensive leak detection, prevention and cleanup program for underground storage tanks. The program regulates underground storage tanks containing petroleum products and certain hazardous substances, and is primarily administered at the state level. The act requires registration of most underground tanks, bans the installation of unprotected tanks, establishes federal technical standards for all tanks, coordinates regulatory efforts between the states and the federal government, and provides for federal inspection and enforcement. Exempt from regulation are farm or residential tanks of 1,100 gallons or less which are used for storing motor fuel, tanks used to store heating oil for consumption on the premises, pipeline tanks regulated under federal laws, and storage tanks in an underground area that are above the surface of the floor. *42 U.S.C. § 6991 (2008).* The RCRA also has been held to not apply to the regular, intended use of lead shot on a shooting range. *See, e.g., Cordiano, et al. v. Metacon Gun Club, Inc.,* 575 F.3d 199 (2d Cir. 2009).

A 1986 amendment created a petroleum underground storage tank response program. The amendments give the federal government authority to respond to petroleum spills and leaks, and provide a leaking underground storage tank fund to clean up leaks from petroleum storage tanks. The trust fund is funded primarily through federal taxes on motor fuels. The 1986 amendments also directed the EPA to establish financial responsibility requirements for underground storage tank owners and operators to cover the costs associated with any corrective action and to compensate third parties for injury and property damage caused by leaking underground storage tanks.

Dump sites located on farms and ranches may be subject to the permitting requirements of RCRA. While RCRA contains a pesticide exemption for farmers, the scope of the exemption is unclear. The original purpose of the pesticide exemption for farmers was to exempt farmers from RCRA liability for disposal of FDA-approved pesticides. *40 C.F.R. § 264.1(g)(4).* It is critical, however, that farmers dispose of pesticides properly for the exemption to apply. The EPA requires farmers to follow disposal instructions provided by the pesticide manufacturer. While this exemption appears to provide protection for most, if not all, farmers, the EPA lists pesticides and herbicides as constituting the predominant waste at nearly one-fifth of all hazardous waste sites on the government's national priorities list. This means that even if a particular farmer avoids liability under RCRA, the farmer still may be liable under CERCLA. In addition, *ranchers* may not be able to avail themselves of the exemption, and the exemption may not cover fertilizers.

Also, it is important to note that many states regulate the disposal of solid waste. *See, e.g., Littleton v. Whatcom County,* 86 P.3d 1253 (Wash. Ct. App. 2004). In *Littleton,* the court determined that agricultural manure used in an agricultural operation was not "solid waste" under the state solid waste management statute. Thus, a worm farmer utilizing chicken manure in his worm farming operation was not required to obtain solid waste handling permit.

## B.   CHEMICALS

### 1. Federal Insecticide, Fungicide, and Rodenticide Act

The Federal Insecticide, Fungicide, and Rodenticide Act (FIFRA) takes a preventative approach with respect to air, water and land pollution. The Act is administered by the EPA and requires registration of all pesticides intended to prevent, destroy, repel or mitigate certain pests. FIFRA also regulates pesticide use and requires certification of pesticide applicators. However, pesticide-treated seeds are not subject to FIFRA registration. *Anderson v. McCarthy,* No. C16-00068 WHA, 2016 U.S. Dist. LEXIS 162124 (N.D. Cal. Nov. 21, 2016). The EPA administrator must assess the risks of using a pesticide at the time of registration and the submission of scientific data to aid in that decision. The Act requires that pesticide registrants disclose expert opinions on adverse effects of pesticides to the EPA, along with all other "factual information" so that EPA can reach a proper determination concerning potential registration. *American Crop Protection Association v. United States Environmental Protection Agency,* 182 F. Supp.2d 89 (D. D.C. 2002).

FIFRA is also a unique environmental law in that the EPA uses a risk/benefit assessment when applying the standard which takes into account the economic, social and environmental cost and benefits of a pesticide.

At the time of registration, the administrator must classify a pesticide as to use. Classification may be for general use, restricted use, or both. *7 U.S.C. § 136a(d)(1)(A) (2008).* The EPA administrator may also issue an experimental use permit if the administrator determines that the applicant needs the permit in order to accumulate information necessary to register a pesticide under FIFRA. *7 U.S.C. § 136c (2008).* A general use pesticide is one that the EPA administrator determines will not cause "unreasonable adverse effects" on the environment when used as directed or in accordance with commonly recognized practices. Restricted use pesticides are those determined to have the potential to cause adverse environmental effects. In addition, restricted use pesticides may be applied only by individuals who are approved by the EPA as certified applicators. FIFRA defines a certified applicator as any individual who is certified under the Act to use or supervise the use of any pesticide which is classified for restricted use. *7 U.S.C. § 136(e)(1) (2008)*. A certified applicator may be either a private applicator or a commercial applicator. To be certified as a private applicator, the applicant must possess a practical knowledge of the pest problems and control practices associated with agricultural operations, being familiar with the proper handling, use, storage and disposal of pesticides and containers as well as related legal responsibility. A state may submit a plan for certification of applicators to the EPA administrator for approval. The EPA administrator will approve a state's certification plan if it designates a state agency to administer the plan and contains assurances, among other things, that the agency has the necessary legal authority, personnel, and funding to execute the plan.

The EPA cannot register a pesticide for use (or approve its label) unless it determines the product will not have "unreasonable adverse effects on the environment." *7 U.S.C. § 136a(c)(5)(D) (2008)*. More specifically, in registering any pesticide, EPA must conclude that the product does not pose any "unreasonable risk to man or the environment, taking into account the economic, social, and environmental costs and benefits of [its] use." *7 U.S.C. § 136(bb) (2008)*. Pesticides are registered for a five-year period. Registrations will be cancelled at the end of that period unless the registrant (or other interested person with the consent of the registrant) requests, in accordance with regulations, that the registration be continued in effect. The sale of an unregistered pesticide is a violation of FIFRA.

If a pesticide registration is denied, the applicant must be notified of the denial and given the reason and factual basis for the denial. The applicant must also be given 30 days to correct the application, and the notice of the denial and the reasons for the denial must be published in the Federal Register. A registration denial constitutes a final order of the administrator and is subject to judicial review, as well as a public hearing and scientific review of the administrator's order. *7 U.S.C. § 136(d) (2008).*

The EPA can review pesticides which have previously been registered if there is a concern the product is causing environmental problems or human injury. This procedure is known as a "special review."

FIFRA also makes it unlawful to sell or distribute any pesticide that is not registered, that differs in composition from that described in the registration forms, or any pesticide that is misbranded or adulterated. In addition, the penalties do not apply to any person who has received a guarantee, from either the immediate seller or the registrant, that the pesticide was registered. This exemption also extends to carriers which lawfully ship or transport pesticides, public officials in possession of pesticides during the performance of official duties, and persons using pesticides under an experimental use permit or in tests solely to determine the pesticides' toxicity or other properties. Under the rule, pesticides applied in accordance with FIFRA were exempt from the CWA's permitting requirements. FIFRA's preemption provision is not all-inclusive and does not preempt claims for defective manufacturing or express warranty and negligence claims not based on inadequate labeling. *See, e.g., Kawamata Farms v. United Agri Products,* 86 Haw. 214, 948 P.2d 1055 (1997); *Netland v. Hess & Clark,* 284 F.3d 895 (8th Cir. 2002), *cert. den.,* 537 U.S. 949 (2002).

Any registrant, commercial applicator, wholesaler, dealer, retailer, or other distributor who violates any of the provisions of FIFRA may be assessed a civil penalty not exceeding $5,000 for each offense. *7 U.S.C. § 1361(a)(1) (2008).* In addition, any private applicator or other person who violates FIFRA after receiving a written warning from the EPA or following a citation for a prior violation, may be assessed a civil penalty not exceeding $1,000 for each offense. *7 U.S.C. § 1361(a)(2) (2008).* Any registrant who knowingly violates FIFRA and is convicted is subject to a fine of not more than $50,000, or one year imprisonment, or both. *7 U.S.C. § 1361(b)(1)(A) (2008).* Any commercial applicator, wholesaler, dealer, retailer or other distributor who knowingly violates FIFRA is guilty of a misdemeanor and subject on conviction to a fine of not more than $25,000 or one imprisonment, or both. *7 U.S.C. § 1361(b)(1)(B) (2008).* Other persons, including private applicators, who knowingly violate FIFRA may be fined not more than $1,000, or imprisoned for not more than 30 days, or both. *7 U.S.C. § 1361(b)(2) (2008)*. In addition, any person who with fraudulent intent uses or reveals trade secrets protected under FIFRA may be fined not more than $10,000 or imprisoned for not more than three years, or both. *7 U.S.C. § 1361(b)(3) (2008)*.

However, compliance with FIFRA does not necessarily guarantee compliance with other federal laws. For example, in *Headwaters, Inc. v. Talent Irrigation District,* 243 F.3d 526 (9th Cir. 2001), the court held that the registration and labeling of pesticides under FIFRA did not preclude the need for a CWA permit. The court noted that the failure of the label to specify that a permit was required did not mean that the CWA did not apply to the discharge of pesticides and herbicides sprayed directly into or over water where the chemicals were used to control weeds and plant growth in an irrigation canal that was a water of the United States by virtue of being a tributary to other CWA jurisdictional waters. The United States Court of Appeals for the Second Circuit has reached the same conclusion. *No Spray Coalition, Inc. v. City of New York,* 351 F.3d 602 (2d Cir. 2003), *further proceeding at,* No. 00 CIV. 5395 (GBD), 2005 U.S. Dist. LEXIS 11097 (2d Cir. Jun. 8, 2005). The EPA, in its *Interim Statement and Guidance on Application of Pesticides to Waters of the United States in Compliance with FIFRA*, dated July 11, 2003, opined that the CWA does not require a permit where the application of the pesticide complies with FIFRA because pesticides applied consistent with FIFRA (i.e., over land) are not "chemical wastes." In a subsequent opinion in a different case, the U.S.

Court of Appeals for the Ninth Circuit held that the pesticide antimycin, when applied to surface water to eliminate pestilent fish and when applied in compliance with FIFRA, is not a "pollutant" under the CWA and, therefore, no NPDES permit is required. *Fairhurst v. Hagener,* 422 F.3d 1146 (9th Cir. 2005). The court distinguished its opinion in *Headwaters* on the basis that antimycin left no residue after it had performed its intended function. The court gave deference to EPA's position on the matter as set forth in the EPA's July 11, 2003, interim guidance. Also, in *Peconic Baykeeper, Inc., et al. v. Suffolk County,* 600 F.3d 180 (2d Cir. 2010), the court held that an NPDES permit is not required for the application of pesticides that is consistent with all relevant requirements under FIFRA for land-based pesticide application. In early 2009, however, the U.S. Court of Appeals for the Sixth Circuit held that the EPA's final rule providing an exemption from the CWA permitting requirements for pesticides applied in accordance with FIFRA was not a reasonable interpretation of the CWA. The court held that the EPA exceeded its authority when it determined that residues of pesticides discharged by point sources were nonpoint source pollutants. *The National Cotton Council of America, et al. v. United States Environmental Protection Agency,* 553 F.3d 927 (6th Cir. 2009).

In addition to registering pesticides, FIFRA gives the EPA the power to regulate how registered pesticides are used and applied through the control of pesticide labeling and packaging. The EPA must approve the label directions which control on what crops and pests the product can be used and which establish any other use restrictions. FIFRA makes it unlawful to use any registered pesticide in a manner inconsistent with its labeling. This "label use" provision gives the EPA authority to assess civil penalties against producers who use pesticides improperly or damage the environment. FIFRA also limits the ability of an individual to bring a state court action for negligence against a pesticide manufacturer or vendor on an inadequate labeling claim or wrongful death claim.

In *Bruce v. ICI Americas, Inc.,* 933 F. Supp. 781 (S.D. Iowa 1996), the plaintiffs owned and operated a large grain farm. The plaintiffs applied to their corn crop a rootworm pesticide manufactured by the defendant. After the pesticide failed to control rootworm, the plaintiff sued for breach of implied warranty of fitness for a particular purpose, breach of warranty of merchantability, breach of express warranty, and in strict liability. The defendant argued that the claims were all barred by preemption of FIFRA and that, in any event, the disclaimers of implied and express warranties barred the claims. The court found that a portion of the plaintiff's claims on both the breach of warranty claims was based on representations made by the defendant in advertising, sales literature and a trade name. The court held that to the extent the claims were not label-based, the claims were not preempted by FIFRA. However, the court held that the disclaimers were conspicuous and barred the non preempted claims.

FIFRA contains a worker protection standard designed to reduce the occupational risk of pesticide poisonings and injuries among agricultural workers and pesticide handlers. The worker protection standard requires pesticide safety training, notification of pesticide applications, use of personal protective equipment, restricted entry intervals into fields following pesticide applications, decontamination supplies, and emergency medical assistance. The FIFRA worker protection standard requires that employers of covered farm workers post required information about the pesticides being applied to their fields, along with other safety-related information, in a centrally located and easily accessible area for workers. In 2003, the EPA levied a civil penalty of $231,990 against a Colorado vegetable farm for 229 violations of the FIFRA worker protection standard. The farm had placed all of the required information in a binder in the reception area of the farm's business office rather than posting the information in a centrally located and easily accessible area for workers.

A state may regulate the use and sale of pesticides only if, and to the extent that, its laws and regulations do not permit any sale or use otherwise prohibited by FIFRA. Presently, all states have enacted pesticide use laws. Most of the state statutory provisions follow the same general pattern and require classification of pesticides, the licensing of pesticide dealers, the regulation of the storage and disposal of pesticides and pesticide containers and the prohibition of acts relating to the improper use of pesticides. In general, enforcement of state pesticide laws is delegated to state agricultural departments. In addition, pesticide use is typically controlled by state licensing and certification of pesticide applicators.

The Food Quality Protection Act of 1996 (FQPA) *(21 U.S.C. § 346 et seq. (2008))* amended both FIFRA and provisions of the Federal Food Drug and Cosmetic Act which pertain to pesticide chemical residues in food. The FQPA substantially changes the way pesticides are evaluated for health effects. Under prior law, the EPA was prohibited from approving a food additive if it were found at any level to "induce cancer" in experimental animals or man. Any pesticide that concentrates in processed food is considered a food additive and, thus, became subject to the zero-risk standard. The zero-risk standard took effect in 1958. Since 1958, significant advances have been made such that the EPA, FDA and independent scientists recommended changing the zero-risk standard to one of "negligible risk." Under a negligible risk standard, the risk of a substance is so low that it is considered trivial or nonexistent. Under the FQPA, the EPA may establish or leave in effect a tolerance for a pesticide chemical residue in or on a food if the EPA determines that the tolerance is safe. In essence, the EPA must determine that there is a reasonable certainty that no harm will result from aggregate exposure to the pesticide chemical residue, including all anticipated dietary exposures and all other exposures for which there is reliable information. The FQPA also requires EPA to take into account "the variability of the sensitivities" of "major identifiable subgroups" when establishing, modifying, leaving in effect, or revoking a tolerance or exemption. While EPA is required to ensure to a reasonable certainty that no harm will result to any children as a result of their aggregate exposure to pesticide, EPA has never addressed whether farm children are subject to a heightened risk of pesticide exposure.

## 2. Toxic Substances Control Act

While the Congress enacted the Toxic Substances Control Act (TSCA) in 1976 to regulate the use of industrial chemicals, the Act is a catchall for the control of all chemicals which potentially could be harmful to the environment and, specifically, to the public water supply. *See 15 U.S.C. §§ 2601 et seq. (2008).* The Act places primary responsibility on industry to develop data concerning the environmental effects of chemicals. In addition, the Act empowers the EPA with authority to prevent unreasonable risks of injury to health or the environment, and allows this authority to be exercised so as "not to impede unduly or create unnecessary economic barriers to technological innovation while fulfilling the primary purpose of [the] Act to assure that . . . such chemical substances . . . do not present an unreasonable risk of injury. . . ."

The Act empowers the EPA to adopt rules requiring testing by manufacturers of substances. The rules must be based on a finding that insufficient data are currently available concerning the substance, and that the substance may "present an unreasonable risk," "enter the environment in substantial quantities," or present a likelihood of "substantial human exposure."

The TSCA also requires a manufacturer to give notice to the EPA before manufacturing a new chemical substance or an old substance for a "significant new use." For substances not covered by the Act, but listed by the EPA as possibly hazardous, the manufacturer must submit data it believes shows the absence of any unreasonable risk of injury. The Act also authorizes the EPA to obtain emergency judicial relief in case of "imminent hazards."

## C. PLANTS, FISH AND WILDLIFE

### 1. Endangered Species Act

The Endangered Species Act (ESA) establishes a regulatory framework for the protection and recovery of endangered and threatened species of plants, fish and wildlife. *16 U.S.C. § 1531 et seq. (2002)*. The U.S. Fish and Wildlife Service (USFWS), within the Department of the Interior, is the lead administrative agency for most threatened or endangered species.

The ESA has the potential to restrict substantially agricultural activities because many of the protections provided for threatened and endangered species under the Act extend to individual members of the species when they are on private land. Many endangered species have some habitat on private land.

Under the ESA, "fish and wildlife" species are defined as any member of the animal kingdom, including without limitation any mammal, fish, bird ... amphibian, reptile, mollusk, crustacean, arthropod, or other invertebrate. *16 U.S.C. § 1532(8) (2002)*. "Plants" are defined as any member of the plant kingdom. *16 U.S.C. § 1532(14) (2002)*. An "endangered species" is a species which is in danger of extinction throughout all or a significant part of its range other than a species determined by the USFWS to constitute a pest whose protection under the provisions of the Act would present an overwhelming and overriding risk to humans. *16 U.S.C. § 1532(6) (2002)*. A "threatened species" is a species which is likely to become endangered within the foreseeable future throughout all or a significant portion of its range. *16 U.S.C. § 1532(20) (2002)*. The term "species" includes any subspecies of fish or wildlife or plants and any distinct population segment of any species of vertebrate fish or wildlife which interbreeds when mature. *16 U.S.C. § 1532(16) (2002)*.

## i. The Listing Process

The Secretary of the Interior (Secretary) determines when a species is to be listed as either threatened or endangered. The Secretary's determination to list a species must be published in the Federal Register. *16 U.S.C. § 1533(c)(1) (2002)*. As of March 18, 2017, 1,652 species in the United States had been listed under the ESA, with 1,276 species listed as endangered and 376 listed as threatened. An endangered or threatened listing is to be made on the basis of the best available scientific and commercial data without reference to possible economic or other impacts after the USFWS conducts a review of the status of the species. *16 U.S.C. § 1533(b)(1)(A) (2002); 50 C.F.R. 424.11 (2002).*

The USFWS considers species for listing on its own initiative, but the ESA also provides a listing petition process for "interested persons" to force evaluation and listing of a species. Within 90 days of receiving a petition for listing, the USFWS must determine whether the petition presents substantial information to warrant listing of the species. *16 U.S.C. § 1533(b)(3)(A) (2002).* The USFWS defines "substantial information" as "that level of information that would lead a reasonable person to believe that the measure proposed in the petition may be warranted". *50 C.F.R. 424.14(b) (2002).* If the USFWS concludes that the petitioned action is warranted, it then conducts a review of the species' status and must determine within one year of the receipt of the petition whether to propose formally the species for listing. *16 U.S.C. § 1533(b)(3)(B) (2002).* The 90-day and one-year deadlines are bright lines. *Biodiversity Legal Foundation v. Badgley,* 284 F.3d 1046 (9th Cir. 2002).

The Secretary's decision to list a species as endangered or threatened is based upon the presence of at least one of the following factors; (1) the present or threatened destruction, modification, or curtailment of a species' habitat or range; (2) the over-utilization for commercial, sporting, scientific or educational purposes; (3) disease or predation; (4) the inadequacy of existing regulatory mechanisms; or (5) other natural or manmade factors affecting a species' continued existence. *16 U.S.C. § 1533(a)(1) (2008).* The USFWS may decline to list a species upon publishing a written finding either that listing is unwarranted or that listing is warranted, but that the USFWS lacks the resources to proceed immediately with the proposal. *16 U.S.C. § 1533(a)(1) (2008).* Under the ESA, all USFWS decisions to decline listing a species are subject to judicial review.

When a species is listed as endangered or threatened, the Secretary must consider whether to designate critical habitat for the species. "Critical habitat" is the specific area within the geographical range occupied by the species at the time of listing that is essential to the conservation of the species. Critical habitat may also include specific areas outside the geographical area occupied by the species at the time it is listed if the USFWS determines that such areas are essential for conservation of the species. However, critical habitat need not include the entire geographical range which the species could potentially occupy. *16 U.S.C. § 1532(5) (2008).* In making a critical habitat determination, the USFWS must consider economic impacts and other relevant impacts, as well as best scientific data. *New Mexico Cattle Growers Ass'n. v. United States Fish and Wildlife Service,* 248 F.3d 1277 (10th Cir. 2001). Also, the failure to consider the economic and social impacts of a critical habitat designation at the time of the designation can be cause to set aside the designation. *Home Builders Association of Northern*

*California, et al. v. United States Fish and Wildlife Service,* 268 F. Supp. 2d 1197 (E.D. Cal. 2003). The USFWS may exclude any area from critical habitat if the benefits of the exclusion outweigh the benefits of specifying the area as critical habitat, unless the USFWS determines on the basis of best scientific and commercial data available that the failure to designate an area as critical habitat will result in the extinction of the species. *16 U.S.C. § 1533(b)(2) (2008).*

## ii. Recovery Plans

The USFWS must prepare a recovery plan for species listed as endangered or threatened, unless a recovery plan would not promote a species' conservation. *16 U.S.C. § 1533(f) (2008).* Recovery plans must include site-specific management actions considered necessary for conservation and survival of the species, establishment of objective, measurable criteria for downlisting or delisting of a species, and an estimation of the time and cost for implementing the recovery measures as needed. *16 U.S.C. § 1533(1)(B) (2008).* A recovery plan may also specify measures for habitat acquisition and maintenance, species propagation, live trapping and transplantation and measures to relieve species' population pressures. *16 U.S.C. § 1532(3) (2008).* Recovery plans are designed to bring any endangered or threatened species to the point at which ESA protections are no longer necessary. Recovery plans are subject to public notice and an opportunity for public review during the development of the plan.

### iii. The Prohibition Against "Taking" Species

Once a species has been listed as endangered or threatened, the ESA prohibits various activities involving the listed species unless an exemption or permit is granted. For example, with respect to endangered species of fish, wildlife and plants, the ESA makes it unlawful for any person to import or export such species, deliver, receive, carry, transport or ship in interstate or foreign commerce by any means whatsoever, and sell or offer for sale in interstate or foreign commerce any such species. The ESA, with regard to endangered species of fish or wildlife, but not species of plants, makes it unlawful for any person subject to the jurisdiction of the United States to "take" any such species. *16 U.S.C. §§ 1538(a)(1)(B), (C) (2008). 50 C.F.R. 17.31(a) (2008)* extends the prohibition to species listed as "threatened." The ESA defines the term "take" to mean harass, harm, pursue, hunt, shoot, wound, kill, trap, capture, or collect, or to attempt to engage in any such conduct. The prohibition against "taking" an endangered species applies to actions occurring on private land as well as state or federal public land.

The ESA provides for civil penalties up to $25,000 per violation for each knowing violation of the taking provision. *16 U.S.C. § 1540(a)(1) (2008)*. The Act also provides for criminal penalties for each knowing violation of the taking provision or fines up to $50,000 and/or one year in prison. *16 U.S.C. § 1540(b) (2008)*. The Act establishes a defense for both civil and criminal penalties such that no penalty may be imposed if the defendant can show that the defendant acted on the good faith belief that the defendant was protecting a family member or any other individual from bodily harm from any endangered or threatened species.

1982 amendments to the ESA establish an incidental take permit process that allows a person or entity to obtain a permit to lawfully take an endangered species "if such taking is incidental to, and not the purpose of, the carrying out of an otherwise lawful activity." *16 U.S.C. § 1539(a)(1)(B)*. A person may seek an incidental take permit from the U.S. Fish and Wildlife Service (FWS) by filing an application that includes a Habitat Conservation Plan which includes a description of the impacts that will likely result from the taking, proposed steps to minimize and mitigate those impacts, and alternatives to the taking that the applicant considered and the reasons why those alternatives were not selected. If the permit is issued, the FWS will monitor the project for compliance with the HCP and the effects of the permitted action and the effectiveness of the conservation program. The FWS may suspend or revoke all or part of an incidental take permit if the permit holder fails to comply with the conditions of the permit or the laws and regulations governing the activity.

The denial of an incidental take permit involving habitat modification of an underground cave bug of no known human commercial value and only found in two Texas counties has been upheld against a Commerce Clause challenge. *GDF Realty Investments, LTD, et al. v. Norton,* 326 F.3d 622 (5th

Cir. 2004), *reh'g en banc denied,* 362 F.3d 286 (5th Cir. 2004), *cert. denied,* 545 U.S. 1114 (2005). Likewise, in *Rancho Viejo, LLC v. Norton,* 323 F.3d 1062 (D.C. Cir. 2003), *reh'g en banc denied,* 334 F.3d 1158 (D.C. Cir. 2003), *cert. denied,* 540 U.S. 1218 (2004), a different court held that the ESA extended to the Southwestern Arroyo Toad even though the Arroyo Toad only resided in southern California and never has been an article of commerce. In 2009, a commercial wind farm was enjoined from further development until receipt of an incidental take permit due to the project's impact on the endangered Indiana bat. The court held that it was a "virtual certainty" that Indiana bats would be "harmed, wounded or killed" by the wind farm in violation of the ESA during times that they were not hibernating. *Animal Welfare Institute, et al. v. Beech Ridge Energy LLC, et al.,* 675 F. Supp. 2d 540 (D. Md. 2009).

An important issue for farmers and ranchers is whether habitat modifications caused by routine farming or ranching activities are included within the definition of the term "take." In 1975, the Department of Interior issued a regulation defining "harm" as "an act or omission which actually injures or kills wildlife, including acts which annoy it to such an extent as to significantly disrupt essential behavior patterns, which include, but are not limited to, breeding, feeding or sheltering; significant environmental modification or degradation which has such effects is included within the meaning of 'harm'." *50 C.F.R. § 17.3; 40 Fed. Reg. 44412, 44416.* The regulation was amended in 1981 to emphasize that actual death or injury to the listed species is necessary, but the inclusion of "habitat modification" in the definition of "harm" led to a series of legal challenges. *50 C.F.R. § 17.3; 46 Fed. Reg. 54748.* The regulation was upheld by the Ninth Circuit Court of Appeals in 1988 in a case involving an endangered bird species whose critical habitat was on state-owned land in Hawaii. *Palila v. Hawaii Dept. of Land & Natural Resources,* 639 F.2d 495 (9th Cir. 1981). The court held that the grazing of goats and sheep threatened to destroy the endangered birds' woodland habitat and resulted in harm and a "taking" of the endangered bird. The court ordered the Hawaii Department of Land and Natural Resources to remove the goats and sheep from the birds' critical habitat. In subsequent litigation, the plaintiffs sought the removal of an additional variety of sheep from the birds' critical habitat. The defendant argued that, under the ESA, "harm" included only the actual and immediate destruction of the birds' food source, not the potential for harm which could drive the bird to extinction. However, the Ninth Circuit held that "harm" is not limited to immediate, direct physical injury to the species, but also includes habitat modification which *may* subsequently result in injury or death of individuals of the endangered species. *Palila v. Hawaii Dept. of Land & Natural Resources,* 852 F.2d 1106 (9th Cir. 1988).

In 1994, the U.S. Court of Appeals for the District of Columbia held that the USFWS rule defining "harm" was neither clearly authorized by Congress nor a reasonable interpretation of the statute, and was therefore invalid. *Sweet Home Chapter of*

*Communities for a Great Oregon v. Babbitt,* 17 F.3d 1463 (D.C. Cir. 1994). Upon review, the Supreme Court reversed, holding instead that the "harm" regulation is reasonable on its face because the ordinary definition of "harm" includes causing injury, and in the context of the ESA that includes habitat modification resulting in actual injury or death to members of a listed species. The court also noted that the broad purpose of the ESA supported the prohibition of activities that cause the precise harms the Act was intended to avoid. However, the Supreme Court did not reach the crucial issue of how to determine when habitat modification has resulted in a "harm" rising to the level of a prohibited taking. The court noted that whether a harm has occurred must be determined on a case-by-case basis. *Babbitt v. Sweet Home Chapter of Communities for a Great Oregon,* 515 U.S. 687 (1995).

Shortly before the Supreme Court rendered its decision in *Sweet Home,* the Federal District Court for the Northern District of California addressed the question of whether a violation of the ESA existed based on the threat of future harm. *Marbled Murrelet v. Pacific Lumber Co.,* 880 F. Supp. 1343 (N.D. Cal. 1995). In the California case, an environmental group sued to prevent the proposed harvest by the defendant of 137 acres of its first-growth redwood and Douglas fir trees in an isolated 440-acre stand located 22 miles inland from the Pacific Coast. The plaintiffs alleged that the logging would result in a "take" of marbled murrelets in violation of the ESA. The court found that the plaintiffs proved by a preponderance of the evidence that marbled murrelets "occupied" the area because the area was deemed to be suitable habitat for the marbled murrelet and evidence demonstrated approximately 100 detections of the species at the location throughout the birds' breeding season for a period of three consecutive years. Thus, the court concluded that the defendant's proposed logging would both "harm" and "harass" the murrelets in violation of the ESA. As such, the court granted the plaintiff's motion for a permanent injunction and awarded the plaintiffs over a million dollars in attorney's fees and costs. On appeal, the Ninth Circuit Court of Appeals affirmed the lower court's decision. *Marbled Murrelet v. Babbitt,* 83 F.3d 1060 (9th Cir. 1996). and the Supreme Court declined to review the case. *Id., cert. denied,* 519 U.S. 1108 (1997).

In *State v. Sour Mountain Realty, Inc.,* 714 N.Y.S. 2d 78 (N.Y. App. 2000), a landowner built a snakeproof fence near a timber rattlesnake den. The court held that this modified the snake's habitat and constituted a "taking" of the protected species under the ESA. In addition, the court held that enjoining the landowner's use of the fence was not a taking of the landowner's property without just compensation. The court found that the fence interfered with the normal migratory patterns of the species and that the land was rural and undeveloped and, therefore, the economic harm to the landowner in losing the fence was "tenuous at best."

Thus, the ESA authorizes the federal government to regulate private property to protect endangered species, and has also been held to allow the government to restrict actions of individuals in the exercise of their state-granted water rights where the removal of the water from a particular source of supply may threaten endangered species. *See, e.g., United States v. Glenn-Colusa Irrigation District,* 788 F. Supp. 1126 (E.D. Cal. 1992). In addition, the ESA's "taking" provision has withstood a constitutional challenge on commerce clause grounds in a case where the Delhi Sands Flower-loving Fly (a listed species) forced the relocation of a county hospital at a cost of $3.5 million. *See National Assoc. of Home Builders v. Babbitt,* 130 F.3d 1041 (D.C. Cir. 1997), *cert. denied,* 524 U.S. 937 (1998).

### *iv. Citizen Suits*

Under the ESA, any person may file a civil action to enjoin any person, including the United States, who is alleged to be in violation of any provision of the ESA. *16 U.S.C. § 1540(g)(1) (2008).* Such an action can be undertaken to compel the Secretary to apply prohibitions with respect to the taking of a listed species, or can be made against the Secretary for any failure to list a species or its habitat. While this language appears broad enough to provide any citizen with access to the courts to seek redress for an alleged ESA violation, the Ninth Circuit Court of Appeals ruled in 1995 that only those persons who allege an interest in *preserving* a species have standing to sue. *Bennett v. Plenert,* 63 F.3d 915 (9th Cir. 1995). In early 1997, the Supreme Court unanimously overturned the Ninth Circuit's opinion and concluded that the plaintiffs did have standing to challenge the government's alleged failure to consider the economic impacts of its determination that the habitat constituted a critical habitat. *Bennett v. Spear,* 520 U.S. 154 (1997).

### v. Exemptions

The ESA contains several exemptions to the statutory prohibitions discussed above. These exemptions include an "undue economic hardship" exemption that is available to any person who enters a contract with respect to a species of fish, wildlife, or plants before the date of publication in the Federal Register of a notice that such species are being considered for classification as endangered. *16 U.S.C. § 1539(b) (2008).* More importantly, perhaps, the ESA was amended in 1982 to provide for the incidental taking of individual members of listed species under certain circumstances pursuant to a permit issued by the USFWS. *16 U.S.C. § 1539(a)(1)(B) (2008).*

An applicant for an incidental taking permit must submit a habitat conservation plan (HCP) to the USFWS that specifies the impact likely to result from the taking, the steps the applicant will take to minimize and mitigate these impacts and the funding available to implement the steps, alternative actions to the proposed action and reasons why the applicant is not taking the alternative actions, and other measures the Secretary may require as necessary and appropriate for the purposes of the HCP. *16 U.S.C. § 1539(a)(2)(A) (2008).* The ESA requires federal agencies to consult with the USFWS to determine if an agency action, including funding and permitting of activities on private land, might jeopardize the continued existence of an endangered or threatened species or result in the destruction or modification of critical habitat of the endangered species. *16 U.S.C. § 1536(a)(2)*. See, e.g., *Sierra Club v. Bosworth,* 352 F. Supp. 2d 909 (D. Minn. 2005); *National Wildlife Federation, et al. v. Brownlee,* 402 F. Supp. 2d 1 (D. D.C. 2005); *Forest Guardians v. Johanns,* 450 F.3d 455 (9th Cir. 2006). After such a consultation, the USFWS may issue an incidental take permit to the federal agency and/or private permit applicant. An incidental take permit allows limited destruction or modification of habitat or destruction of individuals of a listed species if the effect of the permitted activity on the listed species is incidental to, and not the purpose of, an otherwise lawful activity. The incidental taking must not jeopardize the continued existence of the listed species. However, before an incidental take permit can be issued, the USFWS must have evidence that protected or endangered species actually inhabit the area at issue or that the proposed activities would "take" the species. *Arizona Cattle Growers' Association v. United States Fish and Wildlife Service,* 273 F.3d 1229 (9th Cir. 2001).

### vi. Constitutional Issues

The ESA does not provide compensation for restrictions on private land use resulting from application of the Act or for destruction to private property caused by endangered or threatened wildlife. There are very few reported cases alleging that an ESA regulation restricting land use has resulted in an unconstitutional taking of private property. However, in *Tulare Lake Basin Water Storage District, et al. v. United States,* 49 Fed. Cl. 313 (2001), the court held that the plaintiff's contractual right to use water was unconstitutionally taken when the defendant imposed water use restrictions under the ESA to protect two species of fish. Thus, just compensation was required to be paid. But, the same court rejected the underpinnings of its *Tulare Lake* decision four years later. In that case, *Klamath Irrigation District v. United States,* 67 Fed. Cl. 504 (2005), the court noted that it may have awarded just compensation "for taking of interests that may well not exist under state law." *See also Orff v. United States,* 545 U.S. 596 (2005). But, the United States Court of Appeals for the Federal Circuit held in 2008 that a federal requirement imposed on a local water district under the ESA was an unconstitutional taking of private property. *Casitas Municipal Water District v. United States,* 543 F.3d 1276 (Fed. Cir. 2008). In later litigation in the same case, the court held that the required construction of a fish ladder at a cost of $9.5 million was a regulatory taking, but that the loss of water did not involve the loss of a property right because the water right is limited by state law and the plaintiff failed to show any loss of beneficial use of water. *Casitas Municipal Water District v. United States,* 708 F.3d 1340 (Fed. Cir. 2013). Under the facts of the case, the government's order that a water district divert water to a fish ladder to allow passage for ESA-protected fish species was held to be a physical taking. The government conceded that the district had a property right to the water.

Lawsuits brought by private landowners under the Fifth Amendment for property losses attributable to federally protected wildlife are more common, but generally are not successful. *See, e.g., Christy v. Hodel,* 857 F.2d 1324 (9th Cir. 1988), *cert. denied sub. nom., Christy v. Lujan,* 490 U.S. 1114 (1989); *Moerman v. State of California,* 17 Cal. App. 4th 452, 21 Cal. Rptr. 2d 329 (1993), *cert. denied,* 511 U.S. 1031 (1994); *Boise Cascade v. United States,* 296 F.3d 1339 *(Fed. Cir. 2002, cert. den.,* 538 U.S. 906 (2003); *Seiber v. United States,* 364 F.3d 1356 (Fed. Cir. 2004), *cert. denied,* 543 U.S. 873 (2004).

## D. LIVESTOCK

The federal government regulates much of the ranching activity that occurs in the western United States. This is primarily because the federal government is a substantial owner of land in the western United States, owning 47 percent of the land in the eleven western contiguous states.

The Homestead Act of 1860 allowed homesteaders to lay claim to 160 acres. This acreage was thought to be sufficient to support a family farm, and, indeed, worked quite well throughout the eastern and central United States. However, the 160-acre allotments did not support family operations in the western United States due to the lack of moisture that made the land ill-suited for traditional row crop farming. Consequently, western settlers tended to homestead land near water sources and transportation routes and utilized the open range as necessary. As settlements increased and pressure for open range grew, substantial overgrazing of the western range resulted.

## 1. Taylor Grazing Act

The Taylor Grazing Act (TGA) of 1934 had as its purpose the prevention of rangeland resource degradation and the promotion of the stabilization of the domestic livestock industry. *43 U.S.C. § 315 et seq. (2008).* The years immediately preceding the passage of the TGA were characterized by the worst recorded drought in United States history and declining cattle prices. As a result, greater numbers of cattle were held from market and left to graze on depleted lands resulting in increased environmental damage to the range. This abuse of the range had been held earlier to be legal. In 1890, the Supreme Court held that ranchers had an implied license to use the public domain, subject only to use by homesteaders. *Buford v. Houtz,* 133 U.S. 320 (1890).

The TGA revoked prior federal practices and policies that allowed "indiscriminate" grazing on federal rangeland. The Congress later revoked any implied license to graze national forest lands. Under the TGA, a federal grazing permit must be obtained before cattle can be grazed on federal land. Also, the TGA confers only a benefit of being first in line for holders of water rights when a grazing permit is offered

Under the TGA, ranchers, where family homesteads were historically established on public lands, are given a "preference" for a specified number of their livestock to graze federal land other than National Forest Service land. The Secretary of the Interior (Secretary) may issue permits for grazing on unreserved lands of the public domain. *43 U.S.C. § 315b (2008)*. The Secretary has discretion to issue permits to bona fide settlers, residents, and other stockowners engaged in the livestock business that live within or near a grazing district. The permit system establishes the carrying capacity of the land, and permits are only issued to ranchers with sufficient "base" property or water rights to utilize legitimately the associated federal land.

The TGA regulates grazing on federal land under the control of the Bureau of Land Management (BLM). Presently, on BLM lands, an average of 11.1 acres can sustain one cow and her calf for a month. Thus, if a settler had homesteaded 160 acres of average BLM land and grazed livestock year-round, the settler's herd would have been limited to that particular cow/calf pair. As such, private ranches in the western United States are dependent upon access to large amounts of federal land in order to retain economic viability.

Permits issued under the TGA are for a period of not more than ten years and may be renewed. During periods of range depletion due to severe drought or other natural causes, or in case of a general epidemic or disease occurring during the life of the permit, the Secretary is authorized to reduce, refund in whole or in part, or authorize postponement of payment of grazing fees so long as the emergency exists.

In early 1995, the Interior Department proposed
new regulations that were designed to tie federal
rangeland management policy with ecosystem
management. The regulations proposed, in part,
federal government ownership of improvements
(such as fences and water developments) built on
federal rangeland since August 1995, 43 C.F.R.
§ 4120.3–2(b) (1995). the elimination of a grazing
permit preference for the grazing of a certain number
of livestock, 43 C.F.R. § 4100.0–5 (1995), the granting
of permits for uses other than grazing *Id.*, the
qualification for a grazing permit by individuals or
entities not engaged in the livestock business, 43
C.F.R.     §§ 4110.1,     4110.2(a)(1)     (1995),     and
administration by the federal government of water
rights for the purpose of livestock watering on federal
rangeland. *43 C.F.R. § 4120.3–2(d) (1995).* Before the
regulations were scheduled to take effect, a group of
cattle industry organizations filed a lawsuit
challenging the regulations as being in violation of
the TGA. In 1996, the federal district court for the
district of Wyoming in *Public Lands Council v.
United States,* 929 F. Supp. 1436 (D. Wyo. 1996), set
aside a major portion of the 1995 regulations. On
appeal, the Tenth Circuit Court of Appeals upheld
the regulation allowing individuals not engaged in
the livestock business to qualify for a grazing permit.
*Public Lands Council v. Babbitt,* 154 F.3d 1160 (10th
Cir. 1998), *amended on reh'g,* 167 F.3d 1287 (10th
Cir. 1999), *aff'd,* 529 U.S. 728 (2000). The court also
upheld the regulation eliminating grazing permit
preferences for the grazing of a specified number of
livestock, and the regulation giving the federal

government ownership of improvements. However, the court did uphold the district court's opinion invalidating the regulation that would have granted permits for uses other than grazing. The U.S. Supreme Court unanimously affirmed the Tenth Circuit's opinion.

> **Note:** The preference issue is particularly important to ranchers. To establish credit for operating loans, ranchers must establish BLM-granted preferential rights to grazing permit renewals. When assessing the qualifications of a rancher for an operating loan, lenders take into account the future stability and earning potential of the ranch, which is dependent on grazing permits.

## 2. Federal Land Policy and Management Act

The Federal Land Policy and Management Act (FLPMA) of 1976 gives the federal government broad control over public lands. *43 U.S.C. § 1701 et seq. (2008).* The Act specifies grazing fees, grazing leases, and grazing boards as applied to the national forests. The FLPMA is administered by the United States Forest Service (USFS) which has promulgated regulations establishing the criteria necessary for the issuance of grazing and livestock use permits as well as fees to be charged for livestock grazing on National Forest System lands. Permits to graze livestock on National Forest System lands are issued by the USFS under rules promulgated by the Secretary of Agriculture. The permits are issued for ten year periods, and may be renewed at the end of the term. The regulations also specify the amount and type of livestock allowed to graze under temporary (one-year) permits. *36 C.F.R. §§ 222.3(c)(2)(ii)(A), (F)*. The permits require that a rancher's "base property" must be of sufficient size to support the livestock when it is not on forest system lands. The chief administrator of the USFS has the authority to cancel grazing permits in the event of an eminent domain proceeding, or upon the permittee's failure to comply with the regulations or pay grazing fees. Allowing unauthorized livestock to graze on National Forest Service land without a permit may result in criminal prosecution for violation of grazing regulations. *See, e.g., United States v. Larson,* 746 F.2d 455 (8th Cir. 1984).

Grazing fees are charged for all livestock grazing on National Forest System and BLM land. The grazing fee is charged for each animal unit month of grazing and is determined in accordance with a formula, but cannot fall below a prescribed amount. Thus, the fee for grazing one animal unit for one month on National Forest System or BLM land is the greater of the amount determined by the formula or $1.35. However, any annual increase or decrease in the grazing fee for any given year is limited to not more than plus or minus 25 percent of the previous year's fee.

**Note:** The following constitute an animal unit: each cow, bull, heifer, horse, or mule six months of age or older at the time entering National Forest System lands for grazing or which become twelve months old during the grazing period, and each weaned cow, bull, steer, heifer, horse or mule regardless of age, and five adult sheep or goats (or five weaned goats or sheep regardless of age).

The grazing fee formula is established in accordance with the Public Rangelands Improvement Act of 1978, and attempts to represent the economic value of the use of the land to the user. Under the formula, the grazing fee (GF) equals the $1.23 base established by the 1966 Western Livestock Grazing Survey multiplied by the result of the annually computed forage value index (FVI) added to the combined index (beef cattle prices index (BCPI) minus the price paid index (PPI)) and divided by 100. *42 U.S.C. § 1905 (2008).* However, the annual increase or decrease in the grazing fee for any given year cannot fluctuate above or below more than 25% of the previous year's fee. The formula is specified as follows:

$$GF = \$1.23x \frac{FVI + BCPI - PPI}{100}$$

The grazing fee formula for any particular year is based upon the index numbers from the previous year as published in the Agricultural Prices, National Agricultural Statistics Service, USDA. Thus, the 2017 grazing fee (effective March 1, 2017) is determined on the basis of the FVI, BCPI and PPI for 2016 which were as follows: FVI: 542; BCPI: 534; and PPI: 924. Thus, if a rancher wanted to graze 1,500 cattle on federal land for six months in 2017, the grazing fee formula would yield a total cost per animal unit of [(542 + 534 − 924)/100] × $1.23 = $1.8696. So, the grazing fee would be $1.87 × 1500 × 6 = $16,830. The fee for the 2016 grazing season was $2.11 per animal unit. Thus, the $1.87 fee per animal unit for 2017 is within 25 percent of $2.11 and is not further adjusted. Thus, the grazing of 1,500 cattle on federal land for six months in 2017 would be $16,830.

## i. Constitutional Issues

An individual acquiring a permit from the Secretary to graze livestock on BLM land acquires only a privilege, which may be withdrawn by the United States at any time. Withdrawal of a permit does not trigger a Fifth Amendment taking because the permits do not create a property right in the land, but are merely licenses revocable at will. *See, e.g., Bowman v. Udall,* 243 F. Supp. 672 (D. D.C. 1965), *aff'd, Hinton v. Udall,* 364 F.2d 676 (D.C. Cir. 1966); *Klump v. United States,* 30 Fed. Appx. 958 (Fed. Cir. 2002). Likewise, the withdrawal or cancellation of a permit to graze livestock on National Forest System lands does not create a property right in the land and, as such, does not trigger a Fifth Amendment taking.

Until approximately the mid-1970s, federal approval of a grazing permit was routine. Federal policy at the time was that the best use of federal rangelands was to graze livestock and that only ranchers could acquire permits. However, as environmental concerns moved to the forefront beginning in the mid-1970s, the relationship between ranchers and federal officials deteriorated. As a result of legislation and court rulings, federal officials began aggressively regulating the issuance of grazing permits and the manner in which ranchers could use their federal grazing allotments. Simultaneously, nonagricultural interests expressed an increasing desire to use federal lands for recreational purposes. As a result, attempts to issue or reassign grazing permits are presently likely to draw comment from recreational and environmental interests.

*Hage v. United States,* 35 Fed. Cl. 147 (1996) is the lead case arising from this increasingly strained relationship between ranchers and federal officials responsible for administering grazing on federal land. In 1978, the plaintiffs purchased 7,000 acres of Nevada land for $2 million and acquired grazing allotments and water rights on 752,000 acres of surrounding federal land. The ranch covers approximately 1,100 square miles (the size of Rhode Island). Average annual rainfall is less than five inches, and at the peak of its operation, the ranch ran 2,400 head of cattle. In the 1980s, the Forest Service began piping water that was subject to the plaintiff's water rights to a nearby ranger station. In addition, the Forest Service began introducing nonindigenous elk into the area which competed with the plaintiff's cattle for forage. In 1988, the Forest Service ordered the plaintiffs to reduce the number of cattle on a portion of their Forest Service allotment, which agency officials contended had been overgrazed. Upon the plaintiffs' refusal to remove the cattle, federal agents impounded and auctioned 104 head of cattle. Contending that they could not continue to run the ranch economically with fewer cattle, the plaintiffs sold off the rest of the herd and filed a $28 million takings claim in the United States Court of Claims. The court, in ruling for the government, cited longstanding precedence that a federal grazing permit does not create any property interest in federal rangeland. *See also, Diamond Bar Cattle Co. v. United States,* 168 F.3d 1209 (10th Cir. 1999).

In a subsequent action, *Hage v. United States,* 51 Fed. Cl. 570 (2002), the Court of Federal Claims ruled that Hage had vested water rights under Nevada law in more than 20,000 acre-feet of water in his grazing allotment. In addition to the vested water rights, the court held that Hage had vested water rights in ten ditches under the 1866 Ditch Rights-of-Way Act, 43 U.S.C. § 661 et seq., and that the scope of the right was 50 feet on either side of the ditch. Thus, Hage's livestock had the right to use the forage adjacent to the ditch right-of-way. In addition, the court found that the Forest Service could not require Hage to obtain a special permit in order to maintain the 1866 ditches, and could not adjudicate title to the 1866 ditch right-of-way. Accordingly, the court held that the government cannot deny Hage access to his vested water rights without providing Hage a way to divert the water to another beneficial purpose if one exists. The government had constructed fences around springs and streams on the federal land that Hage had the right to use which Hage claimed greatly limited cattle access to the water and prevented Hage from performing maintenance on streambeds. The court held that the government cannot cancel a federal grazing permit and then prohibit the former permit holder from accessing the water to redirect it to another place of valid beneficial use. Perhaps the most important aspect of the case was the court's rejection of the BLM and Forest Service argument that ranchers have no property rights on their grazing allotment.

During the takings phase of the litigation the court
ruled that Hage had no right to compensation based
on the loss of the grazing permit *(See also Smithfork
Grazing Association v. Salazar,* 564 F.3d 1210 (10th
Cir. 2009))*,* but that surface waters flowing from
federal land to patented lands had been taken. *Estate
of Hage v. United States,* 82 Fed. Cl. 202 (2008). In
addition, the court ruled that the 1866 Act irrigation
ditches had been taken. Accordingly, the court ruled
that Hage's estate (Hage died during the litigation)
was entitled to $2,854,816 for the water rights that
had been taken, plus $904,400 for fences, $458,065
for roads and trails and $3,150 for improvements at
seven springs and wells. That made the total award
$4,220,431, plus interest, from the date of the taking,
plus attorney's fees and costs. In late 2009, the court
refused to grant the defendant's motion for partial
reconsideration. *Estate of Hage v. United States,* 90
Fed. Cl. 388 (2009). However, on appeal, the United
States Court of Appeals for the Federal Circuit held
that Hage did not prove that he had title to the
improvements that they had constructed or improved
on the federal land. *Estate of Hage v. United States,*
687 F.3d 1281 (Fed. Cir. 2012)*, cert. den.,* 133 S. Ct.
2824 (U.S. 2013). Instead, the court determined that
the evidence established that the improvements were
property of the federal government. Thus, without
establishing ownership of the improvements, Hage
could not establish a property interest that had been
taken and could not properly pose a claim for loss of
value for the range improvements on his private
property stemming from the cancelation of the
permits. The court also ruled that Hage's regulatory

takings claim and claim for compensation were not ripe. Thus, the court vacated the lower court's damage award and held that to the extent Hage's claim for physical taking relied on fences constructed in 1981 or 1982 it was not timely. To the extent the takings claim was based on fences constructed in 1988–1990, the court reversed the lower court due to a lack of evidence that water was taken that Hage could have put to a beneficial use. The court also ruled, as did the lower court, that Hage was not entitled to any prejudgment interest. The case was remanded for further proceedings.

## 3. Federal Grazing Permits and the Clean Water Act

Section 401 of the Clean Water Act (CWA) requires state certification for any applicant applying for a federal license or permit for any activity that may result in a discharge of pollutants into the navigable waters of the United States. Historically, § 401 has only applied to point source discharges such as from city sewage treatment plants or factories. State certification under Section 401 has been held applicable to the operation of a dam to produce hydroelectricity because the dam raised the "potential" for discharge under the CWA which triggered the application of Section 401 of the CWA. *S.D. Warren Company v. Maine Board of Environmental Protection, et al.,* 547 U.S. 370 (2006). Hence, the USFWS policy is to issue grazing permits without requiring the permittee to first obtain state certification that the grazing will not violate state water quality standards. The pollution, if any, caused by livestock grazing is believed to be a nonpoint source pollutant not subject to § 401 of the CWA. *Oregon Natural Desert Association v. Dombeck,* 151 F.3d 945 (9th Cir. 1998), *rev'g.,* 940 F. Supp. 1534 (D. Or. 1996).

# CHAPTER 10
# REGULATORY LAW

## I. OVERVIEW

Agriculture is one of the most heavily regulated industries in the United States. Almost every activity of a farmer or rancher is somehow regulated by federal or state government. Government programs exist concerning matters such as marketing and quality standards, inspections, animal and plant health, crop insurance, soil conservation, commodity exchanges, credit and farm financing, food production, safety, quality, livestock and stockyard regulation, irrigation regulation, and export/import programs.

## A. FEDERAL AND STATE REGULATION

In some situations, both federal and state regulations apply to the same agricultural activity. When federal and state laws conflict, federal law usually preempts state law. In general, if a federal law concerns a dominant federal interest or creates wide-ranging regulations, a court will find the federal law to prevail over the conflicting state law. *See, e.g., Wisconsin Public Intervener v. Mortier,* 501 U.S. 597 (1991).

An example of an activity of interest and potential benefit to agriculture that is regulated by both the federal government and the states involves the use of unmanned aerial vehicles (UAVs), more commonly referred to as drones. Drones, like other aircraft, are regulated by the Federal Aviation Administration (FAA).

The FAA issued regulations effective December 21, 2015, requiring the registration of small drones (those weighing more than .55 pounds and less than 55 pounds—including such things as cameras) that are used for hobby or recreational purposes. Final regulations were issued on June 21, 2016 which allow for the greater commercial operation of drones in the National Airspace System. At its core, the Final Rule allows for increased routine commercial operation of drones compared to what had been previously allowed. The Final Rule (FAA-2015-0150 at 10 (2016)) adds Part 107 to Title 14 of the Code of Federal Regulations and applies to unmanned "aircraft" that weigh less than 55 pounds (that are not model aircraft and weigh more than 0.5 pounds). The Final Rule became effective on August 29, 2016.

Although the authority to regulate airspace and airworthiness rests with the federal government, not the states, states may regulate the aeronautical activities of their own institutions and departments. Pursuant to this authority, some state laws prohibit evidence obtained by law enforcement using a drone from being admissible in a criminal or civil trial unless it was obtained pursuant to a search warrant or in a manner consistent with state and federal law.

## B.    ADMINISTRATIVE AGENCIES

At the federal level, the Congress enacts basic enabling legislation, but leaves the particular administrative departments (such as the USDA) to implement and administer congressionally created programs. As a result, the enabling legislation tends to be vague with the administrative agencies (such as the USDA) needing to fill in the specific provisions by promulgating regulations. The procedures that administrative agencies must follow in promulgating rules and regulations, and the rights of individuals affected by administrative agency decisions are specified in the Administrative Procedures Act (APA). *5 U.S.C. §§ 500 et seq.* The provisions of the APA constitute the operative law for many of the relationships between farmers and ranchers and the government.

Usually, a farmer or rancher's contact with an administrative agency is in the context of participation in an agency-administered program, or being cited for failure to comply with either a statutory or administrative rule. Consequently, farmers and ranchers may find it beneficial to have a general understanding of how administrative agencies work and the legal effects of their decisions. In general, disputed matters involving administrative agencies must first be dealt with in accordance with the particular agency's own procedural rules before the matter can be addressed by a court of law, unless a facial challenge is made to the regulation at issue. *Gold Dollar Warehouse, Inc. v. Glickman,* 211 F.3d 93 (4th Cir. 2000). This is known as exhausting administrative remedies. Thus, participating carefully in administrative proceedings can be vitally important to a farmer or rancher, especially in terms of properly preserving a record for subsequent court review.

Typically, an appeal to a court of law is made only on the basis of the record generated in the administrative proceeding. Courts are limited in the extent to which they can substitute their judgment for that of an administrative agency regarding the facts of the dispute. Thus, it is critical to preserve all disputed factual and legal issues in the record of the administrative proceeding so that they can later be considered by a court. In addition, the exhaustion of administrative remedies, as a general rule, also requires that legal issues must be raised during the administrative process so as to be preserved for judicial review. *See, e.g., Ballanger v. Johanns,* 495 F.3d 866 (8th Cir. 2007).

Courts generally consider only whether the administrative agency acted rationally and within its statutory authority. Consequently, a particular farmer or rancher bears the burden of insuring that the record is adequate for the appeal of the issues involved before the matter leaves the administrative process. Otherwise, an appeal of an administrative agency's decision must be based solely on arguments that the agency acted arbitrarily, capriciously, beyond legal authority or that it abused its discretion. In general, when dealing with administrative appeals from a federal agency such as the USDA, the court generally defers to the agency's interpretation of its regulations as contained in the agency's interpretive manuals.

Prevailing in court against an administrative agency can be quite difficult. However, in *Christensen v. Harris County,* 529 U.S. 576 (2000), the U.S. Supreme Court ruled that statutory interpretations made by governmental agencies in pronouncements that do not have the force of law, such as opinion letters, policy statements, agency manuals, and enforcement guidelines, are not entitled to such great deference. This is a significant case for the agricultural sector because the USDA often makes interpretations of the laws they administer in formats that do not have the force of law. Similarly, in another case the court noted than an agency is not entitled to deference simply because it is a governmental agency. *Meister v. United States Department of Agriculture*, 623 F.3d 363 (6th Cir. 2010).

The Equal Access to Justice Act (EAJA) 5 U.S.C. § 504 (2008) and 28 U.S.C. § 2412(d)(2)(A) (2008), provides that a party who prevails administratively against government action can recover fees and expenses if the administrative officer determines that the government's position was not substantially justified. However, the USDA's longstanding position is that the EAJA does not apply to administrative hearings before the USDA's National Appeals Division (NAD) because NAD proceedings are not adversarial adjudications that are held "under" the APA. But, the United States Court of Appeals for the Eighth Circuit rejected the USDA's position in 1997. *Lane v. United States Department of Agriculture*, 120 F.3d 106 (8th Cir. 1997). The Ninth Circuit ruled similarly in 2007, *Aageson Grain and Cattle, et al. v. United States Department of Agriculture*, 500 F.3d 1038 (9th Cir. 2007) as did the Seventh Circuit in

2008. *Five Points Road Venture, et al. v. Johanns,* 542
F.3d 1121 (7th Cir. 2008).

## II.   ANTITRUST LAWS

Section 10.08 addressed antitrust laws in the
context of agricultural cooperatives. This section
addresses antitrust issues involving resale price
maintenance, the Packers and Stockyards Act, and
the Agricultural Fair Practices Act.

### A.   RESALE PRICE MAINTENANCE

### 1.  In General

One of the most interesting developments in the
antitrust field has been the subject of resale price
maintenance. Resale price maintenance involves the
specification by manufacturers of prices below which
retailers may not sell their products. Unless there is
some basis for an antitrust exemption, an agreement
between a seller and its buyer fixing the price at
which the buyer may resell the product is a *per se*
violation of Section 1 of the Sherman Act. Such an
agreement, which courts view as an unreasonable
restraint on alienation, forecloses price competition
among buyers on the resale of the product. In
agriculture, this has been and can be an issue with
respect to chemicals, seeds and other inputs that are
sold to farmers.

In 2007, the U.S. Supreme Court issued one of its
most noteworthy antitrust decisions in decades when
it held that all vertical price restraints are to be
judged by the Sherman Act's rule of reason standard

rather than being deemed to be per se illegal. *Leegin Creative Leather Products, Inc. v. PSKS, Inc.,* 551 U.S. 877 (2007). The case involved a manufacturer who had instituted a retail pricing and promotion policy, refusing to sell to retailers that discounted its goods below suggested prices. The manufacturer planned to introduce expert testimony describing the pro-competitive effects of its pricing policy, but the trial court excluded the testimony, relying on the rule that it was per se illegal under the Sherman Act for a manufacturer to agree with its distributor to set the minimum price the distributor could charge for the manufacturer's goods. The appellate court agreed, but the Supreme Court reversed. The Court determined that the rule of reason was the appropriate standard to judge vertical price restraints and vertical minimum resale price maintenance agreements because (1) pro-competitive justifications existed for a manufacturer's use of resale price maintenance; (2) the primary purpose of the antitrust laws was to protect interbrand competition; (3) administrative advantages were not sufficient in themselves to justify the creation of per se rules; and (4) stare decisis did not compel the Court's continued adherence to the per se rule.

The Court's opinion seems likely to have a direct impact on manufacturers, distributors, and retailers of goods. These parties may now consider resale price maintenance agreements in an effort to improve competitiveness and increase sales. However, the magnitude of the change likely will turn on a number of factors including whether business practices will change in traditional distribution channels, and how negotiations concerning intellectual property licenses will be impacted. State laws are another source of potential constraint on changes in distribution practice.

Clearly, the decision does not settle this area of the law, but it does lay the framework for future antitrust litigation involving resale price maintenance and what circumstances could lead to anticompetitive effects.

## B.  PACKERS AND STOCKYARDS ACT

Government regulation of stockyards is designed to protect the producer from the abuses of middlemen and to assure consumers adequate supplies of red meat. The Packers and Stockyards Act (PSA) (*7 U.S.C. § 181 et seq. (2008)*) is enforced by the USDA's Packers and Stockyard Administration, the regulator of the country's livestock and poultry marketing system. The PSA's purpose is to assure the free flow of livestock from livestock farms and ranches to the marketplace. *See, e.g., Stafford v. Wallace,* 258 U.S. 495 (1922). The PSA regulates both packers and stockyards.

### 1.  History of the Act

President Harding signed the PSA into law on April 15, 1921. While the PSA was "the most far-reaching measure and extend[ed] further than any previous law into the regulation of private business with few exceptions," 61 Cong. Rec. 1872 (1921) and the powers given to the Secretary of Agriculture were more "wide-ranging" than the powers granted to the

FTC, the Act was upheld as constitutional in several court cases from 1922 to 1934. Unquestionably, the PSA extends well beyond the scope of other antitrust law.

## 2. Provisions of the Act

### i. *Registration Requirement*

The PSA requires all marketing agencies that handle livestock to register with the USDA which has the authority to suspend registration for violations of the Act for insolvency. *7 U.S.C. § 181 et seq.*

### ii. *Prompt Payment*

The PSA also provides for failure to make prompt and full payment for livestock. For instance, before the close of the next business day following the purchase of livestock, the packer, market agency or dealer must deliver a check or wire funds to the seller. Under the PSA a "dealer" is "a person who buys or sells livestock in commerce on his or her own account or for another person. . . ." If a commission is charged, such person is a "market agency." *7 U.S.C. § 201.*

This provision was added in 1976 and it is specifically exempted from the Bankruptcy Act so even though a packer goes into bankruptcy, the proceeds of livestock sales are held in trust out of bankruptcy away from the creditors to assure payment to the cash seller of the livestock. *7 U.S.C. § 196(b)* provides that "All livestock purchased by a packer in cash sales, and all inventories of, or receivables or proceeds from meat, meat food products, or livestock products derived therefrom, shall be held by such packer in trust for the benefit of all unpaid cash sellers of such livestock until full payment has been received by such unpaid seller." Written notice must be given to the purchaser and the USDA if payment is not made or an instrument of payment is dishonored. Unpaid cash sellers of livestock have priority over holders of perfected security interests of the purchaser as to the purchaser's assets. A cash sale is defined in the PSA as "a sale in which the seller does not expressly extend credit to the buyer." Mailing a check is not an extension of credit. However, the unpaid cash seller must preserve its claim by giving notice to the packer and filing a proof of claim promptly (e.g., within 15 business days after receipt of notice of dishonor) with the USDA Secretary.

> **Note:** While the PSA trust provision protects unpaid cash sellers of livestock to a covered packer, sales to packers are rarely in cash. However, the PSA and the associated regulations create a presumption of a cash sale. For instance, a mere delay in payment does not create a credit sale because, under 7 U.S.C. § 196(c), all sales are presumed to be cash sales unless the seller "expressly extends credit to the buyer." Similarly, a trust is created when a livestock buyer pays a market agency that sells on a commission basis. *9 C.F.R. § 201.42.* Payments to a market agency are held in trust by the market only for the benefit of the seller to the market agency. Under 7 U.S.C. § 201(c), a "market agency" is "any person engaged in the business of buying or selling in commerce

livestock on a commission basis; or furnishing stockyard services."

Nothing but "an express agreement in writing" can operate as a waiver of the seller's right to next-day cash payment for livestock. Proof of delay or a course of dealing is not sufficient to constitute a waiver. However, with a written agreement to defer the payment or pricing of livestock, there is a danger of waiving the right to prompt next-day payment and becoming no more than an unsecured creditor.

The record-low prices for hogs experienced in 1998 gave rise to a number of concerns with respect to long-term hog marketing contracts and the PSA. More than one-half of hog production in the United States is sold under a long-term (typically three to ten years) marketing agreement between the producer and the packer. Certain types of these contracts establish a minimum price that the producer receives for the hogs. If the market price rises above the floor, the producer receives the floor price and the extra amount is credited to a "ledger" account with the packer. If market price is beneath the floor, the producer receives the floor price and the difference is subtracted from the ledger balance. Because of the record low prices for hogs experienced in 1998, negative balances built-up to substantial levels in many accounts. From a PSA standpoint, these long-term hog contracts appear to involve payment even though payment may take the form of a credit against an existing negative balance. Similarly, questions exist as to whether the guaranteed price aspect of the contracts violates the

PSA by restricting access to packers, and whether the contracts could be construed as credit sales under the prompt next-day payment provision or as a loan to the packer.

### iii. Bonding

Packer bonding is required except for those with average annual purchases of $500,000 or less. Thus, there is a danger posed to persons or entities selling livestock to relatively small buyers. Selling to a local locker does not provide the protection that the PSA affords had the sale been to a packer purchasing at least $500,000 worth of livestock per year.

### iv. False Weighing

False weighing of livestock is also prohibited. False weighing of livestock had been a serious longstanding problem. "Back balancing" had been a relatively common practice (failure to empty the scales to show a balanced condition). False weighing is viewed as a serious offense and the regulations impose several detailed requirements to discourage false weighing. *See 9 C.F.R. §§ 201.49–201.99.*

### v. Gratuities

The Packers and Stockyards Act also prohibits the practice of a stockyard owner or market agency giving gratuities to truckers, consignors or shippers. Providing free trucking to consignors as an inducement to consign livestock to a particular market is an unfair practice and a willful violation of the PSA, and discriminates against those consignors not given free trucking. The practice also constitutes an unfair and unjust practice against competing markets, forcing them to give free trucking in order to remain in business.

### vi. Coordinated Buying

The "turn system" of selling livestock has been held to violate the PSA. *Berigan v. United States,* 257 F.2d 852 (8th Cir. 1958). Under the "turn system" of selling livestock, livestock dealers engage in the practice of flipping coins to establish the "order" or "turn" in which they would look at, bid on and have the opportunity to buy stocker and feeder cattle consigned for sale to a market agency. This method of selling livestock limits the number of buyers or prospective buyers which increases the value of the position or turn of those not eliminated with the effect of restricting competition and depressing the market.

### vii. Bribery

The PSA also prohibits the bribery of weighmasters. Likewise, bribing employees of a market agency by a dealer to obtain favored treatment in sale of livestock has been held to violate the PSA. *See, e.g., In re McNulty,* 13 Agric. Dec. 345 (1954). Other violations of the PSA include market agencies purchasing animals from consignments for resale, price discounts being offered to some purchasers of meat products, and the use of "bait and switch" tactics in selling meat.

## viii. Recordkeeping

The PSA requires that books and records be kept. Penalties for failure to do so include a $5,000 fine or three years in prison or both. Private actions may be brought for "reparations" under the Act by filing a complaint with the USDA within 90 days after the cause of action accrues. USDA issues the order requiring payment.

## ix. Price Manipulation

Section 202 of the PSA (*7 U.S.C. §§ 192(a)* and *(e)*) makes it unlawful for any packer who inspects livestock, meat products or livestock products to engage in or use any unfair, unjustly discriminatory or deceptive practice or device, or engage in any course of business or do any act for the purpose or with the effect of manipulating or controlling prices or creating a monopoly in the buying, selling or dealing any article in restraint of commerce. This is a distinct concern in the livestock industry. In recent years, numerous courts have addressed the issue of whether the statutory language requires a producer to prove that a packer's conduct had an adverse impact on competition. For example, in late 2001, a nationwide class action lawsuit was certified against Iowa Beef Processors (subsequently acquired by Tyson Fresh Meats, Inc.) on the issue of whether Tyson's use of "captive supply" cattle (cattle acquired other than on the open, cash market) violated Section 202 of the PSA. *Pickett v. IBP, Inc.,* No. 96-A-1103-N, 2001 U.S. Dist. LEXIS 22453 (M.D. Ala. Dec. 26, 2001). The class included all cattle producers with an ownership interest in cattle that were sold to Tyson, exclusively on a cash-market basis, from February 1994 through and including the end of the month 60 days before notice was provided to the class. The claim was that Tyson's privately held store of livestock (via captive supply) allowed Tyson to need not rely on auction-price purchases in the open market for most of their supply. Tyson was then able to use this leverage to depress the market prices for independent producers on the cash and forward markets, in violation of the PSA. In early 2004, the federal jury in the case returned a $1.28 billion verdict for the cattle producers. However, one month later the trial court judge, while not disturbing the economic findings that the market for fed cattle was national, that the defendant's use of captive supply depressed cash cattle prices and that cattle acquired on the cash market were of higher quality than those the defendant acquired through captive supplies, granted the defendant's motion for judgment as a matter of law, thereby setting the jury's verdict aside. The trial court judge ruled that Tyson was entitled to use captive supplies to depress cash cattle prices to "meet competition" and assure a "reliable and consistent" supply of cattle. *Pickett v. Tyson Fresh Meats, Inc.*, 315 F. Supp. 2d 1172 (M.D. Ala. 2004). On appeal, the U.S. Court of Appeals for the Eleventh Circuit affirmed. *Pickett v. Tyson Fresh Meats, Inc.*, 420 F.3d 1272 (11th Cir. 2005), *cert. den.*, 547 U.S. 1040 (2006). See also *Been, et al. v. O.K. Industries*, 495 F.3d 1217 (10th Cir. 2007), *cert. den.*, 131 S. Ct. 2876 (2011).

Most of the other courts that have considered the issue have also determined that Section 202 of the PSA requires a producer to prove that a packer's conduct adversely impacted competition. *See, e.g., Been v. O.K. Industries, Inc.,* 495 F.3d 1217 (10th Cir. 2007), *cert. den.,* 131 S. Ct. 2876 (2011); *London v. Fieldale Farms Corp.,* 410 F.3d 1295 (11th Cir. 2005), *cert. den.,* 546 U.S. 1034 (2005); *Adkins v. Cagle Foods, JV, LLC,* 411 F.3d 1320 (11th Cir. 2005); *Terry v. Tyson Farms, Inc.,* 604 F.3d 272 (6th Cir. 2010), *cert. den.,* 131 S. Ct. 1044 (2011). While the United States Court of Appeals for the Fifth Circuit, in a contract poultry production case, ruled that the plain language of Section 202 does *not* require a plaintiff to prove an adverse effect on competition in *Wheeler, et al. v. Pilgrim's Pride Corp.,* 536 F.3d 455 (5th Cir. 2008), the court granted en banc review with the full court later reversing the 3-judge panel decision. *Wheeler, et al. v. Pilgrim's Pride Corp.,* No. 07–40651, 2009 U.S. App. LEXIS 27642 (5th Cir. Dec. 15, 2009). See also *Terry v. Tyson Farms, Inc.,* 604 F.3d 272 (6th Cir. 2010), *reh'g. den.,* 2010 U.S. App. LEXIS 13116 (6th Cir. Jun. 23, 2010), *cert. den.,* 2011 U.S. LEXIS 1031 (U.S. Jan. 24, 2011).

In 2009, contract poultry growers in Texas, Arkansas, Oklahoma and Louisiana brought a PSA price manipulation case against the company that provided them with chicks, feed, medicine and other inputs. *City of Clinton v. Pilgrim's Pride Corporation,* 654 F. Supp. 2d 536 (N.D. Tex. 2009). The company had filed for Chapter 11 bankruptcy and, as part of reorganizing its business activities closed certain facilities and terminated some grower contracts. The terminated growers claimed the defendant's actions violated Section 192(e) of the PSA as actions that had the effect of manipulating the price of chicken by terminating those growers that were not near another poultry integrator so that they couldn't sell their chickens to one of the defendant's competitors, and terminating those growers who would not upgrade their chicken houses to include cool-cell technology even though not required by grower contracts. While the court held that the defendant could have a legitimate business reason for its decisions and might be able to show that the plaintiffs were not harmed by its actions, the court determined that the plaintiffs' pleadings were sufficient to survive a motion to dismiss. In addition, the court held that the Texas growers had posed legitimate claims under the Texas Deceptive Trade Practices Act.

### x. Other Prohibited Practices

The Act prohibits any "unfair, unjustly discriminatory, or deceptive practice or device. *7 U.S.C. § 192(a). See, e.g., Kinkaid v. John Morrell & Co.,* 321 F. Supp. 2d 1090 (N.D. Iowa 2004*).*

### xi. Enforcement

Enforcement of the PSA is either by a civil action, initiated by the person aggrieved by the violation of the PSA, or by an action taken by the U.S. Attorney upon request of the Secretary of Agriculture. Jurisdiction is in the federal district court.

## C.  AGRICULTURAL FAIR PRACTICES ACT

While technically not an antitrust law, farmers and ranchers have generally been protected since 1967 against unfair trade practices by handlers under the Agricultural Fair Practices Act. *7 U.S.C. §§ 2301 et seq.* Under the Act, unfair trade practices include coercing any producer into joining or not joining an association of producers, or refusing to deal with any producer because the producer joins such an association. Similarly, discriminating against any producer with respect to price, quantity, quality or other terms of purchase or handling of agricultural products because of the producer's membership in or contact with an association of producers is prohibited. The Act also prohibits the coercion or intimidation of any producer to enter into, maintain, breach, cancel or terminate a membership agreement or marketing contract with an association of producers, or a contract with a handler. Likewise, the Act prohibits the paying or loaning of money, giving anything of value, or offering any other inducement to a producer for refusing or ceasing to belong to an association of producers. Also prohibited is the making of false reports concerning the finances, management, or activities of associations of producers or handlers and the conspiring, combining, agreeing or arranging with any other person to do, or aid or abet the commission of, any unlawful act.

## D.   FEDERAL MARKETING ORDERS
## AND CHECK-OFFS

The Agricultural Marketing Agreement Act (AMAA) of 1937 regulates the handling of agricultural commodities in interstate or foreign commerce.

Marketing orders are established under the AMAA, and are designed to ensure that consumers receive an adequate supply of a commodity at a stable price. Marketing orders also maintain and enhance product prices by controlling the amount and quality of products that can be marketed in a given location. Marketing orders have long been used in the fruit, nut, vegetable and milk industries. Typically, an order requires that a handler (dealer) pay a fixed minimum price to the producer of a commodity, and that the marketing of a commodity follow a system of rules. Many marketing orders have received an antitrust exemption.

Separate legislation has established mandatory assessments for promotion of particular agricultural products. An assessment (or "check-off") is typically levied on handlers or producers of commodities with the collected funds to be used to support research promotion and information concerning the product. Such check-off programs have been challenged on First Amendment free-speech grounds. For example, in *United States v. United Foods, Inc.*, 533 U.S. 405 (2001), the U.S. Supreme Court held that mandatory assessments for mushroom promotion under the Mushroom Promotion, Research, and Consumer Identification Act violated the First Amendment. The assessments were directed into generic advertising, and some handlers objected to the ideas being advertised. In an earlier decision, *Glickman v. Wileman Brothers & Elliott, Inc.*, 521 U.S. 457 (1997), the Court had upheld a marketing order that was part of a greater regulatory scheme with respect to California tree fruits. *Glickman v. Wileman Brothers & Elliott, Inc.*, 521 U.S. 457, *rev'g*, 58 F.3d 1267 (9th Cir. 1995). In that case, producers were compelled to contribute funds for cooperative advertising and were required to market their products according to cooperative rules. In addition, the marketing orders had received an antitrust exemption. None of those facts was present in the *United Foods* case, where the producers were entirely free to make their own marketing decisions and the assessments were not tied to a marketing order. The Supreme Court did not address, however, whether the check-offs at issue were government speech and, therefore, not subject to challenge as an unconstitutional proscription of private speech.

In *Horne, et al. v. United States Department of Agriculture*, No. CV-F-08-1549 LJO SMS, 2009 U.S. Dist. LEXIS 115464 (E.D. Cal. Dec. 11, 2009), the court held that the plaintiff, a raisin grower, was a "handler" who "acquired" raisins and was subject to the AMAA and the order regulating the "Handling of Raisins Produced from Raising Variety Grapes Grown in California. The marketing order's reserve requirements did not violate the constitution's due process clause or amount to an unconstitutional taking of plaintiff's private property without just compensation. On appeal, the court affirmed on the "handler" issue and determined that only the U.S. Court of Federal Claims had jurisdiction on the takings issue. However, on further review, the U.S. Supreme Court reversed. *Horne, et al. v. United States Department of Agriculture,* 133 S. Ct. 2053 (2013). On remand, the Ninth Circuit held that the reserve requirements in the marketing order do not violate the Fifth Amendment's Takings Clause. *Horne v. United States Department of Agriculture,* 750 F.3d 1128 (9th Cir. 2014). But, the Supreme Court reversed that decision. *Horne v. United States Department of Agriculture,* 135 S. Ct. 2419 (2015). In another case involving a takings claim involving the raisin marketing order, the U.S. Court of Federal Claims then held that the Supreme Court's reversal of the Ninth Circuit in *Horne* tolled the statute of limitations as applied to the claims in the later case and, as a result, the plaintiff's taking claim was not barred by the running of the statute of limitations for any of the crop years at issue. *Lion Farms v. United States*, No. 15-915, 2016 U.S. Claims LEXIS 1812 (Fed. Cl. Nov. 29, 2016).

The courts have addressed the government speech issue with respect to agricultural check-off programs.

- The beef checkoff was upheld as constitutional in *Johanns v. Livestock Marketing Association,* 544 U.S. 550 (2005), *rev'g., Livestock Marketing Association v. United States Department of Agriculture,* 335 F.3d 711 (8th Cir. 2003) (beef checkoff upheld as government speech).

- Mandatory assessments under the Avocado Act that were used for generic advertising were upheld because the advertising did not mention specifically the plaintiffs, and an internet survey showing that consumers attributed the advertising to the plaintiffs was deemed not reliable. In *Avocados Plus, Inc., et al. v. Johanns,* 421 F. Supp. 2d 45 (D. D.C. 2006), opinion on further review of attribution issue at *Avocados Plus, Inc. v. Johanns,* No. 02-1798, 2007 U.S. Dist. LEXIS 4572 (Jan. 23, 2007).

- In *In re Washington State Apple Advertising Commission,* 257 F. Supp. 2d 1290 (E.D. Wash. 2003). the court granted challengers to the Washington apple checkoff a preliminary injunction against the checkoff, pending trial. The court found that the apple industry was highly regulated but that the regulation did not collectivize the marketing of apples and that no government speech was involved.

- In *Tampa Juice Services, Inc. v. Florida,* No. 6C-6-00-3488 (Fla. Cir. Ct. Mar. 31, 2003), the Florida citrus "box tax" unconstitutional because the advertising purchased with the "box tax" was not government speech and no comprehensive regulation of the citrus industry was found.

- The Louisiana Fur and Alligator Public Education and Marketing Fund and the Louisiana Alligator Resource Fund has been held unconstitutional for the same reasons.

*Pelts & Skins, L.L.C. v. Jenkins,* 259 F. Supp.
2d 482 (M.D. La. 2003). But, the United States
Court of Appeals for the Fifth Circuit later
vacated and remanded the case for
development of the record in light of the
Supreme Court's opinion in the beef check-off
case. *Pelts & Skins, LLC v. Landreneau,* 448
F.3d 743 (5th Cir. 2006).

- The California grape checkoff has been held
  unconstitutional because the court found no
  collectivization of the marketing aspects of the
  industry, and 90% of assessment money was
  spent on generic advertising of grapes. *Delano
  Farms Co. v. California Table Grape
  Commission,* 318 F.3d 895 (9th Cir. 2003).
  But, on remand, the trial court held that the
  California Table Grape Commission was a
  governmental entity, and that it had engaged
  in government speech within the meaning of
  *Johanns,* 546 F. Supp. 2d 859 (E.D. Cal. 2008).
  On further review, the Ninth Circuit affirmed.
  *Delano Farms Co. v. California Table Grape
  Commission,* 586 F.3d 1219 (9th Cir. 2009).

- The California Court of Appeals has held the
  California Plum Marketing Program
  unconstitutional. However, the California
  Supreme Court, upon review, concluded that,
  under California law, the compelled funding
  of generic advertising should be tested by the
  intermediate scrutiny standard for
  commercial speech. *Gerawan Farming, Inc. v.
  Kawamura,* 33 Cal. 4th 1 (2004). Thus, the

Court remanded the case to the trial court for further fact finding to determine whether the program involved a substantial governmental interest under California law, whether the program directly advanced that interest, and whether it was narrowly tailored in light of the availability of less restrictive alternatives.

- The same analysis has resulted in the dairy checkoff being ruled unconstitutional. *Cochran v. Veneman,* 359 F.3d 263 (3d Cir. 2004), *rev'g,* 252 F. Supp. 2d 126 (M.D. Pa. 2003). The court specifically noted the extensive regulation of the marketing aspects of the dairy industry concerning price and production.

- No constitutional violation of the California Pistachio check-off was found in *Paramount Land Company, LP v. California Pistachio Commission,* 491 F.3d 1003 (9th Cir. 2007), because the Secretary of the California Department of Food and Agriculture retained sufficient authority to control both the activities and the message under the Pistachio Act.

- Milk producer assessments used for generic advertising to stimulate milk sales have been held to be constitutional under the *Johanns* rationale. *Gallo Cattle Co. v. A.G. Kawamura,* 159 Cal. App. 4th 948, 72 Cal. Rptr. 3d 1 (2008).

## E.　ANTITRUST AND CONCENTRATION IN AGRICULTURE

Antitrust deals almost exclusively with the power of sellers and injuries to consumers. Agricultural producers, however, face oligopsony power which involves the exercise of market power to reduce the price paid to sellers, such as meatpackers colluding to keep prices low. This has proven to be very elusive to antitrust investigators who look favorably upon markets when prices are falling. Likewise, a monopsonistic arrangement may also remain competitive in the output market, further camouflaging collusive activities directed toward input sellers. *But see, Mandeville Island Farms, Inc. v. American Crystal Sugar Co.,* 334 U.S. 219 (1948). *See also National Macaroni Manufacturers Assoc. v. Federal Trade Commission,* 345 F.2d 421 (7th Cir. 1965) (by fixing composition of a blend of durum and hard wheat, defendant substantially affected price of durum wheat). But, in *Toys "R" Us, Inc. v. Federal Trade Commission,* 221 F.3d 928 (7th Cir. 2000), the plaintiff coordinated a horizontal agreement among toy manufacturers which took the form of a network of vertical agreements between the plaintiff and manufacturers to restrict the distribution of the manufacturers' products. The court held that the plaintiff violated antitrust law even though having only a 20 percent market share.

Much of the concern in agriculture has been on alleged price fixing by increasingly concentrated input suppliers and output processors, handlers and shippers. The major question in price fixing litigation is what must be shown to establish that price fixing has occurred. In a civil price fixing case, the plaintiff's burden of proof is the preponderance of the evidence standard.

In *In re High Fructose Corn Syrup Antitrust Litigation,* 295 F.3d 651 (7th Cir. 2002), *reh'g denied,* 2002 U.S. App. LEXIS 16149 (7th Cir. Aug. 5, 2002), *cert. denied,* 537 U.S. 1188 (2003), the court held that Section 1 of the Sherman Act is broad enough to apply to a price fixing agreement that did not involve any actual communication among the parties to the agreement. The court noted that, without explicit evidence of an agreement to fix prices, clear and convincing circumstantial evidence must be presented from which a price fixing agreement can be inferred. The court cited prior caselaw for the notion that "if a firm raises prices in the expectation that its competitors will do likewise, and they do, the firm's behavior can be conceptualized as the offer of a unilateral contract that the officers accept by raising their prices." The required evidence, the court stated, can be established by showing a market structure that would be conducive to price fixing, and evidence that the market behaved in a noncompetitive manner. Even if some of the transactions occurred at a lower price than that set by the alleged price fixing activity, that is not a sufficient defense because, the court noted, the price could later become unreasonable due to market conditions. The court agreed with the plaintiffs that the structure of the high fructose corn syrup market was conducive to price fixing, and that the defendants limited price competition. Thus, the court reversed the trial court's grant of summary judgment and remanded the case for trial on the issue of whether a price fixing antitrust violation occurred. On remand, the court held that the plaintiffs' evidence of price fixing was "marginally sufficient" to show concerted action to fix price. *In re High Fructose Corn Syrup Litigation,* 261 F. Supp. 2d 1017 (C.D. Ill. 2003).

## III. REGULATION OF ANIMALS AND PLANTS

### A. ANIMAL WELFARE ACT

The major provisions of the Animal Welfare Act (AWA) legislation include licensing of those who handle pets, and retail pet stores that sell small mammals commonly referred to as "pocket pets" must be licensed as a dealer. *See 7 U.S.C. § 2131 et. seq.* The AWA also requires licensing of all persons who sell exotic or wild animals for research, exhibition, or for use as a pet. "Pocket pets" are considered to be exotic or wild animals for this purpose. *63 Fed. Reg. 3,017 (1998).* In addition, the AWA covers those who handle animals that might be used for research and ultimate dealers, exhibitors and auction operators. The purchase of dogs and cats for research purposes is prohibited except from authorized operators. The AWA covers warm blooded animals used for research and experimentation. Humane standards are imposed for the handling, care and transportation of animals covered by the Act. Health certificates are required. A five-day waiting period applies before dogs and cats can be sold by dealers and exhibitors. Animals must be marked or otherwise identified.

## B.   HORSE PROTECTION ACT

The Horse Protection Act of 1970 [*15 U.S.C. §§ 1821 et seq. (2008)*] was intended to end the inhumane practice by owners, trainers and exhibitors of deliberately making sore the feet of the Tennessee Walking Horse. This type of horse is characterized by high stepping of the forelegs. Trainers "sore" the horses either by applying chemicals or by placing a painful collar around the top of the hoof that causes the animal to step up in a pronounced fashion. The Horse Protection Act outlawed those procedures and made it an inhumane practice if it was done in interstate commerce.

While the Act does not prohibit the soring of horses, it does prohibit sored horses from being entered in horse shows, exhibitions, sales and auctions and moving in interstate commerce or substantially affecting commerce. The Act was extended in 1976 to intrastate commerce. If a horse has the appearance of being scarred, the scar itself is enough to indicate that the horse has been sored, triggering the statute's application. Violations of the Act are subject to civil penalties and suspension from showing horses for a period of at least one year. *15 U.S.C. § 1825(b)(1)*. Knowing violations are subject to criminal penalties." *15 U.S.C. § 1825(a)*.

Under the Act, liability can extend to trainers, for entering a sored horse in a show, and owners who "allow" sored horses to be entered. *See, e.g., Derickson v. United States Department of Agriculture,* 546 F.3d 335 (6th Cir. 2008). Whether an owner is liable for the entry of a sored horse regardless of knowledge or fault is an unsettled issue in the courts. The USDA's position is that an owner is liable regardless of knowledge or fault for a sore horse. Thus, the USDA interprets the Act in a manner that does not require them to prove that the owner is somehow responsible for the soring (either by direct authorization or otherwise). However, the statute appears to differentiate between those who directly enter, show or exhibit horses and those who do not. See *15 U.S.C. §§ 1824(2)(B)* and *(2)(D) (2008)*. See also, *Lewis v. Secretary of Agriculture* 73 F.3d 312 (11th Cir. 1996).

In late 2003, the U.S. Court of Appeals for the Tenth Circuit adopted the USDA's position that an owner is liable regardless of knowledge or fault for a sore horse on the basis that 15 U.S.C. § 1824(2)(D) means that entering, showing or exhibiting a horse in a horse show results in owner liability if the horse turns out to be sore. *McCloy v. United States Department of Agriculture,* 351 F.3d 447 (10th Cir. 2003), *cert. denied*, 543 U.S. 810 (2004)

## C.   "28 HOUR LAW"

The original Act was passed in 1873 to prevent cruelty to animals in interstate commerce by common carrier. The act was repealed in 1906 and replaced with the "28 Hour Law." *45 U.S.C. §§ 71–74*. The Act, sometimes referred to as the "Food and Rest Law," prohibits some carriers from transporting animals beyond certain time limits. For example, common carriers engaged in interstate commerce must unload animals for rest, water and feeding into properly equipped pens every 28 hours for at least five consecutive hours. The Act applies to cattle, sheep, swine and other animals. The Act does not apply, however, to the transport of animals by truck or by airplane. In essence, the act applies to transport by rail or boat. Upon request, the time may be extended to 36 hours. Similarly, if the time period was exceeded because the unloading of animals was prevented "by storm or other accidental or unavoidable causes which cannot be anticipated or avoided by the exercise of due diligence and foresight," the requirement does not apply.

A special rule exists for sheep. Sheep do not have to be unloaded when the 28-hour time period expires at night. In that event, the sheep can be continued for 36 hours without written consent. A similar exception applicable to all animals is that no unloading is required if the animals have proper food, water, space and an opportunity to rest. However, that is not usually the case with railroads and with other kinds of carriers. However, the Act does not apply to all types of carriers.

## D.   SEED SALES

### 1.  Federal Seed Act

Originally enacted in 1939, the Federal Seed Act 7 U.S.C. §§ 1551 et seq., has two major purposes: (1) to correct abuses in the merchandising of agricultural and vegetable seed in interstate commerce; and (2) to

prevent the importation of adulterated or
misbranded seed. The Act is essentially a truth-in-
labeling law that protects buyers against purchasing
mislabeled or contaminated seed by imposing
stringent labeling requirements under which the
class and variety of seed must be specified on the
label of the seed product. Seeds are deemed to include
"agricultural," "vegetable," or "weed" seeds. In
general, the labels must disclose the variety name
and kind of seed, and the percentage by weight of
each variety of seed representing over 5 percent of
the total weight of the container. Hybrid seeds must
be designated, and the label must also contain the lot
number, origin (state or nation) of the seed,
percentage by weight of weed seeds, the kind and
rate of occurrence of noxious weeds, the percentage of
germination, the date of the germination test, and
the date after which any inoculant used on the seeds
may be ineffective. The Act establishes seed
certifying agencies that have the power officially to
certify seeds as meeting purity, packaging and
processing standards established by the Secretary of
Agriculture. Without certification, any
representation of purity is deemed to be a false
representation. *7 U.S.C. § 1562.*

Violations of the Act may result in having the seed
seized, and civil and criminal penalties imposed. Any
violation of the Act or rules and regulations
committed with knowledge or as the result of gross
negligence is considered a misdemeanor and subjects
the offender to fines. Any other violation of the Act or
rules and regulations, even though committed
without knowledge or actual negligence, also subjects

the violator to a fine for each violation. Any act, omission, or failure by an officer, agent, or employee also binds the company, principal, or employer, as the case may be. The Act does not directly create a private civil remedy for the buyer who may be harmed by a violation, but buyers may recover damages against the seed seller or distributor under general tort or contract law, or by claiming a breach of warranty. If the problem related to the seeds stems from the failure of the producer or seller to comply with the Act, that will generally be a major factor in resolving the lawsuit.

Seed imported into the United States is also subject to inspection and sampling requirements under the Act. *See 7 U.S.C. § 1581.* The Collector of Customs is authorized to draw samples of all seeds and screenings so they may be tested and analyzed to insure their fitness for use in the United States. The Act establishes requirements regarding importation of seed into the United States and when seeds may be denied entry. Certain seed which is declared to be imported for the seeding of roses is subject to the import provisions of the Act. Seed that is adulterated or deemed to be unfit for seeding purposes may be prohibited from importation. Unfit or adulterated seed may be cleaned or processed under the supervision of a USDA employee. If, after careful analysis, it is determined that the clean seed meets the requirements of the Act, the seed may be admitted into the United States.

## 2. Plant Patents

Article I, Section 8, Clause 8 of the U.S. Constitution gives the Congress the power to grant patents. A patent is a grant by the federal government to an inventor of the right to exclude others from making, using or selling the invention for a limited time. Patent law creates ownership rights in the results of innovation, and provides an economic incentive for the development of new products. A patent is a claim describing the boundary of the inventor's property right that contains a written description of the invention, how the invention is made and used, and a series of drawings. The written description must be clear enough to enable any person skilled in the art to make and use the invention. *35 U.S.C. § 112.* The purpose of this requirement is to ensure that, after the patent term expires, the public will enjoy the advantage for which the patent was granted. *See, e.g., Grant v. Raymond,* 31 U.S. 218 (1832). To be patentable, an invention must consist of patentable subject matter, and be useful, novel and nonobvious. *35 U.S.C. §§ 101–103.* Whether an invention is nonobvious is determined on a case-by-case basis with judges permitted to use their own common sense rather than relying solely on objective evidence or testimony. *KSR International Co. v. Teleflex, Inc., et al.,* 550 U.S. 398 (2007).

### i.  Plant Patent Act

Before 1930, it was generally believed that plants and other living organisms were not eligible for patent protection because they were products of nature and were not thought amenable to the written description requirement of patent law. The Plant Patent Act (PPA) of 1930 35 U.S.C. §§ 161–164 (1982), addressed both of these concerns. The PPA statutorily recognized that plant breeders created products that were more than mere products of nature, and specifically exempted plant patent applications from the written description requirement of the patent law. As a result, the PPA extended patent protection not only to inventors, but also to "discoverers" of eligible subject matter.

The grant of a plant patent gives the patent owner who reproduces a distinct and new variety of plant the right to exclude others from asexually producing the plant or selling or using the reproduced plant. In *Imazio Nursery, Inc. v. Dania Greenhouses,* 69 F.3d 1560 (Fed. Cir. 1995), the court construed the term "variety" to limit PPA protection to a single plant and its asexually reproduced progeny. As such, infringement requires proof of asexual reproduction of the actual plant patented, and evidence of independent creation is a valid affirmative defense to plant patent infringement. However, protection is limited to plants and plant varieties that have already reproduced asexually. An asexual plant is one that lacks functional sex organs and reproduces by cell division, spore formation or budding. In addition, bacteria is excluded from the Act. Consequently, the PPA requires that a plant be "distinct and new" to be protected. The term "new" simply means that the plant did not exist previously in a capacity in which it could reproduce itself. The term "distinct" is intended to require that a variety covered by a plant patent must be distinguishable from any other previous variety of that plant. As a result of these limitations, the PPA did not grant patent protection to plant species comprising most of commercial agriculture and was generally unavailable to plant breeders.

## ii. Plant Variety Protection Act

The Plant Variety Protection Act of 1970 (PVPA) 7 U.S.C. §§ 2321 et seq., grants "copyright-like" protection to developers of novel varieties of sexually reproducible plants. The PVPA is, in many respects, parallel to the PPA for protection of plant varieties that are sexually reproduced. The PVPA, among other things, authorizes the Secretary of Agriculture to issue a certificate of plant variety protection (certificate of protection) to the breeder of any novel variety of sexually produced plants. The plant variety certificate protection extends to both the plant and its seeds. By contrast, the plant variety patent extends only to the plant. Thus, the grant provides the plant patentee with "the right to exclude others from asexually reproducing the plant or selling or using the plant reproduced." *35 U.S.C. § 163.*

It is unlawful to sell or grow a protected plant variety without permission of the holder of the plant variety protection certificate. As originally enacted, protection under the PVPA extended for 18 years. The major disadvantage of the original PVPA to plant breeders was the so-called "saved seed" or "farmer exemption" that permitted farmers to sell the protected variety to other farmers who would use it as seed, thereby eliminating their need to buy the protected variety directly from the seed company or authorized seed producer/seller. As originally enacted, the PVPA statutory exemption for saved seed contained no limits on the amount of seed that could be sold under the exception. The exception is of no consequence for corn because any seed saved from the first generation of production after the cross breeding to produce a commercial variety lacks the performance of the original seed. However, the exception is of great importance for soybeans and other crops where saved seed performs almost as well as the parent seed.

In 1983, the Fifth Circuit Court of Appeals limited the use of the exemption in the original PVPA by holding that farmers may sell saved seed directly to other farmers, but not through intermediaries such as farm cooperatives and grain elevators. *Delta & Pine Land Co. v. Peoples Gin Co.,* 694 F.2d 1012 (5th Cir. 1983). However, in *Asgrow Seed Co. v. Winterboer,* 982 F.2d 486 (Fed. Cir. 1992), the appellate court noted that the statute did not limit the amount of seed a farmer can save under the "saved seed" exception, but acknowledged that the statute imposed several limitations on such sales. In essence, the court held that the "saved seed" exception permitted up to 50 percent of a farmer's crop produced from a protected novel plant variety to be sold as seed in competition with the owner of the novel variety. But, the Supreme Court, in *Asgrow Seed Co. v. Winterboer* 513 U.S. 179 (1995), held that the "saved seed" exception of the PVPA did not permit up to 50 percent of a farmer's crop produced from a protected novel plant variety to be sold as seed in competition with the owner of the novel variety. The Court limited the right to save seed to the seed needed to plant the farmer's next crop.

In a 2013 decision, a federal district court held that infringement under Section 2541(a)(3) of the PVPA could be proven via sexual multiplication. *Florida Foundation Seed Producers, Inc. v. Georgia Farms Services, LLC, et al.,* 977 F. Supp. 2d 1336 (M.D. Ga. 2013). The plaintiffs in the case argued that the defendants' contracting with farmers to grow the peanuts at issue in the case and receiving a crop from farmers constituted sexual multiplication based on the Supreme Court's *Asgrow* decision. On that point, the court disagreed, noting that the defendants did not plant and harvest seeds themselves, but contracted the process of sexually multiplying the seeds and such conduct was not a "step in marketing" as required for patent infringement. Under the facts of the case, the defendants did not sell or intend to sell seeds and did not propagate a new crop in violation of Section 2541(a)(5) of the PVPA.

In 1994, the Congress amended the PVPA (effective April 6, 1995) and repealed the provision allowing a farmer to sell "saved seed" to other persons for reproductive purposes without authorization from the PVPA certificate holder. *PVPAA, 108 Stat. 3142 (1994), amending 7 U.S.C. § 2543.* However, the amendment does not diminish the right of a farmer to save grain produced from the purchased seed for replanting, to save all or part of the purchased seed as seed for planting the following season on owned and rented acreage or to sell the grain produced from the purchased seed for other than reproductive purposes (e.g., into the grain trade). In short, this change in the PVPA means that farmers can no longer sell or buy "brown bagged" seed, which is the common term for seed sold from a PVPA-protected variety without authorization from the holder of the PVPA certificate. The 1994 amendments also extended the protection period from 18 to 20 years and provided for infringement actions against makers of "essentially derived" varieties. The "essentially derived" language is designed to prevent breeders from copying protected varieties by incorporating them into their own lines with only slight cosmetic changes. No court has interpreted the meaning of "essentially derived."

While the PVPA, as enacted, protected sexually reproducible plants, the Supreme Court, in *Diamond v. Chakrabarty*, 447 U.S. 303 (1980), determined that living things such as genetically engineered microorganisms could be patented under general patent law so long as they satisfied the statutory criteria. The Court's language was sufficiently broad to suggest that even plants that could be protected under the PPA or the PVPA could be the object of a general utility patent. This position has been confirmed in a case involving genetically engineered corn. *See Ex parte Hibberd*, 227 U.S.P.Q. (BNA) 443 (Bd. Pat. App. & Interferences 1985). Indeed, in *J.E.M. Ag Supply, Inc. v. Pioneer Hi-Bred International, Inc.*, 534 U.S. 124 (2001), the Court specifically held that newly developed plant breeds fall within the terms and scope of general utility patent law, and that neither the PPA nor the PVPA limits the scope of coverage of the general utility patent law. The Court noted that the Congress has not given any indication of narrowing the scope of the general utility patent law's application to plants since the *Chakrabarty* decision and that the United States Patent and Trademark Office has issued nearly 2,000 utility patents for plants, plant parts and seeds since 1985. The Court held that something that can be protected under the PVPA may also qualify for patent protection as a utility patent under the general patent laws. Accordingly, with the development of techniques for genetic engineering, many other new varieties of agricultural plants may be patented rather than being protected by the PVPA. A patent would essentially give the developers an exclusive monopoly over their varieties for a period of 20 years without the problem of the "farmer exemption."

Even though general patent protection is possible, the strict requirements of the patent law must be satisfied. Thus, an item must be shown to be "novel," "nonobvious," and must be shown to have "utility" to society. However, even if a patent is granted, the patent only allows the holder to exclude others from making, selling or using the invention. In addition, patented seed that has been lawfully purchased can be resold before planting without violating the PVPA. Similarly, where the patented variety is planted and then harvested, the offspring of the patented variety could certainly be sold as a crop without violating the statute.

**Note:** Patenting is not necessarily limited to genetically-modified varieties. Conventional varieties may also be patented. For example, Monsanto provides the following written warning to soybean seed buyers:

"Saving seed from this year's soybean crop to plant in [a following year] is a great temptation. It is especially tempting to save seed from Roundup Ready varieties because of their popularity in premium performance. But remember, all Roundup Ready varieties are patented, as are STS (DuPont non-GMO variety) and all newer conventional varieties in the seed industry. Legally, no seed from these varieties may be saved for planting purposes."

DuPont/Pioneer utilizes the following language:

"If the tag or the top of the bag indicates this product or the parental lines used in producing this product are protected under one or more US patents, Purchaser agrees that it is granted a limited license thereunder only to produce oil seeds or grain or forage for feeding or processing. Resale of this seed or supply of saved seed to anyone, including Purchaser, for planting, is strictly prohibited under this license. . . . By opening the container, you acknowledge that you read and understood these terms and that you agree to be bound by them to the extent allowable by applicable laws."

Monsanto aggressively enforce its seed patents and licensing agreements. *See, e.g., Bowman v.*

*Monsanto Co., et al.*, 133 S. Ct. 1761 (2013), *aff'g, sub nom., Monsanto Company and Monsanto Technology, LLC v. Bowman*, 657 F.3d 1341 (Fed. Cir. 2011); *Monsanto v. Trantham*, 156 F. Supp. 2d 855 (W.D. Tenn. 2001); *Monsanto v. McFarling*, 302 F.3d 1291 (Fed. Cir. 2002), *cert. denied*, 537 U.S. 1232 (2003); *Monsanto Co. v. Scruggs*, 459 F.3d 1328 (Fed. Cir. 2006), *aff'g*, 342 F. Supp. 2d 602 (N.D. Miss. 2004). See also *Monsanto Co. v. Strickland*, 604 F. Supp. 2d 805 (D. S.C. 2009); *Monsanto Co. v. McFarling*, 363 F.3d 1336 (Fed. Cir. 2004) (construing Missouri law), *cert. denied*, 545 U.S. 1139 (2005), *aff'd*, 488 F.3d 973 (Fed. Cir. 2007), *cert. den.*, 552 U.S. 1096 (2008).

It is worth noting that damages arising from patent infringement are unlikely to be covered by the typical farm liability policy. *See, e.g., Ralph, et al. v. Pipkin, et al.*, 183 S.W.3d 362 (Tenn. Ct. App. 2005). Also, farmers must take caution when making statements during the litigation of such patent infringement cases. *See, e.g., Monsanto Co. v. Dragan*, No. 05CV786S, 2006 U.S. Dist. LEXIS 75670 (W.D. N.Y. Oct. 18, 2006).

### iii. Trade Secrets

For many crops in the United States, true-to-type seed is not usually sold to farmers because if one can make specific crosses between two different inbred varieties of plants, the first-generation progeny from that cross will be a larger, more vigorous plant than either of its parents. As a result, first generation hybrids have become popular in certain crop species. Selling hybrid seeds is attractive to the seed producer because seed from hybrid plants, if saved, typically does not yield comparable plants. For a crop that is sold principally as hybrid seed, it becomes possible to protect as trade secrets the inbred parent plant lines which are necessary to make the hybrid. Trade secret law protects "secret" business information from unauthorized duplication. Trade secrets derive economic value from not being generally known and readily ascertainable by other persons. Trade secret protection is based on state tort law and is designed to protect commercially valuable trade secrets from misappropriation. The trade secret itself is sometimes referred to as a type of property, but it is different than other commercial intangibles that can be subjected to misappropriation. For example, a trade secret is not in the public domain unless the defendant's tort places it there. *Restatement of Torts § 757, Comment b.* This is a critical point for plant breeders attempting to use trade secret law to protect germplasm from piracy activities. Germplasm protected as a trade secret is not deemed to be part of the public domain, and can only become part of the public domain through the tortious conduct of another party attempting to appropriate the protected germplasm.

The practice of protecting inbred parent seed as trade secret has been adopted as a strategy by several breeders of proprietary lines of inbred lines. In *Pioneer Hi-Bred International v. Holden Foundation Seed*, 35 F.3d 1226 (8th Cir. 1994), the court held that the "genetic message" of a proprietary inbred line may be maintained as a trade secret and a right of action for trade secret theft may be pursued against an unlawful appropriator. Consequently, the enforceability of a trade secret right in a plant line offers an alternative form of protection to consider for those plant materials which are not sold as a product in that form. The tort of conversion may also apply to the misuse of germplasm. A subsidiary holding of the federal district court in *Holden* was that the defendant had converted the genetic quality or genetic message of Pioneer's inbred line.

While trade secret protection can be of potentially infinite duration, the protection ends as soon as the innovation is no longer secret, whether by accidental disclosure or a competitor's successful reverse engineering of the invention. Thus, reasonable precautions must be undertaken to maintain trade secret status. This may include the use of confidentiality provisions in purchase agreements and labels on seed bags. Hybrid seed varieties may be kept secret by keeping the parental lines under lock and key and selling only the seed that results from crossing the two lines. It is difficult to determine the exact characteristics of two parents from the resulting seed, but not impossible.

## E.   GENETICALLY MODIFIED ORGANISMS

### 1.  Federal and State Regulation

Genetically modified crops These crops are engineered to be resistant to insect pests and herbicides, but have the potential to disrupt ecological systems, may contain novel proteins with allergenic or toxic properties, and may contain higher concentrations of oversprayed pesticides, herbicides, or both. Consequently, genetically modified crops are appropriate subject matter for regulation.

The governing principle behind the regulation of genetically modified organisms (GMOs) is a concept called "substantial equivalence." Under this concept, a genetically modified crop can be considered the same as a conventional crop. When the concept is applied, regulating agencies only examine a genetically modified product. No scrutiny is given to the manufacturing process. Unfortunately, it is the manufacturing process that makes GMOs unique and serves as the basis for some of the world's concerns over genetically modified organisms.

Under the Federal Food, Drug, and Cosmetic Act (FFDCA) of 1938 and the Food Quality Protection Act (FQPA) of 1996, the EPA is responsible for establishing tolerance levels for the herbicide and pesticide residues on raw and processed foods. Tolerance is defined as the amount of the pesticide that may legally remain on the crop after harvesting. The USDA's Animal and Plant Health Inspection Service (APHIS) is the administrative agency responsible for genetically modified crops, and regulates the planting, distribution and harvesting of the plants. APHIS establishes a permit process for review and approval of genetically modified crops. However, a major criticism of APHIS is that APHIS has granted bio-tech companies permission to field test new genetically modified crops without prior regulatory review. Indeed, several significant genetically modified crops are no longer regulated.

The EPA also attaches terms and conditions to the commercial registration of a plant-incorporated pesticide. For example, growers of genetically modified corn must plant buffer zones and refuges of conventional corn in an effort to prevent or delay pests from developing resistance to the insecticide incorporated in the plant. However, as to enforcement, third party companies contract with the registrant to annually survey growers to ascertain whether they are following the planting rules.

In recent years, numerous attempts have been made at the state and local levels to regulate GMOs. Various limitations banning GMO crops have also passed in several counties in California, but have failed to pass in others. Ordinances banning GMOs have been struck down in *Hawaii, Shaka Movement v. County of Maui, et al.*, 842 F.3d 688 (9th Cir. 2016); *Syngenta Seeds, Inc. v. County of Kauai*, No. 14-16833, 2016 U.S. App. LEXIS 20689 (9th Cir. Nov. 18, 2016).

In response to these attempts at the local level to restrict GMOs, legislation has been introduced in 16 states that would bar local control of plants and seeds. Fourteen of these states have passed the provisions into law. The 14 states are: AZ, FL, GA, KS, ID, IN, IA, ND, OH, OK, PA, SD, TX and WV. The Iowa provision is typical of the various statutes and preempts local legislation relating to the production, use, advertising, sale, distribution, storage, transportation, formulation, packing, labeling, certification or registration of any agricultural seed. *H.F. 642, amending Iowa Code Ch. 199.*

## 2. Labeling of Genetically Modified Organisms

United States' law and the food labeling system is designed primarily to address only proven food risks. If there is no evidence of a health risk, the weight of food labeling law is against labeling. Thus, in the United States, there is no established consumer "right to know." This policy is evidenced in the approach of the three government agencies responsible for regulating genetically modified organisms.

The FDA position, since 1992, is that foods containing genetic organisms are equivalent to conventional foods and do not require labeling. Because the FDA does not view GMOs as a food additive, no special tests or labels are required for foods made from GMOs. Consequently, FDA does not investigate the effect eating GMOs has on people. In 1998, a coalition of scientists, clergy and others filed a lawsuit challenging the FDA position. The court upheld the FDA position. *Alliance for Bio-Integrity v. Shalala,* 116 F. Supp.2d 166 (D. D.C. 2000).

The USDA investigates the effect of GMOs, but only on other plants. Thus, field release and pollen drift are the primary issues instead of issues relating to human consumption. In addition, USDA approvals for new field experiments are generally routine and based largely upon safety information provided by industry.

The EPA's involvement is triggered upon a product being classified as a "bio-pesticide." The EPA's primary concern is the development of pest resistance and environmental impacts rather than safety testing. In the EPA view, if a pesticide is safe to spray *on* plants it is safe to put *in* plants.

At the state level, Vermont is the only state to enact a GMO labeling law. The law requires that specified food products produced with genetic engineering must be labeled as such effective July 1, 2016. However, federal legislation enacted shortly after the Vermont law took effect invalidated the provision.

## IV.  REGULATION OF AGRICULTURAL COMMODITIES

### A.  PERISHABLE AGRICULTURAL COMMODITIES ACT

Agricultural producers who raise specialty crops such as fruits and vegetables often use contracts to lock in their markets. When the commodity involved is highly perishable, any disruption of the contract, such as the failure of the buyer to accept the goods, can be economically devastating. While the producer's rights can be protected under general contract principles, the involvement of a broker as intermediary makes the matter substantially more complex. The Congress enacted the Perishable Agricultural Commodities Act (PACA) in 1930 to address unfair and fraudulent practices in the marketing of perishable agricultural commodities in interstate and foreign commerce. *7 U.S.C. §§ 499a et seq*. A perishable agricultural commodity includes fresh, frozen and iced fruits and vegetables of every kind and character, and cherries in brine. *7 U.S.C. § 499a(4)*. While PACA applies only to the interstate marketing of perishable agricultural products, the courts have generally interpreted the statute broadly.

## 1. Covered Persons

Under PACA, a "commission merchant" is a person who receives covered commodities for the purposes of sale for or on behalf of another, and who receives a commission for the service. "Dealers" are defined as persons who buy or sell such commodities in wholesale or jobbing quantities. However, producers who sell their own products as well as retailers whose invoice price of their purchases of fruits and vegetables does not exceed $230,000 in any calendar year are not defined as a "dealer". Similarly, persons buying commodities, except potatoes for canning or processing in the state where grown, unless the product is frozen, packed in ice or consists of cherries in brine, are not considered to be dealers. "Brokers" are covered by PACA and are persons who negotiate purchases and sales of covered commodities on behalf of the purchaser or vendor. The definition of "broker" under PACA excludes independent agents who negotiate sales of frozen commodities having an invoice value of not more than $230,000 per year.

A "dealer" is defined as "any person engaged in the business of buying or selling in wholesale or jobbing quantities . . . any perishable agricultural commodity in interstate or foreign commerce." *7 U.S.C. § 499a(b)(6)*. By regulation, USDA defines "wholesale or jobbing quantities" to mean "aggregate quantities of all types of produce totaling one ton or more in weight in any day shipped, received, or contracted to be shipped or received." *7 C.F.R. § 46.2*.

While the USDA has a long history of not enforcing PACA against restaurants, restaurants that purchase wholesale produce in sufficient quantity have been held to be a "dealer" subject to PACA. *Magic Restaurants, Inc. v. Bowie Produce Co.*, 205 F.3d 108 (Bankr. 3d Cir. 2000); *In re Country Harvest Buffet Restaurants*, 245 B.R. 650 (Bankr. 9th Cir. 2000); *In re Old Fashioned Enterprises, Inc.*, 236 F.3d 422 (8th Cir. 2001); *Royal Foods, Inc. v. RJR Holdings, Inc.*, 252 F.3d 1102 (9th Cir. 2001). Thus, any money owed to produce suppliers is entitled to statutory priority in repayment.

## 2. Provisions of the Act

PACA requires all brokers and dealers in perishable agricultural commodities to obtain a license from the U.S. Secretary of Agriculture. However, licenses will not be issued to applicants who are not financially responsible, or who have demonstrated character defects of the type likely to result in PACA violations. Licensees may not fail or refuse "truly and correctly" to account and make "full payment promptly" with respect to a transaction, or fail without reasonable cause to perform specifications or duties, express or implied, arising out of transactions. The "full payment promptly" provision is defined by the regulations to mean full payment within a specified number of days (depending on the circumstances) of the transaction unless there is an express agreement between the parties at the time the contract is made that payment should be made under different terms. *7 C.F.R. § 46.2(aa)*.

The proceeds of sale of perishable commodities are held in trust by the dealer for the benefit of the unpaid seller until full payment is made. *7 U.S.C. § 499e(c)(2)*. But, PACA trust protections do not extend to brokers of PACA sellers. See *Onions Etc., Inc., et al. v. Z&S Fresh, Inc., et al.,* No. 1:09-CV-00906-OWW-SMS, 2010 U.S. Dist. LEXIS 64047 (E.D. Cal. Jun. 25, 2010); see also *Sweet Ones, Inc. v. Mercantile Bank,* No. 1:09-CV-1092, 2010 U.S. Dist. LEXIS 39980 (W.D. Mich. Apr. 23, 2010. Thus, once an unpaid seller learns that a PACA trustee has become insolvent, the PACA trust funds are to be escrowed for pro rata distribution among all PACA trust beneficiaries. *Fresh Kist Produce, LLC v. Choi Corp., Inc.,* 223 F. Supp. 2d 1 (D. D.C. 2002). The assets in a PACA trust are excluded from the bankruptcy estate of a bankrupt buyer.

In addition, a PACA trust is created whenever a seller or supplier of perishable commodities provides those products to a covered person on credit. In order to preserve its benefits under the trust, the seller must give the buyer written notice of intent to preserve the PACA trust benefits, and file that notice with the Secretary within a prescribed period of time.

*7 U.S.C. § 499a(c)(3)*. Once the unpaid seller has given written notice to the Secretary of its intent to preserve the trust benefits, an action may be brought in federal district court to enforce payment from the trust and/or prevent the trust assets from being dissipated.

Alternatively, a beneficiary may use ordinary and usual billing or invoice statements to provide notice of the supplier's intent to preserve the trust. *7 U.S.C. § 499e(c)(4)*. The bill or invoice must contain particular language clearly evidencing the supplier's intent to preserve the trust. Sellers who fail to include such language in their notices will not preserve their trust claims. *In re Quality Sales, LLC*, No. 12–200008, 2013 Bankr. LEXIS 3378 (Bankr. D. Conn. Aug. 20, 2013). This provision is designed to provide a simpler and less expensive way for suppliers to preserve their trust rights, and does not redefine what constitutes the corpus of a PACA trust. *See In re Kelly Food Products, Inc.*, 204 B.R. 18 (Bankr. C.D. Ill. 1997).

Licensees may also not "misrepresent by word, act, mark, stencil, label, statement, or deed, the character, kind, grade, quality, quantity, size, pack, weight, condition, degree of maturity," or place of origin of covered commodities. *7 U.S.C. § 499b(5)*. PACA also prohibits other unfair conduct such as intentionally making a false or misleading statement involving any perishable agricultural commodity. *7 U.S.C. § 499b(4)*. Violation of this provision may result in a 90-day license suspension.

## 3. Enforcement Proceedings

Violations of PACA give the producer that has been harmed access to reparation proceedings. The reparation proceedings are designed to resolve contract disputes and establish enforcement proceedings to penalize persons who violate its provisions. A disaffected person may file a petition with the Secretary within nine months of the time a cause of action accrues, alleging facts arising out of a business transaction that would constitute unfair conduct. If the Secretary, on the basis of the complaint, determines that further action is necessary, a copy is forwarded to the broker, dealer or commission merchant involved, who is then given a reasonable time to satisfy or answer the complaint. A hearing may then be held. If liability is found, a reparation order may be issued. This order directs the respondent to pay the amount of damages determined by the Secretary as a result of the violations of the act. This payment must be made on or before the date fixed in the order.

An appeal may be taken from a final reparation order to the federal district court for the district in which the hearing was held. If the case was heard without a hearing, an appeal may be taken to the federal district court for the district where the respondent is located. The appeal must be filed within 30 days from the date the Secretary's order is issued. Enforcement of a reparation order may be had by petition, within three years of date of issuance of the order, to any state court having general jurisdiction of the parties or to the federal district court for the district in which the party seeking enforcement resides or in which the principal place of business of the party against whom such order runs is located.

PACA is also enforced through accounting and recordkeeping requirements. Under PACA, licensed parties must keep records, accounts and memoranda that fully and correctly disclose all transactions involved in the business. Failure to keep the required records may result in suspension of the license.

PACA also empowers the Secretary to employ and license inspectors who may inspect and certify the class, quality and condition of commodity shipments. This inspection may be performed even if no complaint has been filed under the act.

## B.   UNITED STATES GRAIN STANDARDS ACT

The United States Grain Standards Act 7 U.S.C. §§ 71 et seq., was enacted in 1916 as a means of eliminating confusion resulting from the use of many different sets of grain standards applied by many different grain inspection organizations without national coordination and supervision. The Act was amended in 1956 and again in 1968 and 1976,

The Federal Grain Inspection Service is responsible for establishing the policies, guidelines and regulations necessary to carry out the Act. The administrator is authorized to establish standards of "kind, class, quality and condition for corn, wheat, rye, oats, barley, flax seed, sorghum, soybeans, mixed grain and such other grains as in the administrator's judgment the usages of the trade may warrant and permit. The administrator is also authorized to develop standards or procedures for accurate weighing and weight certification and controls for grain shipped in interstate or foreign commerce.

The Act also establishes certain performance requirements for grain inspection and weighing equipment. The regulated equipment generally includes laboratory balances, barley pearlers, grain dividers, dockage testers, mechanical samplers, moisture meters, sieves, and test weight apparatus. These types of equipment must satisfy general design requirements, and grain weighing equipment must meet specified design and performance requirements.

The Act requires that the Secretary provide, by regulation, "for the registration of all persons engaged in the business of buying grain for sale in foreign commerce, and in the business of handling, weighing, or transporting of grain for sale in foreign commerce." 7 U.S.C. § 87f–1(a). Exempt from this requirement are persons who only incidentally or occasionally sell, handle, weigh or transport grain for sale in foreign commerce and who are not engaged in a "regular business" of this nature. Also exempt are producers of grain who only occasionally sell or transport grain which they have purchased, along with persons who transport grain for hire and who have no financial interest in the grain they carry. Also exempt are persons who buy grain for feeding or processing and only incidentally or occasionally sell the grain as grain. Registrants must provide their name and principal address, the names of directors of the business, the names of the principal officers of the business, the names of all persons in a control relationship with respect to the business, a list of locations where the business conducts substantial operations, and any other information as the administrator deems necessary to carry out the purposes of the Act.

## C. UNITED STATES WAREHOUSE ACT

The United States Warehouse Act (USWA) 7 U.S.C. §§ 241 et seq., authorizes the Secretary of Agriculture to license warehousemen engaged in the business of storing agricultural products. The Secretary is also authorized to license persons to weigh, inspect, sample, or classify agricultural products stored or to be stored in licensed warehouses.

The USWA was originally enacted in 1916, but was later amended in 1919, 1923 and 1931. It is independent of any state warehouse legislation. As a result, whenever state warehouse laws and the USWA collide, the USWA controls. *See, e.g., Rice v. Santa Fe Elevator Corp.,* 331 U.S. 218 (1947).

The USWA is quite limited in scope and application. As mentioned above, the Act leaves the decision of being regulated up to a particular warehouse, and only certain types of products that are capable of being stored are covered by regulations issued by the Secretary. Presently, licenses may be issued for the storage of cotton, grain, tobacco, wool, dry beans, nuts, syrup and cottonseed.

Every applicant for a warehouseman's license must furnish a bond to secure faithful performance of the obligations as a licensed warehouseman. However, since some state programs no longer include a bonding program, a bond is required under the federal program. The USDA sets the bond at between $20,000 and $500,000.

Whenever grain moves into or out of a warehouse, it is weighed and a scale (weight) ticket is issued. The scale ticket issued upon delivery into the facility will state the date, the name of the deliverer, the type and gross weight of the commodity, and sometimes the moisture content. However, most scale tickets do not state the number of bushels or the quality. Grain, to be accepted for storage, must be below a specified moisture content. Drying can cause shrinkage and the test weight of bushel can vary according to the quality of the grain. Typically, it is after issuance of the scale ticket that the warehouse determines moisture content, quality, test weight and presence of foreign matter.

Federally licensed warehouses are required to issue warehouse receipts for stored grain, but some state licensed facilities do not issue them, except at the request of the bailor. State licensed warehouses are required in most jurisdictions to issue warehouse receipts upon request. Federally licensed warehouses must use sequentially numbered USDA-supplied warehouse receipt forms. Many states have a similar procedure.

Generally, warehouse receipts are documents of title and represent ownership of the grain. Federal warehouse receipts must indicate the name of the warehouse, its location, the date the receipt was issued, the name of the person to whom redelivery is to be made, the storage charge (tariff), and a description of the agricultural commodity delivered, including quality and quantity. The receipt must be signed by the operator.

The security provisions of the Act require that grain must be paid for within 30 days unless the grain was sold under either a deferred payment or a deferred pricing contract. With a deferred pricing contract, the seller has a stated number of days or weeks or months to set the price. Under a deferred payment contract, the grain sale is complete, but payment has not been made. Deferred payment contracts are the more common, and are typically entered into before fall delivery of the crop. While delivery occurs in the fall, payment is usually withheld until after the first of the next year. A major reason for the use of deferred payment contracts is to defer income for income tax purposes. But, persons who sell grain to a buyer on a deferred payment basis become unsecured creditors of the buyer.

Warehouse receipts must be issued within six months unless a statement is signed that the seller does not desire a warehouse receipt. Grain sold under scale ticket only is considered to be in open storage.

# V. REGULATION OF FOOD PRODUCTS

## A. IN GENERAL

The government agencies with primary responsibility for ensuring the safety of the U.S. food supply are the USDA (through the Food Safety and Inspection Service (FSIS)) and the Food and Drug Administration (FDA). While neither agency has the authority to mandate a recall of unsafe food, they have developed general oversight procedures and protocol for voluntary food recalls by private companies. The USDA is generally responsible for the regulation of meat, poultry and certain egg products, while the FDA has responsibility for the regulation of all other food products including seafood, milk, grain products, fruits and vegetables, and certain canned, frozen and otherwise packaged foods that contain meat, poultry and eggs that USDA does not otherwise regulate.

## B. FOOD ADULTERATION AND MISBRANDING

The regulations generally proscribe the adulteration and misbranding of food. In general, a food is considered adulterated if it contains a harmful substance that may pose a safety risk, contains an added harmful substance that is acquired during production or cannot be reasonably avoided, contains an unapproved substance that has been intentionally added to the food, or if it has been handled under unsanitary conditions that presents a risk of contamination that may pose a safety threat. Under the Federal Food, Drug, and Cosmetic Act (FFDCA), 21 U.S.C. §§ 301–399, the manufacture, delivery, receipt or introduction of adulterated food into interstate commerce is prohibited. The Act provides that any food that is "in whole or in part, the product of a diseased animal" shall be deemed "adulterated." USDA regulations, through the end of 2003, defined "dying, diseased or disabled livestock" as including animals displaying a "lack of muscle coordination" or an inability to walk normally or stand." However, the USDA regulations initially did not prevent the introduction into the human food chain of meat from downed livestock. *See, e.g., Baur v. Veneman*, 352 F.3d 625 (2d Cir. 2003). However, the rules were modified effective October 1, 2007, to prohibit the slaughter of non-ambulatory cattle in the United States (except that veal calves that cannot stand due to fatigue or cold weather may be set apart and held for treatment and re-inspection). *72 Fed. Reg. 38699 (July 13, 2007).* Also, the spinal cord must be removed from cattle 30 months of age and older at the place of slaughter, and records must be maintained when beef products containing specific risk materials are moved from one federally inspected establishment to another for further processing. Countries that have received the internationally recognized BSE status of "negligible risk" are not required to remove specific risk materials.

While neither the USDA nor the FDA can order a private company to recall unsafe food products, they can issue warning letters, create adverse publicity, seize unsafe food products, seek an injunction or begin prosecuting criminal proceedings.

For food products over which the FSIS has jurisdiction, upon learning that a misbranded or adulterated food item may have entered commerce, the FSIS will conduct a preliminary investigation to determine whether a voluntary recall is warranted. If a recall is deemed necessary, a determination is made as to the degree of the recall and the public is notified. For food products subject to the FDA's jurisdiction, a similar procedure is utilized.

## C.   ORGANIC FOODS

Organic foods are produced according to certain production standards. For crops, "organic" generally means they were grown without the use of conventional pesticides, artificial fertilizers, human waste, or sewage sludge, and that they were processed without ionizing radiation or food additives. For animals, "organic" generally means they were raised without the use of antibiotics and without the use of growth hormones. *See, e.g., In re Aurora Dairy Corp., et al.,* 621 F.3d 781 (8th Cir. 2010); *International Dairy Foods Association, et al. v. Boggs,* 622 F.3d 628 (6th Cir. 2010). In most countries, organic produce must not be genetically modified.

Organic food production is legally regulated and, in the United States, a producer must obtain certification in order to market food as organic. Under the Organic Food Production Act (OFPA) of 1990 (*7 U.S.C. §§ 6501–23*), USDA is required to develop national standards for organic products. USDA regulations (*7 C.F.R. Part 205*), are enforced through the National Organic Program (NOP) governing the manufacturing and handling of organic food products. As enacted, the statute provides that an agricultural product must be produced and handled without the use of synthetic substances in order to be labeled or sold as "organic." But, under USDA regulations, a "USDA Organic" seal can be placed on products with at least 95% organic ingredients. The 95 percent rule was challenged by a Maine organic blueberry farmer as being overly tolerant of non-organic substances and inconsistent with the statute, and the United States Court of Appeals for the First Circuit agreed, invalidated several of the regulations while scaling back the scope of other regulations. *Harvey v. Veneman,* 396 F.3d 28 (1st Cir. 2005). In response to the court's opinion (and while the case was on appeal) the Congress amended OFPA. Upon further review, the court determined that OFPA, as amended, permitted the use of synthetics as both ingredients in and processing aids to organic food. *Harvey v. Johanns,* 494 F.3d 237 (1st Cir. 2007).

## D.   VETERINARY FEED DIRECTIVE (VFD)

The FDA, in 2015, revised existing regulations involving the animal use of antibiotics that are also provided to humans. *21 C.F.R. Part 558.* The new rules arose out of a belief of bacterial resistance in humans to antibiotics. Effective January 1, 2017, veterinarians must provide a "directive" to livestock owners seeking to use or obtain animal feed products containing medically important antimicrobials as additives. A "directive" is the functional equivalent of receiving a veterinarian's prescription to use antibiotics that are injected in animals. Antibiotics that are covered by the VFD rule include Neomycin and Terramycin, drugs that are commonly used to treat diarrhea in calves (commonly known as calf scours). Other covered drugs include Tylosin (used to treat colitis in small animals, as well as acute mastitis in cattle and mastitis in sheep and goats, and infectious arthritis in swine), Chlortetracycline (used to treat conjunctivitis in cats), Oxytetracycline (used to treat breathing disorders in livestock, and generally prevent disease and infections in livestock and poultry) and Virginiamycin (used to prevent and treat infections in livestock, and in the fuel ethanol industry to prevent microbial contamination).

Under the rule, obtaining feed containing a covered antibiotic will require a prescription. The prescription (a VFD form) must be obtained either in-person, via email or fax, from a veterinarian licensed to practice in the particular state. In addition, mixing of antibiotics will not be allowed in any product and extra label of feed additive antibiotics will remain be prohibited. A prescription (VFD form) is valid for up to six months, and VFD records must be maintained for at least two years by the veterinarian, feed supplier, and the user. Farmers that mix feed and supply it to another party can only do so after obtaining a distributor's license and completing all necessary forms. In addition, other requirements might apply. A VFD form an only be approved if there is a valid veterinarian-client relationship (as defined by state law) with the livestock producer. In addition, the form must identify the feed mill or other source of the medicated feed and the animals (by group or individually) that receive the feed, and must contain specific information concerning the animals being treated and the farm(s) on which they are located. The VFD form must also list the antibiotics authorized to be used under the prescription (form), any applicable feeding rates and treatment duration. The protocols basically mean that the companies producing feed medications will be barred from selling medications that are labeled only for growth promotion. Thus, any covered antibiotic that is contained in feed for growth promotion purposes will no longer be commercially available. In addition, as noted above, covered antibiotics will require a VFD form for usage.

## E.   PRODUCE SAFETY RULE

The Food Safety Modernization Act (FSMA) of 2010. 21 U.S.C. § 301 et seq., gives the FDA expansive power to regulate the food supply, including the ability to establish standards for the harvesting of produce and preventative control for food production businesses. Beginning in 2018, the new rules will significantly impact many growers and handlers of fresh produce.

The FMSA also gives the FDA greater authority to restrict imports and conduct inspections of domestic and foreign food facilities. To implement the requirements of the FMSA, the FDA had to prepare in excess of 50 rules, guidance documents, reports under a short time constraint. Indeed, the timeframe was so short FDA complained that they didn't have enough time to do the job appropriately. That led to lawsuits being filed to compel the FDA to issue several rules that were past-due. A federal court agreed. *Center for Food Safety v. Hamburg,* 954 F. Supp. 2d 965 (N.D. Cal. 2013). As a result, the FDA issued four proposed rules with comment periods that ended in November of 2013. One of the most contentious issues involved the rule FDA was supposed to develop involving intentional adulteration of food. FDA said it needed two more years to develop an appropriate rule, but the court ordered them to develop it immediately. The hope, at that time, was that the Congress would step in and modify the deadlines imposed on the FDA so that reasonable rules could be developed rather than being simply rushed through the regulatory process for the sake of meeting an arbitrary deadline.

In late 2015, the FDA issued its Final Produce Safety Rule that has application to growers and fresh produce handlers (those that pack and store fresh produce). The rule is designed to reduce the instances of foodborne illnesses. Effective, January 16, 2016, the rule generally covers the use of manure or compost as fertilizer, allowing (at least for the present time) a 90 to120-day waiting period between the application of untreated manure on land and the time of harvest. That timeframe is in accordance with USDA National Organic Program Standards. Relatedly, the rule requires that raw manure and untreated biological soil amendments of animal origin must be applied without contacting produce and post-application contact must be minimized. Also, the rule addresses water quality and establishes testing for water that is used on the farm such as for irrigation or handwashing purposes. Under the rule, there must be no detectible generic E coli in water that has the potential to contact produce. The rule establishes a timeframe for noncompliant growers to come into compliance with the water requirements. The rule also addresses scenarios that could involve contamination of food products by animals, both domestic and wild, and establishes standards for equipment, tools and hygiene. As for potential contamination by wild animals, the rule requires farmers to monitor growing areas for potential contamination by animals and not harvest produce that has likely been contaminated. In addition, the rule establishes requirements for worker training, health and hygiene, and particular rules for farms that grow sprouts.

Under the rule, farms that sell an average of $25,000 or less of produce over the prior three years are exempt. Similarly, exempt are farms (of any size) whose production is limited exclusively to food products that are cooked or processed before human consumption. For producers whose overall food sales average less than $500,000 annually over the prior three years where the majority of the sales are directly to consumers or local restaurants or retail establishments, a limited exemption from the rule can apply. However, these producers must maintain certain required documentation (effective Jan. 16, 2016) and disclose on the product label at the time the product is purchased the name and location of the farm where the food product originated. In addition, the rule also allows commercial buyers to require that the farms from which they purchase produce follow the rule on their own accord.

## VI.   FEDERAL LABOR LAWS IMPACTING AGRICULTURE

### A.   THE FAIR LABOR STANDARDS ACT

The Fair Labor Standards Act of 1938 (FLSA) (*29 U.S.C. §§ 201 et seq.*), as originally enacted, was intended to alleviate some of the more harmful effects of the Great Depression. In particular, the Act was intended to raise the wages and shorten the working hours of the nation's workers. Since 1938, the FLSA has been amended frequently and extensively. While the FLSA is very complex, not all of it is pertinent to agriculture and agricultural processing.

### 1.  Wage Requirements

The FLSA requires that agricultural employers who use 500 man-days or more of agricultural labor in any calendar quarter of a particular year must pay the agricultural minimum wage to certain agricultural employees in the following calendar year.

Man-days are those days during which an employee performs any agricultural labor for not less than one hour. The man-days of all agricultural employees count in the 500 man-days test, except those generated by members of an incorporated employer's immediate family. *29 U.S.C. § 203(e)(3)*. Five hundred man-days is roughly equivalent to seven workers working five and one-half days per week for thirteen weeks ($5.5 \times 7 \times 13 = 501$ man-days). Under the FLSA, "agriculture" is defined to include "among other things (1) the cultivation and tillage of the soil, dairying, the production, cultivation, growing and harvesting of any agricultural or horticultural commodities; (2) the raising of livestock, bees, fur-bearing animals, or poultry; and (3) any practices (including any forestry or lumbering operations) performed by a farmer or on a farm as an incident to or in conjunction with such farming operations, including preparation for market, delivery to storage or to market or to carriers for transportation to market." *29 U.S.C. § 203(f)*. For related entities, where not all of the entities involve an agricultural trade or business, the question is whether the business operations are so intertwined that they constitute a single agricultural enterprise exempt from the overtime rules. *See, e.g., Ares v. Manuel Diaz Farms, Inc.,* 318 F.3d 1054 (11th Cir. 2003) (employee of landscaping company performed fumigation services on farm owned by defendant and operated by another corporation; defendant and plant and tree farm constituted since agricultural enterprise exempt from overtime rules).

The minimum wage must be paid to all agricultural employees except: (1) members of the employer's immediate family, unless the farm is incorporated; (2) local hand-harvest, piece-rate workers who come to the farm from their permanent residences each day, but only if such workers were employed less than 13 weeks in agriculture in the preceding year; (3) children, age 16 and under, whose parents are migrant workers, and who are employed as hand-harvest piece-rate workers on the same farm as their parents, provided that they receive the same piece-rate as other workers; and (4) employees engaged in range production of livestock. *29 U.S.C. § 213(a)(6)*. Where the agricultural minimum wage must be paid to piece-rate employees, the rate of pay for piece-rate work must be sufficient to allow a worker reasonably to generate that rate of hourly income.

When the minimum wage must be paid, the FLSA allows the employer to include, as part of the compensation paid, the reasonable cost of meals, housing and other perquisites actually provided, if they are customarily furnished by the employer to the employees. Also, the costs of employee travel, visa cost and immigration costs that are incurred for the employer's benefit cannot be shifted to the employee if that would result in the employee's net gain from the employment being less than the FLSA minimum wage. *See, e.g.*, *Arriaga v. Florida Pacific Farms, L.L.C.*, 305 F.3d 1228 (11th Cir. 2002).

The FLSA requires covered employers to compensate employees for activities performed during the workday. But, the FLSA does not require that compensation be paid to employees for activities performed outside the workday such as walking, riding or traveling to and from the actual place of performance of the employee's principal activity, and for activities which occur before and after the employee's principal activity. On the question of whether an employee is entitled to compensation for time spent waiting at stations where required safety and health equipment is distributed, donned and doffed, and traveling to and from these stations to work sites at the beginning and end of each workday, the U.S. Supreme Court has ruled that such activities are indispensable to an employee's principal activity and are, therefore, a principal activity itself. *IBP, Inc. v. Alvarez, et al.*, 546 U.S. 21 (2005). See also *De Asencio v. Tyson Food, Inc.*, 500 F.3d 361 (3d Cir. 2007), *cert. den., sub nom. Tyson Foods, Inc. v. De Asencio*, 553 U.S. 1093 (2008). See also *Arnold, et al. v. Schrieber Foods, Inc.*, 690 F. Supp. 2d 672 (M.D. Tenn. 2010). However, the Court ruled that unless an employee is required to report at a specific time and wait to don required gear, the time spent waiting to don gear is preliminary to the first principal activity of the workday and is not compensable unless compensation is required by the employment agreement or industry custom and practice. *See, e.g., Adams, et al. v. Alcoa, Inc.*, No. 7:07-CV-1291 (GHL), 2011 U.S. Dist. LEXIS 110718 (N.D. N.Y. Sept. 28, 2011); *Bouaphakeo, et al. v. Tyson Foods, Inc.*, No. 5:07-CV-04009-JAJ, 2011 U.S. Dist. LEXIS 86437 (N.D. Iowa Aug. 4, 2011). Section 203(o) of FLSA exempts compensation for employee time spent changing "clothes" if such exemption is contained in a collective bargaining agreement. Lower courts are divided on the definition of "clothes" and the U.S. Supreme Court did not address the issue in *Alvarez. See Andrako, et al. v. United States Steel*

*Corp.*, No. 07–1629, 2009 U.S. Dist. LEXIS 52235 (W.D. Pa. Jun. 22, 2009); *Johnson, et al. v. Koch Foods, Inc.*, 670 F. Supp. 2d 657 (E.D. Tenn. 2009) *See also, Sepulveda, et al. v. Allen Family Foods, Inc.*, 591 F.3d 209 (4th Cir. 2009); *Atkinson, et al. v. House of Reaford Farms, Inc.*, No. 6-09-CV-01901-JMC, 2011 U.S. Dist. LEXIS 42942 (D. S.C. Apr. 20, 2011).

The FLSA requires payment of an enhanced rate of at least one and one-half times an employee's regular rate for work over 40 hours in a week. However, an exemption denies persons employed in agriculture the benefit of mandatory overtime payment. *See, e.g., U.S.C. § 213(b)(12)*. The agricultural exemption is broad, defining "agriculture" to include "farming in all its branches and the production, cultivation, growing, and harvesting of . . . horticultural commodities and any practices performed by a farmer or on a farm as an incident to or in conjunction with farming operations." *See, e.g., Elliott v. Custom Apple Packers, Inc.*, 228 P.3d 20 (Wash. Ct. App. 2009). As such, the exemption covers nonagricultural activities incidental to exempt activities. *See, e.g., Rodriguez v. Whiting Farms, Inc.*, 360 F.3d 1180 (10th Cir. 2004); *Pacheco v. Whiting Farms, Inc.*, 365 F.3d 1199 (10th Cir. 2004) A hatchery that occasionally uses fertilized eggs from outside sources is engaged in primary agriculture because FLSA provides that a hatchery engaged solely in procuring eggs for hatching and selling chicks is agriculture. See *Bynum v. Cal-Maine Farms, Inc.*, No. 3:10-CV-862-DPJ-FKB, 2012 U.S. Dist. LEXIS 104046 (S.D. Miss. Jul. 27, 2012). However, workers on Christmas tree farms have been held to *not* be employed in agriculture and, thus, are entitled to overtime wages in accordance with *29 U.S.C. § 207(a)(1)*. *United States Department of Labor v. North Carolina Growers Association, Inc.,* 377 F.3d 345 (4th Cir. 2004) In addition, FLSA exempts from the enhanced overtime wage rate employees who are employed in an executive capacity. *See, e.g., Davis, et al. v. Mountaire Farms, Inc.,* 453 F.3d 554 (3d Cir. 2006), *rev'g,* No. 04-414-KAJ, 2005 U.S. Dist. LEXIS 12543 (D. Del. Jun. 28, 2005). The 500 man-days test is irrelevant in this context. In addition, there are specific FLSA hour exemptions for certain employment that is not within the FLSA definition of agriculture.

An agricultural employer who is required to pay the federal agricultural minimum wage can apply for an administrative waiver permitting the employment of children of others, ages 10 and 11, outside of school hours and for not more than eight weeks in the calendar year. *29 U.S.C. § 213(c)(4)*. Applicants for the waiver must submit objective data showing a crop with a short harvesting season, unavailability of employees ages 12 and above, a past tradition of employing younger children, and the potential of severe economic disruption if this work force is not available. In addition, the applicant must demonstrate that the level and type of pesticides and other chemicals used will not have an adverse effect on the health or well-being of the individuals to whom the waiver would apply. Compliance with adult field worker standards will not necessarily satisfy this requirement.

## 2. Joint Employment

A common scenario in many agricultural settings is that a farmer will have crops harvested by an independent contractor. In this situation, the farmer is considered to be a joint employer with the contractor who supplies the harvest hands if the farmer has the power to direct, control, or supervise the work, or to determine the pay rates or method of payment for the harvest hands. *29 C.F.R. § 780.305(c).*

In both, *Gonzalez-Sanchez v. Int'l. Paper Co.,* 346 F.3d 1017 (11th Cir. 2003) and *Castillo v. Givens* 704 F.2d 181 (5th Cir. 1983) both the Eleventh Circuit and the Fifth Circuit determined whether joint employment existed based on the economics of the relationship of the parties and who controlled the employment situation. However, the Fourth Circuit in *Salinas v. Commercial Interiors, Inc.,* No. 15-1915, 2017 U.S. App. LEXIS 1321 (4th Cir. Jan. 25, 2017), *rev'g.,* No. JFM-12-1973, 2014 U.S. Dist. LEXIS 160956 (D. Md. Nov. 17, 2014), determined whether joint employment existed under the FLSA based on a two-step process. The court held that the test under the FLSA for joint employment involved two steps. The first step involved a determination as to whether two or more persons or entities share or agree to allocate responsibility for, whether formally or informally, directly or indirectly, the essential terms and conditions of a worker's employment. The second step involves a determination of whether the combined influence of the parties over the essential terms and conditions of the employment made the worker an employee rather than an independent contractor. If, under this standard, the multiple employers were not completely disassociated, a joint employment situation existed.

The increased use of contract production of agricultural commodities and livestock in recent years has raised additional issues with respect to categorizing employment in different levels of vertically integrated agricultural operations. A vertical integrator is an enterprise that owns or controls two or more stages involved in putting a commodity into the retail marketplace—from on-farm production to processing and sales to retailers. Under the FLSA, the focus is on the integrator's business rather than that of the contract farmer when determining the status of the integrator's employees. *See, e.g., Coleman v. Sanderson Farms, Inc.*, 629 F.2d 1077 (5th Cir. 1980). But, that court's decision was overruled in 2003. *Sanderson Farm, Inc., v. National Labor Relations Board*, 335 F.3d 445 (5th Cir. 2003).

## 3. Prohibited Acts

In general, the FLSA prohibits the employment of a child under age 16 unless that child is employed by a parent. In this context, the term "employment" is defined broadly to include allowing a child to help out without pay, "suffering or permitting to work" as well as hiring with pay. *29 C.F.R. § 570.70(c)(2)(iii).* However, in agricultural situations, an individual age 14 or 15 may be employed, and an individual 12 or 13 years old may be employed with parental consent. Children under age 12 may be employed with parental consent, but only on farms not required to pay the agricultural minimum wage to any employee. *29 U.S.C. § 213(c)(1)(A)*. The Act also contains a long list of hazardous tasks that may not be assigned to an agricultural employee under age 16. These tasks range from the operation of most tractors and farm machines to working around female animals caring for newborn offspring. However, children age 14 or 15 can be assigned some of these hazardous jobs if they have completed a pertinent 4-H or other approved training program.

The assigning of actual handling of most agricultural chemicals to children under age 16 is prohibited, except where the employer is the parent. *29 C.F.R. § 570.71(9)*. Unless an exemption applies, children must be paid the agricultural minimum wage.

If state child labor laws are more stringent than the FLSA, state law controls. State laws can absolutely prohibit employment of children under an age such as 12 or 14, rule out employment during certain hours of the day, and limit the number of hours a child may work during a set period of time. State school attendance laws also apply even when the parent is the employer.

## 4. Enforcement Proceedings

The FLSA authorizes three causes of action. First, an employee may sue the employer for unpaid overtime, unpaid minimum wages, and, subject to the discretion of the court, up to an additional equal amount in liquidated damages. Second, the Secretary of Labor may sue on behalf of employees to recover such amounts. Third, the Secretary may sue to enjoin violations of the FLSA. Criminal penalties may apply for situations involving willful or repeat offenses. Also, state laws that extend minimum wage or overtime protection to workers not covered under the FLSA are not preempted and must be observed. Similarly, states can enact and enforce wage and hour benefits for agricultural workers at levels more favorable than under the FLSA.

## B. MIGRANT AND SEASONAL WORKER PROTECTION ACT

The Congress addressed the problem of exploitation of migrant farm workers and producers of agricultural products with enactment of the Farm Labor Contractor Registration Act of 1963 (FLCRA). The legislation regulated the activity of farm labor contractors, and required crew leaders to register with the Department of Labor. The crew leader was also required to provide proof of public liability insurance, or proof of financial responsibility, for all vehicles used in the business. Further, crew leaders were required to keep proper payroll records and accurately inform workers about employment terms and anticipated earnings. The FLCRA was amended in 1974 and repealed and replaced by the Migrant and Seasonal Agricultural Worker Protection Act (MSAWPA) in 1983. *29 U.S.C. §§ 1801 et seq.* The MSAWPA does not preempt state laws regulating farm labor contractors.

## 1. Covered Employers

Under the MSAWPA, both growers and farm labor contractors have duties and responsibilities concerning worker protection and can be held liable for violations. Farm labor contractors are required to register with the Department of Labor and carry a certificate of registration at all times.

The MSAWPA broadly defines the term "farm labor contractor" to apply to three classes of persons: agricultural employers, farm labor contractors and agricultural associations. An "agricultural employer" is any person who owns or operates a farm, ranch, processing establishment, cannery, gin, packing shed or nursery, or who produces or conditions seed, and who either recruits, solicits, hires, employs, furnishes, or transport any migrant or seasonal agricultural worker. An "agricultural association" is a nonprofit or cooperative association of farmers, growers, or ranchers, incorporated or qualified under applicable state law, which engages in any of the activities listed in the preceding sentence. A "farm labor contractor" is any person, other than an agricultural employer or association, or an employee of either, who, for a fee, performs any farm labor contracting activity such as recruiting, soliciting, hiring, employing, furnishing or transporting migrant or seasonal agricultural workers. *29 U.S.C. § 1802(7)*. The focus of the Act is on itinerant middlemen who move about the country supplying crews for agricultural operations. Accordingly, agricultural employers and associations are exempt from the Act's registration requirements. However, agricultural employers and associations remain responsible for worker protection along with farm labor contractors.

## 2. Covered Employees

The MSAWPA protects two types of agricultural workers. Migrant agricultural workers are persons engaged in agricultural employment of a seasonal or other temporary nature who are required to be away overnight from their permanent residence. *29 U.S.C. § 1802(8)(A). See, e.g., Lopez v. Lassen Dairy, Inc.,* No. CV-F-08-121 LJO GSA, 2010 U.S. Dist. LEXIS 80308 (E.D. Cal. Aug. 10, 2010). Also protected are seasonal agricultural workers. These persons are employed in specific agricultural employment of a seasonal or temporary nature, but are not required to be absent from home overnight. *29 U.S.C. § 1802(10)(A).* Seasonal agricultural workers are further classified into one of two groups. The first group contains those workers employed on a farm or ranch performing field work related to planting, cultivating, or harvesting, regardless of how they travel to and from work. The second category includes those employed in canning, packing, ginning, seed conditioning or related research, or processing operations, but only if transported to or from the place of employment by a day-haul operation. However, seasonal agricultural workers do not include migrant agricultural workers, immediate members of the family of the agricultural employer or farm labor contractor, and temporary nonimmigrant aliens who are authorized to work in agricultural employment in the United States under the Immigration and Nationality Act. *29 U.S.C. § 1802(10)(B)*.

## 3. Worker Protections

Under the MSAWPA, employers of migrant and seasonal agricultural workers must disclose to each migrant and seasonal agricultural worker information concerning the place of employment, the wage rate, the crops and activities on which the worker may be employed, the period of employment, the transportation, housing or other employee benefits to be provided and the cost to the worker, as well as the existence of a strike or other concerted stoppage, slowdown or other interruption by employees at the place of employment. Covered employers must also disclose to each migrant and seasonal agricultural worker the existence of any arrangements with any owner or agent of any business in the area of employment under which the employer is to receive a commission or any other benefit resulting from sales by the business to the workers. The disclosure must be made in the worker's common language. All of this information is to be disclosed at the place of recruitment to seasonal agricultural workers recruited through use of a day-haul operation.

Covered employers of migrant and seasonal workers must post in a conspicuous place a poster provided by the Secretary of Labor setting forth the rights and protections afforded migrant and seasonal workers under the MSAWPA, including the right to request additional information. The poster must use the language common to the workers. *29 U.S.C. § 1821(g)*. Employers of migrant agricultural workers who provide housing for any migrant workers are to post a statement of terms and conditions of occupancy of such housing.

Covered employers must also make and keep for three years' records on each worker concerning the wage rate, the number of piece-work units earned if the worker is paid on a piece-work basis, the number of hours worked, the total pay period earnings, the amount and purpose of each amount withheld and the net pay. *29 U.S.C. §§ 1821(d)(1), 1831(c)(1)*. Also, the employer must provide an itemized statement of this information for each pay period to each migrant and seasonal agricultural worker. The recipient of this information is to retain it for three years after the end of employment.

Each person who owns or controls the housing facility for migrant agricultural workers is responsible for ensuring that the housing complies with federal and state housing safety and health standards. The applicable federal standards are those promulgated by the Employment and Training Administration at 20 C.F.R. § 654.404 et seq. and the Occupational Safety and Health Administration at 29 C.F.R. § 1910.142; 29 C.F.R. § 500.132. Housing facilities must be certified by a state or local health authority as meeting safety and health standards and the certification must be posted at the site. Uncertified facilities may be occupied by migrant agricultural workers if a request for inspection has been made at least 45 days before occupancy.

However, the housing safety and health requirements do not apply to persons who, in the ordinary course of business, regularly provide housing to the general public of the same character and terms as is provided to migrant agricultural workers.

Vehicles that are used by farm labor contractors, agricultural employers and associations subject to the MSAWPA to transport one or more migrant or seasonal agricultural workers are subject to safety and insurance requirements. However, if the migrant or seasonal workers are covered under state workers' compensation coverage as employees of the farm labor contractor or agricultural employer or association, insurance coverage is not required.

## 4. Defenses to Liability

The courts have accepted two defenses to liability under the MSAWPA—that the worker is an independent contractor or that the worker is employed solely by an independent contractor. These are strong defenses for growers. The MSAWPA only provides protection against illegal grower actions to *employees* of growers, not independent contractors or employees of independent contractors. While an agricultural migrant or seasonal worker may still be able to bring an action against a crew leader on the theory that the worker is an employee of the crew leader, recovery may be difficult to achieve because of the transient nature and lack of resources of many crew leaders.

Under the MSAWPA, a farm labor contractor who supplies a crew and the farmer on whose property the work is being performed, have the potential of being joint-employers. If a joint-employment situation exists, both employers are responsible for observing worker protection requirements. Joint employment relationships are common in agriculture. Under the MSAWPA, several factors are considered in determining the presence of joint employment. The regulations specify the following factors: (1) the nature and degree of control of the workers; (2) the degree of supervision, direct or indirect, of the work; (3) the power to determine pay rates or the methods of payment of the workers; (4) the right, directly or indirectly, to hire, fire, or modify the employment conditions of the workers; and (5) the preparation of payroll and the payment of wages. *29 C.F.R. § 500.20(h)(4)(ii). See, e.g., Ricketts v. Vann,* 32 F.3d 71 (4th Cir. 1994).

## 5. Exemptions

Numerous exemptions from coverage under the MSAWPA exist. Employers who did not use more than 500 man-days of labor during any calendar quarter during the preceding calendar year that employ immediate family members to perform farm labor contracting activities are exempt from the MSAWPA. The activities must be performed, however, only for a farm, processing establishment, seed conditioning establishment, cannery, gin, packing shed or nursery which is owned or operated exclusively by the individual or an immediate family member. *29 U.S.C. § 213(a)(6)(A).* Likewise, persons, other than farm labor contractors, to whom the man-day exemption for agricultural labor under the FLSA applies, are not subject to the MSAWPA. In addition, the MSAWPA does not apply to common carriers that transport migrant and seasonal agricultural workers, certain labor organizations, certain nonprofit charitable organizations and public or private educational institutions, a person engaged in farm labor contracting activity within a 25-mile intrastate radius of the person's permanent place of residence and for not more than 13 weeks per year, custom combining, hay harvesting and sheep shearing operations, as well as custom poultry harvesting, tobacco and seed production operations. The MSAWPA also does not apply to persons whose principal occupation is not agricultural employment and who supply or are supplied full-time students or other individuals whose principal occupation is not agricultural employment to detassel, rogue or otherwise engage in the production of seed, unless the workers are required to be away from their permanent residence overnight or individuals under 18 are providing transportation. Likewise, employees of any parties exempt from the MSAWPA are also exempt when performing farm labor contracting activities within the scope of their employer's exemption and exclusively for the employer.

## 6. Penalties

Violations of the MSAWPA can result in either criminal or civil penalties or both. *29 U.S.C. §§ 1853–1854.* In addition, aggrieved workers have a statutory cause of action for money damages against a noncomplying regulated party. *29 U.S.C. § 1854.* The MSAWPA prohibits the use of the services of a farm labor contractor to supply migrant or seasonal agricultural workers without first determining that the farm labor contractor possesses a valid certificate of registration authorizing the farm labor contracting activity for which the contractor is utilized. Also proscribed is discrimination against a migrant or seasonal agricultural worker because the worker has, with just cause, filed a complaint, instituted a proceeding, or testified or was about to testify in connection with an alleged statutory violation. Any migrant or seasonal agricultural worker believing that they have been discriminated against in violation of the MSAWPA may file a complaint with the Secretary of Labor. An employer may be ordered to hire, rehire or reinstate with back pay a migrant or seasonal agricultural worker if it is determined that the worker was discharged or discriminated against because of the filing of an MSAWPA complaint or engaging in activities such as testifying or planning to testify in MSAWPA proceedings.

Willing and knowing violations of the Act or its regulations are subject to a fine not to exceed $1,000 or imprisonment for not more than one year or both. The lack of knowledge of the MSAWPA has been held not to constitute a defense for intentional violation. *Bueno v. Mattner,* 829 F.2d 1380 (6th Cir. 1987), *cert. denied sub nom., Mattner v. Bueno,* 486 U.S. 1022 (1988). Intent is necessary only as to the action rather than as to the violation of the Act. Additional violations are punishable by a fine of up to $10,000 or imprisonment for not more than three years or both.

If a farm labor contractor violates the MSAWPA when the contractor does not have a certificate of registration, the violation is punishable by a fine of not more than $10,000 or imprisonment for not more than three years or both. Civil penalties may also be assessed up to $10,000 for each violation.

## VII. FOREIGN OWNERSHIP OF AGRICULTURAL LAND

### A. IN GENERAL

In the 1970s, the issue of foreign investment in and ownership of agricultural land received additional attention because of several large purchases by foreigners and the suspicion that the build-up in liquidity in the oil exporting countries would likely lead to more land purchases by nonresident aliens. The lack of data concerning the number of acres actually owned by foreigners contributed to fears that foreign ownership was an important and rapidly spreading phenomenon.

### B. STATE RESTRICTIONS

State statutes designed to restrict alien ownership of real property are generally of three types: (1) outright restrictions on the acquisition of certain types of property; (2) limitations on the total amount of land that can be acquired; and (3) limitations on the length of time property can be held. Acquisition restrictions are common in the agricultural context, with the restriction generally applying only to the acquisition of farmland, as defined by the law.

Exceptions are common for the acquisition of land for conversion to nonagricultural purposes, land acquired by devise or descent, and land acquired through collection of debts or enforcement of liens or mortgages. Acreage restrictions allow foreign investment, but place a premium on having an effective method of discovering and preventing multiple acquisition by the same individuals through the use of various investment vehicles. Time restrictions generally do not apply to voluntary acquisition of the land by foreign investors, but are associated with involuntary acquisitions. Some states require the disclosure of information concerning the land acquired and the investors.

The statutes of states having major restrictions on foreign ownership are surveyed below. The states having minor restrictions on foreign ownership of and investment in agricultural land are: Arkansas, California, Connecticut, Florida, Georgia, Idaho, Kansas, Maryland, Mississippi, Montana, Nevada, New Jersey, New York, North Carolina, Oregon, Pennsylvania, South Carolina, Virginia and Wyoming.

## 1. Illinois

The Illinois statute generally restricts the ability of aliens to hold title to land. *Ill. Ann. Stat. Ch. 6, § 1 et seq. (Smith-Hurd).* Aliens are granted full rights to acquire interests in lands, and can hold these interest for either six years or for six years after the alien's twenty-first birthday, whichever occurs later. After that, the lands are subject to an action by the county attorney for the county where the lands are situated to compel sale of the land. In 1979, Illinois adopted a reporting law identical to federal legislation.

## 2. Indiana

Aliens may acquire and hold up to 320 acres of real estate in Indiana. Aliens that acquire more than 320 acres of land, in any manner, must dispose of the excess within five years, or the excess land is subject to escheat to the state. *Ind. Code Ann. § 43–2–8–1.* The state attorney general has the duty to bring proceedings to recover any escheated property.

## 3. Iowa

The Iowa restrictions date back to statehood in 1846 when a provision was placed in the Iowa Constitution stating that foreigners who became residents could enjoy the same rights as native born citizens as to property ownership, but that aliens living outside Iowa could not take or hold real property.

Presently, Iowa has the most restrictive limitation on nonresident alien ownership of any state in the United States. *Iowa Code § 172C.7.* The Iowa restriction provides that a "nonresident alien, foreign business, or foreign government, or an agent, trustee or fiduciary thereof, shall not purchase or otherwise acquire agricultural land in this state." *Iowa Code § 567.3(1).* A major exception exists that allows restricted parties to acquire up to 320 acres of agricultural land for "an immediate or pending use other than farming" if the conversion is completed within five years, and annual reports on the progress of the conversion are made. In addition, during the five-year period, the land can only be farmed on lease to a family farm, a family farm corporation, or an authorized farm corporation. *Iowa Code § 567.3(3)* and *§ 567.8.* The Iowa law also provides that agricultural land acquired by nonresident aliens by devise or descent must be divested within two years. However, if the land is acquired by devise or descent from another nonresident alien, it need not be divested, unless the nonresident alien originally acquired the land in the six months preceding enactment of the law. For purposes of the Iowa restriction, a nonresident alien is defined as "an individual who is not a citizen of the United States and who has not been classified as a permanent resident alien by the United States Immigration and Naturalization Service." *Iowa Code § 567.1(2).*

## 4. Kentucky

In Kentucky, resident aliens are restricted in taking and holding land for residential, occupational, business, trade or manufacturing purposes for up to 21 years. In addition, nonresident aliens who inherit real estate can only hold it for up to eight years. *Ky. Rev. Stat. § 381.330.* Corporations may not hold real estate for longer than five years, "except as may be proper and necessary for carrying on a legitimate business." *Ky. Const. § 192.* In 1980, the Kentucky legislature adopted a reporting measure requiring the Kentucky Commission of Agriculture to regularly submit to the legislative research commission a comprehensive report providing detailed information concerning foreign investment in Kentucky farmland. The report is to contain the names of the foreign investors and the location and acreage of the land they own.

## 5. Minnesota

Under the Minnesota law, no natural person (unless a United States citizen or a permanent resident alien of the United States) can acquire, directly or indirectly, any interest in agricultural land, including leaseholds. *Minn. Stat. Ann. § 500.221.1.* Foreign corporations cannot, either directly or indirectly, acquire or obtain any interest in title to agricultural land unless at least 80 percent of each class of stock issued and outstanding or 80 percent of the ultimate beneficial interest of the entity is held, directly or indirectly, by United States citizens or permanent resident aliens. Land can be acquired by devise, inheritance, as security for indebtedness, by process of law in the collection of debts, or by enforcement of a lien, but land acquired in these fashions must be divested within three years of acquisition. Similarly, land or interests acquired in connection with mining and mineral processing operations are permissible but, pending development for mining purposes, the land can only be used for farming on lease to a family farm, family farm corporation or authorized farm corporation. Another exception exists for agricultural land operated for research or experimental purpose if the total acreage does not exceed that held on May 27, 1977.

## 6. Missouri

Missouri law prohibits aliens and foreign businesses from acquiring by grant, purchase, devise or descent, agricultural land in the state. *Mo. Rev. Stat. §§ 442.560–442.592.* Under the legislation, "alien" is defined as any person who is not a citizen of the United States and who is not a resident of the United States or its holdings. *Mo. Rev. Stat. § 442.566(2).* A "foreign business" is defined as "any business entity whether or not incorporated, including but not limited to corporations, partnerships, limited partnerships, and associations in which a controlling interest is owned by aliens." *Mo. Rev. Stat. § 442.566(4).* Agricultural land is defined as any tract consisting of more than five acres whether inside or outside the corporate limits of any municipality, which is capable of supporting an agricultural enterprise including production of agricultural crops, livestock, poultry and dairy products. Farm leasehold interests of ten years or longer or a lease renewable at the lessee's option for greater than ten years are treated as the acquisition of agricultural land.

An exception exists for agricultural land acquired for immediate or potential use in non-farming purposes, but the exception is limited to that amount of land necessary for the nonfarm business operation. While the nonfarm activity is being developed, the land may only be farmed under lease to a family farm unit, family farm corporation, or a registered alien or foreign business. The Missouri legislation also contains a reporting requirement requiring any foreign person holding any interest (other than a security interest) in agricultural land to submit a detailed report to the Director of Agriculture within 60 days, except for land used for the production of energy-related minerals. The information required to be submitted includes the name and address of the foreign person, the citizenship of foreign individuals, the type of interest in acquired land held or transferred, a legal description of the land, the purchase price or consideration paid or received, information concerning transferees, and the declaration of the type of agricultural activity engaged in or the nonfarm purpose for which the land was acquired. Failure to file a required report is subject to civil fine.

## 7. Nebraska

Nebraska law prohibits aliens and foreign corporations from acquiring title to, or taking or holding interest in, any land or leasehold interest of more than five years, either by devise, descent, purchase or otherwise. An exception exists for real estate within the corporate limits of cities or villages or within three miles. *Neb. Rev. Stat. § 76–414.* Other exceptions exist for land acquired in connection with manufacturing or industrial establishments, real estate necessary for the construction and operation of railroads, public utilities and common carriers, land acquired by enforcement of a lien or by collection of a debt (subject to divestment within ten years), land inherited by resident aliens provided it is divested within five years subject to escheat, land acquired in connection with the production of oil, gas or other hydrocarbon substances, and land held by aliens before March 16, 1889, that is acquired by widows or heirs by devise or descent, provided it is divested within ten years, subject to escheat. Corporations involved in agriculture must file an annual report disclosing any aliens who have an interest in or are involved in the management of the business.

## 8. North Dakota

Under the North Dakota legislation, persons who are not citizens of the United States or Canada, or permanent resident aliens of the United States, may not acquire, directly or indirectly, any interest in agricultural land. *N.D. Cent. Code § 47–10.1–02.* The legislation defines agricultural land broadly to cover any land capable of use in agricultural production, but excludes any interest in oil, gas, coal or other minerals underlying the land. The restriction also applies to partnerships, limited partnerships, trusts or other business entities unless the ultimate beneficial interest of the entity, in the agricultural land, is held directly or indirectly by citizens of the United States or permanent resident aliens. Exceptions exist for agricultural land acquired by devise, inheritance, as security for indebtedness, or by process of law in the collection of debts or enforcement of liens. Land acquired in the collection of debts or by enforcement of a lien or claim must be disposed of within three years of acquisition, if that acquisition would otherwise violate the statute.

## 9. Oklahoma

Oklahoma law prohibits any alien or person who is not a United States citizen from acquiring title to or owning land in the state. *Okla. Stat. Ann. tit. 60 § 121.* Exceptions exist for land owned by aliens as long as they are held by the present owners, and any alien who is or who shall take up a bona fide residence in Oklahoma during the continuance of the residency. If the residency ceases, the land must be divested within five years. Likewise, land acquired by nonresident aliens by devise, descent, or by purchase upon a foreclosure of a lien held by the alien, must be divested within five years. Failure to divest subjects the land to escheat proceedings.

## 10. South Dakota

The South Dakota provision limits the amount of agricultural land that can be acquired by nonresident aliens to no more than 160 acres. Land acquired by devise or descent or acquired by process of law in the collection of debts or enforcement of a lien or claim thereon must be disposed within three years. Failure to divest subjects the land to escheat proceedings. An exception exists for nonresident aliens who are or become bona fide residents of any state or territory of the United States to acquire and hold agricultural land during the continuance of the residence upon the same terms as South Dakota citizens. *S.D. Comp. Laws § 43–2A–5.*

## 11. Wisconsin

The Wisconsin statute prohibits nonresident aliens and foreign corporations from acquiring, holding, or owning more than 640 acres of land. *Wis. Stat. Ann. § 710.02.* Exceptions exist for the acquisition of land by devise, inheritance or in good faith in the collection of debts by due process of law. The acreage limitation applies to corporations or associations having more than 20 percent of their stock owned by a nonresident alien. The word "association" has been interpreted to include a limited partnership. *Lehndorff-Geneva, Inc. v. Warren,* 74 Wis.2d 369, 246 N.W.2d 815 (1976).

## C.   FOREIGN INVESTMENT DISCLOSURE ACT

In 1978, the Congress enacted the Agricultural Foreign Investment Disclosure Act (AFIDA). *7 U.S.C. 3501 et seq.* Under AFIDA, the USDA obtains information on U.S. agricultural holdings of foreign individuals and businesses. In essence, AFIDA is a reporting statute rather than a regulatory statute. The information provided in reports by the AFIDA helps serve as the basis for any future action Congress may take in establishing direct controls or limits on foreign investment in agricultural land and provides useful information to states considering limitations on foreign investment. The Act requires that foreign persons report to the Secretary of Agriculture their agricultural land holdings or acquisitions. The Secretary assembles and analyzes the information contained in the report, passes it on the respective states for their action and reports periodically to the Congress and the President.

AFIDA requires reports in four situations: (1) when a foreign person "acquires or transfers any interest, other than a security" in agricultural land; (2) when any interest in agricultural land, except a security interest, is held by any foreign person on the day before the effective date of the Act; (3) when a nonforeign owner of agricultural land subsequently becomes a foreign person; and (4) when nonagricultural land owned by a foreign person subsequently becomes agricultural land.

AFIDA defines "agricultural land" as "any land located in one or more states and used for agricultural, forestry, or timber production purposes. . . ." *7 U.S.C. § 3508(1)*. The regulations define agricultural land as "land in the United States which is currently used for, or if idle and its last use within the past five years was for, agricultural, forestry, or timber production, except land not exceeding one acre from which the agricultural, forestry, or timber products are less than $1,000 in annual gross sales value and such products are produced for the personal or household use of the person or persons holding an interest in such land." *44 Fed. Reg. 7117 (1979); 7 C.F.R. § 781.2(b)*. In 1980, the Secretary proposed a change in this definition to increase the acreage amount to ten acres, while preserving the gross sales test. However, the proposed change has not yet become effective.

The reporting provisions of the AFIDA require the disclosure of considerable information regarding both the land and the reporting party. The information must be reported on Form FSA-153 and includes: (1) the legal name and address of the foreign person; (2) the citizenship of the foreign person, if an individual; (3) if the foreign person is not an individual or government, the nature of the legal entity holding the interest, the country in which the foreign person is created or organized, and the principal place of business; (4) the type of interest in agricultural land that the person acquired or transferred; (5) the legal description and acreage of the agricultural land; (6) the purchase price paid, or other consideration given, for such interest; (7) the agricultural purposes for which the agricultural land is being used and for which the foreign person intends to use the agricultural property; and (8) such other information as the Secretary of Agriculture may require by regulation. *7 U.S.C. § 3501(a)(9).*

# INDEX

### References are to Pages

---

**WEEDS**
Noxious weeds, liability for spread of, 457
Liability for negligent control of, 458

**WIND ENERGY**
Leases, suggested provisions, 47–49

**WISCONSIN**
Foreign ownership on agricultural land, restrictions on, 765

**WORKERS' COMPENSATION**
Agricultural exemption, 471
Assumption of risk as defense, 469
Benefits, 470
Co-employee's negligence as defense, 470
Common law duties of farmer
     Generally, 467–469
  Competent employees, farmer's duty to hire, 468
  Safe tools doctrine, 467
  Safe workplace, duty to provide, 467
  Warnings, duty to give proper, 468
Contributory negligence as defense, 470